A HISTORY OF THE HARLEM RENAISSANCE

The Harlem Renaissance was the most influential single movement in African American literary history. The movement laid the groundwork for subsequent African American literature, and had an enormous impact on later black literature worldwide. In its attention to a wide range of genres and forms – from the *roman à clef* and the *Bildungsroman* to dance and book illustrations – this book seeks to encapsulate and analyze the eclecticism of Harlem Renaissance cultural expression. It aims to re-frame conventional ideas of the New Negro movement by presenting new readings of well-studied authors, such as Zora Neale Hurston and Langston Hughes, alongside analysis of topics, authors, and artists that deserve fuller treatment. An authoritative collection on the major writers and issues of the period, *A History of the Harlem Renaissance* takes stock of nearly a hundred years of scholarship and considers what the future augurs for the study of the "New Negro."

RACHEL FAREBROTHER is Senior Lecturer in American Studies at Swansea University. She is the author of *The Collage Aesthetic in the Harlem Renaissance* (2009), which was awarded honorable mention in the 2010 British Association of American Studies book prize. Her essays have appeared in *Journal of American Studies*, *MELUS*, and *Modernism/modernity* and various edited collections including Fionnghuala Sweeney and Kate Marsh's *Afromodernisms: Paris, Harlem, and the Avant-Garde* (2013) and Peter Brooker and Andrew Thacker's *The Oxford Cultural and Critical History of Modernist Magazines: Volume II, North America* (2012).

MIRIAM THAGGERT is Associate Professor of English, Department of English, at SUNY-Buffalo. She is the author of *Images of Black Modernism: Verbal and Visual Strategies of the Harlem Renaissance* (2010), an examination of African American literature and photography and the depiction of an early black modernism. Her essays have appeared in *African American Review*, *American Literary History*, *American Quarterly*, *Feminist Modernist Studies*, *Meridians* and the edited volume *The New Modernist Studies*. Her research has been supported by the Ford Foundation, the Newberry Library, and the Virginia Humanities.

A HISTORY OF THE HARLEM RENAISSANCE

EDITED BY

RACHEL FAREBROTHER

Swansea University

MIRIAM THAGGERT

SUNY-Buffalo

CAMBRIDGE
UNIVERSITY PRESS

CAMBRIDGE
UNIVERSITY PRESS

University Printing House, Cambridge CB2 8BS, United Kingdom

One Liberty Plaza, 20th Floor, New York, NY 10006, USA

477 Williamstown Road, Port Melbourne, VIC 3207, Australia

314–321, 3rd Floor, Plot 3, Splendor Forum, Jasola District Centre,
New Delhi – 110025, India

79 Anson Road, #06–04/06, Singapore 079906

Cambridge University Press is part of the University of Cambridge.

It furthers the University's mission by disseminating knowledge in the pursuit of
education, learning, and research at the highest international levels of excellence.

www.cambridge.org
Information on this title: www.cambridge.org/9781108493574
DOI: 10.1017/9781108656313

First published 2021

Printed in the United Kingdom by TJ Books Limited, Padstow Cornwall

A catalogue record for this publication is available from the British Library.

ISBN 978-1-108-49357-4 Hardback

In Memoriam:
Cheryl A. Wall
1948–2020

Contents

Illustrations

Notes on Contributors

KATHARINE CAPSHAW is Professor of English and Africana Studies affiliate at the University of Connecticut and author of *Children's Literature of the Harlem Renaissance* (Indiana University Press, 2004) and *Civil Rights Childhood: Picturing Liberation in African American Photobooks* (University of Minnesota Press, 2014). With Anna Mae Duane, she edited *Who Writes for Black Children? African American Children's Literature before 1900* (University of Minnesota Press, 2017). She has authored dozens of articles on race and childhood, and is currently writing a book on children's theater during the Black Arts Movement.

CLARE CORBOULD is Associate Professor of History at Deakin University, Melbourne. She is author of *Becoming African Americans: Black Public Life in Harlem, 1919–1939* (Harvard University Press, 2009) and co-editor of *Remembering the Revolution: Memory, History, and Nation-Making from Independence to the Civil War* (University of Massachusetts Press, 2013). Recent work on interwar Harlem includes "Race, Photography, Labor, and Entrepreneurship in the Life of Maurice Hunter, Harlem's 'Man of 1,000 Faces'" in *Radical History Review*, vol. 132 and "Class, Gender, and Community in *Harlem Sketches*: Representing Black Urban Modernity in Interwar Newspapers," in *Race Capital? Harlem as Setting and Symbol*, ed. Andrew M. Fearnley and Daniel Matlin (Columbia University Press, 2018).

HANNAH DURKIN is a Lecturer in Literature and Film at Newcastle University. Her research focuses on twentieth-century Black Atlantic literary and visual cultures with a particular emphasis on anthropology, cinema, dance, and slavery. She is currently working on two book-length projects. The first centers on Sally "Redoshi" Smith (*c.* 1848–1936) and other survivors of the slave ship *Clotilda*. The second examines early black and Jewish women ethnographic filmmakers' pioneering contributions to art and anthropology. She is the author of *Josephine Baker and Katherine Dunham: Dances in Literature and Cinema* (University of Illinois Press, 2019); co-author with Celeste-Marie Bernier, Alan Rice, and Lubaina Himid of *Inside the Invisible: Memorialising Slavery and Freedom in the Life and Works of Lubaina Himid* (Liverpool University Press, 2019); and co-editor with Celeste-Marie Bernier of *Visualising Slavery: Art Across the African Diaspora* (Liverpool University Press, 2016).

RACHEL FAREBROTHER is a Senior Lecturer in English Literature and American Studies at Swansea University, UK. She is the author of *The Collage Aesthetic in the Harlem Renaissance* (Ashgate, 2009). Her work has appeared in various venues including the *Journal of American Studies*, *MELUS*, *Modernism/modernity*, and *Afromodernism: Paris, Harlem and the Avant-Garde*, ed. Fionnghuala Sweeney and Kate Marsh (Edinburgh University Press, 2013).

CAROLINE GOESER is W. T. and Louise J. Moran Chair of Learning and Interpretation at the Museum of Fine Arts, Houston (MFAH) and oversees the Museum's educational and public programs and university partnerships. She is the project director for the Institute of Museum and Library Services grant, "From Cradle to Hub: Advancing Visitor Engagement at the MFAH." She is spearheading a leading-edge study on audience engagement with Slover Linett Audience Research, designed to grow and diversify the Museum's constituents. Prior to her work at MFAH, she was Associate Professor of Art History at the University of Houston. Her publications include *Picturing the New Negro: Harlem Renaissance Print Culture and Modern Black Identity* (University Press of Kansas, 2007), and "The Blare of God's Trombones: Modernizing Biblical Narratives in the Work of Aaron Douglas," in *Beholding Christ and Christianity in African-American Art*, ed. James Romaine and Phoebe Wolfskill (Pennsylvania State University Press, 2017).

MAUREEN HONEY is Professor Emeritus of English and Women's and Gender Studies at the University of Nebraska-Lincoln, specializing in American Women's Literature, the Harlem Renaissance, and Women in World War II. She is considered one of the leading scholars in Harlem Renaissance and Modernist Studies and has published numerous essays on these and other subjects. She is the editor or author of nine books, including *Shadowed Dreams: Women's Poetry of the Harlem Renaissance* (Rutgers University Press 2006, 1989); *Bitter Fruit: African American Women in World War II* (University of Missouri Press, 1999); *Creating Rosie the Riveter: Class, Gender and Propaganda during World War II* (University of Massachusetts Press, 1984); and *Double-Take: A Revised Harlem Renaissance Anthology* (with Venetria K. Patton, Rutgers University Press, 2001). Her most recent book is the critical monograph *Aphrodite's Daughters: Three Modernist Poets of the Harlem Renaissance* (Rutgers University Press, 2016), which focuses on the lives and lyric poetry of Angelina Weld Grimké, Gwendolyn B. Bennett, and Mae V. Cowdery.

WENDY MARTIN is Professor of American Literature and American Studies at Claremont Graduate University and Chair of the Department of English. The author of numerous articles on American literature and culture, she founded and continues to edit *Women's Studies: An Interdisciplinary Journal.* Her books include *An American Sisterhood* (Harper & Row, 1972); *An American Triptych: Anne Bradstreet, Emily Dickinson and Adrienne Rich* (University of North Carolina Press, 1984); *New Essays on The Awakening* (Cambridge University Press, 1988); *We Are the Stories We Tell* (Pantheon, 1990); *Colonial American Travel Narratives* (Penguin, 1994); *The Cambridge Companion to Emily Dickinson* (Cambridge University Press, 2002); *More Stories We Tell* (Pantheon, 2004); *The Art of the Short Story* (Pearson-Longman, 2006), *The Cambridge Introduction to Emily Dickinson* (Cambridge University Press, 2007); *All Things Dickinson: An Encyclopedia Of Emily Dickinson's World* (Greenwood, 2014); *The Gilded Age and The Progressive Era* (with Cecelia Tichi, Greenwood, 2016); and *The Routledge Introduction to American Women Writers* (with Sharone Williams, Routledge, 2016); *The Concise Oxford Companion to American Literature* (with Danielle Hinrichs, Oxford University Press, 2020).

DEBORAH E. MCDOWELL is a scholar of African American/American literature and the Alice Griffin Professor of Literary Studies and Director of the Carter G. Woodson Institute for African American and African Studies at the University of Virginia, where she has been a member of the faculty since 1987. Her publications include *"The Changing Same": Studies in Fiction by African-American Women* (Indiana University Press, 1995); *Leaving Pipe Shop: Memories of Kin* (Norton, 1998); as well as numerous articles, book chapters, and scholarly editions. She is co-editor (with Claudrena Harold and Juan Battle) of *The Punitive Turn: Race, Inequality, and Mass Incarceration* (University of Virginia Press, 2013). Extensively involved in editorial projects pertaining to the subject of African American literature, she founded the African American Women Writers Series for Beacon Press and served as its editor from 1985 to 1993. This project oversaw the reissue of fourteen novels by African American women writers from the nineteenth and twentieth centuries. She also served as a period editor for the *Norton Anthology of African-American Literature*, contributing editor to the *D. C. Heath Anthology of American Literature*, and co-editor with Arnold Rampersad of *Slavery and the Literary Imagination*. Her service on various editorial boards has included *PMLA*, *American Literature*, *Genders, and African-American Review, Modern Fiction Studies*, and *Tulsa Studies in Women's Literature*.

NOELLE MORRISSETTE is Associate Professor of English at the University of North Carolina-Greensboro and Director of the Program in African American and African Diaspora Studies. She is the author-editor of *New Perspectives on James Weldon Johnson's The Autobiography of an Ex-Colored Man* (University of Georgia Press, 2017) and the author of the scholarly monograph, *James Weldon Johnson's Modern Soundscapes* (University of Iowa Press, 2013).

SINÉAD MOYNIHAN is Associate Professor in American and Atlantic Literatures at the University of Exeter. Her research focuses on twentieth- and twenty-first century American and Irish literatures, especially African American literature, the literature of racial passing, and literatures dealing with questions of race and racialization in a transatlantic context. She has published three monographs and her fourth, *"The View from the Kitchen": Domestic Workers in American Literature, 1942–1974*, is a work in progress. She has published numerous articles in venues such as *MELUS, African American Review, Callaloo, Studies in the Novel*, and *Studies in American Fiction*.

JONATHAN MUNBY is a Senior Lecturer in the Lancaster Institute for the Contemporary Arts (LICA) at Lancaster University, UK. He has published widely on African American film, literature and popular culture. His current research on the writer and filmmaker Julian Mayfield explores the relationship between African American art and activism by those who attempted to internationalize the freedom struggle after World War II. He is the author of *Public Enemies, Public Heroes: Screening the Gangster Film from Little Caesar to Touch of Evil*

(University of Chicago Press, 1999) and *Under a Bad Sign: Criminal Self-Representation in African American Popular Culture* (University of Chicago Press, 2011).

JAK PEAKE is a Fulbright scholar and literature lecturer in the Department of Literature, Film, and Theatre Studies at the University of Essex. He is the author of *Between the Bocas: Towards a Geography of Western Trinidad* (Liverpool University Press, 2017). His current research examines Caribbean-New York literary, political, and artistic networks in the early twentieth century. He has published recently on this topic in *Radical Americas* ("'Watching the Waters': Tropic Flows in the Harlem Renaissance, Black Internationalism and Other Currents," 2018) and has co-edited a 2017 special issue of *Comparative American Studies*, "American Networks: Radicals under the Radar (1840–1968)" with Wendy McMahon. He also has a book chapter, "Cyril Briggs: Guns, Bombs, Spooks and Writing the Revolution," forthcoming in *The Red and the Black: Revolutionary Lives of the Red and Black Atlantic*.

KATHLEEN PFEIFFER is Professor of English and Creative Writing at Oakland University in Rochester, Michigan. She has published a monograph, *Race Passing and American Individualism* (University of Massachusetts Press, 2001), an edited collection, *Brother Mine: The Correspondence of Jean Toomer and Waldo Frank* (University of Illinois Press, 2010), and has edited and introduced the re-issue of two Harlem Renaissance novels, *Nigger Heaven* by Carl Van Vechten, and *Holiday* by Waldo Frank. Her scholarship has appeared in *Women's Studies*, *African American Review*, *Legacy*, and *Modernism/modernity*, and she has written numerous biographical essays for the Scribner's American Writers Supplements. She was awarded the Kresge Artist Fellowship in 2012, and she won the Michigan Writers Chapbook Contest in 2018 for her memoir *Ink*.

SONYA POSMENTIER is Associate Professor of English at New York University. She is the author of *Cultivation and Catastrophe: The Lyric Ecology of Modern Black Literature* (Johns Hopkins University Press, 2017) and is a recipient of the MLA's William Sanders Scarborough award. She is at work on a new book, *Black Reading*, about the intersecting histories of black cultural studies and modern lyric theory. Her essays and articles have appeared in *The New York Times Book Review*, *American Literature*, *American Literary History*, *Public Books*, and *Syndicate*.

MARIEL RODNEY is an interdisciplinary scholar of Black Atlantic diasporic literature, performance, and visual culture. Her research and teaching interests span the literature of the Americas and the Caribbean, examining histories of race, gender, and sexuality. Her book manuscript explores the routes to freedom explored by artists and writers of the New Negro era. She currently teaches at SUNY Purchase.

JAMES SMETHURST is a Professor of Afro-American Studies at the University of Massachusetts Amherst. He is the author of *The New Red Negro: The Literary Left and African American Poetry, 1930–1946* (Oxford University Press, 1999), *The Black Arts Movement: Literary Nationalism in the 1960s and 1970s* (University of North Carolina Press, 2005), *The African American Roots of Modernism: From Reconstruction to the Harlem Renaissance* (University of North Carolina Press, 2011), and *Brick City Vanguard: Amiri Baraka, Black Music, Black Modernity* (University of Massachusetts Press, 2020). He also co-edited *Left of the Color Line: Race, Radicalism and Twentieth-Century Literature of the United States* (University of North Carolina Press, 2003), *Radicalism in the South Since Reconstruction* (Palgrave Macmillan, 2006), and *SOS – Calling All Black People: A Black Arts Movement Reader* (University of Massachusetts Press, 2014).

FIONNGHUALA SWEENEY works on African American and Caribbean literature and culture, with particular interests in slavery, emancipation, and anti-colonial radicalism. She has published widely on the work of Frederick Douglass, Ireland, and the Black Atlantic, afromodernisms, the visual arts, and the slave narrative, including the monograph *Frederick Douglass and the Atlantic World* (Liverpool University Press, 2007), and she is currently completing a book on Afromodern London. She teaches American and Black Atlantic literature at Newcastle University, UK.

MIRIAM THAGGERT teaches African American Literature in the Department of English at SUNY-Buffalo. She is the author of *Images of Black Modernism: Verbal and Visual Strategies of the Harlem Renaissance* (University of Massachusetts Press, 2010). Her essays have appeared in *African American Review*, *American Literary History*, *American Quarterly*, *Meridians*, and *Feminist Modernist Studies*.

SHANE VOGEL is Ruth N. Halls Professor of English at Indiana University. He is the author of *Stolen Time: Black Fad Performance and the Calypso Craze* (University of Chicago Press, 2018) and *The Scene of Harlem Cabaret: Race, Sexuality, Performance* (University of Chicago Press,

2009). He is co-editor (with Soyica Diggs Colbert and Douglas A. Jones, Jr.) of *Race and Performance after Repetition* (Duke University Press, 2020).

ANDREW WARNES is Professor of American Studies at the University of Leeds, UK. His work focuses on US literature, food studies, and the cultural traditions of the African Diaspora in the USA. He is the author of *How the Shopping Cart Explains Global Consumerism* (University of California Press, 2018), *American Tantalus* (Bloomsbury, 2014), and *Savage Barbecue: Race, Culture and the Invention of America's First Food* (University of Georgia Press, 2008).

MARK WHALAN was educated at the University of Warwick, the University of Durham, and the University of Exeter, and holds the Robert and Eve Horn Professorship of English at the University of Oregon. He is the author of *Race, Manhood, and Modernism in America: The Short Story Cycles of Sherwood Anderson and Jean Toomer* (University of Tennessee Press, 2007), *The Great War and the Culture of New Negro* (University Press of Florida, 2008), *American Culture in the 1910s* (Edinburgh University Press, 2010), and *World War One, American Literature, and the Federal State* (Cambridge University Press, 2018). He also edited *The Letters of Jean Toomer, 1919–1924* (University of Tennessee Press, 2006). His work has appeared in the *Journal of American Studies*, *American Literary History*, *Modernism/modernity*, *Modern Fiction Studies*, *American Art*, *MELUS*, and *African American Review*. He is currently at work editing *The Cambridge History of American Modernism*.

DANIEL G. WILLIAMS is Professor of English Literature and Director of the Richard Burton Centre for the Study of Wales at Swansea University. He is the author of *Wales Unchained: Literature, Politics and Identity in the American Century* (University of Wales Press, 2015), *Black Skin, Blue Books: African Americans and Wales 1845–1945* (University of Wales Press, 2012), and *Ethnicity and Cultural Authority: From Arnold to Du Bois* (Edinburgh University Press, 2006).

Acknowledgments

We are deeply indebted to the contributors for their sterling work, dedication, and patience. We owe a huge debt of gratitude to Deborah E. McDowell, a pioneer in the field of Harlem Renaissance studies, for her patience and insightful, thought-provoking afterword. We also wish to thank Ray Ryan, Edgar Mendez, and Natasha Burton at Cambridge University Press for their support, guidance, and patience.

We first met at a Modernist Studies Association roundtable organized by Adam McKible. We thank him for his warm friendship and dogged commitment to fostering collaborations among Harlem Renaissance scholars within the MSA.

Rachel would like to thank Ned Allen, David Anderson, Alice Barnaby, Celeste-Marie Bernier, Alan Bilton, Kirsti Bohata, Mick Gidley, Fiona Green, Nicole King, Roberta Magnani, Sarah Meer, Liz Herbert McAvoy, Eoin Price, Jay Prosser, Alan Rice, Fionnghuala Sweeney, Andrew Warnes, and Daniel G. Williams for their support. She would like to thank the Stuart A. Rose Library at Emory University and the Beinecke at Yale University for generous fellowships where she benefitted from the expertise and kindness of Randall K. Burkett and Melissa Barton. A big thank you is also due to her family and friends for their unflagging support.

Miriam would like to thank Bluford Adams, Florence Boos, Lori Branch, Corey Creekmur, Kathleen Diffley, Claire Fox, Nicole Morris Johnson, Teresa Magnum, Dee Morris, Judith Pascoe, Laura Rigal, Phillip Round, Anne Stapleton, Janette Taylor, and Doris Witt for their friendship and support. A fellowship at the Newberry Library was a wonderful opportunity that provided time, space, and supportive colleagues during the early stages of the volume. The Developmental Sciences Hybridoma Bank of the University of Iowa, which offers research fellowships for humanities projects, and the Virginia Humanities also provided fellowship support during the creation of this volume. Miriam would like to offer her deepest gratitude to her family and friends for their humor, generosity, and continuing support.

Introduction: Revising a Renaissance

Rachel Farebrother and Miriam Thaggert

In the popular imagination, the Harlem Renaissance is closely associated with the Jazz Age, with rent parties, clubs, cabarets, jazz, and blues. Langston Hughes did much to cement such views of the period, announcing in his autobiography *The Big Sea* (1940) that "it was the period when the Negro was in vogue," a spectacular cultural boom that came to a sudden halt with the onset of the Depression.[1] In fact, the Harlem Renaissance, or New Negro Movement, was characterized by remarkable diversity that cannot be limited to a linear narrative of boom and bust, and more fiction by black authors was published in the 1930s than in the 1920s.[2] The unprecedented flowering of black cultural production in visual art, literature, dance, and music from the late 1910s to the 1930s encompassed jazz and blues poetry by Sterling A. Brown and Langston Hughes, Zora Neale Hurston's lyrical renderings of folk culture in the South, George Schuyler's unusual blending of satire and science fiction in *Black No More* (1931), militant editorials in the *Messenger*, and modernist cover designs by such artists as Aaron Douglas and Laura Wheeler Waring.

From the outset, participants in the cultural awakening debated whether they were part of a movement and what that movement should be called; they also questioned the location, scope, and political implications of what some writers and intellectuals named the "Negro renaissance." Alain Locke's *The New Negro* (1925), a landmark anthology that brought together some of the most significant cultural figures of the era, including Countee Cullen, Rudolph Fisher, Zora Neale Hurston, Helene Johnson, Jean Toomer, Eric Walrond, and the artist Aaron Douglas, secured its canonical status by reinforcing the cultural nationalist agenda of the Harlem Renaissance. Locke sought to document a generational shift from white-authored representations that supplied a "mere external view [that is] . . . *about* the Negro rather than of him" toward "self-portraiture," "self-expression and the forces and motives of self-determination."[3] Framing the anthology with a dedication to "the Younger Generation" and the score

I

and lyrics of a line from a spiritual, "O, rise, shine for Thy Light is a' com-ing," Locke implied that his portrait of African American culture – which encompassed poetry, prose, drama, artwork, critical essays, art criticism, anthropology, folklore, and sociology – heralded a new era. For Houston A. Baker, Jr., the volume was "perhaps our first *national* book, offering not only a description of streams of tendency in our collective lives but also an actual construction within its pages of the sounds, songs, images, and signs of a nation."[4]

Locke's cultural nationalism chimed with James Weldon Johnson's famous statement in his preface to *The Book of American Negro Poetry* (1922) that the "final measure of the greatness of all peoples is the amount and standard of the literature and art they have produced,"[5] but plenty of their contemporaries were skeptical of such boosterism. Hubert Harrison, St. Crucian émigré and renowned Harlem radical, dismissed the idea of a "Negro Literary Renaissance" as the invention of "Greenwich Village neurotics" who exploited the vogue for black cultural expression "not for the black brothers' profit but for their own" and remained "blissfully ignorant of the stream of literary and artistic products which have flowed uninterruptedly from Negro writers from 1850 to the present."[6] In his 1926 essay "The Negro-Art Hokum," the novelist and journalist George Schuyler went so far as to condemn the very idea of "Negro art" for, as Darryl Dickson-Carr puts it, "unwittingly buying into the same racialist thinking as the Ku Klux Klan."[7] As well as courting controversy by calling the African American "merely a lampblacked Anglo-Saxon," Schuyler saw little evidence of a cultural renaissance: "Eager apostles from Greenwich Village, Harlem, and environs proclaimed a great renaissance of Negro art just around the corner waiting to be ushered on the scene. . . . Skeptics patiently waited. They still wait."[8] Younger artists, who rejected racial propaganda in favor of defiant self-expression and established new, if short-lived, magazines such as *Fire!!* (1926) and *Harlem* (1928), often deployed the term "New Negro" in quizzical, not wholly flattering terms. In her August 1926 "The Ebony Flute" column for *Opportunity* magazine, Gwendolyn Bennett even noted that Rudolph Fisher fêted his newborn son as "the new Negro."[9]

Notwithstanding such skepticism and sly, self-deprecating humor, the Harlem Renaissance was characterized by innovation and experimentation across a variety of disciplines and genres – in visual culture, magazines, poetry, drama, children's literature, music, and dance. It was shaped, in often quite complex ways, by the Great Migration, the Red Summer (the name given to the anti-black violence of 1919), the emergence of Boasian anthropology, the Great War, and the Depression. These forces gave rise to some of the best known and most widely studied African American literature to emerge in the twentieth century, including Zora Neale Hurston's *Their Eyes Were Watching God* (1937), Nella Larsen's *Passing* (1929), Jean Toomer's *Cane* (1923), and Langston Hughes's poetry. The fragmentation and warping of familiar genres that is so distinctive of *Cane*, for instance, stems, at least in part, from what Kobena Mercer has called "an understanding of African American identity as something that has itself been 'collaged' by the vicissitudes of modern history."[10] Take, for example, the startling, surreal description of "eddying," "swirling" blood overwhelming the "whitewashed"[11] order of "Seventh Street" in Washington, DC. Toomer's disorientating imagery at once captures the galvanizing impact of black migrants from the South upon modern urban culture[12] and recalls the Washington, DC "race riot" of 1919, in which African Americans resisted violent state repression, prompting leftwing newspapers like the *Crusader* and the *Messenger* to speculate on "the potential for revolutionary action in the display of black militancy."[13]

The literature, artwork, and music that emerged from the Harlem Renaissance or New Negro movement has occupied a central position in African American literary studies. As Cheryl A. Wall has explained, the first period courses in African American literature in the USA focused on the Harlem Renaissance at a time (the early 1970s) when "the very idea of a 'period' course in black literature seemed anomalous."[14] The reasons for this abiding fascination are complex, but many of the significant developments or "turns" in the field (relating to debates about the politics of representation, vernacular theories of black literature, black radicalism, transnationalism, feminism, and performance studies) have been developed through close analysis of Harlem Renaissance cultural expression. To take just one example, the vernacular-centered literary criticism pioneered by Henry Louis Gates, Jr. and Houston Baker, Jr. in the 1980s cast figures like Hurston and Hughes as exemplars of larger patterns and preoccupations within African American literature. In *The Signifying Monkey: A Theory of African-American Literary Criticism* (1988), for instance, Hurston's *Their Eyes Were Watching God* is showcased as a prime example of "the speakerly text," a term developed to describe a long tradition of black writers exploring the creative and political "possibilities of representation of the speaking black voice in writing."[15]

Essays such as W. E. B. Du Bois's "Criteria of Negro Art," Langston Hughes's "The Negro Artist and the Racial Mountain," and George Schuyler's "The Negro-Art Hokum" – which make respective cases for art as propaganda, the cultural distinctiveness of black American art, and the absence of any fundamental differences between black and white American art – lay bare some of the key disagreements that continue to animate debates about the politics of representation. Marita Bonner's 1925 *Crisis* essay "On Being Young – a Woman – and Colored," with its eloquent insistence that any examination of the relationship between art and politics must attend to questions of sexuality and gender, anticipates critical approaches developed by pioneering black feminists, including Barbara Christian, Akasha (Gloria) Hull, Deborah E. McDowell, Claudia Tate, and Cheryl A. Wall, from the 1970s. Indeed, an enduring tendency to sideline Bonner and other black women writers in critical accounts of Harlem Renaissance debates about "art or propaganda" signals the continuing salience of the black feminist project of "engendering the Harlem Renaissance [by] undoing perimeters that exclude women and their writing."[16]

This sense of debate – of revising and remaking a renaissance – is also evident in a long critical tradition of questioning the terminology, location, and time period of the movement. Sterling A. Brown was famously hostile to the term "Harlem Renaissance" because he viewed Harlem as "the show-window, the cashier's till" for a broader "New Negro movement [that] had temporal roots in the past and spatial roots elsewhere in America."[17] His criticism of a tendency to conflate the New Negro Renaissance with Harlem at the expense of more nuanced understanding of a cultural movement that extended from major urban centers like Washington, DC, Chicago, and New York to the urban and rural South, and the rural Midwest became a familiar refrain as critics discussed the merits of such terms as the Harlem Renaissance and the New Negro Renaissance. In 2013, Davarian Baldwin and Minkah Makalani's *Escape From New York: The New Negro Renaissance Beyond Harlem* situated black modernist literature and visual arts "within a much broader field of political resistance and cultural revolution that extended far beyond Harlem"[18] to Mexico City, Chicago, Havana, Kingston, Berlin, Colón, Paris, and London. In that collection, analysis of the New Negro movement as part of broader global political and cultural currents was developed in tandem with an examination of political, cultural, and intellectual aspects of the movement that have been obscured because of limiting assumptions about class, gender, and time period.

As Andrew Fearnley reminds us, the "'Harlem Renaissance' was neither a term nor a concept used by those who lived and wrote during the years it is now said to describe."[19] Most writers, artists, musicians, and performers conceived of the era in terms of aesthetic choices, political alignments, and generational differences. Reference to the Harlem Renaissance became more prevalent as historical notions of cultural periodization took hold in the academy from the 1940s, but it was institutionalized in academic scholarship in the 1970s, against the backdrop of the establishment of Black Studies programs across the USA.[20] It was in this context, according to Arnold Rampersad, that Nathan Huggins's landmark book *Harlem Renaissance* (1971) "virtually invented a sub-field in American and African-American intellectual history."[21] Later, David Levering Lewis's best-selling cultural history *When Harlem Was in Vogue* (1981) popularized a particular version of the Harlem Renaissance, "which has tended to emphasize U.S.-bound themes of cultural nationalism, civil rights protest, and uplift in the literary culture of the 'Harlem Renaissance.'"[22]

These influential monographs must be read alongside the writings of prominent black feminist scholars whose path-breaking research helped to redefine the period. In a 2001 retrospective on the Harlem Renaissance and how gender impacted the scholarly reconstruction of the period, Cheryl A. Wall surveys the scant engagement with women writers in the tomes by Nathan Huggins and David Levering Lewis, and the new critical frameworks developed by black feminist scholars to interpret writers like Zora Neale Hurston and Nella Larsen. In so doing, she demonstrates that "feminist interventions have changed our sense of what the Harlem Renaissance was."[23] Arguably, there is no other period in African American literary history that has benefitted so richly from the black feminist study of women writers in the 1970s and 1980s. After years of critical neglect, Jessie Fauset, Zora Neale Hurston, and Nella Larsen now occupy a central place in the canon. In the wake of this transformative scholarship, Hurston became so pivotal to black feminist writing in the 1980s and early 1990s that Ann duCille went so far as to coin the term "Hurstonism" to describe a cultural phenomenon that itself provoked critical commentary from Hazel Carby and Michele Wallace, among others.[24] In an ironic echo of the dismissive reviews of Hurston's fiction by Sterling A. Brown and Richard Wright in the 1930s, Carby turned to politics to explain Hurston's popularity, claiming that "representation of African-American culture as primarily rural and oral" facilitated a retreat from engagement with racism and structural inequality in late twentieth-century US society.[25]

Since the 1920s, retrospective accounts of the Harlem Renaissance have continued to debate the terminology, focus, and political and cultural impact of the movement. Langston Hughes's description of the Harlem Renaissance in *The Big Sea* as a "vogue" – propelled into motion by the "pre-Charleston kick" of the popular musical *Shuffle Along* before it "spread to books, African sculpture, music, and dancing"[26] – sought to take stock of the movement with the benefit of hindsight. Looking back at the 1920s from the perspective of 1940, when social protest fiction by the likes of Richard Wright was in the ascendant, Hughes presented the Harlem Renaissance as somewhat superficial because it neither disrupted the de facto segregation of New York nor impinged upon the lives of working-class American Americans. "The ordinary Negroes hadn't heard of the Negro Renaissance," he famously wrote. "And if they had, it hadn't raised their wages any."[27] In fiction, Wallace Thurman's *Infants of the Spring* (1932), a *roman à clef* about a whole household of aspiring artists, singers, and writers from the younger generation, tells a rather pessimistic story of failed promise, decadence, and untapped potential, which culminates in the suicide of the most talented artist of the group, the queer painter Paul Arbian. Presenting his suicide as a kind of performance piece, Paul has decorated the "dingy calcimined wall" of his bathroom with a group of his portraits and "carpeted the floor with sheets of paper" from his unfinished novel before slitting his wrists.[28] Sadly, this attempt to garner publicity for his work is doomed because the manuscript has turned into an illegible, "sodden mass" (186). A "gruesome yet fascinating spectacle" (185), Paul's suicide accords with Thurman's broader critique of the destructive impact of the "white light of publicity" upon black artists (128).

The twenty-first century has witnessed a series of remarkable "discoveries" of previously unpublished or lost works by significant figures, which capture the shifting parameters of Harlem Renaissance studies, its endless capacity to make and remake itself. The list of newly found material includes Zora Neale Hurston's *Barracoon* (composed in 1927 and 1931, and published in 2018), Claude McKay's *Amiable with Big Teeth* (written in the late 1930s and published in 2017), and *Romance in Marseille* ("buried in the archive," according to its publisher, and published in 2020), Edward Christopher Williams's *The Letters of Davy Carr* (published anonymously in the *Messenger* in 1926 and republished in 2004 under the title *When Washington was in Vogue*), and several Langston Hughes poems written on the flyleaf of the 1929 *An Anthology of Revolutionary Poetry* (published in *Poetry* in 2009). These posthumously published texts underline how conceptions of the Harlem Renaissance have been shaped and reshaped by an urgent project of recovering and honoring a lost, neglected archive, but they also embody what William J. Maxwell has seen as a "transtemporal turn" that is attuned to the cultural and political possibilities of "various models of elongated renaissance time."[29]

In this spirit, the Harlem Renaissance – which was perhaps the first time when it was possible to discern the "emergence of an African-American literary and artistic *field* as such, with many competing positions and new forms of institutional support"[30] – has continued to inspire artists, filmmakers, and writers across the twentieth and into the twenty-first century. In an essay on "Richard Bruce Nugent and the Queer Memory of Harlem," Dorothea Löbberman concentrates on "queer moments of 'touch' between the early and late twentieth century," analyzing Nugent's novel *Gentleman Jigger*, which was begun in the 1920s, but published only in 2008, and the "queer temporalities" of films about the Harlem Renaissance, such as Isaac Julien's *Looking for Langston* (1989) and *Brother to Brother* (2004), directed by Rodney Evans.[31] This kind of creative reinterpretation of the Harlem Renaissance, which overlays diverse referents and historical moments to disrupt linear chronology, is not limited to narratives about queer Harlem. Racial passing narratives of the 1920s have inspired diverse creative responses from Heidi Durrow's subtle revision of Larsen's *Passing* in her novel about interracial girlhood, *The Girl who Fell From the Sky* (2010), to the inventive amalgamation of the genres of the passing novel and detective fiction in Mat Johnson's and Warren Pleece's graphic novel *Incognegro* (2008) to the narrative hints of *Passing* in Karla F. C. Holloway's mystery tale *A Death in Harlem* (2019). LaShonda Katrice Barnett's historical novel *Jam on the Vine* (2015) has explored the transnational dimensions of the New Negro movement in a manner that resonates with contemporary debates about black masculinity, the New Jim Crow, and mass incarceration.

Creative re-imaginings of the Harlem Renaissance initiate a complex process of re-reading, which demands engagement with the specific historical and cultural contexts from which New Negro culture emerged and a fluid, capacious critical framework for analyzing its reception, revision, and reinterpretation. The enduring potency of Harlem Renaissance literature – the protean qualities that prompt contemporary poets such as Evie Shockley to draw upon black feminist modernist writers like Anne Spencer to disrupt narratives of progress[32] underscores the extent to which formulations of the New Negro were characterized by fluidity and dynamism from the outset.

Even those writers associated with the more conservative wing of the Harlem Renaissance placed considerable stress upon the inner diversity and dynamism of black culture as they defined the contours of a cultural renaissance. In the past few decades, Alain Locke has quite rightly been taken to task for scant engagement with "the material foundations of racism,"[33] which included a studied refusal to acknowledge Harlem's position as a transnational hub for black militancy and radicalism that flourished in the wake of the October Revolution of 1917 and the Red Summer of 1919.[34] Yet Locke's careful curation of the "ripening forces as culled from the first fruits of the Negro Renaissance"[35] in *The New Negro* entailed insistent emphasis upon diversity. For Locke, Harlem – a transcultural black capital galvanized by the migration of black southerners to New York, the relocation of downtown black New Yorkers into what "is – or promises at least to be – a race capital,"[36] and immigration from across the black diaspora, most notably the Caribbean[37] – symbolized a broader process of cultural reconfiguration: "what began in terms of segregation becomes more and more, as its elements mix and react, the laboratory of a great race-welding."[38] This famous statement is typical of Locke's glancing engagement with segregation and racism, but it also encapsulates his characterization of the New Negro as a figure in transition, in process, and in the making. In retrospective discussions of the 1920s, Locke consistently defended what he saw as the guiding philosophy of the New Negro movement: fluid, dynamic cultural representations that resisted what James Weldon Johnson called the "fixing effects"[39] of US racial ideologies based upon segregation and separation.

Over and again, Locke identified fluidity and expansiveness as foundational concepts: "The most deliberate aspect of the New Negro formulation – and it is to be hoped, its crowning wisdom – was just this repudiation of any and all one-formula solutions of the race question."[40] Taking issue with blanket dismissals of the New Negro movement as politically quietist, he asserted that the "indefiniteness" of the figure was "due to a deliberate decision not to define the 'New Negro' dogmatically."[41] Looking beyond Locke, a stress upon dynamism and cultural complexity emerges as a cardinal principle in Harlem Renaissance expression more broadly. In her landmark essay for Nancy Cunard's *Negro* (1934) anthology, "Characteristics of Negro Expression," for instance, Zora Neale Hurston hailed improvisation and assemblage as guiding principles of black cultural expression. Hurston's essay, which examines drama, dialect, the jook, dancing, and folklore, argues that African American culture comprises "segments" that do not quite cohere: "There is always rhythm," she writes, "but it is the rhythm of segments. Each unit has a rhythm of its own, but when the whole is assembled it is lacking in symmetry."[42]

Notwithstanding such capaciousness, there is sometimes a tendency to be somewhat dismissive of the field of Harlem Renaissance studies. Perhaps this is because, when compared to other fields of African American literature, the stakes of the debate that animated both the Harlem Renaissance and its subsequent scholarly analysis were not life and death as is the case for other period studies of African American literature. The Harlem Renaissance debated not freedom or incarceration, mortality and memory, but rather "art or propaganda." Yet there is something troubling about dismissing Harlem Renaissance studies – whether one calls it that or the more "serious" name of the New Negro movement. The period was the first in African American literary history in which artists and writers boldly claimed and exhibited, collectively, a self-confidence in their representation of blackness that would not be replicated until, arguably, the Black Arts Movement of the late 1960s and 1970s. Hughes's statement, in "The Negro Artist and the Racial Mountain," that the younger artists "stand on top of the mountain, free within ourselves"[43] – an image that is suggestive of the liberatory possibilities of self-expression – prefigures Black Arts Movement scholar Stephen Henderson's recognition that poets such as Amiri Baraka and Larry Neal value "the process of self-definition made clearer and sharper" because it could be "raised to the level of revolutionary thought."[44]

For all the emphasis upon failure in early scholarship, the Harlem Renaissance has been, to some extent, a victim of its own success. As Cherene Sherrard-Johnson notes, the Harlem Renaissance is a powerful "brand" that "continues simultaneously to conjoin utopia and lament."[45] Even so, the romanticized story of the Harlem Renaissance (and the ensuing suspicion of the field that has followed in its wake) has left its imprint on critical interpretations of the period. For one thing, the assumption that publication was an easy feat for the black writer was not correct, as Langston Hughes reminds us: "All of us know that the gay and sparkling life of the so-called Negro Renaissance of the '20s was not so gay and sparkling beneath the surface as it looked."[46] Langston Hughes was one of the few Harlem Renaissance writers who managed to make a living as a writer, and the economic precariousness of his position is on full display in *The Big Sea*, which is animated by a sustained preoccupation with the various ways that a lack of money curtailed artistic experimentation.[47] Such precarity was even more acute for black women writers and artists. The writer, artist, educator, and activist Gwendolyn Bennett, for instance, faced considerable constraints upon her ambitions as an artist, including family demands, economic uncertainty, FBI surveillance, and the debilitating effects of what Jessie Fauset, in a 1922 essay entitled "Some Notes on Color," called "the teasing uncertainty" generated by racism.[48] Fauset's poignant observations about how "the puzzling, tangling, nerve-wracking consciousness of color envelops and swathes us"[49] resonate with Bennett's anxious letters to Langston Hughes about her artistic ambitions when she was studying in Paris in the mid-1920s, and her determined efforts, in "The Ebony Flute" column for *Opportunity* (1926–1928), to foster a collaborative, nurturing artistic community by way of "literary chit-chat and artistic what-not."[50] More broadly, in spite of the popular fascination with "the gay 20s," many of the now canonical books of the period – including Larsen's *Quicksand* and *Passing*, and Thurman's *The Blacker the Berry* and *Infants of the Spring* – are populated with characters suffering from trauma, depression, and melancholy. Another paradox is that the most humorous writer of the period, Rudolph Fisher, was until recently one of the least studied.

The scope of scholarship on the Harlem Renaissance has been transformed by the insights of transnationalism and diaspora studies, queer theory, performance theory, feminisms, leftist criticism, and periodical studies, among others, and each generation has re-made the field in line with its own preoccupations. Such reassessments have prompted some critics to jettison the familiar but contested moniker the "Harlem Renaissance" because of its cultural nationalist and exceptionalist connotations.[51] For all of the debate about terminology, there is a durable utility to this particular phrase. As Sherrard-Johnson notes, the Harlem Renaissance remains useful as "a field-defining term," "not only because of its currency in academic and popular culture, but because of its suppleness."[52] *A History of the Harlem Renaissance* aims to expand the boundaries of the subject further in ways that reflect developments in contemporary scholarship: by examining the significance of the eclecticism and variety of Harlem Renaissance expression in literature, visual culture, popular culture, music, dance, and politics; by going beyond well-known genres to explore genre fiction, film, children's literature, the *roman à clef*, the bildungsroman, biography, and the short story; by revising conventional assumptions about the period, such as location, time period, and terminology; and by attending to tensions and fissures that animate New Negro culture and politics, especially with reference to gender and sexuality. Substantial attention is also paid to the performative aspects of the period (such as dance and music) and the art and aesthetic practices of the movement. Taken as a whole, the volume provides new accounts, interpretations, and critical approaches, which attend to the diversity of the period, its distinctive mix of the militant, the satirical, the lyrical, and the modern. Given the range and scope of black expression in the Harlem Renaissance period, and its multiple cultural and political legacies, the volume could hardly aim for comprehensiveness. Instead, it seeks to capture in its dynamics some of the ways in which contemporary critics participate in a long tradition of revising, re-reading, and remaking the Harlem Renaissance.

A central aim of *A History of the Harlem Renaissance* is to reconsider the significance of genre and form to Harlem Renaissance cultural expression. In its attention to magazines, letters, sculpture, fine art, dance, the essay, the manifesto, children's literature, the *roman à clef*, the *Bildungsroman*, the magazine, drama, book jacket designs and illustrations, and newspaper advertisements, the *History* seeks to at once encapsulate and analyze the eclecticism of Harlem Renaissance cultural expression. Early scholarship on the Harlem Renaissance tended to privilege fiction and vernacular poetry over other genres, but more recent criticism has been attuned to the political, social, and aesthetic significance of writers' and artists' formal choices. Much of this scholarship has explored the dynamic interplay between word and image, especially in collaborative illustrated anthologies and magazines, including *Opportunity*, *The Crisis*, *Fire!!*, and *The New Negro*.[53] This focus on the visual culture of the period has emerged alongside a growing interest in the politics of genre in black Atlantic literature.[54]

Inspired by these new interpretive foci, the volume is animated by a concerted effort to remap and reconsider conventional ideas about the New Negro movement and to enrich the study of African American, US, and black diasporic literatures by offering diverse approaches and readings. This commitment to various critical approaches also characterizes the treatment of specific authors and topics, which are explored across the whole collection from multiple critical perspectives, including gender theory, queer theory, transnationalism and diaspora studies, and performance theory. Although some chapters are devoted to a single author or topic, individual works or authors are often examined from more than one angle, an approach that takes it cue from James Weldon Johnson's insistence, in *Black Manhattan* (1930), that multiple perspectives are fine "so long as one view is not taken to be the whole picture."[55]

The volume is divided into four sections that spotlight how a project of remaking and reinterpretation animates both New Negro cultural expression and the contributors' readings of the New Negro Renaissance. The first section, "Re-reading the New Negro" provides a variety of interpretative lenses through which to reassess the Harlem Renaissance. Daniel G. Williams takes aim at an enduring tendency to view nationalism as an ideology based on notions of purity and segregation, addressing cultural nationalism and cosmopolitanism in works by Duke Ellington, Jean Toomer, and Zora Neale Hurston. Clare Corbould details how New Negro poets explored the topic of enslavement, creating in the process a new archive of enslaved people's experiences and narratives. Kathleen Pfeiffer examines the complex ways in which interracial friendships shaped some Harlem Renaissance literature, with a particular focus on Jean Toomer and Waldo Frank, and Nella Larsen and Carl Van Vechten. Mark Whalan assesses the *Bildungsroman* as an important site for African American authors to consider the Jim Crow logics of what childhood and maturation meant in the USA. In the final chapter of this section, Caroline Goeser turns her attention to visual artists such as Aaron Douglas, Gwendolyn Bennett, and Richard Bruce Nugent, who worked alongside writers, cultural leaders, editors, and publishers to radically re-picture Black American identity – to make the modern Black.

The second section, "Experimenting with the New Negro," explores various kinds of innovation in New Negro writing and its cultural after-lives, with a particular focus on black women writers who have tended to occupy a marginal position in debates about the avant-garde. Sonya Posmentier tracks the lasting influence of Harlem Renaissance writers on Gwendolyn Brooks's poetry, tracing in Brooks's work the development of a tradition of black migratory poetics: poetry that formally and imagina-tively enacts human transnational movement. Sinéad Moynihan focuses on *romans à clef* of the Harlem Renaissance. She argues that Wallace Thurman's *Infants of the Spring* (1932) and Richard Bruce Nugent's *Gentleman Jigger* (2008), read together, foreground the tensions between originality and derivativeness, individual "genius" and collaboration that were being negotiated more broadly in modernist art of the period. Fionnghuala Sweeney interprets Eslanda Goode Robeson's *Paul Robeson, Negro* (1930) as a rare instance of modernist biography, one in which the politics of manhood sits center stage. She situates the narrative as a pioneering act of authorship that engages with broader debates about the politics of art – by constructing Paul Robeson as an exemplary mascu-line subject – while also introducing a shadow narrative that lays bare the hidden costs of such gendered formulations of black cultural and political leadership. Through analysis of poetry by Angelina Weld Grimké, Gwendolyn Bennett, and Mae V. Cowdery, Maureen Honey contends that the erotic lyric or erotically charged pastoral verse largely defined for

New Negro women poets what it meant to be a modern (and modernist) writer. Finally, Katharine Capshaw explores the variety of literature available to young people during the Harlem Renaissance, focusing on periodicals, community theater, black-owned publications, and mainstream publishing houses with an interracial audience. Texts embraced a new vision of African American children as sophisticated, capable, knowledgeable, and courageous; because literacy rates for young people often outmatched those of adults, children were imagined as cultural leaders who would help reinvent the black community.

The third section, "Remapping the New Negro," intervenes in critical debates about the significance of place in Harlem Renaissance culture, juxtaposing analyses that explore the movement in relation to the transnational, the national, and the local. It begins with James Smethurst's examination of the interplay between black political and cultural activists in Britain and the USA during the New Negro era and the creation of black internationalist networks as a subset of what he calls the Black Bolshevik Renaissance. Jak Peake turns to Harlem, noting that New York in this period was part of a Caribbean network that is both represented, and partially downplayed, in New Negro writing and historiography. He analyzes a rarely discussed Caribbean backstory to the symposium on Negro art that W. E. B. Du Bois ran in *The Crisis* through much of 1926. Noelle Morrissette interprets James Weldon Johnson's *God's Trombones* (1927) as an endeavor to draw upon "symbols from within" African American folk and vernacular forms, and also from within the nation's regions, to advance a national African American culture. Turning from the national and the regional to the local, Jonathan Munby argues that Rudolph Fisher – who was unique among Harlem Renaissance writers in making Harlem itself the exclusive focus of his writing – demonstrated keen powers of social observation in revealing how class, regional, phenotypical, and generational distinctions defined Harlem.

The final section, "Performing the New Negro," reaches beyond literature to examine the performative aspects of the period (such as dance and film) and the visual art and aesthetic practices of the movement. There is a particular focus upon interartistic texts and the productive creative tensions generated by the interplay of different aesthetic modes and techniques. Mariel Rodney examines Hurston's early plays, arguing that they are a testing ground for the theories about culture she would later develop in her novels and essays. Hannah Durkin offers another revisionist reading of Hurston, exploring Hurston's film footage of the US South in counterpoint to her first ethnography *Mules and Men*

(1935) to elucidate some of the connections between Hurston's anthropological and creative work. Andrew Warnes examines the literary portrayal of music to illuminate the term "orinphrasis," or the description of sound or music in narrative or poems. Rachel Farebrother studies the literary representation of dancers, particularly child dancers, in Harlem Renaissance fiction and visual culture, arguing that this focus can help explore anxieties about generational conflict, gender, sexuality, tradition, and urban life. Wendy Martin's chapter provides an overview of the role of jazz during the period, noting the musical genre's beginnings in African music patterns and its migration to unexpected areas such as Chicago and California. Shane Vogel details Alain Locke's contributions to value theory and its relationship to the overall cultural project of the Harlem Renaissance. Vogel argues that Locke viewed the New Negro Renaissance and the transvaluation of black árt – that is, the re-estimation of its value according to new principles of judgment – as one moment in a deeper and ongoing axiological transformation. To do so, the essay looks at Locke's writings on African American spirituals and his "cultural retrospectives" of the 1930s and 1940s (annual reviews that took stock of the year's work in black themes) as exemplary instances of such transvaluation. In these writings, Locke continually revised the significance and boundaries of the Harlem Renaissance.

The volume closes with an afterword by one of the leading scholars of the study of the Harlem Renaissance, Deborah McDowell, whose research has been instrumental in shaping the field. Using her sharp feminist eye, McDowell assesses the chapters in the volume and examines what, collectively, they portend for the future of Harlem Renaissance or New Negro studies.

As we approach nearly a hundred years of reading about the New Negro, we need to understand how new interpretations of the New Negro movement can be woven and threaded with, or challenge, the other, more familiar versions of the Jazz Age to anticipate what a new century augurs for the study of "the New Negro." Perhaps we should view the term "renaissance" not as a limiting description of the period of black creativity but in its more literal meaning of revival or re-birth. For the New Negro Renaissance, to combine the terms by which the period is best known, is in fact still being renewed and re-read. The twenty chapters that follow capture something of the excitement of this contemporary revision. The New Negro Renaissance or New Negro Movement or Harlem Renaissance has lived up to its name: it is continually being re-born, re-made, and revisited.

Notes

1. Langston Hughes, *The Big Sea* (1940; New York: Hill and Wang, 1993), 228.
2. George Hutchinson, "The Novel of the Negro Renaissance," in *The Cambridge Companion to the African American Novel*, ed. Maryemma Graham (Cambridge: Cambridge University Press, 2004), 51.
3. Alain Locke, "Foreword," in *The New Negro* (1925; New York: Touchstone, 1997), xxv.
4. Houston A. Baker, Jr., *Modernism and the Harlem Renaissance* (Chicago: University of Chicago Press, 1987), 85.
5. James Weldon Johnson, "Preface," in *The Book of American Negro Poetry*, ed. James Weldon Johnson (New York: Harcourt, Brace, 1922), vii.
6. Hubert Harrison, "No Negro Literary Renaissance" [1927], in *A Hubert Harrison Reader*, ed. Jeffrey B. Perry (Middletown, CT: Wesleyan University Press, 2001), 354, 352.
7. Darryl Dickson-Carr, *Spoofing the Modern: Satire in the Harlem Renaissance* (Columbia: University of South Carolina Press, 2015), 50.
8. George S. Schuyler, "The Negro-Art Hokum" [1926], in *The Norton Anthology of African American Literature*, ed. Henry Louis Gates, Jr. and Nellie Y. McKay (New York: Norton, 2004), 1219.
9. Gwendolyn Bennett, "The Ebony Flute," *Opportunity* (August 1926): 261.
10. Kobena Mercer, "Romare Bearden, 1964: Collage as Kuntswollen," in *Cosmopolitan Modernisms*, ed. Kobena Mercer (Cambridge, MA: MIT Press, 2005), 125.
11. Jean Toomer, *Cane*, ed. George Hutchinson (New York: Penguin Classics, 2019), 51.
12. See Farah J. Griffin, *Who Set You Flowin'?: The African-American Migration Narrative* (New York: Oxford University Press, 1995) for an illuminating account of the emergence of the African American migration narrative and migratory poetics during the New Negro Renaissance.
13. Barbara Foley, *Jean Toomer: Race, Repression, and Revolution* (Urbana: University of Illinois Press, 2014), 224.
14. Cheryl A. Wall, "Histories and Heresies: Engendering the Harlem Renaissance," *Meridians* 2, no. 1 (2001): 63.
15. Henry Louis Gates, Jr., *The Signifying Monkey: A Theory of African-American Literary Criticism* (Oxford: Oxford University Press, 1988), xxv. See, also, Baker, *Modernism and the Harlem Renaissance*.
16. Wall, "Histories and Heresies," 68.
17. Sterling A. Brown, "The New Negro in Literature (1925–1955)," in *A Son's Return: Selected Essays of Sterling A. Brown*, ed. Mark A. Sanders (Boston: Northeastern University Press, 1996), 185.
18. Davarian L. Baldwin, "Introduction: New Negroes Forging a New World," in *Escape from New York: The New Negro Renaissance Beyond Harlem*, ed. Davarian Baldwin and Minkah Makalani (Minneapolis: University of Minnesota Press, 2013), 19.

19. Andrew M. Fearnley, "When the Harlem Renaissance Became Vogue: Periodization and the Organization of Postwar American Historiography," *Modern Intellectual History* 11, no. 1 (2014): 62.

20. Jak Peake, "'Watching the Waters': Tropic Flows in the Harlem Renaissance, Black Internationalism and Other Currents," *Radical Americas* 3, no. 1 (2018): 24.

21. Ibid., 25.

22. Brent Hayes Edwards, *The Practice of Diaspora: Literature, Translation, and the Rise of Black Internationalism* (Cambridge, MA: Harvard University Press, 2003), 3.

23. Wall, "Histories and Heresies," 62.

24. Ann duCille, *The Coupling Convention: Sex, Text, and Tradition in Black Women's Fiction* (Oxford: Oxford University Press, 1993), 11.

25. Hazel Carby, "The Politics of Fiction, Anthropology, and the Folk: Zora Neale Hurston," in *New Essays on Their Eyes Were Watching God*, ed. Michael Awkward (Cambridge: Cambridge University Press, 1990), 76.

26. Hughes, *The Big Sea*, 224.

27. Ibid., 228.

28. Wallace Thurman, *Infants of the Spring* (1932; London: X Press, 1998), 186. Hereafter cited parenthetically.

29. William J. Maxwell, "Questionnaire Response," *Modernism/modernity* 23, no. 3 (2013): 447.

30. George Hutchinson, "Harlem Central," *American Literary History* 23, no. 2 (2011): 407.

31. Dorothea Löbberman, "Richard Bruce Nugent and the Queer Memory of Harlem," in *Race Capital? Harlem as Setting and Symbol*, ed. Andrew M. Fearnley and Daniel Matlin (New York: Columbia University Press, 2019), 223.

32. Evie Shockley, *the new black* (Middletown, CT: Wesleyan University Press, 2012).

33. Barbara Foley, *Spectres of 1919: Class and Nation in the Making of the New Negro* (Urbana: University of Illinois Press, 2003), 153.

34. New York was home to the headquarters for Marcus Garvey's United Negro Improvement Association, the Brotherhood of Sleeping Car Porters, the African Blood Brotherhood, and the black socialist groups around the *Messenger* magazine. As Winston James has shown, the remarkable concentration of radical newspapers in Harlem – including the *Crusader*, the *Messenger*, and the *Negro World* – demonstrates that it had "developed a rich and radical print culture as one facet of a 'black public sphere' of unrivaled scale and intricacy." Winston James, "Harlem's Difference," in *Race Capital?*, ed. Fearnley and Matlin, 125.

35. Locke, "Foreword," in *The New Negro*, xxvii.

36. Locke, "The New Negro," in *The New Negro*, 7.

37. In the 1920s, approximately one in four black Harlemites was born outside the USA. See Fearnley and Daniel Matlin, "Introduction," in *Race Capital?*, 4.

38. Locke, "New Negro," 7.
39. Johnson, "Preface," xl.
40. Alain Locke, "The Negro: 'New' or Newer: A Retrospective Review of the Literature of the Negro for 1938" [1939], in *The Critical Temper of Alain Locke: A Selection of His Essays on Art and Culture*, ed. Jeffrey C. Stewart (New York: Garland, 1983), 272.
41. Ibid.
42. Zora Neale Hurston, "Characteristics of Negro Expression" [1934], in *Zora Neale Hurston, Folklore, Memoirs, and Other Writings*, ed. Cheryl A. Wall (New York: Library of America, 1995), 835.
43. Langston Hughes, "The Negro Artist and the Racial Mountain" [1926], in *The Norton Anthology of African American Literature*, ed. Gates, Jr. and McKay, 1314.
44. Stephen Henderson, *Understanding the New Black Poetry: Black Speech and Black Music as Poetic References* (New York: William Morrow and Company, 1973), 16.
45. Cherene Sherrard-Johnson, "Introduction: Harlem as Shorthand: The Persistent Value of the Harlem Renaissance," in *A Companion to the Harlem Renaissance*, ed. Cherene Sherrard-Johnson (Chichester, UK: Wiley-Blackwell, 2015), 4.
46. Hughes, *The Big Sea*, 227.
47. Take, for example, his account in *The Big Sea* of the economic burden carried by Wallace Thurman and some other contributors as a result of their involvement in the experimental magazine *Fire!!*: "That taught me a lesson about little magazines. But since white folks had them, we Negroes thought we could have one, too. But we didn't have the money" (238).
48. Jessie Fauset, "Some Notes on Color," *The World Tomorrow* (March 1922): 76–77. Repr. *Harlem Renaissance: A Gale Critical Companion, Vol. 2*, 366. http://encyjudaica.com/pdf/samples/sp666181.pdf.
49. Ibid., 367.
50. Bennett, "The Ebony Flute," 260.
51. In *The Practice of Diaspora*, Brent Hayes Edwards consistently signals his wariness of the term "Harlem Renaissance," noting in a footnote that he occasionally uses the term, but primarily as "a means to approach critically the scholarship that has accepted it." Edwards, *The Practice of Diaspora*, 322, n. 8.
52. Sherrard-Johnson, "Introduction: Harlem as Shorthand," 2–3.
53. See, for example, Anne E. Carroll, *Word, Image, and the New Negro: Representation and Identity in the Harlem Renaissance* (Bloomington: Indiana University Press, 2005); Caroline Goeser, *Picturing the New Negro: Harlem Renaissance Print Culture and Modern Black Identity* (Lawrence: University Press of Kansas, 2007); Cherene Sherrard-Johnson, *Portraits of the New Negro Woman: Visual and Literary Culture in the Harlem* Renaissance (New Brunswick: Rutgers University Press, 2007); Miriam Thaggert, *Images of Black Modernism: Verbal and Visual Strategies of the Harlem Renaissance* (Amherst: University of Massachusetts Press, 2010).

54. See, for example, Yogita Goyal, *Romance, Diaspora, and Black Atlantic Literature* (Cambridge: Cambridge University Press, 2010) and Sonya Posmentier, *Cultivation and Catastrophe: The Lyric Ecology of Modern Black Literature* (Baltimore: Johns Hopkins University Press, 2017).

55. James Weldon Johnson, *Black Manhattan* (1930; New York: Arno Press, 1968), 281.

PART I

Re-reading the New Negro

CHAPTER I

Cultural Nationalism and Cosmopolitanism in the Harlem Renaissance

Daniel G. Williams

Ishmael Reed, whose fascination with the Harlem Renaissance informed his celebrated novel *Mumbo Jumbo* (1972), claims that "multiculturalism in the United States has come to mean everybody but blacks."[1] While "white" America is subdivided into various hyphenated identities – Italian-American, Irish-American, and so on – "black" or "African American" functions to homogenize that which Reed describes as the most multi-ethnic group of all.[2] This chapter attempts to explore the relationship between cultural nationalism and cosmopolitanism during the Harlem Renaissance in the light of Reed's claim.

Two common metaphors have been deployed in order to illustrate the opposing positions within the debate on multiculturalism. The first is the "melting pot," a metaphor for the assimilationist ideal in which peoples jettison their particularities and blend into one culture. The second is the "salad bowl." This is preferred by contemporary multiculturalists for it is not based on assimilation, but rather on the co-existence of different cultures.[3] The ingredients within the salad can cohabit within the same space, but can also retain their distinctiveness. Both symbols speak to significant strains within liberal and progressive cultural thought, and both are threatened by exclusionary forms of racism. Yet Reed's comment forces us to ask a more fundamental question: what constitutes the "pot" or the "bowl" itself?

Werner Sollors has noted that the "very language used to create national unity and a sense of coherence" via the assimilationist "melting pot" can also serve "to support the ethnogenesis of regional and ethnic groups that could challenge national unity."[4] Minorities may resist assimilation by claiming a distinctive pot or bowl of their own, thus emphasizing their own internal diversity and ability to integrate others. Indeed, the desire to foreground their hybrid, multicultural credentials has been a characteristic of minority literatures. Alain Locke, for example, described Harlem as "the laboratory of a great race-welding" and attempted to capture its diversity in his seminal *The New Negro* (1925) anthology that seemed to offer a catalogue of the intra-ethnic diversity of African America.[5] In Harlem, African America was itself the "bowl" or "pot" with the potential to confer what Locke described as "culture-citizenship" on its members.[6] Later critics, such as Houston A. Baker, have described Locke's anthology as an unambiguously "nationalist" text, constructing within its diverse pages the sounds, songs, images, and signs of a distinctive African American "nation."[7]

If *The New Negro* anthology seemed to gesture toward a form of "culture-citizenship," Locke's term also draws our attention to the lack of a distinctive territorial, linguistic, or political frame for African American claims to "nationhood." Indeed, the grounds on which Locke could make his famous statement of 1925 that "Harlem has the same role to play for the New Negro as Dublin has had for the New Ireland or Prague for the New Czechoslovakia" were somewhat unclear.[8] That sentence's first clause is often omitted. It reads: "Without pretense to their political significance." However, had Prague not become the capital city of the new Czechoslovakia in 1918 following the collapse of the Hapsburg Empire, and had Dublin not become the capital of the Irish Free State in 1922, what "role" precisely would these cities have played? Can cultural activity be seen to be "nationalist" if it is not projecting some form of political independent statehood? If their "political significance" is occluded, on what basis is the comparison between Harlem, Prague, and Dublin made? Given that African American nationalism could not lead to the kind of independent statehood achieved by Czechoslovakia and Ireland, did it in fact amount to what W. E. B. Du Bois described as "assimilation *through* self-assertion"; an emphasis on the "gift" or "contribution" that black America could make to the larger American nation?[9] Or, again adopting Du Bois, was the nationalism of the Harlem Renaissance primarily engaged in the "conservation" of the race; a cultural resistance to assimilation into the American melting pot?[10] The ways in which these questions were answered tell us much about the relationship between cultural nationalism and cosmopolitanism within the Harlem Renaissance.

Black, Brown and Beige: Duke Ellington

In an article of 1934 entitled "Towards a Critique of Negro Music," Alain Locke called for "constructive criticism and discriminating appreciation" so that the standard of Negro music could be raised "far above the curb-stone values of the market-place," making it "far more exacting than the easy favor of the multitude."[11] In both its aspirations for African American art and its denigration of "the multitude," Locke's article was a late expression of the cultural values informing the more conservative wing of the Harlem Renaissance. While writers such as Langston Hughes would seek to root their works in the lives of the "multitude," the dominant view had been established by writers such as James Weldon Johnson who famously prefaced his *Book of American Negro Poetry* (1922) by noting that the "final measure of the greatness of all peoples is the amount and standard of the literature and art they have produced," an argument reinforced by Locke who believed that the "greatest rehabilitation" of the "Negro" would be "in terms of his artistic endowments and cultural contributions."[12] In the "Foreword" to *The New Negro*, Locke emphasized that "nine-tenths" of the "voluminous literature" on the Negro is "about" rather than "of" him, and encouraged a shift from external observation to "the internal world" of "artistic self-expression."[13] Sitting among the capacity crowd of 3,000 at Carnegie Hall on January 23, 1943, listening to Duke Ellington perform his new forty-five minute "tone parallel to the History of the American Negro" entitled *Black, Brown and Beige* at a benefit concert for Russian War Relief, Locke might have considered that the cultural aspirations that had informed his writings for over twenty years had now been realized.[14] For, in keeping with Locke's desire for a shift of perspective from external observation to internal exploration, Ellington described the composition as an attempt to

> rescue Negro music from well-meaning friends. . . . All arrangements of historic American Negro music have been made by conservatory-trained musicians. . . . It's time a big piece of music was written from the inside by a Negro.[15]

To compose "from the inside" did not, however, require conformity to pre-ordained conceptions of what African American culture should be.

Indeed, the reviews of Ellington's most ambitious composition fell short of the "constructive criticism" that Locke desired, partly because it was deemed to be insufficiently authentic. The young white editor of *Jazz* magazine, Bob Thiele, felt that the "over rich layer of cake and ideas and tones" manifest in *Black, Brown and Beige* were "in direct opposition to the fundamentals of jazz."[16] Record producer, talent scout, and promoter of African American music John Hammond agreed in asking whether the Duke was "deserting jazz," and in wondering why Ellington would seek to "tamper with the blues form" in such a way that he "alienated a good part of the dancing public." In hoping that Ellington "would be able to find himself again" sometime in the future, Hammond alludes to the fact that Ellington was well established by 1943.[17] Having moved from Washington, DC to New York in 1923, Ellington and his orchestra had become associated with Harlem to the extent that Langston Hughes recalled that when he "first came up out of the Lennox Avenue subway" he instinctively "looked around in the happy sunlight to see if I saw Duke Ellington on the corner of 135th street."[18] *Black, Brown and Beige* was a late product of the Harlem Renaissance, begun in 1930 as an "opera" named "Boola" inspired by wide reading in the works of Alain Locke, Joel A. Rogers, and others that Ellington claimed was best "concealed" as the "heavily underlined paragraphs about the exploits of Nat Turner and Denmark Vesey" would not add to his "popularity in Arkansas, say."[19] By desiring that Ellington should "find himself again," John Hammond was exposing his ignorance of Ellington's long-standing ambitions, and unconsciously foregrounding the cultural straitjacket in which African American musicians were expected to operate by the predominantly white commentariat.[20]

What Hammond described as Ellington's "tampering" is most prominent in the final part of the "Brown" movement, where Betty Roche's vocal lament, written by Ellington, is a series of negations:

> The Blues,
> The Blues ain't,
> The Blues ain't nothing,
> The Blues ain't nothin' like nothin' I know.[21]

Roche's singing is almost rubato, and the piece certainly "ain't nothin' like" a blues until Ben Webster enters on tenor saxophone, but even then the harmonic structure oscillates between the keys of C minor and D flat and, as Harvey G. Cohen notes, "there is no relief, no spirited reprise of the tonic chord" at the end of "The Blues" as would be typical of a big-band performance.[22] Ambiguity and alienation are the dominant moods evoked, and this reflects the veiled message with which Ellington introduced his second movement. "The Blues" he announced, resulted from "the many love triangles that developed in the life of the great Negro heroes of the Spanish-American War."[23] There is little in the music that evokes the battle of San Juan Hill, but the idea that the blues was created by returning heroes rather than rural folk musicians was a subtle critique of those, such as John Hammond, who located the roots of African American music in the rural south. Ellington was surely also addressing wartime ideological considerations, not least the "Double V" campaign which called for a simultaneous struggle against fascism abroad and racism at home. In introducing "Beige," Ellington was more explicit in his description of African American disaffection. He clothed his social critique in a patriotic "veneer" that is perhaps similar to the aesthetic primitivism that, he suggests, hid the reality of African American lives. If Alain Locke advocated a shift from writing "about" to being "of" the African American community, then Ellington's interpretation of the Harlem Renaissance "from the inside" encouraged his audience to question surface appearances:

> The first theme of our third movement is the inculcation, or the veneer that we chip off as we get closer and find that all these people who are making all this noise and responding to the tom toms, are only a few people making a living, and they're backed really by people who, many don't have enough to eat and a place to sleep, but work hard and see that their children are in school. The Negro is rich in education. And it develops until we find ourselves, today, struggling for solidarity, but just as we are about to get our teeth into it, our country is at war and in trouble again, and as before, we, of course, find the black, brown, and beige right in there for the red, white, and blue.[24]

To "chip off" the "veneer" is to remove the primitivist mask imposed upon African Americans (including Ellington himself, whose compositions were described as "jungle music" in the 1920s) to reveal the inner lives of individuals; a shift, in Locke's terms, from speaking "about" a people at a distance of alleged objectivity, to manifesting "the internal world" of "artistic self-expression."[25] If a surface "veneer" might render all pieces of furniture homogeneously alike, to chip it away would entail revealing the diverse gradations of color. Culturally, this act of "chipping" may be seen embodied in the transition that takes us from Paul Whiteman's performance of his "symphonic jazz" by an all-white ensemble at Carnegie Hall in 1928, to Ellington's performance of *Black, Brown and Beige* with an African American ensemble at the same venue in 1943.[26] Having removed the veneer, however, the description of what is revealed in the second half of the quotation from Ellington is ambiguous. The patriotic expression of fighting for a common cause is clear enough, but to equate the "black, brown and beige" with the "red, white and blue" seems to suggest national distinctiveness; it is as though below the surface propaganda promoting wartime unity, African Americans have a nation and flag of their own. Duke Ellington's son, Mercer, recalled that *Black, Brown and Beige* was his father's criticism "of his own race, and their prejudices within itself. There were these different castes: the black, the brown or tan ones and the ones light enough to pass for white."[27] David Schiff suggests that the title "might simply be a description of the range of flesh tones in the Ellington Orchestra, or it might stand for the entire nonwhite population of the planet."[28] Yet Ellington himself said in 1956 that the title referred to a "state of mind, not the color of the skin," explaining that the self-image of African Americans "gradually . . . got lighter" after emancipation, "but it never got quite white."[29] Do the three shades of Ellington's title represent a sequence of increasing assimilation and acceptance in an American melting pot, or do they co-exist within an African American crucible? Is the "Black Brown and Beige" a diachronic sequence marking a development over time, or a synchronic spectrum of coexisting colors in the present? These questions speak to one of the key tensions that define the literature and culture of the Harlem Renaissance.

In Solution: Jean Toomer

In the works of Ellington's fellow-Washingtonian, Jean Toomer, the "black, brown and beige" would represent a diachronic sequence; an inevitable process of racial and cultural intermingling. Duke Ellington's claim in 1943 that his movement "Black" sought to "chip off" the primitivist "veneer" imposed on African American culture by those people "making all this noise and responding to the tom toms," was a late expression of a widespread desire – informed by Freudian explorations of the psyche and anthropological excavations of "buried cultures" – to "dig up" historical roots, or to return to a "repressed" past existing beneath the shiny surfaces of modernity.[30] Toomer produced a template for this process of probing and revelation in his novel *Cane* of 1923. *Cane*, as has been well documented, was the product of a "visit to Georgia" where Toomer "heard folksongs come from the lips of Negro peasants. . . . And a deep part of my nature, a part that I had repressed, sprang suddenly to life and responded to them."[31] The first third of the multigenre novel seeks to probe this "repressed" dimension of the self, for it is set in the South, and largely seen through the eyes of a narrator who, like the author, is a northerner who repeats the urban African American's journey "to the soil of his ancestors." He shares the story of "Fern" with a northern audience "against the chance that you might happen down that way."[32] The whole section is pervaded by a sense of tropical otherness, dominated by erotic and primitivized female characters with the opening of the first story, "Karintha," setting the tone: "Her skin is like dusk on the eastern horizon / . . . When the sun goes down."[33]

The second section shifts to an urban, vibrant world of "jazz songs and love, thrusting unconscious rhythms" into the rather sterile, urban North represented by "the white and whitewashed wood of Washington."[34] Ellington seems to be a presence here in the figure of the pianist "Dan" who "turns to the piano and glances through a stack of jazz music sheets" before creating a music that is both modernist and primitivist, and is evoked phonetically as "Ji-ji-bo, JI-JI-BO!"; the music of a "crude new life" that is Negro only "in the boldness of its expression."[35] The final section seeks to offer a synthesis in the form of "Kabnis," a northern intellectual returning to his southern roots in Georgia where, in Father John, he encounters the "dead blind father of a muted folk who feel their way upward to a life that crushes or absorbs them."[36] African American culture seems to have no distinctive future of its own in *Cane*, a novel conceived by Toomer as a "swan-song" to African American cultural distinctiveness.[37]

Toomer described himself as having "seven blood mixtures: French, Dutch, Welsh, Negro, German, Jewish, and Indian." Drawing on this multi-ethnic background, he envisaged a future transcendence of cultural differences:

> [T]he Negro is in solution . . . . If one holds his eyes to individuals and sections, race is starkly evident, and racial continuity seems assured. One is even led to believe that the thing we call Negro beauty will always be attributable to a clearly defined physical source. But the fact is, that if anything comes up now, pure Negro, it will be a swan-song.[38]

For Toomer, African America is "in solution," facing absorption but not yet wholly dissolved and therefore still available for exploration and documentation. The stories of Karintha and Fern he noted, were "derived from a sense of fading, from a knowledge of my futility to check solution."[39]

Sadness and melancholia are the dominant moods that pervade the novel. Judith Butler argues that gender identity – especially among those who identify as heterosexual – is melancholic. In repressing queer leanings the heterosexual constructs an identity that is socially permissible, but is haunted by that loss and repression.[40] Anne Anlin Cheng adapts this argument for racial identity, noting that the binary black/white terms in which race is understood in the USA results in the marginalization of interracialism which remains in the nation's repressed memory.[41] *Cane* enacts such forms of marginalization, perhaps most explicitly in the story

of "Becky" who gives birth to "mulatto" boys and is ostracized as
a scapegoat by both white and black communities. Scenes of lynching
in *Cane* also foreground the extent to which the color line is violently
policed and the prospect of interracial relationships regarded impermis-
sible. In the final section, any hope for an integrated future, suggested
as the "soft belly of a pregnant Negress, throbs evenly against the torso
of the South," is undercut by an earlier description of white lynchers
murdering a mother for attempting to hide her husband, before impal-
ing her living black fetus to a tree.[42] Robyn Wiegman argues that "the
lynch scenario" in literature forces a recognition of "the symbolic force
of the white mob's activity as a denial of the black man's newly
articulated right to citizenship."[43] This is the case in *Cane*, though
here the psychic effects of lynching permeate even the most intimate
of relationships, as in "Portrait of Georgia":

> Hair – braided chestnut,
>   coiled like a lyncher's rope,
> Eyes – fagots,
> Lips – old scars, or the first red blisters,
> Breath – the last sweet scent of cane,
> And her slim body, white as the ash
>   of black flesh after flame.[44]

In its fusion of two people, a white woman and a lynched black male, the
poem seeks to construct a new identity after trauma. George Hutchinson
argues that the poem "embodies both a union of black male and white
female and the terrifying method of exorcising that union to maintain
a racial difference the poem linguistically defies."[45] This is a shrewd reading, suggesting that the logic of the poem could take us toward an intensified division of the races, or a potential union. *Cane* continually testifies to
the terrible consequences of crossing the color line, as embodied in the
isolated lives of mixed-race characters such as Fern and Esther. Yet the
novel's narratives continually seek to cross the racial boundary.

   "Bona and Paul" is an interesting meditation on such crossing, a story
said to be based on a relationship between Toomer and a young woman
that came to an end due to rumors of his African American ancestry.[46] In
its emphasis on gradations of color, the story seems to reach aesthetically
toward a world beyond the binary of black and white. Art is a "pale purple
facsimile of a red-blooded Norwegian," Paul's "dark" skin turns "rosy"
with embarrassment as the "white" skins and surfaces turn "crimson" and
"greys" become "lavender" in the sunset.[47] Yet, while the story aims to

transcend racial binaries, it also enacts the effects of American racial hierarchies:

> Suddenly he knew that people saw, not attractiveness in his dark skin, but difference. Their stares, giving him to himself, filled something long empty within him, and were like green blades sprouting in his consciousness.[48]

Paul finds his potential multicultural identity replaced by an awareness that his "black" ancestry is his "cloudy, but real" self. While others ask whether he is "a Spaniard, and Indian, and Italian, a Mexican, a Hindu or a Japanese," Paul finds the possibility of sustaining several simultaneous identities increasingly difficult.[49] It seems that to be American is to face a racial division, and to be forced to embrace one's "real" race on either side of that black and white binary.

Walter Benn Michaels reads the story as a manifestation of a shift that he traces from the "progressive nationalism" of the late nineteenth- and early twentieth-centuries to the nativism of the 1920s. The "Progressive nationalism" of the earlier period entailed a hierarchy of races and desired the assimilation of racial "others" into a dominant national culture. By contrast, 1920s nativism was plural and anti-assimilationist. "Bona and Paul" reflects the logic of the shift from progressive racism to nativism in that it depicts a process by which the "mulatto vanishes" by "being made black." The desire "not to produce mulattoes," notes Benn Michaels, "is fulfilled by the assertion that there are no mulattoes. And the discovery that there are no mulattoes marks the literally definitive defeat of the melting pot."[50] Michaels's argument is supported in historical terms by the fact that the term "mulatto" was removed from US census forms in 1920.[51] Yet Toomer resisted forms of nativism, and *Cane* is therefore an odd choice of text for exemplifying the alleged shift from assimilationism to nativist pluralism in the 1920s. In its evocation of the in-between states of dusk and twilight and its focus on characters of mixed race, *Cane* gestures toward a form of identity beyond black and white. Toomer imagined himself to belong to a "new race" that "is neither white nor black nor red nor brown."[52] Far from marking the "death of the melting pot," Toomer's work may be read as one of the most advanced forms of its articulation. In conceiving of African Americans "in solution," Toomer ultimately denied that he had any black ancestry, and refused to be advertised as a "Negro" writer. There is some legitimacy, then, to Henry Louis Gates Jr.'s claim that in this denial of his African American self, Toomer exemplified the assimilationist consequences of his universalist vision.[53]

No "the Negro" Here: Zora Neale Hurston

If Toomer described *Cane* as a "swan-song," Zora Neale Hurston was to emphasize the living contemporary vitality of African American culture and folk practices. She argued that "Negro folklore is not a thing of the past" for "it is still in the making" and its "great variety shows the adaptability of the black man: nothing is too old or too new, domestic or foreign, high or low, for his use."[54] "There is no 'the Negro' here" stated Hurston, challenging the simplifying, homogenizing, primitivist view of the outsider.[55] While she registered a widespread view that "the Negro is easily imitated," such an impression could only be based on a ridiculously narrow view of what constituted "Negro behavior." In fact, "nothing is further from the truth" noted Hurston, developing her argument in relation to the Paul Whiteman jazz orchestra that she believed offered a white imitation of a musical culture that was already creatively imitative:

> Paul Whiteman is giving an imitation of a Negro orchestra making use of white-invented musical instruments in a Negro way. Thus has arisen a new art in the civilised world, and thus has our so called civilisation come. The exchange and re-exchange of ideas between groups.[56]

If Whiteman was imitating and adding a respectful veneer to the music of African American musicians, the most celebrated African American band-leader, Duke Ellington, embraced a view of cultural pluralism that was similar to that advanced by Hurston. We can turn again to *Black, Brown and Beige* to witness this process of imitative "exchange and re-exchange." The composition's most celebrated theme, "Come Sunday," is initially introduced in the first movement "Black" by chimes ringing in the distance over the brass section's organ-like chorale, suggesting that this original spiritual is being heard from the distanced perspective of the enslaved listening to a service outside the chapel walls. The theme returns at the end of the "Beige" section in the form of an adopted and adapted African American spiritual and, as David Schiff notes, "an emblem of Harlem's living piety, not as a vestige of the past."[57] To read Ellington's vision of culture from a Hurstonian perspective is thus to see it as cross-pollinating and hybrid, but not based on the desire to assimilate outwards, for black culture also has the capacity to integrate inwards. This perspective resists the notion that cultures are "in solution" within a single American melting pot. Rather, distinctive cultures constitute pots of their own, able to integrate and assimilate others in their own terms. Hurston's cultural vision is based on a pluralist model of an "exchange" between distinctive "groups." The "black, brown and beige," from her perspective, was a synchronic spectrum.

Hurston therefore repudiated those who thought that acquiring degrees and losing their dialect were marks of intelligence and deplored "the intellectual lynching we perpetrate on ourselves; in emulating white."[58] Education, Hurston argued, should not be seen as a vehicle for assimilation, and she suggested that an African faculty be brought to America to teach music and dancing to black Americans.[59] In keeping with this philosophy, Hurston was the only major black writer to attack the first important Supreme Court decision for integration, the 1954 *Brown vs. The Board of Education*. The core of her controversial position was that what black and white liberals had legislated was an insulting assimilationism that implicitly said the best way to educate blacks was to whiten them. For Hurston, the survival of African American culture is predicated upon its internal, and evolving, diversity. It is the inner hybridity of minorities that Hurston seeks to foster in her writing, creating a cultural space where exchange and interaction between groups is possible, while sustaining a black cultural difference which is a necessary logical prerequisite for any such interaction to happen in the first place.

Indeed, it was in her access to the cultural basis of that difference that her anthropology tutor at Columbia University, Franz Boas, located the significance of her work. In the revealing preface that he wrote for her ethnography *Mules and Men*, he described the way in which

> she entered into the homely life of the southern Negro as one of them and was fully accepted as such by the companions of her childhood. Thus she has been able to penetrate through that affected demeanor by which the Negro excludes the White observer effectively from participating in his true inner life.[60]

Hurston offered a more qualified and complicating account of the consequences of "insiderness" for her anthropological practice. In the body of *Mules and Men*, Hurston warned her readers that

> Folklore is not as easy to collect as it sounds. The best source is where there are the least outside influences and these people, being usually underprivileged, are the shyest. They are most reluctant at times to reveal that which the soul lives by. And the Negro, in spite of his open-faced laughter, his seeming acquiescence, is particularly evasive. You see we are a polite people and we do not say to our questioner, "Get out of here!" We smile and tell him or her something that satisfies the white person, because, knowing so little about us, he doesn't know what he is missing.[61]

The shift from "these people" to a "we" who address a distanced "you" is significant in this passage as the tone shifts from scientific objectivity to identification, from "speaking of" to "speaking for." This tension between being spoken for by others and of speaking for oneself is dramatized in *Mules and Men* when an informant, Robert Williams, tells the story of a young woman who goes to college. Upon her return to Eatonville, Florida, she is asked to transcribe a letter dictated by her illiterate father. As the educated daughter transcribes the story, she finds that she is unable to convey on paper the clucking sound that her father uses to coax a mule to work. To the father's question "Is you got dat?" she answers

> "Naw suh, Ah ain't got it yet."
> "How come you ain't got it?"
> "Cause Ah can't spell (clucking sound)."

> "You mean to tell me you been off to school seben years and can't spell (clucking sound)? Why Ah could spell dat myself and Ah ain't been to school a day in mah life. Well jes' say (clucking sound) he'll know what yo' mean and go on wid de letter."[62]

The scene is clearly a self-reflexive consideration of the problem of ethnographic representation, suggesting that African American difference has a linguistic element that lies beyond written representation in the English language.

This notion is developed in "Characteristics of Negro Expression" where Hurston argues that readers no longer need to believe the "writers of Negro dialect and the burnt-cork artists" for they "may go directly to the Negro and let him speak for himself."[63] This argument is seen by the critic Hazel Carby to result in a "theoretical paradigm" that directed Hurston "toward rural, not urban, black culture and folk forms of the past, not the present."[64] Whereas Carby valorizes Langston Hughes's role in shaping a "discursive category of the folk in direct response to the transformative social process of migration to urban cities and industrialisation," she accuses Hurston of having "constructed a discourse of nostalgia for a rural community," and whereas Hughes's use of the blues, jazz, and popular cultural forms "represented a communal sensibility . . . embodied in the conditions of cultural transformation," Hurston "assumed that she could obtain access to, and authenticate, an individualized social consciousness through a utopian reconstruction of the historical moment of her childhood in an attempt to stabilize and distance the social contradictions and disruptions of her contemporary moment."[65] It may be more accurate to think of Hurston's attempts at sustaining the living vitality of African Americans as a response to, rather than an evasion of, the "contradictions" of her contemporary world that, in her view, could not be reconciled through a process of assimilation. Any elements of rural pastoralism in Hurston's work are consistently undercut by an awareness of power relationships within society. The scene in which her mother dies in the autobiographical *Dust Tracks on a Road* depicts a rural society that is coercive and frustrates, in the name of folk custom, the daughter's attempt to fulfill her mother's final wish to keep a pillow beneath her head.[66] Hurston's play, *Color Struck*, depicts both the racial diversity of the African American community and the destructive consequences of internal hierarchies of pigmentation as Emmaline, described as "a black woman," refuses to call a black doctor preferring a Caucasian to treat her "very white" daughter. The daughter dies due to the delay in treatment.[67] Hurston's works are therefore not vindicationist accounts of the worthy authenticity of folk life. She is writing against the metropolitan biases of an urban modernism that assumed it represented progress, and viewed rural life as racially homogeneous and as a static, backward, "other" (a bias that is repeated in Carby's influential critique). Hurston lamented "the white majority's indifference, not to say skepticism" to the "internal lives" of minorities.[68] Her works foreground the internal diversity of those lives.

Conclusion

There is a broad consensus that the Harlem Renaissance was a cultural nationalist movement.[69] Yet, as I suggested at the outset, the implications of Alain Locke's comparison between the nascent centers of nationalist renaissances – Harlem, Dublin, and Prague – are somewhat unclear. The cultural nationalism of the Harlem Renaissance could not have independent political statehood as its goal, but against the static, homogenized, primitivist views of African Americans that predicated their ultimate assimilation into the American melting pot, many authors sought to emphasize the internal diversity of their people. This constituted a significant strain within the African American cultural nationalism of the Harlem Renaissance. To seek national separation is often less a reversion to tribal, atavistic forces than a desire to establish a particular culture's internal cosmopolitanism, and its ability to confer rights on its members and to incorporate "others." Locke's emphasis on "culture-citizenship" may be considered an African American form of the desire to create a frame, bowl or pot that allows the hybrid and multicultural credentials of a minority group to be established and fostered. In "What White Publishers Won't Print" (1950), Zora Neale Hurston noted that publishing houses tended to reject love stories about blacks or Jews unless such works involved racial tension. She emphasized that "for the national welfare, it is urgent to realize that the minorities do think, and think about something other than the race problem. That they are very human and internally, according to natural endowment, are just like everybody else."[70] Thus while Jean Toomer sought to transcend the binary of "black and white" in the creation of a "new race," Ellington and Hurston believed that the universal resided within the particular and its achievement did not entail a homogenizing assimilationism. They attempted to construct a distinctive pot for African America that would contain the black, brown, and beige; its own diversity of unassimilable voices. Establishing and celebrating the internal cosmopolitan diversity of the African American people was one of the results of the cultural nationalism informing the Harlem Renaissance.

Notes

1. Ishmael Reed, *Mumbo Jumbo* (New York: Doubleday, 1972). Ishmael Reed, "The Celtic in Us," *Comparative American Studies* 8, no. 4 (December 2010): 332.
2. Ishmael Reed, "Is Ethnicity Obsolete?," in *The Invention of Ethnicity*, ed. Werner Sollors (Oxford: Oxford University Press, 1989), 227.
3. On these notions, see Werner Sollors, *Beyond Ethnicity: Consent and Descent in American Culture* (Oxford: Oxford University Press, 1986), 66–101; Andy Bertsch, "The Melting Pot vs. the Salad Bowl: A Call to Explore Regional Cross-cultural Differences and Similarities within the U.S.A," *Journal of Organizational Culture, Communications and Conflict* 17, no. 1 (2013): 131–148.
4. Sollors, *Beyond Ethnicity*, 99.
5. Alain Locke, *The New Negro: An Interpretation* (1925; New York: Touchstone, 1997), 7.
6. Alain Locke, *Race Contacts and Interracial Relations: Lectures on the Theory and Practice of Race*, ed. Jeffrey C. Stewart (Washington, DC: Howard University Press, 1992), 99. See Rachel Farebrother, *The Collage Aesthetic of the Harlem Renaissance* (Farnham: Ashgate, 2009), 50–69.
7. Houston A. Baker, Jr., *Modernism and the Harlem Renaissance* (Chicago: University of Chicago Press, 1987), 73–75.
8. Locke, *New Negro*, 7.
9. W. E. B. Du Bois, *The Souls of Black Folk*, ed. David W. Blight and Robert Gooding-Williams (1903; Boston: Bedford/St. Martins, 1997), 67. W. E. B. Du Bois, *The Gift of Black Folk: Negroes in the Making of America* (Boston: Stratford, 1924).

10. W. E. B. Du Bois, "The Conservation of Races" [1897], in *Writings*, ed. Nathan Huggins (New York: The Library of America, 1986), 815–826.
11. Alain Locke, "Towards a Critique of Negro Music," *Opportunity* 12 (November 1934): 328.
12. James Weldon Johnson, "Preface," in *The Book of American Negro Poetry*, ed. James Weldon Johnson (New York: Harcourt, Brace, 1922), vii. Locke, *New Negro*, 15.
13. Locke, *New Negro*, xxv.
14. Harvey G. Cohen, *Duke Ellington's America* (Chicago: University of Chicago Press, 2010), 210.
15. Alfred Frankenstein, "'Hot is Something about a Tree,' Says the Duke," *San Francisco Chronicle* (November 9, 1941). Quoted in Cohen, *Duke Ellington's America*, 204.
16. Bob Thiele, "The Case of Jazz Music," *Jazz* (July 1943): 19–20. Repr. Mark Tucker, *The Duke Ellington Reader* (Oxford: Oxford University Press, 1993), 176.
17. John Hammond, "Is the Duke Deserting Jazz?," *Jazz* (May 1943): 15. Repr. Tucker, *The Duke Ellington Reader*, 172.
18. Langston Hughes, "Harlem and its Negritude," *African Forum* (Spring 1966): 11–20. Repr. *The Langston Hughes Review* 4, no. 1 (Spring 1985): 30. In *The Big Sea* (1940; New York: Hill and Wang, 1993) Hughes reveals that he first arrived in Harlem in 1921 (81). Ellington did not move from Washington, DC to New York until 1923. Hughes's erroneous recollection reflects the extent to which Ellington has become associated with Harlem in retrospect.
19. Richard O. Boyer, "The Hot Bach," in *The Duke Ellington Reader*, ed. Tucker, 238. On "Boola," see Cohen, *Duke Ellington's America*, 215–228.
20. Hammond in *The Duke Ellington Reader*, ed. Tucker, 173.
21. "Black Brown and Beige: A Tone Parallel to the History of the American Negro" appears on *The Duke Ellington Carnegie Hall Concerts: 1943*, Prestige Records, 1977.
22. Cohen, *Duke Ellington's America*, 224.
23. Duke Ellington, "Introduction to Black" (1943). Transcribed from the Prestige recording of *Black, Brown and Beige* by the author.
24. Duke Ellington, "Introduction to Beige" (1943).
25. On "jungle music," see Terry Teachout, *Duke Ellington: The Life of Duke Ellington* (London: Robson Press, 2013), 90.
26. Gerald Early, "Pulp and Circumstance: The Story of Jazz in High Places," in *The Jazz Cadence of American Culture*, ed. Robert G. O'Meally (New York: Columbia University Press, 1998), 393–430.
27. Wayne Enstice and Paul Rubin, *Jazz Spoken Here: Conversations with 22 Musicians* (New York: Da Capo Press, 1994), 121.
28. David Schiff, *The Ellington Century* (Berkeley: University of California Press, 2012), 216.
29. Quoted in Teachout, *Duke Ellington*, 238. From the unpublished interviews with Carter Harman, 1956.

30. See Raymond Williams's discussion of these tendencies within modernism in *The Politics of Modernism: Against the New Conformists*, ed. Tony Pinkney (London: Verso, 1989), 58–60. "The Negro Digs Up His Past" is an essay by Arthur Schomburg in Locke, *The New Negro*, 231–237.

31. Jean Toomer to the *Liberator* (August 19, 1922). Quoted in Michael North, *The Dialect of Modernism: Race, Language and Twentieth-Century Literature* (Oxford: Oxford University Press, 1994), 166.

32. Jean Toomer, *Cane* (1923; New York: Penguin, 2019), 24.

33. Ibid., 1.

34. Ibid., 51.

35. Ibid., 76. Jean Toomer to Waldo Frank, undated. Mark Whalan, ed., *The Letters of Jean Toomer*, 1919–1924 (Knoxville: University of Tennessee Press, 2006), 115. Before he moved to New York in 1923 Ellington was a mainstay on the lively "Black Broadway" of Washington, DC.

36. Toomer, *Cane*, 142.

37. Jean Toomer to Waldo Frank, undated, *The Letters of Jean Toomer*, 115.

38. Ibid.

39. Ibid., 116.

40. Judith Butler, *Gender Trouble: Feminism and the Subversion of Identity* (New York: Routledge, 1990).

41. Anne Anlin Cheng, *The Melancholy of Race: Psychoanalysis, Assimilation, and Hidden Grief* (Oxford: Oxford University Press, 2001).

42. Toomer, *Cane*, 119, 104.

43. Robyn Wiegman, *American Anatomies: Theorizing Race and Gender* (Durham, NC: Duke University Press, 1995), 83–84.

44. Toomer, *Cane*, 36.

45. George Hutchinson, "Jean Toomer and American Racial Discourse," in *Interracialism: Black-White Intermarriage in American History, Literature, and Law*, ed. Werner Sollors (Oxford: Oxford University Press, 2000), 378.

46. Walter Benn Michaels, *Our America: Nativism, Modernism and Pluralism* (Durham, NC: Duke University Press, 1995), 63.

47. Toomer, *Cane*, 97, 101, 98, 95.

48. Ibid., 100.

49. Ibid., 100.

50. Michaels, *Our America*, 64.

51. George Hutchinson, "Jean Toomer and the New Negroes of Washington," *American Literature* 63 (December 1991), 687.

52. Jean Toomer, "The Americans," in *A Jean Toomer Reader: Selected Unpublished Writings*, ed. Frederick L. Rusch (Oxford: Oxford University Press, 1993), 107–108.

53. Henry Louis Gates, Jr., *Figures in Black: Words, Signs, and the "Racial" Self* (Oxford: Oxford University Press, 1987), 202.

54. Zora Neale Hurston, "Characteristics of Negro Expression," in *Zora Neale Hurston: Folklore, Memoirs, and Other Writings*, ed. Cheryl A. Wall (New York: Library of America, 1995), 836.
55. Hurston, *Dust Tracks on a Road* [1942], in *Hurston: Folklore, Memoirs*, ed. Wall, 733.
56. Hurston, "Characteristics," 838.
57. David Schiff, *The Ellington Century* (Berkeley: University of California Press, 2012), 221.
58. Quoted in Robert E. Hemenway, *Zora Neale Hurston: A Literary Biography* (Urbana: University of Illinois Press, 1980), 206.
59. Ibid.
60. Franz Boas, "Preface" to *Mules and Men* [1935], in *Hurston: Folklore, Memoirs*, ed. Wall, n.p.
61. Hurston, *Mules and Men*, in *Hurston: Folklore, Memoirs*, ed. Wall, 10.
62. Ibid., 43–44.
63. Hurston, "Characteristics," 845–846.
64. Hazel Carby, "The Politics of Fiction, Anthropology, and the Folk: Zora Neale Hurston," in *New Essays on Their Eyes Were Watching God*, ed. Michael Awkward (Cambridge: Cambridge University Press, 1990), 80.
65. Carby, "The Politics," 77, 78.
66. Hurston, *Dust Tracks*, 617–618.
67. Zora Neale Hurston, *Color Struck*, in *Zora Neale Hurston: Collected Plays*, ed. Jean Lee Cole and Charles Mitchell (New Brunswick: Rutgers University Press, 2008), 35.
68. Hurston, "What White Publishers Won't Print" [1950], in *Hurston: Folklore, Memoirs*, ed. Wall, 951.
69. This argument is articulated most strongly by Baker, *Modernism and the Harlem Renaissance*.
70. Hurston, "What White Publishers Won't Print," 952.

CHAPTER 2

Making the Slave Anew: History and the Archive in New Negro Renaissance Poetry

Clare Corbould

One of the central preoccupations of members of an African American intelligentsia during the interwar years was history, specifically slavery and its legacy. When boosters of a group of African American artists, writers, scholars, and activists dubbed the group the "New Negroes," they proclaimed a break with both the past and simultaneously their enduring relationship to history.[1] It is significant that African American creative producers of the 1920s and 1930s did not call themselves modernists or, say, black moderns or black modernists. While their relationship to history, especially enslavement, was complex, most of them did not wish to wash away the past.[2] If anything, the ambivalence with which writers, artists, and performers regarded the term "New Negro" signaled their ongoing relationship with black people in the past.

Writers in the New Negro Renaissance came up hard against widespread popular and scholarly accounts of slavery, which were deeply racist. Efforts on the part of "Harlem Renaissance" writers and scholars might be thought of as being bookended by two epic, massively popular films: D. W. Griffith's 1916 *Birth of a Nation* and David O. Selznick's *Gone with the Wind* in 1939. Both films told tales of slavery, the Civil War, Reconstruction, and Jim Crow segregation in ways that appealed to white Americans' fantasies of white supremacy and black inferiority, and to their nostalgia for a supposedly golden age. The interwar decades were also among those during which the heralding of southern life during slavery and in the years of the Confederacy reached its peak. Public history efforts, often led by white women's community groups, were legion at this time.[3] In the scholarly realm, one need only consider former history professor Woodrow Wilson's famed remark that Griffith's film was like "writing" or "teaching history with lightning."[4] That Wilson was at that time the nation's president says much about the dominance of his way of thinking about the past.

Black Americans undertook a wide range of activities to construct an alternative history closer to the truth. These included the creation of an archive that would support anti-racist accounts of African diaspora history, including the more recent American past. Tenacious individuals raised funds for the cause to support organizations such as the Association for the Study of Negro Life and History, founded in 1915. From the following year, that association published the important quarterly *Journal of Negro History*, which often included previously obscure documents in order to make an archive of black history available to researchers and especially black schoolteachers.[5] By 1920, the association's director, Carter G. Woodson, launched the signal Associated Publishers for black history books, and in 1926 began an annual Negro History Week, which drew attention and bolstered significant efforts nationwide to improve black school students' knowledge of black history, including slavery.[6] In black tertiary institutions, newly established social science departments supported historical research, including the collection of testimony from formerly enslaved people.[7] Black weekly newspapers, which circulated nationwide and helped create a sense of a cohesive community among African Americans, were also vital sites for the creation of a fresh archive of black history, whether in reports, editorials, features, or even cartoon series. In the simple act of printing advertisements for new books in black history, newspapers played a key role in generating a thorough-going critique of academic, popular, and public history that claimed American slavery was a benign institution that benefited Africans and their American-born descendants.

African Americans who were engaged in creative work also came to consider the flaws of existing archives and historical narratives. Some were proud of the way that Africans and their American-born descendants had endured bondage. They sought to recuperate the reputation of enslaved people by drawing attention to the beauty and brilliance of hitherto underappreciated black culture. A second group, by contrast, regarded enslavement as an ordeal whose legacy was at best mixed and at worst a continuing trauma. For this group, the New Negro generation had a responsibility to spare their own children by finding a way to discard slavery's traumatic legacy. A third group called into question the very discipline of history by critiquing existing archives and norms about historical expertise. Men and women in this group used their creative work to show that the supposed objectivity of professional historians rested on deeply racist structures that determined what constituted "legitimate" evidence. These New Negro writers and artists critiqued historical practice and the archive of US slavery in ways taken up in much recent scholarship.[8]

Genre and Publishing in the Effort to Make New Histories

African American creative authors and artists of the interwar period used a full range of genres to treat slavery and its legacy, but among published writing it was poetry that lent itself most readily to direct engagement with these topics. There are two likely reasons for this: first, as a genre that is neither fiction nor nonfiction, poetry had the flexibility appropriate to a consideration of history and the archive;[9] second, there was a relatively substantial market for black poets. Poetry appeared in black monthly magazines including the long-running *The Crisis* and *Opportunity* and shorter-lived ones such as *Messenger* and *Fire!!* Occasionally a long poem might get a run, and a page with three or four short poems appeared often. Most of all, however, a short poem would fill the space – usually about a one-third of a page – left after an article was typeset. Poetry also featured in most editions of the weekly black newspapers published in a dozen major cities and distributed nationwide.

The major new book publishing houses, by contrast, do not seem to have been particularly supportive of creative writing by African Americans that directly treated the history and legacy of slavery. When publishers such as Knopf, Boni and Liveright, and Harcourt Brace did support African American poets, they tended to publish volumes of "blues poetry" that improved the publishing houses' reputations as avant-garde – and even these lost money.[10] African American novelists, including Jessie Fauset and Nella Larsen, negotiated this reluctance to publish work directly related to slavery by treating the topic either obliquely or by analogy (and perhaps this was their preference, too). Nonfiction authors also had trouble publishing their research about slavery and its legacy; even the era's most influential scholars, ranging from W. E. B. Du Bois to Charles S. Johnson (and white authors such as U. B. Phillips), paid subventions to have their books appear.[11] When Zora Neale Hurston, now the most famed author of the era to deal with the long legacy of enslavement, tried to publish her scholarly work, she was rejected. She abandoned several manuscripts and found other outlets for the material. The most commercially successful of these was her mid-1930s ethnography *Mules and Men*, whose tone, form, and marketability echoed Hughes's "blues poetry."[12]

The Slave Past as Creative Wellspring

It was possible, suggested one group of interwar African American artists and activists, that the archive created by enslaved people was already the most valuable cultural artifact in the USA. James Weldon Johnson, one of the "renaissance's" vital boosters and a celebrated poet and lyricist (as well as being a former school principal, one of the first black diplomats, and in the 1920s a key member of the civil rights organization the National Association for the Advancement of Colored People), argued that the best and most innovative of American poetic forms had their roots in the experience of enslavement. Johnson compiled a landmark series of anthologies of black American poetry and spirituals published between 1922 and 1926, which were among the few best-sellers of black-authored books during the decade.[13] "In the 'spirituals,' or slave songs," Johnson asserted, "the Negro has given America not only its only folk songs, but a mass of noble music. . . . Take, for instance, 'Go Down, Moses'; I doubt that there is a stronger theme in the whole musical literature of the world."[14]

Far from a source of shame, slave culture, according to Johnson and others, ought to be a source of pride and be recognized as the wellspring from which American popular culture sprang. Ragtime, which had become an international sensation, had its roots, wrote Johnson, in the forms and sentiments of enslaved poets Jupiter Hammon and Phillis Wheatley. Johnson also noted the growing international acclaim for the brilliance of black poetry, spirituals, folk tales, and music. Just as the Irish Renaissance came from a now-venerated folk culture, so too did the New Negro Renaissance. It was high time, Johnson argued, that white Americans also came to appreciate and value the art forms created by their black fellow citizens. Such recognition, he hoped, would challenge the basis of racism. As Johnson wrote, "Once that power" – of the "pure beauty" of the spirituals – "is conceded, the idea of absolute inferiority cannot hold."[15]

Johnson even went so far as to conjure up in his own poetry imagined enslaved songmakers. In doing so, he repudiated the tendency in the mainstream press to depict "ex-slaves" as feeble and popular cultural depictions of the enslaved as comical, mischievous, untrustworthy, and/ or stupid. Johnson's poem, "O Black and Unknown Bards," appeared in the 1922 anthology he compiled and opened the lengthy preface to the 1925 collection. In it, the present-day narrator addressed enslaved people in the second person, with awe and respect. He marveled that such art could spring from "darkness" and "from degraded rest and servile toil." The spirituals, the narrator of the poem announced, were superior to the creations of every other group of oppressed people:

> O black slave singers, gone, forgot, unfamed,
> You – you alone, of all the long, long line
> Of those who've sung untaught, unknown, unnamed,
> Have stretched out upward, seeking the divine.[16]

When poets such as Johnson honored the endurance of enslaved people, they continued a tradition that had existed among African Americans since emancipation, in which they paid tribute to the quiet heroism of those who survived enslavement.[17] The slave songs might not have overturned the institution in the way of armed rebellion, but their existence signaled that enslaved Africans and their descendants had not acquiesced to their enslavement. Nor had they believed or succumbed to racist caricatures of blackness and black people. This was a history of which to be proud and an archive to bring to the light.

Discarding Slavery's Traumatic Legacy by Transcending the Past

Just as Johnson was compiling the first of his anthologies, Jean Toomer was also exploring the relationship between slavery and the present day in a series of published and unpublished poems, plays, and prose pieces that within a couple of years would coalesce into his critically acclaimed, genre-bending book *Cane* (1923). Toomer's biography and its relationship to *Cane* has been told often yet is worth repeating in the context of this study of slavery in the poetry of the Harlem Renaissance. Raised in the elite black circles of Washington, DC, Toomer found his first trip South- to Sparta, Georgia in the fall of 1921 to serve as a temporary school principal- a complete revelation. Where Johnson would argue that to an inquiring mind it was self-evident that contemporary artistic forms such as ragtime and swing originated in southern black culture of earlier generations, for the narrator of *Cane*, this link was a fresh discovery. Yet where Johnson and others argued for slave culture as a source of pride and inspiration, for Toomer this was a much more complicated legacy. As he portrayed it in *Cane* – and as his own life's trajectory after the book's publication seemed to bear out – slavery's aftermath was something that his own generation had a responsibility to face and dispense with, so as to spare successive generations the continuing trauma he had endured.[18]

Cane shared with contemporary journalists, scholars, and folklorists an urgency borne of a sudden realization that the last generation of the formerly enslaved would soon enough be dead and with their deaths would go an untapped storehouse of knowledge and culture dating back to before the Civil War.[19] In fact, purported folklorists had been "capturing" and publishing the stories and songs of "old-time Negroes" for decades. Yet changes in the academic disciplines and methods of anthropology and sociology provoked a new generation to seek out and "record" data in innovative ways and with a sometimes more sympathetic attitude.

Toomer differed from these groups in being much more ambivalent about the value of excavating the archive of a history – slavery – steeped in trauma. Take the poem "Song of the Son," which in 1922 was the first of the pieces in the eventual book to be published.[20] The unnamed narrator notes that he has "returned" to the South just "In time, for though the sun is setting on / A song-lit race of slaves, it has not set . . . it is not too late yet / To catch thy plaintive soul soon gone." Like a literary gerontologist, the narrator discerns the value of the culture of formerly enslaved people. With the poem's only use of the first person, the narrator establishes himself this culture's legatee. Yet the narrator expresses no particular joy or relief at having reached the South in time:

> O Negro slaves, dark purple ripened plums,
> Squeezed, and bursting in the pine-wood air,
> Passing, before they stripped the old tree bare
> One plum was saved for me, one seed becomes
>
> An everlasting song, a singing tree,
> Caroling softly souls of slavery,
> What they were, and what they are to me,
> Caroling softly souls of slavery.[21]

Where others such as Johnson held black folk culture, borne of slavery, up to the light for a reappraisal that would promote respect for African Americans more generally, Toomer hoped to bring it to light in order to vanquish its power. In *Cane*'s third and concluding section, named for its narrator, Ralph Kabnis, Toomer assayed the ambivalent effects of dallying with history, particularly a traumatic one such as enslavement.

In "Kabnis," the action returns to the South following a second section set in Washington, DC and Chicago. The title character, after some wrangling, is forced to reckon with the past. That past, including slavery, is represented by Father John, who inhabits a cellar known as "the hole," a spatial metaphor for the history that had been repressed. Kabnis, a writer, goes through something of a rebirth in John's presence and is nursed by a woman named Carrie K. Yet the end result of these exertions is deliberately unclear. Kabnis ascends from the hole but "with eyes downcast and swollen, trudg[ing]."[22] Whether the experience has revitalized his language and art is not clear. In the meantime, the women of the book, such as Carrie, have mostly given succor to men and their own futures are equally hazy.

In Toomer's view, the consequences of tangling with repressed trauma might be mixed or even harmful. The remedy for this tortured legacy, in his view, was to repudiate the very idea of race and racial difference and to embrace the opportunity that modernity had brought: an opportunity to forge a new people – an "American" race, beyond white, black, and native. Famously, trying to escape the hardening color line that defined life in the North and South, Toomer headed to the West. These beliefs and decisions hampered his writing career in a nation with a hardening color line, where marketing required a racial identification and a targeted audience.[23] Whether or not it was because of the waning of Toomer's star, his idea that addressing the past might have harmful effects was not taken up directly by other poets in the New Negro moment.

Creating an Alternative Archive of Black History in Poetry

In the face of the failures of academic, popular, and public history to tell the truth about the past, a third group of New Negro writers used poetry to probe the question of what precisely constituted slavery's archive and black history. This group was far larger than either the boosters such as Johnson or the elegists such as Toomer. While their poetry explicitly critiqued mainstream and popular historiography, as Johnson had done, they only implicitly suggested the black past be a source of pride. Nor did they advocate for the deliberate shedding of the past, as Toomer had done. They used poetry to muse upon the kinds of stories that dominated accounts of US history and on the kinds of evidence that were absent from histories of slavery. In doing so, these black poets brought to life oral history as a legitimate archive for making history.

Sometimes, black poets simply called out the shameless racism and greed that underpinned historical accounts of white benevolence and black inferiority. Anne Spencer was one. A librarian in a black high school for twenty years in Lynchburg, Virginia, Spencer was well known throughout town for her refusal to ride segregated public transport.

Probably less well-known among Lynchburg's white residents was that Spencer was a respected poet whose work was anthologized frequently and who was the first African American poet included in the *Norton Anthology of Poetry*.[24] In 1930, Spencer was enraged when she read a *National Geographic* article titled "Louisiana, Land of Perpetual Romance." Its ninety pages were steeped in the Acadian myth-making that was becoming central to the state's tourism industry.[25] In touting the place's economic and cultural riches, the reporter failed to mention that all of its success lay in the labor and lives of African Americans, past and present. Specific references to black Louisianians were limited to a few hackneyed photographs – for example, one that portrayed a group of five black men and boys, each with a half-eaten slice of watermelon and with a caption promising that none of them would sacrifice the pleasure of the fruit for a meal in one of New Orleans' fine restaurants.[26]

Spencer took particular umbrage at the public history efforts in Louisiana included in the article, which were typical of interwar local and national societies, all aiming to venerate the slaveholding South and Confederacy. These were the years when such groups, hoping to drown out the rising roar of civil rights activism, raised funds for hundreds of statues and plaques commemorating white founders of towns, leaders in the war, and even the supposedly faithful and loyal "darkies" of the past. The most egregious of these campaigns came quite close in 1923 to raising a statue to honor "the faithful colored mammies of the South" on the Washington, DC mall – an effort stymied by civil rights activists and black newspapers.[27] In Natchitoches, Louisiana, as the *National Geographic* reported, planter and banker J. L. Bryan commissioned the design and production of a bronze statue of a short, stooping man doffing his hat. Its caption read "Erected by the City of Natchitoches in grateful recognition of the arduous and faithful services of the Good Darkies of Louisiana." The statue, erected in 1927, soon became known to locals as "Uncle Jack."[28]

Spencer responded with a scorching seven-line poem that called to account not only those who had enslaved Africans and their descendants but also those – including white women – who besmirched the memory of enslaved people and burnished that of the enslavers. As with all of her poems whose themes were explicitly about black people or about racism, Spencer elected not to publish "The Sévignés."[29] In this poem, Spencer skewered fantasies of white southern paternalism by likening Louisiana's slaveholders to a brutal French seventeenth-century aristocrat, Madame de Sévignés, whose indifference to poor classes was legendary. Had

a published version of this poem reached her white Lynchburg neighbors,
Spencer may well have suffered:

> Down in Natchitoches there is a statue in a public square,
> A slave replica – not of Uncle Tom, praise God,
> But of Uncle Remus . . . a big plinth holding a little man bowing humbly to
>   a master-mistress.
> This shameless thing set up to the intricate involvement of human slavery,
> Go, see it, read it, with whatever heart you have left.
> No penance, callous beyond belief,
> For these women who had so lately fled from the slavery of Europe to the
>   great wilds of America.[30]

In the line that implored Americans to go see the statue with "whatever heart you have left," Spencer, as John Anstey has observed, drew
a line between present-day white Americans and those responsible for
slavery. They, like their ancestors, were "callous beyond belief."[31]
Spencer drew attention to the important role white women played
in public commemoration of the so-called "Lost Cause" of southern
and American history.

   Other poets found solace in portraying the private – and counter-public
– efforts of African Americans to commemorate the past in ways that
honored enslaved people. Langston Hughes, the most prolific poet of the
era, took up the question of slavery and its legacy in a number of poems.[32]
In "Aunt Sue's Stories," one of Hughes's earliest published poems, he
brought to life the precise way that so many black Americans testified to
learning about enslavement: sitting on southern porches with their aging
relatives, usually women, and feeling the experiences and people of the past
"mingle themselves softly" with the present through the power of oral
storytelling:

> Aunt Sue has a head full of stories.
> Aunt Sue has a whole heart full of stories.
> Summer nights on the front porch
> Aunt Sue cuddles a brown-faced child to her bosom
> And tells him stories.
>
> Black slaves
> Working in the hot sun,
> And black slaves
> Walking in the dewy night,
> And black slaves
> Singing sorrow songs on the banks of a mighty river
> Mingle themselves softly

In the flow of old Aunt Sue's voice,
Mingle themselves softly
In the dark shadows the cross and recross
Aunt Sue's stories.

And the dark-faced child, listening,
Knows that Aunt Sue's stories are real stories.
He knows that Aunt Sue
Never got her stories out of any book at all,
But that they came
Right out of her own life.

And the dark-faced child is quiet
Of a summer night
Listening to Aunt Sue's stories.[33]

Hughes's critique of contemporary mainstream historiography, whether scholarly or public, was muted but there nonetheless: black Americans "never got [the] stories out of any book at all." Rather, they were passed on by voice, within families and communal groups. If history books had failed to include Aunt Sue's "stories" – indeed if American historiography was steeped in a mythology that made her account of enslavement impossible for most white people even to hear – then the idea of what constituted legitimate historical evidence needed adjusting.

Still other New Negro poets recognized that there was some experience – for example, that of enslaved women, especially those who were no longer alive – for which the archive was always going to be mere traces. In this instance, it might be necessary to let imagination serve as a legitimate method of historical recovery. Or, to put this another way, to make a virtue of the act of imagining of the past, which was already a part of historical work, no matter how much academic historians insisted that their art was a science, based on verifiable and repeatable data.[34] Poetry could serve to fill that need. (Later, when black diaspora writers were able to publish novel-length work addressing the same issue, they would do so.[35])

Jessie Fauset, who would go on to become the most prolific novelist of the Harlem Renaissance, addressed the question of the historical record of enslaved women's experiences in a 1920 poem, "Oriflamme," which appeared in *The Crisis* (Figure 2.1).[36] The poem opened with an epigraph, which at eighty words was more than twice the length of the two-quatrain poem. The epigraph was a quotation by famed former slave and abolitionist Sojourner Truth. In it, Truth recalled her childhood, asking her mother why she was so mournful. Truth's African-born mother

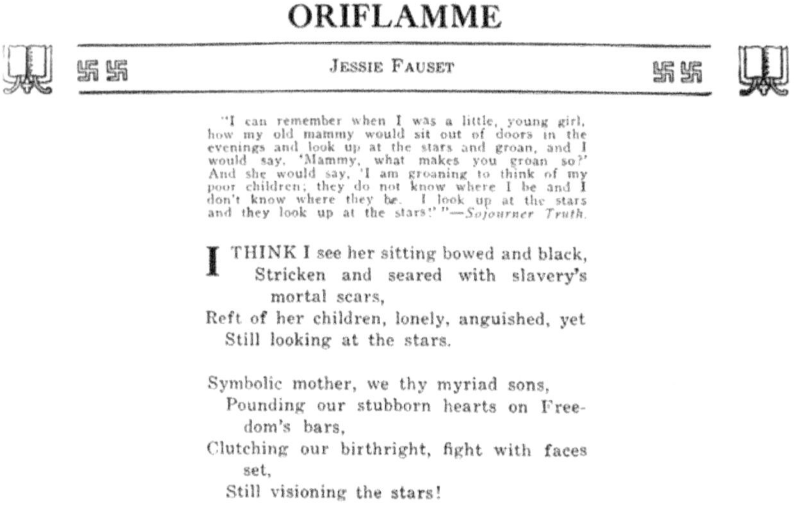

ORIFLAMME

JESSIE FAUSET

"I can remember when I was a little, young girl, how my old mammy would sit out of doors in the evenings and look up at the stars and groan, and I would say, 'Mammy, what makes you groan so?' And she would say, 'I am groaning to think of my poor children; they do not know where I be and I don't know where they be. I look up at the stars and they look up at the stars!' "—*Sojourner Truth.*

I THINK I see her sitting bowed and black,
    Stricken and seared with slavery's
        mortal scars,
Reft of her children, lonely, anguished, yet
    Still looking at the stars.

Symbolic mother, we thy myriad sons,
    Pounding our stubborn hearts on Free-
        dom's bars,
Clutching our birthright, fight with faces
    set,
    Still visioning the stars!

Figure 2.1 Jessie Fauset, "Oriflamme," *The Crisis* 19, no. 3 (January 1920), 128.

lamented, with quotation marks within quotation marks, "I am groaning to think of my poor children; they do not know where I be and I don't know where they be. I look up at the stars and they look up at the stars!" In the ensuing poem, Fauset put into verse the legacy of slavery's catastrophic effects on families separated from one another. In the second stanza, she proclaimed that "Symbolic mother, we thy myriad sons, / Pounding our stubborn hearts on Freedom's bars, / Clutching our birthright, fight with faces set, / Still visioning the stars!" The skies under which the struggle for freedom continued long after emancipation were both geographically and metaphorically similar, with the racism that gave shape to slavery continuing to sculpt black life in the USA.

    Fauset took Truth's words from an account of meeting Truth that Harriet Beecher Stowe published in the *Atlantic* magazine in 1863, but, recognizing the likelihood that Stowe had already manipulated Truth's words, Fauset altered them further. The epigraph appeared in *The Crisis* without any of the spellings and punctuation that denoted so-called black dialect, as Stowe had rendered Truth's speech. Fauset also omitted the final half-sentence in Stowe's account of Truth's recollection of her mother's words; rather than finishing with the romantic idea that at the very least mother and children stared upon the same star-filled night, in Stowe's account Truth's mother ended her short speech with the mournful words "but I can't tell where they be."[37]

In her efforts to reclaim Truth's voice outside of Harriet Beecher Stowe's rendering of her speech, Fauset had an ally: W. E. B. Du Bois. The epigraph to "Oriflamme" appeared in print almost simultaneously in Du Bois's mixed-genre book *Darkwater: Voices from within the Veil.*[38] Fauset's poem appeared in *The Crisis* in January 1920; *Darkwater* was published the very next month, with the manuscript having been sent off the previous September.[39] We do not know when Fauset wrote "Oriflamme," and whether the effort to alter the archive of Truth's words was her idea, Du Bois's idea, or one that the two of them – at the time working closely together at *The Crisis* – decided to embark on together. Du Bois quoted Truth in a chapter in which he paid tribute to African and black diaspora mothering, declaring that "The great black race gave the world not only the Iron Age, the cultivation of the soil, and the domestication of animals, but also, in peculiar emphasis, the mother-idea."[40] In short, Du Bois threw his considerable intellectual weight and reputation behind the archive of Truth's speech as created simultaneously in print by both him and Fauset. Together, they represented black history in such a way as to venerate the enormous effort of enslaved Africans and their descendants, especially black women, to make, maintain, and remake kinship ties, even in the face of the extraordinary violence of enslavement.[41]

Conclusion

Some have argued that the presence of slavery in Harlem Renaissance texts waxed and waned around a dynamic of remembering and forgetting. Yet the era's major writers nearly all dealt with this aspect of black history and US history in some way, if not directly in novels. So too did visual artists and performers. When it came to the less well-known figures who gave breadth and depth to the era and to the black public sphere that made the whole period so important, slavery was a major topic.

Harlem Renaissance poets wondered at the nature of the legacy that slavery had left African Americans, and considered its value and cost. For some, the culture that enslaved Africans and their American-born descendants had generated in such adverse circumstances was something to marvel at and to celebrate. For others, that culture was a dying relic, whose passing might be mourned but would also provide an opportunity to make anew the American race, healed of the wounds of the past. A majority of interwar black poets, perhaps the most pragmatic of the three groups, saw the political uses to which dominant tales of southern history were put and opposed them in their work. The poetry of these "New Negroes" drew attention to the self-aggrandizing mythology of most American history and stressed instead the violence and disruption upon which the nation lay. They also suggested that without a more creative approach to history-writing and history-making – one that recognized that the rules of evidence among professional historians served white supremacy and myth-making about "happy darkies" and benign slave-owners – the truth might never be told.

Notes

For excellent suggestions as I wrote and revised this chapter, my thanks to Rachel Farebrother, Melinda Harvey, and Deakin's School of Humanities & Social Sciences Writing Group. Thanks too to the Australian Research Council for its generous support of my research.

1. Emily Bernard, "The Renaissance and the Vogue," in *The Cambridge Companion to the Harlem Renaissance*, ed. George Hutchinson (New York: Cambridge University Press, 2007), 28–40.

2. On modernists' impulse to shed history, including metaphorical matricide, see Ann Douglas, *Terrible Honesty: Mongrel Manhattan in the 1920s* (New York: Farrar, Straus and Giroux, 1995).

3. W. Fitzhugh Brundage, *The Southern Past: A Clash of Race and Memory* (Cambridge, MA: Belknap Press of Harvard University Press, 2005); Karen L. Cox, *Dixie's Daughters: The United Daughters of the Confederacy and the Preservation of Confederate Culture* (Gainesville: University Press of Florida, 2003); Julie Des Jardins, *Women and the Historical Enterprise in America: Gender, Race, and the Politics of Memory, 1880–1945* (Chapel Hill: University of North Carolina Press, 2003); Joan Marie Johnson, "'Drill into us . . . the Rebel tradition': The Contest over Southern Identity in Black and White Women's Clubs, South Carolina, 1898–1930," *Journal of Southern History* 66 (2000): 525–562; Ethan J. Kytle and Blain Roberts, *Denmark Vesey's Garden: Slavery and Memory in the Cradle of the Confederacy* (New York: New Press, 2018); Stephanie E. Yuhl, *A Golden Haze of Memory: The Making of Historic Charleston* (Chapel Hill: University of North Carolina Press, 2005).

4. Mark E. Benbow, "Birth of a Quotation: Woodrow Wilson and 'Like Writing History with Lightning,'" *Journal of the Gilded Age and Progressive Era* 9 (2010): 509–533.

5. Jacqueline Goggin, "Countering White Racist Scholarship: Carter G. Woodson and the *Journal of Negro History*," *Journal of Negro History* 68 (1983): 355–375.

6. Earl E. Thorpe, *Black Historians: A Critique* (New York: William Morrow, 1971), 108–133; August Meier and Elliott Rudwick, *Black History and the Historical Profession, 1915–1980* (Urbana: University of Illinois Press, 1986); Jacqueline Goggin, *Carter G. Woodson: A Life in Black History* (Baton Rouge: Louisiana State University Press, 1993); Pero Dagbovie, *The Early Black History Movement, Carter G. Woodson, and Lorenzo Johnston Greene* (Urbana: University of Illinois Press, 2007); Clare Corbould, *Becoming African Americans: Black Public Life in Harlem, 1919–1939* (Cambridge, MA: Harvard University Press, 2009), 106–110; Jeffrey Aaron Snyder, *Making Black History: The Color Line, Culture, and Race in the Age of Jim Crow* (Athens: University of Georgia Press, 2018).

7. *Unwritten History of Slavery: Autobiographical Account of Negro Ex-Slaves*, Social Science Source Documents No. 1 (Nashville, TN: Social Science Institute, Fisk University, 1945); and *God Struck Me Dead: Religious Conversion Experiences and Autobiographies of Negro Ex-Slaves*, Social Science Source Documents No. II (Nashville, TN: Social Science Institute, Fisk University, 1945).

8. New Negro movement writers and artists might be considered forerunners of scholarly critics of historians' archival practices. For examples in the historiography of Atlantic slavery, see Michel-Rolph Trouillot, *Silencing the Past: Power and the Production of History* (Boston: Beacon Press, 1995); Saidiya V. Hartman, *Scenes of Subjection: Terror, Slavery, and Self-Making in Nineteenth-Century America* (New York: Oxford University Press, 1997); Saidiya Hartman, "Venus in Two Acts," *Small Axe* 26 (2008): 1–14; and Marisa J. Fuentes, *Dispossessed Lives: Enslaved Women, Violence, and the Archive* (Philadelphia: University of Pennsylvania Press, 2016). Also see three recent collections/special journal issues: Jennifer Brier, Jim Downs, and Jennifer L. Morgan, eds., *Connexions: Histories of Race and Sex in North America* (Urbana: University of Illinois Press, 2016); Brian Connolly and Marisa Fuentes, eds., *History of the Present* 6, no. 2 (2016); and Laura Helton, et al., eds., "The Question of Recovery: Slavery, Freedom, and the Archive," *Social Text 125* 33 (2015).

9. The same argument might also be made for visual culture; interwar artists certainly addressed enslavement and its legacy, from the prints that appeared in Associated Publishers books to Aaron Douglas's monumental murals on the walls of the New York Public Library, Harlem YMCA, Fisk University, and elsewhere.

10. George Hutchinson, *The Harlem Renaissance in Black and White* (Cambridge, MA: Belknap Press of Harvard University Press, 1995).

11. Aaron W. Marrs, "New Introduction," in Ulrich Bonnell Phillips, *A History of Transportation in the Eastern Cotton Belt to 1860* (Columbia: University of South Carolina Press, 2011), xv; Claire Parfait, "Rewriting History: The

Publication of W. E. B. Du Bois's *Black Reconstruction in America* (1935),"
Book History 12 (2009): 266–294.

12. On Hurston's efforts to publish her scholarly and nonfiction accounts of slavery
and its legacy, see Deborah G. Plant, "Introduction," in Zora Neale Hurston,
Barracoon: The Story of the Last Slave (London: HQ, 2018), xxi; Carla Kaplan,
"Introduction," in Zora Neale Hurston, *Every Tongue Got To Confess: Negro
Folk-tales from the Gulf States* (New York: HarperCollins, 2001), xxi–xxxi;
Carla Kaplan, ed., *Zora Neale Hurston: A Life in Letters* (New York: Random
House, 2002), 52, 164 and relevant letters. Cf. Rebecca Panovka, "A Different
Backstory for Zora Neale Hurston's 'Barracoon,'" *Los Angeles Review of Books*,
July 7, 2018, https://lareviewofbooks.org/article/different-backstory-for-zora-
neale-hurstons-barracoon/ (accessed June 30, 2019); and Hannah Durkin,
"Finding Last Middle Passage Survivor Sally 'Redoshi' Smith on the Page
and Screen," *Slavery and Abolition*, 40, no. 4 (2019): 631–658.

13. James Weldon Johnson, ed., *The Book of American Negro Poetry* (New York:
Harcourt, Brace and Company, 1922); ed., *The Book of American Negro
Spirituals* (New York: Viking Press, 1925); and ed., *The Second Book of
Negro Spirituals* (New York: Viking Press, 1926). On sales, see Hutchinson,
The Harlem Renaissance in Black and White, 342–386; and George
Hutchinson, "Publishers and Publishing Houses," in *Encyclopedia of the
Harlem Renaissance*, ed. Cary D. Wintz and Paul Finkelman (New York:
Routledge, 2004), 1000–1004.

14. Johnson, ed., *The Book of American Negro Poetry*, 17.

15. Johnson, ed., *The Book of American Negro Spirituals*, 14.

16. James Weldon Johnson, "O Black and Unknown Bards," in *The Book of
American Negro Poetry*, ed. Johnson, 123–124. Originally published in *Century*
magazine, 1908.

17. Narratives by formerly enslaved people published after the Civil War show
the same tendency, celebrating the sheer survival of slavery as opposed to the
heroic escape that formed the centerpiece of "slave narratives" published with
the support of abolitionists in the antebellum era. See William L. Andrews,
"Slave Narratives, 1865–1900," in *The Oxford Handbook of the African
American Slave Narrative*, ed. John Ernest (New York: Oxford University
Press, 2014), 219–232.

18. Scholarship on *Cane* and Toomer is substantial, but see in particular Paul
Allen Anderson, *Deep River: Music and Memory in Harlem Renaissance
Thought* (Durham: Duke University Press, 2001), 65–77;
Rachel Farebrother, *The Collage Aesthetic in the Harlem Renaissance* (2009;
Oxon: Routledge, 2016), 79–109; Matthew Pratt Guterl, *The Color of Race in
America, 1900–1940* (Cambridge, MA: Harvard University Press, 2001),
176–183; and George Hutchinson, "Introduction," in Jean Toomer, *Cane*,
ed. George Hutchinson (New York: Penguin, 2019), xiii–xxxii.

19. John W. Blassingame, *Slave Testimony: Two Centuries of Letters, Speeches,
Interviews, and Autobiographies* (Baton Rouge: Louisiana State University
Press, 1977); John B. Cade, "Out of the Mouths of Ex-Slaves," *Journal of*

Negro History 20 (1935): 294–337; Catherine A. Stewart, *Long Past Slavery: Representing Race in the Federal Writers' Project* (Chapel Hill: University of North Carolina Press, 2016), 11–13, 28–34.

20. Jean Toomer, "Song of the Son," *The Crisis* 23, no. 6 (April 1922): 261. For a list of the dates of publications of eighteen of the pieces that were later included in the book, sometimes in altered form, see Toomer, *Cane*, 159–161.

21. Toomer, *Cane*, 15–16.

22. Ibid., 158.

23. On the color line in this era, see Earl Lewis and Heidi Ardizzone, *Love on Trial: An American Scandal in Black and White* (New York: Norton, 2001); Guterl, *The Color of Race in America*; and Mae M. Ngai, *Impossible Subjects: Illegal Aliens and the Making of Modern America* (Princeton: Princeton University Press, 2004).

24. Biographical details from J. Lee Greene, *Time's Unfading Garden: Anne Spencer's Life and Poetry* (Baton Rouge: Louisiana State University Press, 1977).

25. W. Fitzhugh Brundage, "Le Réveil de la Louisiane: Memory and Acadian Identity, 1920–1960," in *Where These Memories Grow: History, Memory, and Southern Identity*, ed. Brundage (Chapel Hill: University of North Carolina Press, 2000), 271–298.

26. Ralph A. Graves, "Louisiana, Land of Perpetual Romance," *National Geographic* LVII (1930): 393–482.

27. Micki McElya, *Clinging to Mammy: The Faithful Slave in Twentieth-Century America* (Cambridge, MA: Harvard University Press, 2007), 116–159.

28. The article misquoted the plaque as reading "Good Darkeys." On the statue's genesis and afterlife following its removal in 1968, see Fiona J. L. Handley, "Memorializing Race in the Deep South: The 'Good Darkie' Statue, Louisiana, USA," *Public Archaeology* 6 (2007): 98–115; Gretchen Victoria Klobucar, "Thinking Outside the (Wooden) Box: A Rhetorical Analysis of the Ethical Complexity of the Uncle Jack Statue," MA thesis, University of North Carolina, 2011.

29. Evie Shockley, *Renegade Poetics: Black Aesthetics and Formal Innovation in African American Poetry* (Iowa City: University of Iowa Press, 2011), 121–144.

30. Anne Spencer, "The Sévignés," in *Shadowed Dreams: Women's Poetry of the Harlem Renaissance*, 2nd ed., ed. Maureen Honey (New Brunswick, NJ: Rutgers University Press, 2006), 261–262.

31. John C. Anstey, "Anne Spencer: A Conventional, Yet Unconventional, Harlem Renaissance Poet," MA thesis, Longwood University, 1999, 49.

32. See "The Negro Speaks of Rivers" (1921) and "Proem" (also called "Negro") (1926), which both portrayed slavery as something almost inherited in the body; "Mulatto" (1926), which formed the basis of the play of the same name that ran successfully on Broadway in 1935; and "Remember" (*c.* 1930), in which Hughes suggested that present-day oppression shared many characteristics with American slavery. Hughes also criticized white forms of commemoration, much as Anne Spencer had done, in his short story, "Slave on the

Block," *Scribner's* (Sept., 1933), reprinted in Langston Hughes, *The Ways of White Folks* (New York: Knopf, 1934), 19–31.

33. Langston Hughes, "Aunt Sue's Stories," *The Crisis* 22, no. 3 (July 1921): 121.

34. For a recent history of African American women's lives that takes this approach, see Saidiya Hartman, *Wayward Lives, Beautiful Experiments: Intimate Histories of Social Upheaval* (New York: Norton, 2019).

35. Scholars have made similar arguments for prose, for example, Maboula Soumahoro, "Story, History, Discourse: Maryse Condé's *Segu* and Afrodiasporic Historical Narration," in *Toward an Intellectual History of Black Women*, ed. Mia Bay, et al. (Chapel Hill: University of North Carolina Press, 2015), 178–194.

36. Jessie Fauset, "Oriflamme," *The Crisis* 19, no. 3 (January 1920): 128.

37. Harriet Beecher Stowe, "Sojourner Truth, The Libyan Sibyl," *Atlantic* (April 1863), available at www.theatlantic.com (accessed June 29, 2019).

38. Du Bois, *Darkwater: Voices from within the Veil* (New York: Harcourt, Brace and Howe, 1920), 176.

39. David Levering Lewis, *W. E. B. Du Bois: The Fight for Equality and the American Century, 1919–1963* (New York: Henry Holt, 2000), 11.

40. Du Bois, *Darkwater*, 166.

41. Hortense J. Spillers, "Mama's Baby, Papa's Maybe: An American Grammar Book," *Diacritics* 17, no. 2 (1987): 65–81.

CHAPTER 3

The New Negro among White Modernists

Kathleen Pfeiffer

Wednesday, March 24, 1926: a random, but representative single day as recorded in Carl Van Vechten's daybook reveals a few of the overlapping social circles through which white modernist writers and New Negroes influenced each other. Van Vechten first notes that his work day consisted of writing part of the jacket copy for his novel *Nigger Heaven* (1926) and drafting a review of the novel *Flight* by Walter White. Van Vechten continues:

> At 5 Blythe Daly & Donald Angus came in. Rebecca West gives a dinner at the Pullman Porters. Mrs. Somerset Maugham (met), Marinoff, Walter & Gladys White. . . . Then we went to Whites' where we were joined by Taylor Gordon. Marinoff goes home. Gladys very morose. The rest of us go to Small's where we see Covarrubias & Blanche Knopf with a handsome young man, & take Mrs. Maugham & Rebecca to Lucile Harper's. She won't let us in. Chop Suey at the Far East restaurant. Then home at 3.[1]

Van Vechten believed that he could achieve meaningful racial progress by, among other things, orchestrating integrated parties, and on March 24, we see this in action. The day brings together British, Mexican, and American friends, black, brown, and white: a group that includes authors, actresses, a designer, vocalist, activist, artist, and publisher, ending with a visit to his bootlegger's wife. Many New Negroes met white writers, publishers, readers, and critics, as well as potential mentors, supporters, and patrons, at the West 55th Street apartment shared by Van Vechten and his wife, actress Fania Marinoff. "He and Fania had prodigious and eclectic guest lists," notes Emily Bernard, "which included painter Salvador Dali, singer Bessie Smith, and publisher Horace Liveright."[2] These parties, ranging from the drunken and raucous to the cleverly themed, gleefully leapt over barriers of race and class and offered a model for social politics in action.

Yet for many of Harlem's New Negro writers, friendships with whites carried precarious implications. While these connections provided invaluable access to publishers, patrons, financial opportunities, and social power, they also required artists to navigate whites' racially limited expectations about black identity, expression, and behavior. White modernist writers struggled against the racist and racialist beliefs of their era with varying degrees of success, while New Negro writers chafed against the unconscious racism of their white friends and mentors. For some New Negroes, the "trickster" tradition offered a strategy for playfully disrupting the limitations of a racist social order. For others, when Langston Hughes declared, "We younger Negro artists who create now intend to express our individual dark-skinned selves without fear or shame,"[3] the words resonated. If progressive whites like Van Vechten expressed appreciation for black culture in ways that are seen today as fetishizing racial otherness, and as delighting in the exotic and the primitive, such modernists were also earnest in undertaking ways to comprehend and represent the black experience. Correspondence from these interracial friendships show that white writers sought genuine intimacy; they wanted to know about the interior lives and experiences of their black friends; and they offered not only reciprocal friendship, but also publishing connections and professional subvention in return.

Some New Negro writers developed deep and significant friendships with their white modernist colleagues with whom they shared aesthetic values, supportive collaboration, and authentic sympathetic engagement. In 1922, Jean Toomer wrote to Waldo Frank that "No one in this country . . . [understands me] but you my brother."[4] Frank and Toomer both identified as revolutionary artists, and both strove to create innovative literary forms and designs (terms which were often capitalized in their correspondence, a noted contrast to their use of lower-case letters in discussing "god" or "america"). Jean Toomer's career offers a case study in the porousness of the geographical, racial, and aesthetic boundaries which both joined and separated white and black writers in equal measure. Though *Cane* (1923) has long been identified as a signature text of black lyric genius, Toomer deliberately and consciously apprenticed himself to white modernist writers while he was composing it. Jean Toomer has long occupied an outsized place in Harlem Renaissance studies, and yet, Toomer once wrote that "to try and tie me to one of my parts is surely to loose [*sic*] me."[5]

The parts we have of Toomer are disparate and contradictory. For instance, in the unpublished autobiographical reflections he composed later in life, we see an account that is often at odds with the contemporaneous historical record. Barbara Foley notes, "Too often critics have imposed on the Toomer who wrote *Cane* the Toomer they discerned in later years – whether race traitor, proto-deconstructionist, or mystic seeking psychological wholeness."[6] Toomer's racial self-identification, which shifted throughout his life, seemed especially fluid during the years of *Cane*'s germination. Wesley Beal argues for a "logic of network" governing the politics, formal arrangement, and aesthetics in *Cane*[7] and it is important to note that Jean Toomer's writing life was also, likewise, deeply influenced by the social framework of geography, neighborhood, and friendship. In detailing the complex interracial social relations of this time and place, Michael Soto has noted that "Jean Toomer was one among many Villagers lured there by the charm and romance of its recent past."[8] Toomer's involvement with the Greenwich Village network of white modernist writers was initially cultivated by Lola Ridge, whose parties offered space where the avant-garde could gather; there, Toomer met and mingled with a number of influential writers, artists, editors, and critics. Ridge had been an enthusiastic advocate for modernism during her tenure at the modernist little magazines *Broom* and *Others*, soliciting, encouraging, and advising writers whose experimentation in form, subject, and approach helped to expand the American aesthetic idiom. "Famous and not-so-famous writers and artists and activists poured into her apartment," explains Terese Svoboda, "to discuss the future of art in America and its various freedoms: literary, sexual, and political."[9] Over the years, her guests included William Carlos Williams, H.D., Marianne Moore, Evelyn Scott, Hart Crane, and many others.

In 1919 and 1920, Toomer lodged in Greenwich Village, just a few doors away from the East Ninth Street apartment of Harold and Marjorie Content Loeb, the basement of which would function as the New York office of *Broom* magazine a year later. In its November 1921 first issue, *Broom*'s manifesto declared its intention to become "a sort of clearing house where the artists of the present time will be brought into closer contact."[10] The "closer contact" among artists who *Broom* advocated certainly encouraged Toomer's creative development, and Lola Ridge's generally underappreciated influence on Toomer contributed significantly to his distinctive lyric style. His early letters to her detail his emerging vision, "the rhythm of peasantry [*sic*] with the rhythm of machines. A syncopation, a slow jazz, a sharp intense motion, subtilized [*sic*], fused to a terse lyricism" (qtd in Svoboda, 195). Ridge understood Toomer's poetry as "delicately impressionistic" with "whimsical fancy and a sense of form (unity) as well as of cadence" (134). Toomer read Lola Ridge and was influenced by her poetry, and she, in turn, read and encouraged him.

Toomer became her "protege," and by the time *Broom* published his "Seventh Street" in its December 1922 edition at Ridge's insistence, "she had been critiquing Toomer's poetry for several years" (195). Toomer's friendship with Ridge drew him into *Broom*'s orbit, which buzzed with radical politics, a dedication to free expression and numerous vivacious social interactions.

In 1920, the year Toomer and Frank met at one such Lola Ridge party, they shared critical sensibilities, were mutually committed to formal aesthetic experimentation, and held likeminded progressive political views, though each man had traveled to his particular spiritual, philosophical, and artistic identity along distinctly different paths. In nomenclature alone, we see a hint of each writer's future: consider Waldo David Frank, named after Ralph Waldo Emerson and Henry David Thoreau, who lived his life dedicated to the pursuit and expression of the carefully considered individualism espoused by those writers. Even as a high school student, his intellectual ambitions were clear, and were clearly aligned with the American literary tradition. "I was already keeping notebooks, filling them with exalted resolutions," he writes. "I put down about this time: 'All the books that I shall write shall be proofs of God.' This, of course, was pure Walt Whitman."[11] Nor was his aesthetic ambition solely literary: he was a dedicated, lifelong, amateur cellist, having been raised in a family that valued arts and culture generally. Frank's Jewishness rendered him something of an outsider at Yale, yet he excelled academically, earned a combined BA and MA in just three years, graduated Phi Beta Kappa in 1911, and was named an honorary fellow of the university.

Looking back on his college-aged self, Frank recalls that "modern America was whirling too fast for the young man to find a base there for his vision" (43). Frank's ambition to write novels that "were to be 'proofs of God', who is revealed to every human being when he has the experience of love and calls it beauty" (102) was particularly strong when he and Toomer met. While Waldo Frank seems to have imbibed the racial essentialism of his era, he maintained a sympathetic sensitivity around race that distinguished him from many whites – a legacy, perhaps, of his deeply rooted individualism. While traveling the South as a guest speaker at the Tuskegee Institute, Frank noted the devastating impact of segregation, observing how "these Negro peasants of Alabama were exiles on their own soil, barred from its politics, its universities, held in subjection by the reigning culture" (103). Yet during his lecture (on "Negro music and its relation to America"), Frank marveled at the "unbroken attention" of the Tuskegee student body, as the pupils "with their eyes multiplied a thousandfold into a single eye of spirit . . . as if they were aristocrats with a long heritage of command in their blood, while listening to the message of an envoy from a hostile neighboring country" (102–103).

In addition to several novels, Frank published journalism and criticism in the 1910s, particularly the influential *Our America* (1922), in which he intended to critique national culture in the manner of Whitman's *Democratic Vistas*. With his fellow founding editors of the *Seven Arts* literary magazine, he celebrated the era's "renascent period" in which "the arts cease to be private matters; they become not only the expression of the national life but a means to its enhancement."[12] The *Seven Arts* helped launch a particular style of politically engaged and spiritually informed literary modernism, one imbued with a pluralist, progressive nationalism, goals that were sometimes contradictory, and were joined under the moniker Young America. The magazine not only published Claude McKay's poetry as early as 1917, but under Waldo Frank's influence also it celebrated, and thereby created a receptive audience for, the sort of cultural pluralism that would find its fullest expression in the New Negro movement.

Was there a similar sense of nomenclatural destiny for the man who, in 1920, claimed the name Jean Toomer? Called Nathan Eugene Pinchback Toomer by his parents at birth, he underwent a series of name changes that reflected not only the battle for control to which he was subjected as a child, but also the peripatetic nature of his early adulthood. When his father, Nathan Toomer, abandoned his mother, Nina Pinchback, soon after their only son was born, Toomer's maternal grandparents rhetorically erased his father; thereafter, Nathan's name was not spoken in their home, and his son was addressed as "Eugene Pinchback." Even before this abandonment, Toomer's maternal grandparents had long objected to their only daughter marrying a man twenty-seven years her senior, a man who had been married twice before. As a Pinchback, rather than a Toomer, the boy was aligned with his mother's socially prominent African American family. He was also steeped in the race pride of his grandfather, P. B. S. Pinchback, a man whose political work on behalf of civil rights connected the family to an inescapable public role. His mother's untimely death in 1909 essentially solidified his identity as a Pinchback, which also brought rigorous expectations against which he would chafe as a young man. Rudolph P. Byrd and Henry Louis Gates note that "during the 1930s and 1940s, Toomer published under the name of N. J. Toomer, initials for Nathan Jean,"[13] an indication that even well into adulthood, Toomer adopted alternative monikers which disguised, and thereby distanced him from, his grandfather's legacy.

When, as a young man, he chose "Jean" for himself, it was not intended to evoke the "Eugene" of his birth name, but rather in homage to Romain Rolland's 1913 *Jean Christophe*. The eponymous fictional character served as an inspiration to Toomer and Frank both, not only in Jean Christophe's identity as a musician, but also in the deeply spiritual nature of his artistic struggle. Toomer had presented himself to Frank as an aspiring musician when they first met in 1920, and Frank had offered him an introduction to the composer Ernest Bloch. Yet in their initial correspondence, Toomer was already trying his hand as a writer, and Frank complimented the effort: "Your paper was a remarkably clear and keen piece of work ... you are doubtless, by your own findings a musician, but you have a mind that does not show to disadvantage in writing, either."[14] Toomer developed a keen appreciation for Frank's literary experimentation, celebrating precisely those aspects of Frank's 1922 lyric novel *Rahab* that eschew traditional forms. "But how you have spiritualized it!" Toomer enthuses. "I get a sense of mass movement; a sense of something that is inevitable and permanent. You give horizons; a consciousness of life not simply of the present, but of the past and future, not merely of life as confined and limited by town or race or country, but of life as related to the universe" (28). Even in this early exchange, we not only see that, as Mark Whalan argues, Toomer "engaged in a more substantial way than any other figure of the New Negro Renaissance with the ideas of the white avant-garde,"[15] but perhaps more powerfully, that he strives toward a literary expression of spiritual universality.

Toomer and Frank struggled together with the question of how abstract concepts can be manifested through literary form. Frank's aesthetic and political influence can be seen in *Cane*'s formal logic. Wesley Beal argues that "the spirit of *unanimisme*" informs *Cane*'s shape as a network: "Toomer's experiments with networks of form and content indicate the network's central role in the aesthetics of American modernism and demonstrate how American moderns were beginning to rely on the network as a conceptual tool to rethink their changing milieu – and in Toomer's case, the dynamics of race in America."[16] Toomer's social network also played a powerful role in his aesthetic choices, and his correspondence with white modernist writers illustrates that the influence was often reciprocal and multidirectional. *Cane* was composed alongside of – and in conversation with – Waldo Frank's own southern novel, *Holiday* (1923). This important historical fact bears on each work's formal logic, racial politics, and aesthetic achievement. "I cannot think of myself as being separated from you in the dual task of creating an American literature, and of developing a public, however large or small, capable of responding to our creations," Toomer wrote to Frank. "Those who read and know me, should read and know you" (Pfeiffer, 58–59). In Waldo Frank's foreword to *Cane*, he discusses Toomer's poetics and formal choices using much of the same language that Toomer himself uses in describing both his aesthetic and his transcendent goals. "You not only understand CANE; you are *in* it," Toomer assured Frank, "specifically here and there, mystically because of the spiritual bond there is between us" (100).

The two friends critiqued each other's work in matters that were quotidian as well as spiritual, technical as well as aesthetic. "I am wide open to you for criticism and suggestion," Toomer notes (86). Frank, in return, sought Toomer's help in representing his black characters accurately and authentically:

> May I ask you, aside from giving me your general aesthetic impressions, to go into details with me? as to language, 'business', anything else that occurs to you. You know, the spirit of this world is nearer to me than its body. If you can help me, where I may have gone off as regards the body, I shall be indeed obliged. (97)

Frank's early criticism of the pieces that would become *Cane* identifies a "deadness of the texture" that needs "rewriting rather than reconstructing" in order to enhance the "very beautiful colorful glow of life" which is an evident, but inconsistent strength. Frank assures Toomer that he has "a vision . . . the start of a true Form, but that the Form is not yet there." He continues, "Your whole aim is so new, that the work of formulation must needs be absolutely independent: and to create Form out of chaos, as must all true american artists, takes time time time" (34–35). Perhaps Frank's apparent disregard for traditional punctuation and capitalization in these critiques simply reflects the uncorrected quality of a hastily typed letter; nevertheless, it also underscores the message at its heart, highlighting *Form*, rendering *american* as uncapitalized adjective, and rendering the drumbeat of time time time without pausing for commas. Similar rhapsodies are certainly evident in Toomer's response to Frank's critique. His lengthy letter exalts "the Negro peasant, strong with the tang of fields and soil," describing his Georgia experience with the kinds of sensual details that are often celebrated as examples of Toomer's lyric genius. Still, he accepts

Frank's practical stylistic advice: "I am certain that I would get more inner satisfaction from a free narrative form," he avers (38).

Toomer's formal innovations consistently engaged the agrarian dimensions of southern slavery, yet the natural imagery contained significant personal associations as well. As Barbara Foley notes, "While Toomer was obviously currying favor with his newfound modernist acquaintances – and papering over his criticisms – it bears noting that he consistently deployed the *combinatoire* of seed, soil, root, plant, fruit, and harvest to describe, and insert himself within, the project of creating a nationally based modern literature."[17] Foley's attention to these repeated images of root, tree, and branch connect to her important recent biographical discoveries about Jean Toomer's extended family, and in particular, his sister Mamie Toomer, whose "buried history," she argues, "is contained in the cracks and interstices of *Cane*."[18]

The friendship and collaboration between Toomer and Frank unraveled shortly after *Holiday* and *Cane* appeared in print. Frank's marriage dissolved and he sailed to Europe, unaware that Toomer had become romantically involved with his soon-to-be-ex-wife, Margaret Naumberg. Toomer and Naumberg's intimacy, which likely began around the time of *Holiday* and *Cane*'s joint publication in the late summer of 1923, continued until the spring of 1926, when Toomer ended the relationship. They shared a mutual and intense devotion to the spiritual teachings of George Gurdjieff, a popular mystic; it had been a serious relationship and they even discussed marriage for a time. Jean Toomer was especially drawn to Gurdjieff's promise that "cosmic consciousness" might be achieved through esoteric practice, and, in time, this spiritual quest ultimately supplanted his literary ambition. Nevertheless, Toomer remained involved with white modernists as well as New Negroes during the time he lived in New York; Carl Van Vechten's daybooks record a number of instances where Toomer joined his parties. Indeed, on the evening when Van Vechten first met Toomer in early 1925, Countee Cullen made history: it was a rare occasion when the normally reserved poet was seen dancing the Charleston.[19]

Critical engagement with Carl Van Vechten's life and legacy often pauses on his well-documented desire to generate marketable interest in Harlem-based literature. "Are Negro writers going to write about this exotic material while it is still fresh," he once asked, "or will they continue to make a free gift of it to white authors who will exploit it until not a drop of vitality remains?" In this oft-cited passage responding to the 1926 *Crisis* magazine symposium "The Negro in Art: How Shall He Be Portrayed?"

Van Vechten extolled the commercial opportunities awaiting black authors. "The squalor of Negro life, the vice of Negro life, offer a wealth of novel, exotic, picturesque material to the artist," he writes, revealing his fetishistic attraction to the "primitive" aspects of Negro life.[20] Yet Van Vechten's passion for black arts, black culture, and black people was a deeply rooted and lifelong one, and he deployed that passion in a dedicated effort to bring black voices into the modernist literary canon. He delivered manuscripts from Langston Hughes, Rudolph Fisher, and Nella Larsen to his friend, the publisher Alfred A. Knopf.

While it is true, as John K. Young has noted, that "what sets the white publisher-black author relationship apart is the underlying social structure that transforms the usual unequal relationship into an extension of a much deeper cultural dynamic," it is also true that Van Vechten worked tirelessly to promote the work of black writers throughout the 1920s, and his influence was felt on many levels.[21] In the fall of 1925, for example, Jessie Fauset wrote to ask for Van Vechten's help with a novel she was having trouble placing. Then titled "Marker," the manuscript had been rejected by Liveright and was under review at Viking, which ultimately declined as well.[22] In later years, Fauset would attribute her difficulty finding an appreciative publisher to the fact that her fiction tended to feature aristo-cratic characters and genteel values, both of which were at odds with the edgy, jazz-inflected scenes that often drew white audiences to Harlem writing. "White readers just don't expect Negroes to be like this," she lamented.[23] Jessie Fauset thus turned away from those in the New Negro movement who offered a racialized commentary on modernism's cry to "Make it new!" Instead, she manipulated the familiar, by rendering ostensibly nineteenth-century tropes with subtle critiques of racism and sexism; yet modern audiences craved the novelty of twentieth-century aesthetic innovations, and this was a distinction of which Van Vechten was well aware.

Did Van Vechten have Jessie Fauset's work in mind as he began writing his own "Negro novel"? While he had been planning his book as early as May 1925, he struggled to get launched. On November 3, 1925 – just two weeks after receiving, and presumably reading, Fauset's manuscript – Van Vechten noted, "I begin work on Nigger Heaven and write most of the first chapter before lunch."[24] On the day Van Vechten received inspiration for the title *Nigger Heaven*, he partied at the Renaissance Casino and Ballroom in a group that included Jessie Fauset.[25] Nevertheless, once she read *Nigger Heaven*, Jessie Fauset was so offended that she stopped speaking to Van Vechten altogether, and cut him off her guest lists.[26] Later, when Fauset's own novel was published in 1929 as *Plum Bun*, it contained the subtitle "A Novel without a Moral," which George Hutchinson describes as "a direct slap, apparently, at *Nigger Heaven* (which had been reviewed positively in the *New York Age* under the heading 'A Novel with a Moral')." By then, whatever sympathy Van Vechten may have had for Fauset had long since disappeared; he privately, and cruelly, wrote that he found *Plum Bun* to be an "idiotic book."[27]

Like Van Vechten himself, *Nigger Heaven*, his controversial, best-selling 1926 novel, hovers over the Harlem Renaissance. A multifaceted pastiche merging fact and fiction, *Nigger Heaven* employs a collage aesthetic to shape character, and raises questions about how literature constructs individual, racial, and social identity. Structurally, the inclusion of instructive footnotes and a "Glossary of Negro Words and Phrases" invites readers to view the text as an academic or anthropological study, rather than a traditional novel. *Nigger Heaven* also juxtaposes its own unique fictional characters such as Adora Boniface and Lasca Sartoris (identifiably caricatures of A'Lelia Walker and Nora Holt) alongside the serial Van Vechten character Gareth Johns (a thinly veiled portrait of the author himself, who appears in several Van Vechten novels), in scenes peopled with Mimi Daquin (a fictional character from Walter White's 1926 novel *Flight*). While protagonist Mary Love is a rather one-dimensional character, she personifies Van Vechten's collage aesthetic, reciting long passages of Wallace Stevens from memory, offering didactic monologues about Christophe, and recommending carefully curated reading lists of African American writers. Even as these characters resist familiar categorizations, a subplot involving Dick Sill's passing for white underscores Van Vechten's challenges to American paradigms of racial classification.

Commercial interests notwithstanding, Van Vechten's involvement in Harlem was informed by his long-standing artistic investment in and intense fondness for black culture. Raised in Cedar Rapids, Iowa by racially progressive parents, Van Vechten was taught from childhood to respect and appreciate the dignity and humanity of African Americans. He was drawn to cosmopolitan life and the avant-garde, and he sought out black music, theater, art, and, indeed, black company whenever possible. Nevertheless, his early, appreciative reviews were often tinged with unexamined racial stereotypes. A review of "The Darktown Follies" celebrates a performance which seeks "to present the Negro as he is," creating, he writes, "a sort of spontaneity and effectiveness" which comes when "chorus men and women LIKE what they are doing, and as a result they do it well. . . . they scream with delight; they giggle intermittently; they wave their hands; they shriek."[28] An essay on "The Negro Theatre" likewise offers a nuanced appreciation while also commenting, "How the darkies danced, sang, and cavorted. Real nigger stuff, this, done with spontaneity and joy in the doing."[29]

Van Vechten felt entitled to use racist language, and that complicated legacy will always haunt his involvement in the Harlem Renaissance. He resisted all warnings that *Nigger Heaven*'s title would offend, and insisted that its aesthetic imperative mattered more. Although Langston Hughes had tried to dissuade Van Vechten from using the epithet, the poet ultimately provided the novelist and his book with incalculable practical and artistic support. A few months after *Nigger Heaven* was published, Van Vechten faced a lawsuit for copyright infringement: he had neglected to obtain permission to reproduce song lyrics that appeared throughout the work. Tense and distraught, he turned to Hughes, who responded without hesitation to his friend's request for help. Hughes traveled from Lincoln University to Van Vechten's New York apartment in order to compose, line for line, substitute lyrics for the passages in question. (Soon thereafter, Van Vechten provided Hughes with much appreciated support in kind, by steadfastly defending Hughes's own controversial aesthetic choices, when his title, *Fine Clothes to the Jew*, came under fire at Knopf.) Certainly, Van Vechten wanted a title that would draw attention, and he disregarded its potential to insult and to wound. It is representative of Van Vechten's peculiar racial myopia that when he wrote to Langston Hughes, "you and I are the only colored people who really love *niggers*," he meant it as an expression of love.[30] If Langston Hughes was offended by this, he appears not to have said so. Throughout the years, Hughes used the epithet himself in their correspondence, such as in a letter that signs off, "With a house full of niggers to you."[31] Still, Van Vechten seems to have learned a bitter lesson from the title. "When reviewing his old notebooks in the 1940's prior to committing them to academic archives," Edward White notes, "he even crossed out some uses of 'nigger' and wrote 'Negro' over the top, embarrassed that he had once used the word so indiscriminately."[32]

Van Vechten's influence on Harlem Renaissance artists and writers can be seen across genres: in the Miguel Covarrubias caricature of him depicted in blackface and titled "A Prediction"; in Zora Neale Hurston's declaring him a "Negrotarian," and her announcement that, "If Carl was a people instead of a person, I could then say, these are my people."[33] Harold Jackman's note to Van Vechten after meeting him articulates a sentiment felt by many. "You are the first white man with whom I have felt perfectly at ease," Jackman wrote. "You are just like a colored man! I don't know if you will consider this a compliment or not, but that's the only way I can put it."[34] Several of Van Vechten's African American friends were not only *not* offended by his "honorary Negro" status, they were actually quite supportive of him. The reciprocal influence that resulted from his friendship with Nella Larsen is particularly impactful. "Larsen was a willing pet of Van Vechten," Michelle Dean notes. "In a biographical sketch she gave her first publisher, she described her hobbies as 'bridge and collecting Van Vechteniana.'"[35] Larsen praised *Nigger Heaven* without reservation. "Was it you or another who told me of the shocked horror of one of your friends because 'Carl Van Vechten knows a Negro?'" Larsen wrote to him,

> Well! What will she say when she reads this shy story, with its air of deceptive simplicity and discovers that Carl Van Vechten knows the Negroe [*sic*]?
>
> It is a fine tale, this story of the deterioration and subsequent ruin of a weakling who blames all his troubles on that old scapegoat, the race problem. Dangerous too. But with what exquisite balance you have avoided the propagandistic pitfall. But of course, *you* would. Like your Lasca Sartoris, who so superbly breasts the flood of racial prejudices (black and white). . . . You see it's too close, too true, as if you had undressed the lot of us and turned on a strong light, Too, I feel a kind of despair. Why, oh, why, couldn't we have done something as big as this for ourselves? Fear, I suppose. It is big, big in its pity, big in its cruelties.[36]

Nigger Heaven's influence on Larsen is abundantly evident in her 1929 novel *Passing*, which explicitly echoes Van Vechten's structure, themes, and character development. Physically a "typical . . . Knopf novel," *Passing* was identical in "dimensions, typography, and binding" to her debut novel *Quicksand*, and it also matched *Nigger Heaven*'s dimensions and Caslon type. George Hutchinson remarks upon the impressive presence of "Larsen's bold dedication, 'To Carl Van Vechten and Fania Marinoff,' centered a bit above the middle of the page and spread out over four lines in large type."[37] The dedication reflected Larsen's genuine and appreciative regard for the Van Vechtens, who had become intimate friends by this time, and it also reflected her novel's deep engagement with the man and his work. John K. Young notes, "*Passing*'s (type)face is grounded in an implicitly white American history, even if its content challenges the racial assumptions growing out of that history."[38]

Passing cites the same Countee Cullen poem, "Heritage," that serves as *Nigger Heaven*'s own epigraph. The structure of Larsen's novel employs the same architecture as Van Vechten's, ordered into three sections

(Encounter, Re-Encounter, Finale), which offer transitions and closure parallel to that in *Nigger Heaven* (Prologue, Book One, Book Two) and which underscore that circularity through parallel images of motion. Similar trajectories of plot enhance the effect: *Passing*'s action begins as Irene rides an elevator up into a cool rooftop escape from the sweltering crowds in Chicago's brutal heat and ends with Clare's brutal fall from a penthouse window into the snow of a winter night. *Nigger Heaven*'s bracketing scenes, those for which, as Larsen well knew, Van Vechten was most harshly criticized as "noise and brawling,"[39] both depict raunchy, gin-soaked cabaret life. Both novels end with a sudden, violent death, and the subsequent appearance of a police officer: in Van Vechten's, "a coat of blue buttoned with brass"[40] and in Larsen's "a strange man, authoritative and official."[41] The working title for *Passing* was "Nig," an explicit association with Van Vechten's work, and the strength of Larsen's identification with the man and his novel cannot be underscored too strongly. She regularly updated him about her work on the novel and conceived of it, even in the planning stages, as a tribute to him. In a letter to Van Vechten on March 7, 1927, Larsen writes of her relief at having completed *Quicksand*, her first novel: "Heaven forbid that I should ever be bitten by the desire to write another novel! Except, perhaps, one to dedicate to you. For, why should Langston Hughes be the only one to enjoy notoriety for the sake of his convictions?"[42] George Hutchinson has noted numerous similarities between Nella Larsen herself and *Nigger Heaven*'s protagonist Mary Love: their bookshelves are appointed with all the same volumes; both read and admire Stein's "Melanctha"; both are self-restrained, and each feels torn between her white and black sides. So, too, do several notable similarities echo back from *Passing*: in Clare Kendry's cat-like nature, Larsen's "descriptors derive almost verbatim from Carl Van Vechten's writing about cats."[43] Clare and Carl both favor purple ink, and both write with an "almost illegible scrawl"[44] on unusually sized stationery.

In *Passing*, Clare's return to Harlem takes place against a background of race and class displacement that challenges race's role in defining communities. For as much as Clare Kendry embodies the sort of radical individualism made manifest by the Nordic Van Vechten's interloping forays uptown, Irene Redfield is a creature of her New Negro community in precisely the ways that W. E B. Du Bois promoted. Nella Larsen herself was cattily critical of the presumptuousness that sometimes surrounded the great man. In one instance, she received solicitation for a $100 donation toward Du Bois's birthday present, a collective $2500 gift. "Some nerve I say," she wrote Van Vechten. "I'm about to celebrate a birthday too and

I feel like writing and telling them that. I could use $2500 myself. In fact I think it will do me more good at thirty five than him at sixty."[45] She similarly betrayed her biting cynicism about pretentious race affairs, particularly those associated with National Association for the Advancement of Colored People (NAACP) social events, which she derided as "dicty," the popular Harlem slang word used to describe the swells of the so-called talented tenth. Larsen's own disgust with such hypocrisy is everywhere evident in correspondences, such as when she advised Van Vechten, "About the Spingarn Medal. If you got it, you'd be lynched – by Negroes. Take my advice, refuse it, 'graciously but firmly.'"[46]

While Nella Larsen criticized elitism within the New Negro social order, she certainly remained aware of racism and white supremacy, and *Passing* takes both to task. Yet by linking key tropes in her own novel with the very aspects of *Nigger Heaven* that caused the greatest turmoil for Van Vechten, Larsen attacks the hypocrisy in Irene Redfield's brand of priggish and blind race loyalty; and by killing off the magnificent, vivacious, and passionate Clare Kendry, she both illustrates and laments what is lost. In her life, as in her fiction, Larsen could be quite biting in her criticism of such double standards, particularly among race people. "Have you noticed that when Nordics talk against the admission of Negroes to their homes, etc., it is rank predjudice [*sic*]," she once wrote to Van Vechten, "but when we take the same attitude about white folks it is race loyalty?"[47] Larsen's critique grows as much out of her resistance to the Harlem Renaissance's racial politics as from her sympathetic alignment with Van Vechten, whose influence on her life and her writing ought not be underestimated. It was in a letter to Carl Van Vechten, after all, that Nella Larsen celebrated the modernist moment that surrounded them. "It is nice to find someone writing as if he didn't absolutely despise the age in which he lives," she writes. "And surely it is more interesting to belong to one's own time, to share its peculiar vision, catch the flying glimpse of the panorama which no subsequent generation can ever recover."[48]

Carl Van Vechten's friendship supported Nella Larsen through several painful humiliations after *Passing* was published. Both Nella and her husband Elmer Imes sought Van Vechten's confidential counsel after Nella discovered Elmer's extramarital love affair (with a white woman, no less), a rupture that strained the couple's lives for several years and resulted in their 1933 divorce. Van Vechten also defended Larsen during the escalation of public shaming after she was accused of plagiarizing her short story "Sanctuary," which appeared in *Forum* magazine in early 1930. Gossip about Larsen's alleged theft was widespread, biting, and sustained. "All literary Harlem knows about it," Harold Jackman dished in a letter to

Countee Cullen. "Nella's benefactor, Carl Van Vechten, is trying to justify his protégéé but his arguments are so weak and in this case *so* stupid."[49] The scandal cast an ignominious shadow over what would otherwise have been wonderful news, when she won a Guggenheim fellowship. In the end, Nella Larsen's ability to capitalize on publishing opportunities available to the New Negro proved short-lived, but Carl Van Vechten's dedication to her, both personally and professionally, remained consistent and lasted well past the New Negro vogue, even as many in Harlem shunned her.

Racial solidarity was never a given for Harlem's writers, as misogyny, class conflict, professional jealousy, and other human weaknesses challenged the most earnest efforts at community building. Nella Larsen's biography suggests, counterintuitively, that a white man's friendship offered meaningful support in the face of conflicts fueled by misogyny and classism, most evident in Harold Jackman's competitive bile. In the end, Edward White's assertion that Larsen "was arguably a greater influence on Van Vechten than the other way around"[50] deserves serious consideration, both for its contributions to understanding her biography and for its unexpected metaphorical resonance. In some ways, New Negroes struggled against the presence of white mentors, patrons, and friends, but not always; there were books to be published by writers who had the ambition, capacity for creative innovation, and personal resilience to seize the moment.

Notes

1. Carl Van Vechten, *The Splendid Drunken Twenties: Selections from the Daybooks, 1922–1930*, ed. Bruce Kellner (Urbana: University of Illinois Press, 2003), 114.
2. Emily Bernard, *Carl Van Vechten and the Harlem Renaissance: A Portrait in Black and White* (New Haven, CT: Yale University Press, 2012), 61.
3. Langston Hughes, "The Negro Artist and the Racial Mountain," *The Nation* (June 23, 1926), 694.
4. Kathleen Pfeiffer, ed., *Brother Mine: The Correspondence of Jean Toomer and Waldo Frank* (Urbana: University of Illinois Press, 2010), 92.
5. Ibid., 92.
6. Barbara Foley, *Jean Toomer: Race, Repression, and Revolution* (Urbana: University of Illinois Press, 2014), 51.
7. Wesley Beal, *Networks of Modernism: Reorganizing American Narrative* (Iowa City: University of Iowa Press, 2015), 13.
8. Michael Soto, *Measuring the Harlem Renaissance: The U.S. Census, African American Identity, and Literary Form* (Amherst: University of Massachusetts Press, 2016), 30–1.

9. Terese Svoboda, *Anything That Burns You: A Portrait of Lola Ridge, Radical Poet* (Tucson: Schaffner Press, 2016), 128. Hereafter cited parenthetically.

10. Index of Modernist Magazines: *Broom*, http://modernistmagazines.org/american/broom/

11. Waldo Frank, *Memoirs of Waldo Frank* (Amherst: University of Massachusetts Press, 1973), 11. Hereafter cited parenthetically.

12. Quoted in Casey Nelson Blake, *Beloved Community: The Cultural Criticism of Randolph Bourne, Van Wyck Brooks, Waldo Frank & Lewis Mumford* (Chapel Hill: University of North Carolina Press, 1990), 132.

13. Rudolph P. Byrd and Henry Louis Gates, Jr., "Introduction," in *Cane: Authoritative Text, Contexts, Criticism*, ed. Rudolph P. Byrd and Henry Louis Gates (New York: Norton, 2011), xxix.

14. Pfeiffer, *Brother Mine*, 26. Hereafter cited parenthetically.

15. Mark Whalan, "Jean Toomer and the Avant-Garde," in *The Cambridge Companion to the Harlem Renaissance*, ed. George Hutchinson (Cambridge: Cambridge University Press, 2007), 74.

16. Beal, *Networks of Modernism*, 66–67.

17. Foley, *Jean Toomer*, 93.

18. Ibid., 142.

19. Van Vechten, *The Splendid*, 74.

20. Van Vechten, *Keep A-Inchin' along: Selected Writings of Carl Van Vechten about Black Art and Letters*, ed. Bruce Kellner (Westport, CT: Greenwood Press, 1979), 65.

21. John K. Young, *Black Writers, White Publishers: Marketplace Politics in Twentieth-Century African American Literature* (Jackson: University Press of Mississippi, 2006), 4.

22. Carolyn Wedin, *Jessie Redmon Fauset, Black American Writer* (Troy, NY: Whitston Pub. Co., 1981), 73.

23. Ibid., 73.

24. Van Vechten, *The Splendid*, 99.

25. Bernard, *Carl Van Vechten*, 102.

26. George Hutchinson, *In Search of Nella Larsen: A Biography of the Color Line* (Cambridge, MA: Belknap Press of Harvard University Press, 2006), 211.

27. Ibid., 315.

28. Van Vechten, *Keep A'Inchin*, 21.

29. Ibid., 24.

30. Bernard, *Carl Van Vechten*, 46.

31. Ibid., 83.

32. Edward White, *The Tastemaker: Carl Van Vechten and the Birth of Modern America* (New York: Farrar, Straus and Giroux, 2014), 201.

33. Fannie Hurst, "Zora Neale Hurston: A Personality Sketch," *Yale University Library Gazette* (July 1960): 19.

34. Quoted in Hutchinson, *Searching*, 179.

35. Michelle Dean, "Passing Through: Nella Larsen made a career of not quite belonging," April 3, 2015, www.laphamsquarterly.org/roundtable/passing-through

36. Quoted in Hutchinson, *In Search*, 210.

37. Hutchinson, *In Search*, 318.

38. Young, *Black Writers*, 41.

39. W. E. B. Du Bois, "Critiques of Carl Van Vechten's *Nigger Heaven*: W. E. B. Du Bois," in *The Portable Harlem Renaissance Reader*, ed. David Levering Lewis (New York: Penguin, 1994), 107.

40. Van Vechten, *Nigger Heaven*, ed. Kathleen Pfeiffer (1926; Urbana: University of Illinois Press, 2000), 284.

41. Nella Larsen, *Passing*, in *Quicksand and Passing*, ed. Deborah McDowell. (1928; London: Serpent's Tail, 1989), 241.

42. Hutchinson, *In Search*, 241.

43. Ibid., 303.

44. Larsen, *Passing*, 143.

45. Quoted in Kathleen Pfeiffer, *Race Passing and American Individualism* (Amherst: University of Massachusetts Press, 2002), 142.

46. Quoted in ibid., 143.

47. Quoted in ibid., 143.

48. Quoted in ibid., 136.

49. Quoted in Hutchinson, *Searching*, 345.

50. White, *The Tastemaker*, 216.

CHAPTER 4

The Bildungsroman *in the Harlem Renaissance*

Mark Whalan

As Robert Stepto observes, the African American prose tradition is "dom-inated by autobiographical and *Bildungsroman* impulses."[1] Yet even amongst that long-standing centrality, the Harlem Renaissance stands as a moment when the coming-of-age novel assumed particular significance. Arna Bontemps, W. E. B. Du Bois, Jessie Fauset, Langston Hughes, Zora Neale Hurston, James Weldon Johnson, Nella Larsen, Wallace Thurman, and Walter White all wrote *Bildungsromans*, often borrowing extensively from their autobiographical writings to do so.[2] The genre is conventionally understood – in a famous definition – as a novel that "portrays all but two or three of a set list of characteristics," including "childhood, the conflict of generations, provinciality, the larger society, self-education, alienation, ordeal by love, the search for a vocation and a working philosophy."[3] Yet it suited – and shaped – this movement for several reasons. Its popularity reflected the movement's extensive ties to German Romanticism and Idealism, which flowed most influentially through Du Bois and shaped much of the discourse around education and aesthetics in New Negro circles. (Indeed, Du Bois had studied under the first major scholar of the *Bildungsroman*, Wilhelm Dilthey, in Berlin.) With its plot characteristic-ally advanced by significant "scenes of instruction," the genre reflected how New Negro politics had both centered education as crucial terrain for the fight for fuller black civic enfranchisement and citizenship, but had also recognized American racism as possessing its own kind of pedagogy. As the genre whose classic narrative structure mapped the struggle to harmonize self-definition with successful socialization, it seemed the perfect vehicle for showcasing a civic situation where achieving the enfranchised maturity of full citizenship seemed endlessly deferred for many black Americans.

Perhaps most importantly, the *Bildungsroman* modeled and augmented the New Negro movement's prioritization of youth as its central symbolic and political motif. As Alain Locke suggested, the "Young Negro, in his poetry, his art, his education and his new outlook," was providing "the promise and warrant of a new leadership."[4] Indeed, youth served as one of the most contested and significant terms of the Renaissance's many manifestoes and proleptic essays – from Locke's own "Negro Youth Speaks" to Langston Hughes's "The Negro Artist and the Racial Mountain," from Marita Bonner's "On Being Young, a Woman, and Colored" to the avantgardist rhetoric of *Fire!!* That youth carried such talismanic freight was partly because of the moment's re-energization of what Henry Louis Gates famously called the "trope of the New Negro," but also reflected the rapid changes to the social and cultural *mores* of youth occurring nationwide. The Harlem Renaissance coincided with the emergence of an agesegregated social sphere of youth, forged in a series of new commercial entertainment venues and social practices (from dating to movie-going, car-rides to amusement parks) governed less by familial rules than by peergroup regulation. In middle-class African American communities, this helped effect a definite shift in hegemonic gender identities that was frequently experienced as intergenerational conflict. This was true of both masculinities and femininities. For men "in the postwar period, achieving manhood became less dependent on imbibing the producer values of industry, thrift, sobriety, self-control, and character; rather, individuals constructed a masculine sense of self that was tied to the consumer goods they owned, the leisure practices they engaged in, and their physical and sexual virility."[5] As Saidiya Hartman has recently discussed, at this moment "young black women were in open rebellion," deploying "radical imagination and wayward practices" in a struggle to create "autonomous and beautiful lives."[6] Although several important critics have stressed the importance of intergenerational collaboration in the Harlem Renaissance, nonetheless this broad cultural shift informed the movement's well-known intergenerational arguments over what the literary responsibilities of youth should be. The clash of generations, the question of what model of racial leadership was best suited to this moment of American modernity, and how to navigate through a frequently baffling and hostile urban, consumer-oriented environment, were staples of the several *Bildungsromans* produced by the Harlem Renaissance's major authors.

Education was central to that story, as it was to the entire ethos of the New Negro Renaissance. For Du Bois, "all our problems center in the child," and his magazine, *The Crisis*, carried an annual education number as well as prominently featuring adverts from education institutions of all kinds.[7] As Katharine Capshaw Smith has noted, a faith in education was consistent across the many strains of uplift ideology operative in the period.[8] Yet most Harlem *Bildungsromans* saw educational institutions as sites of struggle between pedagogies of liberation and pedagogies of oppression. Indeed, they regularly featured two types of "scenes of instruction" in schools or colleges – the first, the idealist strain, showcased institutional learning as an exhilarating and delocalized experience of Humboldtian *Bildung*, wherein self-cultivation, growth, and achievement occurred through access to a universalist realm of great ideas and knowledge. The second type portrayed the lessons so memorably enshrined in Richard Wright's "The Ethics of Living Jim Crow," the racial and territorialized knowledges of how to live as a black social being according to the complex civic (and spatial) logics of white supremacy. Often, these scenes were tightly juxtaposed to illustrate the personal and political possibilities of formal education for African Americans as well as how its American institutionalization consistently reproduced an inequitable racial order. Du Bois's *Dark Princess* (1928), for example, opens with his protagonist Matthew Towns angrily departing from the University of Manhattan and his medical studies, after being barred from registering for a required course in obstetrics by a prejudiced and newly appointed southern Dean. Yet Towns also waxes nostalgic about his earlier educational successes, where hard work sees him win "prize after prize" and for a while proves his "life theory" that "character and brains were too much for prejudice."[9] In Wallace Thurman's *The Blacker the Berry*, his dark-complexioned protagonist Emma Lou Brown is eager to attend the University of Southern California, which she hopes will be free of the small-town prejudices she endured in Boise, Idaho; she idealistically imagines that "here, in the colored social circles of Los Angeles ... she would find many suitable companions, intelligent, broad-minded people of all complexions, intermixing and being too occupied otherwise to worry about either their own skin color or the skin color of those around them."[10] Yet instead, she is ostracized, and ultimately forced out of the university by exactly those prejudices. In Jessie Fauset's novel *Plum Bun* (1928), the protagonist, Angela Murray, is perceived as white while enrolled at the Philadelphia Academy of Fine Arts, and is welcomed there; her instructors promise that "there's no telling where your talents and tastes will lead you, – to Europe perhaps and surely to the formation of new and interesting friendships" among "artistic folk" who are "the broadest, most liberal people in the world."[11] Yet when her African American background is revealed, those promises evaporate. Such scenes illustrate a persistent faith in the possibility of liberatory education, but also a grim understanding of the realities of what Du Bois influentially called "caste schooling," a nationwide system that worked to fulfil the needs of a racial-capital order to "teach individuals from both the white and dark worlds how to understand and *live* as caste subjects as well as the value of social life attached to each."[12] Notably, the most pessimistic of Harlem Renaissance *Bildungsromans* – Thurman's *The Blacker the Berry* – has a grimly ironic take on the socialization of Emma Lou, who finishes the novel working as a public school teacher in Harlem and replicating the kind of anti-black pedagogies she experienced as a student in Idaho. Her over-use of cosmetics to hide her dark skin sees her nicknamed "Blacker'n me" by her pupils, aware as they are of her racial self-loathing, which in itself becomes a form of "caste education."[13] Eventually, she seeks a transfer to a school on the East side, to "the Italian section where she would not have to associate with so many other colored teachers."[14]

It salient that as Langston Hughes was writing *Not without Laughter* (1930) he was enrolled at Lincoln University and involved in a nationwide wave of campus activism aimed at challenging just such "caste education" in America's historically black colleges and universities. As he remembered in *The Big Sea*, his final project in Robert Labaree's sociology class was a survey of conditions at Lincoln, including race relations – with a particular focus on Lincoln's all-white faculty and all-white Board of Trustees.[15] His survey found that 63% of Lincoln's 129 upper-classmen preferred an all-white faculty; and as Hughes penned in his devastating report, these figures indicated that "the college itself has failed in instilling in these students the very quality of self-reliance and self-respect which any capable American leader should have – and the purpose of the college, let us remember, is to educate 'leaders of the colored people.'"[16] Controversy ensued when the report reached the press, with many black schools asserting they would no longer hire graduates from "a student body that did not believe Negroes capable of teaching themselves."[17] Perhaps accordingly, Hughes's *Bildungsroman* is centrally concerned with the cultivation of black racial pride, and education for race leadership. The childhood of the protagonist, James "Sandy" Rogers, is freighted with familial ambition that he "get ahead ... in this white man's country" to "help the black race" – his grandmother and his two aunts do all they can to keep him in school in the hope that he will become a "great man" in the mold of Booker T. Washington, Du Bois, Frederick Douglass, or Paul Laurence Dunbar.[18] The novel tracks Sandy from fourth grade to age sixteen, and concludes with him moving to Chicago, working as an elevator operator, and trying to save money to complete high school. The prevalence of female guidance and mentorship in his coming-of-age, as well as the immersive, quiet, and often passive nature of Sandy's acculturation, recalls Erica Edwards's observation that "African American cultural texts have existed in constant tension with charismatic leadership as a scenario of black political modernity," and indeed in "constant tension" with the autobiographical texts of the notable "race men" that often informed those scenarios.[19] As Marlon Ross notes, that Sandy's education and acculturation happens largely through his relationships with women instead of with his largely absent father helps him "develop a subtle orientation to the world that strands [him] between masculine and feminine as conventionally opposed principles of experience and outlook," a "stranding" that challenges "the assumptions of dominant masculinity as a code for measuring male heroism."[20]

If Sandy's subtle gender orientation represented an unconventional model for leadership, so too did the nature of his education, which Hughes conceives of in a holistic sense that carries its own quiet radicalism about the resiliency and complexity embedded in black vernacular culture. Indeed, despite Sandy's family's investment in the rhetoric of education for leadership, his immersive acculturation is often in tension if not outright conflict with his formal schooling, a dynamic that renders *Not without Laughter* pessimistic about formal education as the singular route to maturity and race man status. The novel showcases only one day of Sandy's experiences in a classroom, namely his introduction to racially "integrated" schooling in the fifth grade in his hometown of Stanton, Kansas. The black children in the class are assigned to desks at the rear of the classroom by their teacher after all the white students have been seated in alphabetical order, an action that makes Sandy "feel like crying."[21] Later, Sandy ruminates on the pictures of "ugly" Africans in his geography textbook, who have "bushy heads and wild eyes" – but considers that "Aunt Hager said his mother was an African, but she wasn't ugly and wild; neither was Aunt Hager; neither was little dark Willie-Mae, and they were all black like Africans."[22] As both subject and object of formal schooling, Sandy's blackness is positioned as excluded from the norms of white, ascriptive citizenship, norms which see blackness as ugly, undisciplined, and unassimilable to the collective national body.

In contrast to this highly limited consideration of Sandy's formal schooling, the novel's episodic, picaresque structure ranges extensively across his experiences of acculturation into black cultural, religious, sexual, linguistic, performance, and leisure practices. When considered together, these form a counter-pedagogy of African American civic and cultural subjectivity to what Sandy learns in school. This acculturation occurs in revival tents, dance halls, pool rooms, barbershops, vaudeville theaters, churches, brothels, hotels, and apartment blocks. It is fundamentally black, aural, and modern; as Andy Oler suggests, *Not without Laughter* pushes back against the "meteronormativity" of many accounts of modern black sonic culture by presenting rural Kansas as "a modern space in which the sounds and material apparatus of early twentieth-century jazz music compose the [novel's] cultural field."[23] As Sandy visits traveling carnivals, listens to his father playing blues guitar on the porch of his grandmother's house, and is taken by his aunt Harriet to see an early traveling jazz band play one of the town's dance halls, he gains immersive experience in the secular sonic cultures of black modernity. Yet he also absorbs much of the cultural practices of the black Baptist church, from revival meetings to Sunday school, and above all his grandmother's credo that "hate makes yo' heart ugly. . . . there ain't no room in this world fo' nothin' but love," a powerful iteration of what Darnell Moore has classed as the "Black Radical love" that has always grounded the "Black freedom movement."[24] For much of the novel, Sandy seems strangely passive in his relation to such performances – sitting quietly at the edge of communal gatherings, lying on the floor, looking down from a gallery, or more often than not listening to (or eavesdropping on) the extended passages of everyday dialogue that comprise the majority of the book's early chapters. Such quiet, self-abnegating listening contrasts with the interiorized reflectiveness common to the classic *Bildungsroman*, and also with the kind of agential, masculine self-fashioning so common to Edwards's "scenarios of charismatic leadership." Yet at the end of the novel, passages of interior monologue become more frequent, and indicate his immersive acculturation has informed a sophisticated understanding of the relation between black culture and American racial formation. As he ruminates, "was that why Negroes were poor, because they were dancers, jazzers, clowns? The other way round would be better: dancers because of their poverty; singers because they suffered; laughing all the time because they must forget. . . . It's more like that, thought Sandy."[25] Attentive, evaluative, and balancing the lessons gleaned from his immersive acculturation against the racialized pedagogies of his formal schooling, the novel ends with Sandy's future uncertain but hopeful – he determinedly commits to a "great" future characterized less by charismatic masculine leadership than by a self-formulated ethics of cultivating a widening circle of compassionate empathy and a plan for truthful self-expression.

Although *Not without Laughter* ends with a tentative optimism about Sandy's future maturity, nonetheless that maturity remained unrealized; and many of the novel's initial reviewers lamented that Hughes failed to extend Sandy's future into one of more conventional race leadership. Alain Locke and George Schuyler wished the novel had been expanded to form the first part of a trilogy, and V. F. Calverton grumbled that Hughes could "have made of Sandy's ambition to emancipate his race . . . a more stirring motif."[26] This issue reflects one of the determining stresses on the Harlem Renaissance *Bildungsroman*, pulled between a racial politics urging stories of successful maturation on one hand against a broader generic drift toward what Jed Esty has called "unseasonable youth" on the other.[27] As Douglas Mao observes, "European and North American writers in the twentieth century turned away from the nineteenth century's delight in narrating how young people mature and devoted themselves instead to stories about how young people do not mature, about how life in the modern world is an affair of stagnation or regress."[28] The reasons provided for this generic shift into arrested youth, or defaulted maturity, are complex and varied. They range from arguments about how imperial geopolitics had fractured linear chronologies of personal and national progress, to suggestions that the liberal individualism so often thought to underpin the early genre had been eroded by various forms of social incorporation and institutionalization. Yet it was also true, for African American writers, that presenting "unseasonable youth" risked reconfirming a white supremacist discourse of racial infantalization, of black civic immaturity that precluded African Americans acceding to the responsibilities of full citizenship.

Du Bois's two *Bildungsromans* were forceful on that score, as his protagonists regularly face down and personally disprove arguments questioning black civic aptitude, arguments often explicitly framed in the language of (im)maturity. For example, *The Quest of the Silver Fleece* (1911), Du Bois's major fiction on the politics of black education in the South, begins with the new white teacher of the black protagonists Bles and Zora being told by a local white storeowner that "we just have to carry [the local black population] and care for them like children."[29] When the teacher-activist Sarah Smith claims her school's purpose is to "furnish [black] men and women who can work and earn an honest living, train up families aright, and perform their duties as fathers, mothers, and citizens," the local representative of the white plantocracy counsels her that "the whites can attend to the duties of citizenship without help," a credo he sees as perfectly compatible with a desire to help "these [black] people to develop as far as they can."[30] In such circumstances it is no accident that both novels end with their heterosexually paired dual protagonists achieving a triumphant maturity – with marital union and accession to race leadership, and in the case of *The Dark Princess*, prophetic parenthood. As we are told of Zora's transformation at the end of *The Quest of the Silver Fleece*, "the girl was a woman, well-rounded and poised, tall, straight, and quick. And with this went mental change: a self-mastery ... a subtle air as of one looking from great unreachable heights down on the dawn of the world."[31]

Although these novels are often indexed as evidence of Du Bois's feminist commitments, the Harlem *Bildungsromans* written by female authors read quite differently. They often staged highly critical engagements with not only the marriage plot but also the passing plot as potential routes to fully socialized maturity, a pattern indicative of the limited range of options available for black women to successfully navigate the era's respectability politics. As Deborah McDowell notes, "both passing and marriage are naïve, fantasy-ridden attempts by blacks and women to avoid the structural inequalities that disempower them ... both marriage and passing are the means by which these two disenfranchised groups hope to gain access to power."[32] That both marriage and passing for white are invoked only to be dislodged as the *telos* from so many of the Harlem *Bildungsromans* with female protagonists signals a broadly shared feminist commitment among the era's women novelists to expand the range of socially sanctioned professional, sexual, and social options open to African American women. This feminist reworking of narrative convention also reinvigorated the genre of the African American female *Bildungsroman* by shunting it out of the domestic sphere. As Kathleen Pfeiffer observes of Fauset's *Plum Bun*, "explicit invocations of literary genre frame Angela's decision to pass for white, aligning her rejection of blackness with a rejection of the sentimental tradition of domestic fiction," a tradition that "was often used by the generation of black women writers preceding Fauset; these women presented the domestic ideal to affirm community and family as sites where women have social and civic presence."[33]

As well as feminist pushback against a previous era's sentimental idealization of the domestic sphere, Jim Crow logics of maturation most clearly exerted a warping pressure on classic *Bildungsroman* structures through the passing plot. Many African American coming-of-age stories critically explored the natural extension of those logics – that full maturation (with its corollary of material success and full civic enfranchisement) in a white supremacist America might necessitate becoming white.

Accordingly, the passing novel pushed the *Bildungsroman*'s structuring tensions between the conflicting but necessary conditions of the self within modern capitalist democracy – its pull between Franco Moretti's imperatives of "freedom and happiness, identity and change, security and metamorphoses" – to the point of outright fracture.[34] Such novels often posit passing as the route to full socialization but the death-knell of authentic selfhood; where classic *Bildungsromans* ended in balanced compromise between Moretti's conflicting imperatives, passing plots become zero-sum games. In *Plum Bun*, Fauset contends that the African American *Bildungsroman* must engage the passing plot in the novel's third paragraph, with her genre-signaling reflection that "the satisfied ambition of maturity is a foil for the restless despair of youth."[35] Yet in a white supremacist society, the only untrammeled field for the free exercise of that "restless-[ness]" is whiteness; as whiteness set the terms (and limits) of full access to financial and social success and mobility, it condenses into the sign of that success and mobility for Angela. As she reflects, "all the good things were theirs," because "for the present they had the power and the badge of that power was whiteness," and "she possessed the badge."[36] In the first third of the novel, this "badge" affords her the dream of a liberal individual freedom that she knows is racially circumscribed, but is all the more appealing for that: "she was seeing the world, she was getting acquainted with life in her own way without restrictions or restraint; she was young, she was temporarily independent, she was intelligent, she was white."[37] Yet even that vision is immediately further qualified by her realization of gender inequality, an understanding that "men had a better time of it than women," which means that "all that richness, all that fullness of life which she so ardently craved would be doubly hers" if she aimed to "marry . . . a white man."[38] As such, even before the novel unfolds its failed marriage plot with just such a white man, Angela intuitively understands that the promise of both freedom and security that whiteness seems to offer will be so heavily circumscribed that it might in fact offer neither.

If Fauset's use of "richness" and "fullness" here suggests that a uniquely privileged access to wealth accumulation and the free exercise of social mobility was restricted to white middle- and upper-class men in the period, it is interesting that later in the novel she uses the same phrases to denote Harlem, which thereby comes to represent a contrastive and redefined version of those things. For Harlem is "fuller, richer [than downtown], not finer but with the difference in quality that there is between velvet and silk"; later, "again she sensed that fullness, richness, even thickness of life that she had felt on her first visit to Harlem."[39] This contrast serves as one of several in Harlem *Bildungsromans* in which white bourgeois lifeways, coded as acquisitive, materialistic, atomistic, and emotionally and culturally emaciated, are compared unfavorably to the social and cultural milieu of Harlem. This narrative turn is also found in Larsen's *Passing*, in Clare Kendry's longing for Harlem, at the conclusion of Walter White's *Flight*, and – albeit temporarily – in Larsen's *Quicksand*. Such turns recall Martin Japtok's observation that "group consciousness . . . is more pronounced in ethnic [minority] texts than in the more protagonist-dominated traditional versions [of the *Bildungsroman*] that provided models for ethnic authors."[40] Yet it is not just an atomized versus a communitarian vision that separates these racialized options. For Harlem as a potential space for individual development both carries with it a different (and disruptive) temporality that troubles the smooth narrative emplotment to maturity of the classic *Bildungsroman*, and, relatedly, frequently engages a cosmopolitan dimension that the white characters in these novels shun.

Fauset, White, and Larsen are keen to stress that Harlem is both a "city within a city" with a relative autonomy to the rest of New York, and that its opposition to the atomized and materialist nature of mainstream white America is partly organized through the temporalization of social experience.[41] For example, Angela Murray reflects that the "stream of life" in Harlem ran "thicker, more turgidly than that safe, sublimated experience" of her downtown life.[42] Helga Crane finds Harlem entirely separate from the "sober mad rush of white New York."[43] Walter White's Mimi Daquin, the heroine of *Flight* who passes for white for much of the novel's final third only to re-identify as African American following an epiphanic visit to Harlem and a recitation of spirituals at Carnegie Hall, reflects that only African Americans in the USA have "successfully resisted mechanization" through the temporalities of black music.[44] When listening to jazz in a Harlem cabaret, a form "all wrong when judged by conventional music standards," she hears in its "weird and oddly exciting cacophony of chords and exotic rhythms" "a freedom from rules, a complete disregard of set forms."[45]

It is worth, here, recalling recent scholarship on the modernist *Bildungsroman*, which has focused on how imperial and colonial logics shattered the traditional *Bildungsroman*'s typical narrative temporalities of gradual, accretive character progress. Rooted in these classic *Bildungsromans* were in traditions of Herderian nationalism with its purview of ethno-racially homogenous and bounded nation states, they often hewed to smooth, linear emplotments of "narrative-historical time."[46] As Tobias Boes notes, many modernist *Bildungsromans* engage this colonial dimension by "undermin[ing] the historicist foundations of traditional narrative thinking, according to which national communities are characterized by the preservation of a common formative drive."[47] Yet such undermining typically takes place in the metropolis, wherein "global processes shatter the integrity of national-historical time and create a number of local temporalities."[48] An aligned dynamic of temporalization is at work in *Plum Bun* and *Flight*, for as well as the reflections on Harlem's idiosyncratic temporalities mentioned previously, similarly disruptive to the "integrity of national-historical time" are the narrative trajectories of Angela and Mimi, who both reject the normative *telos* of a life of passing and marriage to white men at their respective novels' close. It is telling that after Angela's climactic decision to publically identify herself as a Negro in front of a group of reporters, her admiring sister remarks that "you certainly have the art of concealing time's ravages, for you not only look young but you have the manner of someone who's just found a million dollars."[49] Angela's decision, therefore, reverses the linear temporality of the *Bildungsroman* by restoring her youth, effectively neutralizing the chronological span of her abortive pursuit of marriage to the white, wealthy, and bigoted Roger Fielding that had preoccupied much of the novel. Moreover, as nationalism becomes reformulated as nativist in these texts – parochial, bigoted, patriarchal, and embodied in the white love interests of both Angela and Mimi – then the traditional *Bildungsroman* emplotment toward marriage so closely allied with that social form is contaminated by association, and therefore rejected for more uncertain futures by both protagonists.

Nonetheless, one convention of the classic *Bildungsroman* remains in several Harlem Renaissance coming-of-age novels – namely, the prominence of aesthetic education. As Moretti puts it, "Instead of directly confronting the great powers of social life, [aesthetic education] creates a new realm of existence in which those abstract and deforming forces penetrate less violently, and can be reconstituted in syntony [*sic*] with the individual aspiration toward harmony."[50] Notably, Moretti observes that in later European *Bildungsromans* such education becomes reformulated as the more exacting, devotional idea of vocation, an idea that increasingly becomes associated with ethnic affiliation and politics. This idea plays an important role in Harlem *Bildungsromans*. Near the end of Du Bois's *Dark Princess*, for example, Matthew Towns becomes less concerned with right and wrong than he does with beauty and ugliness; his immersion in labor activism rather than his hopelessly compromised Chicago political career coincides with his avid re-reading of *Hamlet*, visits to modern art

exhibitions, and even the purchase of a Matisse. It is strongly hinted that
Sandy's incipient maturity will coincide with his beginnings as an artist in
Not without Laughter. James Weldon Johnson's "failed" *Bildungsroman,
The Autobiography of an Ex-Colored Man* (1912), situates its protagonist's
defining error as a failure to devote his career to the development of racial
art, choosing instead to pursue a bland corporate career passing for white –
a decision that leaves him ruefully wondering whether he has "chosen the
lesser part, sold my birthright for a mess of pottage," in the novel's famous
concluding phrase.[51] In *Plum Bun,* Angela's decision to return to the
African American community and renounce passing is closely tied to her
growing vocation as an artist. Indeed, the conclusion to the novel is driven
by her having "gained in the power to compose, a certain sympathy,
a breadth of comprehension, the manifestation of that ability to interpret
which she had long suspected lay within her," moral developments which
also inform her decision to reveal her African American background in one
of the novel's climactic scenes.[52] As this quotation suggests, the growing
power of her work is tied to her increasing cultivation of a social ethic of
"sympathy," particularly evident in sketches she terms her "Fourteenth
Street Types," portraits based on the "sprawling, half-recumbent, dejected
figures" she observes sitting around Union Square for hours on end.[53] Her
involvement with these figures is closely bound up with an awareness of the
ethics of objectification and typification; while she initially feels
a condescending excitement at having found a store of artistic material in
these figures, she quickly worries that her own social positionality renders
her similarly vulnerable to such aesthetic exploitation, pondering "if there
were people more alive, more sentient to the joy, the adventure of living,
even than she, to whom she would also be a 'type.'"[54] Later, when her
"sympathy and knowledge had waxed," she reflects "how fiercely she would
have rebelled had anyone from a superior social plane taken her for copy!"[55]
Her simultaneously moral and aesthetic maturity reflects the Harlem
Renaissance's relentless instrumentalization of aesthetics for the sphere of
political activism, and its allied interest in "exploring the status of 'the
beautiful' in relation to social justice."[56] Moreover, Angela's explicitly anti-
typological aesthetic – which invokes the objectifying, classificatory, and
hierarchical modalities of the aesthetic "type" only to explode them
through a commitment to individuation and sympathetic leveling – was
a key anti-racist strategy for the Harlem Renaissance more generally,
situated as it was in a national media environment saturated with racial
and ethnic caricature. Angela therefore becomes exactly the kind of "prophetic youth" Alain Locke heralded, a nationally successful artist whose

anti-racist humanism will help push the vanguard of social progress and help ameliorate the failures of such progress in the legislative sphere.

Yet such optimism is tempered by Russ Castronovo's reminder that writers like Du Bois, Fauset, and Walter White "frequently asked when beauty had ever stopped a lynching" and were constantly worrying over the limits of instrumentalizing the aesthetic.[57] This worry is manifest in the frequency with which the Harlem *Bildungsroman* stakes hope in the *future* artwork, in the ability of a yet-unrealized novel or painting to help challenge a national discourse of race that seemed so violent and intractable in the present. It is also manifest in the extended considerations of the political limits of the aesthetic sphere in two of the Harlem Renaissance's most pessimistic takes on the *Bildungsroman*, Nella Larsen's *Quicksand* and Wallace Thurman's *Infants of the Spring*. Larsen's Helga Crane invests great belief that her "rare and intensely personal taste" might be the road to self-actualization, that clothes and surroundings organized in accord with what she calls her "aesthetic sense" will literally furnish a solution to the protracted frustrations of nonbelonging she experiences throughout the novel.[58] Yet as Rafael Walker observes, although Helga invests great hope in the aesthetic sphere, she relentlessly encounters it as an arena committed to her own objectification, and her tragic predicament is that "she struggles to exist as a desiring subject in a world furnishing only the means for her to exist as a desired object."[59]

In contrast, Wallace Thurman worried that the Renaissance's prioritization of a proleptic faith in black artistic youth could kick the can of aesthetic agency down the road, deferring the issue of how far black interventions in the cultural sphere could ever both reach a mass audience or change hegemonic and disenfranchising understandings of black life. His *Infants of the Spring* represents a *roman à clef* dealing with the various artistic inhabitants of "Niggerati Manor" – all youths in a state of arrested development, with un-narrated childhoods and no clear path to maturity, and all incapable of producing the artworks their patrons and community hope for. Indeed, youth becomes less a sign of promise in the novel than an excuse for nonproductivity; when the patron-landlady of "Niggerati Manor" expresses impatience with its star artist, with his failure to deliver the "monument to the New Negro" she hopes for, she is told "he's still very young. Someday he will surprise us all."[60] Significantly, hers is one of only two child experiences we have detailed in the book, and it hinges on a moment of shocking racial violence that causes her lifelong trauma – her recollection of being sent away to school in rural Georgia and expecting to meet the school bus straight from the train, only to encounter the sight of a black man lynched on a telegraph pole.[61] The other childhood – of George Jones, who renames himself Pelham Gaylord – is one where his adoptive grandmother instructs him that servitude to the descendants of the white family that owned her in slavery is his natural role, and that "schools were for white folk."[62]

Thurman's point is twofold: first, that a cultural politics cannot, and should never be expected to, redress a social and political situation so violent and extreme; and second, that the entire normative understanding of childhood – characterized by innocence, education, and safety – was, as Robin Bernstein has influentially observed, raced white and often rendered unavailable to black children through social practices of white supremacist violence.[63] (Instead of the schooling she expects, Euphoria's "scene of instruction" is lethal white vigilantism; and Pelham's lack of schooling is directly linked to the paucity of his artistic achievement.) Moreover, Thurman's unwillingness to grant either childhoods *or* maturity to his main protagonists signals his awareness of both the interventionist and the overburdened nature of the *Bildungsroman* in the Harlem Renaissance, a movement which had staked so much on the political aesthetics of youth. Like *Quicksand*, his novel saw the binary logics of Jim Crow childhood as a fearsome barrier to a successful black maturity set according to the terms of full citizenship; and like *Quicksand*, it worried that an overinvestment in the politics of culture was a mark of desperation. Yet even the bleak assessments of Larsen and Thurman demonstrate how the *Bildungsroman*'s rich heritage afforded some of the major authors of the Harlem Renaissance space to explore the raced and gendered dynamics of some of American culture's most important and influential social scripts of childhood and maturation, and in doing so to craft some of the movement's most memorable and engaging characters.

Notes

1. Robert Stepto, *From Behind the Veil: A Study of Afro-American Narrative* (Urbana: University of Illinois Press, 1991), 147.
2. See Zora Neale Hurston, *Their Eyes Were Watching God* (1937; Urbana: University of Illinois Press, 1987); Nella Larsen, *Quicksand*, in *Quicksand and Passing*, ed. Deborah McDowell (London: Serpent's Tail, 1989); Langston Hughes, *Not without Laughter* (1930) in *The Collected Works of Langston Hughes: The Novels: Not without Laughter and Tambourines to Glory*, ed. Dolan Hubbard (1930; Columbia: University of Missouri, 2001); Wallace Thurman, *The Blacker the Berry* (1929; New York: Scribner, 1996); Jessie Fauset, *There is Confusion* (1924; Boston: Northeastern University Press, 1989), and *Plum Bun* (1928; London:

Pandora, 1985); Walter White, *Flight* (1926; Baton Rouge: Louisiana State University Press, 1998); James Weldon Johnson, *The Autobiography of an Ex-Colored Man*, ed. Jacqueline Goldsby (1912; New York: Norton, 2015); Claude McKay, *Banana Bottom* (1933; London: Serpent's Tail, 2005); and W. E. B. Du Bois, *The Quest of the Silver Fleece* (1911; New York: Dover, 2008), *Dark Princess* (1928; Jackson: University Press of Mississippi, 1995), and the *Black Flame Trilogy* (1957–61): *The Ordeal of Mansart* (1957; Oxford: Oxford University Press, 2007); *Mansart Builds a School* (1959; New York: Oxford University Press, 2007); *Worlds of Color* (1961; Oxford: Oxford University Press, 2014).

3. Jerome H. Buckley, *Season of Youth: The Bildungsroman from Dickens to Golding* (Cambridge, MA: Harvard University Press, 1974), 18; and Tobias Boes, "Modernist Studies and the *Bildungsroman*: A Historical Survey of Critical Trends," *Literature Compass* 3, no. 2 (2006): 231.

4. Alain Locke, "Enter the New Negro," *Survey Graphic* (March 1925): 631.

5. Martin Summers, *Manliness and its Discontents: The Black Middle Class and the Transformation of Masculinity, 1900–1930* (Chapel Hill: University of North Carolina Press, 2004), 156–157.

6. Saidiya Hartman, *Wayward Lives, Beautiful Experiments: Intimate Histories of Social Upheaval* (New York: Norton, 2019), xiii.

7. Michelle Phillips, "The Children of Double Consciousness: From *The Souls of Black Folk* to *The Brownies' Book*," *PMLA* 128.3 (2013): 592.

8. Katharine Capshaw, *Children's Literature of the Harlem Renaissance* (Bloomington: Indiana University Press, 2004), xvi.

9. Du Bois, *The Dark Princess*, 12–13.

10. Thurman, *The Blacker the Berry*, 36.

11. Fauset, *Plum Bun*, 65.

12. Clayton Pierce, "W. E. B. Du Bois and Caste Education: Racial Capitalist Schooling from Reconstruction to Jim Crow," *American Educational Research Journal* 54, no. 1 (2017): 23–47.

13. Thurman, *The Blacker the Berry*, 210.

14. Ibid., 211.

15. Langston Hughes, *The Big Sea* (1940; New York: Hill and Wang, 1993), 308; Arnold Rampersad, *The Life of Langston Hughes Vol. I, 1902–1941* (Oxford: Oxford University Press, 1986), 169.

16. Hughes, *The Big Sea*, 308.

17. Ibid., 309.

18. Hughes, *The Collected Works of Langston Hughes*, 208.

19. Erica Edwards, *Charisma and the Fictions of Black Leadership* (Minneapolis: University of Minnesota Press, 2012), x.

20. Marlon Ross, *Manning the Race: Reforming Black Men in the Jim Crow Era* (New York: New York University Press, 2004), 330.

21. Hughes, *Not without Laughter*, 98.

22. Ibid., 127.

23. Andy Oler, "'Their Song filled the Whole Night': *Not without Laughter*, Hinterlands Jazz, and Rural Modernity," *College Literature* 41, no. 4 (2014): 95.
24. Hughes, *Not without Laughter*, 132; Darnell Moore, "Black Radical Love: A Practice," *Public Integrity* 20, no. 4 (2018): 327.
25. Hughes, *Not without Laughter*, 202.
26. See *Langston Hughes: The Contemporary Reviews*, ed. Tish Dace (Cambridge: Cambridge University Press, 1997), 148.
27. Jed Esty, *Unseasonable Youth: Modernism, Colonialism, and the Fiction of Development* (Oxford: Oxford University Press, 2011).
28. Douglas Mao, *Fateful Beauty: Aesthetic Environments, Juvenile Development, and Literature, 1860–1960* (Princeton: Princeton University Press, 2008), 10.
29. Du Bois, *The Quest of the Silver Fleece*, 24.
30. Ibid., 133.
31. Ibid., 294.
32. Deborah McDowell, "Introduction: A Question of Power or, The Rearguard Faces Front," in Fauset, *Plum Bun*, xi.
33. Kathleen Pfeiffer, "The Limits of Identity in Jessie Fauset's *Plum Bun*," *Legacy* 18, no. 1 (2001): 84.
34. Franco Moretti, *The Way of the World: The Bildungsroman in European Culture* (Verso, 1987), 9.
35. Fauset, *Plum Bun*, 12.
36. Ibid., 73.
37. Ibid., 87–88.
38. Ibid., 88.
39. Ibid., 98, 216.
40. Martin Japtok, *Growing Up Ethnic: Nationalism and the Bildungsroman: African American and Jewish American Fiction* (Iowa: University of Iowa Press, 2005), 26.
41. Fauset, *Plum Bun*, 98.
42. Ibid.
43. Larsen, *Quicksand*, 45.
44. White, *Flight*, 282.
45. Ibid., 293–294.
46. Tobias Boes, *Formative Fictions: Nationalism, Cosmopolitanism, and the Bildungsroman* (Ithaca: Cornell University Press, 2012), 141.
47. Ibid., 140.
48. Ibid., 141.
49. Fauset, *Plum Bun*, 349.
50. Moretti, *The Way of the World*, 32.
51. Johnson, *The Autobiography of an Ex-Colored Man*, 110.
52. Fauset, *Plum Bun*, 208.
53. Ibid., 240.
54. Ibid., 89.
55. Ibid., 240.

56. Russ Castronovo, *Beautiful Democracy: Aesthetics and Anarchy in a Global Era* (Chicago: University of Chicago Press, 2007), 107.
57. Ibid., 118.
58. Larsen, *Quicksand*, 1, 44.
59. Rafael Walker, "Nella Larsen Reconsidered: The Trouble with Desire in *Quicksand* and *Passing*," *MELUS* 41, no. 1 (Spring 2016): 173.
60. Wallace Thurman, *Infants of the Spring* (1932; London: The X Press, 1998), 31.
61. Ibid., 46–47.
62. Ibid., 75.
63. Robin Bernstein, *Racial Innocence: Performing American Childhood from Slavery to Civil Rights* (New York: New York University Press, 2011).

CHAPTER 5

The Visual Image in New Negro Renaissance Print Culture

Caroline Goeser

A "Dynamic" Artistic Enterprise: Material Texts of the New Negro Renaissance

In the collaborative arena of New Negro Renaissance print culture, visual artists worked alongside writers, cultural leaders, editors, and publishers to animate the pages and covers of journals, little magazines, and books with graphic images. In creating a new visual expression in this body of work, Aaron Douglas, Gwendolyn Bennett, Richard Bruce Nugent, and many others developed visual strategies from seemingly untenable subject positions in 1920s America to radically re-picture Black American identity – to make Black modern. Their images enhanced texts that called for new interpretations and portrayals of Black identity and history, which stood in contrast to the demeaning Black stereotypes that continued to circulate on the pages of modern print culture. Their illustrations in the National Association for the Advancement of Colored People's (NAACP) *The Crisis* and the National Urban League's *Opportunity* embellished messages of racial uplift championed by their editors, W. E. B. Du Bois and Charles S. Johnson. Their visual art extended the impact of the poetry of Langston Hughes, the essays of Alain Locke, and the novels of Claude McKay. Providing visual components integral to Harlem Renaissance texts, Douglas and his fellow artists revised older illustrative methods that relied solely on mimicry of specific lines from a text. Strategically creating a dynamic interplay between word and image, they engaged with texts in a double-voiced narrative, wielding an independent visual language in active dialog with New Negro prose and poetry to form a new iconography of Black agency.

While this vital visual material has often been lost from the record, illustrated texts in original form or as reprints can bring to life the work of New Negro Renaissance writers and visual artists, who worked together to create a new, modernist expression that was vibrant and resilient. In 1925, Aaron Douglas wrote to Langston Hughes that it was time to "establish an art era." "Let's do the impossible," he declared, "Let's create something transcendentally material, mystically objective ... Spiritually earthy. Dynamic."[1] Douglas's language gave voice to new collaborations between Black writers and visual artists in creating an animated space where word and image could productively collide. Indeed, scholars of Harlem Renaissance visual and literary culture have often cited Douglas's clarion call for a revolutionary artistic production in 1920s America. I have characterized Douglas's paradoxical language as an appeal "for a modern black expression that would comprise a rich amalgam of seeming opposites," which would draw "anew on an ancient past to participate with vigor in shaping contemporary American culture."[2] Analogously, Rachel Farebrother saw in the language of Nella Larsen's *Quicksand* (1928), as voiced by her protagonist Helga Crane, a strategic call for a way to give form to the heterogeneity of Black culture: "For the hundredth time she marveled at the gradations within this oppressed race of hers. A dozen shades slid by ... a fantastic motley of ugliness and beauty ... a moving mosaic."[3] Farebrother explored what she called the "collage aesthetic" in critical New Negro texts, which employed the formal properties of "revision, intertextuality, pastiche, parody" to "delineate a specifically African American culture."[4] Throughout his career in art history and visual culture studies, Richard Powell has identified the distinctive "Blues aesthetic" and "Afro Deco" formal qualities employed by Aaron Douglas and other New Negro visual artists, and more broadly has understood New Negro expression "through the lens of urbanity and a kind of hybrid, part organic, part architectonic paradigm."[5]

Framing this chapter's investigation of the visual image in New Negro Renaissance print culture, three iconic illustrated publications issued between 1925 and 1927 can serve to introduce the varied ways in which illustrations shaped a newly dynamic and hybrid idiom, composed as a modernist collage of disparate fragments. The first is Alain Locke's unprecedented anthology, *The New Negro: An Interpretation* (1925), in which visual material in varying forms functioned to signal the modernity and diversity of New Negro identity. From the moment readers picked up the book, they encountered arresting images by German immigrant artist Winold Reiss that ran the gamut from pure geometric abstraction to modernist documentation. In his vibrant, nonrepresentational dust jacket image, a succession of abstract shapes – dark blue triangles framed by parallel bands of red and pink – emanate downward like arrows. The visual effect is of shimmering movement, suggesting a seismic shift and spatial opening for a newly modern force. The figurative frontispiece image of a modern Madonna – a young, Black mother gently holding her child – and Afro-geometric decorations and lettering on the title page visually introduced Locke's collection of essays, short stories, and poetry by a diverse group of notable authors. These images supported Locke's aim "to document the New Negro culturally and socially," providing "ample evidence of a New Negro in the latest phases of social change and progress."[6] Peppered throughout the volume and printed in audacious color, Reiss's portraits of *New Negro* contributors provided newly modern depictions of African American physiognomy and varying skin tones. "By the simple but rare process of not forcing . . . a foreign convention upon a racial tradition," Locke wrote of Reiss, "he has succeeded in revealing some of the rich and promising resources of Negro types," which Locke hoped the younger African American artists, like Reiss's student Aaron Douglas, would use as a guide.[7]

At this time in 1925, two non-Black artists – Reiss and Miguel Covarrubias (with two illustrations included in *The New Negro*) – were the primary artists to give visual form to the New Negro Renaissance. Yet Locke wisely followed the advice of New York women's rights leader Elise McDougald to also feature work by a Black visual artist in *The New Negro*.[8] Significantly, he included sketches by the young Douglas rather than the work of more established artists like Laura Wheeler, whom Locke associated with a "generation of Negro artists" that he felt "fell short" in developing a "racial expression which was only experimental."[9] Through his inclusion of Douglas's early Afro-Deco experiments, like his simple, beautifully integrated silhouettes in *The Poet*, Locke demonstrated his belief that the young artist's work evinced "the promising beginning of an art movement."[10]

By contrast, in 1926, Wallace Thurman edited an entirely different publication, *Fire!! A Quarterly Devoted to the Younger Negro Artists*, in association with Gwendolyn Bennett, John P. Davis, Aaron Douglas, Langston Hughes, Zora Neale Hurston, and Richard Bruce Nugent. The images by Douglas and Nugent barraged their readers with a cacophony of styles and subjects that signaled critique of the "New Negro." Douglas's searingly militant, red and black cover, with interlocking silhouettes of a stern, primitivist head and an Egyptian sphinx, prepared the reader for the foreword's incendiary position against the Black establishment, proclaiming freedom of expression as a cleansing "FIRE . . . flaming, burning, searing . . . a cry of conquest . . . burning wooden opposition with a cackling chuckle of contempt."¹¹ The interior drawings – Nugent's haggard, sassy "primitives" and Douglas's working-class caricatures – introduced readers to the new forms of vernacular prose and poetry by Hurston and Hughes, and the more transgressive subjects of prostitution and gay male sex of Thurman and Nugent. Both artists injected their Black figures with satire and comic relief, quite absent from images in *The New Negro*. Nugent's first drawing riffs on Thurman's "Cordelia the Crude," showing a haggard nude with drooping breasts, leaning on a palm tree in a primitivist setting – as if satirically foretelling the fate of Thurman's protagonist, the young prostitute Cordelia. Nugent adorned the head of his figure with spiky, tightly curled hair, openly flirting with demeaning stereotypes that Locke, Du Bois, and other New Negroes wished to abolish. At the center of the little magazine, Aaron Douglas's three contour drawings "chuckle" at respectable racial representations, poking fun at three types: an outmoded, Bible-thumping preacher; a New Negro artist primly dabbing his paintbrush on his canvas, worried he might soil his three-piece suit; and "an ogling cabaret waitress with her stockings suggestively rolled below her knees."¹²

Thurman ridiculed the "bourgeois" critics of *Fire!!* who cast its illustrators "in disfavor: . . . Douglas because of his advanced modernism and raw caricatures of Negro types, Bruce [Nugent] because of his . . . decadent types and the kinks he insists on putting upon the[ir] heads." He added sardonically, "Negroes, you know, don't have kinky hair; or, if they have, they use Madame Walker's straightening pomade."¹³ The willingness in 1926 of *Fire!!* contributors to laugh at themselves, poke fun at their elders, and engage with the art of caricature reflected deep divisions among New Negro cultural leaders, who would either come to entertain or flatly reject caricature within the context of Black representation.

As editor of *Opportunity* magazine, Charles S. Johnson assembled *Ebony and Topaz: A Collectanea*, a volume of essays, poetry, and illustrations published in 1927. Though not as well known today, it found a dynamic place between publications like *The New Negro* and *Fire!!* in contents and editorial method. With a witty jab at the more controlling editorial styles of Locke and Du Bois at *The Crisis*, Johnson explained, "This volume, strangely enough, does not set forth to prove a thesis, nor to plead a cause, nor stranger still, to offer a progress report on the state of Negro letters." Instead, he characterized the compilation as "a venture in expression" by contributors "much less interested in their audience than in what they are trying to portray," which suggested a kinship with the younger artists of *Fire!!*. His conclusion insisted, "Those seeking set patterns of Negro literature will in all likelihood be disappointed for there is no set pattern of Negro life."[14]

From his editorial position of anti-stance, Johnson allowed the writings and illustrations to speak for themselves – fiction and prose drawing from Black vernacular expression, anthropological and sociological essays on race, as well as writings and images addressing hotly debated topics of mixed-race identities, mixed-race sexual relations, and rape, which had not been addressed in *The New Negro*. The most transgressive component of *Ebony and Topaz* was its visual material by white artist Charles Cullen and Richard Bruce Nugent, which addressed the taboo intersection of mixed-raced identity, gay male relationships, and ambiguous sexuality – topics that Du Bois and others found "a blow in the face" to respectable African American readers.[15] However, the artists made their images palatable for varying audiences, readable on multiple levels through coded imagery. Cullen's cover image, with idealized dark and light-skinned figures who gaze toward a bright sun above, at first glance suggested a message of racial uplift. However, the figures' suggestive physical interactions and ambiguous gender conveyed a gay male subtext. Similarly, two of Nugent's illustrations depicted dancing "flappers" who on closer inspection are double-sexed, with campy dance steps and poses that typify drag performance. As in *Fire!!*, this visual material approached subjects shunned by the Black "bourgeoisie," but in its visual coding, it appealed to a wider range of readers.

In each of these three New Negro publications, images functioned to underscore the diversity and modernism of their material texts through an independent visual language that pictured African American identity as new, authentically Black, and capable of shifting between abstraction and figuration, vernacular expression and caricature, racial uplift and campy drag. Further investigation of illustrations in related publications can clarify the strategies visual artists used to practice a new Black modernism that dynamically connected the old and new, worked the interstices between race, gender, and sexuality, engaged in satirical coding, gave visual form to sound, and leveraged religious iconography in the service of social justice.

The Ancient-Modern Continuum

In varying ways, New Negro Renaissance artists Aaron Douglas, Joyce Carrington, and Charles Dawson created a new modernist iconography that radically collapsed normative binary distinctions between the ancient

Figure 5.1 Aaron Douglas, *The Young Blood Hungers*, cover of *The Crisis* (May 1928). Yale Collection of American Literature, Beinecke Rare Book and Manuscript Library, Yale University. © 2020 Heirs of Aaron Douglas / Licensed by VAGA at Artists Rights Society (ARS), NY.

world and the modern urban environment. On the May 1928 *Crisis* cover, Aaron Douglas established a privileged continuum between ancient Egypt and modern America as a setting for two African American figures (Figure 5.1). He combined overlapping shapes in a shallow space, with concentric circles forming a backdrop for a turbulent arrangement of ancient Egyptian pyramids, modern tall buildings, silhouetted Black heads, and flowing waves of water. A single arc of light traverses this imagery from the concentric circles in the distance, to the closest tall building fragment in the foreground, suggesting an electric volt that has set these motifs in motion. Just as Du Bois's scholarship and *Crisis* editorials sought a usable past for modern Black people, Douglas's bold image portrayed an origin story for his African American figures, who dynamically connected their ancestry, amidst the pyramids of ancient Egypt, with their present cultural moment among the modern tall buildings of the American urban environment.

This architectural continuum was a feature of 1920s Euro-American art and advertising images in the Art Deco style, in which the essence of the new was pictured through the dynamic intersection of ancient and modern architecture. However, the ancient-modern continuum Douglas and other New Negro artists created carried political and racial assertions.[16] These are made particularly clear in Charles Dawson's *Drawing with Five Great Negro Buildings*, published on the cover of the August 1927 "Education Number" of *The Crisis*. A female figure wearing an ancient Egyptian-styled headdress and breastplate and a young Black male graduate donning a mortar board parade across the composition as if in a modern pageant. Behind them are five buildings: in the distance an ancient Egyptian temple with a pylon façade looms as the ancestor of four contemporary businesses owned and operated by African American entrepreneurs, including Poro College and the People's Finance Corporation in St. Louis. Dawson's choice to illustrate Poro College highlighted the role of Black women in the commercial economy. Annie Turnbo Malone, who developed her own line of beauty products for African American women, established Poro College as "more than a business enterprise," which was "consecrated to the uplift of humanity – Race women in particular."[17] Repeatedly in illustrations by Douglas, Dawson, and others, the daring and highly contested reclamation of ancestry in ancient Egypt for contemporary African Americans laid the foundation for an equally bold political claim to rightful participation in the modern American economy.

On the September 1928 *Crisis* cover, Joyce Carrington employed an even more intrepid iconography, which Douglas had also honed in his illustrations to dispel stereotypes that linked African American and "primitive" identity (Figure 5.2). Carrington's Black female figure is shown in bust length dominating the foreground, with an ancient Egyptian pyramid in the background at left, and a palm tree at right. These were normally contrasting signs in 1920s America for the birthplace of civilization in ancient Egypt on the one hand and "primitive," sub-Saharan Africa on the other. With these visual juxtapositions, Carrington's modern figure radically bridged the typically assigned tropes that divided nature and culture. Through her fashionably bobbed and Marcel-waved hairdo and a chic neo-Egyptian necklace, Carrington's figure achieved an ultra-modern status, in contrast to stereotypes that contemporary African

Figure 5.2 Joyce Carrington, cover of *The Crisis* (September 1928). General Research & Reference Division, Schomburg Center for Research in Black Culture, The New York Public Library, Astor, Lenox, and Tilden Foundations.

Americans, particularly Black women, were America's "primitives." Carrington's modernist figure was both civilized and primitive, ancient and modern – a therapeutic connector between nature and culture.

Intersections of Race, Gender, and Class

New Negro Renaissance artists also refined this new modernist iconography to address intersections between race, gender, and class. For example, James Lesesne Wells provided a bold Art Deco dust jacket for

Lorenzo Greene and Carter G. Woodson's *The Negro Wage Earner*, published by Woodson's Association for the Study of Negro Life and History in Washington, DC (1930). On both the front and back of the dust jacket, Wells created New Negro male figures within architectonic environments that visualized their gender and class. In the front image, he depicted the head and shoulders of an African American man looming large, dressed in a suit and tie. Behind the figure, Wells created a multilayered urban scene with industrial buildings and smokestacks, train engines, and men at work. The figure's formal dress and the scene of labor behind him suggest the range of Black wage earners, from labor to management, which Greene and Woodson documented in the book.

On the back of the dust jacket, Wells created a captivating vignette of an African American waiter standing on an ancient Egyptian pyramid in a cluttered urban environment filled with activated tall buildings. Bending his knees, deftly at the ready for his work, he balances his serving tray filled with miniature city buildings. As a modern African American man, Wells's figure brings his heritage in ancient Egypt into dialog with his modern work. As a contemporary Black wage earner who fueled the urban economy, Wells's male figure metaphorically "serves up" the urban environment. In other publications, Aaron Douglas and E. Simms Campbell presented New Negro workers in settings that connected the urban and industrial landscapes. Douglas's heroic worker on the 1928 cover of *The American Negro: The Annals* leans majestically on a shovel between animated tall buildings and sprawling factories,[18] and Campbell's dynamic workers stride boldly through a fragmented urban, industrial environment on the September 1930 cover of *Opportunity.*

In contrast to the range of New Negro male figures pictured as educated graduates, managers, and workers by Dawson, Wells, and others, the intersectionality of racism and sexism led Joyce Carrington and other women artists to "frame their circumstances" by visualizing a far more restricted subject position for Black women.[19] In the case of Carrington's *Crisis* cover, the female figure's fashionable hair, jewelry, and light brown skin with applied cosmetics were signs of the extreme constraints Black women experienced in attaining status within American consumer citizenship, especially middle-class beauty culture. From *Crisis* cover photographs and illustrations to advertisements for Madame C. J. Walker's Egyptian Brown Face Powder and Glossine, Black women were repeatedly advised that light brown skin and "silken hair" amounted to "alluring perfection."[20]

Breaking marginally with these narrow strictures, Gwendolyn Bennett's evocative July 1926 *Opportunity* cover depicts a stylish, light-skinned Black woman whose facial features are racialized and curly hair worn naturally. She is a dynamic figure who holds in tension her modern identity and her imagined heritage. Her body sways sensually in front of a backdrop with an Africanist tableau showing active, silhouetted dancers that recall lines from Bennett's earlier poem "Heritage," describing her desire to connect with a forgotten past in Africa, to "see the slim palm trees" and "lithe Negro girls, / Etched dark against the sky."[21] In contrast to the active dancers, the sway of Bennett's figure appears reserved. Her head and eyes turn in toward her body in deep reverie, signaling connection with the pervasive theme of longing in the related novels by Jessie Fauset and Nella Larsen that addressed the theme of female passing. In refusing her accessibility to the viewer and portraying her difference from the dancers in the tableau, Bennett accords the figure rare agency in her process of self-determination.

One of the most overlooked women artists of the New Negro Renaissance, Laura Wheeler was a prolific illustrator whose work appeared frequently in *The Crisis*. Her delicate pen and ink drawings ranged broadly in style and subject, but two types emerged from the intersection of race and gender. On the one hand, in the November 1920 issue of *The Crisis*, her sober scene of strong Black women who sought education and the right to vote anticipated the pastels of Winold Reiss in their depiction of dark skin and racialized features.[22] On the other hand, her inverted fairy-tale images for Jessie Fauset's short stories visualized the specter of racism that threatened to shatter the dreams of their light-skinned female protagonists.[23]

Sexuality, Visual Coding, and Satire

The illustrations of Charles Cullen and Richard Bruce Nugent in *Ebony and Topaz* emerged from the intersectionality of racism and homophobia, but they used coded imagery to negotiate these strictures. In his frontispiece for the volume, Cullen celebrated an idealized, nude Black male body, glistening with reflected light as if oiled for an ancient athletic event. The youthful figure stretches across the composition, reaching for the stars etched in the sky – a metaphorical sign of racial uplift. However, upon closer inspection, there is a campy quality to the figure's surroundings – a star with full smiling lips just above his head, and lush foliage that drips and blossoms in exaggerated fashion. With his back to the reader, the Black youth displays his nude body before an ambiguously gendered figure in the

lower left, partly hidden by sumptuous leaves. With female accoutre-
ments – bobbed hair and jewelry, the figure's chiseled chin and thick
neck appear masculine, suggesting a man in drag who gazes passionately
upward at his male lover. With a wily snake dangling from the tree at right,
Cullen has drawn association with the Garden of Eden, perhaps playfully
recasting Eve as queer. Elsewhere in this volume, Nugent's *Drawings for
Mulattoes* recounted a satirical history of mixed-race individuals that
concluded in a nightclub, the figures' campy poses making allusion to
the performers of Harlem's infamous drag balls, at clubs where mixed-race,
same-sex relations were celebrated. As Nugent later declared, "'male' and
'female' impersonation was at its peak as night club entertainment . . . and
gender was becoming more and more conjectural."[24]

In the same drawing series, Nugent wielded his chicanery to riff on
debates regarding the superiority of "Mulattoes" to Blacks. In his *Drawing
Number 2*, a small "Mulatto" figure is born like Venus on the half shell, but
pictured literally half white and half black. Behind the figure, a topsy-turvy
composition completely flips stereotypical assumptions about the black
and white "halves" of "Mulatto" identity. At the center of Nugent's
composition, a Janus-faced head is half white and half black, mischievously
sporting a black "ancient Greek" profile at left, and a white "primitive"
profile at right. Further disrupting visual norms, tall urban buildings frame
the white "primitive" profile, and "primitive" palm trees flank the black
"ancient Greek" profile. By defying normative racial and color assigna-
tions, Nugent tricked the stereotypes that presumed "Mulattoes" were
superior to Blacks. Through satire and humor, Nugent prepared the reader
for the sociological study by E. B. Reuter that followed in the *Ebony and
Topaz* text, which argued that the so-called exceptionalism of
"Mulattoes . . . should be understood as a simple and obvious consequence
of the historic circumstances that have favored them."[25]

Aaron Douglas often shared with Nugent a trickster approach in his
illustrations, especially in his signature Afro-Deco silhouettes that hid as
much as they revealed. In these flat figures, he typically delineated the crisp,
angular contours of the head and body but not the details of skin color or
clothing. Further, he tended to place his silhouetted figures between two
distinct settings that seemed to suggest oppositional forces, at the same
time that his silhouetted tricksters ultimately repressed the implied dual-
ities. In his dust jacket for James Weldon Johnson's *The Autobiography of
an Ex-Colored Man* (1927), Douglas placed a silhouetted male figure
between a dark hill with plantings at left and bright tall city buildings at
right. Yet his cunningly misleading black silhouette portrayed Johnson's

light-skinned protagonist, who decided to abandon fixed categories of race that would pit nature against culture. Instead, he "would neither disclaim the black race nor claim the white race" but "let the world take me for what it would."[26] In his dust jacket for Claude McKay's *Home to Harlem* (1928), Douglas situated McKay's protagonist Jake between a modern tall building at left and an old, Gothic-style church façade at right. In stance and form, his silhouetted protagonist seemingly demarcated contrasting forces in Harlem between vice and purity, when in fact revealing collage-like word fragments – for "Numbers" and "Cabarets" – in the space between the buildings. These fragmented signs denoted Harlem's bustling nightlife of cabaret performances and gambling – at the heart of McKay's novel, and the source of its bourgeois critique.

As Douglas used wit and satire to connect with an author's sensibility, at times he also "smiled satirically" at a racist text.[27] His final set of illustrations for Locke and Montgomery Gregory's *Plays of Negro Life* (1927) accompanied the transcription of Eugene O'Neill's play *The Emperor Jones*, which many Black critics decried as trading on stereotypes of Blacks as "inferior, superstitious, half-ignorant."[28] In his first illustration, Douglas created dynamic surroundings for his figure of Brutus Jones, with layered and fragmented forms thrown into motion: the checkerboard floor pattern careening into the distance, the fragmented throne, the cropped view of arched windows that look onto flowing waves of water. For his silhouetted protagonist at the center of this enervated scene, Douglas followed O'Neill's characterization of the Emperor's flashy uniform and boots. However, he playfully animated the figure with an agile, bent-knee dance step, which can be associated with depictions of blackface minstrels. Seemingly confirming the buffoonery of O'Neill's protagonist, Douglas's satirical dance step also subverted O'Neill's atavistic tale of Brutus Jones, just as black minstrels and performers like Bert Williams had parodied the tradition of blackface minstrelsy.[29]

Aural-visual expression

One of the most pervasive forms of creative inspiration for New Negro Renaissance poets and visual artists came from vernacular cultural forms, especially blues music. In their evocation of sound through visual geometry, illustrators created responses to the blues poetry of Langston Hughes and Sterling Brown, comprising a dynamic aural–visual expression of fragmented and exaggerated forms. Three illustrations for Hughes's blues-inspired poetry, created between 1925 and 1926, reveal different approaches to aural–visual expression. In the October 1926 issue of *Opportunity*, editor Charles S. Johnson published a double-paged spread, titled "Two Artists," with blues poems by Hughes and pen and ink drawings by Aaron Douglas. In his *Play De Blues*, illustrating Hughes's "Misery," Douglas created a captivating composition of silhouetted forms focused on a blues singer and her piano player, each swaying to the blues tunes represented graphically as parallel, wavy bands emanating from the top of the upright piano. The fragmented forms and flowing movement of Douglas's composition gave visual form to the blues music that inspired Hughes's vernacular lines: "Play de blues for me. / No other music / 'Ll ease ma misery. . . . Black gal like me / 'S got to hear a blues / For her misery."[30]

A year earlier, in the August 1925 issue of *Forum*, Winold Reiss created a very different illustration for Hughes's poem "The Weary Blues." In his cacophonous composition, which brought European modernism into dialog with African American vernacular expression, Reiss responded to both the melodic sweetness and the painful dissonance of Hughes's lines in the languid, yet haunted figure of the blues singer, "Droning a drowsy, syncopated tune, / Rocking back and forth to a mellow croon, / I heard a Negro play."[31] Reiss pictured specific elements from Hughes's poem: the "old gas light" behind the singer at left, and the "rickety stool" that tips with the weight of the seated performer. He approximated the sounds of the blues through a complex network of Cubist triangular shafts that extend up and fan out, three-dimensionally from the piano pedal, and as fragmented sheets of music from the singer's lips – visual signs of Hughes's transliteration of the blues. The disjointed and compressed environment surrounding the blues singer visually pulses in tune with the music's syncopation.

For the publication by Alfred A. Knopf of Hughes's first volume of poetry, *The Weary Blues* (1926), the young Mexican artist Miguel Covarrubias received the commission for the dust jacket design. Creating his cover image based on Hughes's title poem, Covarrubias included just three images in his closely cropped composition – a blues musician, an upright piano, and "the old gas light" shining brightly to illumine the scene.[32] The original color-printed jacket had a stunning red background, with contrasting black silhouetted figures and forms, and the light tan paper showing through in the aura of the lamp. Covarrubias gave visual form to the blues music and lyrics through the strong tilt forward of the piano, and the exaggerated size of the musician's gnarled hands and his broadly racialized facial features. Though his figure veered toward the kinds of searingly comic caricatures for which he was famous,

Covarrubias also imbued the blues player with a counteractive dignity in his musical absorption. In fact, the musician seems carried away beyond his music, with hands up, head thrown back, lips loosely parted – as if in a silent, syncopated moment between notes.

E. Simms Campbell, who created boldly modernist woodblock prints to illustrate covers of *Opportunity* in the early 1930s, provided some of the most striking collage-inspired images that gave visual form to the blues. In 1932, he illustrated *Southern Road*, a volume of poems by Sterling Brown, who explored what he perceived as an actively modern, vernacular blues expression, "linked with the itinerant blues musician" of the US South.[33] In his illustration for Brown's title poem, Campbell's active, fluctuating patterns of strongly contrasting black and white fragments resist legibility (Figure 5.3). A heavy chain, a jumble of muscular workers, a cropped view of prison bars, and a slice of a roadside vignette clutter the composition

Figure 5.3 E. Simms Campbell, illustration in Sterling Brown, *Southern Road* (New York: Harcourt Brace, 1932), frontispiece for Part 1. Special Collections, University of Houston Libraries.

with the chaos of a modernist collage. These fragments give strident, rhythmic force and aural–visual form to Brown's blending of a chain-gang work song with blues poetry: "Swing dat hammer – hunh – / Steady, bo' / Swing dat hammer – hunh – / Steady, bo' / Ain't no rush, bebby / Long ways to go."[34] Campbell's chaotic image captures the ceaseless brutality experienced by the southern chain gang, at the same time that the protective embrace shared by his foreground figures suggests the "communal self-preservation" and resistance to white oppression that the chain-gang work song effected.[35]

In this and his other collage-like illustrations for Brown's book, Campbell's fragmented figural forms with exaggerated hands and facial features both flirted with stereotypes of Black physiognomy and invented new, modernist vernacular stylizations that point toward Jacob Lawrence's audacious black and white drawings for Hughes's *One-Way Ticket* (1949).[36] Campbell's images are distinctive as some of the very few examples of New Negro Renaissance illustrations associated with southern cultural production.

In his gouache designs for James Weldon Johnson's *God's Trombones* (1927), Douglas applied an aural–visual aesthetic to religious subjects.[37] For Johnson's poem, "The Prodigal Son," Douglas's illustration recast the biblical, wayward youth and his urban temptresses as modern Black revelers in a Harlem cabaret. He followed sections of Johnson's text, based on African American preaching styles, which recounted the prodigal son's arrival in Babylon to squander his inheritance. There he witnessed a modern city with "brass bands . . . a-playing," and he "spent his nights in the gambling dens, / Throwing dice with the devil for his soul."[38] However, Douglas embroidered beyond the text to create a modern "conception of indulgence," as Richard Powell has aptly described, with "montagelike, beyond-the-composition's-edge renderings of paper currency, a playing card, gambler's dice, and a gin bottle."[39] These image fragments, along with the cropped horns of two trombones above, form a jagged frame surrounding the central black silhouettes of the Prodigal Son and two women, who dance and party in a Harlem cabaret. With every rhythmic line and contour, Douglas created a visual analog to the frenetic movement and cacophonous clatter of the cabaret experience in Harlem. As Powell writes, "*The Prodigal Son* throbs with the relentless beat of snare drums and the feet of shuffling dancers, accentuated by soulful trombones and the high pitched clinking of gin bottles."[40] Douglas's illustration celebrated the modern moment of sensory pleasures, making the biblical parable of the Prodigal Son relevant for the 1920s reader.

Religion and Social Justice

In the late 1920s and early 1930s, Harlem Renaissance artists developed powerful new strategies to employ historical religious imagery to address contemporary instances of political oppression and violence. Roscoe Wright was one of several artists who linked African American experiences of oppression with Christ's crucifixion. In his *Negro Womanhood* on the January 1928 cover of *The Crisis*, Wright's female figure assumes the posture of Christ on the cross, with arms spread wide. A chain at right also links the figure with the history of slavery in America. In his radically modern Black female crucifixion, Wright has suggested an ancestry of suffering shared across time by contemporary Black women.

Another group of artists carried this iconography a step further, linking the historical sacrifice of Christ on the cross with the atrocity of modern lynching. Charles Cullen provided a powerful frontispiece image for Countee Cullen's *The Black Christ and Other Poems* (1929), grafting a Black victim of lynching onto an image of Christ's crucifixion. With this visual superimposition, Charles responded to Countee's lines from his title poem, "How Calvary in Palestine, / Extending down to me and mine, / Was but the first leaf in a line / Of trees on which a Man would swing."[41] In 1931, Langston Hughes composed the poem "Christ in Alabama" in response to the case of the Scottsboro Boys, in which nine young Black men were falsely accused of gang-raping two white women on a freight train in northern Alabama, imprisoned, and sentenced to death. They were finally released after nineteen long years, and their protracted imprisonment was dubbed a legal lynching in the progressive press. Zell Ingram and Prentiss Taylor provided illustrations for separate printings of Hughes's poem "Christ in Alabama," each casting a lynched Black youth as the figure of Christ who was, in Hughes's scathing lines, "Beaten and black – / . . . Of the bleeding mouth: / Nigger Christ / On the cross of the South."[42] Rather than superimposing a Black victim of lynching on a white Christ, as had Charles Cullen, Ingram radically created a Black Christ holding up his hands to reveal white stigmata, just as the Scottsboro Boys would carry wounds of their abuse by a corrupt white legal system in the US South.

White artist Prentiss Taylor, introduced to Hughes through Carl Van Vechten, provided the second image for "Christ in Alabama," published in Hughes's collection of poetry and a play, *Scottsboro Limited* (1932; Figure 5.4). While Taylor's image of a Black youth on

Figure 5.4 Prentiss Taylor, "Christ in Alabama," in Langston Hughes, *Scottsboro Limited* (New York: Golden Stair Press, 1932). Collection of Joseph R. Quiroz.

a white cross articulated Hughes's metaphor of crucifixion for the Black youths who faced death in a Scottsboro jail, his lithograph also worked broadly as a vernacular image lamenting the fate of all southern Black Christs. His Black figure of Mary mourning at left stands in for the multitude of African American mothers who have decried the injustice of their sons' exploitation by a corrupt American legal system. The cotton growing at right resituated the biblical crucifixion in the US South, epitomizing the toil of Black workers in the southern fields – a visual icon of their exploited labor.

Looking Forward

Of all the images created by New Negro artists, it is perhaps those that connect religion and social justice that seem most relevant today. During the last five years, we have become increasingly sensitized to pervasive political injustices in the USA through the activism of groups like Black Lives Matter, the student-led March for Our Lives, and Rev. William Barber's Moral Mondays movement and Poor People's campaign. As these groups have reinvigorated a culture of protest and advocacy, and have made Black lives and religion matter, we can find kindred spirits among New Negro artists who creatively gave voice to the collective outrage at the continued lynching of Black men in the American South.

More broadly, it is the strategies of resistance that New Negro Renaissance illustrators employed that continue to wield power. Deftly defying expectations, they employed a vibrant visual language of seeming opposites, thereby signifying on racial stereotypes and other cultural norms. Through the agency of Carrington's modern Black figures and Nugent's tricksters, the imagined rupture between history and modernity, nature and culture became fluid and dynamic; in the most transgressive images, race and gender became conjectural. Through inspiration from Black vernacular forms like the blues, Douglas, Campbell and others produced cacophonous collage that demanded ears and not just eyes respond. The Black Christs of Ingram and Taylor awakened a remote religious iconography to picture the modern horror of lynching.

In 2016, William Villalongo and Mark Thomas Gibson organized the compelling exhibition *Black Pulp!*, which explored illustrations in New Negro books and magazines, mid-century Black comic books, and contemporary art that drew inspiration from this body of work. In this visual material, Villalongo saw a continuum of Black artists engaged in speaking truth to power through "cunning acts of resistance, punchy expressions of Black agency, joy, and desire."[43] Identifying the roots of this continuum in New Negro Renaissance material texts, Villalongo and Gibson productively placed them in dialog with contemporary art by Kara Walker, Kerry James Marshall, Trenton Doyle Hancock, and others, who continue to use drawings, prints, and mixed media on paper to wield their trickster critique.

Notes

1. Caroline Goeser, *Picturing the New Negro: Harlem Renaissance Print Culture and Modern Black Identity* (Lawrence: University Press of Kansas, 2007), 1.

2. Ibid.
3. Rachel Farebrother, *The Collage Aesthetic in the Harlem Renaissance* (Farnham: Ashgate, 2009), 16.
4. Ibid., 17.
5. Richard J. Powell, "Paint that Thing! Aaron Douglas's Call to Modernism," *American Studies* 49, no. 1/2 (2008): 108.
6. Alain Locke, ed., *The New Negro: An Interpretation* (New York: Albert and Charles Boni, 1925), xv.
7. Ibid., 419.
8. Jeffrey C. Stewart, *The New Negro: The Life of Alain Locke* (New York: Oxford University Press, 2018), 485.
9. Locke, *The New Negro*, 266.
10. Ibid.
11. Wallace Thurman, ed., *Fire!! A Quarterly Devoted to Younger Negro Artists* (November 1926): 1.
12. Richard J. Powell, "The Aaron Douglas Effect," in *Aaron Douglas: African American Modernist*, ed. Susan Earle (New Haven: Yale University Press, 2007), 57.
13. Wallace Thurman, "Negro Artists and the Negro," *New Republic*, August 31, 1927, 37–39.
14. Charles S. Johnson, ed., *Ebony and Topaz: A Collectanea* (New York: *Opportunity* and the National Urban League, 1927), 11, 13.
15. Caroline Goeser, "Black and Tan: Racial and Sexual Crossings in *Ebony and Topaz*," in *Little Magazines and Modernism: New Approaches*, ed. Suzanne W. Churchill and Adam McKible (Aldershot: Ashgate, 2007), 155.
16. Powell, "Paint that Thing!," 114–115.
17. Kathy Peiss, *Hope in a Jar: The Making of America's Beauty Culture* (New York: Henry Holt, 1998), 93.
18. Powell, "The Aaron Douglas Effect," 64–65.
19. Kimberlé Crenshaw, "Why Intersectionality Can't Wait," *The Washington Post*, September 24, 2015; www.washingtonpost.com/news/in-theory/wp/2015/09/24/why-intersectionality-cant-wait/?utm_term=.2559e04c3285.
20. Madam C. J. Walker, "Advertisement for Egyptian Brown Face Powder and Glossine," *The Crisis* (January 1928).
21. Gwendolyn Bennett, "Heritage," *Opportunity* (December 1923): 371.
22. Laura Wheeler, "Ruth Is Not Coming Out of College," illustration in Willis Richardson, "The Deacon's Awakening," *The Crisis* (November 1920): 13.
23. Mar Gallego, *Passing Novels in the Harlem Renaissance: Identity Politics and Textual Strategies* (New Brunswick: Transaction, 2003), 154; Goeser, *Picturing the New Negro*, 200–204.
24. Thomas H. Wirth, ed. *Gay Rebel of the Harlem Renaissance: Selections from the Work of Richard Bruce Nugent* (Durham: Duke University Press, 2002), 221–223.
25. E. B. Reuter, "The Changing Status of the Mulatto," in *Ebony and Topaz: A Collectanea*, 110.

26. James Weldon Johnson, *The Autobiography of an Ex-Colored Man*, ed. Jacqueline Goldsby (1912; New York: Norton, 2015), 99.
27. Alain Locke, "Introduction: The Drama of Negro Life," in *Plays of Negro Life: A Source-Book of Native American Drama*, ed. Montgomery Gregory and Alain Locke (New York: Harper and Brothers, 1927), n.p.
28. Benjamin Brawley, "The Negro in American Fiction," *Dial* 60 (1916): 445.
29. Goeser, *Picturing the New Negro*, 282–284.
30. Aaron Douglas and Langston Hughes, "Two Artists," *Opportunity* (October 1926): 315.
31. Langston Hughes, "The Weary Blues," *Forum* (August 1925): 239.
32. Ibid.
33. James Smethurst, *The New Red Negro: The Literary Left and African American Poetry, 1930–1946* (New York: Oxford University Press, 1999), 64.
34. Sterling A. Brown, *Southern Road* (New York: Harcourt Brace, 1932), 46.
35. Smethurst, *The New Red Negro*, 65.
36. Langston Hughes, *One-Way Ticket* (New York: Alfred A. Knopf, 1949).
37. Caroline Goeser, "The Blare of *God's Trombones*: Modernizing Biblical Narratives in the Work of Aaron Douglas," in *Beholding Christ and Christianity in African American Art*, ed. James Romaine and Phoebe Wolfskill (University Park: Pennsylvania State University Press, 2017), 45–49.
38. James Weldon Johnson, *God's Trombones: Seven Negro Sermons in Verse* (1927; New York: Penguin, 1990), 23–24.
39. Powell, "The Aaron Douglas Effect," 62.
40. Powell, "Paint that Thing!," 111.
41. Countee Cullen, *The Black Christ and Other Poems* (New York: Harper and Brothers, 1929), 69.
42. Langston Hughes, "Christ in Alabama," *Contempo: A Review of Ideas and Personalities* (December 1, 1931): 1.
43. William Villalongo, "Strange Material: Black Pulp!," in *Black Pulp!*, ed. Mark Thomas Gibson and William Villalongo (New Haven: Yale School of Art, 2016), 10.

PART II

Experimenting with the New Negro

CHAPTER 6

Gwendolyn Brooks: Riot *after the New Negro Renaissance*

Sonya Posmentier

In 1938 a young Gwendolyn Brooks sent James Weldon Johnson "a little typewritten group of my poems, which I hope you will think enough of to read and keep,"[1] which she had collected into an elegant, hand-sewn square booklet with a blue-speckled triangular cover page.[2] Brooks was just shy of 21 and Johnson, nearly 67, would live only a few more months after their correspondence. Brooks had sent Johnson poems a year before, in response to which he praised her "unquestionable talent and feeling for poetry," encouraged her to keep reading and writing, and offered marginal feedback and critique.[3] In her fragmented autobiographical book *Report from Part One*, Brooks describes his response as "Patient Interest. Generosity."[4] Now, having placed several poems in significant publications, including the *Chicago Defender*, *The Crisis*, and a collection of American Women's writing, she wanted to publish a book, and once again sought the assistance of a pioneering literary elder of the New Negro movement. Johnson read and kept the booklet (which now lives among his effects at the Beinecke Rare Book and Manuscript Library), but responded frankly that "I did not find anything sufficiently outstanding to interest a first-rank publisher."[5] It was not Johnson but the much younger writer Richard Wright, Brooks's fellow Chicagoan, who ultimately helped to pave the way to publication as an anonymous reader of *A Street in Bronzeville*, the book Brooks would finally publish, to great acclaim, with Harper Brothers in 1945. Yet Brooks's urgent correspondence with the editor of the influential *Book of American Negro Poetry* as well as other writers of the Harlem Renaissance generation indicates their significant influence on her career and her poetry.

It makes sense to think of Brooks as a transitional figure between the New Negro movement that James Weldon Johnson helped to usher in and the Chicago Renaissance and Black Arts Movements with which she became associated later in life. She was taught, inspired by, and actively reading the New Negro poets early in her career, including Langston

Hughes, Countee Cullen, and Claude McKay, all of whom figure prominently in her accounts of becoming a poet. According to Brooks's autobiographical writings, both McKay and Cullen recognized the
accomplishment of *A Street in Bronzeville*. McKay attended a party of
Brooks's at the South Side Community Art Center in Chicago and wrote
to her later to "welcome you among the band of hardworking poets who do
have something to say," and Cullen similarly reached out with praise and
good wishes.[6] By 1950 Brooks shared the pages of a special *Phylon* issue on
Black writing with some of these writers but felt ready to declare a new
aesthetic freedom for Black poetry. In 1967 she was famously transformed
by her encounter with the younger Black Arts poets at the Fisk University
Writers's conference. In the words of Brooks's most recent biographer,
Angela Jackson, 1967 was like a "personal earthquake"[7] after which "nothing was the same" for Brooks.[8] While underscoring the radical shift that
Brooks's contact with younger poets produced, a shift Brooks herself
remarked upon in many contexts, Jackson wisely resists bifurcating
Brooks's career into before and after Fisk, rendering instead a life and
work that was full and developed, rich and varied, multiply influenced and
endlessly influencing.

With this nuanced understanding in mind I wish to follow the lasting
influence of the New Negro writers on Brooks's poetry, including poetry
written after the break. Specifically I turn to *Riot*, the work Brooks
published immediately after Fisk, in 1969, to think about its continuity
with the poetry most closely associated with the "New Negro
Renaissance." I do so not for the sake of periodizing Brooks as part of
the earlier generation of the Harlem Renaissance, or to detach her later
work from its formation in and of the Black Arts Movement. Rather,
I identify and trace in Brooks's work the development of a particular
tradition, perhaps even one apotheosis of that tradition, of Black migratory
poetics.

A migratory poetics is related but not identical to what Jahan Ramazani
calls traveling poetry (poetry that formally and imaginatively enacts human
transnational movement).[9] Migratory poetry might include any of the
following: poems that travel across national and intranational borders;
poems by people or groups of people who travel; and poetic forms, genres,
formats transformed by their circulation. I use migration and migratory
here (rather than "traveling" or "transnational," Ramazani's preferred
terms) as key words that allow us to recognize how the movements of
certain people can be forced, curtailed, constrained, and propelled by
violence and by state and rogue practices of labor, separation, and

incarceration. Migratory poetry as I understand it illuminates, transforms, and at times dismantles that violence and constraint, but also, as we shall see, turns its back on these borders, attempting to find, create, define, and take up space (in land, sea, and imagination) beyond the nation state.

Foregrounding migratory poetics as a necessary inheritance from the Harlem Renaissance, I build on work by previous scholars that has emphasized not particular places but movement from place to place in Black modern literature. Along with earlier studies by Robert Stepto, Hazel Carby, and others, Farah Griffin's *Who Set You Flowin'* transformed the field of Black literary study by insisting that the "migration narrative" was constitutive of twentieth-century Black cultural production.[10] Griffin argues that migration (generally referring, in her study, to migration from the rural US South to the urban US North, with some variations on that theme) is not only a significant historical experience and theme of Black life and art, but also key to understanding how Black art, music, and literature themselves have travelled since the beginning of the twentieth century. In the same decade of scholarship, scholars of Black literature and structure also sought models for theorizing the relationship between *transnational* circulation (as well as migration and immigration) and Black cultural production, perhaps most notably Paul Gilroy's formulation of "the Black Atlantic as a Counterculture of Modernity" and Brent Edwards's rethinking of diaspora as an articulation of transnational difference made particularly visible and audible by translation among languages, media, and forms.[11]

Brooks's poetry would seem ill fitted at first analysis to cosmopolitan frameworks for mobility. After her family's migration from Kansas (where she was born) to Chicago, Brooks would live most of her life in that city and became deeply associated with its south side. It would be sacrilegious and downright incorrect to dislodge Brooks's poems from their rightful role as intricate anthems of Chicago, or Brooks herself from her rightful place as the city's literary queen. In fact, Brooks's capacity to capture the movements of people and ideas *into* Chicago was exemplary of the Chicago Renaissance. As Liesl Oslen puts it, "Here was a poet who saw vivid strains of black folk experience threaded through the urban condition."[12]

Yet to read Brooks's full oeuvre as not only place-based but also migratory is to trace another significant continuity between generations of poets from the Harlem Renaissance or New Negro Renaissance, to the Chicago Renaissance, to the Black Arts Movement, and, as I will address in my conclusion, to our present day. Griffin's reading of Brooks's "Kitchenette Building" and "We Real Cool" as negotiating the possibilities of "homespace" or "safe space" in the context of the violent histories of migration and urbanization[13] – and in the poetic context of Harlem Renaissance poets like Jean Toomer – has long offered a foundation for thinking of Brooks's poetry in this way. Reading *Riot* in a related light, we can extend Brooks's inheritance of a migratory poetic tradition into the "post-break" phase of her career.

Like many of Brooks's other poems, early and late, the sequence of poems that make up *Riot* inhabit the geography of the city. As a group of poems that account for white supremacist violence in the face of Black movement, *Riot* carries on the work of another great Chicago "riot" poem, one focused on the anti-Black violence of the so-called Red Summer of 1919, Claude McKay's "If We Must Die."[14] "If We Must Die" is often heralded as a salient example of poetry's mobility. The sonnet responds defiantly to white rioters' anti-Black violence in midwestern USA. As William J. Maxwell aptly puts it in his introduction to the *Complete Poems*, the form of the sonnet offers McKay "an exceptionally transnational design,"[15] and the poem was published in the USA and the UK, in white publications and Black, as well as years later in McKay's home country of Jamaica. There is a famous but likely apocryphal story about Winston Churchill reading the poem aloud to rally the British troops against Nazis.

In a recent essay in *Jacket2*, Jules Boykoff and Kaia Sand tell another remarkable story of the poem's travel, one that highlights the poem as a link *between* movements.[16] In a September 1971 report on the Attica uprising, a *Time* magazine reporter noted his discovery of a "crude-but-touching" poem apparently written by an "unknown prisoner" passed "clandestinely" among the rebel prisoners, including a stanza of the hand-written poem in the article.[17]

It was none other than Gwendolyn Brooks who wrote to *Time* magazine correcting the reporter's erroneous nonattribution. Amongst other letters employing the very language of dehumanization McKay's poem reverses, Brooks writes: "Sir: Please tell the poetry specialist who gave us the above that his 'find' is a portion of one of the most famous poems ever written – known to Hitler, elementary school children to say nothing of Winston Churchill. The poem is entitled 'If We Must Die,' and the black poet is Claude McKay (1890–1948)."[18]

If the *Time* magazine reporter unwittingly incarcerated the famous poet, while also rendering him nameless, as if a belated punishment for the crime of lyricizing revolt, Brooks liberated McKay from the narrow prison of white reportage. It is fitting that she did so, as yet another

Black poet of riot. Her "Riot" chronicles the uprising across the country, and particularly in Chicago, that followed the assassination of Martin Luther King, Jr. in 1968, nearly fifty years after the Red Summer, and just a few years before the Attica uprising. Mainstream media representations of these "riots" often delegitimized and dismissed their significance as a form of social protest. Brooks's poems directly engage media representations while at the same time offering an alternative to them, what Tonya Foster calls "another music" and Amber Rose describes as *itself* a riot, in which "sensory overload" is "a way of speaking that doesn't require translation or transmediation."[19]

"Riot," the first poem in the chapbook of the same name is well understood as a discourse on white supremacy. In the figure of John Cabot, a fictional white victim of the riot's violence – historians agree that all of the fatalities of the 1968 Chicago Riots were Black – she locates anti-Black violence in the origins of the USA, as far back as the fifteenth-century explorer John Cabot, who claimed North America for England, and the Boston Brahmin of the same name.

One salient feature of the violent anti-Black rhetoric Brooks wishes to engage and dismantle is the use of natural imagery to describe and deride human migration:

> Because the Negroes were coming down the street.
> Because the poor were sweaty and unpretty
> (not like Two Dainty Negroes in Winnetka)
> and they were coming toward him in rough ranks. In
> seas. In windsweep. They were black and loud. And not
> detainable. And not discreet.[20]

Cabot experiences Blackness as invasion, contagion, catastrophic environmental phenomenon. Yet Brooks intersperses among these negative descriptors more neutral natural figures like "seas," "windsweep," and even "breath." White supremacist discourse uses such figures to essentialize and biologize hatred and difference but here they have other potential.

These figures were a central feature of modernist thought and discourse during the period after World War I, of the Great Migration, which was also the period of Gwendolyn Brooks's childhood. A well-known example is Lothrop Stoddard's "The Rising Tide of Color: The Threat against White-World Supremacy," the 1920 anti-immigrant, anti-Black screed that inspired a reference in Fitzgerald's *The Great Gatsby*. Referring to a fictionalized version of Stoddard's book (which was published by Fitzgerald's publisher, Scribner's), Fitzgerald's character, Tom Buchanan,

echoes the oceanic metaphor or Stoddard's treatise, worrying that, "the
white race will be – will be utterly submerged."[21] Such rhetoric also informs
the language of population as waste in T. S. Eliot's "The Waste Land,"
a poem often cited as an influence on Brooks and especially the second
poem in *Riot*, "The Third Sermon on the Warpland." With particular
attention to Eliot's early drafts of the poem, Michael North reads the
experimental techniques of quotation and juxtaposition in "The Waste
Land" as derived from the blackface minstrel show. In North's analysis,
Eliot does not so much offer up an enabling model for Black dialect writers
(as Henry Louis Gates, Jr., Kamau Brathwaite and others have argued) as
he appropriates Black idiom, participating in a "deliberate deterritorialism
of language" that produces "debilitating alienation." According to North's
exhaustive archival research, one of Eliot's sources for Black language was
the lyrics of a song written by none other than Brooks's reluctant mentor,
James Weldon Johnson.[22] "There's a certain irony," North points out, to
Eliot's borrowing of Johnson's "Under the Bamboo Tree," through which
Eliot forces this subversive popular song "back into minstrel stereotypes."[23]
As North acknowledges, however, Eliot could not entirely control the
breadth and length of the influence of his conflicted idiomatic voice.
"Even after Eliot though he had put dialect aside, the racial irony of
Modernism had another turn left in it,"[24] through which Black writers
heard in Eliot one basis for Black expression.

    The second poem in Brooks's lyric trilogy, "Third Sermon on the
Warpland," might be read as evidence of such a turn. The title of the
poem pays obvious homage to Eliot and explores the thematic and linguistic dialectic between Black and white speech, but the poem also rejects
Eliot's depiction of human reproduction, proliferation, and movement as
waste, offering up instead a vision of darkness as abundance. The discourse
between Black and white is personified in Brooks's poem in the figures of
the Black Philosopher who narrates the uprising and its history, uttering
the poem's last words –

> "There they came to life and exulted,
> the hurt mute.
> Then it was over.
> The dust, as they say, settled."[25]

– and the White Philosopher who, earlier in the poem, responded meekly
to the fire the first poem, "Riot,"[26] has set to white supremacy: "It is better
to light one candle than curse the / darkness." The poem reminds us,
significantly, that "White Philosophy" (perhaps something like the very

philosophy of waste that drives Eliot's poem), has been brought to light and burned to the ground. Brooks imagines a Black poetic idiom not of ruin and waste, but of the warpland that rises from its ashes.

We might understand Brooks's trilogy, then, as indebted not only to Eliotic experimentation with fragmentation, quotation, and idiomatic speech, but also to New Negro descriptions of Black migration, growth, and aesthetics, which were in some cases experimental borrowings and transformations of white supremacist discourse. One influential instance of such transformation was Alain Locke's portrayal of migration as the very basis of modern Black artistic practice in his landmark *New Negro* anthology, published in 1925, the same year as *The Great Gatsby*. Here, Locke knowingly echoes and transforms Stoddard's racist figure into a figure of liberation:

> The wash and rush of this human tide on the beach line of the northern city centers is to be explained primarily in terms of a new vision of opportunity, of social and economic freedom of a spirit to seize, even in the face of an extortionate and heavy toll, a chance for the improvement of conditions. With each successive wave of it, the movement of the Negro migrant becomes more and more like that of the European waves at their crests, a mass movement toward the larger and the more democratic chance – in the Negro's case a deliberate flight not only from countryside to city, but from medieval America to modern.[27]

From the New Negro writers, Brooks inherits this sense of migration as a linking force between global anti-colonial and decolonial movements and Black futurity. If we remember that in 1968 Brooks still had McKay in mind, the "riot" of her poem – which is to say both the movement and the growth of people throughout the three poems and the riot of the poem itself – reads as part of this "mass movement toward a larger, more democratic chance." The poem is a "successive wave" following the tide of the earlier poet. Indeed, we might consider migration – that is, seas, windsweep, and breath – as the chronotope of Brooks's *Riot*.

The title poem "Riot" takes language that at first seems interior to Cabot, pervaded with the fearful consciousness of white supremacy and transforms it into something else. Through the mocking depiction of Cabot, the references connecting him to historical colonists, and the debased ugliness of his quoted speech, Brooks creates an ironic distance from the naturalized and biologized language for describing Blackness. Yet earlier in the poem, through the use of free indirect discourse, she empowers the "sea" and "wind" of Blackness, rendering "It" capital, beautiful, and, in her word, "thrilling":

> But, in a thrilling announcement, on It drove
> and breathed on him: and touched him.
> In that breath the fume of pig foot,
> chitterling and cheap chill, malign,
> mocked John.[28]

The "fume" through which Cabot articulates his racist disgust is also his downfall (that which maligns and mocks him, as the poem does). Yet on its own, marked off by enjambment and by the perfect limits of its pentameter, the preceding line describes the contact with breath as a form of intimacy. Through its movement as water and wind, Blackness,

> $\qquad\qquad\qquad\qquad\qquad$ It drove
> and breathed on him, and touched him. In that breath $\qquad$ (10)

The line also speaks to the capacity of poetry itself – that is, breath – to "touch." Brooks's poetic refiguration of interwar metaphors for migration and Black population growth does not idealize physical or linguistic violence. The first poem in *Riot* ends with Cabot going "down in the smoke and fire / and broken glass and blood," and crying out a racial epithet, hardly a Romantic scene (10). Rather, by ironizing and redistributing the ecopolitical and biopolitical language of white supremacy that accompanied, haunted, and taunted the Great Migration, Brooks places herself with Locke and McKay in this tradition of what we might think of as Black migratory poetics, just as the second wave of the Great Migration is reaching its crest. In doing so, she extends a poetic counter-discourse that reclaims language of human migration as *natural*, inevitable, and right.

Through its linguistic confrontation with ecological descriptions of migration, "Riot" clears the way for the remaining poems to claim the warped land of this warpland for Black dwelling. Brooks initiates the second poem, "The Third Sermon," with a dictionary definition of "Phoenix" as an epigraph: "In Egyptian mythology, a bird which lived for five hundred years and then consumed itself in fire, rising renewed from the ashes."[29] This middle poem in the book, the longest and most fragmentary, traces a movement both formal and ideological from the consciousness of the white man whose consciousness dominates the first poem in the sequence, to the lover whose voice takes center stage in the last. It is possible to read this poem as the process of renewal, from the consuming fires of "Riot" to an earth of renewed beauty which the poem goes on to describe: "Watermirrors and things to be reflected. Goldenrod across the little lagoon" (11). Some have understood renewal and transformation in *Riot* as indicative of Brooks "having rejected a white cultural context" (her previous publications with Harper & Row) and "crafted an alternative [Black] context" (her shift to Black publisher Broadside Press) in which Black people can read poetry and understand their immediate circumstances.[30] In other words, Brooks enacts renewal through her disruption of the supposed universal humanism of whiteness, "as she exchanged a high literary idiom for a decidedly more demotic one."[31] The poem stages this drama in the tension between two central speakers, the White Philosopher and the Black Philosopher, and in the proliferation of more disparate voices, such as "the children in ritual chatter" (15).

However, "Third Sermon" also continues the thematic and formal preoccupations of Brooks's earlier oeuvre. The poem is one of three such "sermons," the first "Sermon on the Warpland" having been published pre-Fisk, and "The Second Sermon on the Warpland" in *In the Mecca*, Brooks's final book with Harper & Row, published in 1968. The poem refers to long-standing aesthetic and political commitments through its very title, indicating its place in an ongoing sequence (third) as well as its genre (sermon). So too, as Carl Phillips has argued, Brooks's *formal* experimentation marks the connection to and development of her earlier work and the lasting influence of the New Negro Poets. In a surprising reading of Brooks's three "Sermons on the Warpland" (of which only the third appears in the sequence *Riot*), Phillips identifies all three poems in terms of their participation in, variation upon, and at times rejection of traditional English prosody – a move most surprising of all when it comes to the "Third Sermon," which most scholars read as the harbinger of Brooks's "post-break" oeuvre. Phillips notes that "the English pentameter that figured prominently in the first sermon, then seemed intertwined with demotic speech in the second, here becomes the minority; more often than not, what pentameter there is seems incidental, as it is in conversation."[32] Given the structure of philosophical debate that governs the poem – in which the Black philosopher warns of impending violence in response to oppression, imploring readers to listen for the "rattle" of "our chains" – he asks if perhaps the turn away from pentameter in the "Third Sermon" is a straightforward formal manifestation of the poem's "break" from white oppression: "So, black rioting against white oppression = the eradication of English/white prosody, each an enactment of the other?" he wonders aloud. His answer is "not quite." For, he observes, Brooks's formalism does not so easily yield its grasp. Rather, "Near the end of the third sermon, I detect a sonnet."[33] The poem, part of the fractured, descriptive sequence that makes up "The Third Sermon," is "A Poem to Peanut," a eulogy for the deceased leader of the Blackstone Rangers, whom Brooks describes as

"A Signature. A Herald. And a Span" who "will not let his men explode" (18). While not adhering to the pentameter that shapes some of Brooks's earlier, more conventional sonnets, this one is nonetheless, as Phillips points out, largely iambic and employs a rhyme scheme approaching Petrarchan patterns.

Like Phillips, I see Brooks's experiments with traditional poetic forms as a marker of her development as a poet rather than the disintegration of "craft" in her work. However, whereas Phillips represents Brooks's formalism largely in relationship to English prosody and rhyme patterns, I wish to underscore her education in the work of the New Negro poets, who had already established a strong tradition of modernist experimentation with sonnets, ballads, and other older English forms. Brooks echoes not only the riotous theme of McKay's "If We Must Die," but also its rhythms and lines, and, in turn the "exceptionally transnational design" of the sonnet form (reframed yet again) that was so appealing to both poets.

In the context of "The Third Sermon on the Warpland" as a whole, "A Poem to Peanut" registers as one short fragmentary lyric in a linked sequence of ten. Along with the amended sonnet, "The Third Sermon" names, describes, and brings to life multiple other genres of sonic expression: including "a rattle," (11) "the *black*blues," (11) jazz, the names of several musicians, a radio stolen for listening to said music ("a radio, sit to hear James Brown / and Mingus, Young-Holt, Coleman, John, / on V.O.N.") (14), citations of lyrics ("what/ is going on/ is going on") (14), "The children in ritual chatter," and sirens (15). Collectively these lyrical expressions constitute alternatives to the discourse of the Black and White philosophers (rendered here as speech) and the language of other characters, named and unnamed. Like the people moving through the Chicago streets during the riot, musical and literary forms migrate into the urban space of Chicago. This sonic migration, made possible through and with the tradition of Black poetics in which Brooks writes, makes the "earth" "a beautiful place"; makes the difference between "wasteland" and "warpland" (a place that is twisted or misshapen or, on the other hand, in constrained motion, like a ship tethered to land).

Thus, migratory poetry not only moves us from one place to another, but also transforms our relationship to spaces and places by moving through and in them. "The Third Sermon on the Warpland" begins simply, "The earth is a beautiful place," proceeds to describe how "The young men run" and "the children scatter," and ends, in the Black Philosopher's voice, "The dust, as they say, settled." The poem narrates riot *as migration*: diaspora (scattering) followed by settlement. This is what enables the trajectory from riot to love, what we might think of as the poem's structural migration from the perspective of John Cabot in the first poem to that of two lovers facing dawn in the last:

> The final poem begins, again simply:
> It is the morning of our love.[34]

And ends with two lovers walking:

> in different directions
> down the imperturbable street.[35]

Just as the children pursued by police and military in "The Third Sermon," "scatter upon / their Own and old geography" (making geography at last "their own"), the lovers are inspired on "the morning of our love" to "go / in different directions," suggesting that any direction is available to them.[36] Which is to say that part of what *Riot* achieves is to authorize the rising tide, the coming ashore, the filling up of streets.

Here is where Brooks's poetry draws another intergenerational line, this time from the early part of the twentieth century into the twenty-first. Brooks's presence in our present can be felt not only in contemporary poets' delightful and diverse formal experiments – homages to Brooks by mid-career Black writers like Major Jackson, Terrance Hayes, Evie Shockley, Quraysh Ali Lansana – but also in a successive wave of work by Black, immigrant, and Indigenous poets who use the poetic line to push up against the borders of land and sea, to make the "old geography" "their Own," work by poets like Tonya Foster, Layli Long Soldier, Warsan Shire, and Javier Zamora.

Through Brooks's *Riot*, we can follow the speaker of McKay's 1919 "If We Must Die," facing the "murderous, cowardly pack" of anti-Black race riots[37] into Major Jackson's twenty-first century imagination of a fugitive up against a "phantom mob" in "Migration" (2008),

> *Lord of My Feet.* A country of overnight deputies, everyone had a knot
> To endeavor. I read oaks and poplars for signs: charred branches,
> Tobacco leaves strung up to die, swamp soil in my soul.
> Ever trace the outline of a phantom mob, even if you were late arriving?[38]

into Zamora's "Citizenship," whose speaker, a young Salvadoran boy approaches the Mexico-US border

> up to that invisible line visible thick white paint
> visible booths visible with the fence starting from the booths

booth road booth road booth road office building then the fence
fence fence fence

it started from a corner with an iron pole
always an iron pole at the beginning[39]

Jackson's speaker experiences the transitory landscape as a text and as
a danger, as he "read[s]" trees "for signs" of violence. In its plaintive
closing, the poem turns to the reader to ask: "Ever trace the outline of
a phantom mob"? To read and write about (or "outline") migration is to
encounter said violence, often naturalized and neutralized through literary
genre (the poem begins by evoking "the earth eaters who put the pastor in
pastoral."). Jackson suggests that poetic migration requires a constant re-
reading, re-tracing, and re-writing of both genres and places so as to inhabit
the "old geography" in new ways.

Like Jackson, Zamora puns to highlight the relationship between the
line of poetry and the geopolitical "invisible line" of the border. Various
structures and infrastructure ("thick white paint," "visible booths,"
"fence," "iron pole") make "visible" that which is invisible, and Zamora
emphasizes through repetition the *insistence* of that process by which
something fictional and "invisible" becomes visible and real. Just so, we
can think of the writing of a poem as a parallel process of making "invisible
lines" visible (for example, making aural lyrics textual), marking the
corners and poles and beginnings and endings of a geography.

Read together, notwithstanding the very different autobiographical,
geographical, and even generational contexts in which they write,
Jackson and Zamora can both be understood as twenty-first-century
poets of migration who have inherited (among other things) the tradition
of Black migratory poetics which Brooks in turn extended from her New
Negro forbears. One of the legacies of the Harlem Renaissance to Brooks
and to our time was the urgency of creating "home space" on this beautiful
earth.

Notes

1. Gwendolyn Brooks, "Gwendolyn Brooks to James Weldon Johnson,"
   March 21, 1938, Box 4, Folder 59, James Weldon Johnson and Grace Nail
   Johnson Papers.
2. Gwendolyn Brooks, "Poems" (n.d.), Box 4, Folder 59, James Weldon Johnson
   and Grace Nail Johnson Papers.
3. Gwendolyn Brooks, *Report from Part One* (Detroit: Broadside Press,
   1972), 202.

4. Ibid., 202–203.

5. James Weldon Johnson, "James Weldon Johnson to Gwendolyn Brooks," April 4, 1938, Box 4, Folder 59, James Weldon Johnson and Grace Nail Johnson Papers.

6. Brooks, *Report from Part One*, 201.

7. Angela Jackson, *A Surprised Queenhood in the New Black Sun: The Life & Legacy of Gwendolyn Brooks* (Boston: Beacon Press, 2017), 93.

8. Ibid., 99.

9. Jahan Ramazani, *A Transnational Poetics* (Chicago: University of Chicago Press, 2009), 51–70.

10. Hazel V. Carby, *Reconstructing Womanhood: The Emergence of the Afro-American Woman Novelist* (New York: Oxford University Press, 1989); Farah Jasmine Griffin, *"Who Set You Flowin'?": The African-American Migration Narrative* (New York: Oxford University Press, 1995); Robert B. Stepto, *From Behind the Veil: A Study of Afro-American Narrative*, 2nd ed. (Urbana: University of Illinois Press, 1991).

11. Brent Hayes Edwards, *The Practice of Diaspora: Literature, Translation, and the Rise of Black Internationalism* (Cambridge, MA: Harvard University Press, 2003); Brent Hayes Edwards, "The Uses of Diaspora," *Social Text* 66 19, no. 1 (2001): 64–66; Paul Gilroy, *The Black Atlantic: Modernity and Double Consciousness* (Cambridge, MA: Harvard University Press, 1993).

12. Liesl Olson, *Chicago Renaissance: Literature and Art in the Midwest Metropolis* (New Haven: Yale University Press, 2017), 241.

13. Griffin, *"Who Set You Flowin'?,"* 108–111.

14. I have written elsewhere of Brooks's formal environmental modernism in relationship to McKay's, arguing that in "In the Mecca" Brooks reimagines the physical constraint of McKay's plantation geography in urban space. See Sonya Posmentier, *Cultivation and Catastrophe: The Lyric Ecology of Modern Black Literature* (Baltimore: Johns Hopkins University Press, 2017), 90–93. Here, I return to the relationship between McKay and Brooks to highlight instead constraint's dialectical other: movement.

15. William J. Maxwell, "Introduction," in Claude McKay, *Complete Poems*, ed. William J. Maxwell (Urbana: University of Illinois Press, 2004), xxxv–xxxvi.

16. Jules Boykoff and Kaia Sand, "Recasting Poetry: 'The Long Biography of a Poem,'" *Jacket2* (blog), June 10, 2011, https://jacket2.org/commentary/recasting-poetry-0.

17. "War at Attica: Was There No Other Way?," *Time* 98, no. 13 (September 27, 1971): 22. Quoted in Boykoff and Sand, "Recasting Poetry."

18. Gwendolyn Brooks, "Letters," *Time* 98, no. 16 (October 18, 1971): 10.

19. Tonya Foster, Amber Rose Johnson, and Davy Knittle, "Not Detainable," PoemTalk, November 16, 2018, https://jacket2.org/podcasts/not-detainable-poemtalk-130.

20. Gwendolyn Brooks, "Riot," in *Riot* (Detroit, MI: Broadside Press, 1969), 9.

21. F. Scott Fitzgerald, *The Great Gatsby* (New York: Scribner, 2004), 13.

22. Michael North, *The Dialect of Modernism: Race, Language, and Twentieth-Century Literature* (New York: Oxford University Press, 1994), 88.

23. Ibid., 88–90.

24. Ibid., 91.

25. Gwendolyn Brooks, "The Third Sermon on the Warpland," in *Riot*, 20.

26. Ibid., 15.

27. Alain Locke, ed., *The New Negro: An Interpretation* (1925; New York: Touchstone, 1997), 6. In the special issue of *Survey Graphic* upon which Locke's landmark anthology was based, this description appears in an essay called "Harlem"; in the anthology, however, Locke combined "Harlem" and another editorial essay, "Enter the New Negro," into a single introduction to the volume. This transformation itself constitutes an example of the dialectic between place-based or regional understandings of Black modern poetics and migratory or mobility-based frameworks, a dialectic which I am arguing can also shape our understanding of Brooks.

28. Brooks, "Riot," 10. Hereafter cited parenthetically.

29. Brooks, "The Third Sermon on the Warpland," 11. Hereafter cited parenthetically.

30. James D. Sullivan, "Killing John Cabot and Publishing Black: Gwendolyn Brooks's 'Riot,'" *African American Review* 36, no. 4 (2002): 566.

31. Carl Phillips, "Brooks's Prosody: Three Sermons on the Warpland," *Poetry Magazine*, Poetry Foundation, July 16, 2019, www.poetryfoundation.org/poetrymagazine/articles/141970/brookss-prosody-three-sermons-on-the-warpland.

32. Ibid., 250.

33. Ibid., 251.

34. Gwendolyn Brooks, "An Aspect of Love, Alive in the Ice and Fire," in *Riot*, 21.

35. Ibid., 22.

36. Ibid.

37. Claude McKay, *Complete Poems*, ed. William J. Maxwell (Urbana: University of Illinois Press, 2004), 178.

38. Major Jackson, "Migration," in *Holding Company: Poems* (New York: Norton, 2012), 8.

39. Javier Zamora, "Citizenship," in *Unaccompanied* (Port Townsend, WA: Copper Canyon Press, 2017), 63.

CHAPTER 7

Romans à Clef *of the Harlem Renaissance*

Sinéad Moynihan

In the first instalment of Mat Johnson and Warren Pleece's 1920s-set, five-part comic *Incognegro: Renaissance* (2018), journalist Zane Pinchback and his bartender friend, Carl – both light-skinned African Americans – attend the launch party for a new novel, *Nigger Town*, by white writer Arna Van Horn, at the author's home in midtown Manhattan. There they meet Xavier, an African American who had acted as Van Horn's "guide north of the park" and who is embittered about Van Horn having succeeded in publishing a novel about Harlem life when African American writers are routinely denied such opportunities.[1] When Xavier is found with slit wrists in an overflowing bathtub, with his book manuscript in hand, the connections, not only between the *personalities* of the Harlem Renaissance and the comic (Van Horn is a thinly disguised Carl Van Vechten) but also the *literary works* of the Harlem Renaissance and the comic, become clear. As Johnson acknowledges in his afterword to the issue, "the death of a failed writer drowning in a bath tub at a party, leaving only a ruined manuscript behind, was inspired by a scene in one of my favorite novels, Wallace Thurman's *Infants of the Spring*."[2] Thurman's 1932 novel is the most famous *roman à clef* of the Harlem Renaissance,[3] even if the bathtub demise of Paul Arbian (based on Thurman's friend and fellow writer Richard Bruce Nugent) is entirely fictional: Nugent survived Thurman by fifty-three years. What is a suicide in *Infants of the Spring* becomes a murder in *Incognegro: Renaissance*. As the story unfolds over five instalments, we learn that Van Horn plagiarized Xavier's manuscript, with the latter's cooperation, on condition that Van Horn's white publisher, Christopher Gray, would bring out Xavier's next work. When Gray reneges on his promise and Xavier turns up to the launch party armed with his manuscript and determined to expose Van Horn as a fraud, Gray has him murdered.

If *Incognegro: Renaissance* cites and adapts Thurman's *roman à clef*, it also cleverly joins the dots between *Infants of the Spring* and another *roman à clef* of the Harlem Renaissance: Nugent's *Gentleman Jigger* (written between

1928 and 1933, concurrently with the composition of *Infants*, and published posthumously in 2008) by highlighting vexed questions surrounding authorial originality, collaboration, and plagiarism. In one scene in *Gentleman Jigger*, Stuartt Brennan (Nugent) more or less openly accuses Raymond "Rusty" Pelman (Thurman) of plagiarism. When Hal (Harold Jackman) examines pages from Rusty's manuscript describing the bohemian circle that gathered at 267 West 136th Street and notices a strong resemblance to Stuartt Brennan's (Nugent's) own manuscript, an interesting conversation concerning intellectual property ensues. To separate questions – Is this your work? Is this Rusty's work? – Stuartt answers in the affirmative. Stuartt asserts little, if any, authorial ownership of the passage Rusty incorporated into his manuscript. Rusty asks, in response: "How can we help sounding like each other when we are both writing about the same time and the same people?"[4] However, when Hal points out that Rusty used Stuartt's "very words" and Stuartt teases Rusty with an accusation of plagiarism, Rusty becomes defensive and angrily tears pages of the manuscript into tiny pieces (*Jigger*, 166). (As it turns out, this is only the carbon; he still has the original.)

Eleonore van Notten discusses this incident in *Jigger*, and subsequent interviews with Nugent, contrasting what she perceives as Nugent's "largesse" in retrospective accounts, "which excused Thurman's literary 'borrowing' as part and parcel of the unique quality of their friendship" with the incident in *Jigger*, "where his tone is rather less magnanimous and forgiving."[5] In fact, the charge of plagiarism leveled at Rusty by Hal and Stuartt in *Jigger* is far less serious than van Notten suggests and it is perhaps more helpful to see, as Darryl Dickson-Carr does, the "line dividing Thurman's authorship of *Infants of the Spring* from Nugent's composition of *Gentleman Jigger*" as "entirely fluid."[6] The incident is a useful starting point for this chapter, which argues that Thurman's *Infants* and Nugent's *Jigger*, read together, foreground the tensions between originality and derivativeness, individual "genius" and collaboration that were being negotiated more broadly in modernist art of the period. As Jeremy Braddock notes, "The very name 'New Negro Renaissance' . . . asks to be read in relation to Ezra Pound's slogan 'Make It New!' for both its consonances and dissonances."[7] These questions were, of course, particularly charged for African American artists not only because they had faced accusations of imitativeness and derivativeness ever since Phillis Wheatley published *Poems on Various Subjects, Religious and Moral* (1773) but because of an investment on the part of many Harlem Renaissance intellectuals in what Kenneth Warren calls an "indexical" view of literary production "as evidence of the inner nature and capacity of the Negro race."[8] On the one hand, both *Infants of the Spring* and *Jigger* are invested in models of artistry that valorize "individuality"[9] and "genius" (*Infants* 10, 92, 105) over "standardization" (156) and derivativeness. On the other hand, the texts themselves – which explicitly address the question of plagiarism through differently inflected scenes describing the same event – suggest that a model of authorship or artistry that does not accommodate collaboration, borrowing, and even outright theft is gravely deficient.

The *roman à clef* is the perfect vehicle for airing these concerns because of its radically unstable form. For Sean Latham, the *roman à clef* is a "disruptive literary form" that "profoundly troubles any easy attempt at categorization"; it is a form characterized by "tantalizing ambiguity."[10] The *roman à clef*, or novel with a key, always already raises questions about authenticity, realness, and originality. As Thurman wrote in a review of Carl Van Vechten's *Nigger Heaven* (1926) – a novel featuring characters with easily identifiable real-life counterparts that is sometimes described as a *roman à clef* – the novel "will provide high Harlem with a new indoor sport, namely, the ascertaining which persons in real life the various characters were drawn from."[11] In a subsequent letter to William Jourdan Rapp (with whom Thurman co-wrote the 1929 play *Harlem: A Melodrama of Negro Life*), Thurman engages in this "new indoor sport" himself, confidently proclaiming Nora Holt Ray "the original for Lasca in Van Vechten's *Nigger Heaven*."[12] The *roman à clef*, then, rewards and provides pleasure to those readers equipped with a key – or who imagine themselves equipped with the key – to unlock the "real life" and "original" characters and incidents that feature in the text.

However, because the kind of "authentic" detail incorporated into the *roman à clef* relates to intimate relationships rather than provable historical fact, even those knowledgeable readers in possession of the key necessary to unlock the text do not "gain access to a publicly authenticated history preceding entextualization." Instead, "they paradoxically find themselves locked inside a labyrinthine text, finding that though in possession of a key, they cannot be certain which doors open onto fact and which onto fancy."[13] *Infants* deploys very similar language to consider the imaginative struggles faced by Thurman surrogate, Raymond Taylor. During an afternoon spent wandering alone around Central Park in the hopes of "taking stock of himself" (92), Raymond reflects on his ambitions to be a literary trailblazer, "to become a Prometheus, to break the chains that held him to a racial rack and carry a blazing beacon to the top of Mount Olympus so that those possessed of Alpine stocks could follow in his wake" (92). Yet he fears he is merely "a self-deluded posturer" in possession of only "talent" rather than "genius" (93, 92). Returning home, he tries to organize in his head "innumerable subjects, innumerable people ... thoughts [that] were now nebulous and fast fading into obscurity" (92). He finds that there is "no key to the dark labyrinth to which they had fled" (94). The metaphorical key soon transmutes into a literal one: climbing the steps to 267 W. 136th Street, Raymond "fumble[s] in his pocket for his door key" only for the door to be "flung open" by fellow occupant of "Niggeratti Manor," Paul Arbian (94). The implications of this scene are significant: the opening up of the literal door and, by implication, Raymond's labyrinthine imagination is facilitated by both a friend and a fellow artist.

If the tangled threads of Raymond's artistic consciousness, which must be unraveled with the assistance of a collaborator, replicate the labyrinthine structure of the *roman à clef*, then the experience of reading a *roman à clef* is itself essentially collaborative. The form openly invites corroboration, if not collaboration, on the part of the reader, with the knowing reader and the writer entering into a kind of pact that implicitly excludes the unknowing reader. As Latham notes, with the development of mass culture in the twentieth century, "Book reviewers, gossip columnists, journalists, and even dust jacket blurbs, for example, might unlock a roman à clef, inviting the reader to probe more deeply in searching out historical analogues for allegedly fictional characters."[14] In some cases, the over-zealous reader might mis- or over-read the novel, thus raising questions about how "to maintain a firm boundary not only between fact and fiction, but between proper and improper modes of reading and interpretation."[15] The collaborative dynamics of the wink-and-nod relationship between writer and (knowing) reader are approximated in a scene from *Jigger* that describes the closeness that exists between Rusty and Stuartt:

> they were always ready – both of them or either of them – to notice every little nuance and incidental gesture of the other diners, and they would hug it close, exchanging little looks that fenced everyone else out, and would giggle or lift an eyebrow. This secret or impolite malice would make any palefaces at their table self-conscious beneath the imagined focus of the glances of the other diners in this not-too-familiar land, and the slightly tense atmosphere so unintentionally and deliberately created at their table would tickle the senses of both Rusty and Stuartt even further, and they would titter even more. (107–108)

The collusion of Rusty and Stuartt in "secret or impolite malice" is evocative of the way in which the *roman à clef* cultivates a sense of intimacy – here denoted by language suggestive of sensual closeness (hug; tickle) – between knowing reader and author, an intimacy that "fences" others out. Indeed, the distinction between author and knowing reader collapses here: "both of them or either of them" notice and revel in the discomfort of their fellow diners and collaborate in amplifying such discomfort. Moreover, the tense atmosphere at the table is created, para-doxically, "unintentionally and deliberately." As a form that moves uneas-ily between binaries of various kinds – fact/fiction, writer/reader, respectable/disreputable – the *roman à clef* is well placed to confront, and to unsettle, the modernist preoccupation with novelty, originality, and individual talent or genius.

Tradition, Individual Talent, and (Modernist) Originality

Recent scholarly efforts have contested modernism's "portrait of the artist as a lone insurgent and repopulated it with collaborators, coteries, patron-age networks, and canny commercial ventures."[16] Still, as Catherine Keyser notes, "the cult of authorial originality that comes to us by way of modernist literary studies" has proven very difficult to dislodge.[17] Even T. S. Eliot, whose canonical essay "Tradition and the Individual Talent" (1919) asserts the importance of literary history in the formation of a contemporary poet, clarifies that immersion in tradition should not equate to "following the ways of the immediate generation before us in a blind or timid adherence to its successes." Novelty, he notes, "is better than repetition."[18] Like many of their fellow modernists, Harlem Renaissance artists and intellectuals assumed originality and novelty as the benchmark of artistic achievement and were preoccupied with how best to realize it rather than with questioning its status altogether. The Harlem Renaissance debates on how to achieve original expression have been well-rehearsed and much discussed: the "New Negro," Alain Locke proclaimed in 1925, seems suddenly "to be shaking off the psychology of imitation and implied inferiority";[19] African art provides "a lesson in simplicity and originality of expression," a "mine of fresh *motifs*" that might form "the basis for a characteristic school of expression in the plastic and pictorial arts";[20] folk elements must be incorporated into "Negro drama" to enable to "grow in its own soil and cultivate its own intrinsic elements; only in this way can it become truly organic and cease being a rootless derivative."[21] For Langston Hughes, the "urge . . . toward white-ness, the desire to pour racial individuality into the mold of American standardization, and to be as little Negro and as much American as possible" must be relinquished. The "low-down folks" can "furnish a wealth of colorful, distinctive material for any artist because they still hold their individuality in the face of American standardizations."[22] The dissenting voices tended to object to the prescriptive nature of the proposed routes to achieving individual and distinctive expression rather than the goal of individual and distinctive expression itself. In *Infants*, the infamous literary salon organized by Raymond and Dr. A. L. Parkes (Alain Locke) ends in acrimony and chaos when the participants disagree over the question of "Negro Art" and what it should be doing. For Raymond, the differing views expressed by the attendees – who advocate "a wholesale flight back to Africa" or "a wholesale allegiance to communism" or "a wholesale adherence to an antiquated and for the most part propagandistic program" – are all "equally futile and unintelligent" (156). Still, he upholds the ambition of individual expression itself. "There is ample room for everyone to follow his own individual track," he claims: "Individuality is what we should strive for" (156).

There were some, of course, who considered originality in more nuanced terms. Zora Neale Hurston, in "Characteristics of Negro Expression," claims that "What we really mean by originality is the modification of ideas. The most ardent admirer of Shakespeare cannot claim first source even for him. It is his treatment of the borrowed material." Moreover, Hurston notes that although the Negro is "famous as a mimic," this fact "in no way damages his standing as an original. Mimicry is an art in itself."[23] We see evidence of a similarly complex treatment of originality in Thurman's and Nugent's novels. Moreover, writing specifically about the interplay between the Harlem Renaissance and "white" modernisms, Braddock considers James Weldon Johnson's claim in his preface to *The Book of American Negro Poetry* (1922) that "the Negro [is] the creator of the only things artistic that have yet sprung from American soil and been universally acknowledged as distinctive American products."[24] Emphasizing that Johnson's theory of literary production leans heavily on raw materials drawn from vernacular African American culture, Braddock argues that Johnson presents "a theory of artistic production in which the procedures of appropriation, archivization, and assignation of conventional authorship are always preceded by the cultural object's collective production within the community."[25] As Johnson puts it in *The Book of American Negro Poetry*, "The fact is, nothing great or enduring in music has ever sprung full-fledged from the brain of any master; the best he gives the world he gathers from the hearts of the people, and runs it through the alembic of his genius."[26]

If Johnson's conception of artistic production relies upon "the cultural object's collective production within the community," it points toward collaboration and communality as essential aspects of artistic labor. In the past decade or so, important scholarly work has uncovered the nature and the extent of collaborations that brought together image and text during the Harlem Renaissance. Anne Elizabeth Carroll examines "collaborative illustrated volumes" of the moment while Cherene Sherrard-Johnson explores "the artistic collaborations, conversations, and influence of Harlem Renaissance visual art on the writers of the era" and "the collaborative and experimental nature of these artistic endeavors."[27] However, the fact of *literary* collaboration – and the potential for this to spill over into borrowing, appropriation or theft – remains under-examined. In 1931, Zora Neale Hurston and Langston Hughes had a dispute after they collaborated in the composition of *Mule Bone*, a play adapted by the pair from Hurston's short story "The Bone of Contention." As Rachel Rosenberg argues persuasively, Hurston's and Hughes's competing claims to authorship reflected their differing conceptions of what constituted authorship: "Hurston was more committed to and at home with a vernacular model of artistic creation than Hughes was; Hughes associated the writerly acts of selection, outlining, and (hand)writing with authorship."[28]

Perhaps the most extreme form of borrowing or appropriation is plagiarism. The list of writers in the first four decades of the twentieth century accused of – and sued for – plagiarism is long (and the following is indicative rather than exhaustive): H. G. Wells for *The Outline of History* (1919, 1920; sued in 1925); Fannie Hurst for a short story "Mannequin," which was purchased for a film adaptation by Famous Players-Lasky (1925; sued in 1926); Eugene O'Neill for *Strange Interlude* (1928; sued in 1929); Zane Grey for *The Thundering Herd* (1925; sued in 1930); Arthur Torrance for *Jungle Mania* (1933; sued in 1935). However, the issue was particularly fraught in the context of the Harlem Renaissance given, as Charles Lewis puts it, "the larger pattern of reading black literature as an imitation of – or as that which is assigned value in relation to – work by white writers."[29] Famously, Nella Larsen was accused of lifting the structure of and details from a story by British writer Sheila Kaye-Smith that was published in *Century* in January 1922 in her own story, "Sanctuary," that appeared in *Forum* in 1930.[30] When a reader, Marion Boyd, wrote to *Forum* claiming that "Aside from dialect and setting, the stories are almost identical," the periodical published Boyd's letter along with Larsen's response.[31] Larsen's alleged plagiarism has received an inordinate amount of attention from literary critics. In 2012, Erika Renée Williams uncovered what she claims to be a second incidence of plagiarism in Larsen's work: her "nearly verbatim copying" of the opening of John Galsworthy's short story "The First and the Last" (1917) in *Quicksand* (1928).[32] For Williams, the Larsen "apologists" – those critics who recast Larsen's copying as "a kind of aesthetic innovation" – are misguided: "no rhetoric of formalist innovation can mitigate the error of an author's verbatim copying from another author, especially when it involves pointed linguistic echoes."[33] Beverly Haviland, meanwhile, points to (unpublished) collaborative projects that Larsen undertook with a young white writer called Edward Donahue after the "Sanctuary" scandal. She speculates that Larsen's "late experiments" in collaboration "point to possibilities of alternative models of authorship" that could not be accommodated by existing laws surrounding intellectual property and copyright.[34]

The issue of plagiarism is further complicated by the reality that white writers and artists were much more likely to profit (financially and otherwise) from unattributed citations or appropriations of the work of African Americans than vice versa. In 1936, in his "Hectic Harlem" column for the *Amsterdam News* (New York), Roi Ottley reports two anecdotes relating to Louis Sobol, Broadway columnist for the *Evening Journal* (New York). First, he takes issue with Sobol labeling him "Harlem's Mark Hellinger" because to do so is to suggest that Ottley "ape[s] and cop[ies] [Hellinger's] style and methods." Refuting this intimation, Ottley claims that his "idioms and efforts at humor are derived from a pure Negro background" and that the Negro people "are contributing something entirely new to the language in picturesqueness and quaintness of expression." Having challenged Sobol's backhanded compliment, Ottley reinforces his point in a second anecdote: Sobol apparently published a "collection of current Harlem expressions" that originally appeared in *Amsterdam News* but without giving any credit to the original source. Increasingly, "the ofay is lifting the Negro idiom and palming it off as its own. . . . Music and art have been the chief sufferers. . . . Consequently, when a Negro appears at their doors with a piece of work to sell, the ofays contend that 'this is nothing new.'" In other words, by juxtaposing these two anecdotes, Ottley asks the question: "who is plagiarising whom?"[35]

Copy and Counterfeit: *Infants of the Spring* and *Gentleman Jigger*

Infants of the Spring and *Gentleman Jigger* might both be read profitably in the context of larger anxieties surrounding novelty, originality, and individual talent, on the one hand, and collaboration, imitation, and derivativeness on the other. Both novels highlight forms of unoriginal artistic endeavor that run the gamut from influence to imitation to plagiarism. Influence proves the least problematic of these three. In *Infants*, Paul responds to a request by Stephen Jorgenson (Harald Jan Stefansson) to tell him about his drawings by citing his influences: Wilde, Huysmans, Baudelaire, Whistler, Gauguin, and so on (10). When Stephen complains that "that's not telling me anything about your drawings," Paul's retort is "Unless you're dumber than I think, I've told you all you need to know" (10). In *Jigger*, the intellectuals discuss the influence of African art on the work of Howard (Aaron Douglas). Challenging what he sees as somewhat lazy and ill-informed invocations of "African art," Stuartt claims that what the others identify as African elements in Howard's art – "pointed joints and bulbous foreheads" (112) – show not the influence on Howard of African art per se but the influence of his teacher (Winold Reiss) on Howard's work:

> Howard is his teacher. Fortunately, his teacher is an artist, so the copy isn't quite a counterfeit. And it is his teacher who is influenced by African art – African art and Picasso, who is likewise influenced. Howard is a just a sponge. He has absorbed a technique invented, or discovered, as you will, by his teacher. (112)

The distinction between "copy" (as an acceptable form of artistic expression) and "counterfeit" (as invalid) is a suggestive one and echoes Hurston's claim that "What we really mean by originality is the modification of ideas." Stuartt goes on to argue that: "The artist is continually evolving from what he has created in the past. He is a sieve through which all things pass, and only the finest remains to be used and then sieved again" (112). For Stuartt, then, the influence of Howard's teacher on Howard – and, by extension, the influence of Howard's teacher's influences on Howard – can be the very vehicle for originality. In *The Copywrights*, Saint-Amour uses a very similar analogy to consider the issue of literary originality: "By the time we experience an idea or expression *as* original – really, in order for us to experience it that way – it has passed through the sieves and screens of institution and ideology: critical, educational, legal, economic, and political structures of selection and valorization."[36]

If allowing one's art to be influenced by – and even copying – the work of others can potentially be creative and generative, the novels elsewhere condemn copying when it approaches imitation and derivativeness.

Countee Cullen (DeWitt Clinton in *Infants*; Burton Barclay in *Jigger*) is represented as in thrall to white masters – one specific master, in fact – of the poetic form. Raymond conjures "a vivid mental picture of that poet's creative hours – eyes on a page of Keats, fingers on typewriter, mind frantically conjuring African scenes. And there would of course be a Bible nearby" (153–154). In *Jigger*, the narrator describes the poems Burton Barclay contributes to *The Current* (*FIRE!!*) as "done after the manner of Keats" (80). In *Infants*, Eustace Savoy (Service Bell) is an aspiring opera singer who strives to be "a carbon copy of [Enrico] Caruso" (69). In *Jigger*, the only "genius" that the equivalent character, Sterling, boasts is for "fashioning cocktails" (79). In a conversation with his landlady, Euphoria Blake (Iolanthe Sydney), Raymond wholeheartedly endorses Paul Arbian's iconoclasm over what he sees as Pelham Gaylord's formulaic artistic output: "We have too many of them now – too many like both him and Eustace, striving to make a place for themselves in a milieu to which they are completely alien" (*Infants* 31). Rex Goreleigh (after whom Gaylord in *Infants* is modeled; he is Leo Green in *Jigger*) copies his portraits from newspaper photographs (*Infants* 15, 64). As *Jigger*'s narrator notes, he "drew bad pictures and wrote bad poetry" (86). Leo is "another of those persons who are more taken with the glamor of being known as an artist than with the work entailed in actually being one" (87).

Indeed, both novels deploy the Pelham/Leo character to sound a warning bell regarding the perils of fraudulent authorship. When he is charged with raping the young daughter of an actress who also lives at W. 136th Street, evidence of an improper relationship between the two is furnished by the girl's mother in the form of letters written by Pelham/Leo to her daughter. The letters refer to "kissing her in secret places and churning butter in the lily cup," to which Stephen responds – quoting one of Paul's own poems – that this constitutes "plagiarism" (*Infants* 104). Although these letters were unsigned, the actress commissions a signed poem from Pelham, which he duly supplies, and with this proof that the others were in his handwriting, she "hasten[s] to the police station" to have Pelham charged with rape (103). In *Jigger*, the poems are described as "written in the most childishly erotic style. They spoke of sex in terms of exotic flowers. They mentioned sex acts in a manner that disguised them not at all – in a manner that in fact promised more than Leo could ever have fulfilled. They were reproductions of Stuartt's poems" (*Jigger* 121). The attribution of authorship to Leo is what exposes him to legal sanction: "The only thing that was required of the mother was to prove that the notes were in his handwriting" (121). The authentication of Pelham/Leo as the

author of the works is ironic because both *Infants* and *Jigger* deem the
poems to be "plagiarism" or "reproductions" of Paul/Stuartt's work.

It could be argued that what is presented here is a distinction between
influence in the hands of "genius" (the influence of Wilde and Huysmans
on Paul, for example), which may be generative and inventive, and influence in the hands of a charlatan or literary *poseur*, which results only in
a pathetic aping of literary forebears. Indeed, in several of Thurman's
nonfiction writings, the term "sincerity" is used to denote ingenuity of
both intent and execution: most African American readers, according to
Thurman, are "unable to fathom the innate differences between a dialect
farce committed by Octavius [*sic*] Roy Cohen to increase the gaiety of
Babbitts [insincere art], and a dialect interpretation done by a Negro writer
to express some abstract something that burns within his people and sears
him [sincere art]."[37] However, several other aspects of the texts challenge
what the former model of individual talent or genius implies by focusing
on collaborative endeavor in at least three different ways: first, oral com-
munication as creative and essentially communal; second, differently
inflected scenes in both novels; and finally, the novels' invocation of racial
passing as a collaborative endeavor. Each of these will be unpacked briefly
in what remains of this chapter.

As noted above, oral and vernacular cultures are always collaborative and
communal. It is significant, therefore, that *Infants* in particular puts "talk"
on an equal footing with "work," where "work" denotes written output,
though "talk" in both *Infants* and *Jigger* bears a stronger resemblance to the
witty repartee and conversations characteristic of salon culture and bohemian life than it does to the vernacular cultures described by Hurston and
Johnson. For instance, Georgia Douglas Johnson's "Saturday Night"
group in Washington, DC "read their writing aloud, exchanged criticisms,
talked about the latest books they had read, and argued their views on
literature, art, and politics."[38] In a discussion of bohemian narratives,
Michael Soto takes Ernest Hemingway's use of bohemianism in *The Sun
Also Rises* (1926) as "a yardstick of artistic success and failure, of 'real work'
and 'fake talk.'"[39] In other words, according to the logic of *The Sun Also
Rises*, "one is either a bohemian who writes (authentic) or a would-be writer
who dabbles in bohemianism (inauthentic). One works, the other talks."[40]
Jigger asserts a similar opposition between producing artistic output (in
print) and talking. As Rusty and Stuartt make plans for the publication of
The Current, Rusty stipulates that "we'll have to get to work on it. Some
real work, and not just so damn much talk" (*Jigger* 28) and affirms "There's
a lot more to it than just talking about it like this" (30). A distinction

between "real work" and "fake talk" is also suggested by Rusty's musing
that Stuartt's beautiful reading voice lends "various delicate shadings and
superb nuance" to written material that, had Rusty read it to himself first,
he might have considered "less than mediocre" (31). When, after two years'
touring with a stage production of *Catfish Row*, Stuartt looks back on "the
great doings of the Niggeratti," he realizes that their combined writings
amounted to very little and that "they mostly existed in talk" (160).

However, *Infants*, for its part, strongly upholds the importance of talk.
Raymond's conversations with Stephen Jorgenson are endlessly invigorat-
ing and generative: "Their greatest joy came when they could be alone
together and talk. Talk about any and everything. . . . And no matter how
often these conversational communings occurred, no matter how long they
lasted, there always seemed to be much more to say" (16). When a change
comes over Stephen, as Raymond perceives it, it is both talk *and* literary
creativity that suffer as a result. To Raymond's dismay, Stephen tears up his
efforts at describing his "first impressions of Harlem," calling them "trash"
and "Transparent juvenilia" (109). Raymond hopes that Stephen will
confide in him about what led to the destructive gesture and "lean[s]
forward expectantly" to listen. Stephen "started to speak, but whatever
he was about to say remained unspoken" because the pair are interrupted
by the entrance of Paul and Eustace (109). The destruction of Stephen's
written work has its counterpart in their thwarted conversation. Perhaps
relatedly, the novel ends with the destruction of Paul's manuscript: a print
artifact proves just as elusive, just as incapable of being archived, as
Raymond's and Stephen's "conversational communings."

Meanwhile, reading the paired novels in tandem with one another
invites readers to join the dots between events and/or scenes that are
recounted in both novels but that are inflected differently. Reading *Jigger*
in the light of *Infants* (or vice versa) both challenges and empowers readers
to supplement the knowledge they have arrived at by reading a single
source. One of the most significant allusions in both novels is to the artist-
intellectuals' outing to the annual Hamilton Lodge drag ball (described as
"the far famed Alexander Lodge masquerade" in *Infants* [58]). As Monica
L. Miller observes, the Hamilton Lodge's festivities, "in which female
impersonators, black and white, competed for prizes based on fabulousness
of costume and comportment," demonstrated "the fact that at times
Harlem 'was wide open' to those interested in gender performance and
sexual experimentation."[41] In *Infants*, Paul introduces Raymond to
Countess Barbara Nitsky (Fania Marinoff) at the ball. The pair do not
dance that night, but remain in the box and enjoy "point[ing] out choice

costumes or amusing incidents one to the other" (58). After that, they are often in one another's company and a "gay comradeship" develops between them (58). What is framed as interracial sociability between Raymond and Barbara in *Infants* becomes a more explicitly queer encounter in *Jigger*. As the friends discuss the extravagant drag they observed the previous night, Edna comments that she "can't believe that some of [the costumed] were men," to which Rusty responds, "with a little sneer": "They weren't." Stuartt, in turn, adds his rejoinder: "You danced with one. . . . And he wasn't even in costume" (*Jigger* 165). In *Infants*, Raymond explicitly *does not* dance with a white woman and the possibility of one form of forbidden intimacy (interracial) is curtailed. Moreover, gazing down at the dance floor from his box seat, Raymond asserts his distance from the scene below and enacts the "spectatorial privilege" that allows him to "distinguish [himself] from the queers who organized and participated in the affairs."[42] By contrast, *Jigger*'s Rusty *does* dance – with a man (whose race is unspecified). The fantastical charade of heterosexuality – a man dancing with a "woman" (man in drag) – of this scenario is also foregone: Rusty's dance partner was not costumed. Another form of taboo intimacy (queer) is permitted to take place in Nugent's novel. Reading *Infants* in the light of *Jigger* recasts Thurman's account of the evening as one in which queer desire is suppressed, though a trace of it survives in the reference to Countess Nitsky's "boyish figure" (*Infants* 58).

The Hamilton Lodge scene in *Jigger* is also notable for the self-reflexivity apparently embedded into the discussions of the ball. Rusty is regaling their friends with tales of the ball and is annoyed when Stuartt joins them: "Stuartt's presence meant that Rusty would have to dilute his narrative a little. After all, Stuartt had been to the ball also" (*Jigger* 165). Stuartt, then, can affirm or deny, corroborate or repudiate Rusty's account. The pair are collaborating but the nature of their collaboration has changed. Previously, Rusty and Stuartt were "so inseparable as to be almost the same word" (65). Stuartt and Rusty argued "like a machine – a single machine" (38). When the two engaged in lively repartee, Rusty's voice so resembled Stuartt's that, "had all eyes been closed, it would have been difficult to know just where the one had stopped and the other had continued" (39). By the time this scene unfolds, however, Rusty "could no longer depend on Stuartt to help embroider escapes and incidents with vivid and alluring color" for he is "no longer *sympatico*" (165). Just as Stuartt qualifies and corrects Rusty's account of the ball, so the whole scene qualifies and corrects the version offered in *Infants*. Indeed, it could be argued that *Jigger*'s entire Book II, which opens with Stuartt "lounging after his bath" (171), is a rejoinder to the ending of *Infants*, which closes with Raymond finding Paul dead in the bath. Not only does Nugent explicitly resurrect Paul/Stuartt from his bath in Book II of *Jigger* but Book I ends, significantly, with Stuartt "rewriting the last chapter to his novel" and Rusty searching for the beginning of his own (168).

Most significantly, the discussion of the Hamilton Lodge ball leads directly to Hal noticing that Rusty has used Stuartt's "very words" in his book manuscript (166). It is difficult not to make the connection between Stuartt's subsequent needling of Rusty about "plagiarism" – the other people in the room "had never seen anyone so completely expose Rusty before. Always these exposés had been in private" (166) – and Stuartt's "outing" of Rusty as queer on the previous page. Indeed, both *Infants* and *Jigger* try to unpick the relationship between collaboration and dishonest authorial behavior by alluding to the most prominent plot line predicated on the concealment–exposure dynamic in Harlem Renaissance literature: racial passing. Racial passing is an appropriate lens through which to view the tensions between individual genius, collaboration, and fraudulent (authorial) behavior because it has been subject to precisely this range of oscillating interpretations. As Kathleen Pfeiffer notes, passing has often been viewed as a gesture of "renouncing blackness," of replacing "an 'authentic' identity, in favor of whiteness, an 'opportunistic' one."[43] Passers fraudulently assume a social position to which they are not entitled. Indeed, Eva Saks construes the passer's body, which might legally be classified as black but which defies being read as such, as "a forgery by nature."[44] By contrast, Pfeiffer invites us instead to see the passer "as a figure who values individualism, who may be idiosyncratic, self-determining, or inclined towards improvisation."[45] On the continuum between these two poles – passing as deceitful and duplicitous; passing as a legitimate act of creative self-making – we might locate the collaborative aspect of passing. For the success of the enterprise depends, ultimately, on the collaboration of what Amy Robinson calls the "in-group clairvoyant" with the passer. In what Robinson terms the "triangular theater of identity," a passer is subject to different readings by both a "duped" subject, who "misreads" the passer as white, and by an "*in-group clairvoyant*," who knows who and what the passer "really" is.[46] Time and again, the literature of racial passing provides the reader with scenes in which an "in-group clairvoyant" might, but does not, out the passer to the "duped" subject in his/her company. Robinson discusses the triangular scene – featuring Angela Murray, her darker sister Virginia, and Angela's white suitor, Roger – in Jessie Fauset's *Plum Bun* (1928), but there are many others. In

Langston Hughes's epistolary short story, "Passing" (1934), Jack writes to
his mother to apologize for ignoring her when he encountered her in the
street the previous evening: "You were great, though. Didn't give me a sign
that you even knew me, let alone I was your son. If I hadn't had the girl
with me, Ma, we might have talked."[47]

In *Infants*, Thurman wholeheartedly endorses the collaborative aspect of
racial passing. When, toward the end of the novel, Aline confides to
Raymond that she has decided to pass as white permanently, she expresses
a fear that "someone's gonna tell on [her]" (171). Raymond tells her that
this anxious attitude is precisely what will lead to her being "found out":

> Can't you people who cross the line understand that your own fears
> precipitate disclosure? The minute you leave the colored world, you live
> in unholy fear that Negroes you once knew might meet you somewhere and
> recognize you publicly. What if they do? Nine times out of ten that Negro is
> glad to see your change of status. You antagonize him only by ignoring him.
> Surely you've associated with enough white people around New York to
> know that most of them who happen to have colored friends make no effort
> to hide that fact. Why should you? Greet them as you would anyone else.
> Fail to do so and some of them are bound to talk, long and loud. Merely
> knowing a Negro does not necessarily stigmatize you. (*Infants* 171–172)

For Raymond, then, the "in-group clairvoyant" is only too happy to be
complicit in the passer's passing, as long as the latter does not publicly deny
knowing them. The collaborative aspect of racial passing is also a feature of
Jigger. At one of Serge Von Vertner's (Carl Van Vechten's) parties, Stuartt
encounters, and is introduced to, his older brother, Aeon, a poet who is
passing as white. In this scene, the "duped" are a young black woman called
Myra, a Bohemian actress called Thalia, and Rusty; the in-group clairvoyant is Stuartt and the passer is Aeon. As Stuartt pretends to be meeting
Aeon for the first time, "Nothing in [his] tone revealed that Aeon was, in
fact, his brother and was passing for white" (63).

Scenes like this one derive their interest from the (il)legibility of race
and the dynamics of reading. As Robinson argues, it is the spectator who
"manufactures the successful pass."[48] What I want to suggest by way of
conclusion is that the reader of a *roman à clef* endowed (or not) with the
tools to unlock the true-to-life aspects of the novel is analogous to the
spectator observing (whether s/he knows it or not) an act of racial
passing. Aeon scripts himself as white and Stuartt is the reader equipped
with a key to unlock Aeon's identity. Instead, Stuartt collaborates in
Aeon's act of racial passing, a complicity that produces an intimacy
between them "into which the others should not intrude" (137). When

Stuartt maligns white people in Aeon's presence, saying to his brother
"Present company always excluded" (138), it is, of course, the others in
their company, Rusty and Myra, that are "excluded" from the knowing
intimacy that exists between Aeon (author) and Stuartt (reader).
Ultimately, then, the *roman à clef*'s unsettling of boundaries between
authentic/fake, legitimate/fraudulent, and art/theft enables it to sketch
the complex relationship between influence, copying, collaboration, and
plagiarism that has perhaps been obscured by a critical investment in
novelty and inventiveness that replicates that of many Harlem
Renaissance intellectuals themselves. This critical investment can be
explained, partly, as a response to Nathan Huggins's claim in his 1971
book that "The great innocence of the renaissance is most clearly seen in
the irony that, where its proponents had wanted to develop a distinctive
Negro voice, they had been of necessity mostly derivative."[49] In this
context, it is understandable that scholars of the Harlem Renaissance
would wish to identify, explore, and celebrate work that is innovative
and pioneering. Yet such efforts should not gloss over the intricacies of
authorial originality and collaboration debated, explored, and enacted in
the *romans à clef* of Thurman and Nugent.

Notes

1. Mat Johnson and Warren Pleece, *Incognegro: Renaissance* #1 (Milwaukie, OR:
   Dark Horse, 2018), n.p.
2. Mat Johnson, "Sweet Oogly Moogly: Incognegro's Back," in *Incognegro:
   Renaissance* #1, n.p.
3. Other novels often classified as *romans à clef* include Carl Van Vechten's *Nigger
   Heaven*, ed. Kathleen Pfeiffer (1926; Urbana: University of Illinois Press, 2000);
   George Schuyler's *Black No More*, intro. Ishmael Reed (1931; New York:
   Modern Library, 1999); Countee Cullen's *One Way to Heaven* (New York:
   Harper and Brothers, 1932); and Claude McKay's *Amiable with Big Teeth*,
   completed in 1941 and ed. Jean-Christophe Cloutier (New York: Penguin
   Classics, 2017).
4. Richard Bruce Nugent, *Gentleman Jigger* (Philadelphia: DaCapo, 2008), 166.
   Hereafter cited parenthetically (as *Jigger*).
5. Eleonore van Notten, *Wallace Thurman's Harlem Renaissance* (Amsterdam:
   Rodopi, 1994), 290.
6. Darryl Dickson-Carr, *Spoofing the Modern: Satire in the Harlem Renaissance*
   (Columbia: University of South Carolina Press, 2015), 77.
7. Jeremy Braddock, "Race: Tradition and Archive in the Harlem Renaissance,"
   A Handbook of Modernism Studies, ed. Jean-Michel Rabaté (Chichester: Wiley-
   Blackwell, 2013), 90.

8. Kenneth Warren, *What Was African American Literature?* (Cambridge, MA: Harvard University Press, 2011), 10. An important dissenting voice was George S. Schuyler, who argued that the very idea of "Negro Art" risked endorsing the white supremacist idea "that the blackamoor is inferior and fundamentally different," that "he must needs be peculiar" and that "when he attempts to portray life through the medium of art, it must of necessity be a peculiar art" (54). George S. Schuyler, "The Negro-Art Hokum," *The Nation* 122 (1926), repr. *The Norton Anthology of African American Literature*, ed. Henry Louis Gates, Jr. and Nellie Y. McKay (New York: Norton, 2004), 1223.

9. Wallace Thurman, *Infants of the Spring* (1932; London: X Press, 1998), 156. Hereafter cited parenthetically (as *Infants*).

10. Sean Latham, *The Art of Scandal: Modernism, Libel Law, and the Roman à Clef* (Oxford: Oxford University Press, 2009), 7, 9, 14.

11. Wallace Thurman, "A Stranger at the Gates: A Review of Nigger Heaven by Carl Van Vechten," *The Messenger*, September 1926. Repr. in *The Collected Writings of Wallace Thurman: A Harlem Renaissance Reader*, ed. Amritjit Singh and Daniel M. Scott III (New Brunswick: Rutgers University Press, 2003), 192.

12. Wallace Thurman, "Letter to William Jourdan Rapp" [c. July 1929], in *Collected Writings of Wallace Thurman*, 152.

13. Latham, *The Art of Scandal*, 14.

14. Ibid., 8.

15. Ibid., 9.

16. Paul K. Saint-Amour, "Introduction: Modernism and the Lives of Copyright," in *Modernism and Copyright*, ed. Paul K. Saint-Amour (Oxford: Oxford University Press, 2011), 5.

17. Catherine Keyser, "Review of Mary Chapman, *Making Noise, Making News* and Ellen Gruber Garvey, *Writing with Scissors*," *Journal of Modern Periodical Studies* 6, no. 1 (2015): 87.

18. T. S. Eliot, "Tradition and the Individual Talent," *The Egoist* VI, no. 4 (1919): 55.

19. Alain Locke, "The New Negro," *The New Negro: An Interpretation*, ed. Alain Locke (1925; New York: Touchstone, 1997), 4.

20. Alain Locke, "The Legacy of the Ancestral Arts," in *The New Negro*, ed. Locke, 256.

21. Alain Locke, "The Drama of Negro Life," repr. in *The Works of Alain Locke*, ed. Charles Molesworth (1926; New York: Oxford University Press, 2012), 123.

22. Langston Hughes, "The Negro Artist and the Racial Mountain," repr. in *The Norton Anthology of African American Literature*, ed. Henry Louis Gates, Jr. and Nellie Y. McKay (1926; New York: Norton, 2004), 1311, 1312.

23. Zora Neale Hurston, "Characteristics of Negro Expression," in *Zora Neale Hurston, Folklore, Memoirs, and Other Writings*, ed. Cheryl A. Wall (1934; New York: Library of America, 1995), 838.

24. James Weldon Johnson, "Preface," *The Book of American Negro Poetry*, ed. James Weldon Johnson (New York: Harcourt, Brace, 1922), viii.

25. Braddock, "Race: Tradition and Archive," 99–100.

26. Johnson, "Preface," xiv.

27. Anne Elizabeth Carroll, *Word, Image, and the New Negro: Representation and Identity in the Harlem Renaissance* (Bloomington: Indiana University Press, 2005), 15; Cherene Sherrard-Johnson, *Portraits of the New Negro Woman: Visual and Literary Culture in the Harlem Renaissance* (New Brunswick: Rutgers University Press, 2007), xviii, xix.

28. Rachel A. Rosenberg, "Looking for Zora's *Mule Bone*: The Battle for Artistic Authority in the Hurston-Hughes Collaboration," *Modernism/Modernity* 6, no. 2 (1999): 83. The controversy is also discussed at length in Yuval Taylor's *Zora and Langston: A Story of Friendship and Betrayal* (New York: Norton, 2019).

29. Charles Lewis, "Babbled Slander where the Paler Shades Dwell: Reading Race in *The Great Gatsby* and *Passing*," *LIT: Literature, Interpretation, Theory* 18, no. 2 (2007): 184. Two fascinating recent books confront fearlessly the range of appropriations, borrowings, citational practices, and, yes, plagiarisms contained in nineteenth-century African American literature and, in so doing, suggest that anxieties around confronting such material are dissipating somewhat. See Geoffrey Sanborn, *Plagiarama: William Wells Brown and the Aesthetic of Attractions* (New York: Columbia University Press, 2016) and Daniel Hack, *Reaping Something New: African American Transformations of Victorian Literature* (Princeton: Princeton University Press, 2017).

30. Thadious M. Davis, *Nella Larsen, Novelist of the Harlem Renaissance: A Woman's Life Unveiled* (Baton Rouge: Louisiana State University Press, 1996), 165–166 and 351.

31. Marion Boyd, "Letter: Nella Larsen's Story," *Forum* 83, no. 4 (April 1930): 41. Larsen's defense – that she based her composition on a story told to her during her nursing days by an "old Negro woman" and that it is "a tale so old and so well known that it is almost folklore" – strikes me as entirely plausible given the model of "rehabilitated orality" that Saint-Amour theorizes in *The Copyrights: Intellectual Property and the Literary Imagination* (Ithaca: Cornell University Press, 2011), 96. Nella Larsen, "Letter: The Author's Explanation," *Forum* 83, no. 4 (April 1930): 41.

32. Erika Renée Williams, "A Lie of Omission: Plagiarism in Nella Larsen's *Quicksand*," *African American Review* 45, no. 1–2 (2012): 205.

33. Williams, "A Lie of Omission," 205.

34. Beverly Haviland, "Passing from Paranoia to Plagiarism: The Abject Authorship of Nella Larsen," *Modern Fiction Studies* 43, no. 2 (1997): 310.

35. Roi Ottley, "Hectic Harlem: Let's Look at the Record," *Amsterdam News* (New York), February 22, 1936, 13.

36. Saint-Amour, *The Copyrights*, 10.

37. Wallace Thurman, "Negro Artists and the Negro," *New Republic*, August 31, 1927. Repr. *The Collected Writings of Wallace Thurman*, ed. Singh and Scott, 197–198.

38. Elizabeth McHenry, *Forgotten Readers: Recovering the Lost History of African American Literary Societies* (Durham: Duke University Press, 2002), 269.

39. Michael Soto, "Hemingway among the Bohemians: A Generational Reading of *The Sun Also Rises,*" *The Hemingway Review* 21, no. 1 (2001): 6.

40. Ibid., 11.

41. Monica L. Miller, *Slaves to Fashion: Black Dandyism and the Styling of Black Diasporic Identity* (Durham: Duke University Press, 2009), 187.

42. Shane Vogel, *The Scene of Harlem Cabaret: Race, Sexuality, Performance* (Chicago: University of Chicago Press, 2009), 17; George Chauncey, *Gay New York: Gender, Urban Culture, and the Making of the Gay Male World, 1890–1940* (New York: Flamingo, 1995), 259.

43. Kathleen Pfeiffer, *Race Passing and American Individualism* (Amherst: University of Massachusetts Press, 2002), 2.

44. Eva Saks, "Representing Miscegenation Law," in *Interracialism: Black-white Intermarriage in American History, Literature, and Law,* ed. Werner Sollors (New York: Oxford University Press, 2000), 73.

45. Pfeiffer, *Race Passing*, 2.

46. Amy Robinson, "It Takes One to Know One: Passing and Communities of Common Interest," *Critical Inquiry* 20, no. 4 (1994): 716, emphasis in original.

47. Langston Hughes, "Passing," in *The Ways of White Folks* (1934; New York: Vintage, 1990), 51.

48. Amy Robinson, "Forms of Appearance of Value: Homer Plessy and the Politics of Privacy," *Performance and Cultural Politics*, ed. Elin Diamond (London: Routledge, 1996), 241.

49. Nathan Irvin Huggins, *Harlem Renaissance* (New York: Oxford University Press, 1971), 306.

CHAPTER 8

Modernist Biography and the Question of Manhood: Eslanda Goode Robeson's Paul Robeson, Negro

Fionnghuala Sweeney

Paul Robeson, Negro sits uneasily alongside recent reconsiderations of the Harlem Renaissance as a localized if significant instance of wider afromodernist currents in play in the early decades of the twentieth century, and has received little attention in Harlem Renaissance scholarship. Published in London in 1930 by the leftwing publisher Victor Gollancz, and with minor differences in an edition by Harper Brothers in New York and London in the same year, Eslanda Goode Robeson's first book paints a longitudinal, multidimensional, multimedia picture of her husband, the actor and singer Paul Robeson.[1] *Negro* provides a rare instance of modernist biography, one in which the politics of manhood sits center stage. Its innovative recasting of African American traditions of life-writing steps away from the accommodationist position famously outlined in the last of the nineteenth-century slave narratives, Booker T. Washington's *Up From Slavery* (1901), which had helped sustain the educational work and institution building of the progressive era, to tell a new story in which the principal character becomes an exemplary figure of modern possibility. Its emphasis on Robeson as a visible and visualized subject – as an object of the public gaze – likewise distinguishes it from another major account of African American male experience of the early twentieth century, James Weldon Johnson's *The Autobiography of an Ex-Colored Man*, a *roman à clef* first published in 1912, and later in a slightly amended edition in 1927, in which the narrator decides to pass into white society to avoid the violent risks faced by African American men. In the process, the otherwise unnamed "ex-colored man" must give up his desire for a career in music, a trade-off he famously comes to regret as a decision that had him "sell my birthright for a mess of pottage."[2]

This chapter examines *Paul Robeson, Negro* as a reiteration of the significance of life-writing in mediating the relationship between the

African American subject and the world, but also as a pioneering act of
authorship, one that recalibrates the formal mechanisms of earlier biographical models to bring to the surface material that might otherwise, as
protection against collective reputational injury or otherwise, remain sublimated. Goode's story of Paul Bustill Robeson charts the progress of
a subject who, rather than choosing any "lesser part,"[3] moves toward the
representative status that the title suggests. Her work remains invested in
the emancipatory project that underpinned the slave narrative and the
culturalist position espoused in New Negro philosophy, defining the
character of the New Negro as educated, intellectually brilliant, excelling
on the sportsfield and artistically gifted. Robeson's extraordinary abilities
are tied to an aesthetic premise in which he is not only the epitome of
cultural achievement but its exemplary instance as *Negro* charts his growth
from his birth "in the parsonage of the Witherspoon church" (23), through
his early family life, university career, and attempts at establishing
a profession, as well as his emergence as an actor, singer, subject of art,
and a man personifying modern African American culture on the
American and international stage. It stakes a cultural claim to the birthright
of the contemporary subject, including that patrimony emerging in slavery
and often eschewed in the drive to disassociate the art and literature of the
Harlem Renaissance, with its northern, urban character, from cultural
forms emerging from enslaved communities and indelibly associated
with the "Old Negro" and the regressive politics of the rural South.

In this way, the biography engages with broader debates about the
politics of art: rooting itself in a literary legacy formally and thematically
imbued with an aesthetic of social progress, modernized through an iteration of intergenerational progress that writes the contemporary artist into
being as a cultural presence and political force. Yet it introduces a generic
complication by telling two stories: one centered on Robeson as the public
face of post-slavery diasporan achievement; the other identifying its literary
creator, writing from the cultural margins, as an unassimilated source of
political and narrative possibility. Complicated by the intimate relation
that troubles the relationship between teller and told, the narrative is
symptomatic of wider tensions around representative authority, cultural
hierarchies, and the relation to power. *Paul Robeson, Negro* at once constructs Robeson as an exemplary masculine subject and introduces
a shadow narrative that lays bare the hidden costs of such gendered
formulations of black cultural and political leadership.

Negro therefore raises important questions concerning the shifting relationship between African American artistry and the social world in the

interwar decades, a century after the emergence of the slave narrative as a tool of emancipation and vehicle of an emancipatory aesthetic. It challenges generic boundaries as well as innovating within modal forms – deploying what Rachel Farebrother establishes as the "collage aesthetic" of much Harlem Renaissance writing to "subvert . . . and unsettle dominant historical narratives."[4] The book is composed not just of narrative but also of what Peter Bürger calls "reality fragments"[5] – photographic images, reviews, newspaper reports – punctuating and sometimes interrupting a discontinuous series of historical, biographical, autobiographical or ethnographic accounts that together produce a tale of political force and subversive effect. The mythical Robeson who emerges from these pages is an iconic instance of diasporan sovereignty in an era of opportunity and social change – someone who "inspires enthusiasm which can only be expressed in superlatives . . . [a] wonderful, marvelous, great artist, great man" (145).

Robeson's success in concert hall and stage made him a fitting subject for an act of inventive memory mediating the lived experience of the first, definitively post-slavery generation, and authenticating the artist as a renaissance man. In the 1920s, he sang to packed halls across the UK accompanied by pianist Lawrence Brown, and gained a reputation as an actor – as Brutus Jones in Eugene O'Neill's *Emperor Jones* (1925), as Othello (1929), as well as Jim in the celebrated *Showboat* performed in London in 1926. Later, Robeson's romantic roles would place him at the center of an affective revolution that helped define the anticipatory heroism of pan-Africanism and anti-colonial radicalism. As Michelle Ann Stephens puts it, Robeson's portrayals of revolutionary heroes endorsed the "trope of the New Negro as the particular figure for a new modern masculine construction of black subjectivity," one uniquely able to fulfill a contemporary need for "a certain *affective* dimension in black . . . [culture]."[6] At this relatively early stage of his career, however, Robeson's performances emphasized the sentimental availability of the tragic rather than romantic subject, an availability evident in *Negro*, though the version of manhood the narrative authorizes draws on the redemptive possibilities of intimacy and community rather than on sacrifice and restitution. If the Paul Robeson of *Negro* is talented, successful, brilliant, the embodiment of success, he is also part of a wider family and community who share in his achievement.

Although it fabulates Robeson as the idealized face of New Negro achievement, then, the narrative also embeds a politics of the personal that bridges the gap between the public and private person, generating a critical space in which the ideal itself comes under scrutiny. The intimate domain of family reveals the man occupying the unscripted, behind-the-scenes role of husband and father, a man sometimes fallible, unsteady, and in need of guidance – opening up a space of constructive dissent that forces the biographical subject into dialogue with the modes and consequences of his own self-making. If, as Stephen Knadler writes, the disabled body in narratives of racial uplift raises critical questions around authority, authenticity, and meaning, this narrative of exemplary embodiment identifies the problematic of "who is allowed to speak, who becomes representative, what is silenced or repressed, and . . . who and what become a site of political resistance and value."[7]

This narrating voice refuses to relinquish moral authority to its biographical invention. Instead, it inaugurates biographical narrative as a place in which the autobiographical life may manifest itself, positioning its determinative story of the masculine subject as subject to the wifely labor that brings it into the world – as a reflexive creation which mobilizes biography as the means by which the shadow subject of the authorizing narrative may bring itself into being. Although it presents itself as an apparently transparent piece of writing, as a professional and personal endorsement of Paul Robeson written by his wife and business manager, *Negro* also reflects on and responds to the constraints of bourgeois femininity as it was marshaled in support of that contemporary masculine ideal. Simultaneously, it proffers itself as a popular tale, as a cultural pedagogy of racial uplift – a form of modernist re-education operating within the African American protest tradition and reflecting a broader political intention tied to advocacy, example, and attainment.[8] As an instance of life-writing speaking directly to the enabling fiction of the New Negro, the book illustrates the ways in which afromodernist writing drew on and innovated within African American genres that had established their facility in generating emancipatory accounts of lived experience of compelling ethnographic as well as individual significance.

For all that it provides a definitive story of cultural progress, therefore, *Paul Robeson, Negro* proceeds on the premise that something needs fixing. It represents some of the kindred challenges presented by earlier African American life-writing whose subject remained fleeting and elusive beneath the apparently artless surface of the famously unvarnished tale. The book refuses to nominate itself generically – the terms "biography" or "history" are never invoked – or to assign autonomy to a first person narrator. Like the slave narratives of the previous century, it illustrates the tensions surrounding the representation of the relationship between the black subject and the world, in which authority and authenticity are inherently linked, and place particular pressures on the narrating itself, on "the voice that embodies the ... storytelling," which is both "transparently present and in some respects carefully concealed."[9]

Goode's authorship of *Negro* suggests a narrative based on intimate, first-hand knowledge, and her co-option to a political project requiring the sublimation of female cultural agency and desire. Yet the storytelling voice evades any such complicity. The story is narrated in the third person, establishing an uneasy distinction between teller and told. Mrs. Paul Robeson is inevitably included in the unfolding tale, but only occasionally slips into view, in the guise of "Essie," the name by which Goode was familiarly known. The first glimmer of Essie's presence is not seen until chapter 5, "Groping: Law, Theatre, Music," where Paul Robeson busies himself in his early twenties in becoming "part and parcel of Harlem, and ... her ... most beloved son" (69). His rootedness is confirmed a year later, when he marries an unnamed "Harlem girl," becoming as a result "still more closely bound to the community" (69). Essie is almost glimpsed in the following chapter, "London," when, building on his success on the American stage, Paul goes to London with Jimmy Light and Harold McGhee, "to play *The Emperor Jones*." Even then, she is not mentioned by name, with her presence flagged by the somewhat ambiguous observation that "They took their wives along" (93).

The statement conceals and reveals a great deal about the experimental nature of the Robesons' collaborative relationship. Goode had early carved out an autonomous personal and professional space and been recognized as the organizing drive behind Robeson's career. In 1924, *The Pittsburgh Courier* described how she had "Guided Hubby to Fame," and remarked on the surprise of "a number of very experienced managers when they negotiated with her for the services of the star."[10] In real life as well as in the story as it unfolds, Goode provides prosthetic support to Robeson – in the sexual division of labor that sustains his professional success, in procuring access to services and spaces from which he would otherwise be excluded because of his color (Essie is described as occasionally passing for white), and as resolutely forgiving in the face of the damage caused to the marriage and to Robeson's reputation by his extramarital interests. Yet for all that Goode was central to the invention and success of the star of the title, as well as a subject of some press interest herself, *Negro* contains the barest mention of their marriage, and nothing of their courtship, or Goode's role in handling Robeson's career or the "family correspondence and finances."[11] Instead it splits the narrating voice off from its object presence in the world, and marks that narrating off by means of a sublimation, almost to the point of erasure, of the named fact and embodied presence of the wife. Essie remains beyond narrative access in all but the most pressing of life circumstances – illness, the birth of the child, the risk of death, the potential collapse of the marriage – and in brief glimpses of her cultural acuity, literary endeavor, or her commitment to the marital project, as the "Essie [who] was always ready to go anywhere or to stay anywhere," for "Just so I'm with you [Paul], I'm home" (98).

Simultaneously public liaison, negotiator, and intimate partner, the officially named source of the narration and the all but occluded architect of Robeson's professional career, Eslanda Goode Robeson appears only on the narrative margins of what on the surface seems to be an official tale of the progress of the artist toward professional and personal maturity. Yet Essie's occasional appearances, her endorsement of Robeson, and her intervention in the course of life events – her insistence on her desire to have a child for instance – are a thing apart from that most singular creation of the narrative, namely, the disembodied narrating voice whose veiled approaches to its subject are characterized by a slide from the sanctioned performance of biography, of the individual who voices his mission as an artist "using my art for myself, for my race, for the world," (86) to a more subversive account of "what seems at first glance to be almost pathological laziness," and an "instinct . . . which rouses him to tremendous activity . . . in the presence of things . . . important to his development" (72). The proximity of these moments of idealism and indolence provides insight into private life and the private man, while retaining the impression of spousal loyalty intact. Yet it also creates ripples on the otherwise smooth surface of womanly forbearance by suggesting the unspoken presence of a private hinterland where the price of art, and instinct, and manly success, is paid.

In this, ethnographic and biographical tendencies are aligned in a narrative that is more than an act of wifely homage expressing the uncomplicated intention of its author to promote Robeson's career, or to mobilize his image to provide a narrative of uplift. Robeson is proffered as material evidence and symbol of the legitimacy of any claim to cultural and political citizenship, but Goode's portrait disturbs the affective alignment of the male subject with the idealized individual of the mythology in whose service it is apparently written. It plays with convention in ways that reconfigure the act of biography as a method of overwriting, one in which the narrative gaze, directed toward the visible and visualized biographical subject, is a means not only of imagining that subject as a work of art, but also of disguising the vulnerability of the autobiographical act at the heart of the narrative. As attention to the almost absent Essie reveals, *Paul Robeson, Negro* is a nuanced act of renaissance artistry in which the coming-to-be of the subject is shaped by the operations of a clandestine narration. That narration maneuvers against the recurrent but present difficulties of a literary culture in which an emancipatory aesthetic is deeply embedded, but is also imbricated by layers of cultural authority that push the female narrating voice, and some of that which it seeks to represent – the placement of the female subject in the scopic field, the articulation of desire, the experience of female embodiment, the space and structure of the black female voice – into abeyance. As such, the narrative mobilizes a politics of desire as much as of social transformation, one that demonstrates black manhood's operations within a public sensorium to which the black woman has limited and compromised access.

Goode's was not the first version of Robeson's history to appear in print, or to establish a place for him as the embodiment of cultural achievement. Elizabeth Shepley Sergeant's "The Man with his Home in a Rock: Paul Robeson" published in *The New Republic* in 1926, describes him as "not merely an actor and a singer . . . but a symbol. A sort of sublimation of what the Negro may be in the Golden Age."[12] Even at this early stage of Robeson's career, the enticements he offered to eye and ear were evident. Of his acting and singing performances, Sergeant wrote that "Unlike most moderns, Paul Robeson is not half a dozen men in one torn and striving body. He is one, and clear cut, in the Greek or primitive sense," and a vehicle for the "secret and beautiful life that flows from [his] whole person and quickens his audiences," a voice "dusky and mellow, with [the] elemental power of leading men to springs of tragic truth."[13] Robeson himself emphasized the power of the voice and its role in generating meaning for the individual and the cohesion of community. In an autobiographical account published in *The Sunday Sun* in January 1929, "From My Father's Parsonage to My 'Ole Man River' Stage Triumph," Robeson, whose "life-story has been eagerly sought by many newspapers hitherto without success," begins with his "earliest recollections" of his father, "a clergyman with a very considerable following."[14] His father's story concerns inheritance, not of worldly goods, but of physical gifts granting persuasive and seductive power. Robeson senior "possessed a wondrously deep and beautiful speaking voice," and, as "was only natural . . . his greatest dream was that his children should inherit his own vocal powers." Paul is alone of his father's children in doing so, a fact that proves influential in Paul's early life and subsequent career. The power of the voice remains significant in one way or another throughout the article, which ends with Robeson's account of the "violent storm of protest . . . [that blew up] in the papers" around his casting in Eugene O'Neill's *All God's Chillun*, with the result, that "my name was on everyone's lips . . . and I became famous before I had even walked on the stage."[15]

Not only was his name on everyone's lips, his voice, courtesy of the phonograph, was sounding in many ears. Robeson signed a contract with Victor in 1925, making recordings of his singing and Laurence Brown's piano playing available in the USA and further afield. Not only did *Paul Robeson, Negro* enter a cultural field in which images of and discourse around the figure of Paul Robeson were ubiquitous, but also one where his voice had been made tangible and accessible by new technology and the mass market. In this, it was sharply distinguished from earlier instances of African American life-writing, where, although a distinctively speakerly model of narrative was often present (and the visual image played an important role in the articulation of black subjectivity), the pneumatic qualities of the voice itself were unavailable except as aspects of live interaction, public or private, with the subject themselves.

The biography presents a telling instance of modernist anomaly: a fiction of the subject bound to a mode of representation tailored to meet the formal and thematic challenges of an earlier historical moment – slavery and its immediate afterlife – and the dilemmas of embodiment such writing must inevitably face, mobilized in the service of a very different set of political, technological, and aesthetic circumstances. In 1930, the narrative was positioned in relation to a revolutionary soundscape in which the recorded voice provided affective coherence to and a resonating trace of the absent subject. If technologies of sound made Robeson's voice part of the transatlantic modernist vernacular, Goode's work deploys the story of that voice as a central feature of Robeson's life, career, and charisma, as a means of stretching the limits of inherited forms of life-writing in an ongoing play between the visible and the invisible, the vocal and the silent.[16] Much of the originality of the story lies in its mapping of the terrain of the New Negro as both a cultural space constructed across visual, literary, sensory, and sonic spheres, and a life history, temporally constructed from the prehistory of the subject in slavery to the opportunities of freedom and the pursuit of citizenship. Critical friction is produced on two fronts: between the "complicated national organization" (18) of the African American Church, a symbol of structure and tradition, and the "foreign world" entered from the "subway kiosk at One Hundred and Thirty-fifth Street and Lenox Avenue" (45), a space of modernist novelty and improvisation;

and likewise between the public face of the cultural ideal, and the intimate knowledge of its lived reality that its author, as Robeson's wife, was in a unique position to disclose, or not, as the case might be. In the story of Robeson's life lies much previously restricted knowledge, made known because it provides meaning and form to this novel iteration of the modern African American subject. Hence the increase in the narrative scope to include the emergence of gendered institutions and social hierarchies, the configuration of Harlem as the culturally vital heartland of the Afro-diasporan imaginary, and an assortment of public secrets, from the allegedly widespread practice of racial passing, to Robeson's sexual indiscretions, in which Essie is the publicly and privately injured party.

Paul Robeson, Negro underlines the significance of the recorded life in ways that continue to suggest the cultural and political potency of inscribing the individual into history and generating discursive openings that play with the ethnographic possibility that earlier forms of African American life-writing had so forcefully demonstrated. As one reviewer put it, Goode "writing in the third person ... could ... tell her many white friends of Negro family life, of Negro traditions and accomplishments."[17] There is, the review continues, "something very affecting in the generosity with which she exposes these secrets to a gaping white world, but ... also ... great pride."[18] The biographical sections of the narrative display a debt to the emancipatory aesthetic of African American literary forms that emphasize the significance of lived experience and the speaking subject as a repository of archival and artistic material. As in that tradition of representation comprising slave narratives and autobiographies, the narration presents itself opaquely to the critical gaze. Yet it innovates within that tradition by engaging in generic misdirection. Likewise, although apparently fully endorsing New Negro masculinity, it undermines certain of its social, economic, and artistic assumptions. Significantly, the narrative configures chronology to place the individual's ties to community, and paternal origins in slavery, center stage: "The Reverend Robeson was born in Martin County North Carolina, on July 27th, 1845; ... the son of Benjamin and Saba, who were slaves on the Robeson plantation" (21). In parallel to the more exposed individual of the life-story, it presents a photographic narrative comprising sixteen images already circulating in the public sphere, beginning, in the original edition, with Paul Laib's frontispiece photograph, "Head of Paul Robeson by Epstein," through to the superb final portrait, "Paul Robeson" by Joan Craven (136). The story is anchored throughout in the public domain of newspaper articles and theater reviews, in the artless materiality of word and image as authenticating mechanisms – part of the book's creation of an amenable fantasy that appears to conjure a knowable individual and a concrete world. The chapter "London," for example, describes the parties Robeson attended aboard British travel and fiction writer Ralph Stock's yacht on the Thames, and notes the presence of "a young newspaper man . . . among the guests" (94). It goes on to include verbatim the "description of Paul's singing" said newspaper man subsequently published, blurring the distinctions between private life and the public work of performative art.

There are other instances of innovative practice – stepping away from eventfulness in favor of impressionistic, insider's renderings of place and community in "Harlem and the Negro"; narrative that inserts itself seamlessly but ultimately speculatively into lapses in first-hand knowledge and invents emotional and artistic texture – as in the descriptions in "Groping: Law, Theater, Music," of the tentatively homoerotic working environment in Washington Square where Robeson spent a summer posing for "Tony," sculptor Antonio Salleme; or most obviously in Essie's disconcerting autobiographical presence in chapter 8, "Two Pauls," just a page and a half long, which deals with the conception and birth of Paul Robeson Junior; and in the book's finale, "Finding Himself." This last sees Robeson, "with his typically Negro qualities . . . carving his place as a citizen of the world," (146) confirmed as that representative modern subject for which the preceding narrative has been his apprenticeship and Essie his authorization. Such contrivances obscure the outlines of the biographical story by substituting fantasy for retrospection and recurrently gesturing toward the almost obliterated history of the narrating voice. Essie is the tellingly absent presence of the subject who knows, and her fleeting appearances, albeit at critical moments, underline the fictionality of the biographical act, the fractional, provisional, and contextual nature of intimacy and the knowledge assumed to accompany it.

Goode wrote the book while she was resident in the United Kingdom – the couple, their son, and Goode's mother, Eslanda Cardozo Goode, had "settled permanently" (127) in London in the late 1920s. The prompt to write occurred in conversation one evening in Piccadilly, when the couple's mutual friend, "Martha Sampson," made the case for a biography of Robeson, reflecting that "his life would read like a fairy-tale" (127).[19] At the time of Sampson's urging, Goode had already drafted a version that she declared to be "rotten" (127), but was in the process of writing a revised, less rotten copy that would soon find its way into print. In the USA, its fabulous qualities did not go unremarked. The promotional coupon published by Harper in *Opportunity* assured potential audiences that

Robeson's life "reads like a page from the Arabian Nights."[20] In *The Crisis*, W. E. B. Du Bois wrote, somewhat credulously, that "the hero is a little too perfect" but noted that "the ... triumph of a fine black man makes ... something unusual in these days when everything black in literature has to come from the slums, wallow in Harlem, and go to Hell."[21] Du Bois's remarks are telling, not least because they identify Robeson as one of that "aristocracy of talent" destined to provide leadership and example in addressing the obstacle of the color line.[22] The narrative shows both sides of his family to be of impeccable pedigree. Like Johnson's ex-colored man, he has "the best blood of the South in him"[23] and the best of the North. His paternal lineage, traced through his enslaved grandparents, reveals that his father, Reverend William D. Robeson, or "W. D." "was said among the old blacks in Martin County ... [to] resemble ... his royal Bantu ancestors in Africa" (21). In "1860 at about the age of fifteen" the same William Robeson joined the list of heroic self-emancipators by "escap[ing] to the North" (21). On his mother's side, the Bustill family "is one of the most ... highly respected Negro families in Philadelphia; trac[ing] their ancestry back as far as 1608, along Indian-Quaker-Negro stock." Robeson's great great grandfather, Cyrus Bustill, born in New Jersey, was "one of the founders of the Free African Society," and, tellingly perhaps, "is mentioned by name in Benjamin Franklin's original autobiography" (22).

For all his illustrious ancestry and personal achievement, however, the cosmopolitan creature who emerges at the end of the narrative only does so because of Essie's reprieve. The book was written at a time when the Robeson marriage was publicly in trouble and a pall cast over the marital harmony that had until then publicly prevailed.[24] In a scene in which Paul tries to persuade Essie that he is not the perfect man she believes him to be – one of the few sections of the book in which Essie slips into view, and the only one in which she speaks at length – the subject is tackled head on when, in a moment of candor she declares, "I know what you mean about your being unfaithful to me ... . You mean that someone may have fascinated you ... and that you consummated that interest" (133). In what follows, Essie's apparently open disclosure is tempered by evasion, as she refuses to "admit[] anything, even now. Why should I ... if it might not be true" (133). Nonetheless she denies that irreparable damage has been done by any sexual betrayal because she believes that Robeson has remained emotionally committed: "I know that you are faithful to me in all the important spirit of things. We have kept that sacred to us" (133).

Goode's biographer, Barbara Ransby, argues that Essie's narrative is "a deliberately crafted (and consciously altered) story of their lives," one in which, confronted with Robeson's infidelity and forced to decide whether or not to divorce him, "Essie scripted a fictional marital dynamic and played out her desired outcome."[25] If not quite redeemed by the love of a good woman, Robeson is at least absolved of responsibility for his lapses in sexual constancy by Essie's somewhat dubious claim that "If there have been others, they have . . . brought us closer together" (134). In life, Goode did eventually file for divorce, though she later withdrew her suit, declaring herself to be "Terribly Happy" with Paul, and embarking on a series of new writing projects that included a play, a novel, and several essays.[26] In the narrative, the shift in emphasis from sexual infidelity to emotional devotion, with Robeson confirmed "in Essie's mind [as] the most faithful of husbands," astutely sidesteps the most damaging effects of the betrayal and its impact on private and public domains, recalibrating the narrative toward Essie as the ultimate arbiter of Robeson's sexual and moral conduct.[27] The salvaging of the marriage thereby serves to situate the work as a contradictory account of a modern masculine ideal, as "Finding Himself" brings the story of Paul Robeson and the story of *Paul Robeson, Negro*, together, disclosing the organizing intelligence of the narrative and the intimate tension – the threatened disintegration of the Robeson's marriage – that lies at its heart. Only as a result of Essie's absolution of the offence she never quite acknowledges he has committed is Robeson able to complete the business of "finding himself," and occupy that "place [in the modern world] which would . . . have made his slave father proud" (146).

Paul Robeson, Negro performs as a "loyal" text: loyal to Paul Robeson, loyal to African American cultural politics, loyal to the history of its subject and of the race – to the fight "for the enforcement of the Fourteenth and Fifteenth Amendments to the Constitution . . . for the abolition of lynching, for . . . his inalienable rights as a citizen" (58). As such it encapsulates some of the difficulties of position experienced by black women intellectuals in their relation to an afromodernist cultural authority, particularly the nationalist and internationalist vision of the contemporary "race man" as cultural producer, economic powerhouse, and political leader. There was a corresponding truth to life. Goode remained married to Robeson and was committed throughout her life to advancing the cause of civil rights, to a pan-Africanist vision of local and global politics tied to a broader leftwing, anti-colonial agenda. Yet in *Paul Robeson, Negro*, the gendered asymmetries of that loyalty to color, creed, and conjugal bind produce a tension within the text, a dis-ease with the project of sublimation on which the creation of the narrative of Paul Robeson as race man whose "quality of

greatness ... comes through whatever he does" (145) is inevitably contingent. If, as Hazel Carby puts it, the "result of the pursuit of 'race consciousness, race pride, and race solidarity' was the emergence of particular
social types," Goode's faithful and self-consciously exculpatory narrative
renders some of the shortcomings of the type too visible to the naked eye
for an audience wider than just intimate family and friends.[28] More
particularly, in a narrative emphasizing the role of the father in family
life and his significance in the development of the child, underlining
Robeson's unmistakable "Africanness" and its consequences in Jim Crow
America, positioning him primarily as a cultural rather than economic
actor, and standing by him publicly despite his relationships with other
women, Goode surreptitiously produces an internal critique of a reluctance
within black cultural nationalism to reflect on the assumptions underpinning an understanding of black masculinity as somehow representative of
all gendered positions and experiences.

For all that it appears comfortable with the creed of the New Negro, and
complacent about its own thematic focus: Robeson as the representative
instance of masculine achievement – as an artist, cultural ambassador, and
nationalist activist – the book is also the vehicle of an iconoclastic intent.
Running through the narrative are multiple threads that, under cover of
marital fondness, reveal the shortcomings of the paradigm loved despite as
much as because of "his appearance ... his genial smile, his laziness, his
child-like simplicity" (146), as the more questionable consequences of Paul
Robeson's character and conduct are exposed as acutely trying to those
most directly affected and vulnerable in the intimate family circle – are
made visible and exposed to cultural sanction. In this it provides an
instance of modernist retrospection that seeks to embrace the fluidity of
the subject as a shifting moral entity by accommodating personal failure
and moral shortcoming. Moreover, if the Robeson who emerges from its
pages is a race man, he is likewise the singular creation of Eslanda Goode
Robeson, an artifact of a narrative endeavor tracing the active influence of
the narrating subject as organizing intelligence, rather than the developmental progress of the publicly available and socially determined self.

As such, *Paul Robeson, Negro* takes its place as a re-definitional narrative of
the Harlem Renaissance, one that complicates the assuredness with which
male artists and intellectuals might be cast as exceptional yet representative,
and which embedded the significance of individual history as part of an
ongoing project linked to the emergence of an ethical subject in the archetypal
imaginary. As creative labor undertaken on her own behalf, rather than merely
as professional or wifely services rendered, Goode's writing allows an

adjustment of emphasis that positions Paul Robeson the race man and *Paul Robeson, Negro* as linked projects that situate Goode Robeson's work in a longer tradition of African American activism, and literary innovation, that exerted some of its greatest force in the genre of life-writing. It is the pose of biographer that brings the autobiographical subject, the publicly available but privately evasive fiction that is Paul Robeson's wife, into existence as a disturbing supplementarity. Her presence defines the shortcomings of the ideal, and graciously provides it with prosthetic assistance.

Notes

1. The difference is the inclusion of the portrait by Epstein in the Gollancz edition, and the use of different pseudonyms for some of the individuals mentioned. Eslanda Robeson, *Paul Robeson, Negro* (London: Gollancz, 1930), price 10s 6d; Eslanda Robeson, *Paul Robeson, Negro* (New York: Harper and Harper, 1930), price $2.50. Hereafter cited parenthetically.
2. James Weldon Johnson, *The Autobiography of an Ex-Colored Man* (1912/1927; New York: Norton, 2015), 110.
3. Ibid.
4. Rachel Farebrother, *The Collage Aesthetic in the Harlem Renaissance* (Farnham: Ashgate, 2009), 4–8.
5. Peter Bürger, *Theory of the Avant-Garde* (Minneapolis: University of Minnesota Press, 1984), 77.
6. Michelle Ann Stephens, *Black Empire: The Masculine Global Imaginary of Caribbean Intellectuals in the United States, 1914–1962* (Durham: Duke University Press, 2005), 36.
7. Stephen Knadler, "Dis-Abled Citizenship: Narrating the Extraordinary Body in Racial Uplift," *Arizona Quarterly* 69, no. 3 (2013): 100.
8. See Robert Shaffer, "Out of the Shadows: The Political Writing of Eslanda Goode Robeson," *Pennsylvania History: A Journal of Mid-Atlantic Studies* 66, no. 1 (1999): 48.
9. William L. Andrews, "The Novelization of Voice in Early African American Narrative," *PMLA* 105, no. 1 (1990): 23.
10. "Guided Hubby to Fame," *The Pittsburgh Courier*, September 27, 1924, 1.
11. Ibid.
12. Elizabeth Shepley Sergeant, "The Man With His Home in a Rock: Paul Robeson," *The New Republic*, March 3, 1926, 40.
13. Ibid., 40–41, 43.
14. Paul Robeson, "From My Father's Parsonage to My 'Ole Man River' Stage Triumph," *The Sunday Sun*, January 13, 1929, n.p., Paul and Eslanda Robeson Collection, Moorland-Spingarn Archive, Howard University, Washington, DC (PERC).
15. Ibid.

16. Essie's contribution to Robeson's voice, already "quite perfect," (112) but needing a teacher to help him understand how to sing, is the subject of the chapter "Voice Help."

17. "The First Reader," *New York World*, June 25, 1930, 11.

18. Ibid.

19. Martin Duberman identifies Martha Sampson (Marion Griffin in the American edition) as Martha Gruening, civil rights activist, pacifist, editor of the *Dawn*, assistant secretary to the National Association for the Advancement of Colored People (NAACP), and one of several women intellectuals with whom Goode was friends. Martin Duberman, *Paul Robeson: A Biography* (New York: New Press, 2007), 613, n. 33.

20. Harper and Brothers, publishers order coupon, *Opportunity: A Journal of Negro Life*, n.d., n.p., PERC.

21. W. E. B. Du Bois, "The Browsing Reader," *The Crisis* 37 (September 1930): 313.

22. W. E. B. Du Bois, *Writings*, ed. Nathan Huggins (New York: Library of America, 1986), 842.

23. Johnson, *Autobiography*, 12.

24. Robeson began a relationship with British actress Yolanda Jackson in 1930, and another with Peggy Ashcroft in the same year. Barbara Ransby, *Eslanda. The Large and Unconventional Life of Mrs Paul Robeson* (New Haven: Yale University Press, 2014), 65–66.

25. Ibid., 82.

26. Undated newspaper clipping, PERC.

27. Ransby, *Eslanda*, 82.

28. Hazel Carby, *Race Men* (Cambridge, MA: Harvard University Press, 1998), 4.

CHAPTER 9

Modernism and Women Poets of the Harlem Renaissance

Maureen Honey

Although reprints of their poems have been available in anthologies or collections for three decades, women poets of the Harlem Renaissance continue to be understudied in the area of modernism. In their own era, women's poetry was well represented in New Negro publications such as *The Crisis*, *Opportunity*, and period anthologies, while African American critics praised their work as contributing to artistry that was moving the race forward. Once those publishing outlets vanished in the 1930s, however, Black women writers faced increasingly insurmountable obstacles, and poets especially were hurt by critical models at mid-century that valorized a particular kind of poetry by a handful of white, largely male, writers. These critics (T. S. Eliot and Ezra Pound in particular) dominated scholarly conversations about modernist poetry in the decades after World War II, and the poets they prioritized are still often at the center of critical attention, with some important chiseling away of the edifice by scholars unearthing modernism's original democratic and diverse roots.

In this chapter, I explore some of the recent scholarship on Harlem Renaissance women poets to assess whether these limiting and gendered critical analyses of the past are expanding enough to bring them sufficiently into the fold of Modernist Studies where they belong. I curate some of the most significant scholarship to appear since the widespread development of new critical models in Harlem Renaissance and African American feminist literary criticism. I also present a case study of three poets whose work models for us the modernism of New Negro women's lyrical verse, a genre routinely omitted from the modernist canon, and an example of how women poets infused traditional forms with radically modern content: Angelina Weld Grimké, Gwendolyn Bennett, and Mae V. Cowdery. I argue that the erotic lyric or erotically charged pastoral verse largely defined for them, and many of their sister poets, what it meant to be a modern writer, as well as a New Negro artist-activist, in the modernist era.

Conversations about modernism have expanded to include African American poets, but they almost invariably highlight Black male poets who use folk and urban vernacular, a discourse now being explored in current readings as also appearing in women's poetry of the Harlem Renaissance. Helene Johnson's urban poetry of street language and jazz rhythms, for instance, is being recognized as a groundbreaking exception to the New Negro era's gendered literary landscape. Cynthia Davis and Verner D. Mitchell make the important point that Johnson (1906–1995) created an urban *flâneur* who wanders the streets of Harlem making astute observations about city life while using a distinctly urban vernacular that avoids plantation stereotypes. Citing "Poem" (1927), "Sonnet to a Negro in Harlem" (1927), "Bottled" (1927), and "Regalia" (1929), they compare Johnson's themes with those of Eliot's "The Waste Land" (1922) while locating her squarely within modernism. Although her subjects are often male, they point out, Johnson created a female speaker who easily employs the slang and rhythm of 1920s Harlem.[1] Emily R. Rutter also praises Johnson's poetry for its rhetoric of empowerment, but Rutter turns to the unpublished work written between the 1960s and 1980s, as well as the published, asserting that it speaks back to, rather than echoes, the alienation of Eliot's "Prufrock" (1915), "Preludes" (1917), and "The Waste Land."[2] Along with earlier studies of Johnson as a modernist by Nina Miller (1999) and Katherine R. Lynes (2007), we are now seeing a welcome contemporary light being shone on her modern poetic voice as one that dialogues with innovative poetry of her day and that participates in the new vernacular poetry produced by male poets of the Harlem Renaissance.[3]

Other than Johnson, however, women poets continue to suffer from the stereotype that they failed to treat subject matter of the street and rural folk culture, or to experiment with new forms of poetry, such as imagism, free verse, prose poems, or common speech. Countering this prevailing view is scholarship that recuperates the wide range of poetry women actually contributed to the Harlem Renaissance. It is now coming to light, for instance, that Gwendolyn Bennett wrote unpublished ballads in street slang with proletarian subjects and an unfinished novel in which characters speak in southern folk vernacular through recovered pieces recently made available in 2018 by Belinda Wheeler and Louis J. Parascandola.[4] The reprinting in their Bennett collection of the unpublished 1930s long poems, "I Build America," "Sweat," "Wise Guys," "The Hungry Ones," and "[Rapacious women who sit on steps at night]" will help dispel the false notion that women poets did not venture into the new areas of proletarian themes and language. Building on their work, we can revisit one of Bennett's most famous poems, "Song" (1926), which pays homage to slave tunes and jazz bands alike, and become acquainted with her unpublished "Negro Church," which incorporates lines from gospel music in a call and response stanza construction. Similarly, Alice Dunbar-Nelson's little-known "Music" (1925) compares the sound and impact of orchestral instruments to passion for a lover.[5] It has long been known that Angelina Weld Grimké wrote dialect and formally experimental lesbian-themed poetry very early in her career that was left unpublished, but analysis of it is long overdue, while the superb working-class vernacular poetry of Nat Turner's granddaughter, Lucy Mae Turner, has not been studied at all.[6] These are just a few of the many writers who expanded traditional parameters of poetry to include the sounds and cultural diversity of modern American life in their work.

Women poets of the Harlem Renaissance often have been criticized for using standard poetry forms such as the sonnet or quatrain, but scholars are now contextualizing this work in ways that recover its innovative thrust. Melissa Girard, for example, does a close reading of Angelina Weld Grimké's rondeau, "Surrender" (1927), the leading spear with which she skewers J. Saunders Redding's dismissal of African American poets who used traditional forms in his widely influential *To Make A Poet Black* (1939). Singling out Grimké for criticism, along with other Renaissance poets who worked in established forms, Redding labeled them dilettantes so steeped in "imitation worlds of white folks' making" that they had no place in the African American literary canon.[7] Countering Redding's incomplete and misleading citation of Grimké's poem, Girard deftly connects "Surrender" to Paul Laurence Dunbar's iconic rondeau, "We Wear the Mask" (1895). She points out that Grimké's refrain, "We ask for peace," echoes Dunbar's "We wear the mask" and that her rhythms and number of line syllables mirror his as well. Girard concludes that Redding's 1939 critique marks the beginning of women poets being demoted by Black critics from their original prominence during the Harlem Renaissance to minor status in the years that followed and to their ultimate erasure from the modernist canon. In a similar feminist push-back against dismissal of women's traditional forms, Jenny Hyest does a close reading of Anne Spencer's first published poem, "Before the Feast at Shushan" (1920). A dramatic monologue, "Shushan" is for Hyest a feminist disabling of old poetic forms and language by using them as a code for the outmoded patriarchal views and sexual violence articulated by Spencer's speaker, King Ahasuerus, and directed at Queen Vashti when he banishes her.[8]

Another way women writers have been marginalized is the tendency of Harlem Renaissance critical models to cordon off lyric verse from clearly race-centered poetry with an attendant charge that the former is conventionally sentimental. It is indeed the scholarly distinction between protest poems of racial uplift and seemingly de-racialized lyric verse that has so hampered subsequent appreciation of these poets, who have been stereotyped as genteel sentimentalists trapped in Eurocentric white models. This is a racial lens through which the most striking innovations in African American poetry of the era are identified as a blend of modern musical form or the vernacular and clearly delineated Black subject matter. Jane Kuenz characterizes this definition of modern New Negro verse as "a narrative of aesthetic development that moved away from conventional lyrics . . . toward authentically realized folk forms," a narrative, she asserts, that had profound effects on negative critical assessments of Black women poets: "[A]n emergent literary culture . . . broadly characterized their work, as it has [Countee] Cullen's, as bourgeois, racially empty, and feminine."[9]

Use of the lyric has left New Negro women poets open to the charge of sentimentalism, a stereotype applied to white women of the modernist era as well. Girard correctly maintains that African Americans have suffered from their gendered affiliation with their white peers, and insists that they, along with Edna St. Vincent Millay, Sara Teasdale, Elinor Wylie, and other modernist poets, brought lyric experimentation to their exploration of the personal. The label of sentimentality that has been applied to them, she asserts, fails to capture their radical departure from poetry of the nineteenth century. Girard also reminds us that women's lyrical forays into imagism, *vers libre*, the erotic, and expression of mood were at the heart of American modernism, and only a concerted effort by conservative male critics to enshrine so-called high modernists, such as T. S. Eliot, pushed them off stage.[10] Keith D. Leonard specifically frames African American women poets' use of the lyric as a way for them to break out of conventional self-representations into modern dramatizations of interiority, paving the way for later modernists such as Gwendolyn Brooks and Margaret Walker: "This turn inward was one of the most important . . . artistic innovations of mid-twentieth century African American women's poetry."[11]

Critics are also reading New Negro women writers' use of the erotic as an important branch of modernism. Erin Chapman, for example, has pointed to a small group of women prose writers – Jessie Fauset, Nella

Larsen, Marita Bonner, and Elise Johnson McDougald – who depicted sexual expression as both self-defining and modern.[12] Girard's and Miller's analyses of Harlem Renaissance women poets suggests that they too challenged convention by lyrically exploring interior states of ecstasy and desire, while Melissa Prunty Kemp asserts that Grimké's use of the erotic sutures her work definitively to modernist poetry.[13] To define oneself in this way, they argue, was not only a form of resistance to feminine selfless propriety but also a proactive way to be modern, liberated from Victorian shackles of the previous century, even as they infused nineteenth-century formal or thematic structures with modern content.

Moreover, revisionary Harlem Renaissance scholarship has provided an important context for assessing women's lyric poetry in asserting that any woman writer who highlighted erotic experience in the early twentieth century took a considerable risk, but that this step was especially perilous for African Americans, particularly teachers like Grimké, Bennett, and Fauset or society leaders like Cowdery, Dunbar-Nelson, and Spencer. Because Black women were subjected to salacious stereotyping as prostitutes by the dominant culture, New Negro models of conventional femininity became firmly entrenched in Black communities as a response, according to these critics. Miller, for example, asserts that the street was largely a male domain in a New Negro ethos that sought to elevate Black womanhood through middle-class images.[14] More recently, Chapman describes a patriarchal emphasis in New Negro ideology of the 1920s and a motherhood ideal that undermined both female sexual freedom and self-determination.[15] New Negro women poets were well aware of these boundaries, reflected in the large body of erotic unpublished verse by Grimké and Bennett, for example, and Cowdery's poetic silence after she published her collection in 1936. Nevertheless, women writers celebrated sexual desire as a transporting and modernizing force breaking down both gender and race barriers.

Helping to frame the modernism of women's erotic lyricism, contemporary scholarship on images of women at this time describes a new emphasis on the female body in American culture during the modernist era and that Black women's bodies carried double-edged hedonistic messages. Stephanie Batiste and Jayna Brown link sexualized presentations of African American women stage performers and erotic representations of Black women in film, for example, to imperialism and modernism respectively.[16] Chapman interrogates primitivist and consumerist exploitation of Black women's bodies in popular culture of the 1920s, making clearer women writers' need to create positive images of Black women's sexuality.[17] On the positive side, by illuminating further the modern context for this highlighting of the body, Miller frames American women's poetry with Jazz Age emphasis on female sexuality in the 1920s: "The national, mass media-driven culture that had evolved in America by the 1920s ushered in a palpable national erotics: a charged and luminous representational field out of which individuals and groups derived new identities and identifications."[18] Adding to Miller's early view, Laila Haidarali locates a new brown beauty ideal surfacing in urban spaces of the 1920s as central to New Negro modernity for women, putting female sexuality in a more positive light: "[B]eauty eclipsed chastity and demure self-presentation as central tenets in cultivating the image of respectable middle-class African American womanhood . . . [T]he discourse on brown complexions celebrated rather than repudiated the sexual as the domain of respectable New Negro women."[19]

Agreeing with these critics and focusing on the erotic lyric verse of Angelina Weld Grimké (1880–1958), Gwendolyn Bennett (1902–1981), and Mae V. Cowdery (1909–1948), I have explored the way eros largely defined for them, and many of their sister poets, what it meant to be a modern writer as well as a New Negro artist-activist challenging segregation and sexism.[20] As a way of demonstrating how revisionary approaches to the personal subject matter of women's verse can unlock its modernist thrust, I here provide a close reading of their imagist and traditional pastoral poetry that conveys modern sexual themes. Grimké, Bennett, and Cowdery represent three generations of poets who participated centrally in the Harlem Renaissance and were praised as innovators by critics at the time, like Alain Locke, William Stanley Braithwaite, Charles S. Johnson, and others, only to be forgotten in the decades that followed when they were largely omitted from poetry anthologies until the 1980s. Grimké, writing in Boston and Washington, DC, was part of the first generation of New Negro writers emerging in the century's first decades who found success in New Negro journals and anthologies of the 1920s; Bennett, a New Yorker, was one of the young upstarts at the peak of the arts movement from 1923 to 1928; and the now unknown Cowdery, a Philadelphia native, belonged to a third wave of promising very young writers mentored by Langston Hughes whose call for a new modern kind of Black poetry in the mid-1920s led her to publish prize-winning poetry in *The Crisis* and other journals from 1927 to 1930.

I quote their lyric verse at length here in part to give a sense of their boldness in pairing poetry, considered a high art, with erotic expression, considered a domain of the street. "I should like to creep / Through the long brown grasses / That are your lashes," Grimké's speaker declares to a woman in the published "A Mona Lisa" (1927): "I should like to sink down / And down / And down . . . / And deeply drown."[21] Bennett features post-coital ecstasy in the unpublished "Comrades": "Friend, I'll call you . . . . / When the minutes / Pulse more slowly, / And the rich, dark stream / Of your willful love / Has ebbed through / The ravaged quiet / Of my breasts and thighs."[22] Lust animates Cowdery's "Insatiate," a piece from her 1936 collection: "If her lips were rubies red, / Her eyes two sapphires blue, / Her fingers ten sticks of white jade, / Coral tipped . . . and her hair of purple hue / Hung down in a silken shawl . . . / They would not be enough to / To fill the coffers of my need."[23] Their verse displayed the female body with a new frankness, setting them apart from their nineteenth-century predecessors. Grimké focused on women's lips, perfumed hair, enveloping arms, and alluring eyes. "I let you kiss my mouth / Quite through my curtained eyes / I felt your eyes upon my eyes, my mouth / Compellingly and hungrily you fed," her speaker recalls in an unpublished untitled verse: "And then I slipped into your arms / Forgot all else but just your lips upon / My mouth."[24] Bennett draws our attention to her subject's sexual allure in the published "To a Dark Girl" (1927): "I love you for your brownness / And the rounded darkness of your breast. / Something of old forgotten queens / Lurks in the lithe abandon of your walk."[25] Cowdery's 1927 "Longings" from *The Crisis* includes her speaker's desire to feel water against her naked body at dawn: "To plunge – / My brown body / In a golden pool, / And lazily float on the swell / Watching the rising sun."[26] Her speaker in "The Young Voice Cries" (1928) published in *Harlem*, a new journal designed to continue the radicalism of the now defunct *Fire!!* (1926), urges her elders "to see the naked loveliness of things [. . .] earth's breast against the sky": "The young voice cries / For the pagan loveliness / Of a moon / For the brazen beauty / Of a jazz song . . . / The young voice / Is hushed / In silent prayer / At beauty's shrine . . ."[27]

All three defined female sexuality as a dark force of resilience and enlightened change. This concept was often represented by the speaker's worship of an Aphrodite figure who provided her with an inspirational symbol of a new world in which dark beauty triumphed over prejudice, love over hate, and female power over patriarchal rule. Grimké heralds the arrival of this dark goddess in the unpublished "A Trilogy":

> Behold! She comes, the queen of Night!
> A queen indeed in shape and size
> With haunting grace, and haunting eyes. [. . .]

She charms to rest by slow degrees
The birds, the leaves, the trees, the breeze:
And then she sits upon her throne
A figure motionless, alone,
Her solemn, radiant, vigil keeping
Never sleeping, never sleeping – .[28]

Bennett summons a similar poetic muse in the published "Fantasy" (1927): "I sailed in my dreams to the Land of Night / Where you were the dusk-eyed queen, [. . .] Oh, the moon gave a bluish light / Through the trees in the land of dreams and night. / I stood behind a bush of yellow-green / And whistled a song to the dark-haired queen . . . ."[29] Goddesses also animate Cowdery's darkened landscapes. In three of the four linked quatrains in "Four Poems After the Japanese," from her 1936 collection, she presents images of powerful dark female spirits ruling the universe: "Night turned over / In her sleep / And a star fell / Into the sea." "Earth was a beautiful / Snow woman / Until the rain / Washed her face one day." "The moon / Is a madonna / Cradling in the crescent curve / Of her breast / A newborn star."[30]

Grimké, Bennett, and Cowdery created a dark Aphrodite in these lyrics, a mythical figure who symbolizes a key element of modernist poetics: the eroticized female body as a sacred road to beauty and the artist's authentic self. Experiencing the moment in all its sensual splendor released for the poet a beautiful song inspired by truth within. The true artist accessed an unblemished subjectivity unfettered by society's imprisoning restraints through experiencing the moment in all its sensual splendor and pursuing a beautiful truth. The New American Poetry pioneered by Amy Lowell, Ezra Pound, William Stanley Braithwaite, Harriet Monroe, and others in the century's second decade sought to highlight this subjectivity so as to better communicate with the soul and free it from Victorian constraints of duty and conformity. According to its tenets, the true artist accessed the inner self and followed a path outward through poetry that expressed unfiltered emotion without judgment, fear or censure.[31] Aphrodite was a key symbol of this idea, for not only was she a goddess of erotic power, in Greek mythology she was also a ruler of subjectivity, feeling, the body's call to welcome desire. New Negro writers were no less committed than were white modernists to celebrating subjective states, but they also linked the sensual truth of female desire within to defeat of racist patriarchy without.

For Bennett, Grimké, and Cowdery, for instance, an Aphrodite-like goddess models a new kind of power in the modern age to transcend racist patriarchal civilization, a transcendence symbolized by her dark body's emergence at nightfall. Unlike the classic white naked Aphrodite, Grimké's dusk goddess was either clothed or invisible in the night sky, and she inhabited a realm that releases her speakers from false inhibiting roles played out during daytime routines. "I built a shrine one day / Within my inmost heart," her speaker declares in the unpublished "My Shrine" dated 1902:

> I placed it not upon
> The public-way but in
> A spot retired and sweet
> Where I might go alone . . .
> The idol that I placed
> Within my modest shrine
> Was but a maiden small
> But yet divinely pure,
> And there I humbly knelt
> Before those calm, grave eyes,
> Full oft throughout the night,
> And oft at moments sweet
> Purloined throughout the day; . . .
> Sweet idol of my life,
> One little, saintly, maid,
> Who keeps my actions pure
> And makes me see the best
> In all the sinning world
> Through her grave, thoughtful eyes.[32]

Similarly, Bennett's speaker is mesmerized by her night goddess's vulval "velvet soft" gown in her published "Street Lamps in Early Spring" (1926); the veil she wears is a seductively moist screen, "[a]s shimmering fine as floating dew." Contemplating the quiet night sky from a city street, Bennett's speaker is able to see that the universe is animated by erotic female energy, in dramatic contrast to the fast-paced urban power structures of daylight: "And here and there / In the black of her hair / The subtle hands of Night / Move slowly with their gem-starred light."[33] In Cowdery's 1927 "Dusk," the speaker savors her contemplation of a beautiful, possibly naked, woman as night falls: "Like you / Letting down your / Purple-shadowed hair / To hide the rose and gold / Of your loveliness."[34] The dark goddess of beauty and eros rules quietly in the verse of all three, but she is more powerful than the ignorant world of white male power and civilization's ugly prejudice by day.

Although in Greek mythology Aphrodite is a white figure associated with sunlight, she was repositioned by these three writers as a creature of twilight, dawn, and night, her erotic force imagined as part of a shadowy world glimpsed when day was done, in a landscape of silhouettes, watery visions, and the bright star Venus. In nineteenth-century art, Aphrodite's white body is framed by long tresses of hair or gauzy veils while she is attended by cherubs, swans, and doves on ocean waves with white foam. These images of whiteness are racially transmuted, darkened, when Grimké sets her poems at twilight with speakers raptly gazing at a distant star, Bennett creates what Miller calls a Nightwoman who serenely drifts through space,[35] and Cowdery portrays naked lovers at dusk or bathed in moonlight. The goddess of love is darkened, veiled, set loose at night to awaken forbidden states of ecstasy and emotional release. Birds herald the arrival of this goddess of the dark with song, and flowers adorn her earthly path in their poetry, just as they do in legends of Aphrodite, but she emerges in the shadowy mist of nightfall rather than the bright sunshine of Greek mythology. Grimké, Bennett, and Cowdery painted imagistic portraits of trees pointing upward – phallic emblems of endurance and fecundity – and perfumed white flowers or orgasmic bright stars – allusions to racial integration and sexual transport set at twilight, dusk or evening. They portray a female sexual energy that can be safely unleashed in darkness and wedded to a racial liminality impossible to experience in a daytime ruled by segregation. Nature provided an alternative to an urban space symbolic of the ruling order's white male civilization and power. Countering that power in this pastoral space was the woman artist's pure voice nurtured by nature's dark female essence.

All three of these poets framed the body's desire as a pathway to spiritual power, truth, and beauty for the modern female artist, a guiding force of creativity. Grimké created a religion of longing in her verse, populated by bewitching goddesses who float just beyond reach and vanish into an eternal landscape of bruising loss. The Sapphic deity who rules in this ethereal world nonetheless inspires Grimké's speakers to express forbidden same-sex desire in poetic song and the speaker's worshipful gaze. She created a religion of same-sex desire in which the speaker is purified by worship of the beloved who resides in a sphere her speakers can never reach. In Grimké's unpublished "Thou Art So Far, So Far," for instance, the speaker kneels in humble adoration of a woman who fills her with speechless awe: "Thou art to me a lone, white, star, / That I may gaze on from afar; / But I may never, never, press / My lips on thine in mute caress, / E'en touch the hem of thy pure dress – ."[36] Bennett painted luminous nighttime portraits of female sexuality too glorious for most to see, and she explored the truths that could be found in both the pleasure and pain of heterosexual erotic experience. She follows a decidedly secular and heterosexual path, in contrast to Grimké, but intimacy is equally hallowed ground. In the unpublished "Communion," for example, the speaker presents her lover with a splendid table of wine and delicious treats as testament to their rapturous connection, framing the gesture with Christian symbolism: "Break bread with me, I pray you my beloved, / For food and drink to those who love / More sweet communion are than any holy grail, / More consecrated are than any sacred cup."[37] Cowdery set in motion dark oceans of lust, volcanic eruptions of fire that evaporate in an instant but are as riveting as a comet in her bisexual erotic portraits. Her speaker in the 1929 "Farewell," for instance, mourns the loss of her lover in strikingly erotic images: "No more / The feel of your hand / On my breast / Like the silver path / Of the moon / On dark heaving ocean."[38] Whether looking for beauty in male or female lovers, Cowdery's bisexual exploration of her speakers' sexuality affirms the modern artist's freedom to follow her muse wherever it leads.

Furthermore, these three poets, like other New Negro women writers, although residing in urban centers, gravitated toward pastoral settings for their lyrical and sexual poems, which, ironically, led to their becoming stereotyped as genteel sentimentalists trapped in conventional poetic genres. Grimké locates her speaker's naked body in a field, for instance, in the published "Grass Fingers" (1927): "Touch me, touch me, / Little cool grass fingers, / Elusive, delicate grass fingers, / With your shy brushings, / Touch my face – / My naked arms – / My thighs – / My feet."[39] Bennett creates an English countryside to frame her song of love in her published "Song" (1926): "Oh, my sweet, / I shall paint you a picture / And call it Spring . . . . / Cool greens and sheep / Upon a smoke-blue hill, / And now and then / A puff of snow-white cloud."[40] Cowdery focuses on a garden oasis that provides relief from the noisy city in which her speaker resides in the 1936 "Interlude:" "I like this quiet place / Of lawns and trees well kept / And bright geometric gardens / Where droning bees hover and lift / On pollen-burdened wings . . . / Where even sunlight is genteel / And birds are shy and swiftly scarlet. / I love this quiet place / Of sane and placid beauty, / But soon I shall return / To be torn anew / At the bold thrust of skyscrapers / Against a murky sky / And the strident song / Of cars and people rushing by."[41]

Though all three were city women who were drawn to and loved New York, they, like many women poets, most often located their erotic verse neither in Harlem nor any city.[42] Female bodies in their poetry are framed by nature; intimate caresses are veiled in pastoral allusions. With the exception of Helene Johnson's *flâneurs*, it is through references to the natural world, rather than the urban scene of cabarets on which male poets focused, that women writers tended to explore female sexuality. Harlem, of course, was a primary site of sexual activity in the 1920s, its clubs a mecca for bohemians and artists looking for release from convention, uninhibited dancing, illicit trysts. Novelists could get major book contracts for stories set in Harlem, playwrights financial backing for Broadway productions. Black women artists who contributed to Harlem's jazz scene, however, were mainly stage and cabaret performers – Bessie Smith, Ma Rainey, Josephine Baker, Ethel Waters. The most innovative of Harlem Renaissance poets – such as Langston Hughes and Claude McKay – celebrated this female performer, drew sympathetic portraits of her sexual persona, and poetically rendered the allure of cabaret life. This was prob- lematic space for the female literary artist, however, documented by Nella Larsen and other writers, who depict the great divide between New Negro women dedicated to racial uplift and modern Black women seeking sexual autonomy or adventure.[43] As K. T. Ewing describes this gulf: "Both the visibility and popularity of blues women were problematic for [New Negro] clubwomen who were concerned with presenting a morally and sexually pure image of African American womanhood."[44] In response, women poets located an emerging narrative of modernity and power rooted in female sexuality at the center of a Whitmanesque nonman- made space: nature.

Grimké, Bennett, and Cowdery are not the only New Negro women poets who focused on the erotic in modern lyric and pastoral verse while battling racism in protest poems – Georgia Douglas Johnson, Jessie Fauset, Helene Johnson, Anne Spencer, and many others also celebrated a modern dark female sexuality while advocating for racial justice. Fine biographies, as well as editions of their work in some cases, are available that can advance advocacy of women's lyric verse as belonging in the modernist canon.[45] Their lasting legacy is that all these poets brought female sexuality to the forefront of lyric poetry in a transformative modern moment that is at the heart of contemporary feminist artists in our own era linking sexual freedom with rebellion against patriarchal and racist systems of control.

Over the last two decades, recovery of the vibrant connection between modernism and the Harlem Renaissance has helped integrate two fields long separated by a color line that unwittingly replicates the very segrega- tion under which Black artists suffered in the early twentieth century. As Mark A. Sanders says, "a discussion of the New Negro Renaissance and its relation to American modernism begins not with our received New

Critical sense of the era, but with a look at . . . a heterodox modernism in which New Negroes participated fully."[46] Or, as Girard makes clear in her critique of J. Saunders Redding and John Crowe Ransom, "Like Ransom, Redding was willing to leave behind an extraordinary diversity of poetry in the name of formal innovation."[47] New Negro women poets arguably have suffered the most from this narrowing of how we define modernist poetry. As I look across the scholarship on these understudied writers of the modernist era, I am struck by the importance of recovering the context for their work, whether that be literary, political, biographical, or historical. Without that context, women's poetry can be trivialized, misunderstood, distorted, maligned, forgotten. Whereas high modernist art leaned toward the shocking, the abstract, art for art's sake, and New Criticism sought to view the work of art as an autonomous entity, New Negro artists sought connection with the masses and to use art as a weapon against segregation. Poets needed to be accessible, attuned to the ear and eye of readers and listeners. Barred from most media outlets and positions of power by racism, Black women poets declared their modernity by valorizing their truth in passionate embrace of the lived moment as experienced by the dark female body and by seizing their power as artists to create a new more beautiful world. It has taken a while for us to provide that context, and yet more needs to be recovered, but scholarship seeking to restore modernism's diverse, democratic, feminist beginning has made it possible for us to hear those voices once again.

Notes

1. Cynthia Davis and Verner D. Mitchell, "Modernism and the Urban Frontier in the Work of Dorothy West and Helene Johnson," in *A Companion to the Harlem Renaissance*, ed. Cherene Sherrard-Johnson (Chichester, UK: Wiley-Blackwell, 2015), 103–118.
2. Emily R. Rutter, "'Belch the pity! / Straddle the city!': Helene Johnson's Late Poetry and the Rhetoric of Empowerment," *African American Review* 47, no. 4 (2014): 495–509.
3. Katherine R. Lynes, "'A real honest-to-cripe jungle': Contested Authenticities in Helene Johnson's 'Bottled,'" *Modernism/modernity* 14, no. 3 (2007): 517–525; Nina Miller, *Making Love Modern: The Intimate Public Worlds of New York's Literary Women* (New York: Oxford University Press, 1999).
4. Belinda Wheeler and Louis J. Parascandola, eds., *Heroine of the Harlem Renaissance and Beyond: Gwendolyn Bennett's Selected Writings* (University Park, PA: Pennsylvania State University Press, 2018). Bennett composed over fifty unpublished poems in the decade following the 1920s that are housed in

her archive at the Schomburg Center for Research in Black Culture (hereafter cited as SCRBC). Wheeler and Parascandola include fifteen of them, one of which uses urban slang to bring northern working-class male characters to life, "Wise Guys" (1938). Bennett's unfinished novel, *The Call* (1928–1932), features southern female working-class characters who speak in the vernacular.

5. Bennett's "Song" and Dunbar-Nelson's "Music" are reprinted in *Shadowed Dreams: Women's Poetry of the Harlem Renaissance*, ed. Maureen Honey (New Brunswick: Rutgers University Press, 2006), 6–7, 94. "Negro Church" is in Bennett's unpublished poetry file in her archive at the SCRBC.

6. Lucy Mae Turner's collection, *'Bout Cullud Fokses* (New York: Henry Harrison Pub., 1938), makes superb use of the vernacular and shines a light on working-class realities for African Americans. Grimké's vast amount of unpublished poetry is housed at the Moorland-Spingarn Research Center at Howard University (hereafter cited as MSRC). Gloria T. Hull was the first to address Grimké's lesbian-themed unpublished works in *Color, Sex, and Poetry: Three Women Writers of the Harlem Renaissance* (Bloomington: Indiana University Press, 1987).

7. Melissa Girard, "J. Saunders Redding and the 'Surrender' of African American Women's Poetry," *PMLA* 132, no. 2 (2017): 281.

8. Jenny Hyest, "Anne Spencer's Feminist Modernist Poetics," *Journal of Modern Literature* 38, no. 3 (2015): 129–147.

9. Jane Kuenz, "Modernism, Mass Culture, and the Harlem Renaissance: The Case of Countee Cullen," *Modernism/modernity* 14, no. 3 (2007): 507–508.

10. Melissa Girard, "'Jeweled Bindings': Modernist Women's Poetry and the Limits of Sentimentality," in *The Oxford Handbook of Modern and Contemporary American Poetry*, ed. Cary Nelson (New York: Oxford University Press, 2012), 96–119.

11. Keith D. Leonard, "African American Women Poets and the Power of the Word," in *The Cambridge Companion to African American Women's Literature*, ed. Angelyn Mitchell and Danielle K. Taylor (New York: Cambridge University Press, 2009), 177.

12. Erin D. Chapman, *Prove It on Me: New Negroes, Sex, and Popular Culture in the 1920s* (New York: Oxford University Press, 2012), 114–151.

13. Melissa Prunty Kemp, "African American Women Poets, the Harlem Renaissance, and Modernism: An Apology," *Callaloo* 36: 789–801.

14. Miller, *Making Love Modern*, 211–216.

15. Chapman, *Prove It*, 17.

16. Stephanie Leigh Batiste, *Darkening Mirrors: Imperial Representation in Depression-Era African American Performance* (Durham, NC: Duke University Press, 2011); Jayna Brown, *Babylon Girls: Black Women Performers and the Shaping of the Modern* (Durham, NC: Duke University Press, 2008).

17. Chapman, *Prove It*, 78–113.

18. Miller, *Making Love Modern*, 152.

19. Laila Haidarali, *Brown Beauty: Color, Sex, and Race from the Harlem Renaissance to World War II* (New York: New York University Press, 2018), 28.

20. Maureen Honey, *Aphrodite's Daughters: Three Modernist Poets of the Harlem Renaissance* (New Brunswick: Rutgers University Press, 2016).

21. Angelina Weld Grimké, "A Mona Lisa," in *Caroling Dusk: An Anthology of Verse by Negro Poets of the Twenties*, ed. Countee Cullen (New York: Harper & Brothers, 1927), 42.

22. Gwendolyn B. Bennett, "Comrades," Unpublished Poetry, Gwendolyn Bennett Papers, SCRBC.

23. Mae V. Cowdery, "Insatiate," in *We Lift Our Voices and Other Poems* (Philadelphia: Alpress, 1936), 57.

24. Angelina Weld Grimké, "[I let you kiss my mouth]," Unpublished Poetry, Angelina Weld Grimké Collection, MSRC, Howard University.

25. Gwendolyn B. Bennett, "To a Dark Girl," in *Caroling Dusk*, ed. Cullen, 157.

26. Mae V. Cowdery, "Longings," *The Crisis* (December 1927): 337.

27. Mae V. Cowdery, "The Young Voice Cries," *Harlem* (November 1928): 14.

28. Angelina Weld Grimké, "A Trilogy," Unpublished Poetry, MSRC.

29. Bennett, "Fantasy," in *Caroling Dusk*, 158.

30. Mae V. Cowdery, "Four Poems After the Japanese," in *We Lift Our Voices*, 12.

31. These tenets of modernism are described in Amy Lowell, *Tendencies in Modern American Poetry* (New York: Macmillan, 1917); Harriet Monroe, *Poets and Their Art* (New York: Macmillan, 1932); and Louis Untermeyer, *The New Era in American Poetry* (New York: Henry Holt & Co., 1919).

32. Angelina Weld Grimké, "My Shrine," February 24, 1902, Scrapbook, box 38–15, file 243, MSRC.

33. Gwendolyn B. Bennett, "Street Lamps in Early Spring," *Opportunity* (May 1926): 152.

34. Mae V. Cowdery, "Dusk," in *Ebony and Topaz: A Collecteana*, ed. Charles S. Johnson (New York: National Urban League, 1927), 23.

35. Miller, *Making Love Modern*, 215.

36. Angelina Weld Grimké, "Thou Art So Far, So Far," Unpublished Poetry, MSRC.

37. Gwendolyn B. Bennett, "Communion," Unpublished Poetry, SCRBC.

38. Mae V. Cowdery, "Farewell," *The Crisis* (February 1929): 50.

39. Angelina Weld Grimké, "Grass Fingers," in *Caroling Dusk*, ed. Cullen, 38.

40. Gwendolyn B. Bennett, "Song," *Palms* (October 1926): 21.

41. Mae V. Cowdery, "Interlude," *We Lift Our Voices*, 44.

42. After her father died in 1930, Grimké moved to the Washington Heights area of New York where she lived until her death in 1958. Bennett went to high school in Brooklyn, spent much time with her parents there after graduating, attended Columbia University as well as the Pratt Institute, and lived in New York from 1930 until her retirement to Kutztown, Pennsylvania in 1968. Born and raised in Philadelphia, Cowdery moved to New York after graduating from high school in 1928 and visited the city frequently even after she moved back to Philadelphia in the 1930s.

43. Nella Larsen's *Quicksand*, in *Quicksand and Passing*, ed. Deborah McDowell (1928; London: Serpent's Tail, 1989) depicts the conflict between respectable New Negro women activists and women who ventured out into Harlem's cabarets.
44. K. T. Ewing, "What Kind of Woman? Alberta Hunter and Expressions of Black Female Sexuality in the Twentieth Century," in *Black Female Sexualities*, ed. Trimiko Melancon and Joanne M. Braxton (New Brunswick: Rutgers University Press, 2015), 102.
45. See, for example, Carolivia Herron, ed., *Selected Works of Angelina Weld Grimké* (New York: Oxford University Press, 1991); Claudia Tate, ed., *The Selected Works of Georgia Douglas Johnson* (New York: G. K. Hall, 1997); J. Lee Greene, *Time's Unfading Garden: Anne Spencer's Life and Poetry* (Baton Rouge: Louisiana State University Press, 1977).
46. Mark A. Sanders, "American Modernism and the New Negro Renaissance," in *The Cambridge Companion to American Modernism*, ed. Walter Kalaidjian (New York: Cambridge University Press, 2005), 130.
47. Girard, "J. Saunders Redding," 287.

CHAPTER 10

Children's Literature of the Harlem Renaissance

Katharine Capshaw

In 1912, W. E. B. Du Bois published an issue of *The Crisis* magazine dedicated to the topic of black childhood, the first of what would become an annual number. He introduced the issue by articulating a theory of inclusivity for child readers:

> This is the Children's Number, and as it has grown and developed in the editor's hesitating hands, it has in some way come to seem a typical rather than a special number. Indeed, there is a sense in which all numbers and all words of a magazine of ideas must point to the child – to that vast immortality and wide sweep and infinite possibility which the child represents.[1]

African American families and communities had always been deeply devoted to their children and to their possibilities, but the Harlem Renaissance was a singular moment for the development of black children's literature, appearing in both periodicals and long-form publications. Major writers of the era, like Langston Hughes and Nella Larsen, published works for young people, as did a range of educators, playwrights, and academics, from Carter G. Woodson to May Miller. Swirling around this surge in black children's literature were new ideas about childhood in the larger cultural milieu; writers were influenced by black uplift commitments to cultural advancement, progressive-era child welfare reform, post-war anti-colonialist sensibilities, and intensified public embrace of social justice through the ascendance of the National Association for the Advancement of Colored People (NAACP) and other organizations. In large part, black children's literature grew from a convergence of these ideologies of progress with access to print venues. Considered broadly, children's literature of the Harlem Renaissance responded to the era's massive cultural shifts by embracing education, child activism, community galvanization, and black citizenship demands.

In response to broad cultural shifts and to the uptick in racial violence after World War I, Du Bois and others across the Harlem Renaissance struggled to define what kinds of material to offer to young people. Should children be sheltered from incidents of racial violence? Should young people be offered the same level of political and social commentary as adults? How might texts for children approach futurity, building a new black nation through psychological and educational preparation of the young? In that first Children's Number, Du Bois included many of the features that would typify his wide-ranging approach to a child audience. A photograph of the toddler son of Charles Young, first black military attaché, sits across from a description of lynchings; the conclusion of Jessie Fauset's "Some Books for Boys and Girls" appears on the same page as an account of October events in black history; and a discussion of African American death rates prefaces a children's folk tale from Uganda. Sprinkled throughout the issue are beautiful photographs of children of various ages. Early in the 1910s, Du Bois recognized the need to include young people in vital political and social conversations, and he moved into the Harlem Renaissance with a deep commitment to the education and edification of all readers of *The Crisis*.

Texts for black children had appeared since the nineteenth century,[2] but it was the Harlem Renaissance that galvanized creative energies around youth. While the ideological currents shaping children's literature were multiple, the sensibility producing such texts insisted on the need for the "New Negro" to arise from a new generation of young people. Many texts for children emerged from the desire from the educated elite to uplift and improve the lower classes, including Silas X. Floyd's revised version of *Floyd's Flowers: Duties and Beauties for Colored Children*,[3] which in 1920 was published with Edward S. Green's *National Capital Code of Etiquette* (1920), aimed at adults. Monroe A. Majors issued *First Steps and Nursery Rhymes* (1920), an innovative collection of poetry, conduct material, and photographs. Yet the racial uplift contingent of the "Talented Tenth" was not the only group invested in young people at the dawn of the Harlem Renaissance. Black Caribbean radicals issued a children's periodical, *Our Boys and Girls* (1919–1920), which was edited by Anselmo R. Jackson, a Virgin Island immigrant to New York, and supported by a group of intellectuals and activists, including Claude McKay, Arturo Schomburg, John Edward Bruce, W. A. Domingo (who had been the editor of Marcus Garvey's *Negro World*), and Hubert Harrison, among others. Only a few issues of the periodical remain in archives,[4] but they reveal the children's magazine's searing critique of US imperialism in the Caribbean and around the world, and an approach to working-class people akin to that of Garvey's Universal Negro Improvement Association. *Our Boys and Girls* appears particularly to respond to the failures of America to promote racial equality in the wake of World War I. From thinkers concerned with etiquette and uplift to those who aimed to develop child radicals, children's writers were deeply invested in creating a new, modern sense of identity among young people, with a variety of incarnations.

Periodicals, Politics, and the Emergence of Black Children's Literature

As Du Bois's initial editorial demonstrates, the issue that propelled such a range of responses to the challenge of writing for young people was the ubiquity of racial prejudice. Like *Our Boys and Girls*, Du Bois's *The Crisis* used the post-war moment to introduce a diasporic sensibility to its readership, decrying European and American colonialism, and supporting the era's pan-African movement. Children were among the readers of Du Bois's political columns, especially those published in the annual Children's Number and annual Education Number. Yet the "Red Summer" of 1919 was a turning point for Du Bois, a moment that propelled him deeper into children's literature through the publication of the landmark *Brownies' Book*.[5] Announcing the new magazine in October 1919, Du Bois laments the effect of exposure to racial violence in *The Crisis*, saying "To educate them in human hatred is more disastrous to them than to the hated; to seek to raise them in ignorance of their racial identity and peculiar situation is inadvisable – impossible."[6] The *Brownies' Book* allowed Du Bois to foster children's sense of self-worth in the face of individual hostility and systemic racism. In creating this separate publication for young people, Du Bois spearheaded the field of black children's literature. His may have not been the first publication for black children, but it was the most substantive and influential, and it retained a political import by reporting on lynching and other racial atrocities, and through depictions of anti-lynching efforts, like the Silent Protest Parade of 1917. Du Bois's monthly "As the Crow Flies" column on world affairs was a signal achievement in children's literature; Michelle H. Phillips notes its "unconventionally mature" perspective in that it "exhaustively recorded the experiences of race-based discrimination the world over."[7]

While the magazine refused to shelter children from the vexed state of race relations, it also embraced a true multiplicity of genres and images for a black child readership. One of the goals of the magazine was to "make colored children realize that being colored is a normal, beautiful thing";[8] Du Bois, and the magazine's literary editor Jessie Fauset, suffused the publication with images of black beauty and attached black childhood to a sense of wonder. From poetry, plays, and short stories, to puzzles, dances, quizzes, folk tales, games, and fairy tales, the *Brownies' Book* aimed to include and involve children in the forms of children's literature and play that were ascendant in the early twentieth century. These forms, however, were always inflected with a black sensibility in the magazine: African fairy tales, princes, and princesses appear on its pages, as does black Santa Claus, children's plays with black fairies, and biographies of Harriet Tubman, Benjamin Banneker, and others. The magazine imagined its reader as capacious, curious, resilient, and ambitious, offering young people content that brings together oral traditions, fairy-tale lore, anthropological descriptions, among other forms. Each issue was also lavishly illustrated by black artists like Marcellus Hawkins, Hilda Rue Wilkinson, and Laura Wheeler (Waring), and included dozens of photographs of black children and young people. In terms of inculcating a sense the reader's racial self-worth, the *Brownies' Book*'s expansiveness allowed readers to embrace a range of definitions of black value and beauty. In this way, Du Bois and Fauset's courageous publication opened up possibilities for black childhood and representation.

Under the sure hand of Fauset, the publication also issued some of the earliest pieces by the luminaries of the Harlem Renaissance, including works by Langston Hughes, Georgia Douglas Johnson, Mary Effie Lee (Newsome), and Nella Larsen. It also printed plays, including those by Willis Richardson who published "The King's Dilemma" (December 1920), "The Children's Treasure" (June 1921), and "The Dragon's Tooth" (October 1921), and went on to become the first African American playwright to stage a serious play on Broadway ("The Chip Woman's Fortune," 1923). The publication ended its two-year run because of a printer's strike, although in fact subscriptions had only approached 5,000, whereas *The Crisis* subscriptions in the late 1910s reached 100,000. Nevertheless, Du Bois continued throughout his tenure at *The Crisis* to publish literature and images for children. Effie Lee Newsome, who wrote from Alabama, far from the "mecca" of Harlem or vibrant Washington, DC, issued nearly every month from March 1925 until November 1930 her *Crisis* "Little Page," which focused on nature writing and also included her illustrations. Du Bois's yearly list of race "Debit and Credit" in 1923 lists four prominent black poets: "Hughes, Cullen, Lee-Newsome, and Toomer."[9] The fact that Du Bois includes Newsome – the only woman on his list – suggests her prominence and wide readership and speaks to the erasure of children's literature from historical memory.

Du Bois's publications for children helped shape activist sensibility and expand readers' conceptions of black identity. Speaking of his childhood in rural Kentucky, Horace Mann Bond – the first black president of Lincoln University and father of Civil Rights leader Julian Bond – addressed the influence of Du Bois's work for children:

> Through the *Crisis* Du Bois helped shape my inner world to a degree impossible to imagine in the world of contemporary children, and the flood of various mass media to which they are exposed. . . . The real truth about a brutal social order, however frightening; the beauty and dignity of black people; these learnings were almost impossible to come by, for children of whatever color or race in the USA, when I was a child. This is what I know that Du Bois did for me.[10]

The Children's Number, *Brownies' Book*, and "Little Page" founded the field of black children's literature, revealing the Harlem Renaissance's deep commitment to building a new generation of black citizens.

Black Children's Drama and Redressing Racial Biases in Education

As the most prominent intellectual of the black community, Du Bois's profound investment in childhood is quite legible. What is more ephemeral, but no less influential, is the Harlem Renaissance's dedication to childhood through grassroots venues, like local theater. Perhaps the most pervasive populist creative endeavor for young people during the 1920s and 1930s was, in fact, drama. Its heart was located in Washington, DC, home to Howard University and the important black high schools, Dunbar, Armstrong, and Cardozo. While *The Crisis* publications had an activist imperative and included a true miscellany of forms, children's drama during the Harlem Renaissance largely responded to the educational and textual inequities experienced by black young people. The 1920s witnessed an upswing in the education of African Americans across the country. As David Levering Lewis reminds us, only 2,132 African Americans attended college in 1917; ten years later, that number had reached 13,580.[11] With the initiation of the Rosenwald school building program in 1914, coupled with the Negro Schools Fund of the Jeanes Foundation, elementary education for black children in the South soared in the 1920s.[12] By 1930, black child literacy in the South approached 80 percent, and nearly 90 percent of black children went to school.[13] Of course, educational parity with whites in terms of facilities, teacher training, books, transportation, and supplies was nonexistent. Particularly jarring for black teachers working in segregated spaces under state control was the depiction of black identity in textbooks. As the February 1921 "The Grown-Ups' Corner" of *The Brownies' Book* noted, for the black child, "All through school life his text-books contain much about white people and little or nothing about his own race. All the pictures he sees are of white people. Most of the books he reads are by white authors, and his heroes and heroines are white."[14]

In response to the degradations of African American culture, both within classrooms and in the larger culture, community members and teachers wrote and produced performances that offered historical correct-ive and spoke to the distinctive cultural contributions of black America, as well as acknowledging the accomplishments of historical figures in Africa and in the Caribbean.[15] Generally, children's drama of the era falls into three categories: pageantry, history plays, and domestic drama. Yet what unifies this body of work is its adherence to the era's respect for black child sophistication and capability. Just as *The Crisis* publication engaged young people in complicated civic and cultural discussions, especially in terms of racial violence, the plays and pageants of the era place the education of children at the heart of definitions of community. These plays and pageants deploy various modes of textual authority, an especially revealing gesture given the ascendance of child literacy and the courage of black schoolteacher playwrights. The performances staged written evidence of black historical accomplishment, often by quoting from legal documents, almanacs, magazine articles, poetry, and novels. In venerating the textual on stage, the plays and pageants made concrete and verifiable the stories, histories, and accomplishments sought by all community members, phrased in terms that would please the literate child audience. It is as though schoolteacher playwrights responded directly to Bella Seymour, who wrote to Du Bois at the *Brownies' Book* to recount her child's question: "My little girl has been studying about Betsy Ross and George Washington and the others, and she says: 'Mamma, didn't colored folks do anything?' When I tell her as much as I know about our folks, she says: 'Well, that's just stories. Didn't they ever do anything in a book?'"[16] Because young people lived in a school culture that embraced the textual and evidentiary, the playwrights made written texts a palpable presence on stage, relying on staged versions of texts to offer proof of black cultural achievements.

Of course, black children also lived in home cultures suffused with oral tradition. Perhaps this doubled literacy is one reason why plays and pageants were the site of community galvanization, offering stories of black history verifiable in text, but oral in transmission so that all members of the audience could access them. The textual emphasis of plays and pageants also extends from the long-standing tradition of public recitation within black communities, particularly of the works of Paul Laurence Dunbar, whose poems are fraught objects on the page (given their indebtedness to the plantation tradition of dialect poetry) but come alive with satirical interpretive possibility when recited. Alice Dunbar Nelson's popular *The Dunbar Speaker and Entertainer* (1920), which is dedicated to "the children of the race which is herein celebrated," contains poems on a range of subjects – from comedic to heroic – as well as suggested programs of poetry recitation along with accompanying music. Also influential on the shape of children's drama was the emergence of progressive-era pageantry as a form of community articulation. The white leaders of the American Pageant Association saw pageantry as "art of the people, by the people, for the people,"[17] which Du Bois himself may have refigured in arguing for drama "about us, by us, for us, and near us."[18] Du Bois staged his pageant, "Star of Ethiopia," from 1913 to 1924, using nearly 1,200 participants in a single production. At the end of the 1910s, pageantry migrated from large-scale efforts to local school productions, and schoolteachers took up the form with enthusiasm.

Black children's pageants typically begin with a female figure, a chronicler or spirit of history, who appears onstage carrying a scroll or tablet from which she reads the record of black achievement. In *Two Races* by Inez M. Burke, a teacher at Charles Young Elementary School in Washington, DC, the Spirit of Negro Progress introduces famous figures like Frederick Douglass and Booker T. Washington, as well as the school's namesake; the Spirit notes of Colonel Young and his black soldiers in the Spanish-American War, "Roosevelt . . . made a splendid speech in praise of their heroism . . . The Negro has proved his bravery."[19] Like Nannie Helen Burroughs's *When the Truth Gets a Hearing*, which was produced four times between 1916 and 1930 at the school Burroughs founded,[20] Edward J. McCoo's *Ethiopia at the Bar of Justice*, first produced in 1924, relies on the premise of a court hearing to debate the status of people of African descent. McCoo's character, Ethiopia, defends herself against the character of Opposition, and witnesses like History, Civil War Veteran, World War Veteran, Labor, and Business offer evidence of black accomplishment. The play concludes with figures representing the Declaration of Independence, the Anti-Lynch Law, and the Thirteenth, Fourteenth, and Fifteenth Amendments who quote from their documents to settle, decisively, the issue of citizenship and civil rights. In addition to quotations and

Chronicler figures who read evidence, the pageants' emphasis on textuality in pageants becomes especially acute in Louise Lovett's unpublished "Forward" (1935), which she wrote when teaching speech at Cardozo High School. This pageant records the struggles of nineteenth-century figures to establish schools for black children, and uses a range of textual documents, from speeches to Board of Education records. Textuality as a concept gets materialized when the pageant concludes with two "Pages" who dress as sheets of paper; their costumes consist of statistics about black education.[21] Similarly, May Miller's unpublished "The Guide Book" brings to life a text that shaped scholarly and behavioral expectations at Baltimore's Frederick Douglass High School where Miller taught for many years. A character embodies the book, and the stage directions read: "The Guide Book walks slowly and deliberately on the stage. She is a tall, commanding student bearing on her breast an open booklet that is a replica of the Guide Book."[22] For writers like Lovett and Miller, the theater enabled communities to value the textual by extending the reach and embrace of the written word, while at the same time venerating oral and performative traditions.

History plays are similarly invested in documentation of black achievement, but with perhaps less structural alignment with classroom authority. Often authored by educators as a mode of resistance, history plays are intensely revisionary. They take up a site in history that has been overlooked, misinterpreted, or disparaged. Two important anthologies of plays include children's drama alongside adult pieces – *Plays and Pageants from the Life of the Negro* (1930), edited by Willis Richardson, and *Negro History in Thirteen Plays* (1935), edited by Richardson and May Miller – collections that attest to the centrality of work for the young to drama of the period. The children's plays chafe against inherited histories. For example, the 1935 volume contains two dramas about Haiti, a site which by the mid-1930s would be familiar ground for black artists,[23] especially those drawn to heroes and militancy. Yet Helen Webb Harris's *Genifrede: The Daughter of L'Ouverture* and May Miller's *Christophe's Daughters* allow us to recognize the interrogative critical stance of black children's literature during the Harlem Renaissance. The plays disrupt preconceptions about male Haitian revolutionary heroes in order to create a novel perspective on the past and on representation. The plays' feminist perspective fuses with an anti-colonialist undercurrent, since the plays comment not only on the forgotten female agents of history, but also embrace black self-determination in the wake of the US military occupation of Haiti (1915–1934). Other history plays of the era, like Willis Richardson's *Near Calvary* (1935), use history as an analogue to the twentieth-century anti-lynching efforts. Richardson's play focuses on Simon the Cyrenian, an African man who helps Jesus carry the cross. The play considers Simon within the domestic sphere, as is typical of anti-lynching dramas; the setting emphasizes his value to an extended family at home who wait for repercussions from white characters for Simon's assistance to Jesus. The language repeatedly links blackness to courage: "Uncle Simon is brave and black."[24] When authorities knock on the family's door, they also identify him through color: "We are looking for the black man."[25] Since Simon is not at home, the soldiers take Simon's brother, and the play ends with his child asking, "Father is brave; isn't he, Mother?"[26]

The domestic dramas written for young people during the Harlem Renaissance also commented on the need for education, but frequently included a perspective that reveals the class inequities between generations. For example, Thelma Myrtle Duncan's *Sacrifice* (1930), a play written for eighth grade students, juxtaposes the difficult labor of a washerwoman against her children's moral failings in their pursuit of education and white-collar employment.[27] Aimed at "advanced students in high school" as well as in college, May Miller's *Riding the Goat* daringly includes dialect in depicting the tension between Carter, an educated young man described as a "young upstart,"[28] and his community, as he refuses to lead the black lodge's annual parade because he considers it vulgar and showy. The play's climax reveals the man's girlfriend, Ruth, has led the parade in the disguise of Carter, saving the relationship between the young physician and a community that requires both his attentions and their cultural practices. Alice Dunbar-Nelson's school play, *The Quest* (1920), depicts class tensions provocatively by beginning with a group of young people at high school graduation who plan for careers as teacher, nurse, public speaker, lawyer, musician, and businessman. At that graduation, they virtually ignore a woman whose son is stoned by a mob, and then over the course of twenty-five years, succumb to moral temptations and betray their people. One person, Esther, remains committed to southern communities, challenges the others: "I am choked with horror at the corruption within our own ranks. How can we, how can you, how can any of us hope to rise save by purifying the baseness within ourselves?"[29] As these examples demonstrate, domestic dramas for young people served as a form of community galvanization related to that proffered by pageantry. While pageants included all audience members by making oral the authenticating documents of print culture, domestic dramas embrace the ethos of education as a mode of social change, but caution against snobbishness, elitism, separatism, and betrayal of those who have not had educational opportunities. Plays and pageants for young people during the Harlem Renaissance offered an especially vital location for the articulation of a new vision of black childhood, one immersed in the accomplishments of the past, invested in education for the future, and committed to questioning white classroom and historical authority in order to secure cultural survival.

Carter G. Woodson and the Women Artists of Associated Publishers

Carter G. Woodson, the father of black history, strongly supported children's theater, publishing the two major anthologies through his Washington, DC, Associated Publishers, founded in 1921. Along with Du Bois's *Crisis* publications and children's drama, Woodson's publishing work constitutes a third major thread in the field of Harlem Renaissance children's literature. Woodson is best known for founding the Association for the Study of Negro Life and History (1915), the *Journal of Negro History* (1916), and Negro History Week (1926), but throughout his work he remained committed to youth, perhaps as an outgrowth to his tenure teaching high school in West Virginia as a college graduate, and at Armstrong and Dunbar High Schools from 1909 to 1919. Since Woodson's Association sought broad-based engagement with black history, he issued a children's book first in 1928, *African Myths*, which in correspondence he revealed was, perhaps, overwritten: "Some parts of the book would not be considered clear to children of the third or fourth grade."[30] The Associated Publishers turned to women teachers as authors for books for young people, beginning in 1931 with Sadie Iola Daniel's *Women Builders*.

As in the case of plays and pageants, Woodson's authors sought to rebut racist representations of African Americans in textbooks and literature. Two general types of books emerged from Woodson's publishing house: texts that expressly explore black identity and history, and books of poetry that appear "color blind" in language but often speak of racial pride in images. In terms of the first group, black women hoped to transform the place of African American history within segregated educational structures, and offered texts that are sometimes ideologically problematic. Because Woodson's writers wished to infiltrate classrooms across the country, the books are fundamentally torn between celebrating black distinctiveness and demonstrating the alignment of blackness with white America. One can read their work in the 1930s and 1940s as contributing to the civil rights efforts toward school integration, but often their assertions of affinity with white America prove unnerving to a contemporary audience.

For example, Jane Dabney Shackelford's *Child's Story of the Negro* (1938) seeks to celebrate Africa, but accomplishes it through exoticization and strangeness. Addressing her reader about foodways, she asks, "But how would you like roasted locusts, caterpillars, ants, monkeys, rats, beetles, and elephant's feet? I think I would rather go hungry than eat some of those things, wouldn't you?"[31] Her depiction of enslavement aims to ameliorate racial tensions by offering an imaginative tour of a successful plantation. Shackelford's papers reveal that her original version was even more conciliatory than what appears in print: "I tried to write it in such a way that children would not hate white people because of the institution of slavery. I emphasized not cruel masters, but that happy times some slaves enjoyed in the evening."[32] When she read the chapter to her class, a child asked, "O, Mrs. Shackelford, could we be slaves again?" To her credit, Shackelford revised: "I spent the following weekend rewriting 'Life on a Southern Plantation.'"[33] Similarly, *Word Pictures of the Great*, authored by two teachers and their principal at George Bell Elementary School in Washington, DC, offers beautiful biographies of black artists, musicians, writers, and scientists that are threaded with moments of jarring affection between slave owners and black people, often figuring whites as adoptive parents to enslaved children. Writers' impulses during the era of segregated education sometimes put them at odds with their commitment to racial pride, and as a result such books can appear deeply conflicted to a modern audience.

More successful, perhaps, are the books of poetry Woodson's publishers issued, including a collection by his sister, Bessie Woodson Yancey. Unlike her well-educated and traveled brother, Yancey remained in Huntington, West Virginia for much of her life, and authored perhaps the first black Appalachian book for children, *Echoes from the Hills* (1939), which was heavily indebted to Paul Laurence Dunbar. It offers tribute to West Virginia as a refuge for those who seek independence, and imagines mine work as requiring racial parity. In "Comradery," she writes, "There's one place on this planet where / A man is just a brother . . . Black or white, he's just a comrade, / When a heart is rent and sore."[34] She also writes in dialect about black fatherhood, as in "Negro Lullaby," which concludes in a prayer, "O mek mah chile er man! / (Sleep! mah lil lamb, sleep!)."[35] Other books of poetry barely spoke of racial subjects. *The Picture Poetry Book* (1935) by Gertrude Parthenia McBrown and *Gladiola Garden* (1940) by Effie Lee Newsome, the writer who worked with Du Bois on the *Brownies' Book* and *The Crisis* "Little Page," furnish pleasant verses about flowers, fairies, insects, animals, and weather that do not mention race. Yet both volumes bear images by Lois Mailou Jones, the important black artist who served as Woodson's primary illustrator for the publishing house.

Jones expresses in images what the poets themselves could not say. For instance, McBrown's "Happy Fairies" concludes with "I like to watch the fairies / When they're skipping 'round about; / They're always glad and cheery / When they're dancing in and out."[36] Jones's accompanying illustration depicts seven fairies, some seated on flowers and some dancing beneath, that are clearly coded as black. Throughout the book and across Newsome's work as well, Jones's gorgeous, romantic images of black children and black fairies claim for the reader a stake in the fairy lore that permeated child culture. While Newsome's *Gladiola Garden* does contain a poem that references African American identity in "Spirituals," the illustrations leave a more lasting impression upon the reader; Jones animates largely innocuous poems with astonishing beauty and racial dignity. In fact, Newsome herself wished to infuse the text with a black sensibility, including in her original manuscript such poems as "Bronze Legacy," perhaps her most famous text, which concludes with "I thank God, then, I am brown / Brown has mighty things to do."[37] Woodson, however, excised the race-conscious poems from the collection, deleting even the mention of "Negro" children from the preface, and then promoting the book in his *Negro History Bulletin* as "remarkable in that it is not a book about Negroes, and apparently not written by a Negro in the sense of being racial. . . . Her mind is that of a poet, not that of a Negro."[38] The exchange between Woodson and Newsome prefacing *Gladiola Garden* speaks to the profound dependence of black women writers on male arbiters, especially in the case of Newsome who wrote from Birmingham, Alabama, far from sites of power in Washington, DC and Harlem. The reshaping of *Gladiola Garden* also excavates Woodson's desire for his publishing house to succeed in this intensely difficult moment for black writers who wished to infiltrate white libraries and schoolhouses. While racial claims could not be staged via the written word, images could speak of the value of black identity; Jones's illustrations remain as evidence of Woodson's, McBrown's, and Newsome's commitment to exquisite African American representation and to the idea of the black child at home in nature and in fairyland.

Langston Hughes and Arna Bontemps: Empathy and Mainstream Publishing

A final important site of Harlem Renaissance children's literature is the work of Langston Hughes and Arna Bontemps, major writers who issued books for children from mainstream publishing houses for an integrated audience. Together they published *Popo and Fifina: Children of Haiti* (1932), and authored "The Pasteboard Bandit" (1935), "Bon-Bon Buddy" (1935), and "The Boy of the Border" (1935), which were unpublished in the 1930s. Separately, the authors issued an extraordinary body of work for children across their lives; Hughes's first publications appeared in Du Bois's *Brownies' Book* as a teenager, and his populist aesthetic drew him to youth audiences as he grew older, including his important poetry collection, *The Dream Keeper* (1932). Hughes went on in the 1950s and 1960s to publish extensively nonfiction for children in the Watts' "First Book" series and in Dodd, Mead & Co's First Americans series. He was working on a picture book, *Black Misery* (1969), when he passed away in 1967. Bontemps published a dozen children's books by the mid-1950s, but his work during the Harlem Renaissance included *You Can't Pet a Possum* (1934) and *Sad-Faced Boy* (1937). While *The Crisis* publications directly engage prejudice and racial violence, and the plays and Woodson's texts negotiate historical and cultural defamations of black people, Hughes and Bontemps write with a palpable awareness of their white publishers and interracial audiences. They both sought financial success through children's books, as their correspondence reveals, and wanted the recognition of the Newbery Award. Since they enter a wider literary landscape than other more local children's writers, Hughes and Bontemps address a range of perspectives and approaches, and are often deeply invested in cross-cultural identification and the refutation of stereotype.

Popo and Fifina depicts working people in Haiti, including children, in terms that respect their sense of beauty and artistic expression. Hughes had visited Haiti in 1931 and returned with an intensified interest in class divisions within black cultures; *Popo and Fifina* appeared at the same moment as Hughes's searing *New Masses* essay, "People without Shoes" (1931), which criticized the US occupation of Haiti and the mixed-race ruling class. *Popo and Fifina*, however, depicts the daily life of poor children, but with understated critique of social inequity. The authors aimed to engender a reader's admiration and affection for the characters in order to dispel bias against Haiti. For instance, in depicting the "poor men" who labored for a dozen years to build the Citadel, Haiti's revolutionary fort, the characters put themselves into the minds of the workers rather than celebrating the monument itself, "so that the French might not come and make them slaves again. And that was why the men worked so hard."[39] Across the text, Hughes and Bontemps attempt to engender reader empathy with the characters, whether by describing the children's joy in play, the mother's cooking practices, or the father's labor as a fisherman. A woodcarver character offers a statement on art that is analogous to the approach of the text: "What I am inside makes the design. The design is a picture of the way I feel. . . . And when people look at your design . . . they will feel as you felt when you made the design. That's the fine part. That is really the only way that people can ever know how other people feel."[40] Empathy, especially for the economically and socially disadvantaged, is the express purpose of children's literature for Hughes and Bontemps. Hughes's poetry collection, *The Dream Keeper*, also appeared in 1932, and contains his most important poems, including "The Weary Blues," "I, Too," "The Negro Speaks of Rivers," "Mother to Son," and texts Hughes published in the *Brownies' Book* as well as in collections first aimed at adults. *The Dream Keeper* is structured carefully, beginning with seemingly colorblind poems about fairies and sea travel, and concluding with blues poems and masterpieces of black identity, a structure that perhaps seeks first to entice an interracial audience with what they might expect from a children's book, and ends with poems that call on child participation in social change.

Bontemps's work engages stereotypes about the black south, offering multilayered narratives that deflate assumptions about rural inferiority through playful, animated characterization. Most striking is *Sad-Faced Boy* (1937), a depiction of three children, Slumber and his brothers, who leave Alabama for Harlem. His face an unreadable trickster mask, Slumber at first appears a country bumpkin, lost in the subways, markets, and libraries of New York. Bontemps's commentary on the failures of the city land squarely on the abuses of capitalism; Slumber thinks, "good luck tricks worked very well when he was at home in Alabama and in the country" but they "wouldn't help you to get a cool water ice when you didn't have the nickel."[41] By the end of the book, Slumber and his brothers have decided to leave the city, enacting a reverse "Great Migration" back to Alabama, with its rural beauty and familial comforts.

Vast and various, Harlem Renaissance children's literature sought to engage a young audience in progressive iterations of history and identity. The effort transpired through major voices, like Du Bois and Hughes, and grassroots efforts, like schoolteacher playwrights, and at locations across the country, from Indiana to Alabama, West Virginia to Washington, DC. In all of this generative work, we witness a faith that the newest African Americans will discover their history, embrace their beauty, and claim their civil rights.

Notes

1. W. E. B. Du Bois, "Of Children," *The Crisis* 4, no. 6 (October 1912): 287.
2. See Katharine Capshaw and Anna Mae Duane, eds., *Who Writes for Black Children? African American Children's Literature before 1900* (Minneapolis: University of Minnesota Press, 2017).
3. *Floyd's Flowers* was originally published in 1905, but was revised and reissued across the Harlem Renaissance, including 1920, 1922, and 1925. See Silas X. Floyd, *Short Stories for Colored People Both Old and Young* (Washington, DC: Austin Jenkins, 1920).
4. The Schomburg Center for Research in Black Culture, part of the New York City public library system, holds two issues of *Our Boys and Girls*, dated March 1919 and October 1919. Advertisements for the children's periodical appear in Cyril Briggs's *The Crusader* during the span of 1919. See Katharine Capshaw, "War, The Black Diaspora, and Anti-Colonialist Journalism: The Case of *Our Boys and Girls*," in *Children's Literature and Culture of the First World War*, eds Lissa Paul, Rosemary Ross Johnston, and Emma Short (New York: Routledge, 2016), 77–92.
5. Katharine Capshaw, *Children's Literature of the Harlem Renaissance* (Bloomington: Indiana University Press, 2004).
6. W. E. B. Du Bois, "The True Brownies," *The Crisis* 18, no. 6 (October 1919): 285.
7. Michelle H. Phillips, *Representations of Childhood in American Modernism* (New York: Palgrave, 2016), 120.
8. Du Bois, "True Brownies," 286.
9. W. E. B. Du Bois, "Debit and Credit," *The Crisis* 25, no. 4 (February 1923): 151.
10. Horace Mann Bond, "The Legacy of W. E. B. Du Bois," *Freedomways* (Winter 1965): 16–17.
11. David Levering Lewis, *When Harlem Was in Vogue* (New York: Penguin, 1997), 157–158.
12. Prospects for high school education for African Americans, however, were bleak. On the rise of schooling in the South, see James D. Anderson, *The Education of Blacks in the South, 1860–1935* (Chapel Hill: University of North Carolina Press, 1988).
13. See Eric Anderson and Alfred A. Moss, Jr., *Dangerous Donations: Northern Philanthropy and Southern Black Education, 1902–1930* (Columbia: University of Missouri Press, 1999), 11.
14. "Grown-Ups' Corner," *Brownies' Book* 2, no. 2 (February 1921): 63.
15. See Clare Corbould's discussion of pageantry in *Becoming African Americans: Black Public Life in Harlem, 1919–1939* (Cambridge, MA: Harvard, 2009); also, see plays on Haiti and Cuba in *Negro History in Thirteen Plays*, ed. Willis Richardson and May Miller (Washington, DC: Associated Publishers, 1935).

16. Bella Seymour, "Letter to the Grown-Ups' Corner," *Brownies' Book* 1, no. 2 (February 1920): 45.

17. Naima Prevots, *American Pageantry: A Movement for Art and Democracy* (Ann Arbor: UMI Research, 1990), 1.

18. W. E. B. Du Bois, "Krigwa Players Little Negro Theater," *The Crisis* 32, no. 3 (July 1926): 134.

19. Inez M. Burke, "Two Races," in *Plays and Pageants from the Life of the Negro*, ed. Willis Richardson (Washington, DC: Associated Publishers, 1930), 300.

20. See Murray's discussion of the pageant in light of Burroughs's work at the National Training School for Women and Girls. Alana D. Murray, "Countering the Master Narrative in US Social Studies: Nannie Helen Burroughs and New Narratives in History Education," in *Histories of Social Studies and Race, 1865–2000*, ed. Christine Woyshner and Chara Haeussler Bohan (New York: Palgrave, 2012), 99–114.

21. Louise J. Lovett, "Forward: A Pageant in Five Episodes," Ts. Box 120–2, Folder 100, William A. Joiner Papers, Moorland-Spingarn Research Center, Howard University, Washington, DC.

22. May Miller, "The Guide Book," Ts. Box 17, Folder 12, May Miller Papers, Stuart A. Rose Manuscript, Archives, and Rare Book Library, Emory University.

23. African Americans saw in Haiti a potent source of inspiration as the first independent black nation and as a site of distinct folk identity. Zora Neale Hurston explored Haiti in *Tell My Horse* (Philadelphia: J. B. Lippincott, 1938), and composed her masterpiece, *Their Eyes Were Watching God* (1937; Urbana: University of Illinois Press, 1987), while living in Haiti. On stage, Leslie Pinckney Hill presented *Touissant L'Ouverture* in the late 1920s and Shirley Graham produced a full-scale opera about Haiti entitled "Tom-Tom" in 1932. On film, Josephine Baker starred as a Haitian in *Zou Zou* (1934), and Langston Hughes offered the play *Drums of Haiti* in 1935, which became *Emperor of Haiti* in 1936, and then an opera, *Troubled Island*, in 1949.

24. Willis Richardson, "Near Calvary," *Negro History in Thirteen Plays*, ed. Willis Richardson and May Miller (Washington, DC: Associated Publishers, 1935), 101.

25. Ibid., 105.

26. Ibid., 107.

27. Thelma Myrtle Duncan, *Sacrifice*, in *Plays and Pageants from the Life of the Negro*, ed. Willis Richardson (Washington, DC: Associated Publishers, 1930), 3–24.

28. May Miller, "Riding the Goat," in *Plays and Pageants from the Life of the Negro*, ed. Willis Richardson (Washington, DC: Associated Publishers, 1930), 141–176.

29. Alice Dunbar-Nelson, *The Quest*, Ts. Box 20, Folder 380, Alice Dunbar-Nelson Collection, University of Delaware, Newark (Act 2.11).

30. Carter G. Woodson, Letter to Jane Dabney Shackelford, April 7, 1936, Ts. Jane Dabney Shackelford Collection, Accession Number 780222, Series VI,

folder 1. Community Archives, Vigo County Public Library, Terre Haute, Ind.

31. Jane Dabney Shackelford, *The Child's Story of the Negro* (Washington, DC: Associated Publishers, 1938), 33.

32. Jane Dabney Shackelford, "How I Became a Writer," Ms. Jane Dabney Shackelford Collection, Accession Number 800627, D.C. 1, folder 20, Community Archives, Vigo County Public Library, Terre Haute, Ind.

33. Ibid.

34. Bessie Woodson Yancey, *Echoes from the Hills* (Washington, DC: Associated Publishers, 1939), 22.

35. Ibid., 51.

36. Gertrude Parthenia McBrown, *The Picture-Poetry Book* (Washington, DC: Associated Publishers, 1935), 49.

37. Effie Lee Newsome, "Bronze Legacy (To a Brown Boy)," *The Crisis* 24, no. 6 (October 1922): 265.

38. Carter G. Woodson, "Two Timely and Useful Books: *Gladiola Garden* and *Word Pictures of the Great*, a New Book," *Negro History Bulletin* 4, no. 9 (June 1941): 202.

39. Arna Bontemps and Langston Hughes, *Popo and Fifina: Children of Haiti* (1932; repr. New York: Oxford University Press, 1993), 78.

40. Ibid., 73–74.

41. Arna Bontemps, *Sad-Faced Boy* (Boston: Houghton Mifflin, 1937), 90.

PART III

Re-mapping the New Negro

London, New York, and the Black Bolshevik Renaissance: Radical Black Internationalism during the New Negro Renaissance

James Smethurst

The Bolshevik Revolution in October 1917 energized a wave of Black radical internationalism that traveled to a significant degree on political and cultural circuits (and ships) between the USA, the UK, the Caribbean, the Soviet Union, Asia, and Africa. There was a profound current of Black political and cultural radicalism circulating between Britain, the Caribbean, Africa, and the USA throughout the first half of the twentieth century, including such figures as Claude McKay, Eric Walrond, George Padmore, Jomo Kenyatta, Amy Ashwood Garvey, Paul Robeson, Eslanda Goode Robeson, Esther Cooper Jackson, Kwame Nkrumah, and C. L. R. James. This current featured to varying degrees a convergence of Black nationalism and Marxism, creating an internationalist minded Black radicalism in both Britain and the USA that circulated through overlapping transnational circles of Black nationalism, the Black intelligentsia, and leftwing labor activism. If the notion of a nationalist Black internationalism seems paradoxical, one need only recall the Garvey movement with a million members in the USA and another million in Africa and its diaspora outside the USA to see that this paradoxical combination of the national and the international, a combination that was, in fact, filled with tensions and contradictions, characterized much Black radicalism through the twentieth century, from Garveyism to Black Power and Black Arts. The network of the Third International inspired by the October Revolution and the creation of the Soviet Union appealed to Black radicals on two levels: as a practical alliance of workers and oppressed peoples in the struggle against imperialism in the Leninist sense of the "highest stage of capitalism" as well as in the older colonial sense; and as a model for imagining a Black revolutionary international that was more egalitarian than the Garvey Movement.

This chapter considers the interplay between Black political and cultural activists in Britain and the USA during the New Negro era and the creation of Black internationalist networks as a subset of what I am calling the Black Bolshevik Renaissance. The creation of these networks significantly inflected the trajectory of Black radicalism in the USA and the UK (and the Caribbean and Africa) from the New Negro Renaissance through the Popular Front era to the Black Arts and Black Power movement of the 1960s and 1970s. A significant focus here will be how this internationalism decentered notions of what we might now call a "Black Atlantic" or the "Atlantic World," emphasizing building and strengthening the relationships of Africa and African diasporic communities with non-European peoples in European and North American colonies and semi-colonies of "the East," anticipating what many US Black political and cultural radicals would later term the "Bandung World." This look away from "the West" to "the East" also encompassed the new revolutionary society in the Soviet Union, which, as Kate Baldwin points out, endeared itself to Black radicals by refusing to officially declare itself "European" or "white."[1] After discussing Black Bolshevism and the British-US (and African and Caribbean) connection generally, the chapter will zoom in on work by Claude McKay, C. L. R. James, and Eric Walrond by way of literary illustration.

This chapter is meant to further a conversation rather than be definitive. Brent Edwards no doubt has a point in calling into question Guyanese-born, Black British nationalist Ras Makonnen's suggestion that Britain was at *the* center of Black anti-colonialism in the first half of the twentieth century.[2] Still, much more work needs to be done in the study of Britain, particularly London, as *a* center for a radical Black internationalism in dialogue with diasporic communities in the Americas as well as with Africa. This is especially so in the cultural sphere where there is really no analogue for the scholarly studies that such political historians as Hakim Adi, Marika Sherwood, Susan Pennybacker, and Minkah Makalani have done on Black British radicalism in the interwar period.

In many ways, what these Black radicals imagined was a Black Bolshevik World and a "Black International" – and both "Black" and "Bolshevik" are important here. With the centenary of the October Revolution just past, it is important to remember the liberatory energies released by that event. The terms "Black Bolshevik World" and "Black Bolshevik Renaissance" are used because what is notable about this writing in response to and inspired by the October Revolution is not simply sympathy (or even empathy) with the liberation of another oppressed people (or other oppressed peoples), but also how it imagines

Bolshevism as a political and cultural network that African and African-descended peoples could join and that would have the leverage to end colonialism and white supremacy. The October Revolution suggested the possibility of a Black Bolshevism, though what that would actually mean was yet to be filled out other than the possibility of a viable Black radicalism that combined self-determination, internationalism, and anti-capitalism. As the Jamaican-born W. A. Domingo, the leftwing founding editor of the *Negro World*, the newspaper of the Garveyite Universal Negro Improvement Association (UNIA), wrote in the Black socialist journal *The Messenger* in 1919:

> The question naturally arises: Will Bolshevism accomplish the full freedom of Africa, colonies in which Negroes are in the majority, and promote human tolerance and happiness in the United States by the eradication of the causes of such disgraceful occurrences as the Washington and Chicago race riots? The answer is deducible from the analogy of Soviet Russia, a country in which dozens of racial and lingual types have settled their many differences and found a common meeting ground, a country, which no longer oppresses colonies, a country from which the lynch rope is banished and in which racial tolerance and peace now exist.[3]

One can see the origins of the later "Black Belt Thesis," then, not as simply a Comintern initiative, but issuing from a Black response to Bolshevism and the October Revolution. Domingo by extension here also imagines a truly pan-African Bolshevism in which a Union of African Socialist Republics would be viable, imagining a multi-ethnic, multinational Black state that would allow for Black self-determination without creating a settler colony elite that had previously marred and continued to make problematic Black revolutionary emigrationist schemes.

In addition, the rise of a new post-Bolshevik Revolution Black Left combining nationalism, internationalism, and socialism provided a viable alternative to Garveyism and its promotion of black capitalism that was attractive to many Black radicals while drawing on the supporters, organizations, and communications networks of the Garvey Movement. The St. Croix-born Hubert Harrison, a major figure of the Left of the New Negro Renaissance in Harlem and an important influence on Garvey during Garvey's early days in New York (and never a Communist), argued in "A New International" (1920) in the *Negro World* that the Bolshevik Revolution, and the response of the great imperialist powers to it, was a major catalyst for a "new international" of the colonized and oppressed peoples of the world, especially in Africa and its diaspora:

Why the difference? It is because the international linking up of those peoples is a source of strength to those who are linked up. Naturally, the overlords want to strengthen themselves. And, quite as naturally, they wish to keep their subject masses from strengthening themselves in the same way. Today the great world-majority, made up of black, brown and yellow peoples, are stretching out their hands to each other and developing a "consciousness of kind" – as Professor Giddings would call it. They are seeking to establish their own centers of diffusion for their own internationalism, and this fact is giving nightmares to Downing Street, the Quai d'Orsay and other centers of white capitalist internationalism.[4]

Here Harrison draws on the work of sociologist Franklin Giddings and Giddings's notion of a "consciousness of kind" (in which subjects recognize themselves as fundamentally akin) to suggest Bolshevik internationalism demonstrated that the creation of a common consciousness among geographically, linguistically, and culturally disparate peoples of the colonialized world was possible.[5] This common recognition inspired by the Black Bolshevik Renaissance, generally and often emphatically rejected the reification of the "Atlantic World" that inscribed the connection between Europe and the Americas (and Africa to the Americas by the agency of Europe) as the key global relationship. While Ethiopianism was a common feature of much Black nationalist rhetoric in the nineteenth and twentieth centuries, the rhetoric of Caribbean-born radicals, such as Harrison, Cyril Briggs, Claude McKay, and the Black Bolshevik circles of the African Blood Brotherhood and its newspaper *The Crusader* (as well as Garveyism) was particularly suffused with it. Harrison's transformation of the famous quote from Psalms 68:31 with the oppressed peoples of the world stretching their hands out to each other in mutual recognition instead of to God mirrors a 1918 editorial of Cyril Briggs in the *Crusader*, "Ethiopia shall yet stretch forth her hand to Freedom and God! And Ethiopia is not alone, but ALL the oppressed of the earth."[6] As will be shown later, Claude McKay would take Ethiopianist rhetoric into an even more explicitly revolutionary internationalist direction.

Interestingly enough, this Black Bolshevik Renaissance or Black Bolshevik World emerged, at least initially, outside the local Communist affiliates in the USA and the UK, especially in the case of the Communist Party of Great Britain (CPGB), which resisted Comintern attempts to force it to pay attention to the "Negro Question," both in its colonies and, especially, in Britain itself where thousands of Black marine workers as well as Black artists, intellectuals, and students lived.[7] The key organizational conduit for the international connection of radical Black artists, intellectuals, and workers in the 1920s was the Comintern as it related to such more localized radical Black organizations as the African Blood Brotherhood (USA), the West African Students Union, and the Negro Welfare Association (UK). This is not to say that Black Communists who became important leaders of the Communist Party of the United States of America (CPUSA), such as William Patterson and James Ford, did not play important roles in building radical Black political and cultural networks in Britain, but they generally did so not as representatives of the CPUSA, which had its own problem recruiting Black members in the 1920s, but of the Comintern and its organizations, interacting with Black workers, students, intellectuals, artists, and so on, who saw these Black US radicals as representing an international movement rather than the CPGB.

These circuits of black radicalism did not emerge out of nowhere, but significantly drew on already existing networks, especially the UNIA and its supporters. Margaret Stevens's *Red International and Black Caribbean Communists in New York City, Mexico and the West Indies, 1919–1939* illuminates how the Russian Revolution energized liberation movements around the Black world – though her primary focus is the Western Hemisphere. Among Stevens's many valuable observations is that the rank and file Garveyite and the Left Black nationalists of the African Blood Brotherhood (from which many of the Caribbean-born early Black US Communists came) often participated in the same organizations at the grassroots level and saw no real contradiction in shuttling back and forth between Garveyite Liberty Halls and Communist lectures and schools.[8] It is also during this period, as the Comintern begins to grapple with the national question and its relation to the populations of African descendants in the Western Hemisphere, that Black US Communists start to play important roles as Comintern representatives in the Caribbean and Mexico – and, eventually, the UK.

However, this is not to suggest that this Black radical energy flowed only from the USA to the UK (or from the USSR to the USA and the Caribbean Basin to the UK). Paris, rightly, has received much attention as a center of radical Black internationalism, where Negritude intersected concretely and personally with the New Negro Renaissance, with significant impacts on both movements. London, too, was such a radical Black crossroads. The early twentieth-century Black British community was comparatively small, though with deep historical roots, especially in London, Bristol, Cardiff, and Liverpool. However, because the British Union Jack flew over nearly one-sixth of the world, including huge portions of Africa, Asia, and the Caribbean, London was the Black colonial metropole of the world, even more so than Paris or New York – a fact particularly reflected among its maritime workers of whom a large proportion were of African or Asian descent. As it would be for decades, London was a place where Africa and its diaspora met and was easily accessible linguistically and in terms of travel to Black US artists, intellectuals, activists, and merchant sailors (some of whom, like Langston Hughes and Claude McKay, were all of these at times), especially through the networks of Caribbean-(and to a lesser degree, African-)born radicals, who were such an important segment of the Black Left in both the USA and the UK. Politically, too, London was often far more open to Black radicals and Black radical literature of various stripes than were the British colonies in Africa, Asia, and the Caribbean where colonial authorities worried a great deal about insurrection, labor unrest, and independence movements by Black and brown locals – though such restrictions and exclusions were not unknown in London proper.[9]

While such metropoles as New York, London, and Paris, and such European hubs of global transportation and trade as Hamburg and Marseilles, are places where Africans and African diasporans mix with each other and with various peoples of the European and North American empires, Black radical artists and activists refigure the symbolic geography of the world so as to significantly decenter the relationship between Europe and the Americas. It is telling that in the ending of Claude McKay's *Home to Harlem* (1928) and the beginning of his linked novel *Banjo* (1929), the Haitian intellectual Ray (a major character in both novels) travels from New York City (the setting of most of *Home to Harlem*) to Marseilles (whose "Ditch" or La Joliette/Carré Vieux neighborhood is where most of *Banjo* is set) by proceeding west, which is to say, culturally and ideologically, to and from "the East" through the Caribbean, the Pacific, the Indian Ocean and Red Sea, and the Suez Canal into the Mediterranean (a body of water that is traditionally a link to the "East" in the imagination and imagining of "Europe"). Ray's journey west via the "East" that sets *Banjo* in motion reverses *Home to Harlem*'s beginning where the other major character of that novel, Jake, arrives in Harlem after a period as a docker in London, joining the large community of maritime workers in New York as a longshoreman.

Jake reappears briefly in *Banjo* leaving the sense that his journey to New York (and marriage to a woman) from Europe resulted in a sort of personal stasis while the partnership of Ray and Banjo, who is basically a more musical analogue of Jake (a Black proletarian "natural man" originally from the US South) ends the novel in a refusal to ship out west across the Atlantic like the rest of their Black comrades in "the Ditch," but to "beat it a long ways from here" as untethered Black maritime *flâneurs,* perhaps to one of the great ports of the "East."[10] This homoerotic union of the Black proletarian artist Banjo and the Black intellectual Ray, both from different parts of the diaspora, is seen as productive and liberating.

If one thinks about *Banjo,* its international Black community largely consisting of maritime workers is one that McKay first encountered in London (and describes briefly at the beginning of *Home to Harlem*) rather than in Marseilles where McKay spent relatively little time until the late 1920s. The sort of bifurcation between the Black diasporic life of "The Ditch" and Ray's white friends beyond the port area was something that he had already experienced in London near McKay's apogee as a Black Bolshevik. As McKay himself recalled about his days in London he oscillated between the primarily white Left political and literary circles of the emerging British Communist Movement, the journal *The Workers Dreadnought,* the International Socialist Club, and a club frequented by Black British servicemen drawn across the far-flung empire and Black maritime workers from around the world.[11]

Not surprisingly, the Black Bolshevism that inflects McKay's novels written as he was still on the Left, but drifting from the Communist movement, can be seen even more sharply in his poetry written during his greatest engagement with the African Blood Brotherhood, the CPUSA, the British Communist movement, and the Comintern in the late 1910s and early 1920s. The symbolic geography of the Black "East" and the journey to Europe via the "East" rather across the Atlantic is revealed more clearly in a poem that was first published, and perhaps composed, during McKay's sojourn in London from 1919 to 1921, and was published in a slightly different form under a number of titles: the original "To Ethiopia," "Exhortation," "Exhortation: Summer 1919," and "Summer 1919." As Wayne Cooper, among others, notes McKay is obviously paying tribute to the inspiring example of the October Revolution and the new Soviet Union.[12] At that time, it should be remembered that the Bolsheviks in the Soviet Union were still engaged in a desperate war against counter-revolutionary white armies and foreign military intervention (including by the USA and the UK), which is to say that the revolution was still not a settled matter in 1919 and 1920 (when the poem first appeared in the US Left journal *Liberator* that was at the time edited by the then Communist Max Eastman and would be later edited by McKay and the Communist Mike Gold). As Bill Maxwell also reminds us, in addition to its invocation of the still in process Bolshevik Revolution, it also engaged a long tradition of African American (and Jamaican) Ethiopianism in which that nation in the horn of Africa served as a synecdoche for all African-descended peoples ("Lift your heavy-lidded eyes, Ethiopia! awake!").[13] In other words, the poem might be read as both a call for a Black Bolshevism that sees the October Revolution as a model merging with older Black nationalist notions and a defense of a revolution that was by no means assured of victory:

> Through the pregnant universe rumbles life's terrific thunder
> And Earth's bowels quake with terror; strange and terrible storms break,
> Lighting-torches flame the heavens, kindling souls of men, thereunder:
> Africa! Long ages sleeping, O my motherland, awake![14]

Obviously, there is a sort of millenarian new world a-coming out of the destruction of the old world language that is a familiar theme in Black Christianity in both the USA and McKay's native Jamaica. However, it also references the millenarian aspect of the "Internationale," the socialist anthem that became increasingly associated with the Communist movement as the century wore on. I would argue that McKay's later line "For the big earth groans in travail for the strong, new world in making," engages the original French version and the Russian and US English translations that appeared at the beginning of the twentieth century with the birth of a new world based on new foundations and the destruction of the old prominently featured in the first verse (generally the only one sung on most occasions).[15] This is important because it indicates that McKay is not calling on Africans and African descendants simply to wake up and be inspired, but to actually join an international movement, join the choir, so to speak.

However, it is also significant that McKay chooses to address the poem to "Ethiopia" in that it has already joined the choir of resistance to imperialism – and is, in fact, an international icon of successful Black anti-imperialism. After all, a generation before McKay wrote this poem, Ethiopia decisively defeated an Italian colonial invasion in the First Italo-Ethiopian War, notably at the Battle of Adwa in 1896. While the Ethiopian victory over the Italians was not the first time a colonial European power suffered a catastrophic loss in Africa, it was certainly the most decisive and long lasting triumph of an African nation over a would be colonizer. The point here is that Ethiopia, the nation, not the metonym for Africa and its diaspora, was the most successful example of Black resistance to colonialism, by any means necessary, in the high imperialist era of the early twentieth century.

In addition, not only is it not a "Black Atlantic" nation, but also it is in "the East," geographically (and culturally, as in the Islamic story of early Muslim exiles seeking shelter in Ethiopia before their triumphant return to Arabia) looking across the Red Sea and the Indian Ocean:

> In the East the clouds glow crimson with the new dawn that is breaking,
> And its golden glory fills the western skies.
> O my brothers and my sisters, wake! arise!
> For the new birth rends the old earth and the very dead are waking,
> Ghosts are turned flesh, throwing off the grave's disguise,
> And the foolish, even children, are made wise;
> For the big earth groans in travail for the strong, new world in making–
> O my brothers, dreaming for dim centuries,
> Wake from sleeping; to the East turn, turn your eyes![16]

This yoking of the Bolshevik Revolution and its armed struggle to Ethiopia is particularly significant in the summer of 1919, the Red Summer. One thing that linked Black communities in the USA and the UK is that both suffered massive assaults by racist mobs in that summer. The "race riots" of Chicago, Washington, Knoxville, Omaha, Norfolk, Longview, and numerous other locales in the USA that year have received some considerable attention, both in the popular press and in scholarship. Similar assaults in London, Cardiff, Liverpool, Newport, and other cities with significant Black populations, primarily maritime workers, have received less consideration until recently, and primarily in the UK. However, McKay did reference these racist British assaults in his fiction and his journalism. One of the things that sent Jake back to the USA in *Home to Harlem* was a white racist assault on Black workers in London's docklands.[17] Like the better-known sonnet "If We Must Die," "Exhortation" is a call to self-defense by any means necessary, foregrounding the Red Summer in both the USA and the UK more openly than the famous sonnet, linking this self-defense to successful anti-colonialism, pan-Africanism, and the Bolshevik Revolution. "Exhortation" allows us to read McKay's militant protest sonnets, particularly "If We Must Die," not simply in terms of the mass racist domestic violence in the USA during the "Red Summer" of 1919, but also in that of a Black internationalist resistance to similar violence in the UK as well as solidarity with the new Soviet Union besieged by "White" armies and the forces of the major colonial powers.

Eric Walrond's 1926 *Tropic Death*, a collection of stories, was heralded by participants in the New Negro Renaissance in the USA as, along with Jean Toomer's *Cane*, a prime exemplar of a new avant-garde Black fiction that was emphatically modern without being derivative of white European modernism.[18] Walrond himself embodied the circuits of October Revolution Black radicalism, perhaps even more than McKay. He was born in British Guiana and grew up in Barbados and Panama, one of many Black Anglophone Caribbeans whose families migrated to Panama to work on the construction of the Panama Canal. He moved to New York in 1918 and became a key figure in radical Black cultural circles there.

Walrond was known as one of the chief raconteurs of the Harlem Renaissance, serving as an early guide to Carl Van Vechten.[19] He was also involved with both the Garveyite movement and the new Communist Parties (initially there were two Communist Parties in the USA until their unification in 1921). In his capacity as an associated editor of the *Negro World* from 1923 to 1925, he published essays of Claude McKay reporting on the Black and radical scene in London. Walrond left New York for London in 1929, living the rest of his life in the UK, where mental illness and relative poverty limited his literary and political efforts, though he participated as he could in the Black British cultural circles that developed around Amy Ashwood Garvey (the first wife of Marcus Garvey and herself a key figure of the circulation of Black radicalism of various stripes between the USA, the Caribbean, and the UK from the New Negro Renaissance to the onset of Black Power) and Claudia Jones (the Trinidadian-born US Communist leader who was deported to the UK in the 1950s during the Red Scare and a key figure of Black radicalism in both the USA and the UK).[20]

The stories of *Tropic Death* are set in a variety of locales in the Americas, basically Panama and the Caribbean. The focal point of the collection is Colón, a city founded by US business interests as a railroad terminal serving the California gold trade and later as the anchor of the construction of the canal and its administration after a failed attempt to build a canal across the Panamanian isthmus. While the word "terminal" suggests a sort of ending or endpoint, Colón, the canal, and the Caribbean generally are not so much terminals or dead ends in the sense of an ending, but transit points for a new radical Black internationalism out of the dead end of Jim Crow, racism, colonialism, and, perhaps, capitalism. Colón can be seen as a link between what might be thought of as the Black Atlantic and the Black Pacific in the era of high colonialism, connecting Africans and peoples of African descent to the other colonialized peoples of the world in Asia and the Americas as well as the displaced poor of

Europe. This can be seen in the presence of Chinese and other peoples of the Pacific-Indian Ocean rim in *Tropic Death*:

> Down in the Cut drifted hordes of Italians, Greeks, Chinese, Negroes – a hardy, sun-defying set of white, black, and yellow men. But the bulk of the actual brawn for the work was supplied by the dusky peons of those coral isles in the Caribbean ruled by Britain, France, and Holland. At the Atlantic end of the Canal the blacks were herded in boxcar huts buried in the jungles of Silver City; in the murky tenements perilously poised on the narrow banks of Faulke's River; in the low, smelting cabins of Coco T.[21]

Interestingly, none of the nationalities of the laborers could be said to be "Atlantic," except perhaps the African-descended people in the Cut. Even the European groups named are from what might be thought of as the Mediterranean Rim, which is to say the middle sea between Europe, Africa, and Asia. The Cut is a liminal place of contention between East and West, North and South, various "races" and nationalities, but it is also the sort of place where a "consciousness of kind" is forged out of peoples who are not white or are at least off-white as such things were figured in the USA.

Tropic Death frequently adopts and adapts a term of US imperialism and military intervention in the Caribbean Basin, referring to the Caribbean as the "American Mediterranean."[22] The Mediterranean Sea was in the early twentieth century, and had been since antiquity, a body of transit between Europe, Africa, and Asia, but was also a key link, perhaps the key thoroughfare of French and British colonialism. Even the canals that mark the high imperialism of the modern age in the Caribbean and the Mediterranean (Panama and Suez) mirror each other. In that sense, Walrond's work is connected to that of other Black radicals of the early twentieth century, especially McKay, in his complication of any simple notion of a "Black Atlantic," a concept that in some senses would exclude the major populations of Afro-Columbians, Afro-Peruvians, Afro-Mexicans, and Afro-Ecuadorians clustered on the Pacific Coast of South and Central America, communities of which Caribbean-born radicals, especially those like Walrond and, indeed, Garvey who had spent any time in South or Central America, were very aware. Walrond's engagement with and subsequent rejection of Garveyism and his association with the Communist Left in the 1910s and 1920s bears some resemblance, too, to McKay's trajectory – though without the bitter break with Communism that McKay experienced. McKay also works backward to the "tropics" in his fiction, moving from New York in the at least partially ironically titled *Home to Harlem* to Jamaica in the 1933 novel *Banana Bottom*, a symbolic return from exile for McKay. In other words, not only does *Tropic Death* complicate the north/south axis of domestic politics, but also the old triangle trade model reproduced in various accounts of the "Black Atlantic."

By the early 1930s, the Bolshevik Revolution was more than a decade in the past, the white armies and their interventionist allies defeated, and the Third or Communist International was also more than a decade old. Notions of race, nation, and class long dominant on the Left were being challenged, particularly in the USA and South Africa, with reverberations throughout Africa and its diaspora, by the Comintern's policies and new theoretical understanding of the "national question," particularly during the "Third Period" of the late 1920s and early 1930s. The CPUSA and the Comintern advanced the notion that African Americans in the South, in the largely rural "Black Belt" where Black people constituted the over-whelming majority of the population, were an oppressed nationality entitled to self-determination. This notion of self-determination included the right to form some sort of independent, federated, or autonomous state following the model of the former Russian Empire after the October Revolution from which independent nations (such as Finland), the feder-ated republics of the Soviet Union, and autonomous regions were formed following this principle of national self-determination (whether or not these republics and regions had any true self-governance is another ques-tion). The "Black Belt Thesis," as the Communist position became known, also declared African Americans in the urban North to be a "national minority" that should be integrated into civil society on the basis of full social equality.

This approach to "Negro liberation" was really only applied directly to the USA and in a somewhat different modality to South Africa by the Comintern. However, radicals in African descendant communities across the diaspora, including both colonies and countries where the population was overwhelmingly Black, such as Jamaica and Haiti, multiracial and multinational colonies and countries, but with a large Black population, such as Trinidad and Guyana, and others with actual "Black Belts," such as Cuba and its Oriente Province, adapted elements from the Black Belt Thesis, emphasizing revolutionary Black nationalism *and* internationalism even more prominently than in the immediate period of the Bolshevik Revolution. In the late 1920s and early 1930s during the apogee of the "class against class" "Proletarian" period of the Comintern and its cultural circles, Communists and sympathetic radicals, sought to place Black revolt and revolution, and such heroic figures as Denmark Vesey, Nat Turner,

Toussaint Louverture, and Dessalines, as part of the nonbourgeois trad-ition of revolution along with the Paris Commune and the Bolshevik Revolution.

One of the key texts and events in this tradition of Black revolt and the nonbourgeois revolutionary tradition is C. L. R. James's play *Toussaint*, which he wrote in Britain during the early 1930s, completed in 1934, and staged in 1936 in London with Paul Robeson in the lead role. By the time James completed *Toussaint* in 1934, he was well on his way to his mature identity as a Trotskyist (and later post-Trotskyist) and radical pan-Africanist. While he remained militantly "anti-Stalinist" his entire life (a not surprising move given the CPGB's checkered history regarding race and colonialism) and came to espouse an anti-vanguardist form of Marxism, he admired and became close to individual Black Communists and Communist supporters, such as George Padmore (a childhood friend of James in Trinidad and a leader of Comintern "Negro" work who had not yet broken with the Communist movement when James reconnected with him in 1932), Robeson, and, later, Richard Wright (who, too, was still in the CPUSA when James met him).

In the case of Robeson the fact of the CPGB's indifference to Black Britons and colonial oppression does not mean that encounters with mass organizations and events organized largely by Communists in the UK in the 1920s and early 1930s did not have an impact on him. In 1929 Robeson encountered a column of unemployed Welsh miners in the town of Pontypridd near Cardiff (then a Black British center of the UK) who sang in perfect harmony as they walked to London as part of a national hunger march organized by the Communist-led National Unemployed Workers' Movement. These miners mesmerized Robeson who then joined them much to their surprise and pleasure in what might be seen as Robeson's first significant step toward the organized Left, a progression that led him to be the most visible Black radical figure in the world by the 1940s. Of course, one might say that the particular impact of the miners on Robeson, and his continuing affection for Wales (and the continuing Welsh affection for Robeson), had as much to do with the "national question" as it had with class politics as such, given the particular history of Wales and its relationship to the UK.[23]

James's play, which was an important step toward the research and realization of James's landmark 1938 history of the Haitian Revolution, *The Black Jacobins*, cast the revolt of the slaves as the purest expression of the Jacobin sympathies of the French Revolution, much purer, in fact, than in France where the inheritors of the Revolution attempted to return the black rebels of Saint-Domingue to slavery. In the end, Toussaint's mistake, which he eventually acknowledges is that he trusts too much in revolutionary France and is betrayed by that revolution, rather than believing, as does his lieutenant Dessalines, in the former Black slaves of Haiti. "Oh, Dessalines! Desalines! You were right after all!" cries Toussaint in the penultimate scene.[24] However, that is not where the play ends. Invoking the sacrifice of Toussaint, Dessalines rallies an army of former slaves joined by a mixed-raced army to fight, successfully as we know, the French (and all comers) and establish the first Black republic in the world – and for all practical purposes, the first successful plebeian-led republic in the world. Thus, if the Haitian Revolution is in some senses the purest expression of Jacobinism, it is also something like the first workers' republic (leaving aside for the moment the argument of whether the slaves and free Black artisans were truly "proletarians" or not).

While the play received mixed reviews, both for its content and its actual writing and performance, it was a key moment in what might be thought of as the transition from the Black Bolshevik strain of the New Negro Renaissance with its exchanges between the USA, the UK, Africa, and the Caribbean, to new sorts of radical alliances (and schisms) of the "Red Decade" of the 1930s, the Popular Front, and beyond. It was certainly an epochal moment both for James in his transition to revolutionary Marxism in the Trotskyist mode and for Robeson in his journey toward the CPUSA and its political and cultural world. Certainly, Robeson acted in such a clearly Black radical play by a Black radical author. In part, the different trajectories of James and Robeson – and, indeed, of other Black Leftists with connections to both the USA and UK, such as Padmore, McKay, Walrond, W. E. B. Du Bois, Eslanda Goode Robeson, and others, had to do both with the splits in the Soviet Union and Stalin's consolidation of power in 1932 and the rise of the Popular Front, a subject beyond the scope of this chapter.

However, the point is that the UK–US connection remains an underexplored node of the New Negro Renaissance and the development of radical Black internationalism in the twentieth century. Through such an exploration, we might find new frames for the excellent scholarship already done on the Left of the Harlem Renaissance by Bill Maxwell, Gary Holcomb, and others. It might give us new contexts for considering Du Bois's 1928 novel of Black internationalism and revolution *Dark Princess* (which might be been seen as promoting a Black Bolshevik vision embodied in a union of two individuals much like that of *Banjo*, albeit in a much more normatively heterosexual mode than in *Banjo*) and later

Black Left literature of the 1930s, such as Arna Bontemps's *Black Thunder*, a novel of Denmark Vesey's rebellion haunted by the specter of the Haitian Revolution. This interchange is an important circuit for the development of pan-African radicalisms that quite consciously attempt to escape from the reification of the "Atlantic World" and the notion that the relationship between Africa and the African diaspora and the European and North American imperial powers is more important than the Black relationship to "the East," both the Bolshevik Revolution and the emergent Soviet Union and the peoples of colonized and semi-colonized Asia. Paradoxically in some ways, and not surprisingly in the high age of imperialism in others, these Black Bolshevik–Black nationalist links were made in such European and North American metropoles as Paris, New York, and London – but also in Moscow, its University of the Toilers of the East and other Comintern schools, institutions and organizations, particularly the Red International of Labor Unions and its affiliates, with a profound impact on the development of Black radical politics and culture from the New Negro Renaissance, Negritude, and Negrismo to the Popular Front to Black Power and Black Arts (and beyond).

Notes

1. Kate A. Baldwin, *Beyond the Color Line and the Iron Curtain* (Durham: Duke University Press, 2002), 5.
2. Brent Hayes Edwards, *The Practice of Diaspora: Literature, Translation, and the Rise of Black Internationalism* (Cambridge, MA: Harvard University Press, 2003), 241–242.
3. W. A. Domingo, "Did Bolshevism Stop Race Riots in Russia," in *African American Anti-Colonial Thought, 1917–1937*, ed. Cathy Bergin (Edinburgh: Edinburgh University Press, 2016), 34.
4. Hubert Harrison, "A New International," in *African Anti-Colonial Thought*, ed. Bergin, 41.
5. Franklin H. Giddings, *Readings in Descriptive and Historical Sociology* (New York: Macmillan, 1906), 275–325.
6. Cyril K. Briggs, "Africa for the Africans," in *African Anti-Colonial Thought*, ed. Bergin, 84.
   In this editorial, Briggs, much like Du Bois in *The Crisis*, supports the war effort of the Allied Nations against the Central Powers, but only on the basis that the Allied Nations live up to their promises about democracy, freedom, and self-determination. Of course, Briggs, like Du Bois, was to be disappointed, pushing him (and *The Crusader*) farther to the Left and, ultimately, to the Communist Party of the United States of America.

7. Marika Sherwood, "The Comintern, the CPGB, Colonies, and Black Britons, 1920–1938," *Science and Society* 60, no. 2 (Summer 1996): 137–163; Hakim Adi, *Pan-Africanism and Communism: The Communist International, Africa and the Diaspora, 1919–1939* (Trenton: Africa World Press, 2013), 251–291.

8. Margaret Stevens, *Red International and Black Caribbean Communists in New York City, Mexico and the West Indies, 1919–1939* (London: Pluto Press, 2017), 25.

9. As Margaret Stevens notes, the colonial government of Trinidad was particularly hostile to black radicalism during the Harlem Renaissance era. Ibid., 34–36.

10. Claude McKay, *Banjo: A Novel without a Plot* (New York: Harper and Brothers, 1929), 326.

11. Claude McKay, *A Long Way from Home: An Autobiography* (1937; London: Pluto Press, 1985), 66–72.

12. Wayne F. Cooper, *Claude McKay: Rebel Sojourner in the Harlem Renaissance* (Baton Rouge: Louisiana University Press, 1996), 133.

13. Claude McKay, *Complete Poems*, ed. William J. Maxwell (Urbana: University of Illinois Press, 2004), n.174; Claude McKay, "Exhortation: Summer, 1919," in McKay, *Complete Poems*, 330.

14. McKay, "Exhortation: Summer, 1919," 175.

15. Ibid., 176.

16. Ibid., 176.

17. Claude McKay, *Home to Harlem* (New York: Harper and Brothers, 1928), 7.

18. Langston Hughes, "Marl Dust and West Indian Sun," *New York Herald Tribune*, December 5, 1926, 9; W. E. B. Du Bois, "Five Books," *The Crisis* 33 (January 1927): 152.

19. James Davis, *Eric Walrond: A Life in the Harlem Renaissance and the Transatlantic Caribbean* (New York: Columbia University Press, 2015), 83–154.

20. For a discussion of Claudia Jones and her influence on black British radicalism in the 1950s and 1960s and beyond, see Marika Sherwood, *Claudia Jones: A Life in Exile: A Biography* (London: Lawrence & Wishart, 1999), 130–149.

21. Eric Walrond, *Tropic Death* (New York: Liveright, 2015), 67.

22. Jennifer Brittan, "The Terminal: Eric Walrond, the City of Colón, and the Caribbean of the Panama Canal," *American Literary History* 25, no. 2 (Summer 2013), 301–303.

23. For the best account of Robeson's relationship to Wales (and vice versa), see Daniel G. Williams, *Black Skin, Blue Books: African Americans and Wales, 1845–1945* (Cardiff: University of Wales Press, 2012), 142–207.

24. C. L. R. James, *Toussaint Louverture: The Story of the Only Successful Slave Revolt in History* (Durham: Duke University Press, 2013), 128.

CHAPTER 12

Island Relations, Continental Visions, and Graphic Networks

Jak Peake

In February 1926, W. E. B. Du Bois published a questionnaire in *The Crisis*, the National Association for the Advancement of Colored People (NAACP) journal he edited, on the nature of black representation in the arts. The responses were published in the magazine as part of a long-running symposium that is remembered today as a major Harlem Renaissance event. What is not remembered, however, is the Caribbean backstory to the symposium initiated by controversy over a new edition of a now little-known novel, *The Wooings of Jezebel Pettyfer*, by a largely forgotten British author, Haldane Macfall (Figure 12.1).

Born in 1860, Macfall served as a military officer in Jamaica and West Africa from 1885 to 1892, and later became an illustrator, art critic, and writer. The stepson of feminist writer Sarah Grand, he was apparently paid a backhanded compliment by George Meredith, who purportedly stated that *The Wooings* "was the finest novel of his generation ... [though] it ought never to have been written."[1] Set in both Barbados and Jamaica, Macfall's picaresque novel follows the lives of two "coloured" (mixed race) Barbadians, Jezebel Pettyfer and Jehu "Masheen" Dyle, who briefly become lovers. Refusing to marry Jehu, and suspecting him of infidelity, Jezebel marries Huckleback, a Jamaican owner of a rum store. Living up to the modern associations of her name, Jezebel still seeks out sexual partners when married. Jehu enters into the British West India Regiment in Jamaica, but regularly runs foul of the law and "decent" society; eventually he deserts the army and is arrested.[2]

First published in 1898, *The Wooings of Jezebel Pettyfer* was undoubtedly ahead of its time in terms of its representation of sexual freedom. A shorter alternative version of the novel, published as *The House of the Sorcerer* circa 1900, included a frontispiece illustrated by Macfall of a bare-breasted mixed-race woman, judged as "indecent" by one reviewer (Figure 12.2).[3] Generally early reviewers praised *The Wooings* yet expressed reservations

Figure 12.1 Haldane Macfall by H. S. Mendelssohn, *The Review of Reviews*, Vol.
XVIII (July–December, 1898), 92.

about its characters' morals.[4] Reviews of the novel up until the mid-1920s featured in "white" magazines, and many of these reviewers refer to Afro-Caribbean characters as exotic figures far removed from their audience.[5] With Knopf's 1925 edition of Macfall's novel, however, the book came under intense scrutiny in the black press and served as the catalyst for Du Bois's 1926 symposium.

The aim of this chapter is to relate how *The Wooings* and its Caribbean context contributed to Du Bois's 1926 symposium, and yet were written out of the story – a legacy that still prevails today. The drive here is recuperative in several senses. A "lost" author and text are being brought into the frame, not so much for their individual merits per se, but rather to gain a fuller view of the larger picture. To borrow from Bonnie Kime Scott, this discussion functions as a form of literary history "that searches out a . . . web of connections, allowing for multiple identifications, traditions and communities."[6] It concerns what contemporary writers thought at a time when a number of black periodicals and black writers were attaining considerable status. It also offers a re-evaluation of how literature and art approaching blackface minstrelsy were assessed and related to literary and cultural modernism, even as they were rejected as inauthentic and racist. It is this legacy of the blackface minstrel – still read as all too often

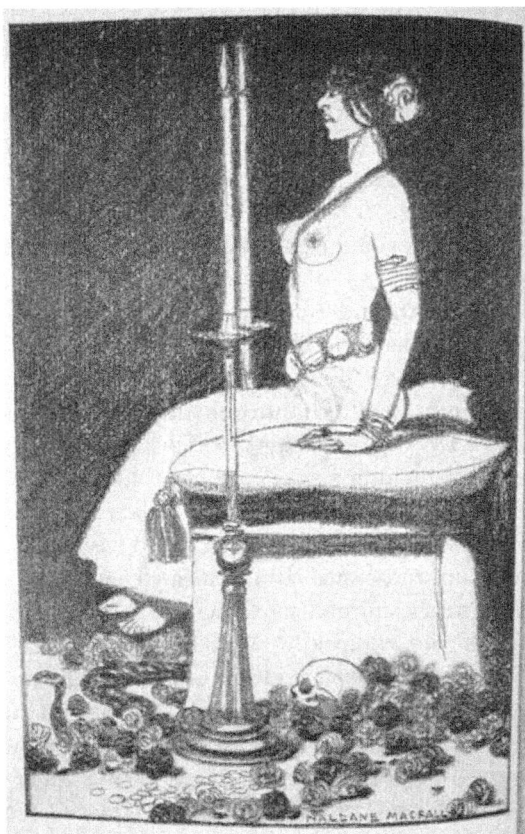

Figure 12.2 Frontispiece, *The House of the Sorcerer* (Boston: R. G. Badger & Co., 1900).

straightforwardly racist and therefore of no literary historical value – that this chapter seeks to complicate. Following in the footsteps of recent scholarship on minstrelsy, it takes the position that literature and visual art approaching this theatrical form, which frequently betrayed racist agendas, was in part driven by an ethnographic impulse to transcribe black culture.[7]

While Du Bois's symposium and mid-1920s dilemmas of "black" representation in art frame the large picture, this chapter focuses on a few specific moments and concerns: the controversies and absences in Alain Locke's richly illustrated Harlem issue of the *Survey Graphic* and *The New Negro*; Eric Walrond's collaboration with Mexican illustrator Miguel

Covarrubias in *Vanity Fair* and his writing over the 1924–26 period more broadly; the promotion of Macfall's novel by Carl Van Vechten, perhaps the most prominent white connoisseur of the black arts in the USA, and reactions to his assessment in the black press; and the concerns reflected in New Negro discourse about dialect, as well as images, which invoked black minstrelsy. Particular consideration is given to the "inter-artistic" relations between text and image, or a variety of mixed media in New Negro publications that has proved a rich seam for Harlem Renaissance studies in recent decades.[8]

In the late nineteenth and early twentieth centuries, the growth in image-laden, mixed-media periodicals was phenomenal. The US magazine revolution of the 1890s saw the price of periodicals lowered, their mass production made easier, and an improvement in the techniques of color print. By 1900, a variety of popular and specialist periodicals were available to the general public, including science journals like *National Geographic*, fashion magazines like *Glass of Fashion* and *Home Arts*, quality monthly magazines like *Harper's* and *Scribner's*, and cheap weeklies.[9]

Modernist writing and visual art permeated and were informed by magazines and the black cultural movement spanning the 1910s through to the 1930s was no exception. While "New Negro" or "Negro Renaissance" publication houses and patronage were often in the hands of a select number of whites, New Negro coverage in magazines was generally more interracial in character. Indeed, one of the most important documents of the "Negro Renaissance," as it was then known, was a March 1925 special issue of *Survey Graphic*, "Harlem: Mecca of the New Negro," which was the result of a collaboration between the journal's white Michigan-born editor, Paul Kellogg, and African American philosopher Alain Locke.[10]

Kellogg and Locke's collaboration itself emerged on account of Charles S. Johnson, a behind-the-scenes operator and editor of *Opportunity*, a mouthpiece of the civil rights organization the National Urban League. Johnson engineered a "coming-out" dinner at the Civic Club on March 21 1924 for a new generation of young New Negro writers. Johnson enlisted Alain Locke, then a Howard professor of philosophy, to act as master of ceremonies. Speeches were given by notable figures from the literary world, including publisher Horace Liveright, W. E. B. Du Bois, and the African American poets James Weldon Johnson, Countee Cullen, Georgia Douglas Johnson, and Gwendolyn Bennett. That night Kellogg approached Locke over the special issue. The "Harlem number" proved incredibly successful. Selling 42,000 copies, it was the journal's best-selling issue. Two months before its publication, publishers Albert and Charles Boni commissioned Locke to produce a book based on the issue. This would become the anthology *The New Negro: An Interpretation*, published in late 1925, which re-used material from the *Survey Graphic* issue and expanded upon it considerably.

Locke's *Survey Graphic* "Harlem number," and its successor, *The New Negro* (1925), heralded the arrival of a black renaissance. Locke defined *The New Negro* as an exemplar of "the first fruits of the Negro Renaissance" and issued a definitive call to arms for a young generation of black artists, asserting "that any vital artistic expression of the Negro theme and subject in art must break through the stereotypes to a new style, a distinctive fresh technique, and some sort of characteristic idiom."[11]

Locke's commitment to overcoming black stereotypes was evident in his two major 1925 publications. In both the *Survey Graphic* Harlem issue and *The New Negro*, Locke championed the work of German illustrator Winold Reiss as the principal artist to illustrate the "characteristic idiom" of the New Negro. The question of how this New Negro should be represented was far from straightforward however. The legacies of colonialism, white hegemony, racism, the emergence of "primitivism," the segregationist Jim Crow laws of the US South, and the rise of the Ku Klux Klan left its toll on the representation of black people – a factor black intellectuals were acutely aware of. Around 1925 and 1926, the matter of how black people should be represented became especially heated.

Reiss's artwork for the March *Survey Graphic* issue was a case in point. In April 1925 at a Harlem branch of the New York Public Library, Paul Kellogg came under fire for selecting Locke, a non-Harlemite to edit the issue, while Reiss's exhibited pictures caused, as Elise Johnson McDougald wrote to Locke, a "furore."[12] One picture, "Two Public School Teachers" (Figure 12.3) provoked controversy, with one spectator ruminating as to whether "the whole art side of the issue were a 'piece of subtle propaganda to prejudice the white reader.'" He added that "he would be afraid of them" if he met them, while one of the teachers in the work, Miss Price, defended the work as a "pretty good likeness."[13]

In an article, "To Certain of our Philistines," that features in the May 1925 issue of *Opportunity*, Locke defended the *Survey Graphic* issue, claiming that the anxious reception to Reiss's artwork was a result of prejudice toward his dark-skinned figures.[14] In Locke's view, Reiss's sketch of the schoolteachers reflected figures from his "own profession" in realistic and symbolic terms. In addition, it presented "a professional ideal" which

Figure 12.3 Winold Reiss, "Two Public School Teachers," *Survey Graphic*,
March 1925, 687.

he was "glad to think representative of both ... [his] profession and
especially its racial aspects" (156).

   Locke's discussion of representatives draws upon the terminology of the
social sciences, an area that had not only influenced Locke's scholarship,
but also informed magazines like *Opportunity* and the *Survey Graphic*,
a richly illustrated version of the sociological magazine the *Survey*. The
Survey Graphic Harlem issue employed "types" in ways which suggested
that the New Negroes in its pages were studies and quite distinct from the
readers and writers of the magazine. For the most part, the types and

portraits in the *Survey Graphic* Harlem issue are African American, but only one representative of the Caribbean features overtly, "A Woman from the Virgin Islands" (685). This visual representation is more US-centric than the range of contributors, four of whom were Caribbean (Claude McKay, Arthur Schomburg, J. A. Rogers, and W. A. Domingo). Domingo's essay "The Tropics in New York" is the most overtly Caribbean piece, raising concerns about Caribbean migrants' lives in New York. Indebted to Claude McKay's poem of the same name, which is included in a framed inset at the bottom left-hand corner, the essay lays emphasis on the uneasy intraracial, interethnic relations between Afro-Caribbeans – predominantly from the British Caribbean – and African Americans. In Domingo's view Afro-Caribbeans' flamboyant dress sense, nonconformism, entrepreneurialism, and radicalism made them the "butt of many a jest" among African Americans.[15] In addition, the article not only outlined the relatively recent life cycle of Caribbean migration to Harlem, but also set this in a long history of Caribbean relocation to and settlement in New York; the conclusion one might draw on reading this prior to the succeeding article, "Harlem Types," is that a not uncommon Harlem type was of Caribbean extraction. This is not apparent in the "Harlem Types" illustrations.[16]

Harold Jackman, a second-generation Barbadian and on-off lover of Countee Cullen, served as the model for "A College Lad" (Figure 12.4). It seems somewhat ironic that this hidden figure of partial Caribbean descent features not as the flamboyantly dressed stereotype of an Afro-Caribbean male but rather as a representative figure of African American sophistication in dress, elegance, and education; in short, an idealized icon of racial uplift. This absence is underlined by Locke's linkage of Reiss's art to Africa in "Harlem Types" as opposed to the wider Americas, and in particular, the Caribbean (653). One reason for this emphasis undoubtedly was related to the fact that the issue was more concerned with interracial than interethnic portrayal. Hence, the black American of the USA and his homeland, Africa, are brought to the fore in ways that mirror discourse on white Americans and Europe as the mother continent.

The success of the Harlem number undoubtedly placed constraints on its successor, *The New Negro: An Interpretation*. African Americans of status, sensing the importance of Locke's project, lined up for representation in his work. Both W. E. B. Du Bois and Robert R. Moton, Booker T. Washington's Tuskegee successor, had sat for Winold Reiss prior to the publication of the *Survey Graphic* Harlem number, presumably hoping to be included. Kellogg pondered the commercial benefits of the inclusion of

Figure 12.4 Winold Reiss, "A College Lad," *Survey Graphic*, March 1925, 654.

their portraits in a letter to Locke. Locke, however, felt their inclusion went against the spirit of their special issue and won the argument as their images were omitted from the issue (Stewart, 473–475). Come the summer of 1925, Locke could not be so choosy. On June 16 that year, Emmett Scott, Secretary-Treasurer of Howard University's Board of Trustees, wrote to Locke to inform him that the university would not renew his contract. Now out of work, but busy with a large editorial project, Locke could ill-afford to make enemies among the black bourgeoisie. The *Survey Graphic* issue had already upset Robert R. Moton who had called the *Survey* offices to complain about lack of coverage of Hampton/Tuskegee-style education, which he had overseen for years (Stewart, 477, 473).

    The dissonance between the presence of Caribbean contributors and the visual signifiers of the New Negro greatly increase from the *Survey Graphic* Harlem number to *The New Negro*. First, the latter presents portraits of an African American elite: Alain Locke, Jean Toomer, Countee Cullen, Roland Hayes, Charles S. Johnson, James Weldon Johnson, Robert

R. Moton, Elise Johnson McDougald, Mary McLeod Bethune, and W. E. B. Du Bois. In addition, a good deal of these were printed in color, an expensive venture that was not replicated in subsequent editions.[17] While the section "Negro Youth Speaks" suggests that the anthology is in part a celebration of a young generation of artists, visually speaking the publication only had two such representatives (Jean Toomer and Countee Cullen), with the rest 40 years old or upwards. The portrait of a Virgin Islands' woman becomes a figure, as her caption states, "From the Tropic Isles" (Figures 12.5 and 12.6), displacing her from her specific Caribbean homeland to a generic tropical milieu. The visual pantheon of elite African Americans in color undoubtedly was included to assert "representatives" in the idealized sense. What readers are confronted by is a visual equivalent of Du Bois's "talented tenth." In doing this, Locke reproduced an "uplift" agenda, while rebuffing the early criticism of Reiss's work. Black America (USA) dominates black representation in the text, while references to Africa and the Caribbean generally appear secondary and tertiary respectively. The interracial dynamics of black and white representation predominate over the intraracial dimensions between different black groups, which perhaps would not translate all too well in a visual form.

Four months prior to the publication of Locke's *Survey Graphic* issue, *Vanity Fair* ran a two-page sketch entitled "Enter, the New Negro, a Distinctive Type Recently Created by the Coloured Cabaret Belt in New York" illustrated by Miguel Covarrubias with captions by Guyanese-Barbadian-Panamanian émigré writer, Eric Walrond (Figure 12.7). Walrond most likely knew of Locke's essay, "Enter the New Negro," prior to publication as he had been closely involved with organizing the Civic Club dinner that resulted in the *Survey*'s editor, Paul Kellogg, approaching Locke with the offer of a special issue. In addition, he had been commissioned to write an essay for the issue that never materialized. The sketch serves as an interesting counterpoint to Locke's version of the New Negro. Collectively, its creators dismiss the figure of the Old Negro, both in the subtitle ("Exit, the Coloured Crooner of Lullabys, the Cotton-Picker, the Mammy Singer and the Darky Banjo-Player, for so Long Over-Exploited Figures on the American Stage") and an introductory editorial, perhaps written by *Vanity Fair* editor Frank Crowninshield ("Not the old type [of Negro], of course. The lullaby singer has gone. Also the plantation darkey."). Yet Walrond's captions and Covarrubias's illustrations, which celebrate the cabaret, are tonally and visually distinct from Locke's oeuvre in various ways. Composed of eight sketches of cabaret figures, the

Figure 12.5 Winold Reiss, "A Woman from the Virgin Islands," *Survey Graphic*,
March 1925, 685.

illustrations and captions are comic and light in tone, skirting close at first
glance to blackface. The everted lips and bared teeth of "dis Strutter,"
a gloved and suited cabaret dandy, who "Tu'n mo' tricks 'n a monkey" may
have unsettled some respectable, senior, or old guard black intellectuals –
and risk troubling associations today.[18]

Reviewing Taylor Gordon's autobiography *To Be Born*, which was illustrated by Covarrubias, in *The Crisis* in 1930, Du Bois stated that he, "could
exist quite happily if Covarrubias had never been born."[19] Du Bois judged
Gordon's work as a "product of the Van Vechten school" and imagined "Carl
[Van Vechten] and Muriel [Draper] splitting their sides with laughter, while
he jiggs and 'yah-yahs!'" Gordon performed in vaudeville acts organized by
B. F. Keith and James Weldon Johnson's brother, J. Rosamund Johnson. The
editorial inference is that Gordon's authorial performance is inauthentic,

From the Tropic Isles

Figure 12.6 Winold Reiss, "From the Tropic Isles," *The New Negro: An Interpretation*.

overdone, and too steeped in "Old Negro" dialect. Ultimately, Du Bois decided that it was "not literature."[20] This dismissal of dialect, vaudeville, and Covarrubias gives a sense of Du Bois's probable judgment of Walrond and Covarrubias's *Vanity Fair* collaboration.

A February 1925 Walrond-Covarrubias sketch in *Vanity Fair*, "The Increasing Vogue of the Negro Revue on Broadway," made reference to "Harlem . . . as the Mecca not only of the Negro poet and creative artist but of the writer of the musical revue." While this text suggests an editorial awareness of Locke's *Survey Graphic* Harlem issue a month prior to its publication, it signals a departure from Locke's vision. Song and dance remain paramount, innovative forms shaping both black and white cultural spheres in Harlem and Broadway. Although the editorial text, possibly authored by Crowninshield, singles out the musical review "writer," the captions written by Walrond focus on the dancers and use dialect.

Figure 12.7 Eric Walrond and Miguel Covarrubias, "Enter, the New Negro,
a Distinctive Type Recently Created by the Coloured Cabaret Belt in New York,"
Vanity Fair, December 1924, 60–61 (© María Elena Rico Covarrubias).

Figure 12.7 (continued)

Accompanying a dapper smiling figure with teeth but no eyes, labeled "Kind O' Reculiar," the caption reads "'Don't nobawdy ca'ah faw me!' – Kigh Sigh Sambo's racially esoteric refrain of a lively old ditty."[21]

The closeness here to blackface both visually and tonally is quite distinct from anything in Locke's 1925 publications. In fact, the blackface performance, if one reads it as such, is complicated by Walrond's racial identity. As an Afro-Caribbean, his performance was double. Introduced in the December 1924 *Vanity Fair* issue as a "talented Negro poet," despite being a prose writer, and as a "Negro writer" in the February 1925 *Vanity Fair* issue, no mention is made of his Caribbean ethnicity, where by contrast the magazine made much of Covarrubias's Mexican identity in numerous issues. If this is to be read in terms of a black mask, then it is that of an Afro-Caribbean adopting African American personae and dialect. There are parallels between Walrond and another Caribbean-American, Bert Williams, a light-skinned blackface star who Walrond admired and who could perform as an African American with no trace of an accent.[22] Similarly, Walrond's Caribbean identity is not flagged in these articles, and so he functions as an authenticator of black culture in a "white" magazine. This particular black mask may have suited Walrond, who perhaps hoped to capitalize on the inability of *Vanity Fair*'s readers to place him.

Dialect itself as a mode of black representation was on tender ground among some senior New Negroes. In his anthology *The Book of American Negro Poetry* (1922), James Weldon Johnson wrote:

> Negro dialect is at present a medium that is not capable of giving expression to the varied conditions of Negro life in America, and much less is it capable of giving the fullest interpretation of Negro character and psychology. This is no indictment against the dialect as dialect, but against the mould of convention in which Negro dialect in the United States has been set.[23]

Johnson was careful not to dismiss dialect as a form of expression, but rather the conventions within which it generally functioned in media. Despite his reservations, the anthology features a mixture of dialect and nondialect poetry. In addition, Johnson's introduction demonstrates some real admiration of dialect, particularly in relation to Claude McKay's early Jamaican poetry, which he conjectured as "more touching and charming" than any other work he would produce (xliv). Just why Johnson so admired McKay's Jamaican dialect, but felt notable anxieties about African American dialect is unclear. It is not hard to see a certain ethnocentrism at work in which the Caribbean is imagined at a distance as a region of picturesque regional speech while the USA – Johnson's homeland – is read as a pitched battleground in which representative racial codes must be fiercely protected.[24] Caribbean writers like McKay and Walrond, not to mention a host of African American writers, including Zora Neale

Hurston, Jean Toomer, and John Matheus, all made use of dialect in their fiction. Their connection to black people in places like Harlem, Washington, DC, the US South, and the Caribbean would have reinforced their awareness of the polyphony of black accents. For Caribbean writers like McKay and Walrond, dialect may have served as an index of ethnic identification, signposting not only the territories they had come from but also their foreignness in the USA. Dialect, therefore, may have been looked upon by Caribbean-Americans writers as a kind of ethnographic "authenticator." In a 1929 issue of the magazine *American Speech*, Nathan van Patten characterized Walrond's use of dialect in his short story collection *Tropic Death* (1926) as offering "remarkable transcriptions of the speech of the Negro in Panama, Honduras, Barbadoes and Guinea [*sic*]. It has a distinct value in any study of Negro speech in these countries."[25]

Around the time that *The New Negro* was hitting the press in the winter of 1925, Locke argued in favor of Covarrubias's comic style in *Opportunity*:

> This typical Latin interest and tradition, with its kindly farce in which there is no hint of social offense or disparagement, no matter how broad or caricaturistic the brush, is familiar to us now in the work of Miguel Covarrubias. It may yet be an antidote for that comic art which is so responsible for the hypersensitive feelings of American Negroes and stands between them and the full appreciation of any portrayal of race types. Surely the time has come when we should have our own comic and semi-serious art, and our own Cruikshanks and Max Beerbohms.[26]

Covarrubias himself did not see his work as caricaturist, but argued that his work was "done from a more serious point of view."[27] Notably, both Covarrubias and Walrond were incorporated into *The New Negro*, though their work was separated out. Walrond's Panama-based short story "The Palm Porch" features in the fiction subsection of "Negro Youth Speaks," while three Covarrubias illustrations appear in the first edition confusingly listed under two titles "Jazz" and "Blues Singer" (225, 227). Two of the three illustrations accompanied Walrond's writing in *Vanity Fair*, with the illustration from the December 1924 *Vanity Fair* issue ("That Teasin' Yalla Gal") republished as the "Blues Singer" being the only Covarrubias illustration to survive in the second 1927 printing – effectively a new edition – of *The New Negro*.[28] If Covarrubias raised eyebrows in *The Crisis*, he was to some extent tamed in Locke's *The New Negro*, as his three illustrations were trimmed to one by its second printing, and the apparent insouciance of the "Blues Singer" was stripped of the cabaret backdrop of the *Vanity Fair* sketches.

In February 1926, Du Bois ran with a questionnaire in *The Crisis*, later packaged as the symposium "The Negro in Art: How Shall He Be Portrayed?," which he put to his readers and significant art world spokespeople over several months.[29] The moment itself could be said to reflect not so much a crisis in the representation of black people, but rather the anxieties of the New Negro literati as the vogue for the Negro expanded. The opening question sets the overall tenor of succeeding questions: "When the artist, black or white, portrays Negro characters is he under any obligations or limitations as to the sort of character he will portray?"[30] The symposium generated numerous responses from various illustrious authors and publishers. In the first printed response that featured in the March issue, Van Vechten defended the freedom of the artist:

> I am fully aware of the reasons of why Negroes are sensitive in regards to fiction which attempts to picture the lower strata of the race. . . . Are Negro writers going to write about this exotic material while it is still fresh or will they continue to make a free gift of it to white authors who will exploit it [?] (219)

Langston Hughes, H. L. Mencken, Charles W. Chesnutt, Walter White, and Mary White Ovington all roughly championed the freedom of the artist. Countee Cullen, Benjamin Brawley, and Jessie Fauset, literary editor of *The Crisis*, were among the few who agreed with Du Bois's argument that the writer should apply restraint.

Interestingly, while most studies of this debate collapse the symposium into what Du Bois in part made it, a black and white issue over black representation in the arts, the roots of the symposium contain a virtually hidden Caribbean component that rarely surfaces in the historiography. The November 1925 issue of *The Crisis* carried a stinging review of Haldane Macfall's novel *The Wooings*. The book had been republished by Knopf in 1925 as part of its Blue Jade Library series, most likely after encouragement from Carl Van Vechten. Van Vechten had a partial or complete hand in scripting Knopf's advertisements of the novel in the *American Mercury* and the *Saturday Review of Literature* in September and October 1925 respectively. Not one to shy away from hyperbole, Van Vechten described Macfall's work as "probably the best novel yet written about the Negro" and claimed it as the work of an "artist," not a "professional humorist." What humor there was belonged to "the Negro" and was not that "of a cartoonist."[31] However, the November *Crisis* reviewer, Emmett J. Scott, noting the enthusiasm for the novel in Knopf's adverts, claimed that Macfall had performed a kind of artificial blackface, comparing him to the writers Octavus Roy Cohen and

Thomas Nelson Page, illustrator E. W. Kemble, and the blackface actor Al Jolson – all white, all criticized for dealing in black stereotypes. Ultimately, for Scott, Macfall belonged to this field and was in his view a "Negro-hater."[32]

Five months prior to this review on June 16, 1925, Scott – Locke's nemesis at Howard – had written to Locke to communicate that his employment at the university was effectively terminated. Then Secretary-Treasurer of Howard, Scott had served as Secretary of Booker T. Washington's Tuskegee Institute between 1912 and 1917, and later as Special Assistant for Negro Affairs to the Secretary of War – making him the highest ranking African American in the War Department. Distinguished and respectable, Scott was also deeply conservative.

In response to Scott's criticism of Macfall's book, Van Vechten wrote to Du Bois on October 29, 1925 in defense of the book and his promotion of it. He wrote of the "explicable tendency" in black people to be "sensitive" with respect to their representation on the page, but argued that such a stance could place "destructive" limits on black writers interested in "speaking any truth which might be considered unpleasant."[33] Du Bois replied on November 5, asking to quote from the letter in a forthcoming article on "the problems of Negro art" that he intended to publish in *The Crisis*.[34] Then a few days later on November 9, Du Bois wrote to Van Vechten again, elated with "a brilliant idea" for "a symposium on freedom in Negro art."[35] Imagining it initially as running for just two issues, he envisaged attaining contributions from Heywood Dubose, Rudolph Fisher, and Winold Reiss.

Just prior to the February 1926 initiation of *The Crisis* symposium, the debate over Macfall's novel was carried out in *Opportunity*. In the December 1925 issue, Countee Cullen opened a review of Du Bose Heyward's *Porgy* accordingly: "A few weeks ago I felt that ... I could match Carl Van Vechten's appraisal of THE WOOINGS OF JEZEBEL PETTYFER as the best novel on the Negro by a white author that I had read. Since then, however, I have read PORGY."[36] Cullen paid deference to Van Vechten, who was very much a part of his social circle by late 1925, while simultaneously knocking Macfall's novel off the top-spot allotted to it. A month later, *Opportunity* carried a glowing review of Macfall's novel from none other than Clarissa M. Scott, the daughter of Emmett Scott. Far from reading this as the work of a "Negro-hater" like her father, Clarissa judged this to be a novel "compounded of laughter and joy, of understanding and discernment." For her, the laughter evoked in the reader was not one of "superiority" but rather "understanding and tenderness and appreciation of human character."[37]

The stage was set for the symposium that ensued in February 1926. In his defense of Macfall to Du Bois in October, Van Vechten admitted, "Whether or not it presents an accurate picture of Negro life in the Barbadoes I have no means of knowing; I have never been in the Barbadoes" – lines which were unaltered in his February 1926 *Vanity Fair* article, "Moanin' wid a Sword in Mah Han'."[38] Van Vechten not only dismissed the setting, but also glossed the fact that much of the novel is set in Jamaica. His response, to a large extent, echoes what happened in the course of the symposium. The Caribbean, or its representation, was barely a reference point, as the burning issue concerned black representation, and, not too implicitly, black representation by whites. However, on May 1, 1926, the *Saturday Review of Literature* published a review of Macfall's novel by Eric Walrond that aimed to address this tropical lacuna. Walrond was careful to reference the positions of both his friends, Van Vechten and Cullen ("I was constrained to admit it the best novel on the Negro that I had read; but since that time 'Porgy' has come," 756), but ultimately read the book as "incapable of achieving a pure view of the tropical life." While Walrond claimed he was "not sensitive" with regards to the "transcriptions of the speech of the West Indian peasantry," he took issue with Macfall's representation of cultured Afro-Caribbeans in the novel. To stress his point, he listed a number of outstanding Caribbean intellectuals as exemplars, including Hector Joseph, the first black attorney general of British Guiana, Albert Marryshaw, the long-serving Grenadian editor of the *West Indian*, and Herbert de Lisser, a prolific Jamaican journalist and author.[39] In the tugs of war over black representation, Walrond generally went against the grain of a Du Boisian agenda of aesthetic uplift. Ironically, here, however, Walrond's aesthetic judgment bears similarities to that of the more senior New Negro wing, in that his objections concern the apparent ill-formed portraits of the "respectable" set. While Macfall's novel is undoubtedly not without its problems in terms of its essentialism and exoticism for the modern reader, a question mark remains as to what type of humor Macfall was aiming for in this work. In Walrond's view, it would have been acceptable had "it [been] conceived in the garb of burlesque." However, he saw the joke as working "at the expense of a people whose culture and moral precepts ought to be intelligible" to the author (756). Whether the jokes went too far or not was obviously down to the reader. At least two black readers – Cullen and Clarissa Scott – thought not, but they were probably, like Van Vechten, unfamiliar with Barbados.

Macfall himself would enter the fray of *The Crisis* symposium a month after Walrond's review came out. Responding principally to Scott's criticisms, Macfall wrote that Scott was "within his rights to find my novel feeble in wit and humour." Yet Macfall rejected the idea that he had "sustained contempt" or "hatred" for black people, recalling the love he inspired in his Afro-Jamaican troops when stationed at Port Royal. The anecdote places him in an imperial frame that hints at a sense of superiority in relation to the soldiers he commanded. Nevertheless, it also indicates some ambiguity. In his *Crisis* article, Macfall made reference to "a bronze god of a man whom they called 'Long' Burke," fictionalized in his novel, whom he feared would attack him. In a tale of mastery, resembling that of *Robinson Crusoe*, Macfall outlined how he gave Burke a light punishment for ill-behavior and essentially won his loyalty, leading to his becoming "the most devoted friend to me for the rest of his service."[40] A friendship that lasts for as long as a contract is probably not the best example of genuine regard; nevertheless, the autobiographical reference establishes his position as a superior in relation to a servant, as well as something like a friend – however unequitable the relationship – to his black associate.

Whatever the differences of perspective, both Walrond and Macfall drew attention to the Caribbean dimension of the latter's novel, extending a hitherto US-centric discussion beyond the shores of the USA. For Du Bois and Van Vechten, Macfall's Caribbean setting was superfluous to the discussion of black representation. As a result, the ensuing *Crisis* symposium barely referenced Macfall's work, or took into account why a novel set in the Caribbean might be read as exotic, or problematically, by black residents in the USA. The matter was collapsed into issues of black and white representation (and this is broadly how the debate is remembered today) instead of being problematized in terms of different geographies with distinct relations of power. Largely under colonial control by European powers in the 1920s, the Caribbean was quite unlike the independent USA; culturally, Afro-Caribbeans and African Americans may have seen themselves as quite distinct, despite their shared legacies of racial exclusion, transatlantic displacement, and slavery.

It is quite possible that these factors, coupled with the absence of Caribbean pictorial or written representation in Locke's 1925 New Negro projects and Du Bois's *Crisis* symposium, prompted Eric Walrond to push for a Caribbean special issue of *Opportunity* in November 1926 while he was business manager of the magazine. Charles S. Johnson's motivation in accepting Walrond's proposition of a Caribbean issue as *Opportunity*'s editor may well have been due to his being left out in the cold – as Du Bois and Locke jostled for authority over the New Negro generation of artists. Johnson, after all, had masterminded the very dinner that had led to Locke's *Survey Graphic* issue, though he was a less obvious beneficiary of the evening. Johnson was probably the most open out of himself, Locke, and Du Bois to a trans-American partnership and, crucially, debate. Bankrolled by the Virgin Islander, Caspar Holstein, a notorious and unusually erudite lottery kingpin, for literary contests in 1926 and 1927, *Opportunity* was by 1926 a partly US-Caribbean venture and hence, unsurprisingly, it fell to Johnson, with prompting from Walrond, and the promise of further funding from Holstein, to address the Caribbean silence of his African American colleagues. While the November 1926 Caribbean special issue of *Opportunity* was perhaps less ambitious, or attention-grabbing than either Locke's or Du Bois's editorial work over 1925 and 1926, it succeeded at least in raising the issue of the Caribbean presence within the New Negro movement, and consequentially, its Renaissance.

Notes

1. Vincent Starrett, "Haldane Macfall, Novelist," *The Double Dealer* I, no. 5 (May 1921): 187–188.
2. Haldane Macfall, *The Wooings of Jezebel Pettyfer* (New York: Knopf, 1925).
3. "Guide for the Christmas Book-Buyer," *The Critic* XXXV (July–December 1899): 1152.
4. See, for example, "Literary Notes," *The Saturday Review*, July 2, 1898. "The Book of the Month," *The Review of Reviews* XVIII (July–December 1898).
5. Grant Richards, "*The Wooings of Jezebel Pettyfer*. By Haldane Macfall," *The Athenaeum*, no. 3691 (1898). G. W., "Women Who Did and Who Do Yet," *The Egoist* 1, No. 1 (January 1, 1914): 16.
6. Bonnie Kime Scott, "Beyond (?) Feminist Recuperative Study," in *Women and Literary History: "For There She Was,"* ed. Katherine Binhammer and Jeanne Wood (Newark: University of Delaware Press, 2003), 226.
7. Louis Chude-Sokei, *The Last "Darky": Bert Williams, Black-on-Black Minstrelsy, and the African Diaspora* (Durham: Duke University Press, 2006), 32. Eric Lott, "Blackface and Blackness: The Minstrel Show in American Culture," in *Inside the Minstrel Mask: Readings in Nineteenth-Century Blackface Minstrelsy*, ed. Annemarie Bean, James Vernon Hatch, and Brooks McNamara (Middletown, CT: Wesleyan University Press, 1996), 24–26.
8. See Martha Jane Nadell, *Enter the New Negroes: Images of Race in American Culture* (Cambridge, MA: Harvard University Press, 2004), 7.
9. Theodore Peterson, *Magazines in the Twentieth Century* (Urbana: University of Illinois Press, 1956), 2–3.
10. "Harlem: Mecca of the New Negro," *Survey Graphic* 6, no. 6 (March 1925).
11. Alain Locke, ed. *The New Negro: An Interpretation* (New York: A. and C. Boni, 1925), xi, 266–267. Hereafter cited parenthetically.

12. Quoted in George Hutchinson, *The Harlem Renaissance in Black and White* (Cambridge, MA: Belknap Press, 1997), 394.

13. Jeffrey C. Stewart, *The New Negro: The Life of Alain Locke* (New York: Oxford University Press, 2018), 480–481. Hereafter cited parenthetically.

14. Alain Locke, "To Certain of Our Philistines," *Opportunity* 3, no. 29 (May 1925): 155. Hereafter cited parenthetically.

15. W. A. Domingo, "The Tropics in New York," *Survey Graphic* 6, no. 6 (March 1925): 650.

16. "Harlem Types: Portraits by Winold Reiss," *Survey Graphic* 6, no. 6 (March 1925): 651–654. Hereafter cited parenthetically.

17. While subsequent editions did not use color, it is worth noting that the second printing of *The New Negro: An Interpretation*, published in 1927 differs quite significantly from the original 1925 printing (making it effectively a new edition in all but name). Both printings use color prints.

18. Miguel Covarrubias and Eric Walrond, "Enter, the New Negro, a Distinctive Type Recently Created by the Coloured Cabaret Belt in New York," *Vanity Fair* 23, no. 4 (December 1924): 60–61.

19. [Du Bois], "The Browsing Reader," *The Crisis* 37, no. 4 (April 1930): 129. Though not signed off by Du Bois, he was the sole editor of *The Crisis* at the time.

20. Ibid.

21. Miguel Covarrubias and Eric Walrond, "The Increasing Vogue of the Negro Revue on Broadway," *Vanity Fair* 23, no. 6 (February 1925): 61.

22. James C. Davis, *Eric Walrond: A Life in the Harlem Renaissance and the Transatlantic Caribbean* (New York: Columbia University Press, 2015), 74–76.

23. James Weldon Johnson, ed., *The Book of American Negro Poetry* (New York: Harcourt, Brace and Co., 1922), xli. Hereafter cited parenthetically.

24. Raised in Florida, with a Bahamian mother and maternal great grandmother from Saint-Domingue (modern-day Haiti), Johnson could be considered Caribbean-American or even Caribbean (as Florida is part of the Caribbean Basin). Nevertheless, Johnson had closer immediate ties – the national, cultural and otherwise – to the United States than he did the Caribbean.

25. Nathan van Patten, "Organization of Source Material for the Study of American English and American Dialects," *American Speech* 4, no. 6 (1929): 428–429.

26. Alain Locke, "More of the Negro in Art," *Opportunity* 3, no. 36 (December 1925): 364.

27. Quoted in Nadell, *Enter the New Negroes*, 103.

28. Alongside the illustration featured in Covarrubias and Walrond's December 1924 *Vanity Fair* sketch "Enter, the New Negro," one of Covarrubias's "Jazz" illustrations accompanies a March 1925 *Vanity Fair* story by Walrond: Eric D. Walrond, "The Adventures of Kit Skyhead and Mistah Beauty: An All-Negro Evening in the Coloured Cabarets of New York," illustrated by Miguel Covarrubias, *Vanity Fair* 24, no. 1

(March 1925): 52, 100. By 1927, Covarrubias's "Jazz" illustrations are replaced by Gwendolyn Bennett's poem, "Song," despite being erroneously included in the list of illustrations as featuring on page 225. Alain Locke, ed., *The New Negro: An Interpretation* (New York: A. and C. Boni, 1927), 225. I am grateful to Peter Hulme for some of the discussion here.

29. "A Questionnaire," *The Crisis* 31, no. 4 (February 1926): 165. Beginning life as a questionnaire in the February issue of *The Crisis*, "The Negro in Art" symposium was only officially announced in the magazine's March issue. Questions and answers to the questionnaire/symposium were published in the magazine from February to June and August to November 1926.

30. "The Negro in Art: How Shall He Be Portrayed?," *The Crisis* 31, no. 5 (March 1926): 219. Hereafter cited parenthetically.

31. "The Borzoi Broadside for September 1925," *American Mercury* 6, no. 21 (September 1925): xx. The Borzoi Broadside advertorial ascribes no author, however, the subsequent *Saturday Review* advert replicates some of the same copy verbatim, attributing Van Vechten as the spokesperson. Knopf, "The Wooings of Jezebel Pettyfer," *The Saturday Review of Literature*, October 3, 1925.

32. Emmett J. Scott, review of *The Wooings of Jezebel Pettyfer*, *The Crisis* 31, no. 1 (November 1925): 32.

33. Van Vechten to Du Bois, October 29, 1925, Du Bois Papers, Special Collections and University Archives, University of Massachusetts Amherst Libraries, MS 312. Hereafter WDB.

34. Quoted in Herbert Aptheker, ed., *The Correspondence of W.E.B. Du Bois: Selections, 1877–1934*, vol. I (Amherst: University of Massachusetts Press, 1997), 324–325.

35. Du Bois to Van Vechten, November 9, 1925, WDB.

36. Countee Cullen, review of *Porgy*, *Opportunity* 3, no. 36 (December 1925): 379.

37. Clarissa M. Scott, review of *The Wooings of Jezebel Pettyfer*, *Opportunity* 4, no. 36 (January 1926): 26–27.

38. Van Vechten to Du Bois, October 29. Carl Van Vechten, "Moanin' wid a Sword in Mah Han'," *Vanity Fair* 25, no. 6 (February 1926): 102.

39. Eric Walrond, "Mr. MacFall's 'Jezebel'," *The Saturday Review of Literature*, May 1, 1926, 756. Hereafter cited parenthetically.

40. "The Negro in Art: How Shall He Be Portrayed?," *The Crisis* 32, no. 2 (June 1926): 73.

CHAPTER 13

"Symbols from Within": Charting the Nation's Regions in James Weldon Johnson's God's Trombones

Noelle Morrissette

In his 1922 "The Negro's Creative Genius," the preface to *The Book of American Negro Poetry*, James Weldon Johnson assigned his African American contemporaries the task of discovering and producing in their poetry "a form that will express the racial spirit by symbols from within rather than by symbols from without."[1] While his declaration was situated in a discussion of dialect's profound limitation for the African American poet (its "two full stops: humor and pathos"[2]), it referenced a far broader framework of national culture upon which the poet must draw: a framework founded and fostered through the nation's regions, its networks of individuals and social, political, and literary group practices. Thus, according to Johnson's preface, the emerging black national self-concept of the New Negro renaissance period rests on the incorporation of "symbols from within" the regions of African American life and culture. While the author's emphasis on such symbols may appear as conservative efforts to constrain and authorize certain expressive modes of African American life over others, potentially excluding all but the most elevated, best-foot-forward racial representations, for Johnson, these internal symbols offered expansive possibility. In geography, form, and practice, Johnson's "symbols from within" expressed ever-broadening cultures of African American modernity. Johnson's lifetime of writing charted this terrain by moving African American culture, history, and modes of expression through southern locales to points further South: the Caribbean, Cuba, and an articulation of African American bilingualism. His poetic work *God's Trombones: Seven Negro Sermons in Verse* (1927), moving between the folk fixture of the black preacher and what Marcellus Blount has called the "preacherly" text,[3] enacted a formal experimentation that simultaneously translated the contemporary political relevance of African American religious culture. Johnson's emphatic use of the performance and text-mobility of his own works drew attention to the contextualization of his writings as expressive practice, carrying them between textual and performed realms.

James Weldon Johnson's legacy as a New Negro Renaissance author should center on his geographic travels to and from the South, which reframe Johnson as a culture-gatherer whose major poetic work *God's Trombones* was created out of regional, North–South–Midwest travel.[4] Out of these regional movements Johnson created a practice-based form of literary culture that drew upon expressive models of African American communion – of place-gathering and collective expression – to create a contemporary political collective. While New Negro culture has often been characterized as making use of a usable folk Negro past, Johnson knew that New Negro culture – often understood as modern and urbane, starkly contrasting folk and regional – needed to contend with everyday folk as practice-based individuals whose inherent nature was political as well as imaginative. Therefore, although dialect poetry held profound limitation for African American poetic expression, vernacular practices – everyday speech and images and self-concept – were political practices with powerful potential. His vernacular project in *God's Trombones* was more than a simple linguistic project to avoid dialect and yet elevate black vernacular, it was an endeavor to draw upon "symbols from within" African American folk forms, and also from within the nation's regions, to advance a national African American culture that exceeded those very boundaries.

The literary-cultural historian Gerald Early has observed that religious culture structured social life for African Americans regardless of geographic location or aspirations to secular identity. In Harlem, African Americans "were trying to create a great, model urban community for the first time in their history, in the very center of the most important English-speaking cultural center of the USA."[5] The modern, New Negro of Harlem and other urban locations was dependent on prior forms of social organization based on the authority of the African American church. "Ironically, for African Americans, the only way to fashion a great secular community like Harlem was through the leadership of black churches,"[6] Early observes. As Johnson was aware, these prior and powerful "folk" forms of worship were everywhere in the nation, originating in their most powerful form of necessity – as political as well as spiritual forums for a people excluded from national life and civic participation. In his preface to *God's Trombones* Johnson says as much:

The old-time Negro preacher ... was an important figure, and at bottom a vital factor. It was through him that the people of diverse languages and customs who were brought here from diverse parts of Africa and thrown into slavery were given their first sense of unity and solidarity ... this power of the old-time preacher ... is still a vital force; in fact, it is still the greatest single influence among the colored people of the United States. The Negro today is, perhaps, the most priest governed group in the country.[7]

Yet more than simply acknowledging this, more than simply appropriating the authority of the preacher for his own ends, Johnson redirects folk forms to political and literary relevance in the modern world, placing African American religious practice and worldview in a contemporary context that renders them politically, and humanly, relevant to modern social and literary discourse. In *God's Trombones*, Johnson renegotiates an authoritative space in national culture for a modern and at times secular African American church culture. At the same time, Johnson creates an authoritative space for himself as a poet and political leader, ministering to his audience through *God's Trombones'* performance. Johnson productively negotiates between American culture and vernacular African American expressive forms to create a theory of poetic expression and linguistic transcription.[8]

Yet, the English-speaking cultural center in the making that was Harlem, New York was not the center of Johnson's linguistic endeavor in *God's Trombones*. Johnson's "symbols from within" expressed everbroadening cultures of African American modernity, and those cultures extended and contradicted any narrow definition of national culture. Johnson's writing charted an African American modernity defined by black cosmopolitanism and a diaspora that contained many nationalities, spoke many languages, and significantly contributed to the national cultural store. This narrative of black modernity did not emphasize a simple, unidirectional story of origins, a usable past for African American culture; instead, it was oriented toward movement and the modern, the practice of blackness in different frames of experience. For Johnson himself this narrative resounded, carrying from his ancestral narrative to the bilingual Jacksonville of his boyhood, and beyond to Venezuela and Haiti, returning South in purpose-directed trips from church to church as Field Secretary of the National Association for the Advancement of Colored People (NAACP).[9] His regional and hemispheric movements situate *God's Trombones* in a global context.

In 1916, Johnson became the NAACP's first African American executive member in the newly created position of Field Secretary. Over the next three years, he was responsible for increasing membership in the organization by over 60,000, and for initiating the establishment of hundreds more branches in the South. This increased membership and regional representation of southern blacks effectively rewrote the organization's profile, as well as its power and significance, making it truly national and black-directed. While Johnson would rise in rank to Executive Secretary in 1920, his first role at the organization deeply shaped this institution's endeavors in social advocacy and social justice. Johnson's travels put him in danger at times in a white South openly hostile to African American equality, but his routes also connected him to a nascent African American political body with powerful cultural practices – African American expressive modes brought together in group practice.

The Call of *God's Trombones*

On a Sunday in Kansas City, Field Secretary Johnson, after delivering a series of talks at black churches on behalf of the NAACP, remained on the platform awaiting a sermon by a famed evangelist. The preacher began to present "a formal sermon from a formal text." It was flat, Johnson recalled. Facing an unresponsive audience and a droning text, the preacher suddenly slammed the Bible shut, "stepped out from the pulpit, and began to preach. He started intoning the old folk-sermon that begins with the creation of the world and ends with Judgment Day. He was at once a changed man, free, at ease, and masterful."[10] Johnson described this scene in his preface to *God's Trombones*; later in his autobiography, *Along This Way* (1933), he elaborated:

> He was free, at ease, and the complete master of himself and his hearers. The congregation responded to him as a willow to the winds. He strode the pulpit up and down, and brought into play the full gamut of a voice that excited my envy. He intoned, he moaned, he pleaded – he blared, he crashed, he thundered. A woman sprang to her feet, uttering a piercing scream, threw her handbag to the pulpit, striking the preacher full in the chest, whirled round several times, and fainted. The congregation reached a state of ecstasy. I was fascinated by this exhibition; moreover, something primordial in me was stirred.[11]

Johnson described the event that marked the birth of *God's Trombones* and the origin of the poet and the preacher in an "ecstatic," "primordial" expression of time before time. Before the preacher had finished his sermon, Johnson took out a slip of paper and jotted down his ideas for his first poem "The Creation." According to Johnson, the genius of the

black preachers was not foremost in "what" they said but in the combination of "how, when and where" of their speech.[12] The words, launched by
the preacher, do not stop in empty space (or on the page). They are
received and brought to fullness by their hearers. *God's Trombones* stands
as a tribute to what Johnson calls the "old-time Negro preacher," the figure
whom Johnson considered to be "the greatest single influence among the
colored people of the United States." Yet it stands even more so as a tribute
to the dynamic expression of the preacher's congregation, the charismatic
leadership of the congregants. In this space, Johnson could make room for
himself as author and his developing concept of the textual and performed
registers of his compositions.

Marcellus Blount coined the term "preacherly text" to provide a critical
term for an aspect of African American poetry, which, neglected and
under-theorized, undergirds long-standing practices of black poetic subjectivity in an African American literary tradition. While African American
poetry has often appeared to practice "a discrete, seemingly fragmented
expression," Blount finds that this in fact "masks its own continuity as
a way of veiling its challenges to the legitimacy of dominant political
institutions and cultural traditions."[13] Read this way, African American
poetics challenge the mainstream authority of American political life and
its literary-cultural values, for example, literary modernism, "as a way of
enacting a new realm of subjectivity." Blount describes preacherly texts as
"written texts that draw on the aesthetics of vernacular performance,"
wherein "the tensions between repetition and improvisation that operate
in a verbal performance are translated into competing structures of creation
and recollection for literary artists and their audiences."[14]

James Weldon Johnson's use of sermonic structures of thought in *God's
Trombones* negotiates an inside and an outside of authority and voice,
providing multiple occasions for audiences to attune themselves to an
interior language of subjectivity "from within": the sermons, put into
practice through performance, create an expansive region of African
American subjectivity that is defined by practice and movement between
texts and speech performance. His prefaces and other writings enhance this
work, offering different framings of a blackness that refuses to be defined
and classified. Confirming Blount's idea of a "preacherly text" that repeats,
improvises, and creates competing structures of creation, *God's Trombones*
alternates between text and performance. It alternates between these modes
in three significant ways: first, in the preacher himself, as he modulates
meaning away from the "formal text" of the Bible and yet through the
idioms and sonority of King James English; second, in the work's preface as

an authoritative stance from within and without, through whose shifting voice mediates a meaning defiant of cultural reduction (to stereotype); and third, in Johnson's extensions and embodiment of *God's Trombones* as its reader in a variety of settings, intimate and public.

In *God's Trombones*, the preacher is a negotiating figure between the black working and middle classes. As they merge, they form a dynamic collective to negotiate with a white middle class. Through the intimacy of the setting in which he shared his readings of *God's Trombones*, Johnson could achieve an embodied relation of preacher and congregation, art and political thought. Johnson's physical bond with his listeners, and his embodiment of preacher and congregation, create a new mythos of the nation – one that acknowledges the "preacherly text" that is the history of African American thought and lives, conveyed through expressive modes and a distinct poetics. He carefully instructed how to listen and interpret the poetic sermons in his preface to *God's Trombones*. His audience must carry their meaning, stirred by innate emotion to the personae and themes of African American religious thought *as* contemporary politics. Through Johnson, the message is clear: the "lay preacher" and his congregants were politicized, demanded acknowledgment – by the black middle class, and by whites as well.

Johnson re-inscribed the role of the black preacher from white dramas such as Paul Green and Marc Connelly's and from poems such as Vachel Lindsay's "The Daniel Jazz." Extended and performed, *God's Trombones* would enter into the world of other moderns who dramatized their works, using their bodies as instruments of expression: Vachel Lindsay and Edna St. Vincent Millay, charismatic, magnetic performers – while *God's Trombones* would also supplant the idea of a simple, static folk existing outside history, instead granting the agents of his sermons an emotional and cultural authority. Working-class religious culture thus, like Johnson himself, embodied an active, speakerly political identity – one that affirmed the interpretative authority of leaders in the black church, whose authority had been called into question as hymnals and texts came to be increasingly linked to the expression of religious culture.

Focusing on the preacher as a mediating figure of cultural and textual authority, Johnson references the recent history in black churches of "lining-out" hymns and the brief introduction of printed hymnals, which the author calls "books of idiotic anthems" in his preface to the *Book of American Negro Spirituals*.[15] As Evelyn Brooks Higginbotham writes, "Lining-out had not required literacy, but only an able song leader to introduce each verse of song, which in turn was followed by the congregation's repetition of verse. The introduction of the hymnals, how-ever, disadvantaged the illiterate, since it reconfigured the collective voice to include the literate only."[16] As he wrote *God's Trombones*, Johnson was acutely aware of the issue of the textual transcription of expressive modes of black culture. He was fascinated with a newly emerging "public voice, indeed, a charismatic authority," writes Higginbotham, that "rivaled the authority of the educated black leadership."[17] In the 1920s and into the 1930s a northern-migrated black working class effected the shift to an emotional folk orality that challenged the cultural authority of the black middle class. *God's Trombones* contested textual authority and its opposite while drawing both stances together as praxis to create a political and cultural authority and a cultural nationality.

The very poems themselves suggested the formal possibility of breath through Johnson's emphasis on the "tempos of the preacher" and the poems, "better intoned than read," "the decided syncopation of speech," and the "pause that is marked by a quick intaking and an audible expulsion of the breath."[18] According to Brent Edwards, in Johnson's sermonic poems

> the revolutionary possibility that opens up here is that Johnson . . . begins to toy with the technique of transferring the swing from the vernacular, performing black body or bodies into the very formal body of the poem; in the manipulations of line, measure, and punctuation, the poem itself begins to be sketched out as a "breathing," "syncopating" body.[19]

The significance of this move is that Johnson's listener and reader encounter "the ethical value of black music," which "transforms belong-ingness and creative originality into a quality that can never be simply owned or possessed; its roots are swung back and forth in the form itself."[20]

God's Trombones honored the creative, spiritual, and political legacy of the black church and its sermonic tradition, a dynamic and sustaining culture for African Americans that could also, in Johnson's view, sustain the nation. In Johnson's 1922 preface to *The Book of American Negro Poetry*, the author observes that "the status of the Negro in the United States is more a question of national mental attitude toward the race than of actual conditions. And nothing will do more to change that mental attitude and raise his status than a demonstration of intellectual parity by the Negro through the production of literature and art."[21] Johnson continues with an assertion: "the Negro has already proved the possession of these powers by being the creator of the only things artistic that have yet sprung from American soil and been acknowledged as distinctive American products."

Johnson listed these four major creations as "the Uncle Remus stories . . . the 'spirituals' or slave songs . . . the cakewalk and ragtime."[22]

Johnson saw his *God's Trombones* as part of this creation story. Recognizing the creative, spiritual, and political power of the black church and the sermonic tradition, *God's Trombones* was like the four creative African American forms: it created a distinctly American art based on African American expressive forms. Centered on the African American sermonic tradition, *God's Trombones* found a form that expressed "the racial spirit by symbols from within rather than by symbols from without." By this, Johnson meant that his poetic sermons would not make use of dialect, language too readily associated with buffoonery and minstrel antics. With advice for his fellow African American poets that he himself followed, Johnson sought "a form freer and larger than dialect, but which will still hold the racial flavor; a form expressing the imagery, the idioms, the peculiar turns of thought, and the distinctive humor and pathos, too, of the Negro, but which will also be capable of voicing the deepest and highest emotions and aspirations, and allow of the widest range of subjects and the widest scope of treatment."[23] To Johnson, the trombone best represented this wide, expressive range of the sermon – not "Gabriel's Trumpet," as his good friend and fellow poet Anne Spencer, who was instrumental in the composition of "The Creation," suggested as the work's title.

The first poem of Johnson's collection, "The Creation," enunciates the ethos of the black church community. God possesses awesome powers "spangling the night with the moon and stars."[24] Yet he also exhibits human-like qualities, from his emotions and observations to his physical form. Even while regarding his creations – "his moon . . . [and] his little stars" (19) – he is lonely, and states as much: "I'm lonely – / I'll make me a world" (17). Beginning with light and with each following phenomenon, God comments on his creation: "And God said: That's good!" (17) God himself takes on an embodied form by the end of the sermon, a "Great God, / Like a mammy bending over her baby, / Kneeled down in the dust / Toiling over a lump of clay / Till he shaped it in his own image; / Then into it he blew the breath of life, / And man became a living soul. / Amen. Amen" (20).

James Weldon Johnson found his language of interior subjectivity not exclusively in Kansas City, but also in Lynchburg, Virginia, in the company of Anne ("Annie") Spencer. Together, they started the Lynchburg chapter of the NAACP, in 1918. Johnson completed his first poetic sermon, "The Creation," shortly after he met Spencer in his travels as Field

Secretary. It was published in early 1920 in *The Freeman*. It was also while visiting Spencer and visiting the church Spencer and her husband attended that Johnson discussed African American religious worship and the poetic form that would allow for the breadth of African American experience and the depth of individual emotion. Their mutually rigorous and appreciative attention to each other's poetic experimentations resulted in Spencer's publication of some of her first poems and Johnson's sustained quest to give full expression to African American preaching in his poems. Johnson would later solicit Spencer's advice on the title of his work as *God's Trombones* went to press, confirming her involvement in conversations about its composition. Anne Spencer played a more important role in the construction of "The Creation" and *God's Trombones* than has been acknowledged. She provided Johnson with a southern locus of New Negro agency and poetics from which to direct his work.

Johnson directed rhythm, meter, breath, and pauses through the poetic form of the sermons. The preface's self-described linguistic project also expanded the concept and potential of African American individual subjectivity and the practices that would enable such cultural articulations, the symbols "from within" that are defined by practice and movement between texts and speech performance. As Johnson asserts his avoidance of dialect, too readily associated with burlesque, he not only avows that his work cannot be read as such. He claims an African American bilingualism:

> The old-time Negro preachers, though they actually used dialect in their ordinary intercourse, stepped out from its narrow confines when they preached. They were all saturated with the sublime phraseology of the Hebrew prophets and steeped in the idioms of King James English, so when they preached and warmed to their work they spoke another language, a language far removed from Negro dialect. It was really a *fusion* of Negro idioms with Bible English; and in this there may have been, after all, some *kinship* with the innate grandiloquence of their old African tongues.[25]

The sublime phraseology of the Hebrews, the idiomatic language of the King James Bible's translation of the Hebrew, the kinship of African tongues in speech: one begins to see the coursing movement of text, translation, and speech. Johnson takes care to distinguish the fusion of expressive forms from dialect as it reflects the problematic "mental attitude" toward black culture: "To place in the mouths of the talented old-time preachers a language that is a literary imitation of a Mississippi cotton-field dialect is sheer burlesque."[26] He further specifies that this reductive attitude places distorting emphasis on "the use of big words by preachers, in fact by Negroes in general ... the laugh being at the exhibition of ignorance involved. What is the basis of this fondness for big words? Is the predilection due, as is supposed, to ignorance desiring to parade itself as knowledge?" He answers succinctly: "Not at all. The old-time Negro preacher loved the sonorous, mouth-filling phrase because it gratified a highly developed sense of sound and rhythm in himself and *his hearers*."[27] Stating it in this way, Johnson drew attention to black expressive existence, its continuity and dynamism, outside and inside the authoritative structure of literary and spiritual value. He also emphasized African linguistic kinship in form and feeling to the familiar text of the Bible.

Moving African American culture, history, and modes of expression through southern locales to points further South, Johnson drew on the expansiveness of black identity that exceeded the definitions of the American nation – its language, religion, geographic boundaries, and peoples. *God's Trombones* fits into Johnson's lifelong endeavor to describe African American identity through a diasporic lens, one that viewed African American modernity from the inception of the transatlantic slave trade and African diaspora. Johnson had written about New World black culture from the expansive geography of his mother's Bahamian and Haitian heritage and his father's experiences as a free black in Virginia who migrated to New York City. He also had access to the geographic, linguistic, and visual diversity of New World black cultures from his hometown of Jacksonville, a port city, and through its Cuban itinerant workers. Johnson's scholarly and multilingual backgrounds, as well as his travel to black churches and communities through the nation's regions as Field Secretary, shaped his view of black modern identity as dynamic and resistant to static categories. Honoring the inside and outside negotiations of authority between speech and text, Johnson sought to animate New World black culture as Johnson had encountered it as a citizen, a diplomat, an author, and an activist on behalf of the NAACP, paving the way for his political, literary, and nonfiction works. Not just *God's Trombones* but also his *Black Manhattan* (1930), which offered a social history of black New York that broadly extended to world citizenship rights for African Americans, and his translations into English of poems by the Cuban author Plácido in *The Book of American Negro Poetry* (1922), characterize Johnson's endeavor to create a black poetic subjectivity through the sermon, a form negotiating structures of authority and voice to create multiple, competing frameworks of blackness. These frameworks were directed at an audience attuned to the dynamism of black expressive culture, its resistance to dominating cultural and political forms of power while creating new structures of creation and recollection. Johnson's excesses draw attention to these processes.

The task Johnson shared with his contemporary African American poets in *The Book of American Negro Poetry* of using "symbols from within" meant asserting and framing these dynamic, multiple concepts of racial blackness – effectively creating a new space for the "American Negro" of Johnson's titled anthology. Brent Edwards, in "The Frame of Blackness," discusses the rhetorical power of anthologies in relation to their introductions/prefaces. An introduction frames the text(s) that follow it, certain abstract and contextual placements produce specified relations and discursive locations.[28] Prefaces to poetic anthologies that chart the terrain of blackness, New Negroness, African Americanness have a different, but related task: to offer multiple points of entry, literary and documentary, to the discourse of the text that follows – to do the complex work of asserting and of "framing race."[29] Prefaces can often present a new space for a text that allows multiplicity and the combination of forms of writing into a new way of thinking about those forms.[30] Edwards finds that the frame of blackness in *The Book of American Negro Poetry* undoes itself: "if *The Book of American Negro Poetry* frames its particular motivating difference by overflowing the nation-state – even while defining national culture through a 'racial gift' – the same framing overflows itself, extending and questioning the limits of its difference. The book splits its own binding."[31] Moving South, outward to the Caribbean, even to Africa, Johnson's New World preacher and congregation's practices present alternative forward-looking potentialities for the nation and for cultural-political definitions in new modes of expression and experience.

By the time of Johnson's revised edition of *The Book of American Negro Poetry*, in 1931, several younger poets of the 1920s had embraced the use of African American folk forms and "dialect," or vernacular, placing it at the center of their innovative formal techniques. Among them, Johnson viewed the work of Langston Hughes and Countee Cullen as exemplary and representative of a new arc of African American poetic expression. In his 1922 preface, Johnson had outlined modern African American poetry through two schools: the first, Paul Laurence Dunbar's minstrel tradition; the second, World War I writers who responded to these conventions through revolt and rejection of stereotype. "Since the original publication of the book a third group has arisen," Johnson now wrote. "The preeminent figures in this younger group are Countee Cullen, who published his first volume, *Color*, in 1925, and Langston Hughes, who published his first volume, *The Weary Blues*, in 1926."[32]

In addition, between 1922 and 1931, Johnson had authored *God's Trombones*:

> Several of the group have dug down into the genuine folk stuff – I mention genuine folk stuff in contradistinction to the artificial folk stuff of the dialect school – to get their material; for example, Langston Hughes has gone to such folk sources as the blues and work songs; Sterling A. Brown has gone to the Negro folk epics and ballads like "Stagolee," "John Henry," "Casey Jones," and "Long Gone John." These are unfailing sources of material for authentic poetry. I myself did a similar thing in writing *God's Trombones*. I went back to the genuine folk stuff that clings around the Negro preacher, material which had many times been worked into something both artificial and false.
>
> ...
>
> An artist accomplishes his best when working at his best with the material he knows best. And up to this time, at least, "race" is perforce the thing the American Negro poet knows best. Assuredly, the time will come when he will know other things as well as he now knows "race," and will, perhaps, feel them as deeply; or, to state this in another way, the time should come when he will not have to know "race" so well and feel it so deeply. But even now he can escape the sense of being hampered if, standing on his racial foundation, he strives to fashion something that rises above mere race and reaches out to the universal in truth and beauty.[33]

Writing ten years after the publication of *God's Trombones*, Sterling Brown underscored the high stakes of cultural authority and original literary expression derived from "symbols from within": "The reading world seems to be ready for a true interpretation of Negro life from within, and poets with dramatic ability have before them an important task. And the world has always been ready for the poet who in his own manner reveals his deepest thoughts and feelings. What it means to be a Negro in the modern world is a revelation much needed in poetry."[34] Brown describes an interpretative authority generated by African American poets interpreting themselves.

Responses to *God's Trombones*

God's Trombones was the work of which Johnson was most proud in his oeuvre, a work that not only served a hefty diplomatic purpose, but which he also described as the potential for a writing life that he could not fully pursue. He imagined, yearned for, a pure-form poetic vocation, one independent of the demands of his challenging work at the NAACP. Yet for years, *God's Trombones* enabled Johnson's diplomatic work of the NAACP. Johnson traveled nationwide to perform and promote his work in *God's Trombones* in new contexts, not only giving lectures on behalf of the NAACP but also giving readings of the sermons in *God's Trombones* – effectively using the text in performance as an act of diplomacy. When traveling, Johnson followed his daily political speeches and activities with an evening reading from *God's Trombones* in the parlor of his hosts. Then, too, Johnson's photograph was offered to NAACP supporters and stood framed in the intimate spaces of more than one white household, his suave grey-green eyes looking outward to the intimate setting of their homes. *God's Trombones* was therefore not only a work with which James Weldon Johnson found an intimate, organic connection, but also a work that mythologized the author, and that, through its performance by Johnson, created a diplomatic and intimate bond with his listeners.

For his readings, he carefully noted such pacing and pitch in his personal copy of the book. For example, notes for the performance of "Go Down, Death" emphasize the rising intensity, slowed to rise once more. The second stanza contains Johnson's marks, "even – with slightly increased intensity – diminishing in last two lines." The third stanza sustains and raises that, with "increased intensity" underlined and "Call me Death!" triple underlined: "Call Death! Call Death!" The poetic sermon's fifth stanza slows the pace and lowers the pitch, as Johnson adds "pause" to the lines, "And she's tired– / And she's weary–." The sixth stanza increases the pace once more, as Johnson indicates "acceleration"; the seventh stanza emphatically underscores that Sister Caroline, facing death, saw what the living "couldn't" see: "Old Death." The pitch lowers, as "Death took her up like a baby," in a "pitch low with slight acceleration with heightening effect in voice." The concluding lines of the second-to-last stanza slow to near silence with the insertion of a "double-pause" between the repeated invocation, "Take your rest [double-pause], take your rest."[35]

Johnson's voice conveyed the meaning, delivering the pacing, rhythm and pauses that he emphasized as crucial beyond the words themselves; forty years of smoking Benson & Hedges cigarettes gave his voice a distinct, complex sonority. As the popularity of *God's Trombones* grew, Johnson increasingly gave broadcasts of his readings, accompanied by nationally recognized choruses such as the Fisk Jubilee Singers, whose major repertoire consisted of the spirituals. Writing to his editor at

Viking, Johnson informed Marshall Best of his Sunday, April 12, 1936, NBC broadcast to London at 1:15 EST: "The broadcast will emanate from Fisk University Chapel. The Jubilee Singers will sing, and I shall read 'The Creation.'"[36]

Eventually, these readings by Johnson were taken into the hands of community performers, as a 1938 letter from poet, Atlanta classmate, and Federal Arts Project coordinator Gwendolyn Bennett indicates. She mentions to Johnson the Harlem choir that performs his sermons: "The Negro Melody Singers, A Federal Music Project Group, do arrangements of your sermons beautifully. Would you consider taking part in a program during which they would sing them and you would speak at the Harlem Community Art Center?"[37] Such performances, which feature Johnson's and other's voices as well as musical and dramatic arrangements, indicate Johnson's desire to adapt his works to voice them through others.

One of the earliest extensions of Johnson's composition was a jazz-infused chamber music piece for high voice and eight instruments by Louis Gruenberg titled "The Creation." The poetic sermon by Johnson with this title was published in 1918 and served as an inspiration to the composer. Once *God's Trombones* was published, the poems within its pages have been set to music many times. Johnson was excited by Gruenberg's work and shared the score with Blanche Knopf, who, as the author's editor and agent at Alfred A. Knopf, had recently arranged for the reissue of *The Autobiography of an Ex-Colored Man*, timed to be released with *God's Trombones*. "I am sending you at the same time the musical setting of one of my poems called 'The Creation.' I thought you might be interested in it. The score is by Louis Gruenberg. Perhaps you know him. It was published in Vienna."[38] Gruenberg's composition, brought out in 1925 by G. Schirmer musical publishers, was a "jazz-influenced chamber work" that, together with a score for the poet Vachel Lindsay's "The Daniel Jazz," published the previous year, brought widespread attention to the composer as a proponent of the "new music." Gruenberg trained as a pianist, had studied at New York's National Conservatory from 1892, at which time it was headed by Antonin Dvořák.[39] A handful of composers who were Johnson's contemporaries – including, but not limited to, Dvořák, Ferruccio Busoni, Dmitri Shostakovich, and Frederick Delius – had identified the value of folk song to national art. Such compositions embraced the influential "nation-building" narrative popularized by the late nineteenth-century French critic Hippolyte Taine: natural environs create a mood, which creates a people who exhibit that mood, a language representative of that place and people, a folk culture that carries these traits, and, at last, the development of that culture into a national culture that is representative of civilization. The ascension of folk culture to civilization marks the birth of a national culture.

The nation-building narrative could either romanticize or dismiss working-class culture, for this is the culture of the "folk." In the hands of everyday, working-class people, the ostensible folk artist is something other than a crude building block – the artist is a moving, human category. While the nation-building narrative emphasized historical progress and transformation, the folk artist as cultural agent emphasized the imperative of present-tense adaptation. Johnson's plans to extend his work on the "old-time Negro preacher" through musical and dramatic scores indicate his desire to enact the role of the folk artist as a human in motion, in multiple, moving contexts.

Johnson planned to extend the entirety of *God's Trombones* in a form similar to Gruenberg's score for "The Creation." Using one of the influential members of his solicited audience for this work, Rebecca West, Johnson sought an introduction to the composer and musicologist Leonard Constant Lambert. He hoped that Lambert would provide a symphonic score of *God's Trombones* in its entirety, while Johnson would write the libretto (1931). "I think it is an inspired choice," she wrote Johnson. "I wish I could send the poems to him straight away, but maybe he had better wait for your libretto."[40] No collaboration occurred, but Johnson's attempt to coordinate such an endeavor indicates his desire to transform and extend his poetic sermons beyond the page, his strategic targeting of audiences and readers of his work, and his effort to create an interracial conversation through music centered on the old and the new, and also a black culture centered on the old and the new. Lambert did acknowledge Johnson in his book, *Music Ho! A Study of Music in Decline*, a work that depicts the rise of the new music and the tensions between "revolutionary" and "conservative" trends in modern music. Lambert acknowledges Johnson as a poet and a composer in his distinctively American milieu.

In the late 1920s, Johnson attempted the dramatization of *God's Trombones* as *A Plantation Sunday*, the working title for his play, looking to his brother for orchestration and to Millard Thomas to design the set. He had in mind the tremendous success of Paul Green's *In Abraham's Bosom* (1926) and Marc Connelly's *The Green Pastures* (1929), both of which won Pulitzers in the years in their production. Two personae introduced in the pages of Johnson's manuscripts who do not make it to the finished work underscore the driving power of Johnson's "call" through the sermons: "Moze" Jackson and Jasper Jones. Johnson uses these characters to enact the *performance* of the sermons; indeed, he envisioned a dramatic performance of his work on a par with Paul Green's and Marc Connelly's plays. Yet rather than be carried by a beatific God figure, Johnson emphasized the preacher and parishioners themselves. Like Wallace Thurman's Cordelia (a figure who appears in the short story "Cordelia the Crude" and his later play, co-written with William Jourdan Rapp, *Harlem: A Melodrama of Negro Life in Harlem* (1928)), Johnson's Moze Jackson persona was meant to carry this larger history of the folk. The folk in turn shaped Johnson's practice as an author, as he animated a poetics of expression that could not be reduced to a text or a people, but instead moved between, residing in the form of the sermon itself. Such a poetics was a radical departure for an age in which the image of the folk preacher was taken to represent a simple past.

The originators of the sermons of *God's Trombones* possess the "wonderful voice" "not of an organ or a trumpet, but rather of a trombone, the instrument possessing above all others the power to express the wide and varied range of emotions encompassed by the human voice – and with greater amplitude."[41] Among Johnson's literary works, *God's Trombones* is particularly cherished. Like "Lift Every Voice and Sing," it continues to be performed with new inflections of culture and experience. This is the difference between a trumpet and a trombone: between a religious authority and the expressive slide of group authority, the people's practice.

Remembrance and mythology

In death, *God's Trombones* became a tribute to Johnson himself – a tribute that took hold in the years following his untimely passing in 1938. The mythology attached to Johnson as his body lay in state for viewing in New York City at Salem Methodist Episcopal Church at 129th Street and Seventh Avenue in Harlem: dressed, according to his wishes, in his writing attire of "lounging robe" and trousers, a copy of *God's Trombones* placed on his chest. He would later be cremated, his ashes joined with his wife Grace after her death. As Johnson was memorialized, so too was *God's Trombones* performed; the author and his text became symbols not just of the author Johnson and his work of art, but also of the perceived community that he forged in his life work as a race leader, poet, and executive member of the NAACP.[42]

The sermon moves between Johnson and his text. James Weldon Johnson and *God's Trombones* are made one, the author's union of *God's*

Trombones with his life, their bond through the ashes of death, and the performative extensions of *God's Trombones* negotiating public discourses to create a dynamic and ethical practice of expression, a new mythos of the nation and of the modern author.

Religious institutions responded to these extensions by affirming Johnson's authority in other institutional religious practices. Johnson's earlier composition with his brother Rosamond, "Lift Every Voice and Sing" – a work of profound significance that Johnson described as a modern-day spiritual that voiced the suffering and striving of African American subjects for civil rights – is now included in the hymnal used in Quaker meeting houses.[43] Johnson was made a saint in the Episcopal church.

"The power of the Negro to suck up the national spirit from the soil and create something artistic and original, which, at the same time, possesses the note of universal appeal, is due to a remarkable racial gift of adaptability; it is more than adaptability, it is a transfusive quality,"[44] Johnson wrote, in his Preface to *The Book of American Negro Poetry*. Johnson's *God's Trombones* was a poetic endeavor to create an evaluative framework for reading African American poetry in the American poetic tradition. This act of sharing was a potentially life-saving act, one that intermingled blood and spirit in making a fully realized, and great, American civilization.

Notes

1. James Weldon Johnson, "Preface," in *The Book of American Negro Poetry*, ed. James Weldon Johnson (New York: Harcourt, Brace, and Co., 1922), xli.
2. Ibid., xl.
3. Marcellus Blount, "The Preacherly Text: African American Poetry and Vernacular Performance," *PMLA* 107, no. 3 (May 1992): 582–593.
4. As I discuss in detail in my book manuscript, "Anne Spencer between Worlds," Johnson traveled frequently to poet Anne Spencer's home at 1313 Pierce Street, Lynchburg, Virginia. Johnson, tasked with assisting in the establishment of local southern chapters of the National Association for the Advancement of Colored People (NAACP) as Field Secretary of the growing institution, met Spencer in his travels through the South in this official capacity; Spencer had helped organize a chapter of the NAACP in Lynchburg.
5. Gerald Early, "Three Notes Toward a Cultural Definition of the Harlem Renaissance," *Callaloo* 14, no. 1 (1991): 143.
6. Ibid.
7. James Weldon Johnson, "Preface," in *God's Trombones: Seven Negro Sermons in Verse* (1927; repr. New York: Penguin, 1990), 2–3.
8. As Brent Edwards has shown, Johnson articulates this theory in his prefaces to the *Book of American Negro Poetry*, the *Book of American Negro Spirituals*, and

the *Second Book of American Negro Spirituals*. See his "The Seemingly Eclipsed Window of Form: James Weldon Johnson's Prefaces," in *The Jazz Cadence of American Culture*, ed. Robert G. O'Meally (New York: Columbia University Press, 1998), 580–601.

9. Johnson was the first African American executive member of the National Association for the Advancement of Colored People. Through this institution he left a lasting legacy of legislative and journalistic endeavors to defend the citizenship and individual rights of African American and African-descended peoples in the New World. Johnson served as American diplomat to Venezuela (1906–1909) and Nicaragua (1909–1913) before leaving the foreign consulate because of race prejudice. In 1920 he traveled to US-occupied Haiti as an informal diplomat and wrote a four-part series for *The Nation* describing American abuses of power.

10. Johnson, "Preface," in *God's Trombones*, 6.

11. James Weldon Johnson, *Along This Way: The Autobiography of James Weldon Johnson* (New York: Viking Press, 1933), 336.

12. Ibid., 338.

13. Blount, "The Preacherly Text," 583.

14. Ibid.

15. James Weldon Johnson, "Preface," in *The Book of American Negro Spirituals*, ed. James Weldon Johnson (New York: Viking Press, 1925), 49.

16. Evelyn Brooks Higginbotham, "Rethinking Vernacular Culture: Black Religion and Race Records in the 1920s and 1930s," in *African American Religious Thought: An Anthology*, ed. Cornel West and Eddie S. Glaude, Jr. (Louisville, KY: Westminster John Knox Press, 2003), 982.

17. Ibid., 985.

18. Johnson, "Preface," in *God's Trombones*, 10–11. Brent Edwards has discussed the way in which Johnson's prefaces to the *Book of American Negro Spirituals* and *God's Trombones* initiate and answer the question of the transcription of expressive culture by using the figure of the body, removed from the figure of music, to capture the elusive nature of musical and aural expression in black culture through the form itself. See Edwards, "The Seemingly Eclipsed Window of Form," 595.

19. Edwards, "The Seemingly Eclipsed Window of Form," 595.

20. Ibid., 598.

21. Johnson, "Preface," in *The Book of American Negro Poetry*, ed. Johnson, vii.

22. Ibid., viii.

23. Ibid., xli.

24. Johnson, *God's Trombones*, 18. Hereafter cited parenthetically.

25. Johnson, "Preface," in *God's Trombones*, 9, my emphasis.

26. Ibid.

27. Ibid., my emphasis.

28. Brent Hayes Edwards, *The Practice of Diaspora: Literature, Translation, and the Rise of Black Internationalism* (Cambridge, MA: Harvard University Press, 2003), 38.

29. Ibid.
30. Ibid., 40.
31. Ibid., 50.
32. James Weldon Johnson, "Preface to the Revised Edition," in *The Book of American Negro Poetry*, ed. James Weldon Johnson (New York: Harcourt Brace, 1931), 5.
33. Ibid., 6–7.
34. Sterling Brown, *Negro Poetry and Drama. No. 7 Bronze Booklet* (Washington, DC: Associates in Negro Folk Education, 1937), 129.
35. Johnson, *God's Trombones*, copy 4, James Weldon Johnson Collection, Stuart A. Rose Manuscripts, Archives, and Rare Book Library, Emory University.
36. Johnson to Marshall Best, April 8, 1936, box 22, folder 510, Series I, James Weldon Johnson and Grace Nail Johnson Correspondence, Beinecke Rare Book and Manuscript Library (JWJ Corr., BRBL). A version of the following discussion appears in Noelle Morrissette, *James Weldon Johnson's Modern Soundscapes* (Iowa City: University of Iowa Press, 2013), 108–110.
37. Gwendolyn Bennett to Johnson, January 4, 1938, box 3, folder 44, Series 1, JWJ Corr., BRBL.
38. Johnson to Blanche Knopf, April 29, 1926, box 12, folder 267, Series I, JWJ Corr., BRBL.
39. Gruenberg wrote "The Creation" while he was studying at the Vienna Conservatory with Ferruccio Busoni, who, like Dvořák, was known for using folk music in his compositions.
40. Rebecca West to Johnson, February 14, 1931, box 23, folder 534, Series I, JWJ Corr., BRBL.
41. Johnson, "Preface," in *God's Trombones*, 5.
42. There is a photograph of Johnson reading "The Creation" to his students at Fisk in the early 1930s. It is an oddly specific reference to the exact work that is being spoken – indicating the signature quality of that first sermonic poem of the collection. James Weldon Johnson reading "The Creation" to his students, Fisk University, *c.* 1931. James Weldon Johnson Papers, Fisk University John Hope and Aurelia Elizabeth Franklin Library Special Collections.
43. Johnson presents this "hymn" as a modern spiritual, suggesting that as a nation we must become attuned to the many voices and experiences that attach themselves to the song. The survival of "Lift Every Voice and Sing" for over a century of expression in various contexts, sung by blacks and whites, children and adults, conveys a truth about us as a nation: We sing far better than we know. See also Noelle Morrissette, quoted in "'Lift Every Voice and Sing': Whether Anthem or Hymn, Song Invokes Pride," *Atlanta Journal-Constitution*, February 1, 2018. www.ajc.com/news/local/lift-every-voice-and-sing-whether-anthem-hymn-song-invokes-pride/oG3m3HPfeeygasa5bbyaTI/
44. Johnson, "Preface," in *The Book of American Negro Poetry*, ed. Johnson, xix.

CHAPTER 14

Rudolph Fisher: Renaissance Man and Harlem's Interpreter

Jonathan Munby

Rudolph "Bud" Fisher, son of a Baptist minister, explored the complexity of having faith in the city and modernity in the most concerted way of all Harlem Renaissance writers. From 1925 until his untimely death at the age of 37 in 1934, Fisher published fourteen short stories, two novels (including the first African American detective novel to be published in book form), a critical essay, and two scientific articles on the relationship between bacteriophage and ultra-violet light. His varied and prolific writings in such a short period gained him significant recognition at the time. As Langston Hughes reflected:

> The wittiest of these New Negroes of Harlem, whose tongue was flavored with the sharpest and saltiest humor, was Rudolph Fisher, whose stories appeared in the *Atlantic Monthly*. His novel, *Walls of Jericho*, captures but slightly the raciness of his own conversation. He was a young medical doctor and X-ray specialist, who always frightened me a little, because he could think of the most incisively clever things to say – and I could never think of anything to answer.[1]

Despite his contemporaneous renown, Fisher's contribution to the Harlem Renaissance was neglected for years. His premature death meant he left no collection of his short stories, which were locked away in magazine archives, and his novels went out of print. As Maria Balshaw points out, this lack of attention would not be resolved "until the revival of publishing interest in African American fiction in the 1980s."[2] The redis- covery of Fisher was particularly important because, as a Harlem Renaissance figure, he was signal in making Harlem itself the exclusive focus of his literary art. As the editor of the first collection of Fisher's short stories, John McCluskey Jr., emphasizes, "startling perhaps is the fact that so few writers used Harlem extensively as a backdrop for their fiction. ... Of all the Renaissance fiction writers, it is to [Fisher] we must turn time and time again to get the flavor ... of the 1920s 'black capitol of the world.'"[3] Fisher himself stated, "if I should be fortunate enough to become known as Harlem's interpreter, I should be very happy."[4]

Fisher's short stories and novels, as well as his 1927 essay, "The Caucasian Storms Harlem" (on how Harlem cabarets increasingly catered to white audiences), capture the rhythmic cadence of the Jazz Age street, the vicissitudes of black social mobility between under-educated lower-class "rats" and educated pretentious bourgeois "dickties," the drama of African Americans arriving as a modern people. His polymath achievements (as an X-ray physician-scientist on one hand, and a writer of fiction on the other) defined him as the epitome of a "renaissance man" and informed how he developed a literary aesthetic adequate to the complexities of African American urbanization. The very encounter between the folkloric and science, superstition and modernity are at the heart of Fisher's mediation of Harlem.

In contemporaneous coverage of the New Negro movement, Fisher is given brief mention as the author of *The Walls of Jericho* (1928) by James Weldon Johnson in *Black Manhattan* (1930). While Johnson grouped Fisher with other writers capitalizing on a general fascination with African American experience, he also highlighted what made Fisher stand out: "And every bit of this fiction – that is, every bit that has been published in a way calculated to reach the general public – has been written by writers of the Harlem group. . . . Rudolph Fisher brought the first light, satirical touch."[5]

By implication, this comment acknowledges how Harlem Renaissance writing exploited white interests in African American experience. Following on from the controversial success of a white author's novel about black Harlem, Carl Van Vechten's *Nigger Heaven* (1926), *The Walls of Jericho* might have been open to criticism as pandering to white readership fantasies. Some forty years later Nathan Huggins would reintroduce Fisher as a significant but overlooked member of the Harlem Renaissance with similar reservations. However, like Johnson, he qualified any sense that Fisher was a literary opportunist by stating that "Fisher wrote the only novel in the decade that exposed class antagonism among Harlem blacks" and that, in the process, he "achieved greater distance from his subject than did Van Vechten, who could not (dared not?) use satire as a device for critical judgment of Harlem blacks."[6]

Fisher's status as satirist initially gleaned positive attention from the bastion of the African American intellectual elite, W. E. B. Du Bois. As editor of *The Crisis*, Du Bois awarded Fisher a $100 prize in August 1925 for his short story, "High Yaller," about the deleterious effect of presumptions about skin hue on the Harlem community.[7] Three years later, however, he wrote a negative review of *The Walls of Jericho*, for its apparently inadequate representation of the black bourgeoisie:

> Mr. Fisher does not yet venture to write of himself and his own people; of Negroes like his mother his sister and his wife. His real Harlem friends and his own soul nowhere yet appear in his pages, and nothing that can be mistaken for them. The glimpses of better class Negroes which he gives us are poor, ineffective make-believes. One wonders why? What does Mr. Fisher fear to use his genius to paint his own kind as he has painted Shine and Linda?[8]

One of the key aspects of Fisher's writing was, precisely, its attendance to the resilience of the black lower classes and the pretentions of the middle classes. Even if he, as an Ivy League trained physician and writer, was a member of Du Bois's "Talented Tenth" (that 10 percent of higher educated African Americans meant to lead the challenge against white racism), Fisher refused to turn a blind eye to the problems of social hierarchy and class privilege that attended this notion. Even though it may have been discomfiting, Fisher provided a candid, yet humorous view of intraracial division as something definitive of a modern black condition.

Short Stories

Fisher's short stories were more than rehearsals for his longer fiction. Eight of them appeared in print between 1925 and 1927, prior to *The Walls of Jericho*. Four were showcased in the one of the nation's oldest and most respected magazines, *The Atlantic Monthly*, including his first, "The City of Refuge." Its title has a contradictory meaning that is played out throughout his fiction. Harlem is at once a destination and refuge away from the segregated South and a black metropolis with distinctly modern problems. King Solomon Gillis emerges from the subway at 135th Street and Lenox Avenue, the heart of Harlem. He is a greenhorn migrant from Waxhaw, North Carolina, who had shot a white man and barely escaped a lynching. Recovering from his first experience of underground transportation, he is overcome by what he sees: "Negroes at every turn" and, most impressively, the traffic (including vehicles transporting white people) at a major crossing being halted and directed by an African American policeman.[9] "Even got cullud policemans" becomes a refrain in the story, one that reminds King Solomon of how, despite all its pitfalls, "in Harlem, black was white" (4).

Far from living up to his name, Fisher makes King Solomon the victim of a confidence trickster, Mouse Uggam, who dupes him into dealing "little white pills" (dope) as "French medicine" (10). Mouse Uggam is also from King Solomon's hometown, Waxhaw. By contrast, however, he is a far more experienced migrant, having fought in France and on return stayed in Harlem rather than return home. Mouse has undergone a modern urban transformation and developed street smarts. Symptomatically, the first exchange between Mouse and King Solomon is inflected by quite different vernaculars that are indicative of how far Mouse has become a Harlemite and how far King Solomon will have to go.

In response to Mouse's offers to help him, King Solomon asks for directions to an address in Harlem: "Wha' dis hyeh at, please, suh?" His Southern accent betrays him as a potential patsy to the street savvy Mouse, who tests out King Solomon's gullibility further by asking, "You from – Massachusetts?" To which King Solomon answers, "No, suh, Nawth Ca'lina." Their conversation literally accentuates a gap between urban North and rural South, with Mouse concluding in street argot that King Solomon was "the shine I been waitin' for . . . a baby jess in from the land o'cotton and so dumb he thinks ante bellum's an old woman" (5–6).

Mouse inveigles himself into King Solomon's confidence by securing him a job at an Italian American grocery, where he supplies certain customers with envelopes of narcotic pills. The story concludes with King Solomon descending into Edwards, a basement speakeasy jazz venue and cabaret, a movement that mordantly parallels his emergence out of the 135th Street subway station at the story's beginning. Here white detectives catch him taking envelopes of pills from Mouse, who in turn betrays him. King Solomon is provoked to fighting the detectives by this and the sight of a female black entertainer being harassed by a white man – but stops when an African American police officer confronts him. The story's ironic conclusion is that King Solomon is not the victim of white prejudice – he's a patsy for a black criminal ruse and arrested by a black cop. King Solomon's epiphany at the end is expressed through his final words as he stops resisting arrest for dope-peddling: "Even – got – cullud – policemans" (16). Harlem as refuge is thus given a candid qualification.

"The City of Refuge" introduces us to a range of elements and tropes that are definitive of Fisher's exposition of Harlem. Harlem is a place of encounter between a variety of African Americans, testament to the way the diversity of the black metropolis holds out dialogical possibility on one hand, and hampering division on the other. Fisher is concerned with the quotidian drama of black-on-black experience (the fact of white racism lurks beyond the borders of Harlem). Sites of intraracial interchange can be positively conceived. The street and cabaret, for example, can be spaces where different classes of black Americans can come together, even as they are spaces that accentuate more negative notions of difference. Here the newly arrived rural greenhorn is taken advantage of by the experienced urban hustler. Southern "wisdom" fails to surface and is threatened by northern avarice. Traditions associated with the migrant seem atavistic or endangered by processes of becoming modern. Vernacular voices articulate and separate Harlem denizens in a tragicomic narrative. "The City of Refuge" initiates readers in Fisher's ear for "Harlemese," with its many registers, idioms, cadences, sparring and musical character, or what M. Michelle Robinson calls his "hybrid enunciation of community."[10]

Published in the same year, "The South Lingers On" developed further the migrant/Harlem relationship. Indeed, perhaps in search of a more generous or heterogenous treatment of this theme, Fisher opted for a format consisting of five vignettes where southern values compete with Harlem's possibilities, good and bad. Like "The City of Refuge," the first vignette deals with the fleecing of new migrants. A gambler converted to charlatan preacher, Reverend Shackleton Ealey, is out to profit from newly arrived black folks at New York's Pennsylvania station by encouraging them to join and sponsor his old-time religion church in Harlem. His scam is undermined by the arrival of the Reverend Ezekiel Taylor who has been forced to leave the South for Harlem in pursuit of his congregation. Taylor rescues his flock, an act that suggests a God-fearing regional inheritance might be able to co-habit with secular iniquity, after all.

Fisher, the son of a Baptist minister, would return to this first vignette's rumination on the possibilities of retaining faith in the city two years later in his stories "The Backslider" and "Fire by Night" (1927). In the former, Eben Grimes is a lapsed Christian, a "sinful backslider" whose love of cabaret and alcohol have led to his expulsion from the church (103–104). The story has an ironic outcome when Deacon Crutchfield, the minister who cast him out, is arrested for being a backsliding gambler caught in a speakeasy. Eben sees this as a redemptive lesson, renounces the Devil and returns to the congregation.

"Fire by Night" is a redemption narrative about Rusty Pride, the fallen son of one of Harlem's most revered preachers (Reverend Daddy Pride), who has become a diffident frequenter of the Club, a pool hall and bootlegging underworld haunt. An upstanding woman, Roma, still carries a torch for him. Three drunk "rats" gate-crash a "dickty dance" evening arranged by "uppity boogies" at the nearby New Casino (where Roma is in attendance) and cause a major fight to break out (124). Class difference is enunciated as dickty erudition ("Private dance ... You can't come in without an invitation") and ratty street slang ("Listen, mistuh. Is anybody ast you what kind o dance dis is? ... we're big time niggers, too") accentuate division and resentment (124). The feral Club denizens, including Rusty, raid the Casino's coatroom, stealing furs and wraps. In the fracas, Rusty defends Roma, and they run away pursued by one of Rusty's foes. The distraction of the riot allows someone with a vendetta against the Club's owner to set it on fire. As the inferno brightens the night sky, the couple unwittingly find refuge in the doorway of Daddy Pride's house. The prodigal son and his newfound love have returned.

The other vignettes in "The South Lingers On" vary in their degree of optimism for a productive relationship between past and present, South and North, supernatural and the secular. In the second vignette, newly arrived Jake Crinshaw, a Virginia farmhand, seeks legitimate urban work to no avail. The way to prosperity is through pimping or picking pockets. In the third, a grandmother laments how Harlem has changed her granddaughter, Majutah, a young woman who enjoys the nightlife and has forsaken the church. In the fourth, a couple argue about how their daughter's education has increased the distance between generations. The mother sees this as a virtue, the father resents it. The mother cajoles his attitude as symptomatic of having "too much cotton field" in him (37). Their daughter, Anna, arrives home with news that she's won a scholarship to go to Columbia. Her father changes his stance and smilingly tells her "You sho' is yo' daddy's chile" (38). In the final vignette, out of curiosity two cynical young bootlegging men decide to attend a church tent service on 138th Street. One of them ends up admitting that the preacher's talk of hell got to him. Collectively, these scenarios reveal how connection (or reconnection) exists alongside separation and distance between the South and Harlem.

McCluskey highlights how Fisher "deepens the theme of transition by introducing the specific figure of the ancestor who actively struggles to keep some sense of integrity clear to her young charges."[11] The grandmother as a southern ancestral maternal figure is central to three stories: "The Promised Land" (1927), "Guardian of the Law" (1933), and "Miss Cynthie" (1933). Respectively, Mammy, Grammie, and the eponymous Miss Cynthie all meet their different Harlem challenges with "mother wit" in attempts to protect the younger urbanized generation.

"The Promised Land" starts with Mammy singing a spiritual which competes with the blues music of a rent party in another apartment across the airshaft. She observes young folks dancing, including her grandsons, Sam and Wesley, and sees an absence of God. She reflects on how Harlem had destroyed their friendship with Sam now earning twice as much as Wesley. Mammy hurls her Bible across the airshaft, smashing the window of the house rent party to prevent a fight breaking out between her grandsons over Ellie, object of their rival interests.

To Mammy, Ellie is very much "a girl of the city" as she is interested in dating Sam because he earns more (even though she fancies Wesley) (52). Mammy is disturbed by this example of "the philosophy of the metropolis ... its ruthless opportunism" (53). Responding to Mammy's criticism of her ungodly attitude, Ellie states, "Pity you old handkerchief-heads would n' stay down South where you belong" (54–55).

Angered, Ellie rejects both Sam and Wesley's advances. Wesley comments that northern girls were "gimme gals" whose "kisses were a commodity" (55–56). He does a window cleaning chore for Mammy requiring him to stand precariously in the airshaft. In a fit of pique thinking that Wesley had put Ellie up to rejecting him, Sam kicks out at Wesley who falls to his death. Mammy covers up the truth by telling the white detectives that it was an accident. Sam's remorse is short-lived as he gets back with Ellie. The story ends with Mammy singing a spiritual, "Bow low! – How low mus' I bow / To enter in de promis' land?" (59). This story's tragic conclusion is reinforced by Mammy's understanding of Harlem as a promised land as just that: "All hit do is promise" (54).

Comparatively, "Guardian of the Law" is more optimistic in tone. Grammie is a snuff-snorting feisty grandmother of Sam, a newly appointed policeman. This story returns to the "even got cullud cops" refrain by King Solomon in "The City of Refuge." Additionally, it recycles the idea of a rivalrous love triangle which is central to "The Promised Land," "Ringtail" (a 1925 story that dramatizes tensions between West Indians and African Americans), "High Yaller," "Blades of Steel" (1927), and "Common Meter" (1930). Officer Sam secured his police job to the cost of rival applicant Grip Beasely. Both men were also competing for the affection of Judy, who settled on Sam once he won the appointment. Grammie senses that this combination of losses would fuel deep resentment in Grip, someone who "would have been just one more hoodlum in uniform. Couldn't help it – too much Harlem in him" (61).

With the help of his friend Cawley, Grip kidnaps Judy and dupes Sam into coming to his apartment. At gun-point, he attempts to make Sam drink a bottle of whisky, get him drunk and turn him in to the police as a rookie officer violating his terms of probation – thus paving the way for

Grip to get the job he lost to Sam. Grammie thwarts the scheme, breaking into the room where Sam is being held. The shock of seeing an old woman "framed on the threshold, a small, terrible angel of vengeance" pronouncing "What kind o' foolishness is this?" distracts Cawley (64). She throws snuff into his eyes and he drops the gun reaching for his face. Sam emerges triumphant from a consequent fight with Grip.

When the cops arrive on the scene, Grammie spins a yarn to cover up her own role in resolving matters and amplify that of Sam. Unlike "The Promised Land," the lies the old maternal figure tells here are positively construed, designed to make Sam the hero of the scene and increase his good standing with the police station. The story's title is productively misleading, for "the guardian of the law" turns out to be Grammie not her rookie cop grandson. The "law" being protected has more to do with ancestral "lore." Her southern mother wit has found a positive calling in the city. As Balshaw puts it, "[t]he figure of the grandmother provides grounding for urban assimilation, but she represents not so much a Southern or rural history kept alive as the redrawing of a tradition within the urban context."[12]

The idea of redrawing tradition through a maternal ancestor is, perhaps, most richly portrayed in "Miss Cynthie." A southern God-fearing grandmother from Waxhaw (like King Solomon) travels to Harlem, to see her grandson, David Tappen. Her hope is that David has found a proper calling as a doctor, or at least as an undertaker (work that would keep him near to the Lord). Unbeknownst to her, however, David, is a secularized debonair song and dance star, whose skills had earned the sobriquet of "Tap."

While impressed by the "swagger" of Harlem black folks (including the quality and speed of Tap's Packard), Miss Cynthie is disconcerted by the amount of theaters, which she believes are the "stronghold of transgression" (75). Tap's challenge is how to break the news to his grandmother about his profession. His girlfriend, Ruth, holds a stereotypical view of southern old folks' conservative ideas. However, Tap retorts, "Yea – but with her you can change 'em. . . . I know her. She's for church and all, but she believes in good times too, if they're right" (73).

The next evening Miss Cynthie lets herself be led "like an early Christian martyr" to the Lafayette Theatre, where she discovers that her grandson is a renowned performer. The show starts with an elegy to the South, featuring a plantation scene with spirituals (74). Against her prejudices, Miss Cynthie becomes entranced by the scene. Her transported state is broken when the music changes, "distorted itself into ragtime," underscoring dance routines for gyrating scantily clad bodies (75). To her deep chagrin, Tap emerges in this scene of iniquity – singing and then dancing with "Ruth, a dancer; not the gentle Ruth Miss Cynthie knew, but a wild and shameless young savage who danced like seven devils – in only a girdle and breast-plates" (77).

Significantly, the scene they perform narrates Tap's migration story to Harlem. Initially duped as a greenhorn, he eventually triumphs as a Broadway headline act with Ruth. While this *mise en abyme* invites reflection on Fisher's use of migration tropes to understand Harlem, it is also an affirmation of how the urban entertainment industry constituted a progressive opportunity for African American advancement. Here a Harlem show becomes an innovative way to exploit the community's own story of modernization by restaging it as a basis for a black popular art.

At the conclusion, a synthesis of otherwise incompatible values is achieved through Tap's encore performance of a song that he had been taught as a kid by Miss Cynthie, "Oh I danced with the gal with the hole in her stockin'." This homage to his grandmother reconciles her to Tap's achievements as good rather than sinful and makes her see the audience no longer as "shriftless sinners" but as "a crowd of children, enjoying the guileless antics of another child" (77).

"Miss Cynthie" corroborates another distinguishing feature of Fisher's mediation of Harlem, namely his musical ear. Fisher was an accomplished musician who had written and arranged songs for Paul Robeson, accompanying him on tour in 1919.[13] In Fisher's writing music is not simply a background score lending color to the Harlem scene. Music is the basis for site-specific gathering and performance. Spirituals vie with blues and jazz as affective modes that best express an African American engagement with modernity and the intergroup conflict it fosters.

"Blades of Steel" centers on conflicts surrounding Harlem's Barber's Ball. Like the barbershop itself, the annual ball constitutes a common ground where "dickties" and "rats" can mix. It also features as a venue where competitive rivalries are orchestrated. In this case, the "yaller" Dirty Cozzens is resentful of the dark hued Eight-Ball's relationship with the "sealskin brown" Effie Wright (136). At the ball, to the syncopation of a "low down" orchestra that specializes in "shouts," Effie rejects Dirty's wish to dance with her, preferring the company of her date, Eight-Ball, when it comes to an immersive dancing experience (137). Dirty tries to knife Eight-Ball later at a grill room. Equipped with a hidden razor in his fingers, Eight-Ball overcomes his foe. At the point of no return, a blues song, "Mercy – Lawd, have mercy" on the restaurant's phonograph awakens Eight-Ball to the situation and causes him to release Dirty (141).

The story which most captures Fisher's discursive understanding of music in the lives of Harlemites is "Common Meter" (1930). Two jazz orchestras at The Arcadia compete for audience popularity – the winner to be determined by length of applause. Fess Baxter's Firemen and Bus Williams' Blue Devils have different approaches to music. "Bus's philosophy of jazz held tone to be merely the vehicle of rhythm" (153). His orchestra knows how to achieve "blueness" (156), how to transport their audience back in time and connect this modern urban romance hungry crowd to slave shouts, lamentation songs, and African rhythms. By contrast Fess has no relationship to the blues: "Contrary to Bus Williams's philosophy, Baxter considered rhythm a mere rack upon which to hang his tonal tricks" (154). Their battle is intensified as both orchestra leaders are also in competition for the attention of the "honey-dew" Miss Jean Ambrose (151). Fess wins the battle through cheating but Jean falls for Bus because he understands that the black community's "unfaltering common meter" is the blues (156).

While music is a preponderant feature of Fisher's stories, so too is his elaboration on skin hue and how it complicates intraracial relations. In "High Yaller," the story that most directly engages this issue, the main protagonist, the ironically named Evelyn Brown, can pass for white (as a "high yellow"). In a tale underscored by a jazz refrain, "Yaller Gal's Gone Out o' Style," Evelyn finds herself accused of only associating with lighter toned African Americans. Hurt by this presumption, she deliberately seeks out a darkly hued boyfriend, Jay Martin. Far from resolving matters, this relationship only compounds things. Now onlookers think Jay and Evelyn represent an unwanted interracial partnership. Jay, accused being a "pink-chaser" (85), is conscious of how the looks he gets communicate contempt about "what that nigger is doing with a white woman," while, in equal measure, Evelyn is seen as a "cheap drab" if she wants to "tag around with a nigger" (92). Caught in a no-win scenario, Evelyn, following the death of her dark-skinned mother, decides to relinquish any association with being black. She would prefer to live by passing as white. The story concludes sardonically with Jay witnessing his loss of Evelyn to a white partner at a cinema, a situation underscored by the ironic repeat of the musical refrain, "Yaller Gal's Gone Out o' Style," which falls on his ears "like a guffaw" (97).

The Walls of Jericho (1928)

Fisher's longer fiction builds on a sensitivity in his short stories to how regional and class differences, while being a vital part of the modern black metropolis, might also hinder the task of finding a "common meter." As Darryl Dickson-Carr highlights, Harlem's messy diversity was at once testament to a democratic possibility for an urban modern future for African Americans, and a threat to the black bourgeoisie's attempt to show "the best of 'the race' to the ever-present white world."[14]

Fisher was important because he satirized this tension most acutely. Dickson-Carr singles out *The Walls of Jericho* "as the first glimpse in fiction of the black literati's division by a member of that group. Fisher lampoons the powerful and influential members of the black bourgeoisie, their white patrons, and – briefly – the artists enjoying a moment of glory in the Jazz Age."[15] The authority of his lampooning was anchored in forensic powers of observation. As Robinson describes, "we might label Fisher a literary sociologist for his thick descriptions of urban experience and distinctive characters."[16]

The Walls of Jericho focuses on diversity and division in black Harlem, on interaction between "rats" and "dickties." As such, the novel's form is driven by character and dialogue, with "rat" street talk or regional dialect sparring with pretentious "dickty" rhetoric. It is also episodic, oriented primarily around Harlem scenes of social intercourse, such as the pool hall, bar room, dance floor, church, and streets for strolling. These spaces are populated by characters representing the variety of Harlem's denizens. Key among these are a couple, Shine and Linda, and a lawyer, Fred Merrit.

The novel's title refers to many things, the walls that sequester Harlem, those that divide it in terms of class, and those that hinder personal development and relationships. Shine's "wall," for example, is his need to keep up his "hard" image. "Every act must be sentimentally airtight" is his mode of self-defense, something that Linda (who is not without her walls either) resents.[17] It takes a sermon by Father Tod on the meaning behind Joshua's bringing down the walls of Jericho (God's message was that Joshua had to stop kidding himself) to bring about an epiphany for Shine: that he should be brave enough to reveal his softer side. While this message obtains to Shine's inflexible masculinity, it also extends to the way different castes and classes of black Harlemites maintain their differences through self-delusion – something that hampers the community's progress.

Shine is the moniker for Joshua Jones, an orphan who had graduated from shining shoes to moving pianos. This deep black hulking "rat" develops a relationship with a striving maid, Linda Young, who becomes Merrit's housekeeper. Merrit is a "dicty" who can pass for white. As such, his status as a bourgeois African American is complicated by his capacity for racial masquerade. Merrit knows that white racism disregards class difference when perceiving black folks. This is most pointedly revealed through his exchange with Agatha Cramp, a patronizing white liberal and object of parody, whose confidence in Merrit (believing him to be white) exposes her bigotry. Merrit's "merit," in the sense of both wealth and light skin hue, allows him to buy property in an otherwise white neighborhood. His merit, however, also leads fellow blacks to mistrust him because of how his fortune is seemingly allied to his light pigmentation.

Positively conceived, phenotopic difference within what is otherwise monolithically labeled "black" puts a lie to racial essentialism. As Fisher celebrates:

> Here is every variation of skin-color, every variety of feature-form, every possible combination of these variations and varieties. And of course every imaginable result, from the most outrageous ugliness to the most extraordinary beauty. Harlem is superlatively rich in diversity (79).

For Fisher, the heterogeneity of blackness is complicated by class interest. Being a "high yaller" may give you social climbing opportunities, while being "eight-ball" dark may give you street credibility. No matter what variation of color might be on display, diversity gives way to division. This problem is depicted typically by Fisher through the collectivity-through-dance-and-music trope and spatial imagery: "Out on the dance floor, everyone, dicty and rat, rubbed joyous elbows, laughing, mingling, forgetting differences. But whenever the music stopped everyone immediately sought his own level" (74).

The Walls of Jericho's denouement derives from a destructive intersection of class resentment and pigment difference. When Merrit's house is burned down, most black folks assume that this was an act by bigoted whites objecting to an African American (who can pass for white) moving into their neighborhood. It turns out, however, that the culprit was the dark-skinned pool hall owner and bootlegger, Henry Patmore, who bears a grudge against the fair-skinned professional, Merrit, having lost a lawsuit to him.

Merrit is important not only because he can cross the color line, but also because he disregards the "dicty"/"rat" divisions within the black community (treating lowly Jinx and Bubber, for example, as equals – something that puzzles them), exposing how class and regional prejudice poisons intraracial relations. At the novel's end, he hires Shine and helps him fulfill the dream of owning his own trucking firm, pronouncing: "What kind of a social structure can anybody have with nothing but the extremes – bootblacks on one end and doctors on the other. Nothing in between. No substance" (283).

Significantly, Fisher included a glossary of "contemporary Harlemese" at the back of the novel. Even as this could be construed as an aid for uninitiated readers who might be white, it is equally valid to see this as an ironic dig at black bourgeois readers who disregarded the richness of street vernacular. As Langston Hughes corroborated in his landmark essay, "The Negro Artist and the Racial Mountain" (1926):

> Let the blare of Negro jazz bands and the bellowing voice of Bessie Smith singing the Blues penetrate the closed ears of the colored near-intellectuals until they listen and perhaps understand. Let Paul Robeson singing "'Water Boy," and Rudolph Fisher writing about the streets of Harlem, and Jean Toomer holding the heart of Georgia in his hands, and Aaron Douglas drawing strange black fantasies cause the smug Negro middle class to turn from their white, respectable, ordinary books and papers to catch a glimmer of their own beauty.[18]

The Conjure Man Dies (1932)

In a radio interview in 1933, Fisher provided clues as to what encouraged him to engage with an established white literary form and write the first detective-mystery novel by an African American:

> Darkness and mystery go together, don't they? The children of the night – and I say this in all seriousness – are children of mystery. The very setting is mystery – outsiders know nothing of Harlem life as it really is . . . what goes on behind the scenes and beneath the dark skins of Harlem folk – fiction has not found much of that yet. And much of it is perfectly in tune with the best of the mystery tradition – variety, color, mysticism, superstition, malice and violence.[19]

Stephen Soitos stresses how Fisher set "new standards for applying detective story conventions to African American concerns."[20] The novel plays with the "whodunnit" format by having the person we think is murdered, an immigrant African prince, N'Gana Frimbo, magically reappear halfway through the novel. Frimbo's character is thus introduced to us only through the various memories of those being interrogated by the investigators. These flashback reports betray the way superstition structures the suspects' thinking and behavior. Frimbo's occupation as a fortune teller is, after all, what attracted those suspected to him in the first place. To the appropriately named Jinx, for example, Frimbo was a mystery because one could not place him nationally or racially: "Didn't talk like an African native certainly. Didn't talk like any black man Jinx had ever heard. Not a trace of a Negro accent, not a suggestion of dialect. He spoke like a white-haired judge on the bench, easily, smoothly, quietly."[21]

Equally, for the investigators, detective Dart and Dr. Archer (both African American), Frimbo is an enigma because his African conjure man sorcery credentials are at odds with his being a Harvard graduate with a keen interest in philosophy, as evidenced in his bachelor degree certificate and the array of books, including Tankard's *Determinism and Fatalism*, Preem's *Cause and Effect*, Dessault's *The Science of History* and Fairclough's *The Philosophical Basis of Destiny*, that adorn his bookshelves (16–17).

Differences in class, caste, region, belief, and language are characterized by the interaction between the three educated middle-class investigators, detective Dart, doctor Archer, and eventually the conjure man himself, and seven suspects from lower-class street or regionally distinct backgrounds. Alongside comic foils Bubber and Jinx, a numbers runner, a funeral home owner's wife, a railway porter, a devout church-working lady, and a drug addict all come under suspicion for murdering someone they thought was Frimbo. The dead man turns out to be a fellow tribesman and servant who periodically posed as Frimbo in order to protect him from possible harm from unhinged clients.

An immigrant African, Frimbo mixes his knowledge of homeland traditions and rituals with his Harvard education. He is at home then with both street and scientific reasoning, able to profit from what I have elsewhere described as Harlem's "fortune economy."[22] Symptomatically, he puts the science of prognostication to successful use in working out what numbers were likely to come up in Harlem's gambling lottery, the policy or numbers racket.

In a pyrrhic denouement Frimbo exposes himself to danger and death in order to apprehend the killer. He is shot and killed by railroad porter Easley Jones, who is in turn caught trying to escape the scene by a trap set by Frimbo. Jones turns out to be Samuel Crouch, the undertaker, in disguise. He killed Frimbo because the latter was having an affair with his wife.

The novel plays out the tensions between rational deductive logic, inductive reasoning and superstition, between modern scientific thinking and atavistic belief in the supernatural. In doing so, it reanimates ideas about Harlem's diversity that define his shorter fiction in a more concerted way. While *The Walls of Jericho* takes the reader on a tour of Harlem's main sites of intermingling demonstrating Fisher's powers of social observation, *The Conjure Man Dies* is itself a reflection on the art of fabulation as it obtains to a distinctly African American world. As a detective novel, it reworks the conventions of the locked-room mystery in the context of African American ways of negotiating the challenges of becoming modern. Logic confronts voodoo, deduction is in tension with prophecy, forensic certainty is undermined by masquerade, the art of dissembling, and belief in luck. Ultimately, the novel dramatizes Fisher's own attempt to balance two worlds, as a specialist in roentgenology and as a writer of fiction.

In providing an X-ray of the Harlem body politic, Fisher's writing augmented his work as a physician in uncovering what makes an African American life "worth living." The origins of this motivation can be traced back some thirteen years prior to the publication of *The Conjure Man Dies*. As Brown University's Commencement orator for the Class of 1919, Fisher, who had graduated with a dual major in biology and English, gave a speech about the relationship between science and religion. Titled "The Emancipation of Science," he proclaimed:

> As thinking Christians, we strive not to bring men to heaven, but to bring heaven to men, and with that the aim of science is identical. It is this oneness of purpose that brings science and religion into harmony – a harmony which permits science to devote its energies not to self-protection, but to the making of life worth living.[23]

Notes

1. Langston Hughes, *The Big Sea* (1940; New York: Hill and Wang, 1993), 240.
2. Maria Balshaw, *Looking for Harlem: Urban Aesthetics in African American Literature* (London: Pluto Press, 2000), 31.
3. John McCluskey Jr., ed., *The City of Refuge: The Collected Stories of Rudolph Fisher* (Columbia: University of Missouri Press, 1987), xix–xx.
4. John Clark, "Mystery Novel Writer Is Interviewed over the Radio," *Pittsburgh Courier*, January 21, 1933, cited in McCluskey, *The City of Refuge*, xxxix.
5. James Weldon Johnson, *Black Manhattan* (New York: Knopf, 1930), 275–276.
6. Nathan Huggins, *Harlem Renaissance* (New York: Oxford University Press, 1971), 119, 121.

7. Letter from W. E. B. Du Bois to Rudolph Fisher, August 6, 1925. W. E. B. Du Bois Papers (MS 312). Special Collections and University Archives, University of Massachusetts Amherst Libraries.

8. W. E. B. Du Bois, "The Browsing Reader, review of *The Walls of Jericho*," *The Crisis* 35 (June 1928): 374.

9. McCluskey, *The City of Refuge*, 3. Hereafter all short story references cited in text.

10. M. Michelle Robinson, *Dreams for Dead Bodies: Blackness, Labor, and the Corpus of American Detective Fiction* (Ann Arbor: University of Michigan Press, 2016), 188.

11. McCluskey, *The City of Refuge*, xx and McCluskey, "Aim High and Go Straight: The Grandmother Figure in the Short fiction of Rudolph Fisher," *Black American Literature Forum* 15 (1981): 55–59.

12. Balshaw, *Looking for Harlem*, 33.

13. McCluskey, *The City of Refuge*, xiv.

14. Darryl Dickson-Carr, *Spoofing the Modern: Satire in the Harlem Renaissance* (Columbia: University of South Carolina Press, 2015), 89.

15. Ibid., 98.

16. Robinson, *Dreams for Dead Bodies*, 179.

17. Rudolph Fisher, *Walls of Jericho* (1928; Ann Arbor: University of Michigan Press, 1994), 197. Hereafter cited in text.

18. Langston Hughes, "The Negro Artist and the Racial Mountain," *The Nation* 122 (June 23, 1926): 694.

19. Quoted in Stephen F. Soitos, *The Blues Detective: A Study of African American Detective Fiction* (Amherst: University of Massachusetts Press, 1996), 100.

20. Ibid., 95.

21. Rudolph Fisher, *The Conjure Man Dies* (1932; London: X Press, 1995), 41. Hereafter cited in text.

22. Jonathan Munby, *Under a Bad Sign: Criminal Self-Representation in African American Popular Culture* (Chicago: University of Chicago Press, 2011), 31–36.

23. *News from Brown*, "Rudolph Fisher '19, physician and literary wit of the Harlem Renaissance," February 11, 2011. https://news.brown.edu/articles/20 11/02/fisher.

PART IV

Performing the New Negro

CHAPTER 15

Zora Neale Hurston's Early Plays

Mariel Rodney

To those who want to institute the Negro theatre, let me say it has
already been established.
                Zora Neale Hurston, "Characteristics of Negro Expression"

On May 1, 1925 Zora Neale Hurston attended an awards dinner hosted by
Opportunity magazine that would introduce her to the literary world as one
of Harlem's rising stars. The well-publicized literary contest attracted over
seven hundred submissions and drew an outstanding guest list that
included Langston Hughes, Countee Cullen, James Weldon Johnson,
Alain Locke, wealthy heiress A'Lelia Walker, Paul Robeson, and Carl
Van Vechten. In her biography of Zora Neale Hurston, Valerie Boyd
writes, "All the present and future luminaries of the Harlem Renaissance
were there."[1] The evening drew together rising and established artists, black
and white critics, and popular figures from Harlem's upper echelons.

In addition to its exceptional scope and star-studded attendance roster,
the night proved particularly gratifying for Hurston. Having just moved to
Harlem earlier that year in the hope that she could launch her career,[2]
Hurston went on that evening to win the most prizes, accepting awards in
the categories for fiction and drama. Hurston's two award-winning short
story submissions included "Black Death" and "Spunk," two pieces that
would grow in popularity over time.[3] Yet, it was the recognition for her
work in the category of drama that most excited Hurston that evening,
with her play *Color Struck* taking second place, and an additional play,
Spears, receiving an award for honorable mention. Both plays combined
her love of storytelling with her ambition for theater and dramatic writing.
Anecdotally, Hurston's exclamations at the dinner have become the stuff of
Harlem Renaissance legend:

> [Hurston] strode into the room – jammed with writers and arts patrons,
> black and white – Zora flung the colorful scarf around her neck with

a dramatic flourish and bellowed a reminder of the title of her winning play: "Coloooooor Struuucckkkk!"[4]

The *Opportunity* contest thus signified for Hurston an induction that could not be overstated. It signaled what scholars have frequently pointed to as a watershed moment in her career. Indeed, scholars speculate that the dinner solidified some of Hurston's most committed contacts.[5] Yet what is frequently lost in discussions of Hurston's Harlem years is an exploration of the genre for which she wrote so ardently and passionately when she first arrived in Harlem in 1925: drama.[6]

In this chapter, I examine Hurston's early dramatic works during the period popularly known as the Harlem Renaissance.[7] In order to fully appreciate Hurston as a Harlem Renaissance figure, the consideration of her early work in the field of drama and black performance is key. The early twentieth century proved to be one of the most vital periods for black theater. The black stage was alternately a wellspring of black creativity and racist vitriol, where some of the most tenuous debates about form, progress, and respectability played out. Hurston's dramas written during the beginning of her career – particularly the first four she published before entering a restrictive contract with patron Charlotte Osgood Mason – exemplify these debates.[8] To situate Hurston as a Harlem Renaissance writer without this context reinforces the erasure of drama from its significant role in shaping black art of the 1920s and beyond.[9] Additionally, this exclusion disregards Hurston's passionate commitment to a genre that she returned to again and again across the entirety of her career, despite the intense challenges and constraints she faced to do so.[10] With the exception of *Mule Bone* and Hurston's well-known feud with Langston Hughes, Hurston's dramatic works receive less attention than any other area of her creative output, despite the fact that Hurston's plays constitute one of her most prolific areas of writing. Only a handful of scholars have ventured to explore Hurston's plays, with even less attending to her plays written at the height of the Harlem Renaissance.[11] Yet, unmistakably, Hurston's early career is nearly exclusively devoted to the collection of a black aesthetic enacted through folk life. Under this context and combined with the fairly recent discovery of her plays, a fuller view of Hurston's efforts becomes possible. As early as 1925, we see Hurston was committed to a project of black life *dramatized.* Her plays thus anticipate what would later become her efforts to sustain, not merely preserve, an embodied folk archive. Given the role of ritual and vernacular folk idioms that would come to dominate her creative writing and her social science career, Hurston's early plays reveal a testing ground for the theory she would later develop in her novels and essays.

Could an attention to black life on the stage depict the "new soul" of the Negro? As black artists and activists sought creative routes to reimagine black futures, black folk culture increasingly emerged as a source of racial pride and an instrument of social justice. W. E. B. Du Bois lauded black folk culture in 1903, writing that "the Negro folk-song . . . remains as the singular spiritual heritage of the nation and the greatest gift of the Negro people."[12] James Weldon Johnson later argued that folk art offered a defining characteristic in human development: "A people may become great through many means," but the Negro's folklore is "the touchstone, it is the magic thing, it is that by which the Negro can bridge all chasms."[13]

Still, the relationship between folk culture and the black stage remained a vexed one and Hurston's relationship to the folk was not uncomplicated. As black artists struggled to define themselves apart from the long legacy of minstrelsy's influence, black intellectuals feared that "unrefined" folk forms bore too close a resemblance to the commodified stereotypes of black life that increasingly drew white crowds. White-authored folk plays added an additional complexity to the questions of representation and black folk culture. Ridgely Torrence and Eugene O'Neill, for example, created black folk life on stage to much success, but such popularity did not satisfy the clarion call for black folk art to be composed by black artists.[14] Alternately, the mass popularity of black-produced shows like Noble Sissle and Eubie Blake's 1921 comedy, *Shuffle Along*, further intensified debates around what Langston Hughes called "the Negro vogue."[15]

The black stage thus occupied the imagination of black and white artists, activists, and intellectuals in the early decades of the twentieth century with a passion that fractured into multiple visions for the future. As ideas about how to build a new black theater developed during the Harlem Renaissance, black artists hotly debated how best to portray black life. They actively mentored scores of young writers, shared correspondences, imagined possibilities, and staged literary contests to encourage and accomplish this end. Two of the leading black periodicals – the National Urban League's *Opportunity* and the National Association for the Advancement of Colored People's *The Crisis* – routinely hosted playwriting contests with cash prizes to seek out and encourage emergent talent. Angelina Weld Grimké's 1916 drama, *Rachel*, saw production as a direct result of winning one such contest. Like Grimké, Hurston's plays hinted at the promise of a new generation for black theater.

Toward these aims, in 1925, W. E. B. Du Bois and Regina Anderson launched the Krigwa Players, a Harlem-based theater group that would

eventually stage plays nationwide.[16] Notably, the folk plays of Eulalie
Spence and Willis Richardson saw production through this theater
group. In an article on the Krigwa Players written for *The Crisis*, Du
Bois defines his vision for a "real Negro theatre." His vision relied upon
four principles that were fundamental to the success of black artistry. For
this success to take root, Du Bois described that a real Negro theatre
must be:

> 1. About us. That is, they must have plots which reveal Negro life as it is. 2.
> By us. That is, they must be written by Negro authors who understand from
> birth and continual association just what it means to be a Negro today. 3.
> For us. That is, the theater must cater primarily to Negro audiences and be
> supported and sustained by their entertainment and approval. 4. Near us.
> The theatre must be in a Negro neighborhood near the mass of ordinary
> Negro people.[17]

Du Bois sought a black theater that could dismantle racism and elevate an
appreciation of black art. Earlier that year however, Alain Locke articulated
his own vision for the black stage in *Theatre Art Monthly*, stating that
"Negro dramatic art" would need to "break with established dramatic
convention of all sorts ... and have the courage to develop its own
idiom, to pour itself into new moulds ... in short, to be experimental."[18]
Where both black intellectuals looked to break away from the long shadow
of American minstrelsy and slavery, each of them sought different means to
achieve that vision. As though in response to both her previous mentors –
Locke and Du Bois – Hurston would write in her essay "Characteristics of
Negro Expression" (1934) the following: "to those who want to institute the
Negro theatre, let me say it has already been established."[19] Indeed,
Hurston's early plays, *Meet the Mamma*, *Spears*, *Color Struck*, and *The
First One*, had already begun the work of crafting her own response to the
question of how black life should be represented.

Hurston's early career – particularly her plays – mark the intense debates
that make up this period. Composed between 1925 and 1927, each of
Hurston's early plays offer profound meditations on community, belonging, and inheritance. Ever interested in the stories we inherit and how they
bind or exclude (African) Americans from each other, Hurston's plays
dramatized a folk modernism[20] that would transform the black renaissance.
Each of her early plays navigates the often-tenuous terrain of belonging and
exclusion, albeit across different modes of theatrical writing. Her creative
range was fluid – she unabashedly moved between musical comedy, tragedy,

and melodrama. Indeed, Hurston's experimentation with playwriting reveals the scope of her imaginative vision and her commitment to black art.

Depicting the Folk

In 1997, the Library of Congress unearthed over a dozen plays and sketches authored by Hurston. The discovery revealed a theatrical output spanning nearly thirty years. Although Hurston would only see two of her plays published over her lifetime,[21] she continued to work in a variety of theatrical capacities throughout her life.[22] Theater scholars Jean Lee Cole and Charles Mitchell note in their introduction of Hurston's plays, "Hurston's first formal education was a theatrical one."[23] In her analysis of Hurston's play *Cold Keener*, Jennifer Cayer notes that Hurston was invited to launch, run, and consult at drama departments in at least two southern colleges; she wrote skits for the Broadway revue *Fast and Furious* in 1931; and she frequently staged several incarnations of her own revue, *The Great Day*. Theater was no accident of Hurston's career. She actively and passionately pursued it.

If, as Alain Locke describes, "the real future of the Negro drama . . . lies with the development of the folk play,"[24] then Hurston's play *Color Struck* asserts black women as central to that future. *Color Struck* takes place in 1901 as a group of black dancers travel to a cakewalking competition in the rural South. The play emphasizes the forms of black vernacular gesture and dialogue that Hurston would eventually make central to her essay "Characteristics of Negro Expression." Act I opens with characters dressed in their "tawdry best"[25] and the play anticipates Hurston's now classic articulation of "the will to adorn."[26] The verbal jest of characters throughout the play also serves to reveal Hurston experimenting with the characteristics she would come to define as essential to black folk culture. In a letter to Langston Hughes in 1928, Hurston lists her early conception of what would later become "Characteristics of Negro Expression":

1. The Negro's outstanding characteristic is drama. That is why he appears so imitative. Drama is mimicry. note gesture is place of words.
2. Negro is lacking in reverence. note number of stories in which God, Church & heaven are treated lightly.
3. Angularity in everything, sculpture, dancing, abrupt story telling.
4. Redundance. Examples: low-down, Cap'n high sheriff, top-superior, the number of times – usually three – that a feature is repeated in a story. Repetition of single simple strain in music.

5.   Restrained ferocity in everything. There is a tense ferocity beneath the
     casual exterior that stirs the onlooker to hysteria. note effect of negro
     music, dancing, gestures on the staid nordic.
6.   Some laws in dialect. The same form is not always used.[27]

Yet *Color Struck* is notable for more than a simple characterization
of the folk. Hurston's use of the cakewalk receives an extended description emphasized through stage direction. Staging one of the most
popular dances of the twentieth century within an all-black rural community in this way suggests Hurston was deeply familiar with the
pleasures and the risks of black folk performance re-appropriated across
various audiences.[28] Nowhere is the point made more explicit than in
Hurston's portrayal of Emma – the dark-skinned black woman at the
heart of the play. While Emma and her beau John are rumored to be "the
bestest cake-walkers"[29] in the region, Emma refuses to dance with John
during the competition on the suspicion that he desires instead to dance
with Effie, a lighter skinned black performer. Emma's refusal to participate in the cakewalk ritual leads to a form of self-exile that Hurston uses
to explore the damning consequences of a community and self now
divided. By turning explicitly to consider the interior life and concerns
of a dark-skinned black female performer, Hurston amplifies the figures
of the New Negro future that Locke's and Du Bois's original vision
seemed to exclude.

Color Struck bears a unique significance to Harlem Renaissance history
in particular due to its inclusion in the iconoclastic literary journal
Fire!!: A Quarterly Devoted to the Younger Negro Artists. Published in
1926, *Fire!!* adopted a radical vision that departed from the leading black
periodicals of the 1920s such as *The Crisis*, *Opportunity*, and *The Messenger*.
The magazine was spearheaded by Wallace Thurman, and co-edited by
Hurston, Langston Hughes, Aaron Douglas, Richard Bruce Nugent, and
Gwendolyn Bennett. This group – dubbed by Hurston as "the Niggerati" –
sought an outlet that could "burn up a lot of the old, dead, conventional . . .
ideas of the past."[30] *Fire!!* rejected a New Negro vision that did not make room
for art that was more than mere propaganda. "Devoted to the younger artists,"
Fire!! thwarted conventional ideals of respectability by commenting on black
sexual desire, colorism, and the working class. A combination of genres –
poetry, short stories, drama, and visual art – *Fire!!* subverted the rigid expectations for folk art. A stunningly complex folk drama, *Color Struck*, reveals
Hurston's willingness to imagine a New Negro future borne of the close
connections formed during *Fire!!*'s premier (and only) issue.

Although *Fire!!* magazine was a short-lived experiment for the Niggerati, Hurston continued to produce plays that experimented with form.[31] Hurston's first published play, *Meet the Mamma* (1925), accomplishes this task in an unconventional way. The play is perhaps best described as a series of plays within a play, thus emphasizing the meta-theatrical nature of the plot and its conceptual underpinnings. Foundationally a black musical comedy, *Meet the Mamma*, follows its characters from New York, across the "high seas,"[32] to an imagined African kingdom in pursuit of an alleged inheritance. As the play moves from scene to scene, characters rehearse various roles (villain, count, princess, and so on) across a range of musical styles and theatrical modes including folk ballads, blues, opera, melodrama, tragedy, comedy, and absurdist drama.

Meet the Mamma serves as a back to Africa fantasy of grand proportions. The plot centers on a young married couple, Pete and Carrie, who run a prominent New York hotel together. Pete's frequent philandering bears the scrutiny of his mother-in-law, Edna, who calls on him to account for his whereabouts from the previous night. Amidst the commotion, Pete receives a telegram notifying him that an uncle in West Africa has discovered a diamond mine amounting to a wealthy inheritance. Excited at such a stroke of luck, Pete, Carrie, Pete's friend Bill, and Edna (as an unexpected stowaway) make the long journey to the kingdom of Luababa to obtain the newfound riches.

Published in 1925, the same year as Locke's canonical anthology, *The New Negro*, Hurston's turn to black musical comedy parodied black caricature and primitive tropes in ways that may have proved discomforting to many black intellectuals. Even today, Hurston's play has seen little to no scholarly attention due perhaps in part to what Cole and Mitchell refer to as her "unapologetic, even gleeful, incorporation of black show conventions such as the jungle dance, hypersexualized black women, and razor-wielding roughs."[33] Still, *Meet the Mamma* reveals Hurston's early attempts to experiment with the form and freedom that a New Negro vision promised.

Where the play begins as a convenient back to Africa scheme, it goes on to stage nuanced questions about diaspora and community. The play problematizes a romanticized return "home" while raising profound questions about inherited traditions of dominance and power. Hurston's attention to this gendered dynamic of community and return are active themes within the play. It in fact reveals how Hurston was continually drawn to the perverse and often violent ironies of domination at work across a diasporic imagination. If Locke's New Negro seized upon mobility and generational difference as central to the new burgeoning spirit of the masses, Hurston's early plays revealed the female lives caught in the heart of those spirited flights away from and toward creative futures. Hurston's plays deliberately centered various "angles"[34] of black life, including her attention to the "Negro farthest down,"[35] and thus legitimized not just the people whose lives she wrote about, but the forms and genres most unexpected to a New Negro project. While Locke's New Negro eschewed melodrama, fantasy, and sentimental fiction, Hurston's plays refused to follow a singular narrative of telos and progress. Instead, she pursued a range of themes and forms that could illustrate black life with the complexity and fervor that it demanded. *Meet the Mamma* was the first published play to do this work and the result is a damning parody of sexual and gendered relationships in the New Negro era. As the play's title hints, meeting the "mamma" provokes a quest for origins at the very moment when a New Negro vision declared its freedom from an inherited past.

Hurston's exposure to the theatrical shows of Washington, DC and New York City re-ignited her interest in the world of theater.[36] In *Meet the Mamma* Hurston seizes on the popularity of black musical theater, vaudeville, and stage revues, but does so with critical difference. Thomas Riis explains that "black musical comedies of the nineteenth century generally consisted of an overture, between ten and twenty songs, and a few dance numbers."[37] In this musical universe songs existed as single units that were not expected to advance the actions of the characters or the plot. Taken together the tableaux of songs often bore a structural relationship to one another, but rarely were they expected to make "dramatic statements"[38] of character or concept. Audiences were often treated to musical numbers at the climactic moment where they could experience demonstrations of syncopation, costume, and melody. Rather than wielding music within the play as convenient spectacle, Hurston deploys musical scenes to forward character development and contribute to the metanarrative commentary of the play. Although songs in traditional musicals were often used as a function of mere interpolation, Hurston composed her melodies *for* her characters as dramatic exposition.

With this key difference, music and dance in Hurston's play serves a critical function in *Meet the Mamma* and seems to rehearse traditional gender divisions. In Act I, for example, the pieces sung by Pete and Carrie solidify their respective values as individuals. Pete launches into his first musical number – a folk ballad that re-interprets a famed biblical figure as a martyr for his lying skills – after bemoaning the lack of a good liar to help him come up with an alibi for his mother-in-law:

> . . . Ananias was a liar
> Much needed in every club
> To fix things to tell your wife
> And alibi in any rub[39]

Pete's ribald admiration for a good storyteller echoes Hurston's own fascination with black vernacular innovation and the practices of myth-making and "lyin' up a nation"[40] in her ethnographic and creative work. Carrie's first songs also offer a vivid portrait of her character and disposition. Carrie's song – a traditional blues ballad – voices the loneliness of mourning an absent, unfaithful lover with wit and awareness. Evoking the blueswoman's plight, Carrie sings:

> I'm blue, I'm blue, so blue,
> I don't know what to do
> Because my man don't stay home;
> Every night he has to roam
> Because I'm his, he thinks me slow
> But other men don't find me so.[41]

On its surface Carrie's song first appears to rehearse rigid gender roles. Upon closer analysis, we might consider Carrie's song as an invocation of the feminist traditions of early twentieth-century blueswomen.[42] As Carrie brazenly calls out her husband's infidelity, she reveals both her dissatisfaction with and her awareness of the gender dynamics shaped by marriage. The last two lines of the refrain slyly mock her husband's ignorance while feigning her own. Read together, Pete and Carrie's songs anticipate the inversions of plot and character later in the play. Moreover, they reveal Hurston's commitment to depicting alternative images of black womanhood in her dramas.

Some of the most notable songs of the play emerge during the second act, which takes place exclusively on an ocean liner as the characters travel to the West African village of Luababa. Following the suggestion that they all "take parts" and "give shows"[43] to pass the time aboard the vessel, the sea-travelers perform mini-plays in the style of an opera, a melodrama, an absurdist drama, and an embedded musical comedy, each with corresponding musical numbers and a supporting chorus. Each character enacts a "part" that provides an analog for their role in the original scenario of the play. For example, in the melodrama, Carrie's mother, Edna, plays a villain (Princess Heebie Jeebie) who seeks to thwart the relationship of the Lady Sweet Patootie (Carrie) and the heroic Count Shake and Roll (Pete). Costumes, props, and a chorus are central to each manifestation of these smaller performances until the final "play" (a musical comedy) is absurdly interrupted by the seasickness of the voyagers, who can no longer maintain their roles without falling over weakly from nausea.

Hurston's interruption of the last "show" – the musical comedy – reflects the intensity with which she wishes to focus on this particular genre. By forcing the characters to embody and then abandon their roles within the embedded musical comedy, Hurston signifies upon the awareness of each character's caricatured roles. The musical comedy is thus reflexive, marking the moment that both the audience and the characters must acknowledge the artificial composition of their once-fixed (gender) roles. That it cannot be maintained without great effect further emphasizes the performative nature of hierarchies of power inflected across gender roles. This reflexive nature is mirrored later in the play once the characters are again called upon to re-orient their roles at the play's conclusion. This comedic reflexivity becomes central to Hurston's development of dramatic practice and black musical comedy would go on to become a feature of Hurston's folk project later in her career in various manifestations. Her later plays and revues, *Cold Keener* (1930), *The Great Day* (1932), *Spunk* (1935), and *Polk County* (1944) would reflect this influence.

Hurston's second play returns to the imagined African kingdom of Luababa. Published the year after *Meet the Mamma*, *Spears* takes place entirely in Luababa as characters struggle against scarcity, drought, and starvation. Departing from the farcical nature of *Meet the Mamma*, *Spears* highlights presumed African idioms and rituals, including a rain dance and a battle scene, seemingly extending Hurston's interrogation of black life in "darkest Africa."[44] Given what we know of Hurston's developing theoretical approach to originality, with its emphasis upon the reworking of "borrowed material," *Spears* gestures toward this "modification of ideas"[45] despite her never having traveled to West Africa. Cole and Mitchell have attempted to describe Hurston's repeated exploration of African idioms as an exploitation of "the then-faddish interest in 'primitive' cultures and peoples that foreshadowed . . . her eventual relationship with Charlotte Osgood Mason, a champion of primitivism who believed that American society could be rejuvenated through contact with African American and African culture."[46] While Cole and Mitchell argue that Hurston "sets her characters dancing to the tom-tom beat . . . seemingly without irony,"[47] we might perhaps consider Hurston's turn again to Luababa as an attempt to continue searching for a folk idiom that could capture a continuity of aesthetic principles across the black diaspora.

Like *Meet the Mamma*, *Spears* is also a play in which characters navigate community and hierarchies of power. As the play begins, we quickly realize the scarcity and hunger facing the tribe if they do not act quickly. As the community voices various plans to alleviate hunger and fend off tribal warfare, the ideas of young warriors are pitted against the wisdom of elders. As some of the men consider "sell[ing] the women that we may live,"[48] the play rehearses discourse that reduces women's bodies to tools of male domination and economic exchange. The layered gender dynamics of the play also anticipate Janie's treatment in Hurston's novel *Their Eyes Were Watching God* (1937). In one scene in which Zaidi, the king's daughter, attempts to speak on behalf of Uledi, the tribe's greatest warrior, she is instructed, "women were not made to counsel men but to serve them."[49] Zaidi refuses to heed this instruction, instead her speech satirizes masculinist discourse, and in it we see the glimmers of the opening lines from *Their Eyes*:

> Zaidi: We women have no minds at all. We know nothing – what we saw yesterday is today forgotten. Each day the sun takes our thought with him into his hut and does not bring them back to us again.[50]

When Zaidi's speech results in the rescue of the tribe's chief warrior, the opposing tribe is defeated, and thunder and lightning signal the end of the drought accompanied by cheers offstage. If read within the context of generational difference and group belonging, *Spears* rewards the wisdom of the youth while also acknowledging loyalty to the tribe. It is difficult not to read the ending of *Spears* alongside Locke's appreciation for "renewed self-respect and self-discipline."[51]

Spears is another Hurston drama that has not been met favorably. Although the play won honorable mention in a 1925 *Opportunity* contest, scholars have wondered, "how [this] play was awarded a prize . . . ?" given its seeming reliance upon a primitivist gaze. Hurston's African imaginary begs more depth than this question implies. By drawing upon an African imaginary, Hurston experiments with, and negotiates the contours of, an evolving black diaspora. Anticipating her later plays, Hurston here is intent on emphasizing the very facets of African culture that would become central to her discussion of the folk later in her career. At first glance *Spears* may not appear to fit the sophisticated, urban edge of the New Negro, but Hurston's plays insist that on pursuing that disjuncture. Upon close reading the play resists being reduced exclusively to the primitive troping reflected on its surface. Indeed, it is possible to read *Spears* beyond the binaries its title suggests: not simply as a covert weapon or instrument of defense, but also as an offshoot – a moment of new growth toward something decidedly different and "new."

Hurston would also experiment with single act plays during her early career. *The First One*, published in 1927 in the anthology *Ebony and Topaz*, combined Hurston's interest in ritual, myth, and origin stories with her love of folk and drama. A folkloric re-imagination of the Ham legend, Hurston's play improvises biblical myth and ritual. Hurston's turn to the popular legend of Ham – a story frequently used to justify the origins of blackness as a curse inflicted upon the son of Noah – uses black folkloric elements to satirize the tale's use as a justification for racial caste systems.

The First One is a play that thematically bears much in common with Hurston's previous play, *Color Struck*, despite the obvious differences in plot and structure. Like *Color Struck*, *The First One* takes seriously the consequences of ritual participation and group exclusion. The climax of the play will see Ham "cursed" with black skin and exiled as punishment, the result of an elaborate scheme by his brother's wives. The play asks that we examine the roots of skin prejudice and dramatizes the biblical origins of Ham's "blackness" and the value of commemorative rituals.

The play opens three years after the Great Flood with the survivors Noah, his wife, their three sons (Ham, Japheth, and Shem) and their wives and children. The family gathers yearly to pay tribute to and to "commemorate [their] delivery"[52] from the catastrophe. Discord and jealousy surface with the wives of Shem and Japheth who accuse Ham of singing and dancing "all during the year" while Shem and Japheth "work always in the fields and vineyards."[53] Throughout the play Ham's frequent association with flowers, song, and dance are cherished by Noah, even over the work of the other brothers. When Mrs. Japheth and Mrs. Shem see an opportunity to stage an act of betrayal that Noah cannot forgive, they do so, causing Noah to curse and exile Ham.

Although the curse and Ham's resulting exile is certainly the climax to the single-act play, its commemorative rituals reveal Hurston's investment in the project of black memory. The beginning of the ritual is described through stage directions: "Noah goes to the heaped up altar . . . he kneels at the altar and the others kneel in a semi-circle at a little distance. Noah makes certain ritualistic gestures and chants."[54] A sacrifice of meat follows as Noah recounts the events of the flood. At the end of his narration, Mrs. Noah and Eve (the only wife whose name stands independent of her husband's) share their memories of the flood:

> MRS. NOAH: (*Feelingly*) Yes, three years ago, all was water, water, water! The deeps howled as one beast to another. (*She shudders.*) In my sleep, even now, I am in that ark again being borne here, there on the great bosom.

EVE: (*Wide-eyed*) And the dead! Floating, floating all about us – We were one little speck of life in a world of death! (*The bone slips from her hand*.) And there, close beside the ark, close with her face upturned as if begging for shelter – my *mother*! (*She weeps, Ham comforts her*.)[55]

The ritual conjures memories of the flood and, significantly, of the shared terror of being on the ship.[56] As though in a trance, both women attempt to communicate the horror of the experience. Mrs. Noah's description of the ark invokes the experiences aboard the ships of the Middle Passage ("all was water, water, water!"). Her description of the "deep howl[ing] as one beast to another" recalls the sounds of the hold and the dehumanizing conditions aboard the vessels.

Eve's response to the ritual conjures a more filial memory. Haunted by the images of the floating dead she states, "we were one little speck of life in a world of death!" Moreover, Eve's remarks reveal that she is forced to abandon her mother during the flood. Mrs. Shem's callous response characterizes a seemingly long-held disdain for Eve:

MRS. SHEM: (*Eating vigorously*) She would not repent. Thou art as thy mother was – a seeker after beauty of raiment and laughter. God is just. She would not repent.[57]

Mrs. Shem's crass comment reveals Hurston's blending of at least two biblical tales. While the legend of Ham's curse is central to the heart of the play, Eve – both as original woman and as the wife of Ham – cannot escape sin in Mrs. Shem's interpretation. By naming Ham's wife Eve, Hurston establishes another lineage of sorts, and thus fuses multiple origin stories together: an accounting of the origins of man, a re-enactment of the transatlantic slave passage, and the invention of race. That Hurston highlights the production of race as a divisive tool used to monopolize wealth transforms the biblical drama into yet another satirical critique.

When Mrs. Shem claims Eve's mother was unrepentant, Eve's rejoinder to Mrs. Shem is equally telling. Eve asks why Jehovah must hate beauty and boldly claims, "the unrepentant are no less loved."[58] Eve's refusal mirrors Hurston's own refusal to reproduce easy binaries within her dramas. This moment foreshadows her loyalty to Ham once the curse is exacted. Unlike the rest of his family, Eve is the one who leads Ham and his child to forge a new life. If Ham is Hurston's quintessential folk musician, it is Eve who preserves that art from the complete disavowal and exile that the curse enacts. The closing lines of the play condemn Noah, Ham's brothers, and the wives left behind. Ham's last words illustrate this point:

HAM: (*Lightly cynical to all*) Oh, remain with your flocks and fields and vineyards, yards, to covet, to sweat, to die and know no peace. I go to the sun.[59]

By writing all of the action as a single-act play, Hurston condenses the biblical narrative and focuses on swift ironic action enacted through dialogue. Here, as we have seen in Hurston's previous plays, we witness the emergence of some of Hurston's most compelling folk heroes and heroines.

Conclusion

Hurston's dramatic practice is at once satirical, experimental, and referential in scope. Her early characters and plots embody the gestures of the folk in ways that would come to mark the fullness of her vision. Traversing genre and plot, Hurston's early plays pursue a deliberately imperfect folk archive brought to life.

Notably, other imperfect archives continue to yield key fragments of Hurston's commitment to theater. In June 1926, Zora Neale Hurston excitedly penned a letter to W. E. B. Du Bois. In the short epistle, Hurston reaffirms her commitment to revising her writing even as she struggles with the "grimy toil" of moving into a new apartment across Harlem. In a flurry of puns, Hurston describes the "hells of moving into a flat" that has left her "flat and flattened." Still, Hurston's passion and eagerness to create new directions for black drama shines in the letter. Of the two new plays referenced in the letter, Hurston promises to revise "at once"[60] a first draft of a play shared with Du Bois and is not shy about her eagerness for comments on the revisions ("Could you, or would you bring it past my place soon?"). The letter closes with a question full of promise and anticipation for an unnamed second play: "Do you think Krigwa would be interested in a play with music?"[61]

Another epistle, dated later in 1928 to Langston Hughes, captures Hurston's continued passion. Hurston writes, "Did I tell you . . . about the new, the real Negro art theatre I plan? Well, I shall, or rather we shall act out the folk tales, however short, with the abrupt angularity and naivete of the primitive 'bama nigger."[62] Hurston's early plays demonstrate her investment in this coterie of values by re-imagining folk life as sophisticated portraits that eschewed the dominant narratives of black modernity. Drama offers a heterogenous medium for Hurston to negotiate "abrupt angularity" and folk values. Though we know now that Hurston's vision for black theater ultimately came to distinguish itself from the vision of Hughes, Du Bois, and even Locke for a New Negro, her early plays depict the zeal with which she had begun imagining a world of black life dramatized in earnest. Through performance, she moved within and against dominant narratives of blackness, including those deemed acceptable by her peers, mentors, and patrons. Indeed, performance is the genre in which we see Hurston exercising her most radical and unconstrained vision as an artist.

Notes

1. Valerie Boyd, *Wrapped in Rainbows: The Life of Zora Neale Hurston* (New York: Scribner, 2004), 97.
2. According to Hurston biographer, Valerie Boyd, Hurston moved to Harlem in January 1925.
3. Notably, Hurston re-cast "Spunk" as a play in 1935.
4. Boyd, *Wrapped*, 98.
5. Ibid. Boyd notes the additional guests in attendance who would later play influential roles in Hurston's career at one point or another: Barnard College trustee Annie Nathan Meyer, novelist Fannie Hurst, Eugene O'Neill, and James Weldon Johnson (previously mentioned) whose brother Rosamund Johnson, Hurston would later enlist to help her work on future plays.
6. Notable exceptions include Valerie Boyd, Carla Kaplan, Soyica Diggs Colbert, Elin Diamond, Jennifer Cayer, and David Krasner.
7. The period known as the Harlem Renaissance has been variously defined as having "multiple" beginnings and endings. See Cheryl Wall, *The Harlem Renaissance: A Very Short Introduction* (Oxford: Oxford University Press, 2016), 7. In his autobiography *The Big Sea*, Langston Hughes offers this classification: "The 1920's were the years of Manhattan's first black renaissance." Langston Hughes, *The Big Sea* (1940; New York: Hill and Wang, 1993), 223. For the purposes of this chapter, I focus my attention on Hurston's plays within this first decade of the 1920s.
8. Hurston entered a contract with patron Charlotte Osgood Mason in December of 1927. The contract extended through the fall of 1932. It provided Hurston with a monthly stipend of $200, a camera and a car. According to Carla Kaplan, it also "denied [Hurston] any autonomy or control over her work ... [a]ny material collected or written by Hurston legally belonged to Mason, who was described as hiring Hurston as her 'agent' in the collection of 'music, folk-lore, poetry, hoodoo, conjure, manifestations of art, and kindred matters existing among the American Negroes.'" Carla Kaplan, ed., *Zora Neale Hurston: A Life in Letters* (New York: Random House, 2002), 48.

9. In "Writing the Absent Potential: Drama, Performance, and the Canon of African American Literature," Sandra L. Richards argues that drama is often excluded from the African American literary canon. In *Performativity and Performance*, ed. Eve Sedgewick and Andrew Parker (New York: Routledge, 1995), 65.

10. As Kaplan suggests, Hurston's collection of folklore was not without intense material constraints that affected her physically and emotionally. Kaplan, *Zora Neale Hurston*, 48.

11. Where Hurston's early plays are given serious consideration, only the play *Color Struck* has received substantial critical attention. See Jean Lee Cole and Charles Mitchell, "Zora Neale Hurston – A Theatrical Life," in *Zora Neale Hurston: Collected Plays*, ed. Jean Lee Cole and Charles Mitchell (New Brunswick: Rutgers University Press, 2008), xv–xxxi; Soyica Diggs Colbert, *The African American Theatrical Body: Reception, Performance, and the Stage* (Cambridge: Cambridge University Press, 2011), 91–122; and David Krasner, *A Beautiful Pageant: African American Theatre, Drama, and Performance in the Harlem Renaissance* (New York: Palgrave Macmillan, 2002), 114–130. Jennifer Cayer, Katherine Biers, and Elin Diamond have contributed to analysis of Hurston's 1930 play *Cold Keener*. See Katherine Biers, "Practices of Enchantment: The Theatre of Zora Neale Hurston," *TDR/The Drama Review* 59, no. 4 (2015): 67–82; Jennifer A. Cayer, "'Roll Yo' Hips - Don't Roll Yo' Eyes': Angularity and Embodied Spectatorship in Zora Neale Hurston's Play, *Cold Keener*," *Theatre Journal* 60, no. 1 (March 2008): 37–69; Elin Diamond, "Folk Modernism: Zora Neale Hurston's Gestural Drama," *Modern Drama* 58, no. 1 (Spring 2015): 112–134. *Meet the Mamma*, *Spears*, and *The First One* have received little more than biographical mentions. See Robert Hemenway, *Zora Neale Hurston: A Literary Biography* (Urbana: University of Illinois Press, 1980); Deborah G. Plant, *Every Tub Must Sit on its Own Bottom: The Philosophy and Politics of Zora Neale Hurston* (Urbana: University of Illinois Press, 1995); Kaplan, *Zora Neale Hurston*.

12. W. E. B. Du Bois, *The Souls of Black Folk* (Boston: Bedford/St. Martins, 1997), 186.

13. James Weldon Johnson, "Preface," in *The Book of American Negro Poetry*, ed. James Weldon Johnson (New York: Harcourt Brace, 1922), vii, xix.

14. Various black artists supported and critiqued the depiction of black folk life by white authors. Du Bois frequently supported the work of Ridgely Torrence's plays, even including his work in multiple issues of *The Crisis*. For an in-depth discussion of the interracial relationships of the Harlem Renaissance within the context of Du Bois's Negro theatre, see George Hutchinson, *The Harlem Renaissance in Black and White* (Cambridge, MA: Belknap Press of Harvard University Press, 1995), 158–166.

15. The portrayal of black dialect and other black vernacular forms added additional layers to these concerns. For black artists of the 1920s, complex debates emerged around questions of audience and authority. For example, James Weldon Johnson described the "problem of double

audience" facing black writers. See James Weldon Johnson, "The Dilemma of the Negro Author," *American Mercury* 15, no. 60 (December 1928), 477. Respectively, Langston Hughes and Du Bois weighted the concerns of the "serious black artist" with the pursuit of commercial success and political advancement; Hughes, *The Big Sea*, 223; Langston Hughes, "The Negro Artist and the Racial Mountain," *Nation* 122 (June 23, 1926): 692–694; W. E. B. Du Bois, "Criteria of Negro Art," *The Crisis* 36, no. 2 (October 1926): 290.

16. The Krigwa Players was an acronym for CRIGWA: Crisis Guild of Writers and Artists. Although the theater group would only last nine years it was later joined by additional theater groups of the period including the Negro Experimental Players (1929), the Harlem Players (1931), and the American Negro Theater.

17. W. E. B. Du Bois, "Krigwa Players Little Negro Theater," *The Crisis* (July 1926): 134.

18. Alain Locke, "The Negro and the American Stage," *Theatre Arts Monthly* (February 1926): 116.

19. Zora Neale Hurston's essay originally appeared in Nancy Cunard's *Negro: An Anthology* (1934). "Characteristics of Negro Expression," in Zora Neale Hurston, *Folklore, Memoirs, and Other Writings*, ed. Cheryl A. Wall (New York: The Library of America, 1995), 845.

20. Elin Diamond, "Folk Modernism: Zora Neale Hurston's Gestural Drama," *Modern Drama* 58, no. 1 (Spring 2015), 112–134.

21. *Color Struck* was published in *Fire!!* in 1926 while *The First One*, was published in *Ebony and Topaz* in 1927.

22. Hurston writes plays well into what has been called "the second half" of the Harlem Renaissance in the 1930s, but I focus my discussion of Hurston's early plays to the first four plays that she composed in the 1920s. This is due in part to the neglect of these plays in scholarly discussions. The remainder of Hurston's Harlem Renaissance plays have been previously studied by a number of scholars. Her later Harlem plays include *Cold Keener* (1930), *De Turkey and de Law* (1930), and *Spunk* (1935). Hurston would also produce a variety of short plays or sketches that were variations of her revue, *The Great Day* (1932).

23. Jean Lee Cole and Charles Mitchell, "Zora Neale Hurston – A Theatrical Life," in *Zora Neale Hurston: Collected Plays* (New Brunswick: Rutgers University Press, 2008), xv.

24. Alain Locke, "The Drama of Negro Life," *Theatre Arts Monthly* 10, no. 2 (October 1926), 703.

25. Zora Neale Hurston, *Color Struck*, in *Zora Neale Hurston: Collected Plays*, ed. Cole and Mitchell, 35.

26. Hurston, "Characteristics," 831.

27. Kaplan, *Zora Neale Hurston*, 115–116.

28. Colbert, "Reenacting the Harlem Renaissance," in *The African American Theatrical Body*, 91–122.

29. Hurston, *Color Struck*, 39.

30. Hughes, *The Big Sea*, 235–236.

31. Hurston manipulates multiple genres across her plays. By attending to their "form," we can recognize how she sees a value in re-purposing popular forms of performance (melodrama, folk drama, musical drama), emphasizing how form and content can signify upon multiple meanings for characters and audiences. My approach to form draws on Sandra Richards's call, in "Writing the Absent Potential," to "analyze what is 'there' on the page" as material absence *and* presence, so that we may better attend to "those meanings we produce based on the multiple discourses in which we and the script are embedded" (72).

32. Zora Neale Hurston, *Meet the Mamma*, in *Zora Neale Hurston: Collected Plays*, ed. Cole and Mitchell, 2.

33. Cole and Mitchell, ed. *Zora Neale Hurston: Collected Plays*, 1.

34. Drawing upon Hurston's interest in angularity as a technique of dance and visual representation, the play presents its characters in a number of different guises and costumes. This enables readers to see them from a number of different angles, so to speak. In this play, Hurston's angularity appears as performative strategy and as rhetorical technique.

35. Hurston, *Dust Tracks on a Road*, in Hurston, *Folklore, Memoirs*, ed. Wall, 689.

36. In *Dust Tracks*, Hurston describes her early working years as formatively shaped by working in theatre. Her pursuit of theatre after her arrival in the North is indicative of her fascination with the genre and enables her to monitor and ultimately develop her own contemporary depictions of staged life.

37. Thomas L Riis, *Just Before Jazz: Black Musical Theatre in New York, 1890–1915* (Washington, DC: Smithsonian Institution Press, 1989), 49.

38. Ibid., 50.

39. Hurston, *Meet the Mamma*, 4.

40. Hurston, *Mules and Men*, in *Folklore, Memoirs*, ed. Wall, 45.

41. Hurston, *Meet the Mamma*, 5.

42. Carrie's song draws on a blueswoman tradition popularized by Mamie Smith (consider, e.g., "Crazy Blues"), Ma Rainey, and Bessie Smith. In her study of black blueswomen, Angela Davis describes the function of similar songs like Ma Rainey's "Misery Blues." Davis argues that these songs "reveal the beginnings of an oppositional attitude toward patriarchal ideology." For more on how twentieth-century blueswomen defined black feminism, see Angela Davis, *Blues Legacies and Black Feminism: Gertrude "Ma" Rainey, Bessie Smith, and Billie Holiday* (New York: Pantheon Books, 1998), 18.

43. Hurston, *Meet the Mamma*, 14.

44. Ibid., 12.

45. In "Characteristics of Negro Expression," Hurston argued against any simplistic notion of "originality," arguing instead that "originality" always involved the "modification" of "borrowed material" (838).

46. Cole and Mitchell, ed., "Introduction to *Spears*," in *Zora Neale Hurston: Collected Plays*, 51.

47. Ibid.

48. Hurston, *Spears,* in *Zora Neale Hurston: Collected Plays,* 54.

49. Ibid., 58.

50. Ibid.

51. Alain Locke, "Enter the New Negro," *Survey Graphic,* March 1925, 631.

52. Hurston, *The First One,* in *Zora Neale Hurston: Collected Plays,* 65.

53. Ibid., 65.

54. Ibid., 66.

55. Ibid., 67.

56. The water imagery in this flood scene is a particularly potent symbol for Hurston. We see similar motifs in her short stories ("John Redding Goes to Sea"), in her later plays, (*Cold Keener*), and most famously in her novel, *Their Eyes Were Watching God.*

57. Hurston, *The First One,* 67.

58. Ibid.

59. Ibid., 74.

60. It has not yet been determined whether or not Hurston received a response from Du Bois.

61. Kaplan, *Zora Neale Hurston,* 116.

62. Ibid.

CHAPTER 16

Zora Neale Hurston, Film, and Ethnography

Hannah Durkin

When Zora Neale Hurston embarked on a twenty-seven-month anthropological research trip through the US South in the late 1920s, she brought along a 16 mm movie camera. At a time when anthropology tended to disregard African American cultures as unworthy of academic study, Hurston was one of the first fieldworkers to document black lives in the US South and West Indies. The fifteen reels of footage that she produced during her trip were perhaps the first professional recordings ever made by an African American woman.[1] Moreover, the material that she collected included some of the first scientific recordings of dance, children's games, and Bahamian cultures, and her lost footage of the 1929 New Orleans Mardi Gras featured some of the earliest moving images of the city's jazz bands. The cinematic portrait of the interwar black South that Hurston created highlighted the region's economic and cultural contributions to US society and spoke back to commercial and educational filmmaking from the period, which framed black southern life straightforwardly as agrarian, and by implication, cut off from modernity. Such footage also had a significant influence on Hurston's creative work. In particular, the Floridian lumber camp community that features heavily in her films was a key focus of her 1935 book on black southern folklore, *Mules and Men*. Equally, her recordings of children's games, laborers, and Bahamian dancing served as the basis for much of her stage work, including her Broadway revue, *The Great Day* (1932). Yet Hurston's celebrated literary career has overshadowed her status as a pioneering black woman filmmaker. Consequently, dialogues as well as tensions between her films and writings have still to be explored.

Between December 1927 and March 1930, Hurston traveled to Alabama, Florida, Louisiana, and the Bahamas with instructions to "seek out, compile and collect all information possible, both written and oral, concerning the music, poetry, folk-lore, literature, hoodoo, conjure, manifestations of art and kindred subjects relating to and existing among the North

American Negroes."[2] Hurston interviewed more than 120 people as part of this project and collected seven volumes' worth of data. Most of this material is thought to be lost, but one volume was published posthumously under the title *Every Tongue Got to Confess: Negro Folk-Tales from the Gulf States*, and a number of her interviewees' stories appeared in *Mules and Men* and two articles for *The Journal of American Folklore*.[3] The footage that Hurston shot served as a cinematic accompaniment to these interviews. Altogether, she recorded a sea baptism, lumber camp labor, men chopping wood, children's games, young girls at leisure, a barbecue, wine-making, Bahamian dancing, a New Orleans Mardi Gras parade, men and women at a baseball stadium, and Oluale Kossola/Cudjo Lewis (*c.* 1840–1935), who until 2019 was the last known survivor of the transatlantic slave trade.[4]

This chapter examines key sections of such footage to explore Hurston's contributions as a black woman to ethnographic cinema and to black southern cinema more broadly, and also to elucidate some of the connections between her anthropological fieldwork and her creative work. The films help illuminate the ways in which Hurston understood and sought to depict black folk cultures on the page and stage. They draw attention to the international focus of her research and show that the textual and cinematic strands of her project should not be read in isolation because they were conceived as a joint corrective to mainstream US distortions of black artistry. Such work represented a mixed-media engagement with African American and African diasporic working lives, religious beliefs, and creative practices. Moreover, the films are rare cinematic documents of the everyday lives of black working-class subjects whose artistry underpinned so much of Hurston's creative work and interwar US culture more generally. The footage is a reminder that there were multiple authorial voices in Hurston's ethnographic writings, and it adds to our understanding of her subjects by providing more detailed information about their lived experiences and artistry than the writings alone reveal.

Hurston's field trip was framed around competing interests. Her films shed light on the expectations that were placed on her as a pioneering black anthropologist who was assumed to have an "insider's" appreciation of her subjects, and consequently her awkward relationship to a black southern community of which she had once been part, but which she was now expected to view through what she termed the "spy-glass of Anthropology."[5] As a recent graduate in anthropology who had been tutored by Franz Boas, Hurston was expected to demonstrate scientific rigor and produce scientific results. As one of the first African American anthropologists, she knew that she had to prove her abilities to the scientific establishment. Yet Hurston was also gathering data on behalf of wealthy white patron Charlotte Osgood Mason, who hired her to amass what Mason perceived to be dying black traditions for consumption as "art." Hurston was expected to collect, but not to interpret, such material and had no ownership over it. Mason gave Hurston a camera for this purpose; she was charged with creating a cinematic document of the African American South for an elderly white woman who was unable physically to satisfy her curiosity first-hand.

However, Hurston had her own agendas too, and her film footage shows that she sought to shed light on a mobile, industrialized, and culturally dynamic world that was at odds with white imaginings of a disappearing black rural folk culture. She also collected material covertly for her own creative purposes. Ostensibly intended to serve as visual "data" of dying African American traditions, Hurston's cinematic documents of African diasporic labor and leisure practices instead played a key role in her effort to create what she termed "the new, the *real* Negro art theatre" that would function as a corrective to mainstream US distortions of black cultures.[6] Hurston used film selectively and the purpose of her recordings evolved during her field trip. Her footage of Kossola was the first film that she made, and it adhered to the collecting requirements specified in her job contract. Mason wanted Hurston to record the man that she believed to be the last living transatlantic slave trade survivor. However, letters between Mason and African American writer Alain Locke, who advised Mason and mentored Hurston, reveal that Hurston's chief interest in the South was not to document slavery, but rather to gather oral material for her fiction and stage work, and she made no effort to film or even openly to identify the other Middle Passage survivor that she encountered on her trip.[7] By contrast, her reels of Bahamian dancing – the final footage that she shot – were recorded without Mason's knowledge and with the intention of introducing West Indian cultural practices to the US stage.

Critical neglect of Hurston's footage has helped to obscure her radical contributions, as a Harlem Renaissance intellectual, to filmmaking. Paula Massood highlights cinema's general absence from the movement's major publications and asserts that "African American intellectuals and artists based their aesthetic judgments on white canonical norms and, therefore, did not consider film to be a legitimate art form."[8] Massood identifies Hurston as the only member of the Harlem Renaissance who engaged meaningfully with cinema in the 1920s, but concludes that, "as her use of the medium suggests, film was valued for its scientific properties not its aesthetic potential."[9] However, Massood's reading sets up a dichotomy between art and science that overlooks the creative purposes of Hurston's collecting activities. Hurston ultimately worked on both ethnographic and commercial film. In 1940, she was hired by anthropologist Jane Belo to record religious worship in a sanctified church in Beaufort, South Carolina, as part of a two-month expedition, co-engineered by Margaret Mead, that sought to compare religious trances across different cultural contexts. She also served briefly as a story consultant for Paramount Pictures in the early 1940s. Hurston left no record of her thoughts about her film work, which means that the precise intentions behind such work are hard to determine. Nevertheless, the immersive filmmaking techniques that she developed in the 1920s and her effort to record scenes that she would later recreate on the page and stage show that she viewed her cinematic fieldwork as a creative as much as a scientific tool.

Hurston's engagement with ethnographic filmmaking in the 1920s, and her willingness to experiment with the genre, was significant because it was so unusual. Pseudo-scientific recordings of non-European communities, in which complex cultural practices were commodified and fragmented for voyeuristic consumption, were prominent features of early cinema. Yet the US anthropological establishment was slow to embrace filmmaking and largely ignored the medium as a potential research tool until after World War II. Leading anthropologists such as Franz Boas privileged language as the only effective in-depth method of scientific study, believing that the visual could capture only the surface of a culture, and did not provide a theoretical framework for cinematic documentation. Expensive, unwieldy equipment and a lack of formal training at a time when anthropology was still striving to achieve legitimacy as a scientific discipline may have deterred would-be filmmakers. However, by foregrounding the single-authored ethnographic text over cinematic representation, anthropologists ensured that complex human encounters were framed around a single witness's literary interpretation, which reinforced hierarchies of power between scientists and their subjects. Alison Griffiths has claimed that, "Ironically, cinema's ability to represent reality with such compelling verisimilitude may have contributed to anthropologists' ambivalence about the medium, since the sense of agency afforded native peoples for the duration of a performance also threatened to undermine the specular authority of an idealized scientific observer."[10] By embracing filmmaking, Hurston granted her subjects a degree of autonomy away from the writer's pen and unsettled such scientific hierarchies. In so doing, she transformed anthropological investigation into a two-way creative encounter that acknowledged her subjects as artists and individuals.

Hurston's footage, which is now nearly a century old, is brief and fragmentary. The fifteen reels, of which only nine survive, represent a handful of silent moving snapshots – lasting from a few seconds to a few minutes – of a two-year recording trip. Yet they still have tremendous historical value as cinematic documents of the interwar African American South. With the exceptions of Eatonville, where she grew up, Africatown and Bogue Chitto, where the two Middle Passage survivors lived, and Eau Gallie, where she rented a cottage to write, her stopping points in the South – Mobile, Loughman, Lakeland, Mulberry, Pierce, Miami, New Orleans, and Bogalusa – were all major centers of industry that attracted jobseekers from across the region in the 1920s, and what is particularly remarkable about Hurston's research project is the geographical diversity of her interviewees. *Every Tongue Got to Confess* reveals that they came not only from Alabama, Florida, and Louisiana, but also from Georgia, Mississippi, South Carolina, Tennessee, Texas, Virginia, the Bahamas, the Cayman Islands, Jamaica, and even West Africa. On *Mules and Men*'s opening page, Hurston outlines such mobility as her reason for conducting research in Florida:

> Dr. Boas asked me where I wanted to work and I said, "Florida," and gave, as my big reason, that "Florida is a place that draws people – white people from all over the world, and Negroes from every Southern state surely and some from the North and West." So I knew that it was possible for me to get a cross-section of the Negro South in the one state.[11]

Such diversity was the result of a rapidly transforming southern economy, and Hurston's attention to and fascination with her subjects' wide-ranging origins highlights her objective to create a culturally and geographically dynamic portrait of black lives.

The world that Hurston explores on screen therefore is not centered on plantations and sharecroppers, but instead on new towns and villages built around phosphate mines, railroads, sawmills, and turpentine production. These industries were just four decades old when Hurston arrived in Florida, having emerged as economic alternatives to the declining cotton industry in the aftermath of the US Civil War. Leigh Anne Duck notes that "Hurston's 'folk' appear surprisingly modern," although she concludes that *Mules and Men* "does not emphasize the modernity of these southern African Americans."[12] The text spends little time considering its subjects' working lives and gives no consideration to their geographical origins, favoring instead a portrait of a seemingly isolated lumber camp. Yet African American southern modernity is exactly what her camera does reveal.

A comparative analysis of *Mules and Men* and Hurston's footage makes it possible to fill in some of the gaps in her textual representation of the South, and therefore to reflect more deeply on the lived experiences of the communities that she documented.

The footage from the lumber camp outside Loughman, Polk County, begins with a point-of-view shot from a moving log train, which Hurston uses as a makeshift dolly to record the wooded landscape of central Florida. The train's fast-paced journey through the forest speaks to Hurston's subjects' itinerant livelihoods and can also be read as a metaphor for a society whose industry is advancing rapidly. Early ethnographic filmmaking privileged fixed camera shots to create a stable – and thus seemingly authoritative – cinematic record of its subjects. Hurston's train footage therefore is creatively radical, as the constantly moving imagery refutes claims to representational authority. This filmmaking technique can be read as a self-reflexive interrogation of Hurston's presumed role as recorder of dying black cultures, as she relies on the log train, and therefore on the lumber camp community's technology, to document the southern industrial landscape. The train moves at such a fast pace that the surrounding trees are barely discernible to the viewer, and the driver stands in front of and obscures the lens when he disembarks; the camera can only give a partial and fleeting impression of the society that it records. A typed, undated note by Mason, which states, "Train too fast at first," highlights the footage's resistance to easy visual consumption.[13] The train is not traveling too fast for its economic purpose, which points up tensions between the film as a presumed visual artifact and the real human labor underpinning the industrial South. In turn, the footage highlights the competing agendas of Mason, who hired Hurston to document apparently dying black traditions for consumption as "art," and her employee, who sought to create a dynamic portrait of the African American South.

Hurston's point-of-view camera shot therefore mimics the world that it records, a world of geographical mobility and industry, which challenges the viewer to rethink popular conceptions of the interwar black South as a space cut off from modernity. The attention that the camera affords to the sawmill as the train reaches the lumber camp reinforces this reading. As Tiffany Ruby Patterson observes, "The sawmill operation [at Loughman] used the most modern techniques. Steam engines did the mechanical work and hoisting machinery was used to handle many tons of lumber with ease."[14] The footage records some of this modern machinery, including the hoisting equipment and a furnace. The sequence concludes with footage of massive tree trunks piled onto moving train wagons, which reveals the

extent of the workers' labor while also hinting at the subsequent geographical circulation of the lumber, which visualizes the community's links to
the wider national economy. Such footage emphasizes that Loughman,
and by extension the African American South, is not a technologically
backward society but rather a region that is very much part of the "modern" world and in fact is fueling its economy.

Hurston situated her fieldwork activity in explicit opposition to theatrical distortions of black southern cultures, and her research was the basis of
her Broadway revue, *The Great Day*, which depicted a day in the life of
a railroad work camp. Yet her portrait of Floridian industry also served as
a visual counter-narrative to dominant cinematic constructions of the
African American South that emphasized the region's apparent racial and
geographical "otherness." *Hallelujah!* and *Hearts in Dixie* (both 1929) were
the first mainstream cinematic portraits of black southern cultures, and
both were made and released during Hurston's field trip. In these productions, African Americans were situated within an apparently timeless rural
South divorced from wider society. Such narratives did not simply dominate commercial cinema but also carried over into government-sponsored
filmmaking. In 1921, the United States Department of Agriculture released
Helping Negroes to Become Better Farmers and Homemakers. This instruc-
tional film, which was made in conjunction with the Tuskegee Institute,
promoted a patronizing portrait of African American rural life that sought
to reinforce racialized social hierarchies. As J. Emmett Winn observes,
"The result shown in the film was that the black tenants' lives were
dramatically improved thanks to the help of white authorities. ... In
maintaining polarizing differences between blacks and whites, the motion
picture supported separate-but-equal laws and customs and communicated
that blacks are inferior to and dependent on whites."[15] By contrast,
Hurston imagined the African American South cinematically as a space
of creativity and industry. In so doing, her films presented a radical
challenge to such socially marginalizing constructions of black southern
lives and revalued their contributions to the national economy.

The movement that Hurston's footage invokes and that its filmmaker
experiences conflict with the everyday lives of her subjects, however.
Hurston rides freely on the log train, presumably at her request and with
permission from the driver who sits alongside her, and she travelled
elsewhere in the South by car. By contrast, the workers that she filmed
were bound to their camps by debt labor and had little economic hope of
traveling with the freedom that Hurston is seen here to enjoy, except by
hoboing in segregated trains. The sequence therefore reveals black

southern workers' contributions to the modern US economy, but it also draws attention to their social exclusion from the consumer economy in ways that perhaps exceeded Hurston's intentions, for *Mules and Men* largely ignored its subjects' working conditions in its effort to document their folk tales. Hurston took artistic license with her written material to meet her publisher's demands. The narrative that holds together *Mules and Men* was fabricated a year after Hurston returned from her southern sojourn and four years after she visited the lumber camp, despite presenting itself as verbatim account of her experiences there. The text privileged its subjects' leisure activities over the arduous, monotonous, and dangerous labor that they were expected to undertake, and it gave the false impression that folk tales that were recorded separately across different Gulf States emerged from a single Florida fishing trip conversation. Poet Sterling Brown criticized the book upon publication for its "socially unconscious" characters and judged it be "singularly *incomplete*," noting that the text "should be more bitter; it would be nearer the truth."[16]

Hurston eventually acknowledged the demanding and dangerous working conditions of southern labor camps in her autobiography, *Dust Tracks on a Road* (1942). Here, she observed that log choppers must work "All day, all night" to feed with logs a physically terrifying mill whose "smokestacks disput[e] with the elements, its boiler room reddening the sky, and its great circular saw screaming arrogantly as it attacks the tree like a lion making its kill."[17] Elsewhere in the text, workers go down the phosphate mines "to make rich land in far places," fell trees to produce the "Paint, explosives, marine stores, flavors, perfumes, tone for a violin bow, and many other things which the black men who bleed the trees never heard about," and beat "nine-pound hammers on railroad steel" because "The world must ride," a world that by implication did not include the workers.[18] This belated engagement with black southerners' vital contribution to a national economy from which they were socially excluded highlights the gaps in Hurston's earlier literary portrait of interwar black southern culture.

Yet the subjects' labor is at the heart of Hurston's film footage and it provides crucial information about the Floridian lumber camp as a lived experience that rectifies some of *Mules and Men*'s "incomplete[ness]." Workers stand perilously close to tree trunks as they are lowered to the ground. Elsewhere, they sit and stand around in boredom as they wait for the log train to arrive and the sawmill to do its work. While *Mules and Men* focuses on folk tales, "lies" (tall tales), and the pleasure of the jook joint, the footage reveals the context in which such leisure activities emerged and hints at the psychological significance of such practices as distractions from daily monotony, exploitation, and danger. The footage therefore has tremendous value for helping to recover the real men and women whose experiences underpinned Hurston's literary and stage work. Hurston interviewed approximately seventeen men and three women between the ages of seventeen and fifty in and around the Loughman lumber camp. Although it is not possible to identify individual subjects in the film footage, with the possible exception of the lone woman in the sequence, who appears to have a bobbed hairstyle much like the woman named "Babe" Hill in the text, *Every Tongue Got to Confess* provides the names, approximate ages, and birth places of her interviewees and thus makes it possible to trace many of these workers across census data.

Moreover, the camera affords Hurston's subjects a chance to return the anthropological gaze in ways that are not possible on the page. Hurston masqueraded as a bootlegger to gain acceptance into the supposedly lawless lumber mill community of Loughman, and it is unclear to what extent her subjects understood why they were being filmed. She admitted in a letter to Langston Hughes of her encounters with "self-conscious Negroes" who "are likely to object to my work."[19] She also alluded to fellow anthropologist Ruth Benedict to "Negroes with 'Race Consciousness' and 'Race pride' drilled into them" who suspected that her collecting project was part of an effort by white people to ridicule them.[20] In this regard, it is striking that the workers' only interaction with the camera is the occasional glance and stare, which suggests no sense of familiarity with the filmmaker and at best ambivalence to being recorded. Hurston shot almost all of her adult subjects from a distance, and it is perhaps no coincide that the solitary woman on screen steps out of the way of a panning shot at the end of the sequence. *Mules and Men* was disparaging about women who lived among the labor camps of Central Florida. As Tiffany Ruby Patterson notes, "According to Hurston, the women who attached themselves to these camps had little to offer in the way of beauty, intelligence, or commitment. They were the refuse society had cast off."[21] Yet this woman's fleeting appearance onscreen and her ultimate refusal of the camera's gaze affords her a brief moment of agency away from such value judgments. On the screen if not the page, the woman has some freedom to assert her humanity on her own terms.

Other surviving film footage underscores the representational tensions that were embedded in Hurston's fieldwork project, but it also shows how she engaged creatively with ethnographic cinema to destabilize scientist-subject hierarchies. One of the most remarkable recordings is a ten-shot staged scene that features two young black girls on the cusp of adulthood.

The footage is edited into a coherent narrative to highlight the girls' daily leisure activities and may be the first film sequence to be staged in such a way by an African American woman. The sequence initially intervenes in pseudo-scientific racist viewing practices, but subsequently unfolds into a seemingly autobiographical portrait of black southern girlhood.

The footage begins with a shot of a young girl wearing a plain, light dress as she steps out of her cabin and walks toward the camera. There is a jump cut and she repeats the same gesture, although the camera is now positioned closer to the cabin so that only the girl's head and shoulders are in the frame. The camera cuts again and the girl now stands with her head and shoulders presented to the viewer. She smiles for the camera. There is another break in the recording and the girl's head is now shown in profile. She turns her head so that the other side of her face is visible and smiles again. As Fatimah Tobing Rony and Cara Caddoo have noted, such a pose recalls the racist practices of early anthropology, in which head measurements were used to illustrate theories of racial difference.[22] Hurston began her anthropological training by measuring the heads of Harlemites to disprove myths of African American intellectual inferiority and the sequence can be read as an extension of such work. The footage underscores the purpose of her field trip, which was to document scientifically black southern communities. However, if the footage initially situates itself within a history of pseudo-scientific display, it engages creatively with racist ways of seeing to underscore the humanity of racialized subjects. The young girl appears to pose willingly, and her serene smile refracts attempts to read her as a physical "type" by instead calling attention to her youthful beauty. Her individuality cannot be contained by the camera.

Moreover, the sequence quickly abandons such documentation practices in favor of artistic experimentation.[23] In so doing, it shows how Hurston resisted her role as "collector" of black folk forms and positioned fieldwork as a creative tool by which to recover individual black experiences. If the footage previously played into racist ways of seeing, here the scientific gaze is broken down, for the sequence transforms into a cinematic narrative of the girl's everyday leisure activities. Here, Hurston creates a portrait of black southern girlhood, possibly for the first time on screen, that celebrates their daily lives. The camera cuts again and the girl is shown returning to her cabin. The camera cuts once more and the girl is shown sitting on the porch bench next to another girl. A medium shot of the same scene captures the girls nudging each other and smiling. The sequence has shifted from pseudo-scientific portraiture to a picture of young female friendship, and the intimacy of the girls' behavior reveals the closeness of their relationship. The camera is showing that these are not racial "types," but rather young women living quiet but sociable lives.

The camera then moves behind a fence and records the same porch from a distance. One of the girls, now wearing a hat and carrying a basket, walks up the steps into the cabin. The camera moves back to the cabin to reveal one of the girls lounging on the porch bench and posing with her chin on her hand. A low-angle camera shot reinforces this visual concern with leisure by revealing the feet of a sleeping cat and one of the girls as she sits in a rocking chair. The camera shifts position one final time to show the same scene from a distance. Unlike the footage of Kossola, the sequence is not a visual document of the living past, but rather is a cinematic meditation on contemporary black girlhood. In her study of nineteenth-century literary representations of African American girlhood, Nazera Sadiq Wright has shown that, while black male writers presented black girls as "flat, two-dimensional figures that modeled the behaviors and attributes male authority figures believed were essential for the progress of the race," black women writers wrote about "girls who had inner desires that should be nurtured and cultivated."[24] Although Wright's study predates the Harlem Renaissance, she identifies Hurston as an inheritor of these women writers' "vision of a world in which black girls could grow up to become women with important things to say."[25] Hurston's footage shows that she articulated this vision not only on the page but also on the screen, as her careful attention to framing and editing results in a meaningful cinematic reflection on interwar black southern girlhood as a lived experience. The footage highlights the extent to which Hurston's filmmaking broke down and resisted the collecting agenda with which she had been charged. The visual shift from scientific encounter to experimental documentation mirrors Hurston's own transition from "collector" to creative interpreter of black southern cultures.

Despite the careful attention with which the film sequence was constructed, Hurston left behind no record of how it was planned or staged. However, a speculative identification of at least one of the two girls in the footage is possible. In the manuscript that would eventually be published posthumously as *Every Tongue Got to Confess*, Hurston kept a note of the people that she interviewed during her field trip. Seventeen-year-old Willie May McClary and 20-year-old Geneva Woods were two of only five women in their late teens and early twenties that Hurston interviewed for the manuscript. They each shared a folk tale with Hurston that appears in the published version of *Every Tongue Got to Confess*. Both young women were born in Georgia, but while Woods' residence is not recorded,

McClary at least was living in Hurston's childhood hometown of Eatonville when Hurston interviewed her, which corresponds to the residential location that is shown on screen. If we assume that the setting of the sequence is Eatonville, and this is a likely possibility given that almost all of her other stopping points were industrial centers, the scene can be viewed as a cinematic reimagining of Hurston's own girlhood experiences. The footage therefore becomes a site in which anthropology, autobiography, and artistic experimentation converge: Hurston is recording a world very similar to that of her own youth. In turn, the sequence can be read as a cinematic precursor to the porch conversation between Janie and her best friend Pheoby that frames Hurston's semi-autobiographical novel, *Their Eyes Were Watching God* (1937).

Anthropology, autobiography, and artistic experimentation converge once more in Hurston's footage of dancing children. Hurston collected a substantial number of children's games around Mulberry, Pierce, and Lakeland in Florida, including activities that had been part of her own childhood, as she acknowledged in both *Mules and Men* and *Dust Tracks on a Road*.[26] Such games featured in *The Great Day* and its various iterations as well as in *Mule Bone: A Comedy of Negro Life*, an unfinished collaborative play on which Hurston embarked with Langston Hughes immediately after her return from the South. In "New Children's Games," an article that was written for the Federal Writers' Project but not published in Hurston's lifetime, she outlined her purpose in recording, and by implication staging, the children's games: to evidence their West African origins. Acknowledging that black children in Florida played "Purely white games that have been learned by Negro children by contact with whites," she nevertheless asserted that they also played "Purely Negro games" and that such games "have been kept alive in America by hand-clapping in the absence of the African drums."[27] Hurston emphasized the centrality of such games, and by extension West African traditions, to African American culture by stating that, "All through Negro life and creation is evident the will to rhythm and it is the thing of Negro children's games. From the Florida east coast comes a sample of almost pure rhythm."[28]

Hurston's recognition of West African survivals in children's play was pioneering, and her observations also anticipated much more recent scholarship that has traced the origins of black popular music to the rhythms and chants learned in the schoolyard.[29] Her attention to children's games can be read as part of a wider effort to uncover hidden black artistry that was key to the development of popular and stage dancing in the early to mid-twentieth century. Hurston was acutely aware of the ways in which black dance cultures were being appropriated, and their origins obscured, by mainstream US society. In "Characteristics of Negro Expression" (1934), she underscored the African American origins of the Charleston, speculating that it dated as far back as the 1890s and was "danced up and down the Atlantic seaboard from North Carolina to Key West, Florida."[30]

Yet what is not stated in Hurston's writings but is revealed on screen is the virtuosity of the child performances that she observed. While Hurston's article frames the children's activities as spontaneous play in ways that risk reinforcing perceptions of black cultural forms as "raw" material readily available for appropriation rather than as innovative artistry in their own right, her camera acknowledges and even mimics visually the creativity on which her study of children's games drew. One young boy's artistry is particularly striking. In the sequence, about twenty children are shot from a distance as they dance in a circle around the boy. The circle of children comes to a halt and begins clapping out a rhythm as the boy starts dancing. The camera then moves to the edges of the circle, adopting the point of view of one of the other children as the boy shuffles, stomps, and jumps and cartwheels into the splits. The camera cuts to a close up of the boy's head and shoulders as he continues to dance. The camera then moves even deeper into the circle, appearing to adopt the boy's point of view as it pans around the other boys and girls, who continue to clap out a rhythm. The camera then cuts to a low-angle shot, which shows the children's feet as they tap out the same rhythm. By imitating the children's point of view, and effectively dancing among them, Hurston's camera records the scene's rhythmic energy and virtuosity, and in so doing, foregrounds the children's artistry. The footage therefore serves as a visualization of the otherwise hidden creative practitioners whose artistry underpinned Hurston's ethnographic writings and stage work and is a reminder that such work was based on human encounters, including those of her own childhood.

The films that Hurston shot in the Bahamas also highlight the connections between her anthropological and artistic work, for much like the children's game footage, they show how she immersed herself in black dance cultures to recover such practices and call attention to their cultural significance. Equally, they demonstrate that she expanded the geographical parameters of her collecting project beyond the confines of the US South to shed light on the region as a space of migration and cross-cultural interaction and visually negate Euro-American misperceptions of the black South as a space adrift from modernity. Hearing Bahaman music and witnessing a Jumping Dance at Liberty City, Florida near the end of her field trip and "entranced" by what she saw, Hurston concluded that, "This music of the Bahaman Negroes was more original, dynamic and African, than American Negro songs. I just had to know more. So without giving Godmother [Mason] a chance to object, I sailed for Nassau."[31] The apparent spontaneity of Hurston's trip signals her determination to assert independence from Mason and engage with black southern cultures on her own terms. Although the footage is lost and it is not possible to tell if her cinematic engagement with the dances was as radical as the footage containing the children's games, Hurston records that she participated in such dance practices not only to document them but also to creatively re-enact them. Once again, boundaries between scientist and subject were broken down as Hurston "took pains" to learn the dances and "resolved to make them known to the world."[32] Hurston's Bahamian material ultimately served as the climax to her Broadway revue, *The Great Day*. The footage therefore played a fundamental role in her effort to create "the new, the *real* Negro art theatre."

In 1932, Hurston premiered *The Great Day* at the John Golden Theatre on Broadway. The production ran for just one night, although she continued to stage versions of the revue under different titles in New York, Florida, and Chicago over the next several years. While preparing for her Broadway show, Hurston begged Mason to view some of the Bahamian footage that she had recorded during her trip: "Godmother, may I show Mr. Colledge the fire-dance films from the Bahamas? I'd see to it that no one saw them outside the Judson offices, and I'd see that they were handled carefully and returned immediately. It would save time if I could . . . Then too, seeing the films would refresh *my* memory on details. Please, may I?"[33] Hurston's imploring letter, to which there is no documented response from Mason, underscores the power relations underpinning Hurston's fieldwork trip, in which not even the researcher let alone her subjects had much control over her material. Yet it also shows how Hurston's ostensible task of amassing "dying" black folk forms transformed into a creative project that sought to showcase the geographical diversity and artistry of African diasporic cultures that she found in and around the US South. Such footage is a radical 1920s exploration of black southern cultures that pays tribute to its subjects' labor and leisure activities and serves as a cinematic challenge to contemporary northern myths of a world cut adrift from modernity.

Notes

1. Gloria J. Gibson makes this point. See Gloria J. Gibson, "Cinematic Foremothers: Zora Neale Hurston and Eloyce King Patrick Gist," in *Oscar*

Micheaux and His Circle: African-American Filmmaking and Race Cinema of the Silent Era, ed. Pearl Bowser, Jane Gaines, and Charles Musser (Bloomington: Indiana University Press, 2001), 206.

2. Contract between Zora Neale Hurston and Charlotte Osgood Mason, December 8, 1927, Box 164–99, Folder 5, Alain Locke Papers, Moorland-Spingarn Research Center, Howard University.

3. See Zora Neale Hurston, *Every Tongue Got to Confess: Negro Folk-Tales from the Gulf States*, ed. Carla Kaplan (New York: HarperCollins, 2001); Zora Hurston, "Dance Songs and Tales from the Bahamas," *The Journal of American Folklore* 43, no. 169 (1930): 294–312; Zora Hurston, "Hoodoo in America," *The Journal of American Folklore*, 44, no. 174 (1931): 317–417.

4. For newly discovered interviews with and film footage of Middle Passage survivor Sally "Redoshi" Smith, who was brought to the USA with and ultimately outlived Kossola, see Hannah Durkin, "Finding Last Middle Passage Survivor Sally 'Redoshi' Smith on the Page and Screen," *Slavery & Abolition* 40, no. 4 (2019): 631–658.

5. Zora Neale Hurston, *Mules and Men*, in *Zora Neale Hurston: Folklore, Memoirs, and Other Writings*, ed. Cheryl A. Wall (New York: Library of America, 1995), 9.

6. Zora Neale Hurston, Letter to Langston Hughes (April 12, 1928), in *Zora Neale Hurston: A Life in Letters*, ed. Carla Kaplan (New York: Random House, 2002), 116. Emphasis in original.

7. For Hurston's reluctance to complete her work on Kossola's story, see Alain Locke, Letter to Charlotte Osgood Mason (June 15, 1931), Box 164–169, folder 5, Alain Locke Papers; Charlotte Osgood Mason, Dictated note entitled "Alain Leroy Locke" (December 6, 1931), Box 164–100, folder 8, Alain Locke Papers; Alain Locke, Letter to "Godmother" (March 14, 1932), Box 164–169, folder 14, Alain Locke Papers. Hurston mentioned in a letter to Langston Hughes that she had found a second Middle Passage survivor, but she did not name her. Zora Neale Hurston, Letter to Langston Hughes (July 10, 1928), in *Zora Neale Hurston*, ed. Kaplan, 123.

8. Paula J. Massood, *Making a Promised Land: Harlem in Twentieth-Century Photography and Film* (New Brunswick, NJ: Rutgers University Press, 2013), 60. Jenny Woodley also notes that, "While there were occasional references to films in the NAACP [the National Association for the Advancement of Colored People] correspondence or reviews in *The Crisis*, the association devoted little attention to the business of motion pictures until the [1930s] drew to a close." However, she attributes this neglect not to cinema's perceived lack of cultural worth, but rather to "the fact that the NAACP had not yet discovered a way into the closed world of the white film industry and that the broader national climate had not yet provided it with the opportunity for action." Jenny Woodley, *Art for Equality: The NAACP's Cultural Campaign for Civil Rights* (Lexington: University Press of Kentucky, 2014), 128.

9. Massood, *Making a Promised Land*, 61. Massood's reading underscores the movement's lack of attention to the aesthetic possibilities of cinema, although it does overlook Paul Robeson's performance in Oscar Micheaux's *Body and Soul* (1925) as well as the close attention that Floyd Covington, Geraldyn Dismond, and Langston Hughes paid to the medium when synchronized sound film emerged at the end of the 1920s. Hughes went so far as to travel to Hollywood in 1928. He also corresponded with Mason on her notes on Hurston's film footage. For a discussion of Covington, Dismond, and Hughes's responses to early sound cinema, see Edward Allen, "Langston Hughes at the Cinema," in *Modernist Invention: Media Technology and American Poetry* (Cambridge: Cambridge University Press, forthcoming 2020), 206–248.).

10. Alison Griffiths, *Wondrous Difference: Cinema, Anthropology, and Turn-of-the-Century Visual Culture* (New York: Columbia University Press, 2002), 168.

11. Hurston, *Mules and Men*, 9.

12. Leigh Anne Duck, "Go There Tuh *Know* There: Zora Neale Hurston and the Chronotope of the Folk," *American Literary History* 13, no. 2 (Summer 2001), 274.

13. Charlotte Osgood Mason, "Notes on Zora's Films," Box 164–99, folder 4, Alain Locke Papers.

14. Tiffany Ruby Patterson, *Zora Neale Hurston and a History of Southern Life* (Philadelphia, PA: Temple University Press, 2005), 132.

15. J. Emmett Winn, *Documenting Racism: African Americans in U.S. Department of Agriculture documentaries, 1921–42* (New York: Continuum, 2014), 107.

16. Sterling A. Brown, "Old Time Tales," *New Masses*, February 25, 1936, 25. Emphasis in original.

17. Zora Neale Hurston, *Dust Tracks on a Road*, in Hurston, *Folklore, Memoirs*, 690.

18. Ibid., 691.

19. Zora Neale Hurston, Letter to Langston Hughes (August 16, 1928), in *Zora Neale Hurston*, ed. Kaplan, 125.

20. Zora Neale Hurston, Letter to Ruth Benedict (*c.* spring 1929), in ibid., 140.

21. See Patterson, *Zora Neale Hurston*, 137.

22. Fatimah Tobing Rony, *The Third Eye: Race, Cinema, and Ethnographic Spectacle* (Durham, DC: Duke University Press, 1996), 204; Cara Caddoo, "Double-Consciousness and the Films of Zora Neale Hurston," in *Theorizing Visual Studies: Writing Through the Discipline*, ed. James Elkins and Kristi McGuire (New York: Routledge, 2013), 108.

23. For a discussion of the creative radicalism of this sequence, see Elaine S. Charnov, "The Performative Visual Anthropology Films of Zora Neale Hurston," *Film Criticism* 23, no. 1 (1998): 46.

24. Nazera Sadiq Wright, *Black Girlhood in the Nineteenth Century* (Urbana: University of Illinois Press, 2016), 3, 180.

25. Ibid., 178.

26. Hurston, *Mules and Men*, 57; Hurston, *Dust Tracks on a Road*, 572.

27. Zora Neale Hurston, "New Children's Games," in *Go Gator and Muddy the Water: Writings by Zora Neale Hurston from the Federal Writers' Project*, ed. Pamela Bordelon (New York: Norton, 1999), 105.

28. Ibid., 100.

29. Kyra D. Gaunt, *The Games Black Girls Play: Learning the Ropes from Double-Dutch to Hip-Hop* (New York: NYU Press, 2006), 1.

30. Zora Neale Hurston, "Characteristics of Negro Expression," in Hurston, *Folklore, Memoirs*, 842.

31. Hurston, *Dust Tracks on a Road*, 700.

32. Ibid., 805, 701.

33. George Leydon Colledge was a concert manager and the Arthur Judson Company was his employer. Zora Neale Hurston, Letter to Charlotte Osgood Mason (October 15, 1931), in *Zora Neale Hurston*, ed. Kaplan, 233. Emphasis in original.

CHAPTER 17

The Pulse of Harlem: African American Music and the New Negro Revival

Andrew Warnes

Before the mythologizing of its literary Renaissance began – and even before Alain Locke's *The New Negro* collection appeared in 1925 – Harlem was already famous for its music. Journeying north of Central Park from the 1910s on meant stepping into a neighborhood where all the industrial rhythms of modern New York – the clatter of its warehouses, workshops, and elevated trains – gave way to a set of more expressive, rehearsed and extemporized sounds. As James Weldon Johnson recalled, "a brilliant parade with very good bands" could seize the major streets of the increasingly African American district on any day of the week, the sound of its calliopes, drums, and cowbells often pulling in "a good part of the crowd" as it marched past.[1] From before dusk until after dawn, boogie-woogie or stride piano riffs could be heard emanating from one of the "parlor socials" or rent parties that Harlem tenants often held to remain solvent or even stave off eviction.[2] For Maud Cuney-Hare among other visitors, the "street-cries of the hucksters and vendors" provided another "class of fragmentary tunes" – and these, in turn, vied for attention with busking bluesmen, with the crackle of phonographic or shellac discs, and even with the calypso beats that followed the arrival of Trinidadians and other Antilleans in the 1920s.[3] The establishment of Abyssinian Baptist and Pentecostal churches in the same decade ensured that the up-tempo hymns of praise, improvised shouts and chants of affirmation which Zora Neale Hurston identified with such "sanctified churches" added further accents and figures to the distinctive medley of Harlem life.[4] Even the popularity of "the Harlem Renaissance," a term that had completely replaced Locke's "New Negro revival" by the 1930s, might have been boosted at some level by the black-run Renaissance ballroom that opened its doors on Seventh Avenue and 139th Street in 1922 and remained a source of what Langston Hughes called the "mellow magic / of dancing sound" long after the interwar period.[5]

All manner and moods of music, drawn from a vast range of diasporic routes, thus enabled black Harlemites to "take possession of the streets," in Richard Wright's phrase, staking a cultural claim equivalent to the economic independence being enacted in the black-run businesses that clustered west of the Mount Morris Park in the years after World War I.[6] Some white visitors to this neighborhood might have found in its bawdier traditions of song and dance a source of moral opprobrium. Others, admiring on the face of it, still heard in even the subtlest and most skillful of jazz solos only formless, primitive outpourings of African passion.[7] Yet the unique soundscape that they encountered also left these prejudiced observers, like others, in no doubt that they were here in the presence of a different culture – a culture already rich in the kind of autonomy with which the leading writers of the Renaissance hoped to imbue their literary works.

Their tributes and explanations, placing black music at the heart of their literary movement, are the focus of this chapter. As we will see, Alain Locke, Zora Neale Hurston, W. E. B. Du Bois, Richard Nugent, Langston Hughes, and Claude McKay all found in African American music a muse of unparalleled interest. All paid close attention to its origins, migrations, and transformations, and all agreed that it offered the best way of understanding "the pulse of the Negro world that had begun to beat in Harlem," as Locke put it.[8] Where the songs of Harlem sprang from, how they had survived a murderous past, and what they might now become: these were critical questions for the writers of the revival, and as they raised them they also faced the existential mystery of music itself, confronting afresh the paradox of a form that could seem so central to human experience yet lie beyond the reach of human language. Indeed, if, as Mark A. Sanders has suggested, "many New Negroes saw folk culture as an essential element of a usable past," then their work characteristically approached this precious heritage as an aural, acoustic resource, saluting its "work songs, seculars, field hollers, shouts, spirituals, blues" among other music lineages said to begin on the plantation.[9] Some of these salutes were imitative, and invented the new genre of blues poetry, for example, via their translation of its time signatures, repetitions, and anticipatable, confirmatory rhymes. Others were descriptive, asserting the historical or cultural importance of African American music within the idiom of the literary novel or magazine essay. Others still mixed imitation and praise: songs sang the "song of waters / Shaken from firm, brown limbs," in Gwendolyn B. Bennett's phrase, while Langston Hughes's *The Weary Blues* (1926) mythologized out-of-hours blues performance even as it devised ingenious textual echoes of the "mellow croon" and "drowsy syncopated tune" held therein.[10] Yet while these acts of recognition thus took varied form, never speaking in a single voice, all drew inspiration from a music that already existed in the night and day of Harlem life, naming it as a vernacular precedent for the acts of independence that the Renaissance would achieve in print. Together, then, these writers created a vast composite acclamation of song in textual form, and the scale of their endeavor – the sheer regularity by which they alternately pondered, praised, and mimicked the music in their midst – established a new genre of cross-cultural reflection which would, in turn, call for us to develop a new critical vocabulary today.

"The gifts divine are theirs": History and Orinphrasis in *The New Negro*

In the years that followed World War I, as numerous arrivals came to Harlem from the US South and the Caribbean, so too did a range of new revolutionary thoughts. The Workers' League, the American Labor Alliance and other socialist groups held several mass rallies in the district, and sought to maximize local interest with speeches that condemned US racism, placed it into global perspective, and denounced "Washington" as "the capital of world imperialism."[11] Other rallies and parades held aloft the red, black, and green flag of Marcus Garvey's proposed African republic, saluting the Jamaican leader in person or in spirit as a savior who would end the forced dispersal of the African diaspora.[12] Radical possibilities like these remained a source of heated debate in post-Armistice Harlem. Although Claude McKay suggested that, by 1922, supporters for Garvey in the neighborhood were "legion," and as "noisy as a tambourine yard party," *New York Amsterdam News* reporters long afterwards faced little difficulty in coaxing criticisms of him, and indeed of various socialist leaders, from other ordinary Harlemites.[13] Yet many of those who thus voiced skepticism or who upheld a patriotic viewpoint sometimes seemed to share with the revolutionists they mocked a rather mechanistic view of culture. An underlying belief that art was a means to an end, of value only inasmuch as it displayed the worth of a nation or group, united pan-Africanist and socialist thought in this period and pervaded discussion in Harlem's major churches as well as the National Association for the Advancement of Colored People (NAACP). Even Du Bois, the Hegelian thinker who had once theorized the power of the slave spirituals or sorrow songs, and who had by this time become a fierce critic of Garveyism, could seem so shaken by the war and the violent consolidation of white power in the USA that he now hesitated over the value of culture itself. His postscript to *Darkwater*, the autobiographical polemic he published in 1920, effectively retracted the work's intermittent bursts of poetry, all of which, he suggested, were "unworthy to stand alone"; as he concluded: "I know not . . . why the book trails off to playing, rather than standing strong on unanswering fact."[14] In the immediate aftermath of chemical warfare in France and racist massacres in Arkansas, the man whose *The Souls of Black Folk* (1903) had offered one of the first serious theorizations of black US song thus found it necessary to adopt a more urgent set of political priorities, denying his own intermittent flurries of lyrical expressivity.

This is the immediate background against which Alain Locke's editorial work on *The New Negro* needs to be weighed. At a time when radicals of different stripes were adopting a rather instrumental view of culture, and when even its old champions had grown doubtful of its power in the face of what *Darkwater* called the "millionaire industrial system," Locke's commissions, arrangements, and introductory essays coalesced into a different kind of revolutionary thought.[15] Against a somewhat utilitarian consensus, as his biographer Jeffrey G. Stewart has observed, Locke focused "his advocacy of the New Negro" on cultural form – on "art, literature, music, dance, and theater" among other "arenas in which queer Black people of color like himself found sanctuary." Using "Beauty to subjectivize Black people," he moved "the discussion of the Black experience toward the creative industries that even racists admitted were mastered by Black people."[16] In so doing he harnessed the performative power he identified in such artistic achievements, using them to announce the existence of a new black citizen on the national stage.

Yet it is also clear that, as he shepherded *The New Negro* toward publication, Locke remained mindful that the artistic forms that Stewart lists ("art, literature, music, dance, and theatre") had all progressed at different speeds in African American history. Nothing ever fascinated Locke personally quite as much as the "plastic arts" of West Africa, a subject that he would return to later in the interwar period and which he would recognize as evidence of the civilization that had flourished there in the centuries before European colonialism.[17] Yet in the early 1920s Locke already saw that the violence of the Middle Passage and the plantation regime had deprived his own American ancestors of the materials, time, and tools by which they might have sustained such "abstract decorative" traditions. Convinced that this "African spirit" remained only a "slumbering gift" in the New World, Locke turned instead to "music and poetry, and to an extent . . . dance," as "the predominant arts of the

American Negro."[18] Objective observation rather than his own personal preferences thus persuaded him to base his call for an artistic renaissance on the historic achievement of African American song:

> The Spirituals are really the most characteristic product of the race genius as yet in America. But the very elements which make them uniquely expressive of the Negro make them at the same time deeply representative of the soil that produced them. Thus, as unique spiritual products of American life, they become nationally as well as racially characteristic. It may not be readily conceded now that the song of the Negro is America's folk-song; but if the Spirituals are what we think them to be, a classic folk expression, then this is their ultimate destiny. Already they give evidence of this classic quality.[19]

Earlier the introduction confirms that, for Locke, this "indelible" contribution is what has allowed the New Negro to herald "an augury of a new democracy in American culture."[20]

> Recall how suddenly the Negro spirituals revealed themselves; suppressed for generations under the stereotypes of Wesleyan hymn harmony, secretive, half-ashamed, until the courage of being natural brought them out – and behold, there was folk-music. Similarly the mind of the Negro seems suddenly to have slipped from under the tyranny of social intimidation and to be shaking off the psychology of imitation and implied inferiority. By shedding the old chrysalis of the Negro problem we are achieving something like a spiritual emancipation. ... With this renewed self-respect and self-dependence, the life of the Negro community is bound to enter a new dynamic phase, the buoyancy from within compensating for whatever pressure there may be of conditions from without. ... From this comes the promise and warrant of a new leadership.[21]

A skeptical view might suggest that these remarks actually reflect more than they upset the consensus of the day. Just as *The New Negro*'s opening marries together a dedication "to the younger generation" with a slave spiritual invoking a coming emancipation ("O, rise, shine for Thy Light is a' coming"), so Locke's editorial work in general might be thought to instrumentalize culture insofar as he "uses" the spirituals as an inspiring precedent for the new "task" facing the descendants of slaves on the verge of democratic transformation.[22] One might add that Locke achieves all this while looking beyond Harlem's immediate soundscape. His own patrician status as a professor of philosophy at Howard University might seem betrayed by his focus on a songwriting canon considerably less sexual and more Christian than any blues or ragtime number to be found in Manhattan or among the "thrusting unconscious rhythms" that his contemporary Jean Toomer overheard on Washington, DC's Seventh Street.[23]

Both of these criticisms contain some truth but hide a deeper complexity. It is true, for example, that Locke has here hitched the "surprise" of old
black song to his vision of an equally unforeseen phenomenon in the
political realm. Unlike other polemicists of his era, however, he is not
confining his interest in culture to its ability to corroborate political values
he already holds. Instead it is, if anything, the other way around. Finding
a transcendent capacity in the cultural sphere – finding that the spirituals
are remarkable because they "transcend emotionally even the very experience of sorrow" – he is trying to mine from it a political basis for "a change
in the Negro far beyond the measurement of the sociologist," as Nathan
Huggins once put it.[24] The distinction was too fine for some. Some
sympathetic readers believed that Locke was in essence celebrating the
spirituals on the grounds that their beauty and sophistication prove the
humanity of the African people, but this was to focus on a single step in
Locke's argument at the expense of his more radical destination. For if
Locke is hoping here to lay to rest the old lie of racial inferiority, this is so
that he can reiterate, and perhaps redeem, *The Souls of Black Folk*'s original
description of the Sorrow Songs as America's "folk-song."[25] Du Bois's
assertion of the unique importance of the spiritual thus justifies Locke
sending his readers on what Stewart calls "an archaeological mission into
the . . . folk heritage of Negroes."[26] A canonical authority has helped him
approach the spirituals as a cultural resource unique enough to vouchsafe
his vision of a New Negro now on the cusp of remaking American
democracy.

Similarly, given the scale of these ambitions, it is unsurprising that
Locke should have looked beyond the syncopated rhythms and passionate
solos of the immediate jazz soundscape in order to focus on a more
venerable body of work. Again, it is true that ragtime, jazz, and the blues
were never to his taste, an unfortunate blind spot for a man at the helm of
black US modernity's defining manifesto. Yet it is also true that, while jazz
continued to be routinely misunderstood as a formless outpouring of
primitive African passion, the Fisk Jubilee Singers among other choirs
had already secured some recognition and respect for the spirituals among
American music lovers. Ignoring what one of Langston Hughes's white
characters calls the "tomtom-like music . . . coming out of" the "grand
piano[s]" of Harlem might have suited Locke's personal tastes.[27] Yet it also
made tactical sense, allowing him to ground his call for political transformation in a body of cultural work whose established credibility inoculated it
to a degree from the simplifications and stereotypes of his intensely
racist era.

It is also apparent that the significance of what Locke produced as a result of this focus was never limited to the subject of that focus, the spirituals themselves, but always resonated among the many tributes his contributors to *The New Negro* paid to music of all kinds. Within a context of intergenerational agreement, indeed, it was through the subtler shifts – the aspects where he departed from Du Bois's view – that Locke began to build this wider resonance. On the uniqueness of the spirituals, for example, both men, as we have seen, agreed; but they did so for different reasons. Uniqueness, for Du Bois, meant unrepeatable: the music of the Sorrow Songs was drawn from "the siftings of centuries," was more "ancient than the words," and their final form was determined by an epic and exceptional meeting of drummed West African chants and choral European hymn.[28] Yet uniqueness, for Locke, meant inauguration, instigation. He explained the spirituals not as the result of a set of unusual historical circumstances but as the first original product of the signature processes of hybridization and cultural progression that were now conditioning African American modernity in general. Vanished here was Du Bois's acute sense of the fragility of the Sorrow Songs, his way of talking about them as if they were heirlooms or remnants all but forgotten in a segregated black US South whose "turbulent proletariat" had "no leisure class" and "no old folks to sit beside the fire and hand down traditions of the past."[29] Against this elegiac tone, when Locke wrote of "the deceptive simplicity of Negro song," and when he described it as "thematically rich, in idiom of rhythm and harmony richer still, in potentialities of new musical forms and new technical traditions so deep as to be accessible only to genius," his use of the present tense spoke volumes.[30] He did not need to mention jazz, let alone affirm it, for his readers to see it was a likely place to find the "new technical traditions," and perhaps even the geniuses, of today. Continuities paramount in what Winston Napier describes as "Locke's call for a black self-referential discourse" rested on a canon of songs Du Bois had spoken of as a marvelous archaeological deposit.[31]

It was by rerouting *The Souls of Black Folk*'s excitement into the contemporary, then, that Locke placed African American music at the heart of black modernity. In Houston A. Baker's words, his "editorial work constitutes a song of a new generation, his attempt to produce a singing book of (and for) a new era in Afro-American expressive history," and this in turn provided a clear de facto rationale for the many tributes to music performance that he placed inside *The New Negro*.[32] Zora Neale Hurston's allusions to how her protagonist Spunk could "stroll the soft dark lanes with his guitar," Rudolph Fisher's description of an underground Harlem club where "the drum and cornet rip out a fanfare, almost drowning the piano," and Langston Hughes's dizzying vision of "a whirling cabaret" where "long-headed jazzers play," all could now seem not just to describe music but also to follow Locke's manifesto in naming it as the fount and precedent for their own cultural creativity.[33] His decision to place the spiritual at the vibrant heart of African American expression even provides an indirect rationale for the jazz performance imagined in Claude McKay's "Negro Dancers" (1919):

> 'Tis best to sit and gaze; my heart then dances
> To the lithe bodies gliding slowly by,
> The amorous and inimitable glances
> That subtly pass from roguish eye to eye,
> The laughter gay like sounding silver ringing,
> That fills the whole wide room from floor to ceiling, –
> A rush of rapture to my tried soul bringing –
> The deathless spirit of a race revealing.

"Negro Dancers," like much else in *The New Negro*, was not a new commission: it had originally appeared in *The Liberator* alongside articles on French socialism, the international labor movement, and other matters of concern to that magazine's Marxist readership. As such, and beyond a brief clichéd preface in which he is said to possess a "more simple and strong gift of poetry than any other of his race," McKay's poems appeared in the magazine as an unexplained interruption to its usual mode of social prognostication.[34] Yet *The Liberator* was far from alone in thus interspersing its long stretches of analysis with occasional bursts of lyrical expression. Unexplained fragments of poetry also appear in many compositions that *The New Negro*'s future contributors themselves produced in the first few years after World War I. True of *Darkwater*, this was also true of "What the Negro is Doing for Himself" (1918); for example, James Weldon Johnson's essay on the emergence of the NAACP likewise interrupts its political chronicle with a lyric from R. C. Jamison but says nothing about the relationship between the two.[35] McKay's own *Liberator* essay on Ireland, meanwhile, speaks of the "art of revolution" but only to mean conventional channels of protest, and leaves unanswered the question of why he himself "did not go in for pugilism instead of poetry."[36] It fell to Locke to see that Ireland could inspire culturally too, providing his New Negroes with an example of a land where "the greatest literary men of our time" had become great precisely because they had tarried among "the humble cabins of the Irish peasants" and gathered the "primitive emotions and traditions" they found within.[37] *The New Negro*'s vision of an equivalent African inherit-ance – an enthralling harvest of music and song – would in time provide a kind of retroactive rationale for "Negro Dancers," theorizing the wonder that gathers and grows as McKay brings his second stanza to a close:

> Not one false step, no note that rings not true!
>   Unconscious even of the higher worth
> Of their great art, they serpent-wish glide through
>   The syncopated waltz. Dead to the earth
> And her unkindly ways of toil and strife
>   For them the dance is the true joy of life.[38]

European literary traditions often reserve special significance for those moments when a poem turns to reflect upon a work of visual art. At such moments of extended description, known as *ekphrasis*, European poetry spirits attention away from its own origins in song, seeking new alliances and affinities with the work of Old Masters among other canon-ical forms thought to permit more "institutionally legitimated modes of aesthetic experience," in Frank Capogna's phrase.[39] Yet this is also a notoriously torturous field. Any comparison between the malleability of paint or clay and the fixed abstract code in which poetry is set down can never quite escape the basic dissimilarity of these forms. Out of ekphrasis, as a field of comparative analysis in the lyrical mode, claims of cultural supremacy often get made. Yet they are often made with uncertainty, or ambiguity; ekphrasis can as often undermine as protect the precise grounds on which civilization is supposed to stand.

One measure of *The New Negro*'s radicalism is how, despite his own interest in West African sculpture, Locke rejects such ekphrastic activity, installing music instead as the chief means to glorify "the artistic skill and historical achievements of a people," as Sneharika Roy has put it.[40] Locke, as we have seen, was always mindful that, for all their mastery, the "plastic arts" of Yoruba and Ibo had not survived the genocidal impact of transat-lantic slavery. Such traditions might now be studied and purposefully rekindled, but they could not in their existing state sustain an ekphrastic sequence vibrant enough to serve his aim of placing the African American people at the vanguard of modernity. The "syncopated waltz" overheard in "Negro Dancers," on the other hand, could. *The Liberator*'s readers, on encountering the first appearance of McKay's poem, could have seen its abundant allusions to John Keats, and to "Ode on a Grecian Urn" (1819) in particular. They could have seen that, like Keats's canonical act of ekphra-sis, "Negro Dancers," too, is written in iambic pentameter; it, too, bathes in wonder; it, too, calls up questions of aesthetic truth. Yet they could also have seen that there was nothing supplicatory about these tributes; McKay was not just draping himself in the garb of a vaunted white canon. Instead his echoes are purposeful, transformative. They reanimate "Ode on a Grecian Urn," exposing it to the night sounds of Harlem. Here, after all, the "Bold Lover" and "Fair Youth" doomed to stasis in Keats's frozen Hellenic world become "lithe bodies," gliding and swaying in syncopated time; even the poet's own "heart dances."[41] It is through such revivifying devices that "Negro Dancers" parallels and enacts Locke's overarching goal, transferring Keats's ekphrastic search for "great art" from the optical to the acoustic field. Woven into a wider editorial project, "Negro Dancers," in reviving Keats's dormant "sensual ear," retains the second part of *ekphrasis* (the Greek word *phrasein* meant "describe" or "speak out") even as it seeks a subject altogether less external (the Greek word *ex* meant "out").[42] Admittedly, as he hears the music inside him but remains still, McKay's own formal structures can seem small, English, a skin so tight he cannot join the dance; the syncopation of the music and the regular iambs of the poetry can seem poles apart. Yet the distance between such formal units also functions, simultaneously, as a sign of the transformational potential that the song holds over the poem and of their final and inescapable difference from each other; and this is to say that it performs a paradoxical function, forever promising and refusing formal convergence, not unlike the distance between paintwork and prosody might, for example, in canons of European ekphrasis.

Upon being republished in *The New Negro*, "Negro Dancers" came to seem less of a curiosity and more like part of a wider movement. Within his collection, indeed, Locke's own reflections on West African art can feel less important and less representative of this movement than the many mediations of and meditations on music with which he surrounded it. All of *ekphrasis*'s arcane dilemmas can, in turn, seem to be replaced entirely as these meditations and mediations revisit what Henry Louis Gates, Jr., once characterized as "the oxymoron" of "the talking book," and reflect, not unekphrastically, on their own "attempt[s] to represent what is not there, to represent what is *missing* or absent."[43] Moreover, as it thus enacts this total replacement – as it returns us to a trope first theorized in *The Signifying Monkey* (1988) – so *The New Negro* might look, with Gates, eastward, urging us to "discover ... analogues and functional equivalents for Western aesthetics in African aesthetics," as Houston A. Baker puts it.[44] Just as Gates, inspired by Wole Soyinka's dramatic vision of Yoruban *orishas*, found in this West African culture the trickster "Esu-Elgebra, keeper of the crossroads," and "guide and guardian" of his "theoretical project," so we might here take up the Yoruban word *orin* – defined as "music produced by singing" – to develop a way of identifying the alternative to ekphrasis presented in Locke's book.[45] *Orinphrasis* – an African American alternative to ekphrasis, produced when writers of the tradition marvel at, puzzle over, and mimic the music in their midst – might, indeed, name the means by which Locke's manifesto performs a new way of thinking in American life.

"Paint Most Wondrous Tune": Orinphrasis and Syncopation

In the years that followed the publication of *The New Negro*, a host of writings likewise lingered and pondered over the meanings of African American music. Nella Larsen evoked profound ambivalence about the "endless moaning verses" and "wailing singing" of a Tennessee church in her metropolitan novel *Quicksand* (1928) while Langston Hughes's landmark collection *The Weary Blues* (1926), as Shane Vogel has shown, "draws from the rhythms, sounds, improvisations, and intimacies of the blues and urban nightlife performance to map the spatio-temporal experience of afterhours."[46] As these acts and gestures of orinphrasis proliferated it became apparent that most were leaving Du Bois's cherished spirituals behind and finding their greatest inspiration, as McKay and Hughes had done in *The New Negro* itself, in the dance music of Harlem cabarets and southern Jooks. "Musically speaking," as Zora Neale Hurston suggested in her essay "Characteristics of Negro Expression" (1934), "the Jook is the most important place in America." It eclipsed the innovations of the "sanctified church" because "in its smelly, shoddy confines had been born the secular music known as blues, and on blues has been founded jazz." Hurston continued:

> In past generations the music was furnished by "boxes," another word for guitars. One guitar was enough for a dance; to have two was considered excellent. Where two were playing one man played the lead and the other seconded him. The first player was "picking" and the second was "framing," that is, playing chords while the lead carried the melody by dexterous finger work. Sometimes a third player was added, and he played a tom-tom effect on the low strings. Believe it or not, this is excellent dance music.[47]

This orinphrasis in prose makes it clear that the music one might hear in this space differed significantly from jazz in the modern sense of the term. The music that Hurston here depicts as an outgrowth of the blues also remained, emphatically, a type of dance music; she evokes what would later be thought of as the heyday of the traditionalists, a period before Louis Armstrong felt forced to "fight them damn beboppers" and "keep music alive." (Praising the easy-going swing of Bunk Johnson's "Franklin Street Blues," Armstrong continued: "That clarinet is trying to tell a story – you can *follow* him. . . . You can dance to it! In bebop, they don't know which way they're going to turn.")[48] In place of the avant-gardism and chromatic complexity that Armstrong disliked, the live band to be found inside Hurston's imaginary Jook, as she suggests, remained functional, and their function was to allow the crowd to dance. Every aspect of their performances was governed by their mutual production of danceable rhythm. Improvisation here still mattered, but not to vent individual genius so much as to upset and reinvigorate that central rhythm all the better to make people move. Remembering how to control your own body, reclaiming it from insult and industrial fatigue, were certainly observable effects of the dances that resulted. In Hurston's Jooks, as Robin D. G. Kelley has suggested, "the black body" became "an instrument of pleasure rather than an instrument of labor."[49] Those who jived and jitterbugged were evidently performing a radical alternative to those European cultural codes, from Platonism to Emersonian Transcendentalism, which vaunted the soul in terms of the escape from or rejection of the body. Even the sheer singularity of a phrase like "the body," indeed, met a challenge in this "most important place." If, onstage, musicians had to work, as Armstrong put it, "like a basketball team, everybody passing the ball just right," then they did so in the hope of getting the whole Jook to dance; the bodily reclamation Kelley describes was on offer to everyone in the room.[50] Exchanges flowing between such an ensemble and an audience of dancers clearly created a cultural scene radically unlike the metropolitan sphere of writing and publication.

   In some ways, indeed, even while she urges this radical alternative upon us, the protocols of Hurston's literary occupation continue to remove her from it. The distance between form and object remains almost as large as in "Negro Dancers." Whereas Hurston's novels often homed in on jazz-style improvisation, her explanatory mode here, never heedless of a white readership, place an inexorable distance between her and the scene she describes. In one sense, the idiomatic conventionality of her essay implies a historical relationship unlike that of "Negro Dancers." McKay's iambs can seem archaic, Keatsian, an old shape he holds onto as he drinks in what Vogel has termed "the totality of the rhythms, gestures, beats, moods, and movements, the perceptible quiver of the air," in Harlem's nocturnal soundscape.[51] But Hurston, by contrast, is offering a backwards glance, a memory of a South that seems to become more remote and mythic even as she remembers it. The occasional formalities her genre requires of her discourage the kind of inventive improvisations she brought to *Their Eyes Were Watching God* (1937), for example, preventing further poetic bursts on a par with that novel's description of a hurricane as a "monstropolous beast [that] had left his bed."[52] The perennial obligation to help white readers navigate African American culture blocks the more radical possibilities that are flowing from it. In particular it closes down the possibility, made manifest in *Their Eyes Were Watching God*, that jazz's innovations of rhythm – what Hughes called its "drowsy syncopated tune" – might find an echo in the black US canon following its extended experiments in orinphrasis.

No such formal limitation is apparent in the case of "Smoke, Lilies and Jade" (1926), the elliptical work of association and desire Richard Nugent first published in *Fire!!*

> the night was so blue . . . how does blue feel . . . or red or gold or any other color . . . if colors could be heard he could paint most wondrous tunes . . . symphonious . . . think . . . the dulcet clear tone of a blue like night . . . of a red like pomegranate juice . . . like Edith's lips . . . of the fairy tones to be heard in a sunset . . . like rubies shaken in a crystal cup . . . of the symphony of Fania . . . and silver . . . and gold . . . he had heard the sound of gold . . . but they weren't the sounds he wanted to catch . . . no . . . they must be liquid . . . not so staccato but flowing variations of the same caliber . . . there was no one in the cafe as yet . . . he sat and waited . . . that was a clever idea he had had about color music . . . but after all he was a monstrous clever fellow.

Through this synesthetic performance, as Vogel suggests, Nugent's protagonist Alex "maps sexual spaces in the city through the nocturnal appropriation of walking."[53] As he wanders, though, his steps also become percussive, projecting rhythms born in Hurston's Jook, with their promise of bodily reclamation, out onto Harlem's streets. Yet, as he does so, the "tremendous sex stimulation" Hurston identified in such spaces ventures outside too.[54] A chance encounter that Nugent describes orinphrastically, as a collaborative improvisation, leads to the open seduction of a beautiful man:

> Alex walked music . . . the click of his heels kept time with a tune in his mind . . . and had an echo . . . sound being tossed back and forth . . . back and forth . . . someone was approaching . . . and their echoes mingled . . .and gave the sound of castanets . . . Alex liked the sound of the approaching man's footsteps . . . he walked music also . . . he knew the beauty of the

narrow blue . . . Alex knew that by the way their echoes mingled . . . and the
echo of their steps mingled . . . they walked in silence . . . the castanets of
their heels clicking accompaniment . . . the stranger inhaled deeply and with
a nod of content and a smile . . . blew a cloud of smoke . . . Alex felt like
singing . . . the stranger knew the magic of blue smoke also . . . they
continued in silence . . . Alex knew he had never seen a more perfect
being . . . his body was all symmetry and music . . . and Alex called him
Beauty . . . long they lay . . . blowing smoke and exchanging thoughts . . .
and Alex swallowed with difficulty . . . he felt a glow of tremor . . . and they
talked and . . . slept.[55]

"Smoke, Lilies and Jade," for Brian Glavey, is above all a work of queer
ekphrasis: it is "ekphrastic" in its "exploration of the gap between the verbal
and the visual," and its "queerness" is manifested in "its refusal of the
categorizing strictures of sexual or racial identity."[56] The ellipses that
structure Nugent's story, for Glavey, may "establish a tempo appropriate
for the story's languorous, dreamlike meditation," but their "importance"
remains "chiefly visual."[57] As one might expect given the interest of this
chapter, however, I take a different view. Nugent, after all, was not the first
modernist writer who experimented with ellipsis. They also preponderate
in Robert Leland DeCamp's "Syncopation" (1919), for example, and the
title of this long poem, also a keyword for Hughes and McKay, suggests
another way of understanding Nugent's experimental punctuation.[58] For
such syncopation, defined as the "use of rests and dotted values, placing
emphasis on the offbeat," was a hallmark of the dance scene that flourished
in Harlem in this period.[59] Such striking "rests" and unexpected emphases
were integral to the rhythmic innovations of Fats Waller, Willie the Lion
Smith, James P. Johnson, and other early Harlem musicians, and in time
they would clearly play a part in the emergence of swing and its familiar use
of "offbeat notes" and "micro-rhythmic variations."[60] One might at the
same time feel that such syncopation manifests another kind of queerness,
a musical technique that flaunts the process by which it subverts expected
form and redefines bodily movement. Certainly we may say that as
syncopation uses "rests" to remake the rhythmic line, so Nugent uses
ellipses to refashion the novelistic sentence, again drawing his own processes to the foreground of the performance. It is not that in doing so
Nugent relinquishes all claim to the ekphrastic mode on which Glavey
focuses. "Smoke, Lilies and Jade" is full of allusion, anything but still. But
it also swings. Its synaesthesia focus attention on the body, its ekphrasis
evokes its relationship to visual aesthetics – but its queer orinphrasis

embeds jazz echoes into the silent, printed text, fulfilling Locke's vision with a new sensory power.

The transformational and liberatory power that music holds over the African American literary tradition remains as apparent today as in the first years of the New Negro Revival. The simple name of Toni Morrison's sixth novel remains exemplary. *Jazz* (1992) is unusual only in being quite so explicit about its efforts to import harmony and rhythm onto the silent, static world of the printed page. Yet where *Jazz*'s formal translations amount to nothing less than an intervention in US history, recasting the Great Migration as a "train-dance" out of Jim Crow penury, it remains at the same time only one of many literary works that follow *The New Negro*'s example.[61] The go-go callouts of Thomas Sayer Ellis's *The Maverick Room* (2005), the diasporic chants of Chris Abani's *Sanctificum* (2010), and even Rita Dove's remarkable "Ludwig von Beethoven's Return to Vienna" (2017) can all be listed alongside *Jazz* as works of the tradition which draw inspiration from musical form.[62] In fact this list is so long, and these African American experiments so numerous, that connoisseurs of the tradition might find it too familiar to mention. Sometimes, though, it falls to critics to name what is in front of them. Orinphrasis is an original element in the African American literary tradition, and its practice is central to the articulation of its history and its difference from the other literatures in the world.

Notes

1. James Weldon Johnson, *Black Manhattan* (New York: Arno Press, 1968), 168–169.
2. On the long working hours of rent party pianists, see Jacob Womack, "Luckey Roberts, Willie 'the Lion' Smith, 'Fats' Waller, and James P. Johnson: An Analysis of Historical, Cultural, and Performance Aspects of Stride Piano from 1910 to 1940," PhD diss., West Virginia University, 2013, 14. Womack defines "boogie-woogie" as a "style of solo piano in which the left hand plays a repeated bass pattern of single notes, usually one- to two-measures" (4).
3. Maud Cuney-Hare, *Negro Musicians and their Music* (New York: Da Capo, 1974), 93. See also Clare Corbould, "Streets, Sounds and Identity in Interwar Harlem," *Journal of Social History* 40, no. 4 (2007): 873.
4. For an analysis emphasizing the centrality of music in Pentecostal worship, see Cheryl J. Sanders, *Saints in Exile: The Holiness-Pentecostal Experience in African American Religion and Culture* (New York: Oxford University Press, 1996), 42–44.

5. Langston Hughes, "College Formal: Renaissance Casino" in *The Collected Works of Langston Hughes: The Poems 1951–1967*, ed. Arnold Rampersad (Columbia: University of Missouri, 2001), 53.

6. Richard Wright, "High Tide in Harlem: Joe Louis as a Symbol of Freedom," in *Speech and Power: The African-American Essay and its Cultural Content From Polemics to Pulpit*, ed. Gerald Early (Hopewell, NJ: Ecco Press, 1992), 15.

7. Ted Giola critiques the Primitivist logic in operation in early French and US jazz criticism in "Jazz and the Primitivist Myth," *The Musical Quarterly* 73, no. 1 (1989): 140–141.

8. Alain Locke, "The New Negro," in *The New Negro*, ed. Alain Locke (New York: Touchstone, 1997), 14.

9. Mark A. Sanders, "African American Folk Roots and Harlem Renaissance Poetry," in *The Cambridge Companion to the Harlem Renaissance*, ed. George Hutchinson (Cambridge: Cambridge University Press, 2007), 97. See also Alexander G. Weheliye, "I Am I Be: The Subject of Sonic Afro-Modernity," *boundary* 30, no. 2 (2003): 103.

10. Gwendolyn B. Bennett, "Song," in *The New Negro*, ed. Locke, 225.

11. Anonymous, "Radicals Ridicule Arms Conference," *New York Times*, November 14, 1921.

12. Anonymous, "Garvey Reviews Big Negro Parade," *New York Times*, August 2, 1924.

13. Claude McKay, "Garvey as a Negro Moses," *The Liberator* (April 1922): 8.

14. W. E. B. Du Bois, *Darkwater: Voices from within the Veil* (Mineola, NY: Dover, 1999), ix.

15. Ibid., 67.

16. Jeffrey C. Stewart, *The New Negro: The Life of Alain Locke* (New York: Oxford University Press, 2018), 8–9.

17. Ibid., 702.

18. Alain Locke, "The Legacy of the Ancestral Arts," in *The New Negro*, ed. Locke, 254.

19. Alain Locke, "The Negro Spirituals," in *The New Negro*, ed. Locke, 199.

20. Locke, "The New Negro," 9.

21. Ibid., 4–5.

22. Locke, *The New Negro*, vii. The spiritual Locke chose recasts a message God gives to the Israelites in the Book of Isaiah, placing it in the future tense. Its source in the King James Bible reads: "Arise, shine; for thy light is come, and the glory of the LORD is risen upon thee." Isaiah: 60:1.

23. Jean Toomer, *Cane* (New York: Penguin, 2019), 51.

24. Nathan Huggins, *Harlem Renaissance* (New York: Oxford University Press, 1971), 57.

25. W. E. B. Du Bois, *The Souls of Black Folk*, ed. David W. Blight and Robert Gooding-Williams (1903; Boston: Bedford/St. Martins, 1997), 186.

26. Stewart, *The New Negro*, 510.

27. Langston Hughes, "The Blues I'm Playing," in *The Ways of White Folks* (London: George Allen and Unwin, 1934), 108.

28. Du Bois, *The Souls of Black Folk,* 187.

29. Ibid., 99, 122.

30. Locke, "The Negro Spirituals," 200.

31. Winston Napier, "Affirming Critical Conceptualism: Harlem Renaissance Aesthetics and the Formation of Alain Locke's Social Philosophy," *The Massachusetts Review* 39, no. 1 (1998): 96.

32. Houston A. Baker, Jr., *Modernism and the Harlem Renaissance* (Chicago: University of Chicago Press, 1987), 72.

33. Zora Neale Hurston, "Spunk," in *The New Negro,* ed. Locke, 108; Rudolph Fisher, "The City of Refuge," in *The New Negro,* ed. Locke, 71; Langston Hughes, "Jazzonia," in *The New Negro,* ed. Locke, 226.

34. Anonymous, "Claude McKay," *The Liberator* (July 1919): 7.

35. James Weldon Johnson, "What the Negro is Doing for Himself," *The Liberator* (June 1918): 32.

36. Claude McKay, "How Black Sees Green and Red," *The Liberator* (June 1921): 18.

37. Quoted in Stewart, *The New Negro,* 87.

38. Claude McKay, "Negro Dancers," in *The New Negro,* ed. Locke, 214.

39. Frank Capogna, "Ekphrasis, Cultural Capital, and the Cultivation of Detachment in T. S. Eliot's Early Poetry," *Journal of Modern Literature* 41, no. 3 (2018): 163.

40. Sneharika Roy, *The Postcolonial Epic: From Melville to Walcott and Ghosh* (London: Routledge, 2018), 137.

41. John Keats, "Ode on a Grecian Urn," in *The Complete Poems,* ed. John Barnard (Harmondsworth: Penguin, 1983), 344–346.

42. Roy, *The Postcolonial Epic,* 138.

43. Henry Louis Gates, Jr., *The Signifying Monkey: A Theory of African-American Literary Criticism* (Oxford: Oxford University Press, 1988), 181.

44. Houston A. Baker, "'The Urge to Adorn': Generational Wit and the Birth of 'The Signifying Monkey,'" *Early American Literature* 50, no. 3 (2015): 834.

45. Ibid., 834. Kayode J. Fakinlede, *English-Yoruba, Yoruba-English: Modern Practical Dictionary* (New York: Hippocrene, 2003), 398.

46. Nella Larsen, *Quicksand* (1928), in *Quicksand & Passing,* ed. Deborah McDowell (London: Serpent's Tail, 1989), 112. Shane Vogel, *The Scene of Harlem Cabaret: Race, Sexuality, Performance* (Chicago: University of Chicago Press, 2009), 120.

47. Zora Neale Hurston, "Characteristics of Negro Expression" (1934), in *Zora Neale Hurston, Folklore, Memoirs, and Other Writings,* ed. Cheryl A. Wall (New York: Library of America, 1995), 841.

48. Louis Armstrong, *Louis Armstrong: In His Own Words,* ed. Thomas Brothers (Oxford: Oxford University Press, 1999), 165.

49. Robin D. G. Kelley, "'We Are Not What We Seem': Rethinking Black Working-Class Opposition in the Jim Crow South," *The Journal of American History* 80, no. 1 (1993): 85.

50. Armstrong, *Louis Armstrong: In His Own Words,* 166.

51. Vogel, *The Scene of Harlem Cabaret,* 118.

52. Zora Neale Hurston, *Their Eyes Were Watching God* (Urbana: University of Illinois Press, 1978), 236.

53. Vogel, *The Scene of Harlem Cabaret,* 221.

54. Hurston, "Characteristics," 842.

55. Richard Nugent, "Smoke, Lilies and Jade," *Fire!!* (November 1926): 35.

56. Brian Glavey, *The Wallflower Avant Garde: Modernism, Sexuality, and Queer Ekphrasis* (Oxford: Oxford University Press, 2015), 83–84.

57. Ibid., 79.

58. Lines on the opening page of Leland's "Syncopation" include: "That half-concealed your beauty … Traffic" and "A Song to Eros … a dance to Syncopa … our symphony of life vivacious … " See Robert DeCamp Leland, *Syncopation* (Boston: Poetry-Drama Company, 1919), 7.

59. Michael C. Thomsett, *Musical Terms, Symbols and Theory: An Illustrated Dictionary* (Jefferson, NC: McFarland and Company, 1989), 188.

60. Howard Spring, "Swing," *Grove Music Online.*

61. Toni Morrison, *Jazz* (London: Picador, 1993), 30.

62. As Keith Leonard observes, *The Maverick Room* derives from Washington, DC's go-go scene "an alternative literary-cultural historiography predicated on the principles of formal repetition, rigorously self-conscious attention to cultural form, conceptions of time as nonlinear, and a notion of blackness as dissident creativity." Keith D. Leonard, "Postmodern Soul: The Innovative Nostalgia of Thomas Sayers Ellis," *Contemporary Literature* 56, no. 2 (Summer 2015): 344.

CHAPTER 18

The Figure of the Child Dancer in Harlem Renaissance Literature and Visual Culture

Rachel Farebrother

The dynamic interplay between literature, music, and visual art in Harlem Renaissance cultural expression has received considerable critical attention, with major studies on the "experimentation with visual and verbal techniques for narrating and representing blackness" by Anne Carroll, Caroline Goeser, Martha Nadell, and Cherene Sherrard-Johnson adding to a large body of scholarship on jazz and blues aesthetics.[1] By contrast, the thematic and formal fascination with dance among black modernist artists and writers has been somewhat neglected.[2] This chapter traces the political, cultural, and aesthetic burdens of an enduring preoccupation with dance in African American modernism by shifting the focus of discussion away from black female dancers who occupied a central place in debates "around miscegenation, cultural heritage, nationalism and the folk, and the consequences of capitalism."[3] The dance of children (and young adults) emerges as a source of fascination and discomfort in the Harlem Renaissance that is neither limited to a particular cultural and political position nor a specific genre or media. In literature, journalism, and photography, dancing children sometimes embody new possibilities for the future and resistant aesthetics that defy categorization, but they make for anxious, loaded imagery that flickers between embarrassment and pride. This is partly because of dance's fraught history in the representation and exploitation of African Americans (both on the stage and beyond it), but it is also linked to unease about the commodification of black culture.

Representations of dance became an important trope for imagining black cultural identity in the 1920s and 1930s, and a means by which to explore anxieties about generational conflict, gender, sexuality, tradition, and urban life. Attending to representations of children opens up a fresh perspective from which to examine the significance of dance in relation both to questions of cultural identity (including black modernists' engagement with the legacies of minstrelsy) and to what Shane Vogel has termed the "sensuous Harlem Renaissance," an aesthetic project that "turned toward the possibilities of feeling, sense, and perception . . . to imagine new experiences of black pleasure and desire."[4] Against the backdrop of a broader preoccupation with black childhood among social scientists, educators, and political activists, which found full expression in W. E. B. Du Bois's 1920 assertion that "all human problems . . . center in the Immortal Child and his education is the problem of problems," representations of child dancers were freighted with contradictory emotions that complicate discourses of racial uplift.[5] The focus on children's experiences of everyday pleasure and discomfort in portrayals of child dancers and children observing dance expands our understanding of the emotional cultural politics of the Harlem Renaissance. It also adds a new dimension to the study of visuality in the period because such scenes are centrally concerned with questions of perception, observation, and spectacle. Taken together, these dynamic representations of children should be read as probing reassessments of modes of interpreting and seeing blackness that reorient perception away from sensationalism toward the dynamics of everyday life. They also prompt a fuller understanding of how shifting attitudes toward dance as both a social practice and a performance affected ways of seeing.

Dance and Racial Uplift

Dance occupied an uneasy position in relation to racial uplift, a program of social change that came to prominence in the 1890s as middle-class African Americans envisioned "embodying respectability, enacted through an ethos of service to the masses."[6] As Kevin Gaines has shown, uplift ideology was animated by contradictions. Its emphasis upon respectability and assimilation amounted to "a limited, conditional claim to equality, citizenship, and human rights for African Americans" that upheld patriarchal, often elitist values.[7] The concept of an educated, respectable vanguard depended upon an understanding of "low" culture as corrupting and decadent.

In this context, it is no surprise that influential cultural arbiters such as Alain Locke and Charles S. Johnson distanced themselves from developments in black social dance of the 1920s – including crazes for the Charleston, the Black Bottom, the Lindy Hop, and the Stomp – and the social space of the cabaret, which, as Wallace Thurman put it, served as "a welcome and feverish outlet" in Harlem "where the struggle to live is so intensely complex."[8] It is difficult to miss Alain Locke's unease about vaudeville in his 1936 Bronze booklet *The Negro and His Music*, not least because the specter of slavery haunts his judgment of "artistic bondage to the ready cash of our dance-halls and the vaudeville stage."[9] Locke's ambivalence about tap-dancing, a hybrid form that evolved from percussive Irish and African diasporic dance traditions,[10] even prompted him to advise readers to obstruct their view of the star Bill "Bojangles" Robinson: "A Bojangles performance is excellent vaudeville, but listen with closed eyes, and it becomes an almost symphonic composition of sounds. What the eye sees is the tawdry American convention; what the ear hears is the priceless African heritage."[11] Evidently, the transformation of vernacular culture into "symphonic" forms (which Locke positions outside the vagaries of the cultural marketplace) required a jettisoning of cultural forms that have been "tarnished with commercialism and the dust of the market-place."[12]

Robinson's considerable fame rested upon virtuoso performances of his signature stair dance, which involved dancing up and down a staircase that was "part set, part drum set."[13] By the 1930s, when Locke published his study, Robinson had become a controversial figure, partly because of a Hollywood career that consigned him to stereotypical roles. By taking aim at Robinson's incorporation into the "American" cultural marketplace, Locke draws distinctions between art and commercialization, highlighting the risks of cultural commodification, primitivism, and spectacle. The most revealing tensions in Locke's commentary, however, cluster around the issue of embodiment. By celebrating Robinson's taps as an "African" symphony, Locke resists a tendency to bracket African Americans with physical rather than cerebral culture. Paradoxically, he seeks to obscure the bodily movement that is so critical to dance, focusing instead on the (disembodied) sounds created by Robinson's feet. It is difficult to miss the irony that Robinson's (invisible) body remains the locus of authentic "African" traditions. Yet Locke's praise of the "symphonic" qualities of Robinson's taps amounts to more than an assertion of parity with European cultural traditions; it attempts to redefine the classical by making room for racial distinctiveness.

Notwithstanding such unease about dance, some prominent vaudeville performers, including the dancer and choreographer Aida Overton Walker, were, as Daphne A. Brooks notes, "openly aligned with black uplift and women's era social and political agendas" and regarded theater as a means through which to transform social attitudes.[14] In a 1905 essay for the *Colored American Magazine*, Walker challenged the tendency among "our so-called society people [to] regard the Stage as a place to be ashamed of," arguing that "our profession does more toward the alleviation of color prejudice than any other profession among colored people," partly because audiences were brought face-to-face with performers' artistry.[15] Walker sought to harness the growing cross-cultural cachet of certain black dances to achieve "the uplift of all."[16] Known as the "Queen of the Cakewalk," Walker was instrumental in infusing this popular dance with associations of grace and modernity, both as a performer with the Williams and Walker Company and as a teacher whose instruction of rich whites underlined the remaking of a dance that originated in black parodies of white dancing on the plantation into a symbol of modern urban sophistication. Nevertheless, she could not completely shake off the cakewalk's complicated history, which summoned up both cultural resistance and the traditions of racial impersonation and caricature embodied in minstrelsy (by the late nineteenth century, the cakewalk had been coopted by black and white blackface minstrels).[17]

In this context, it is hardly surprising that literary representations exploring dance and racial uplift during the New Negro Movement were marked by ambivalence. Jessie Redmon Fauset's *There is Confusion* (1924) is a romantic novel that explores the lives of three black Philadelphian families against the backdrop of World War I. It places considerable emphasis upon Joanna Marshall's difficult transition from the protective domestic environment of her childhood to adulthood. The narrative focus is Joanna's quest for success as a dancer, an ambition that is framed not in terms of modern celebrity but the politics of racial pride. Joanna is raised to believe that "honest effort led invariably to success" and she inserts herself into a tradition of "great women" such as Harriet Tubman, Phillis Wheatley, and Sojourner Truth who "had won their way to fame and freedom through their own efforts."[18] This emphasis upon heroism prompts the question: why does Fauset focus on dance rather than intellectual or educational endeavors in her fictional exploration of the promises and perils of cultural uplift?

In many ways, Joanna's dancing, which begins as she moves toward young adulthood, accords with uplift ideology. Her success rests on a dance with its roots on the street: a circle dance and game performed by children on 63rd Street to the song, "Sissy in the Barn," serves as the basis for her signature piece, *The Dance of the Nations*. The children, who are associated with authenticity and complete absorption in "the spirit of the dance and the abandon of the music" encapsulate a romanticized inclusive image of American identity because "Italians, Jews, colored Americans, white Americans" are among their number (47). They also represent a version of uplift that eschews commercialism and spectacle in favor of a quasi-ethnographic transformation of vernacular culture into what Locke would call "symphonic" styles.

Yet the prominence of dance in Fauset's coming-of-age story introduces unresolved tensions: popular vs. elite dance; art vs. commercialization; idealism vs. reality. If children are associated with futurity and new possibilities, Joanna's emergence as a dancer as she reaches adulthood initiates a painful transition from innocence to experience. Moving into the public sphere forces her to wrestle with the persistent influence of racism upon everyday life and cultural institutions. Imagining life on the stage in idealized terms, Joanna seeks to put clear distance between her artistry, which she distinguishes from "ordinary dancing" in its pursuit of "queer beautiful things," and assumed lower vernacular styles associated with the vaudeville stage (45). To sustain her faith in dance as a vehicle for social uplift, she overlooks the compromises required to obtain adequate training in classical ballet, a style of dance that is traditionally associated with white European culture. Indeed, irony abounds when Joanna's ardent account of her ballet teacher's contention that "if there's anything that will break down prejudice it will be equality or perhaps even superiority on the part of colored people in the arts" is juxtaposed with the fact that Bertully, Joanna's instructor, is only willing to teach her as part of a racially segregated class set up to cater for black students (97).

As Nina Miller points out in an astute interpretation of Fauset's treatment of "the problem of performance" for middle-class African American women, the novel is characterized by a strange reluctance to portray Joanna in the act of dancing.[19] It provides only fleeting glimpses of her "slender flaming body" that emphasize her training in classical ballet, as in a description of how Joanna's "lovely graceful limbs flashed and darted and pirouetted" (229). Moreover, success on the stage results in an exposure to "confusion" and "this problem of being colored in America" that Joanna's sheltered upbringing has done little to prepare her for (283). She eventually recognizes that the realities of racism mean that critical acclaim will do nothing to mitigate the humiliating necessity that she must "consider ordinary vaudeville" to make ends meet as a performer (283). This realization leads her to renounce artistic ambition in the public realm by retreating into the private sphere as a wife and mother.

The novel exhibits uneasiness about public exposure of the ambiguously raced female body on the stage, an anxiety captured in recurring images that juxtapose vulnerability and nakedness with coverings, wrappings, and clothes that provide inadequate protection from invasive spectatorship. Notwithstanding the sincerity of Joanna's desire for social transformation through art, fame is ultimately dismissed as "an empty thing" (274) that results in a proximity to the "garish" (sexualized and commercialized) excesses of the vaudeville stage that is uncomfortable for a bourgeois woman (233). By the end of the novel, Joanna regards her artistic ambitions as a desperate attempt to mask unsettling realities: "she saw life as a ghastly skeleton and herself feverishly trying to cover up its bare bones with the garish trappings of her art, her lessons, her practice, her press-clippings" (233).

The Figure of the Dancing Child and the Legacies of Minstrelsy

If walking the line between socially respectable dance and "ordinary vaudeville" proves impossible for Joanna, the legacies of minstrelsy cast a longer shadow over representations of the figure of the dancing child in Harlem Renaissance literature. There is, of course, a long tradition of seeing New Negro theater as marking a break with minstrelsy. David Krasner, for instance, identifies one "constant" in the diverse output of early twentieth-century black performers, insisting that "black modernity represented a desire to *transform the image of black culture from minstrelsy to sophisticated urbanity.*"[20] In this context, it is telling that the figure of Topsy, the unruly black child from Harriet Beecher Stowe's *Uncle Tom's Cabin* (1852) who was reborn as "a sign of irrepressible black childishness" and the most prominent female figure on the minstrel stage, became a touchstone in formulations of New Negro cultural identity.[21] For many early twentieth-century black intellectuals, Topsy embodied the humiliations of "Old Negro" stereotypes that confined black drama to a grotesque comic mode precluding full expression of emotional complexity. In his essay for Alain Locke's *The New Negro* (1925), for instance, the playwright Montgomery Gregory famously lamented the "baneful influence" of Topsy's "fearful progeny," describing the "descent from sentimentalism to grotesque comedy" as a kind of sickness from which "public taste" had yet to recover.[22]

In an account of the entanglement of cultural constructions of innocence with race, Robin Bernstein has demonstrated that nineteenth-century portrayals of black children as "comically impervious to pain" served to cordon off innocence as a category that applied only to white children: "As childhood was defined as tender innocence, as vulnerability, and as the pickaninny was defined by the inability to feel or to suffer, then the pickaninny – and the black juvenile it purported to represent – was defined out of childhood."[23] Bernstein's observations about the racialized dimensions of who gets to count as a child are astute, but she underestimates the extent to which concepts of (sexual) innocence were part and parcel of an enduring fascination with black children in US popular culture. In a recent article on the 1920s film series *Our Gang*, for example, Katherine Fusco argues that "white identification and affection are tied to the black child's possession of the triumvirate qualities of cuteness, youth, and, most important, sexlessness."[24] For Fusco, white audiences' "aesthetic enjoyment of black childhood" in minstrel shows and popular films depended upon the episodic qualities of narratives that left children "suspended in infancy," separated off from the temporal progression toward adulthood that would require full recognition of their humanity, sexuality, and future citizenship.[25] Notwithstanding the pervasiveness of these narratives of containment, African American performers found potential for resistance in the dance of black children. Training her critical gaze on so-called "pickaninny choruses" and "pickaninnies" on the early twentieth-century vaudeville stage, Jayna Brown argues that, for all their repackaging of minstrel tropes that imagined "slavery as racially innocent fun," the careers of early twentieth-century black child performers (including Josephine Baker) opened the way for alternative interpretations of such imagery.[26] "Topsy is inured to pain and proudly so; in her defiance she refuses humiliation," Brown explains. Consequently, "the twisting body of the dancing girl is a reclaimable trope of black expressive transfiguration."[27]

Read in this context, Zora Neale Hurston's 1924 story "Drenched in Light," which features Isis, a joyful child with an irrepressible urge to entertain, raises more questions than it answers. After indulging in the kind of frolicking that would not be out of place on the minstrel stage – in one incident, Isis prepares to shave off her sleeping grandmother's whiskers with a razor – the sound of the "thudding band" prompts Isis to run off to a barbecue where she gives an impromptu performance that attracts the attention of a white couple.[28] Blessed with "gifted" feet, Isis can "dance most anything she saw," but she also wheels about in the style of a minstrel performer (21). The description of Isis "wheel[ing] lightly about" (22) is a specific reference to Thomas Dartmouth Rice's "Jump Jim Crow" – with its famous line, "Wheel about, an' turn about, an' do jis so; / Eb'ry time I wheel about I jump Jim Crow" – a song that secured his position as the best-known performer of antebellum blackface caricature.[29]

A further layer of complexity is introduced through the (often ironic) portrayal of the white tourists who are so impressed by Isis's "brown little feet doing all sorts of intricate things" that they whisk her off to a hotel to perform for white folks (21). Isis is delighted at the prospect of performing on the stage, but Hurston's portrayal of the white couple recalls the exploitative consumption of racialized caricature and spectacle in minstrelsy. Not only does Helen, the white woman who "saves" Isis from a whipping by taking her to the hotel, describe the child as a "shining little morsel" (24), but she also displays complete self-absorption as she "look[s] hungrily ahead of her," relishing the prospect of Isis shining "a little of her sunshine to soak into [Helen's] soul" (25). References to consumption and appetite highlight Helen's selfish expectation that the child will provide "rejuvenation through joy," to borrow the title phrase from Langston Hughes's satirical short story about the packaging up of black culture for rich whites. Anticipating Richard Wright's later criticism of *Their Eyes Were Watching God* for "*voluntarily*" continuing "the tradition which was *forced* upon the Negro in the theater, that is, the minstrel technique that makes 'white folks' laugh," "Drenched in Light" centers on the dancing child (a stock character in minstrelsy) to expose the uneasy correspondences between minstrelsy and primitivist modernism.[30] Yet it does so in a manner that raises questions about ways of seeing and interpreting blackness. Indeed, Hurston's differentiation of white and black audiences means that what might be interpreted as *joie de vivre* can all too easily slide into something more sinister once the questionable motivations of white spectators come into view.[31]

This uncomfortable proximity between minstrelsy and primitivist modernism helps explain the consistent pairing of dance with respectability and domesticity in the pages of the short-lived children's magazine *The Brownies' Book* (1920–1921). The magazine, which developed as a spin-off from the popular annual children's numbers for *The Crisis* (1912–1934), consolidated Du Bois's pioneering efforts to foster African American children's literature and to rethink notions of black childhood in such a way as to encourage children's racial pride while preparing them for the struggle against oppression. Edited by Jessie Fauset, this groundbreaking magazine not only replicated *The Crisis*'s multigeneric format, but also boasted a contributor list that "reads like a who's who of the Harlem Renaissance."[32] Images of child dancers were common during the magazine's two-year run. The cover of the first issue, for instance, features a photograph of a young dancer on tiptoes with her arms stretched above her head (Figure 18.1). Wearing ballet shoes, a tiara, and a diaphanous white dress, the child's enjoyment of dancing is obvious. The camera lingers on details that identify a child at play rather than a professional dancer, such as creased, wrinkled clothing, the asymmetrical positioning of the girl's head, and her open smile. Such images are incorporated into narratives of racial uplift, but an emphasis on everyday pleasure inserts them into a tradition of vernacular photography through which, as Robin D. G. Kelley explains, viewers "discover in the gaze and gestures of ordinary African Americans a complex and diverse community too busy loving, marrying, dancing, worshiping, dreaming, laughing, arguing, playing, working, dressing up, looking cool, raising children, organizing, performing magic, making poetry to be worried about what white folks thought about them."[33]

More generally, *The Brownies' Book* eschews the visual imagery and limited emotional expression associated with minstrelsy and the vaudeville stage, focusing instead on children's pleasure in learning carefully choreographed steps from ballet and folk traditions. These dances are presented as untainted by commerce, although the photographs inadvertently expose the cost of ballet lessons and clothing. Dance is a constant feature in a regular column entitled "Playtime," which described games, African

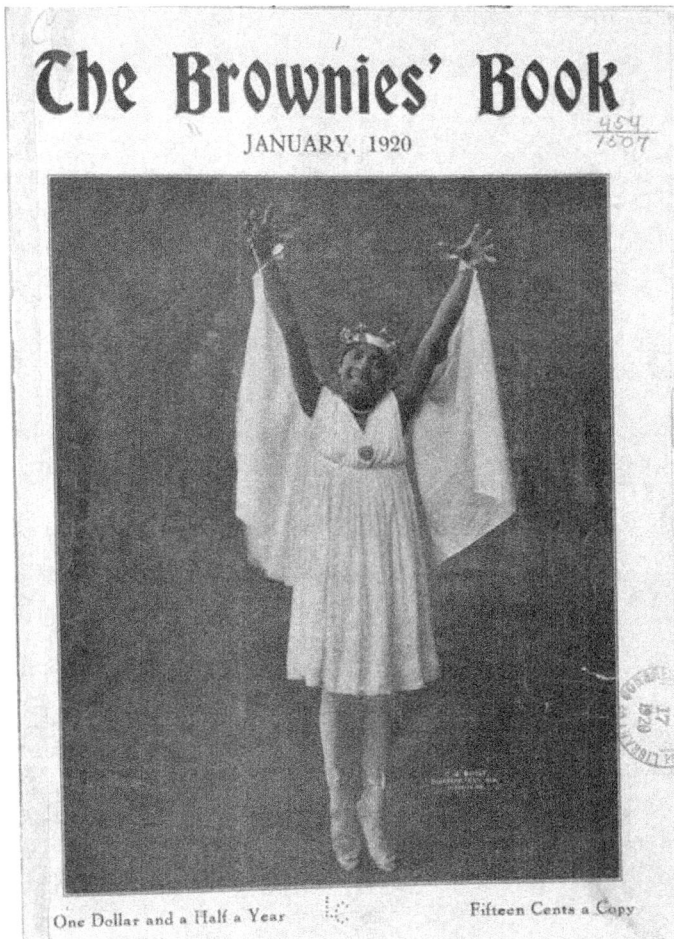

Figure 18.1 Cover of *The Brownies' Book*, January 1920, n. p.

riddles, dances, and activities children could try at home. The dances were presented in a user-friendly format, complete with instructions, diagrams, and musical scores.[34] Illustrations for the "Playtime" column (Figure 18.2), which depict well-dressed, self-contained children holding hands or dancing in a ring, are a far cry from the unruly, spontaneous bodily motion and acrobatics associated with Topsy. To date, scholarship on the "sensuous Harlem Renaissance" has focused almost exclusively on questions of sexuality and gender in such social spaces as the cabaret, but analysis of

20　　　　　　THE BROWNIES' BOOK

it was with great difficulty that Miss Dyson obtained order. Mr. Sellers, President of the School Board, sat by Miss Dyson's desk, looking very large and important, while the other judges sat hard by. After a few whispered words with Miss Dyson, Mr. Sellers arose and stepped ponderously forward.

He wasn't much of a speechmaker, he said,—in fact he couldn't make a speech at all. But the other judges had insisted that he present the prize. As every scholar knew, this prize was a five dollar gold-piece, to be given to the pupil who wrote the most comprehensive review of "Macbeth." After a very careful consideration of all the manuscripts handed in, the judges had come to this conclusion: Most of the reviews were good; two or three were excellent; but the one the judges considered the most deserving of the prize was written by Miss Maude Barstow. Therefore, it was with unqualified pleasure that he presented Miss Barstow the gold.

"HARK, HARK, THE DOGS DO BARK"

A Nursery Rhyme Dance
CARRIEBEL B. COLE

FORMATION—Single circle, facing for walking.

"HARK, hark"

Right hand at ear (listening), walking forward, right and left.

"The dogs do bark"

Hands at sides, four little scuffling steps forward: left, right, left, right.

"The beggars are coming to town"

Left hand over eyes (looking), three steps forward, trunk bending, and looking from side to side.

"Some in rags, and some in tags"

Arms hanging relaxed at sides, four steps forward: right, left, right, left, with high knee bending.

"And some in velvet gowns"

Right arm extended forward, left backward, three stately walking steps forward: right, left, right, left.

"And some in velvet gowns"

Repeat, but much slower, and more stately.

Figure 18.2 Carriebel B. Cole, "Playtime: Hark, Hark, the Dogs Do Bark, A Nursery Rhyme Dance," *The Brownies' Book*, January 1920, 20–21.

THE BROWNIES' BOOK   21

DANCE

1. Touch right toe in front.
2. Touch right toe in front.
1. Change weight to left foot, and point right in front.
2. Change weight to right foot, and point left in front.
3. Change weight to left foot, and point right in front.

Repeat all, but start with touching left foot.

1, 2, 3, Change step forward, starting with left foot.
1, 2, 3, Change step forward, starting with right foot.
1, 2, 3, Change step forward, starting with left foot.
1, 2, 3, Change step forward, starting with right foot.

Repeat the whole dance.

NOTE—Change step: step forward right, bring left to it, and step again right. This resembles the two-step, or is a catch-step.

Figure 18.2 (continued)

representations of children's joy, pleasure, and play in *The Brownies' Book* opens the way for an examination of the commonplace and the everyday that also encompasses writings invested in the politics of respectability.

Dance and Cultural Resistance

Elsewhere in early twentieth-century African American literature, the figure of the dancing child is associated with subversion and defiant expression of cultural difference in the face of what Langston Hughes condemned as attempts to "pour racial individuality into the mold of American standardization."[35] It is significant, for instance, that readers of Du Bois's *The Quest of the Silver Fleece* (1911) first encounter the young character of Zora in the midst of a whirling dance that, in its speed and fluidity, refuses comprehension or categorization. In an act of self-expression that is performed with no expectation of an audience, Zora's "arms twirled and flickered, and body and soul seemed quivering and whirring in the poetry of her motion."[36] Everything about this dance is in motion, suggestive of a subjective and sensory complexity that resists white efforts in the novel to quantify African Americans as "statistics" in order to maximize profit through social and economic exploitation (10). Notwithstanding his position at the forefront of US sociology, Du Bois's first novel is animated by an awareness of the risks of totalizing empiricism. Zora's dance encapsulates modes of representation rooted in the imagination, "formless" and "boundless" styles of expression that elude dominant models for interpreting blackness, including the newly institutionalized academic disciplines of sociology and anthropology (2). Zora's location on the swamp, a space with deep historical associations with resistance to racial terror, is also significant.[37] Although the novel's dominant narrative arc charts Zora's social transformation into an educated community leader, dance connotes an enduring tradition of cultural resistance. The figure of the dancer embodies a defiant resistance to racial terror and white cultural norms that tugs against the strategic assimilation that is central to racial uplift.[38]

Just as in Hurston's story, the portrayal of a dancing child in Du Bois's novel prompts reflection upon the ethics of spectatorship, not least because Zora's "whirring" motion is witnessed by a dumbstruck young black boy named Bles who is "dazzled ... bewildered, fascinated" by the "wild whirl" of "the soul that had called him" (2–3). In this scene, an intimate, emotional connection is established between dancer and observer, which places dancing in the realm of spirituality, romance, and dreaming rather than public entertainment or commercialism. The unreadability of Zora's dance (and the extent to which her inner life remains opaque) challenges southern social and political structures that see African Americans as "statistics" not "folks" (10). As Daniel G. Williams has noted, the novel is governed by "tensions that derive from a belief in the social and cultural uplift of the race, and the desire to preserve a black anti-materialist primitivism," and Zora's dancing, which "resists being reduced to a single interpretation," opens the way for new ways of reading, of observing and being observed.[39]

A more ambivalent portrait of the figure of the female child dancer, in which dancing is expressive of tensions relating to class, gender, and generational identities, enlivens Dorothy West's short story "An Unimportant Man," which was printed in the Boston magazine *The Saturday Evening Quill* in 1928. At the heart of West's story lies the question of how parents should raise their children in the context of a hostile political and social order. It soon becomes clear that Zeb, the "unimportant man" of the title, is frustrated that his life has been dictated by his mother's ambitions for him to leave the South, graduate from high school, and qualify as a lawyer, goals that sit uneasily with his lack of aptitude and commitment. Zeb's mother, Miss Lily, remains a formidable presence in his adulthood, and the narrator pointedly remarks that "she had not learned the pitiable wrongs of living for one's child."[40] This uneasy dynamic between parent and child, in which "restrictive ideas about success and happiness are passed down" the generations, finds its corollary in Zeb's relationship with his bright, if wayward daughter, Essie, whose desire to become a dancer provokes family conflict on such a scale that it is a factor in the death of her mother, Minnie.[41] For Zeb, ambition to become a dancer is associated with "independence" and a willingness to "stand up to people," a challenge to authority that takes a less appealing form in Essie's rudeness to her grandmother and various visitors to the family home (140). Essie's yearning to dance also bespeaks a longing for "beautiful things" (149). Her child's view yields clear-sighted insights on class hypocrisy, most notably when she asks why dancing is seen as a "sin" comparable to "lying and stealing" (148).

In the end, Zeb's insistence that he does not believe "in stifling a child's natural impulse" proves no match for Miss Lily's and Minnie's opposition (147). For both women, this is a matter of life and death. Miss Lily announces that she would "rather see this chile dead ... than a half-naked dancer on the stage" (147) and Minnie resolves to "beat it out of her if it kills me," which it does (156). In the moment of crisis following Minnie's death, Zeb cannot summon the strength to challenge the

repressive forces of bourgeois respectability; instead, he justifies his capitu-
lation to convention by invoking discourses of racial pride, telling himself
that "above all, Essie owed it to her race" (160). Zeb constructs
a redemptive narrative of "sacrifice" where a "broken heart" is a small
price to pay for "a forward step toward the freedom of our people" (160).

Such rhetoric of racial solidarity rings hollow because it is expedient. Yet
West also refuses to romanticize the lot of the female chorus dancer,
acknowledging that Minnie and Lily are justified in their anxiety about
young dancers' vulnerability to predatory men. Although contemporary
readers would have been aware of the successes of bankable stars like
Josephine Baker, the battles over Essie's future (and the narrowing of her
options to a career in teaching) demonstrate that "the child's body becomes
the site on which the character of the new black identity can be staged."[42]
Faultlines relating to gender, class, and generation cluster around the figure
of the child dancer and the ensuing family battle exposes bitter truths about
the limited prospects for middle-class black women in this period.
Notwithstanding stubborn resistance that sees Essie "savagely surveying"
her family, she is set upon a path that confirms the "cold" judgment of
Parker, a family friend who prizes uplift above all else, that "all nice colored
girls are teachers. . . . There's nothing else for a real nice girl to do" (154).

As "An Unimportant Man" draws to a close, Essie's unpredictable, sharp
voice is silenced, disappearing entirely from the story as adults define the
contours of childhood in line with their own prized ideas about innocence
and respectability. Such treatment is sharply at odds with Du Bois's call, in
Darkwater (1920), for child-rearing practices that avoided the pitfalls of
either "shielding and indulgence" or leaving children "to sink or swim in
this sea of prejudice" by providing "intelligent guidance" and "frank, free,
guiding explanation" about the realities of racial inequality.[43] By emphasizing the need to foster children's understanding of "the white world's
attitude and the shameful wrong of it," Du Bois identifies "the life task of
the parent to guide and to shape the ideal; to raise it from resentment and
revenge to dignity and self-respect, to breadth and accomplishment, to
human service."[44] By contrast, the adults in West's story never explain
their motivations to Essie; instead, she becomes the passive vessel of their
vision for the future and her creativity is denied any outlet.

Child Dancers and the Politics of Spectatorship

Some representations of child dancers succeed in capturing the kind of
emotional complexity that is shut down in West's exploration of the

fraught power dynamics between child, parent, and grandparent. Of particular note is James VanDerZee's 1928 photograph of five young girls enjoying a dancing lesson in Harlem. As in *The Brownies' Book*, VanDerZee eschews the sensationalism and commercialism associated with vaudeville, focusing instead on the everyday experience of learning tap. As Constance Valis Hill points out, buck-and-wing or tap was a vernacular dance that had "been developing as a performance art since the turn of the century in traveling medicine shows, carnivals, tent shows, and circuses" and "moved forward with great vigor on the vaudeville stage."[45] VanDerZee provides a glimpse of the "socializing feature of dancing lessons," puncturing fantasies associated with Harlem nightlife by focusing on mundane, everyday experiences of children at play.[46] Moreover, the focus on multiple dancers, who each engage in the lesson in their own particular style (from poised sophistication to private joy), ensures a shift from singularity toward a diversity and complexity that leaves viewers intrigued by the emotional expressiveness of each dancer. Indeed, the girls in the second row have not completely synchronized their movements, and the young girl with her eyes closed seems to be in her own world of enjoyment.

As Thomas F. DeFrantz has argued, such images invite "speculative perusal," not least because of the dynamics between dancer and observer built into their structure, which resonates with a broader interest in the question of how to interpret black culture.[47] As we have seen, images of child dancers in literature often provoked reflection upon the politics of interpretation, with a particular focus on how perception is complicated by commodification, the legacies of minstrelsy, and racial uplift. These are texts that display an enduring preoccupation with the figure of the spectator. Nowhere is this more obvious than in Langston Hughes's *Not Without Laughter* (1930), a *Bildungsroman* that draws heavily upon the author's experience of growing up in Kansas.

Dance becomes a primary means through which Sandy, the young protagonist, forges his identity as he advances toward adulthood. What makes the novel unusual is that Sandy is not a dancer. Instead, it is as an intelligent, sensitive spectator that he reconciles the conflicting demands of racial uplift, education, and vernacular culture, a theme that Aaron Douglas highlights in his striking cover design, with its depiction of a receptive Sandy watching his Aunt Harriett dance before two generations of the family. This crucial shift from the dancer to the observer highlights the agency that Hughes assigns to children in his fiction while bringing questions of interpretation into focus. Departing from notions of childhood as innocent and redemptive, Hughes emphasizes that Sandy's interpretation of dance is governed by an understanding of its entanglement with racism and sexism. One of the most troubling scenes in the novel occurs when a group of southern white men at the hotel where the teenaged Sandy is employed try to force him to dance for them. This demand summons up a long history – on slave ships during the Middle Passage, at the auction block, and on plantations – of whites coercing African Americans to dance in what Katrina Thompson calls "staged performance of race and power."[48] Elsewhere, Sandy registers the potential for sexual exploitation within vaudeville when he spots Harriett at the carnival "prancing in a mad circle of crazy steps" under the lascivious gaze of a white manager who never lifts his eyes from "Harriett's legs."[49]

Sandy receives bitter lessons about the grim realities of American racism and racial violence throughout the novel. Armed with a clear-sighted awareness of the risks of spectacle, exploitation, and coercion, he is positioned as an astute observer who learns to navigate such difficulties in formulating his own cultural identity. In a scene positioned at the heart of the novel, he attends a dance with Harriett and spends the night watching the dancing from a balcony. This bird's-eye view fosters a sophisticated appreciation of the complex emotional temper of the blues, which is at once characterized by entrapment and release, expression and repression, laughter and despondency, all encapsulated in Hughes's description of an elemental beat "that made the dancers move, in that little hall, like pawns on a frenetic checker-board."[50] The novel is punctuated with scenes where Sandy watches and interprets performances, including Harriett's dance to Jimboy's singing and guitar playing in the yard; Aunt Hager's "whirling around in front of the altar at revival meetings"; Harriett's dance in the minstrel-show tent; and Harriett's performance at the Monogram Theatre as "Princess of the Blues."[51] Sandy's perception repudiates sensationalism, firmly rooting interpretations of black music and dance in the novel inside the community. Yet it also allows for the emergence of fresh perspectives, not least when he recognizes the shared emotional impulses and historical forces that underpin the blues and religious worship.

Jayna Brown has identified the figure of the solo female black dancer in Harlem Renaissance poetry of the 1920s as "a central trope used in the discourses of primitivist modernism as New Negroes sought a modern subjectivity and a usable past."[52] Representations of child dancers tap into associations between dance and ancestry as well as engaging with pressing contemporary issues, including cultural commodification, the legacies of minstrelsy, and the pressures of racial uplift. Attention to children's pleasure and play in everyday settings undercuts associations of child dancers with commercialism and the limited emotional compass of minstrelsy. More generally, the figure of the child dancer in Harlem Renaissance cultural expression offers an alternative point of entry to a wider debate about how to interpret black culture. These texts probe the social and cultural meanings of dance in the period and illustrate how the act of dancing, which is so natural to children, is transformed by the white gaze. In addition to exploring the fraught dynamics between spectator and subject, these representations clear a space for children to reinvent themselves and the world. In the penultimate chapter of *Not Without Laughter*, for example, Sandy reflects that black dancers are "captured in a white world," but develop cultural forms infused with a "spirit" of subversion. Although he is represented as an active interpreter of culture and life for much of the novel, alternative possibilities for the child as social agent are imagined by way of dance: "Aunt Hager's dreams for Sandy dancing far beyond the limitations of their poverty, of their humble station in life, of their dark skins," we learn at the end of the novel, have been nurtured by his grandmother's "singing, dreaming, calling up the deep past, creating dreams within the child."[53]

Hughes's recourse to the motif of dancing to imagine a future reconciling racial uplift with a deep commitment to black cultural traditions captures in its dynamics the creative possibilities of representation of the dance of children in Harlem Renaissance cultural expression. Into the 1930s and 1940s, the medium of film captured the emotional complexity of black dance, with a 7-year-old Sammy Davis, Jr. tapping his way out of the racist constraints of the short film *Rufus Jones for President* (1933), and the Nicholas Brothers performing flash dancing with breathtaking virtuosity. However, it was a white child star, Shirley Temple, taught to dance on-screen by Bill "Bojangles" Robinson, who became most famous for her taps, an injustice that would prompt Toni Morrison's young protagonist Claudia McTeer in *The Bluest Eye* (1970) to resent "squint-eyed Shirley" because Bojangles was "*my* friend, *my* uncle, *my* daddy [who] ought to have been soft-shoeing it and chuckling with me."[54]

Notes

The author would like to thank Sarah Meer, Miriam Thaggert, and Daniel G. Williams for providing thought-provoking, invaluable feedback on drafts of this chapter.

1. Miriam Thaggert, *Images of Black Modernism: Verbal and Visual Strategies of the Harlem Renaissance* (Amherst: University of Massachusetts Press, 2010), 3.
2. Notable exceptions include Jayna Brown's *Babylon Girls: Black Women Performers and the Shaping of the Modern* (Durham: Duke University Press, 2008).
3. Ibid., 191.
4. Shane Vogel, "The Sensuous Harlem Renaissance: Sexuality and Queer Culture," in *A Companion to the Harlem Renaissance*, ed. Cherene Sherrard-Johnson (Chichester, UK: Blackwell, 2015), 269.
5. W. E. B. Du Bois, *Darkwater: Voices from Within the Veil* (New York: Dover, 1999), 114. For a discussion of how children's literature became a site for the redefinition of modern black identity, see Katharine Capshaw Smith, *Children's Literature of the Harlem Renaissance* (Bloomington: Indiana University Press, 2004).
6. Kevin K. Gaines, *Uplifting the Race: Black Leadership, Politics, and Culture in the Twentieth Century* (Chapel Hill: University of North Carolina Press, 1996), xiv.
7. Ibid., 4.
8. Wallace Thurman, *Negro Life in New York's Harlem: A Lively Picture of a Popular and Interesting Section* (Girard: Haldeman-Julius Publications, 1928), 33.
9. Alain Locke, *The Negro and His Music* (Washington, DC: Associates in Negro Folk Education, 1936), 4–5.
10. See Constance Valis Hill, *Tap Dancing America: A Cultural History* (Oxford: Oxford University Press, 2010), 1–19 for an account of the hybrid cultural origins of tap.
11. Locke, *The Negro and His Music*, 135.
12. Ibid., 4.
13. Megan Pugh, *American Dancing: From the Cakewalk to the Moonwalk* (New Haven: Yale University Press, 2015), 31.
14. Daphne A. Brooks, *Bodies in Dissent: Spectacular Performances of Race and Freedom, 1850–1910* (Durham: Duke University Press, 2006), 335.
15. Aida Overton Walker, "Colored Men and Women on the Stage," *Colored American Magazine*, October 1905, 571.
16. Ibid., 575.
17. Soyica Diggs Colbert, *The African American Theatrical Body: Reception, Performance, and the Stage* (Cambridge: Cambridge University Press, 2011), 106–109.
18. Jessie Redmon Fauset, *There is Confusion* (Boston: Northeastern University Press, 1989), 149, 14. Hereafter cited parenthetically.
19. Nina Miller, *Making Love Modern: The Intimate Public Worlds of New York's Literary Women* (New York: Oxford University Press, 1999), 183.
20. David Krasner, *A Beautiful Pageant: African American Theatre, Drama, and Performance in the Harlem Renaissance, 1910–1927* (New York: Palgrave, 2002), 10.

21. Sarah Meer, *Uncle Tom Mania: Slavery, Minstrelsy, and Transatlantic Culture in the 1850s* (Athens: University of Georgia Press, 2005), 40.

22. Montgomery Gregory, "The Drama of Negro Life," in *The New Negro*, ed. Alain Locke (New York: Touchstone, 1992), 155.

23. Robin Bernstein, *Racial Innocence: Performing American Childhood from Slavery to Civil Rights* (New York: New York University Press, 2011), 20.

24. Katherine Fusco, "Sexing Farina: *Our Gang*'s Episodes of Racial Childhood," *PMLA* 133, no. 3 (2018): 537.

25. Ibid., 534, 537.

26. Bernstein, *Racial Innocence*, 21.

27. Brown, *Babylon Girls*, 77.

28. Zora Neale Hurston, "Drenched in Light," in *Zora Neale Hurston: The Complete Stories* (New York: HarperPerennial, 1995), 21. Hereafter cited parenthetically.

29. Katrina Dyonne Thompson, *Ring Shout, Wheel About: The Racial Politics of Music and Dance in North American Slavery* (Urbana: University of Illinois Press, 2014), 169.

30. Richard Wright, "Between Laughter and Tears," *The New Masses*, October 5, 1937, 25.

31. This fictional exploration of how racialized ideas about the dancer threaten to displace appreciation of the expressive qualities of dance resonates with Hurston's brief descriptions of her "joyful tendencies" as a young child in "How It Feels To Be Colored Me" (1928). Zora Neale Hurston, "How It Feels To Be Colored Me," in *Zora Neale Hurston, Folklore, Memoirs, and Other Writings*, ed. Cheryl A. Wall (New York: Library of America, 1995), 827.

32. Cheryl A. Wall, *Women of the Harlem Renaissance* (Bloomington: Indiana University Press, 1995), 54.

33. Robin D. G. Kelley, "Foreword," in Deborah Willis, *Reflections in Black: A History of Black Photographers, 1840 to the Present* (New York: Norton, 2000), x.

34. See, for example, Carriebel B. Cole, "Playtime: Hark, Hark, the Dogs Do Bark, A Nursery Rhyme Dance," *The Brownies' Book* 1, no. 1 (January 1920): 20–21.

35. Langston Hughes, "The Negro Artist and the Racial Mountain" [1926] in *The Norton Anthology of African American Literature*, ed. Henry Louis Gates, Jr. and Nellie Y. McKay (New York: Norton, 2004), 1311.

36. Du Bois, *The Quest of the Silver Fleece* (New York: Dover, 2008), 2. Hereafter cited parenthetically.

37. For a detailed discussion of cultural representations of the swamp as "a place of freedom, outside the racial terror of the plantation South," see Mick Gidley and Ben Gidley, "The Native-American South," in *A Companion to the Literature of the American South*, ed. Richard Gray and Owen Robinson (Malden, MA: Blackwell, 2004), 170.

38. My reading of Zora's dancing as a powerful mode of resistance that refuses transparency and legibility draws inspiration from Daphne Brooks's analysis of the subversive effects of Aida Overton Walker's performances of "Salome,"

in which she dances "a spectacularly visible opacity." Brooks, *Bodies in Dissent*, 340.

39. Daniel G. Williams, *Ethnicity and Cultural Authority: From Arnold to Du Bois* (Edinburgh: Edinburgh University Press, 2006), 195, 198.

40. Dorothy West, "An Unimportant Man," in Dorothy West, *The Richer, The Poorer: Stories, Sketches, and Reminiscences* (New York: Random House, 1995), 143. Hereafter cited parenthetically.

41. Cherene Sherrard-Johnson, *Dorothy West's Paradise: A Biography of Class and Color* (New Brunswick: Rutgers University Press, 2012), 64.

42. Katharine Capshaw Smith, "Childhood, the Body, and Race Performance: Early 20th-Century Etiquette Books for Black Children," *African American Review* 40, no. 4 (Winter 2006): 799.

43. Du Bois, *Darkwater*, 120.

44. Ibid.

45. Valis Hill, *Tap Dancing America*, 54.

46. Thomas F. DeFrantz, *Dancing Many Drums: Excavations in African American Dance* (Madison: University of Wisconsin Press, 2002), xi.

47. Ibid.

48. Thompson, *Ring Shout*, 7.

49. Langston Hughes, *The Collected Works of Langston Hughes: The Novels: Not Without Laughter and Tambourines to Glory*, ed. Dolan Hubbard (Columbia: University of Missouri, 2001), 84.

50. Ibid., 75.

51. Ibid., 202, 204.

52. Brown, *Babylon Girls*, 191.

53. Hughes, *Not Without*, 202.

54. Toni Morrison, *The Bluest Eye* (1970; London: Picador, 1994), 13.

CHAPTER 19

Jazz and the Harlem Renaissance

Wendy Martin

The Harlem Renaissance is known as "a flowering" of African American arts and letters between the end of World War I and the mid-1930s, producing works that were consciously informed by the New Negro Movement. In addition, jazz – the most prevalent form of music during that time – became the unintentional (and unlikely) anthem of the New Negro Movement. While the Harlem Renaissance was underway, the great jazz musicians were for the most part unaware that they were changing US culture, resurrecting the world's greatest musical tradition, and creating the New Negro. It is even more unlikely that anyone else thought they were doing this – in fact, some of these artists were outright criticized for "holding back" the progress of the race by, it was thought, engaging in stereotypes and pandering to the mainstream. Yet the fact remains that, whether for personal gain or for love of the art, these innovators took the folk spirit of African American music and crafted it into something widely admired. The stage personas of these musicians were never unequivocally submissive: they knew very well how to reverse negative stereotypes and how to satirize the expectations that were placed upon them; and if they gave the public what it wanted, it was in a way that challenged its preconceived notions.

This chapter will argue that although jazz was not initially thought of as the ideal emblem for the African American experience by relatively conservative African Americans such as Benjamin Brawley, who called jazz "a perverted form of music,"[1] it unmistakably preserved the folk traditions from which it originated, elevating them through innovations in technique and performance. To illustrate this point this chapter will explore the history and qualities of jazz, noting its African foundations and the unexpected US locations that shaped its history. This analysis of the various responses to jazz as an art form concludes by profiling the important jazz artists of the 1920s and 1930s.

The Harlem Renaissance Throughout America

Although initially centered in Harlem, the Renaissance was profoundly felt throughout the nation, particularly in the Midwest with Chicago as its cultural center. The Midwest was the hometown and stopping place for major figures in both literature and jazz: Langston Hughes lived in Lawrence, Kansas, and Cleveland, Ohio, and his early works are heavily influenced by those of Paul Laurence Dunbar, an Ohio native. Richard Wright moved to Chicago in 1927, beginning a vibrant literary circle that included Arna Bontemps and Margaret Walker.[2] In terms of music, Harlem jazz would not have existed if New Orleans musicians like King Oliver and Louis Armstrong had not first brought it to Chicago, and if Chicago musicians, both black and white, had not added the harmonic and rhythmic complexities that constitute Chicago Dixieland. During the Renaissance itself, the South Side of Chicago was a hotbed for musicians like Louis Armstrong, Duke Ellington, and Billie Holiday.

On the West Coast, Los Angeles and San Francisco were the most significant sites of influence despite the relatively low population of African Americans compared with other large urban centers. Although the West Coast was more expensive to live in and harder to reach geographically, the black population there was surrounded by other minority groups (particularly Mexican Americans and Chinese Americans) – as a result, black artists had the benefit of encountering the art forms of other non-Europeans.[3] African American artists such as the painter Sargent Johnson made his career in San Francisco while architect Paul Revere Williams was born in Los Angeles and established his firm there. Wallace Thurman and Arna Bontemps were raised in the West and lived in Los Angeles before moving to Harlem, while Hollywood attracted black entertainers including Bill "Bojangles" Robinson and the Nicholas Brothers.[4]

It was from the West Coast and the South that various dance moves migrated northeast, making jazz dance a category of its own. The shimmy and turkey trot, for example, are supposed to have originated from the West Coast, as well as the Balboa, which was a staple of the Swing Era. These dances are as disparate as can be: the shimmy, which involves fast hip and shoulder shaking, has roots in Haitian dances while the turkey trot is associated with ragtime. The South also made significant contributions such as the Charleston and the cakewalk. The Charleston combines European steps with shimmying motions; it was popular among "flappers" and made famous by Josephine Baker in her *danse sauvage*.[5] The cakewalk, on the other hand, originated during the days of slavery as a blend of African and Seminole Indian dance movements.

Jazz, Underdog of the Harlem Renaissance

During the Harlem Renaissance, music reached distant cities before paintings and poems, thanks to the phonograph, so that the jazz craze was rapidly felt throughout the whole nation. Yet jazz was disparaged by those who regarded themselves as the gatekeepers of music. Jazz was considered not only an incompetent form of music but also one that made its listeners incompetent. Will Earheart, the director of music for Pittsburgh's public schools during the 1910s, wrote, "I do not approve of 'jazz' because it represents, in its convulsive, twitching, hiccoughing rhythms, the abdication of control by the central nervous system -- the brain."[6] Jazz turned respectable citizens incompetent by taking away their self-control, leading to unrespectable behavior.

Yet perhaps what is more significant in the context of this discussion is how the black intelligentsia perceived jazz. These intellectuals were the members of an elite group often referred to as "the Talented Tenth" – a phrase originally used by northern white liberals who sought to establish black colleges in the South at the end of the nineteenth century. In his essay titled "The Talented Tenth," W. E. B. Du Bois redefines the phrase to refer to the elite minority of African Americans endowed with natural talent, a superior education, and the ability to incite social change by setting a positive example. "The Negro race, like all races, is going to be saved by exceptional men," he writes.[7]

According to Kelly King Howes, "Du Bois and the Talented Tenth preferred spirituals because they were sublime in nature and came out of the black folk tradition. Jazz and blues were viewed as uncivilized and vulgar."[8] Yet jazz was not unequivocally despised by all upper-class New Negroes. Although it is easy to divide the Harlem Renaissance into two opposing parties – the elite decriers of jazz and the masses who supported it – one must remember that outright condemnation was rare even among the Talented Tenth. Rather, there was a spectrum of opinions and plenty of debate: critics like George Schuyler believed that there was nothing remarkable or distinctly African American about jazz, that it could have been "produced by any group under similar circumstances."[9] W. E. B. Du Bois, on the other hand, was less dismissive but nonetheless perceived jazz as inferior to the spirituals. Alain Locke, James Weldon Johnson, and Zora

Neale Hurston appreciated jazz from an anthropological standpoint, as a folk art worthy of study, while Claude McKay employed primitivist notions of jazz for his iconoclastic literary agenda. If there was any member of the Talented Tenth who thought of jazz as an intellectually and spiritually superior art form, it was Langston Hughes. Nevertheless he was outnumbered in his time.[10]

In general, these Harlem Renaissance writers had a relatively positive view of jazz and admired it as uniquely African American. James Weldon Johnson appreciated the connections between jazz and folk genres, comparing the role of a trombone to that of a preacher's voice in a church service. Joel A. Rogers made similar conclusions but also thought of jazz as a symbol of the modern age, celebrating its recent forays into popular music. These writers were perceptive enough to separate jazz from vice, eliminating the biggest reason why jazz was not favored among the "Talented Tenth." Rogers denied any inherent connection between jazz and immorality, calling it "a creation for the industrious and dissipator of energy for the frivolous, a tonic for the strong and a poison for the weak."[11] Locke drew a similar distinction: "there is a vast difference between its first healthy and earthy expression in the original peasant paganism out of which it arose and its hectic, artificial and sometimes morally vicious counterpart which was the outcome of the vogue of artificial and commercialized jazz entertainment."[12]

Alain Locke respected the folk origins of the genre, although phrases like "peasant paganism" might sound dismissive to the twenty-first-century reader. According to Locke, jazz was uniquely African but terribly flawed. It was not entirely devoid of the "Negro musical idiom" but nonetheless adulterated by commercialization. Locke and his colleagues dreamed of a symphonic manifestation of jazz that could transcend commercialization – a new jazz developed by an African American Dvořák so that its salient qualities could be enjoyed without the trappings of low culture.[13] According to Locke, some musicians were closer to this ideal than others; his favorites included not only the usual suspects like Duke Ellington, Jimmie Lunceford, and Benny Goodman, but even Fats Waller and Cab Calloway. Unsurprisingly, he pinned much of his hopes on Ellington, "the pioneer of super-jazz and one of the persons most likely to create the classical jazz towards which so many are striving."[14] Yet this "super-jazz" – the long-awaited lovechild of folk and classical forms – had not yet arrived.

Harlem Renaissance fiction dealt more mercifully with jazz, allowing jazz tropes to inform the structure and themes of their literature – though with vastly different effects. Claude McKay, for example, used jazz rhythms and sensual imagery to drive his point home. Jazz serves as the accompaniment for Dionysian encounters in *Home to Harlem* (1928) that offended critics including Du Bois. No writer of the New Negro Movement appreciated jazz the way Langston Hughes did. Unlike the aforementioned authors and critics who saw jazz as a mongrelized form, inseparable from the primitive, Hughes was preoccupied with the spiritual effects of jazz as though it were on par with classical and sacred music. He structured his poems in a way that evokes jazz cadences (for instance, using capital letters in the middle of a line to imitate a syncopated drumbeat) and writes of black music as a form of deliverance. In *Not Without Laughter* (1930), music externalizes the emotions into an aesthetic form and provides meaning in the endless drudgery of existence. Hughes is unapologetic when it comes to defending his zeal before the rest of the Talented Tenth: "Let the blare of the Negro jazz bands and the bellowing voice of Bessie Smith singing blues penetrate the closed ears of the colored near-intellectuals until they listen and perhaps understand."[15] Hughes believed that until the black upper class shed its preconceived notions about jazz, its appreciation of the full and complex range of black life would be significantly lacking.

Hughes's criticism targets not only the opponents of the genre but even the Harlem Renaissance's most liberal thinkers who perceived jazz as a primitive (and compromised) art form. Theirs was a vision of jazz that unintentionally alienated the cabaret and the speakeasy, the rent parties of Fats Waller and the opium dens of Cab Calloway. What did these critics fear more – the encroachment of white capitalism upon the sanctity of black music, or the supposed moral decadence associated with working-class African Americans? Is it possible to have a "pure" form of jazz that avoids both? Locke, for one, was unafraid to admit the inconsistency of his vision, referring to his symphonic ideal as "a somewhat unstable hybrid."[16]

Critics today observe that the Talented Tenth were elitist.[17] Yet Harlem Renaissance intellectuals were cornered in such a way that they could not easily embrace jazz as the representative African American music. Their goal was to elevate the status of the race and they knew very well that any elevation was nearly impossible without the approval of the status quo. We must remember that New Negro intellectuals' involvement in politics was matched only by the jazz musician's lack thereof; perhaps what lurked in the former's mind was the fear that the frivolity of this music directly opposed (and might even undo) any hope of progress.

An Overview of Jazz History

There is most likely no earlier precursor to jazz than the polyrhythm and polyphony of African folk music, which is why critics like Alain Locke and Zora Neale Hurston did not consider jazz a separate category from the folk genre. Polyrhythms – "setting two or more time schemes against one another" – would show up repeatedly in styles as diverse as big-band swing and boogie-woogie.[18]

A later, perhaps most significant, ancestor of jazz is the African American spiritual. Its contributions include the call-and-response pattern, layered polyphony, and highly inflected melodic lines that weave through the harmonies.[19] Then there is the sublime nature of spiritual music – the way it helps the listener escape life's troubles through bodily engagement. By singing, clapping, and stepping in tune, the participant can momentarily transcend life's troubles and grant religious meaning to hardship. Jazz is a decidedly kinetic form of music as shown by Eileen Southern's description of a Sunday meeting:

> The benches are pushed back to the wall when the formal meeting is over, and old and young, men and women ... all stand up in the middle of the floor, and when the "sperichil" is struck up, begin first by walking and by-and-by shuffling around, one after the other, in a ring. The foot is hardly taken from the floor, and the progression is mainly due to a jerking, hitching motion, which agitates the entire shouter, and soon brings out streams of perspiration.[20]

This moment of call and response contains many affinities with jazz performance – the congregation responds vocally and kinetically to the music being played and to the calls of the preacher. A Harlem rent party or a big-band performance is very similar: the preacher (now replaced by the bandleader or rent party pianist) will exhort the dancers with wisecracks and catchy phrases, and the dancers will respond through increased movement, the nonreligious equivalent of an "amen." These performances invite participation as a way not merely of forgetting life's troubles but also of sublimating them by aesthetic means.

This sublimating effect is shared by the younger sister of the spirituals – the blues, which gave to jazz the technique of slurring or bending tones to imitate the sound of the human voice.[21] Like its illustrious descendent, the blues makes use of both music and lyrics to portray sorrow, often involving lyrics that are as romantic and beautiful as they are easy to remember. The formulaic nature of the blues – its eight-bar, twelve-bar, and sixteen-bar forms – makes it accessible to even the most fledgling musician, a form which jazz would borrow from and ultimately transcend through more sophisticated techniques.

The development of jazz from these roots is emblematic of the freedom from slavery. Jazz was created from musical as well as physical and economic freedom: no longer resorting to washboards, jugs, clapping, and foot stomping to accompany singing, African Americans of the late nineteenth and early twentieth centuries were now free to innovate with a range of musical instruments.

If jazz had been gestating for centuries, it was at last given birth with the emergence of five- or six-piece military bands – made popular during World War I and largely based in New Orleans. The marching band eventually became the "jazz band," a similar concept that had the same instrumentation (trombone, clarinet, tuba, banjo, and drums). Both jazz and marching bands borrowed their form from the European minuet – AABBACCDD, each letter representing a musical section. Ragtime, a later concoction created by the black Creoles of New Orleans, would borrow this form but add syncopation, emphasizing the second and fourth beats instead of the first and third. These were the final ingredients before jazz developed as a genre apart, no doubt a momentous event when "some person or persons from the black and black Creole subculture tried the epochal experiment of making the double speed secondary pulse in ragtime explicit."[22] Jazz had begun.

The two salient qualities that make jazz what it is – syncopation and improvisation – represent not only freedom from traditional form but also freedom in the context of African American history. Michel Feith describes the symbolic role of syncopation thus: "By stressing weak beats, it can be said to reveal and valorize the 'shadow' or 'background' of the dominant beat. It can therefore represent an apt metaphor for the situation of a minority, especially as it tries to assert pride and identity through artistic means."[23] In other words, syncopation represents unrepresented people by prioritizing the second beat over the first.

The origins of syncopation might be African or European – if European, we can see its first traces in the Ars Nova composers in the late Middle Ages. Yet it was West African music, with its "fluid" conception of rhythm, that was added to European techniques by ragtime pianists. These musicians combined two traditions, creating a unique sound that expressed the full range of human emotion. They invented a new form of syncopation that, like its West African forebear, is too subtle to notate on paper – for much like the human voice, each ragged note could vary by a fraction of a beat.

Improvisation is even more difficult to trace – we do not have a "missing link" between ragtime and jazz to show us when exactly improvisation began, except perhaps in the ragtime variations of Jelly Roll Morton. In spite of its mysterious origins, improvisation is no less symbolic and empowering. The uncertainties of migration, poverty, and racial violence were reflected in a musical style that was equally precarious in form – after all, adaptability and quick thinking are paramount requirements for a life in which nothing is set in stone. (The "cutting contests" between experienced musicians and fledgling ones attest to this necessity.) Yet inseparable from that precariousness – and far more precious – is the freedom to defy the notes and chords of another person's song. All this is to say that even down to its structural components, jazz was not merely the product of musical genius but also the embodiment of a historical experience.

Jazz officially came to being in New Orleans at the turn of the century (1890) and would hold sway until around 1917. Its earliest known manifestation is Buddy Bolden's band, which was essentially a marching band that combined ragtime syncopation with the bent notes (notes that are varied in pitch) and chord patterns of the blues.[24] His style was picked up by later New Orleans bands that maintained a marching band's instrumentation: cornet, clarinet, trombone, banjo, tuba, and drums.[25] Iconic recordings from this era include Jelly Roll Morton's "Jelly Roll Blues" (1915), King Oliver's "Dippermouth Blues" (1923), Sidney Bechet's "Wild Cat Blues" (1923), and Louis Armstrong's "West End Blues" (1928). (The latter three, although recorded during a later period, are decidedly in the New Orleans style.)

The form of Dixieland jazz was relatively simple: chords were mostly triadic and restricted to the I–IV–V progression, while the rhythm was played in flat-four.[26] The simplicity of this style allowed freedom for melodic and collective improvisation, so harmonic integrity was not prioritized; rather, musicians were free to improvise whatever melody fitted the mood as long as it did not clash with the rest of the band.[27] As a result, everyone had their freedom as long as no one took the spotlight: collective improvisation allowed the musicians to contribute to the polyphony, but only to the extent that all the instruments blended properly; extensive solos were all but absent during this time.

During this early phase of jazz, New Orleans bands performed on various occasions such as funerals, parades, and other communal gatherings. In historical venues like Congo Square, African-based dance styles such as Calinda, Congo, and Carabine flourished and had a profound influence on jazz dance – and although city leaders suppressed public dances at the Square following the Civil War, these styles nonetheless persisted wherever jazz was played.[28] Most notably, however, jazz was heard on a nightly basis in the brothels of Storyville, New Orleans's red-light district. As such, this music would be associated with the nightlife for many decades afterwards.

The reign of New Orleans Dixieland would come to an end, for the most part, when jazz expanded northward and the Harlem Renaissance began. For one, the postwar dance craze required a stationary jazz band with more complicated instrumentation – the double bass instead of the tuba, the piano instead of the guitar.[29] In 1919, Art Hickman added saxophones to his San Francisco band to create a more mellifluous sound for dancers to move to. A new style of jazz had now developed, a style which we refer to as "Chicago Dixieland" since Chicago was the first metropolitan stopping place for jazz musicians coming from New Orleans, as well as a major site of innovation. This second movement of jazz began roughly in 1917 and would last until around 1932, the beginning of the Swing Era. The Chicago scene was dominated by the same musicians from New Orleans – Louis Armstrong and Sidney Bechet, most notably – along with newer innovators including Earl Hines and Jimmy Dorsey; the latter end of this period would witness the rise of bandleaders such as Count Basie, Fletcher Henderson, and Duke Ellington. Famous pieces during this era include Louis Armstrong's "Heebie Jeebies" (1926), Fats Waller's "Ain't Misbehavin'" (1929), and Ethel Waters's "Dinah" (1925).

Chicago Dixieland was more complex and tightly structured than its New Orleans predecessor, and Chicago bands added the flatted third and seventh notes for a richer sound (borrowed from the blues), as well the sixth note to add a hint of unresolved tension. They also abandoned the flat-four rhythm and accentuated the second and fourth beats instead, a hearkening back to ragtime. Performances were much more circum-scribed and fast-paced, with 32-bar choruses and soloists trading bars; improvisation (now more harmonically conscious) was mainly the job of the soloist for whom it was now acceptable to stand out and pioneer their own style.[30]

The Swing Era, roughly from 1932 to 1942, brought another configur-ation of jazz – more streamlined to meet the demands of mass production, and in certain ways hearkening back to its New Orleans roots to achieve a more simplified form. For example, swing bands relied on riffs (repeated motifs over a changing harmony), a technique commonly used by the blues-inflected bands in the Southwest; sometimes, entire sections of a song would be made of riffs.[31] The 4/4 rhythm of New Orleans

Dixieland was also brought back, but with a twist: the third note was "swung" – in other words, delayed (whether as a dotted eighth note or as a triplet) for better dancing.[32] Drummers lightened the rhythm further by using the hi-hat – composed of two cymbals and foot pedal – instead of the snare to play the ground beat; at the same time, the rhythm section was doubled and played in unison to be heard in large dance venues such as the Savoy, the Roseland, and the Blue Bird.[33] The most popular dance styles of the time include the Lindy Hop, Charleston, and Balboa, coming from regions as diverse as Harlem, South Carolina, and Southern California.

The call-and-response pattern, syncopation and improvisation, and blues riffs, to name a few make clear that jazz is a process-oriented music. The individuality and particularity of musical sound is highly prized in jazz, not conformity to a standard or ideal. At the same time, jazz celebrates the collaborative process of the musical group as well as the brilliance of the individual soloist. Jazz honors the community and the individual.

Jazz made itself felt in the lives of people regardless of gender, class, or race, having a profound influence on American language and literature. The lyrics of jazz songs would popularize Harlem slang such as "dig," "jook," "ofay," and "cruising," many of which were used by black and white Americans alike. Jazz inflections would riddle the works of Harlem Renaissance writers, and even those of white writers ranging from F. Scott Fitzgerald to William Faulkner. Jazz musicians would begin their own literary subgenre – the jazz autobiography – in which prominent musicians like Louis Armstrong, Sidney Bechet, Billie Holiday, and Charles Mingus give their own versions of American rags-to-riches stories; these texts explore improvisation as not only a musical form but also as a way of life, reconfiguring what it means to be a successful American. All this goes to show that freedom and individual expression are crucial dimensions of jazz and American literature as well as US ideology and politics.

Jazz Innovators

It would not be an exaggeration to say that Louis Armstrong, with a career that spanned the late 1910s to the 1960s, made Chicago Dixieland and inspired creativity throughout the 1920s and 1930s. Beginning with his famous cadenzas and elaborate codas, he brought attention to himself as an artist, reshaping the jazz band from being a sum of its parts into a collaboration of musicians. In fact, it was because of Louis Armstrong that people began to conceive of the "jazz artist" as an entity. He was unafraid to steal the show; anyone could pick out his style with its triplets and doubletimes.[34] Yet none of it was unrestrained bravado: in his solos, he would give the impression of playing without regard for the band while being keenly aware of its movements, returning to the final beat just in time. This controlled exuberance was manifest in his public persona. His wall-to-wall smile, bug-eyed look, and other comedic capers earned him a fair amount of opprobrium. But he was performing his artistic persona. By putting his audience at ease, perhaps he reinforced some negative stereotypes of African Americans at the time, but he broke a good many more.

Duke Ellington was responsible for bringing Dixieland back to the uniformity of swing, and for bringing much more besides. He was active during roughly the same decades as Louis Armstrong, using the same kind of instrumentation found in New Orleans Dixieland as well as the African rhythms and blues structures that had characterized early jazz. He not only used the same kind of instrumentation found in New Orleans Dixieland but was also faithful to the African rhythms and the blues structures that had characterized early jazz. Although he did not make use of collective improvisation, he involved his musicians in the composition process and often "improvised [a song] into being."[35] As a performer, he introduced his pieces with witty asides; both he and his band were impeccably dressed and maintained a serious demeanor, upending anti-black stereotypes even in problematic settings like the Cotton Club.

An Ellington piece can be easily picked out for its emotional effect, which he heightened in several ways. First, he had a keen sense of balancing and blending the different textures of sound (as opposed to blending the merely quantifiable elements such as volume, chords, and pitch). We see this in his choice of instrumentation for "Mood Indigo" (1930), in which he defies convention by assigning the highest notes to the trumpet, the central part to the trombone, and the lowest notes to the clarinet.[36] Next, Ellington knew how to use dissonances and modulations in a way that was not painful for the listener; for example, "Black Beauty" (1928) begins without a clear tonic until finally settling on B flat, only to uproot itself again and modulate to an uncharacteristic A flat.[37] These effects among many others have contributed to the unmistakably pictorial quality of Ellington's music. His titles speak for themselves – "Sophisticated Lady," "Dusk," and "Sunset and the Mockingbird."

Duke Ellington (with the indispensable help of Billy Strayhorn) brought back the emotional sublimity that had come from the blues and the spirituals, an element that had almost disappeared amid the rigid sectionalization of the Swing Era. Jazz is a celebratory genre, sometimes artificially so when in the hands of commercial interests. Yet the compositions of these two men expanded the emotional palette of jazz, setting the stage for the cerebral and mystical creativity of bebop and the avant-garde.

Cab Calloway is perhaps the most visually unforgettable of the Harlem innovators. With a long career spanning from the 1920s to the 1980s, he was as much a singer and a dancer as he was a bandleader, recognizable by his zoot suit, flopping hair, and lanky figure which he put to full use: "When Calloway came on for the second set," says Albert McCarthy, "he made a remarkably spectacular entry, leaping over chairs, turning somersaults, and indulging in all manner of nonmusical showmanship, while singing."[38] His vocal feats were no less dramatic, ranging from rapid-fire scatting to vaudeville-esque sustained high notes.

Cab Calloway's key to success was his ability to involve the audience with his call-and-response routines. One example is his "hi-de-ho" routine, which was in fact borrowed from his sister Blanche Calloway who may have borrowed it unconsciously from West African antiphonal song (in which the leader and chorus exchange vocal lines: the leader's lines are varied and improvised while the chorus's are not).[39] By inviting the audience to participate in this easy way, Calloway transplanted a religious tradition (the call and response of the spiritual) into the context of entertainment.

Less known is Calloway's skill as a composer. In pieces like *Evening* (1936), we see proof that his band could be every bit as atmospheric as Ellington's, using instruments like the bowed bass, celeste, and muted trumpets. Calloway used these instrumental effects and minor themes to create an image of Harlem street life, anticipating the bebop era with complex chords containing elevenths, thirteenths, and tritones.[40] If Ellington's pieces are often a celebration of nature – the jungle, the sunset, the mist – Calloway's pieces evoked the opium dens and alleys of Harlem.

Billie Holiday did for popular song what Ellington did for big-band jazz – that is, bringing sophisticated artistry into commercial dross. Beginning in the late 1920s until her death in 1959, she was the modernist cynic in a sea of schmaltz, going in the opposite direction to where jazz vocals were heading at the time. Holiday satirized the lyrics of a song by "minimizing" its form; for example, in "What a Little Moonlight Can Do" (1935), she sings at a fast clip and casually throws off the lines without sustaining the last note.

On paper, Holiday did not have the vocal advantages of Ella Fitzgerald or Sarah Vaughan – her range could barely reach one-and-a-half octaves while other singers could easily reach two. She could hardly project her voice.[41] Yet Holiday more than made up for these deficiencies – used them to her advantage, in fact. Her tone was not as smooth as Ethel Waters's but it was perfect for her cynical interpretations of popular songs. As for the softness of her voice, it made the audience listen closely to how she articulated each syllable – every vowel and consonant can be clearly heard in a Billie Holiday piece because not one of them is neglected. Her style is deeply personal, almost confessional, unlike anything else recorded in that era.

No Harlem pianist is as well known and loved as James P. Johnson's protégé, Thomas "Fats" Waller, active from 1918 until his death in 1943. It is through Fats Waller that we can acquire a visceral sense of the Harlem music scene behind the artifice and glamor of the Cotton Club. He brought the Harlem rent party to the ears of privileged listeners by incorporating dialogue and sound effects into his records: in "The Joint Is Jumpin'" (1937), for example, extras engage in party conversation while the piece is performed, followed by police sirens in the background as Waller reassures the guests, "If we go to jail I got the bail." This is one of countless instances in which Harlem life is made real to the listener.[42]

Like Louis Armstrong and Cab Calloway, Waller was a hyperbolic showman, but in a wry sort of way. His expressions might vary from mock surprise to fearsome grimaces; with a cigarette dangling from his mouth he might grumble sarcastic asides to his fellow performers. All of this was done simultaneously with his gymnastic piano playing. He turned the stride genre on its head by complicating it even further, playing behind the beat or switching the roles of the left and right hands – at times he would play the melody with his left and tremolos or riffs on his right, as though he were a one-man orchestra.[43]

Conclusion

Today we cannot conceive of the Harlem Renaissance without jazz; the innovations of Duke Ellington and Louis Armstrong seem as part and parcel of the era as the writings of Langston Hughes and Alain Locke. Although scholars debate whether or not the Renaissance was a success, jazz *did* succeed, wielding an influence as great as its visual and literary counterparts; for if the New Negro Renaissance left a mark on Chicago, Harlem, and other US cities, it was through music – thanks to the dance craze and the record-making business, the first bit of Harlem Renaissance culture to reach distant cities like Los Angeles was jazz. When black literature and art went out of "vogue" after the white public lost interest, jazz remained strong because of its ability to evolve.

What Locke saw as the corrupting influence of popular music and commercial interests does not disqualify jazz from being uniquely African American. Jazz was as affected by commercialization as it was by the Great Migration; it went from expressing the joys and sorrows of the African American experience to expressing those of all humanity. Surely that does not erase the African ancestry of jazz, which remained intact even throughout the Swing Era. Young people flocked to the dance halls to learn the latest moves, while slummers attended rent parties to escape their lives – they likely had no idea that by participating in the call-and-response routines and losing themselves in the drumbeat, they were taking part in cultural forms that had their roots in African American church services and dancing to a West African polyrhythm. Jazz remains a descendent of its folk origins, preserving the principles of improvisation, syncopation, and dissonance within its beating heart.

Jazz was as much a performance of the New Negro as were the arts and literature of the movement. It was not merely performance as a form of self-conscious artifice, though artifice did play a role – for example, the impeccable white suits worn by Duke Ellington's musicians or the synchronized choreography of Jimmie Lunceford's band, which reversed anti-black stereotypes of savagery and slovenliness. More importantly, it was during the Harlem Renaissance that black jazz musicians became known as artists. Louis Armstrong initiated the conception of the jazzman as a memorable persona, as visible to the public as a movie star; Duke Ellington and Billy Strayhorn created pieces as harmonically complex as those of a classical composer; while Billie Holiday brought psychological complexity to the schmaltzy lyrics of Tin Pan Alley. These transformations could not have occurred without the so-called dangers of commercialization that placed these men and women at the fore. The results of the music would exceed its motivations: the freedom in jazz, the respect it demanded, and its capability of expressing the full range of human experience would plant the seeds of dissent and self-reliance as would be seen in bebop, hard bop, and the avant-garde. Jazz was, and always would remain, the music of the New Negro, overtaking other art forms and the expectations of its critics.

Notes

Special appreciation to Eunice Kim, Claremont Graduate University, who contributed to every phase of this essay from research to drafting.

1. Benjamin Brawley, "The Negro Literary Renaissance," *Southern Workman* (January 1927): 177.
2. Cary Wintz and Paul Finkelman, *Encyclopedia of the Harlem Renaissance* (New York: Routledge, 2004), 508.
3. Ibid., 504
4. Ibid., 505.
5. Ibid., 291.
6. Robert Walser, ed. *Keeping Time: Readings in Jazz History* (Oxford: Oxford University Press, 1999), 49.
7. W. E. B. Du Bois, "The Talented Tenth," in *The Negro Problem: A Series of Articles by Representative American Negroes of To-Day* (New York: James Pott & Co., 1903), 33.
8. Kelly King Howes and Christine Slovey, eds., *Harlem Renaissance* (Detroit: UXL, 2001), 87.
9. George Schuyler, "The Negro Art Hokum," *The Nation* (June 16, 1926), 692.
10. Nathan Huggins, *Harlem Renaissance* (New York: Oxford University Press, 1971), 64.
11. J. A. Rogers, "Jazz at Home," in *The New Negro*, ed. Alain Locke (1925; New York: Touchstone, 1997), 223.
12. Alain Locke, *The Negro and His Music* (Washington, DC: Associates in Negro Folk Education, 1936), 85.
13. Kathy J. Ogren, "Controversial Sounds: Jazz Performance as Theme and Language in the Harlem Renaissance," in *The Harlem Renaissance: Revaluations* (New York: Garland Publishing, 1989), 162.
14. Locke, *The Negro and His Music*, 99.
15. Langston Hughes, "The Negro Artist and the Racial Mountain," *The Nation* (June 23, 1926): 693.
16. Locke, *The Negro and His Music*, 85.
17. Kevin K. Gaines explores some of the tensions that animate the ideology of racial uplift in *Uplifting the Race: Black Leadership, Politics, and Culture in the Twentieth Century* (Chapel Hill: University of North Carolina Press, 1996).
18. James Lincoln Collier, *Louis Armstrong: An American Genius* (New York: Oxford University Press, 1983), 47.
19. David W. Megill and Paul O. W. Tanner, *Jazz Issues: A Critical History* (Madison, WI: Brown & Benchmark, 1995), 19–21.
20. Eileen Southern, *The Music of Black Americans: A History* (New York: Norton, 1971), 27.
21. Megill and Tanner, *Jazz Issues*, 31–32.
22. Collier, *Louis Armstrong*, 51–52.
23. Michel Feith, "The Syncopated African: Constructions of Origins in the Harlem Renaissance (Literature, Music, Visual Arts)," in *Temples for Tomorrow: Looking Back at the Harlem Renaissance*, ed. Geneviève Fabre and Michel Feith (Bloomington: Indiana University Press, 2001), 66.
24. Ted Gioia, *The History of Jazz* (New York: Oxford University Press, 2011), 39.
25. Megill and Tanner, *Jazz Issues*, 145.

26. Ibid., 106.
27. Ibid., 196.
28. Edward Branley, "NOLA History: Congo Square and the Roots of New Orleans Music," July 2, 2012, https://gonola.com/things-to-do-in-new-orleans/arts-culture/nola-history-congo-square-and-the-roots-of-new-orleans-music.
29. James Lincoln Collier, *The Making of Jazz* (Boston: Houghton Mifflin, 1978), 48.
30. Gioia, *The History of Jazz*, 156.
31. Ibid., 166.
32. Megill and Tanner, *Jazz Issues*, 61–62.
33. Collier, *The Making of Jazz*, 190.
34. Howes and Slovey, *Harlem Renaissance*, 87.
35. Megill and Tanner, *Jazz Issues*, 192.
36. Collier, *The Making of Jazz*, 248.
37. Alyn Shipton, *A New History of Jazz* (New York: Continuum, 2001), 119.
38. Albert McCarthy, *Big Band Jazz* (London: Barrie and Jenkins, 1974), 211.
39. Alyn Shipton, *Hi-De-Ho: The Life of Cab Calloway* (New York: Oxford University Press, 2010), 19–20.
40. Shipton, *A New History*, 288–289.
41. Gioia, *The History of Jazz*, 161.
42. Kathy J. Ogren, *The Jazz Revolution: Twenties America and the Meaning of Jazz* (New York: Oxford University Press, 1992), 26.
43. Shipton, *A New History*, 181.

CHAPTER 20

Alain Locke and the Value of the Harlem Renaissance

Shane Vogel

What is the value of Blackness in an anti-Black world? Is Black art possible in a world where concepts such as the Good and the Beautiful are keyed to the criteria of whiteness? In one way or another, these questions propelled the Harlem Renaissance and were central to one of its guiding figures: the distinguished philosopher and cultural critic Alain LeRoy Locke (1885–1954). Locke edited the era-defining anthology *The New Negro: An Interpretation* (1925) and promoted younger artists such as Langston Hughes, Countee Cullen, and Zora Neale Hurston. He studied philosophy at Oxford, the University of Berlin, and Harvard, where he earned his PhD, and eventually took a faculty position at Howard University in Washington, DC. By the early 1920s, Locke had achieved national and international prominence as an intellectual and an educator, and from this position he brandished his authority to influence the direction and debates of the Harlem Renaissance. Along with Jessie Fauset and Charles S. Johnson, he was largely responsible for organizing the disparate creative and intellectual work of African Americans in the 1920s into what he hoped would be a transformative cultural movement in Black arts.

Locke's philosophical training and worldview shaped his vision for the Harlem Renaissance. Steeped in the Pragmatist philosophy that was popular at Harvard during his education there, Locke understood philosophy ultimately to be "philosophies of life and not of abstract, disembodied 'objective' reality; products of time, place, and situation, and thus systems of timed history rather than timeless eternity."[1] The relationship between race, value, and culture was of primary concern to Locke's philosophy. Over the course of his career, Locke developed a coherent philosophical program that was based on three related features: cultural pluralism (the preservation and encouragement of distinct cultural identities that can coexist within a dominant national culture, distinct from a "melting pot" notion of assimilation); cosmopolitanism (an international worldview of social inclusion, exchange, and tolerance between nations and cultures); and axiology (the study of values and valuation).

While the first two aspects have been given extensive treatment in relation to his vision of the Harlem Renaissance, Locke's value philosophy has been relatively neglected in these conversations despite the fact that it provides crucial insight into the movement. As we will see, Locke's theories of value as they subtended the Harlem Renaissance called for a shift from a *racial axiology* to the *axiology of race*. The former is a system of evaluation and judgment predicated on a racial distinction that holds whiteness as an absolute, unchanging standard by which to measure the beautiful, the good, and the true, inscribing everything nonwhite as worth less (or worthless). The latter describes the study and destabilization of how race came to be a marker of value in the first place. For Locke value is prior to and makes possible other systems of thought such as ontology or politics, since value allows the concerns of those other domains to become legible as significant, good, or true in the first place. At the same time, Locke understands value not as a metaphysical concept but as a practical and functional dynamic that comes out of concrete, lived experience. This value pluralism underlies Locke's notions of cultural pluralism and is the vehicle for his New Negro revaluing of Blackness as a sign of beauty.

Approaching the Harlem Renaissance through Locke's value theory – commenced in the decades prior to the Harlem Renaissance and more fully developed in the decades following it – can help us to view this cultural movement anew. Locke's academic philosophy and cultural criticism deeply informed one another. As he wrote in the introduction to *The New Negro*, "immediate hope rests in the revaluation by white and Black alike of the Negro in terms of his artistic endowments and cultural contributions, past and prospective."[2] The New Negro Renaissance and the transvaluation of Black art – that is, the re-estimation of its value according to new principles of judgment – was but another moment in a larger and ongoing axiological transformation. This chapter first details Locke's theories of value and their relationship to his overall cultural project. It then turns to his writings on African American spirituals. Composed throughout the Harlem Renaissance across multiple journals and volumes, these writings not only make up a substantial theory of Black musical and performance history but also exemplify the possibilities of aesthetic transvaluation for a deconstruction of racial axiology. In conclusion, it examines Locke's cultural retrospectives of the 1930s and 1940s – annual reviews that took stock of the year's work in Black themes – as exemplary instances of such transvaluation (the reappraisal, reversal, or transformation of dominant values). In these writings, Locke continually revised the significance and boundaries of the Harlem Renaissance. Paradoxically, these retrospectives looked forward more than they looked back: they advanced a characterization of the New Negro as an ever-evolving, unending process of interpretation, one that anticipated the enduring preoccupation with re-reading and re-interpreting the Harlem Renaissance across the twentieth century and into the twenty-first.

From Racial Axiology to the Axiology of Race

Studying value was not an obvious choice for Locke – it was a minor and fairly technical topic then only recently appearing in European philosophical circles and on the peripheries of the philosophy departments at Harvard and Oxford. However, as Locke's biographer Jeffrey C. Stewart indicates, the topic became an unlikely expression for Locke's "emerging sense of being at the vortex of social change" and a fresh way to approach the metaphysics of racial modernity.[3] Western philosophies from antiquity through the Enlightenment have traditionally proposed some universal and transcendental properties, or "ultimates," that define the highest virtues of human experience: beauty (the highest value of the aesthetic), truth (the highest value of science/logic), and goodness (the highest value of morality). For Locke, these ultimates – where they come from, how we recognize them – are "the core problem" of value theory.[4] Rather than seek their origin in a singular, transhistorical foundation (God, for example, or reason/rationality, as previous philosophies had done), he built on Pragmatist traditions to argue that these values were shaped by forces as sweeping as historical context and as intimate as individual temperament. At the same time, however, he was wary of an entirely subjective or anarchic value free-for-all. He recognized that all communities required at least some shared norms in order to function *as* communities, and that such standards were a crucial part of one's identity and everyday lived experience. Seeking a "middle ground between those extremes of subjectivism and objectivism," Locke asked how we might understand norms (or philosophical "imperatives") in a way that can account for the diversity of cultural systems around the world without falling into "dogmatism and absolutism" in our philosophy and "intolerance and mass coercion" in our everyday life.[5] He hoped that such a functionalist approach to value – one that considers how we use and refine our imperatives in the world – might help philosophy to better fathom the core problem of value.

Rather than understand the process of evaluation as the use of judgment and reason to assess what is good, true, or beautiful, Locke offered the original proposition that values emerge first as feelings. In our everyday life, we encounter situations or objects that cause us to have a particular emotional response. This response initiates a particular mode of consciousness he calls a "value-mode." For Locke, examples of value-modes break down along the philosophically traditional domains of morality (good/bad), logic (true/false), and aesthetics (beautiful/ugly), though these modes may have variations and subcategories, and Locke even adds a fourth value-mode – religion, with its polarities of salvation/damnation. Thus, before our evaluation of something is logical or cognitive, it is first affective. A particular "feeling-quality" tips us off to the value-mode we are in: if we feel something as good or bad, we are in the value-mode (or valuing-consciousness) of morality; if we feel it as beautiful or ugly, we are in the aesthetic value-mode; and so on.

Locke believed that demonstrating the origin of valuation in our affective responses would provide an "effective antidote to value absolution" because it indicates that "values are rooted in attitudes not in reality and pertain to ourselves, not to the world."[6] Rather than fixed absolutes that exist objectively in the world, Locke submits that the feeling-quality of our values is mediated by the ongoing interaction of culture and individual disposition. Things become "dispositional," Locke explains, through the "smooth-feeling curve of habit and inner equilibrium" as these are shaped within and against the positive reinforcement of values from external sources (culture, history, family, etc.).[7] Yet such values are not wholly arbitrary. Locke takes some value-modes to be more or less constant across histories and cultures (perhaps even hard-wired into our psychology). All cultures, Locke presumes, have feelings of beauty and ugliness, even if they have different ideas of what objects or images define beauty; all have feelings of right and wrong, even if the content of those moral systems are distinct, and so on.[8] Thus he concludes that "the feeling-quality, irrespective of content, makes a value of a given kind."[9] This was the basis of what he called value pluralism, an axiology that informed his complementary philosophies of cultural pluralism and cosmopolitanism.

From this value pluralism, Locke deduces its two most important corollaries: tolerance and reciprocity. Value pluralism leads to greater tolerance between groups that established their values along different affective registers. Likewise, it can lead to a reciprocal exchange between cultural groups. Given the professional philosophical audience to whom his value theory was addressed and his own temperament,

Locke often pulled his punches when he applied his principles of value pluralism to the contemporary scene, and without further qualification the ideas of tolerance and reciprocity can seem hopelessly naïve – as when he wrote in 1935 that the recognition of value pluralism might lead "Nordicism and other rampant racialisms" toward "historical sanity or at least, prudential common-sense to halt at the natural frontiers of genuinely shared loyalties and not sow their eventual downfall through forced loyalties and the counter-reactions which they now inevitably breed."[10] This accommodationist tenor – the suggestion that white supremacy or Nazism might recognize the reciprocal value of other cultures and thus preserve their own cultural values in some measured and tolerant way – often led many to regard Locke as a quiescent scholar who placed too much faith in culture for political change.

Yet Locke was not unmindful of the role of power and domination in the experience of value. At the root of his approach is a radical skepticism of the purity of categories. By describing values as affects rather than intrinsic properties of objects or situations, Locke contended that the concept of fixed ultimates is indefensible – rather than measuring our experiences to pre-existing criteria, our values derive from our experiences. This resistance to the purity of categories is the same attitude that Locke brought to his regular debunking of race science and archaic anthropologies that described ever refined delineations of race, a task he unwaveringly set himself throughout his career. The historical background for his philosophy as it developed from the 1910s through the 1940s included Jim Crowism in the USA, colonialism across the global south, and fascism in Europe – each of which were substantiated by a racial axiology that posited whiteness as the ultimate of the good, the true, and the beautiful.

More recently, Black Studies scholar Lindon Barrett describes the operation of this racial axiology as producing a double identity: "value as form" – the way the abstract categories of the valued and the unvalued appear to us – and "value as violence" – the disavowed operation that defines the valuable in opposition to its negative other.[11] The universalized value of whiteness in the West simultaneously produces Blackness as disorderly, excessive, and expendable. The role of violence at the foundation of value, Barrett explains, needs to be perpetually renewed and maintained to stabilize the West's racial axiology in the face of contending evidence of Black worth. "In the same way that *valued* whiteness must struggle to occlude its internal mechanisms – the originary and ongoing violences that maintain its privileged status," he writes, "so too it must struggle to occlude competing formations of value sponsored by and within the 'excessive' communities designated as black."[12]

While Barrett more explicitly names the acts of domination and struggle that subtend racial axiology, Locke, too, maintained that value ultimates were at their origin a product and a tool of violence. For Locke, what appear to be transcendental absolutes are nothing other than the rationalization of a preference, and "their tap-root, it seems, stems more from the will to power than the will to know."[13] Locke and Barrett both identify racial axiology as an instrument of domination and force. In dismantling the metaphysical ground of value absolutes by locating the operation of value in affect, culture, and disposition rather than objective reality, Locke replaced a racial axiology with pluralistic and relativistic axiologies of race that not only imagined that different cultural value systems could coexist, but also that they act upon and can transform one another.

It is in this second aspect – that values are not fixed but can change and be changed – that we can understand the special significance of Locke's value theory to the Harlem Renaissance. He identified two kinds of value change: the process of transvaluation, as when something bad or ugly comes to be seen as good or beautiful, and the process of "value-movement," or when feeling-qualities cut across value-modes, such as when a mathematical proof is seen as beautiful or an artwork seen as spiritual. In this latter process, such experiences are more than mere metaphor; they indicate a transformation of the value-mode itself. Locke offered experiments in modernist music as one example for how aesthetic values could be so transformed through the gradual modification of an individual's "smooth curve of habit and inner equilibrium" and of a group's collective recognition of worth. With the help of musical author-ities and institutions, new forms of music "have developed critical criteria appropriate to their idiom and at the same time not inconsistent with the older criteria after habituation. What the modernist styles have done is really, by conditioning, to enlarge both by bringing them into the orbit of the same favorable aesthetic reaction."[14] The result was to convey "into the realm of immediately felt concordance what was previously felt as irregular and cacophonic, and could not, therefore, be apprehended pleasurably and integrated into an aesthetically toned reaction."[15] In other words, the harmonious is not natural but learned. Characteristically, his examples were European composers such as Igor Stravinsky and Paul Hindemith, though he also holds out the possibility that "good jazz, which has devel-oped for jazz idioms and forms more and more professionalized devotees and rigidly normative criteria of taste and critical musical analysis," can also achieve the status of classical music and modify its standards.[16]

With value pluralism, transvaluation, and value-movement in mind, the project of the Harlem Renaissance itself takes on new dimensions. It invites us to understand the New Negro as a process of reinterpretation and revaluation as much as any individual subjectivity, collective figure, or historical formation. The Harlem Renaissance in this sense was an ongoing challenge to the racial axiology of the USA and Western modernity more broadly. More than a representational undertaking that sought to counter negative stereotypes with positive ones, the Harlem Renaissance emerges as an axiological project that sought to deconstruct the very basis on which positive/negative, good/bad, beautiful/ugly, and true/false operate in the first place. In displacing the philosophical notion of universal systems of value, Locke undermined the metaphysical grounds of Jim Crowism and colonialism. The philosopher Leonard Harris calls this "subterranean deconstructive project" of Locke's value theory a vital subtext of his philosophy that worked in the Harlem Renaissance not only to alter cultural depictions of African Americans but also to locate Black culture as the excluded inside – rather than the included outside – of American national identity.[17]

This is where Locke's Black radical philosophy collided with the "smooth feeling curve of habit and inner equilibrium" of his own temperament, as his musical example suggests. Born in 1885 and inculcated with the values of a respected middle-class family in one of Philadelphia's most desirable Black neighborhoods, Locke was suspended between his Victorian upbringing and a modernist yearning that he was born too early to fully inhabit, but nevertheless helped to flourish in a younger generation of writers. Despite his commitment to the New Negro and the radical possibilities of transvaluation, he was a cultural elitist who was personally devoted to European aesthetic standards and drifted toward what many viewed as an accommodationist politics (as a naïve reading of tolerance and reciprocity would suggest). He was also a sensitive and discrete gay man who was dismissive of younger women writers during the Harlem Renaissance even as he was quick to mentor emergent male artists, and many in that movement found him to be a difficult, bitter, and manipulative figure, even on his good days. These biographical details and political contradictions can be disappointing or frustrating to readers searching, then as now, for a more direct confrontation with racial inequality or an uncomplicated cultural hero. Yet it is because of, not despite, these contradictions that Locke's philosophy took the form it did. His theories perform a self-reflexive investigation into the tension between his finely cultivated personal values and his commitment to African American group values. As he put it in a passing aside, "every society, and nearly every soul, is full of conflicts between opposing valuation."[18] Though the conflicts of Locke's soul were never neatly reconciled, they produced an understanding of value as an ongoing process, rather than a fixed thing, and drew blueprints for the radical transformation of even the most entrenched senses of our selves.

Locke's Spiritual Strivings

With Locke's example of modernist music in mind, we can see more concretely how his philosophical investigations and his cultural theory developed together during the Harlem Renaissance. Locke had a very particular vision for the cultural movement he announced with the publication of *The New Negro*. He called on Black artists – poets, visual artists, dramatists, musicians, and novelists alike – to draw on the rich resources of Black folk forms as material for their work, preserving their essence even while developing them in technical, studied, and professional ways. By returning to the folk arts of the undervalued Black American "peasant matrix," he explained, Black artists could elevate, modernize, and transform their cultural inheritance.[19] With the examples of Russian, Hungarian, and Irish folk arts before him, he believed this was a viable path by which African Americans would achieve worldwide recognition for their distinct contributions to culture. The point was not merely for African American art to demonstrate parity with European culture. More significantly, it was for the particularity of Black arts to transcend their local (in Locke's terms, "provincial") contexts and offer their distinct forms and expressions to a cosmopolitan sphere of culture.

While the examples could be multiplied, I turn here to Locke's writings on music to illustrate how his cultural criticism in the Harlem Renaissance nurtured and anticipated his more mature philosophical writings. From 1923 to 1940, Locke wrote a handful of essays about African American spirituals and a short book, *The Negro and His Music* (1936). Throughout these writings (which collectively constitute a substantial contribution to the history and theory of Black music), Locke presented the spirituals as "the most characteristic product of Negro genius to date," its "great folk-gift," and the highest expression of "a people's group character."[20] The spirituals were religious folk songs created by enslaved people that brought African musical sensibilities to the Christian hymns learned in the USA and expressed the conditions of their existence – their sorrow, joy, longing, perseverance, and protest. The history of the spirituals in the half-century after Reconstruction found them arranged into symphonic compositions by the Fisk University Jubilee Singers in 1871 and then renewed by singers such as Roland Hayes and Paul Robeson in the 1920s, Marian Anderson and Dorothy Maynor in the 1930s, and by composers/arrangers such as Hall Johnson, Eva Jessye, William Grant Still, and William Dawson, whose 1934 *Negro Folk Symphony* Locke praised. He called this twentieth-century renaissance of the spirituals a "glorious time" that has "brought our interpretive artists a welcome opportunity, after mastery of the great universal language, to pay their racial homage to the native source of their artistic skill and spiritual strength."[21] For Locke, the spirituals exemplified the axiological possibilities of transvaluation and value-movement that the Harlem Renaissance might achieve.

Black musical traditions (including the incorporation of their rhythms and sensibilities into literature) were at the center of Locke's New Negro axiological project. As Barrett explains, the Black singing voice was "a primary means by which African Americans may exchange expended, 'valueless' selves in the 'New World' for productive, recognized selves."[22] Locke aimed to cultivate this choral sense in the Afro-modernism of the Harlem Renaissance. While W. E. B. Du Bois famously emphasized the spirituals as a record of a Black past in *The Souls of Black Folk* – "the songs are indeed the siftings of centuries; the music is far more ancient than the words" – Locke emphasized them as ground for a Black future.[23] To Locke they were not museum pieces or exotic relics but a vibrant, living form that could be brought out of its folk context and into a cosmopolitan stage. "We cannot accept the attitude that would merely preserve this music," he wrote, "but must cultivate that which would also develop it."[24] In a telling metaphor, he described the spirituals as the "most valuable musical ore in America," figuring it as rich native material to be mined from centuries of Black American history and worked into a new, modern form.[25] Such Black American contributions to the modern art scene would transcend provincialism without losing its ties to racial particularity. The responsibility for this future art fell not only to "the trained musician who has the sense and devotion to study seriously the folk music at its purest and deepest sources" but to the critic as well.[26] It was the critic who was necessary to educate the audience in how to hear these new musical forms and provide the artist with "constructive criticism and discriminating appreciation" lest she fall prey to fad and fashion, stumbling on the "curb-stone values of the market-place" or the "easy favor of the multitude" – the kind of commercial transactions that Locke knew more often than not would leave white racial axiology intact.[27]

Roland Hayes, a favorite performer of Locke's, was the model for this transformation of folk song to art music. The renowned tenor performed recitals of spirituals alongside German lieder and Italian arias and achieved great fame across European capitals. The son of formerly enslaved parents, Hayes grew up immersed in the musical world of his mother's church. He moved to Tennessee after his father's death and continued performing in church choirs, where a pianist who was taken by his voice introduced him to recordings of Italian tenor Enrico Caruso. "That opened the heavens for me," he remembered, "the beauty of what could be done with the voice overwhelmed me."[28] He later attended Fisk University, where he performed spirituals as a Jubilee Singer, and by the dawn of the Harlem Renaissance he was touring internationally and performing programs that combined his own arrangements of spirituals alongside European concert music. Locke appointed him an "ambassador of culture in [sic] our behalf," and Hayes's portrait graced the cover of the Survey Graphic, the journal issue on African American culture that Locke edited and later expanded into The New Negro. To Locke, Hayes was quite literally the face of the New Negro.[29]

Locke's cultural program called less to conform Black music to Western musical standards than it did to alter and expand Western musical standards as such. Hayes performed in a context in which Black vocal performance was registered by many white listeners as a kind of noise that was only intelligible on the variety stage or nightclub floor. Educated white audiences might recognize the talent of performers such as Hayes, but as exceptions or oddities. Locke's promotion of Hayes aimed to continue what Barrett describes as the "'disturbance' of New World configurations of value" posed by the Black singing voice.[30] He hailed Hayes's ambition not to settle for paternalistic success in America and instead "[risk] failure for the single standard of musical Europe" – particularly the musical capital of Vienna, whose "critics are the most exacting" and whose "public one of the most musically enlightened bodies in the world."[31] Locke, who attended Hayes's Vienna performance as his guest, took his triumphant reception there as verification that culture could not be fixed into absolute or unchanging aesthetic categories. Hayes's concert program, in other words, allegorized the cultural reciprocity, value-movement, and transvaluation that Locke later elaborated in his philosophical writings. Opening his concerts with arias by Mozart and Berlioz and closing with his versions of "Go Down, Moses" and "Bye and Bye" was more than an audacious demonstration of aesthetic parity or an early advance for Black performance over the color line of the classical music world.[32] It portended, Locke hoped, a revolution in values that would undermine Western racial axiology and its absolutes.

The juxtaposition of spirituals with German classical music in his Vienna performance, in particular, brought about a palpable movement in values and value-modes that confirmed Locke's view. Watching the Vienna audience stirred by Hayes's performance, Locke described "the transfer from these simple folk-songs to Bach, through an affinity of religious feeling, of a religious quality which makes Mr. Hayes' interpretation of Bach songs a delight to all connoisseurs of that great master."[33] In the proximity and sonic contact between the spirituals and Bach, by way of Hayes's voice, something of the Black folk touches the European tradition. What Locke would call the feeling-quality of salvation proper to religious value transfers to and transforms the aesthetic value of Bach. It is not the spirituals that get whitened here but Bach who is filled with the spirit – a value-movement that would find its pinnacle three-and-a-half decades later in Nina Simone's recording of "Love Me or Leave Me" (1958). Such value-movement and transvaluation disturbs the "value loyalties" that lead to absolutism and bigotry.[34] This description of Hayes's performance, moreover, perhaps points to why Locke later included religion as a fundamental value constant in his philosophy alongside the Enlightenment triad of morality, aesthetics, and logic.[35]

Locke gravitated toward the spirituals rather than the blues and jazz performance that inspired a number of younger writers not out of moral disapprobation but simply out of his own disposition and taste preference for the symphonic. The spirituals' formal adaptability to European musical aesthetics lent themselves to ready presentation on the concert stage where they could be appreciated as music in itself, in contrast to the social music performed in dancehalls and cabarets, where the musical value was as much social as it was aesthetic – a distinction that obviously does not hold up, even in Locke's own writings. By the 1930s, Locke had come to see jazz as equally destined to the concert stage, especially in the figure of Duke Ellington and his Orchestra.[36] As with the spirituals, when jazz returned to the musical ore of folk culture it would produce its own forms and idioms by which it could be appropriately measured. While there are obviously elements of snobbery in his attitude, Locke was also highly vigilant against the commodification that always threatened to reduce the aesthetic value of Black music to a debased exchange value for giddy white consumption in the musical marketplace.

Yet even while he allows that Ellington's jazz might transvalue US racial axiology into a pluralistic axiology of race, it was still the European concert hall that metonymically represented his cosmopolitan vision. As Paul Allen Anderson observes, "the residue of aestheticism figured in Locke's tendencies toward formalism and his enthusiasm for the recruitment of folk materials into the service of purportedly universalist ideals of formal sublimation and pure artistry."[37] We thus see across his musical writings both the shortcomings as well as the possibilities of Locke's axiology. On the one hand, as Jeffrey Stewart puts it, the "sense of a single standard of excellence in the arts set the limit on Locke's cultural relativism. Locke retained a belief in universal values of excellence, even if the content of the aesthetic product was varied, for it was only in the universality of form that true equality was possible."[38] In other words, Locke believed in Beauty, even if he knew it to be variable, and "that was what Europe meant to him."[39] Yet alongside that conviction, Stewart asks us to remember that there was also a strategic use in Locke's petition to European aesthetic standards, since Europe was held by most Americans as the height of developed culture in the early twentieth century.[40] As Hayes himself explained to Locke, his "ultimate intention in coming to Europe, in appealing to European judgment, was eventually to widen opportunity for the Negro artist in America."[41] Occupying European standards of judgment from a minor position within and against them, the dream went, would transform the critical aesthetic judgments of the white institutions and the racial axiology of the West.

The Value of Valuing: Looking Back on the Harlem Renaissance

These writings on the spirituals show us Locke as cultural critic and arbiter of value. This was the primary role he played in Black arts and letters during the Harlem Renaissance and the decades following, particularly in his annual "retrospectives" first published in *Opportunity* magazine (in 1929 and from 1931 to 1942) and then in the journal *Phylon* (from 1946 to 1953).[42] These retrospectives were omnibus reviews that took stock of the past year's publications about Blackness and race relations. Locke was exhaustive: he covered fiction, poetry, drama, children's literature, biographies, histories, travel writing, *belles lettres*, musical scholarship, sociological and anthropological studies, and studies of Africa and the Caribbean. These retrospectives became a venue for Locke to assess and reassess the overall shape and direction of Black culture in the USA. In doing so he took the long view (the sailboat is a favorite recurring metaphor, listing, tacking, and careening in its course over the years). He tracked trends, foregrounded new directions in theme and tenor, assessed where things had been, and offered his own hopes for the future development of African American literature. As arbiter, Locke positioned himself above any particular school of criticism to offer perspective and guard against the inroads of any aesthetic dogmatism or absolutes (though to be sure he could be a particularly severe critic himself).

These retrospectives were more than simple catalogues or summaries. They were entries in the ongoing process of transvaluing the work of the Harlem Renaissance and recalibrating its feeling-tones. Already by his second retrospective, which reviewed the year's work since the stock market crash of 1929, Locke was pointedly reinterpreting the trajectory of Black literary output. Assessing the work of the 1920s as a period of literary "inflation and overproduction" whose value was cheapened, he heralded a "second and truly sound phase of the cultural development of the Negro in American literature and art" that would usher in "more responsible and devoted leadership, a revision of basic values, and along with a penitential purgation of spirit, a wholesale expulsion of the money-changers from the temple of art."[43] Among other things, for Locke this second phase of literary production and race leadership would displace economic value with the deeper spiritual value of a New Negro yet-to-come. Finding the earlier period of literature now to be "merely superficial" in its treatment of Black themes, he determined that "the true Negro is yet to be discovered and the purest values of the Negro spirit yet to be refined out from the alloys of our present cultural currency."[44] Here and across his two-and-a-half decades of retrospectives, the New Negro never arrives but is always charted as a future destination, a process of becoming rather than a fixed or finished figure.

Locke explicitly returned to this theme in his 1938 retrospective, in which he took the occasion of his review to once again revisit and revalue the state of Black culture since the publication of *The New Negro*. By that year, a number of artists had turned against the Harlem Renaissance's cultural program of affirmation and embraced a more radical, often proletarian, politics in their literature. Locke's New Negro suddenly seemed old-fashioned. In response to his critics, he acknowledged that "there was inevitable indefiniteness as to what was meant by the 'New Negro,'" but insisted that this indefiniteness was a "deliberate decision not to define the 'New Negro' dogmatically, but only to characterize his general traits and attitudes."[45] Rather than concede its outdatedness, Locke maintained instead that it was ahead of itself. Describing the work of the mid-1920s as a "first-generation course that was more like a careen than a career," he reviewed the year's work in 1938 as the advent of the movement he conjured in *The New Negro*.[46] Arguing that the critiques launched against the Harlem Renaissance were either misguided or already anticipated, he again presented the New Negro as a prophecy. He pronounced that not only "has it not been superseded . . . it has yet to be fully realized."[47] Three years later, in the retrospective of 1941, Locke reiterated this vision of the Harlem Renaissance as nothing other than the process of "successive emphases" and the "the polemical clash of differing interpretations" that would one day arrive at a vantage point "where the objective truth about the Negro can be pieced together and put into a clear and meaningful perspective."[48] Yet as Locke's annual reviews in their sum make clear, such a day is perpetually deferred. Any "clear and meaningful perspective" will shift with the emphases and differing interpretations required by the current moment, leaving the New Negro an endlessly renewable resource and necessarily unfinished project.

These retrospectives are brilliant instances of Locke's own revaluation of the Harlem Renaissance. In this, Locke heralded successive generations of such reinterpretations. From the moment it was named a movement, critics and scholars have debated the value of the Harlem Renaissance – whether it was a "success" or a "failure"; whether the art it produced was "good" or "bad"; whether it was helpful to Black Americans or harmful; whether its poetry and fiction would be lasting or were merely faddish. Individual works and collective goals are continually judged according to new standards and contexts, and the Harlem Renaissance appears less as a delimited historical *period* or a literary *formation* than an ongoing and unending *process* of transvaluation. The New Negro thus stands as the name of a particular value-movement or feeling-quality that continually transvalues our imperatives. This act of ongoing revision is itself generative of new values and value-movements throughout the twentieth and twenty-first century – what Cherene Sherrard-Johnson describes as the "persistent value of the Harlem Renaissance."[49] The Harlem Renaissance scholarship of the past half-century (those titles that seek to rethink or revisit the Renaissance, or recover its lost aspects) thus takes its cue from the movement itself; such studies are themselves valuations of valuations. As an unending process of transvaluation, with continually recalibrated feeling-qualities and value-modes, the term *renaissance* is remarkably apt and the subtitle of Locke's anthology, *The New Negro: An Interpretation*, is grammatically appositional rather than subordinate – not an interpretation *of* the New Negro but the New Negro *as* interpretation. As an ongoing process of (Black) valuation, Locke's Harlem Renaissance is an ever-renewable engagement and refinement of aesthetic, political, and spiritual values.

Notes

1. Alain Locke, "Values and Imperatives" [1935], in *The Philosophy of Alain Locke: The Harlem Renaissance and Beyond*, ed. Leonard Harris (Philadelphia: Temple University Press, 1989), 34.
2. Alain Locke, "The New Negro," in *The New Negro: An Interpretation*, ed. Alain Locke (New York: Albert and Charles Boni, 1925), 15.
3. Jeffrey C. Stewart, *The New Negro: The Life of Alain Locke* (New York: Oxford University Press, 2018), 154.
4. Alain Locke, "A Functional View of Value Ultimates" [1945], in *The Philosophy of Alain Locke*, ed. Harris, 81.
5. Locke, "Values and Imperatives," 38, 36.
6. Ibid., 46.
7. Ibid., 44.
8. See Locke, "Pluralism and Intellectual Democracy" [1942], in *The Philosophy of Alain Locke*, ed. Harris, 55.
9. Locke, "Values and Imperatives," 40.
10. Ibid., 48.
11. Lindon Barrett, *Blackness and Value: Seeing Double* (Cambridge: Cambridge University Press, 1999), 31–33.
12. Ibid., 56–57; emphasis in original.
13. Locke, "Values and Imperatives," 46.
14. Locke, "A Functional View of Value Ultimates," 90–91.
15. Ibid., 91.
16. Ibid.
17. Leonard Harris, "Rendering the Subtext: Subterranean Deconstructive Project," in *The Philosophy of Alain Locke*, ed. Harris, 279–289. See also Ernest D. Mason, "Deconstruction in the Philosophy of Alain Locke," *Transactions of the Charles S. Pierce Society* 24 (1988): 85–105.
18. Alain Locke, "Value" [*c.* 1935], in *The Philosophy of Alain Locke*, ed. Harris, 125.
19. Locke, "The New Negro," 15.
20. Alain Locke, *The Negro and His Music* (Washington, DC: Associates in Negro Folk Education, 1936), 18; Alain Locke, "Spirituals" [1940], in *The Critical Temper of Alain Locke: A Selection of His Essays in Art and Culture*, ed. Jeffrey C. Stewart (New York: Garland Publishing, 1983), 123.
21. Locke, "Spirituals," 124.
22. Barrett, *Blackness and Value*, 91.
23. W. E. B. Du Bois, *The Souls of Black Folk* (Boston: Bedford/St. Martins, 1997), 187; cf. Locke, *The Negro and His Music*, 25.

24. Alain Locke, "The Negro Spirituals," in *The New Negro*, ed. Locke, 210.
25. Locke, *The Negro and His Music*, 21. Paul Allen Anderson traces Locke's development of this metallurgic metaphor to the writings of the Victorian aesthete Walter Pater. See Paul Allen Anderson, *Deep River: Music and Memory in Harlem Renaissance Thought* (Durham: Duke University Press, 2001), 146–150.
26. Alain Locke, "Negro Music Goes to Par" [1939], in *The Critical Temper of Alain Locke*, ed. Stewart, 118.
27. Alain Locke, "Toward A Critique of Negro Music" [1934], in *The Critical Temper of Alain Locke*, ed. Stewart, 109.
28. Alan Rich, "A Bouncy Seventy-Five: Roland Hayes, Despite His Age, Gives Concerts, Teaches and Reminisces," *New York Times*, June 3, 1962: X7.
29. Locke, "Roland Hayes: An Appreciation" [1923], in *The Critical Temper of Alain Locke*, ed. Stewart, 104.
30. Barrett, *Blackness and Value*, 61.
31. Locke, "Roland Hayes: An Appreciation," 104, 103.
32. Christopher A. Brooks and Robert Sims, *Roland Hayes: The Legacy of an American Tenor* (Bloomington: Indiana University Press, 2015), 109.
33. Locke, "Roland Hayes: An Appreciation," 105.
34. Locke, "Values and Imperatives," 48.
35. Understanding Locke's positing of religion as a fundamental value in his axiology of race provides useful context to Steve Pinkerton's insight that Locke utilizes religious modernity and themes of black messianism in *The New Negro* – what he describes as the anthology's "auto-sacralizing bid" and prophetic impulses. See Steve Pinkerton, "'New Negro' v. 'Niggeratti': Defining and Defiling the Black Messiah," *Modernism/modernity* 20, no. 3 (2013): 541–545.
36. See Locke, "Toward A Critique of Negro Music," 113, and Locke, "Negro Music Goes to Par," 118–119.
37. Anderson, *Deep River*, 118.
38. Stewart, *The New Negro*, 371–372.
39. Ibid., 372.
40. See Stewart, *The New Negro*, 371–373.
41. Quoted in Locke, "Roland Hayes: An Appreciation," 104.
42. These retrospectives are helpfully compiled in Jeffrey C. Stewart, ed., *The Critical Temper of Alain Locke*, 201–393.
43. Alain Locke, "This Year of Grace: Outstanding Books of the Year in Negro Literature" [1931], in *The Critical Temper of Alain Locke*, ed. Stewart, 205, 206.
44. Locke, "This Year of Grace," 206.
45. Alain Locke, "The Negro: 'New' or Newer: A Retrospective Review of the Literature of the Negro for 1938" [1939], in *The Critical Temper of Alain Locke*, ed. Stewart, 271, 272.
46. Locke, "The Negro: 'New' or Newer," 271.
47. Ibid., 278.

48. Locke, "Who and What is Negro?" [1942], in *The Critical Temper of Alain Locke*, ed. Stewart, 313.
49. Cherene Sherrard-Johnson, "Introduction: Harlem as Shorthand: The Persistent Value of the Harlem Renaissance," in *A Companion to the Harlem Renaissance*, ed. Cherene Sherrard-Johnson (Chichester, UK: Wiley-Blackwell, 2015), 1–14.

Afterword

Deborah E. McDowell

"Do we really need another book on the Harlem Renaissance?" Before the editors of this volume could begin to curate and frame this rich collection of work, they had first to answer that vexing (and flatfooted) question asked by one of their colleagues. I confess to having asked myself a similar flatfooted question when they invited me to provide an afterword to the volume: "What is left to say about the Harlem Renaissance?" Now that I have read all the chapters here, I can answer these two questions without equivocation: Yes, we do need another volume and, yes, there is plenty left to say, even when this volume has made its way into print.

As the editors state in their introduction, the tendency to question and debate, contest and dispute – including the very idea of a "renaissance" – has defined considerations of the movement since its very inception, and there is no agreement even on its "inception." Scholars have expanded and contracted the boundaries of the period in multiple directions, depending on who is "telling time," as it were. Across the generations, they have also rehearsed the internal debates and fissures, the clashes of purpose and focus in which artists of the period were embroiled. These tensions, fissures, and debates, which are represented in many of these chapters, account perhaps, for what the editors term the "enduring potency" of the Harlem Renaissance.

The Harlem Renaissance has certainly earned its uncontested distinction, to quote Eric Sundquist, as the "most canonical moment in African American literary history,"[1] stimulating a veritable cottage industry of scholarship – books, critical articles, essay collections – all purporting to "re-examine," "revisit," "review," "remember," "revise," or "reinterpret" the movement. Nearly one hundred years since the Harlem Renaissance was first heralded, it retains its fascination. Indeed, as Shane Vogel notes in his chapter in this volume, the Harlem Renaissance has stimulated "an ever-evolving, unending process of interpretation," one perhaps Alain

Locke set in motion in giving his landmark and "era-defining" 1925 anthology, *The New Negro*, the subtitle, *An Interpretation*.

Most of the texts collected here certainly provide new interpretations of many of the most familiar artists and phases of the movement, while also illuminating the broader interpretive shifts and developments in Harlem Renaissance studies of the last generation. "In the past two decades," as the editors remind us, "the scope of scholarship on the Harlem Renaissance has been transformed by the insights of transnationalism and diaspora studies, queer theory, performance theory, feminisms, left criticism, and periodical studies, among others." Many of these developments inform the chapters here. Taken together, they re-make the Harlem Renaissance or attempt, at least, to make it "new" again by adding to the mix authors, topics, texts, artistic forms, and genres typically absent from standard treatments of the period. Especially welcomed are the chapters that consider the performative dimensions of the period, such as Rachel Farebrother's "The Figure of the Child Dancer in Harlem Renaissance Literature and Visual Culture," and provide new takes on the place of music in the period, as does Andrew Warnes in "The Pulse of Harlem: African American Music and the New Negro Revival."

As much as these chapters introduce new topics into the mix of Harlem Renaissance studies, they also bring new insights and interpretations to familiar discussions and debates, especially those generated during what many regard as the period's inaugural phase, which coincided with the publication of *The New Negro*. Perhaps there is no more familiar debate during this period than the meaning of "the New Negro," a concept that well antedated Locke's volume. While Booker T. Washington, to name but one example, had titled his 1899 volume *A New Negro for a New Century*, the concept has come to be associated with Locke's anthology, which marked, at least for him, the birth of a modern black subject. What constituted that modern subject was also open to endless debate, but, according to the focus and parameters of Locke's collection, the "new Negro" was, almost by definition, northern and urban, distinguishable from the rural agrarian "folk" Negro of the South.

Over the roughly one hundred years of debate about the Harlem Renaissance, much of that debate has found its center in the work of Zora Neale Hurston, in ways not always favorable to her and her artistic projects. In his opening chapter, "Cultural Nationalism and Cosmopolitanism in the Harlem Renaissance," Daniel G. Williams sets the tone for a collection that refreshes this debate. This chapter, which brings sonic and literary studies together, puts Duke Ellington, Jean

Toomer, and Zora Neale Hurston into fruitful conversation with each other, especially as regards the tension between "cultural nationalism" and "cosmopolitanism." While Williams's insights about this tension are engaging, perhaps the chapter's greatest contribution lies in its reassessment of Zora Neale Hurston and her relationship to the "folk." That reassessment involves a re-reading of one of the most influential critiques of Hurston in Harlem Renaissance studies.

Since its publication in 1990, Hazel Carby's classic essay, "The Politics of Fiction, Anthropology and the Folk: Zora Neale Hurston," has been influential in discussions of Hurston, "the folk," and "the New Negro." There, Carby argued that Hurston remained in the grip of a "theoretical paradigm" that directed her "toward rural, not urban, black culture and folk forms of the past, not the present."[2] Unlike Langston Hughes, who managed to shape a "discursive category of the folk in direct response to the transformative social process of migration to urban cities and industrialization," Carby argued, Hurston "constructed a discourse of nostalgia for a rural community" based on her "utopian" childhood.[3] Williams does well to argue that it may be more accurate to think of Hurston's attempts at sustaining the living vitality of African Americans in rural communities as a creative response to, rather than an evasion of, the "contradictions" and racialized power dynamics of their world. Further, the fact that Carby's essay focused on southern to northern migration obscured the internal migration patterns of southern blacks. While many fled the South for northern cities, others migrated from rural to urban, industrialized communities in the South. There, they experienced some of the same social upheaval presumably experienced only by those who had migrated from the hamlets of the South to urban industrial arenas in the North.

Although Williams stops short of considering the ways in which Hurston represented the social process of migration and industrialization that transformed the lives of rural southern communities, Hannah Durkin takes up that question. In "Zora Neale Hurston, Film, and Ethnography," among the richest chapters in the collection, Durkin echoes and reinforces Williams's constructive re-reading of Hurston and the question of the folk, but she also widens the view of Hurston studies beyond her celebrated writings to consider Hurston's pioneering career as an experimental film-maker. Indeed, in placing Hurston's films in fruitful dialogue with her writings, Durkin deepens our discussions both about Hurston and the folk, as well as our understandings of "the new Negro." Finally, Durkin lends more texture and dimension to discussions of Hurston's vexed relationship with her patron, Charlotte Osgood Mason, by placing that relationship within the context of Hurston's conscious critiques of anthropology and its constraining epistemologies.

Durkin argues persuasively that the textual and cinematic strands of Hurston's works should not be read in isolation from each other, especially since they tend to be mutually illuminating. The scenes she filmed would eventually make their way onto the pages of Hurston's fiction and ethnography, as well as into the scripts of her plays. Even when there are tensions between and among the various genres in which Hurston worked, it is useful nonetheless to understand how each enables the other. Although Hurston's work in film was ostensibly in the service of collecting "data" on "dying" black folk forms for Mrs. Mason, Hurston evaded that assignment, notes Durkin, converting it into a "creative project that sought to showcase the geographical diversity and artistry of African diasporic cultures that she found in and around the US South." In other words, Hurston abandoned her assignment as "collector" and assumed the role of "creative interpreter of black southern cultures," the vitality of which challenged the widespread notions that they were dying. With her films, Durkin argues, Hurston established that these black southern cultures and communities in which "the folk" resided were not only vital and dynamic, but also subjects of a modern, geographically mobile, industrializing world that fueled the southern economy. These were no agrarian or romanticized subjects lost in time – or "modernity's" underbelly – but rather, creative souls who lived and worked in "towns and villages built around phosphate mines, railroads, sawmills, and turpentine" camps.

Hurston's pioneering film work, Durkin argues, deepens our understanding of Hurston, the anthropologist, who challenged the prerogatives and methodologies of the field, particularly ethnography. As Durkin notes, the US anthropological establishment had been slow to embrace film as a viable research tool until after World War II, privileging instead the single-authored ethnographic text. Durkin argues persuasively that Hurston "transformed anthropological investigation into a two-way creative encounter that acknowledged her subjects as artists and individuals," possessed of their own creative agency. This "two-way creative encounter," evident in Hurston's footage, featuring scenes from the everyday lives of black working-class subjects, recalls and reinforces now familiar understandings of her narrative technique.

Students of Hurston have long debated the narrative strategies and techniques of her most canonical novel, *Their Eyes Were Watching God* (1937). Henry Louis Gates, Jr.'s discussion of "free indirect discourse" in *The Signifying Monkey*, a technique describing the dual roles of involved storyteller and omniscient narrator, has been among the most influential.[4] Others, Cathy Brigham, for example, have expanded upon Gates by arguing for a "multivocal storying dialectic" involving a "succession of tale-tellers," underscoring Hurston's investments in creating "egalitarian discourse communities."[5] The complex rhetorical – and ritualized – scenes that Hurston stages throughout *Their Eyes*, which underscore relations of power and gender, find their antecedents in Hurston's films. Also featuring "multiple authorial voices," notes Durkin, these films implicitly reject the notion that a single ethnographer could capture complex human encounters. Although, according to Durkin, Hurston left no record of her thoughts about her film work, it is clear from the footage she collected that she sought to intervene in the hierarchies of discursive power between ethnographers and their subjects.

Durkin's chapter on Hurston's pioneering films is in fruitful dialogue with Mariel Rodney's on Hurston's plays. Although in accounts of the Harlem Renaissance, Hurston's reputation has mainly rested on her fiction, Rodney reminds the reader that drama was the genre for which Hurston had perhaps the greatest passion, certainly during her early years in Harlem. While scholars have turned their attention to the controversial *Mule Bone*, they have yet to grant to Hurston's dramatic work the scholarly attention it merits. In much the same way as her films, Hurston's plays work to complicate our canonical readings of "the folk." Among the most valuable insights of Rodney's piece is the distinction she draws implicitly between *preserving* black folk life and *dramatizing* it. Hurston, she suggests, was invested in the latter, an investment she shared with other figures of the Harlem Renaissance. Alain Locke and W. E. B. Du Bois, for example, were equally committed to developing a "Negro dramatic art," in Locke's words, that would be experimental, breaking with established dramatic conventions. Once again, this emphasis on dramatizing black life also reinforces Hurston's break with the anthropological conventions discussed earlier. Blacks would not be treated as "specimens," whether living or dead.

As companion pieces Durkin's and Rodney's chapters perform the valuable and necessary work of complicating the complacent assumptions about the "black folk" experience, long staples in discussions of the period. In so doing, they also implicitly puncture the developmental narratives and logics about black life and history that have worked in tandem with discussions of the "folk" and contributed, in part, to simplistic readings of Hurston's work. Such logics were at work in the writings that have come to define the Harlem Renaissance, perhaps most especially in Locke's essay

"The New Negro," which concludes by heralding a "new phase of group development," a "spiritual Coming of Age."[6]

Daniel G. Williams is right here when he argues that Hurston was writing against this and other "metropolitan biases of an urban modernism that assumed it represented progress, and thus viewed rural life as racially homogeneous, as static, backward, 'other'." While certain scholars have acknowledged – Cheryl Wall among them – the ways in which Hurston's writings have served as a corrective to such misconceptions, adding considerations of her work in film and drama affords a fuller understanding of Hurston's complexities as an artist and intellectual.

If the interpretations of Hurston that Williams, Durkin, and Rodney provide force us to question how we define and periodize "modernity" and the "new," Clare Corbould's "Making the Slave Anew: History, and the Archive in New Negro Renaissance Poetry" invites us to consider the ways in which the frenzied proclamations of the "new" during the Harlem Renaissance illuminated the conflicted relationship some of the era's most celebrated writers bore to slavery. As Corbould notes, "when boosters of a group of African American artists, writers, scholars, and activists dubbed the group the 'New Negroes,' they proclaimed both a break with the past and simultaneously their enduring relationship to history," particularly the history of slavery. Of course, there was perhaps no greater "booster" than Alain Locke, and his titular essay "The New Negro" proclaimed emphatically a break with the past.

If in Locke's conception, the "New Negro" was defined by a "vibrant . . . new psychology" (3), a "spiritual emancipation," a "buoyancy from within" (4), this "self-willed beginning," as Henry Louis Gates has noted, depended fundamentally upon "self-negation, a turning away from the . . . labyrinthine memory of black enslavement."[7] Although Locke never mentions slavery explicitly, its spectral presence is evident in a constellation of references throughout the essay: "'aunties,' 'uncles,' and 'mammies,'" "Uncle Tom," "Sambo" (5), and the "Civil War." The "march of development," Locke insisted, necessitated a "sudden reorientation of view" (4). No longer should the "New Negro" be viewed through "the dusty spectacles of past controversy," but rather, through the clearer, brighter lenses of present possibility (5). Such frames would establish the "New Negro" as "an augury of a new democracy in American culture" (9).

Of course, the millenialist chords Locke struck in these and other passages in "The New Negro" clashed with writings in the same period, though those not typically incorporated into canonical interpretations of the Harlem Renaissance, which have tended to focus on the most recognizable and celebrated writers. Corbould turns her attention to those writers she terms "less well-known," in order to challenge the notion, Locke notwithstanding, that the topic of slavery "waxed and waned around a dynamic of remembering and forgetting" during the Harlem Renaissance era. She argues instead that, across a full range of genres – including editorials, advertisements, and cartoon series – African American creative authors and artists of the period established that "slavery was a major topic," most especially for the poets of the era on whom her chapter focuses. As she notes, poetry appeared not only in black monthly magazines, including *The Crisis*, *Opportunity*, and the *Messenger*, but also in weekly black newspapers with national distributions. The prevalence of poetry in these outlets, she continues, functioned to counter the racist treatment of slaves and slavery saturating the white-dominated public media.

Given the credit Corbould wishes to grant to the poetry of the era within the broader construction of an alternative history of slavery, her sample is perhaps a bit too small to make a persuasive case. While I would quibble with her suggestion that "less well-known" figures of the period provided its "breadth and depth," I would argue that considering them and the venues in which they published does other vitally important work for Harlem Renaissance studies. For example, the work published in the newspapers and little magazines expands the objects of scholarly inquiry in the era beyond the luminaries, beyond the dominant texts, topics, and genres of the period, on which much scholarly interpretation rests. There is interpretive value in bringing that work and its preoccupations into conversation with the work produced by those inside the "magic circle" of influence and acclaim, not least because, as Corbould argues, the poetry of these less well-known writers "drew attention to the self-aggrandizing mythology of most American history." While Locke may have proclaimed the death of "Sambo," "Uncle Tom," and other "plantation darkies," the poets Corbould considers knew that these racist stereotypes remained alive and influential, alongside racist representations of slavery, not just in popular media, but also in professional discourses, history, for example.

Corbould usefully situates the work of these poets within a larger effort to counter the "deeply racist structures" undergirding the work of professional historians, whose writings often "served white supremacy and mythmaking about 'happy darkies' and benign slaveowners." Collectively committed to remembering the tortured past of slavery, these popular poets also underscore the limitations of our conventional literary historical narratives. A more complete history of this period would need to account for the rich and complex store of writings that blacks contributed to *The Crisis, The Negro Quarterly,* and *Opportunity,* and other such outlets that provided a hearing and incentives to black writers who were otherwise closed out of mass circulation magazines. Corbould's chapter encourages us to think about the broad swath of literary activity occurring beneath the conventional literary histories of the Harlem Renaissance we have constructed, activity that took a creative approach to history-writing and history-making, especially about slavery.

While Locke may have proclaimed prematurely the birth of the "new Negro" who had broken the chains of slavery, he fully understood that the institution had left its marks and wounds which required both psychic and discursive repair. For him, as for many self-styled architects of the "Harlem Renaissance," that repair would take many different forms: "inner" work, specifically repair to a "damaged group psychology," but also "outer" work to repair a "warped social perspective" (10). Just whose "social perspective" was "warped" is but one of many delicious textual ambiguities in "The New Negro." Locke's opening references to the "Sociologist, the Philanthropist, the Race Leader" and other "professional observers" (3), certainly imply that *their* perspectives (though not theirs alone) were warped and warranted repair. Such repair, Locke suggested, was already manifesting itself in the "new outlook," the forward-looking stances reflected in the artistic production of youth.

While Locke may have claimed for the "New Negro," a "sense of a mission," a commitment to "rehabilitating the race in world esteem from that loss of prestige for which the fate and conditions of slavery" (14) were responsible, at least two chapters here consider how certain writers of the era responded to this pressure, some chafing under the pressures and burdens of representing "blackness." Both Mark Whalan's "The *Bildungsroman* in the Harlem Renaissance," and Fionnghuala Sweeney's "Modernist Biography and the Question of Manhood: Eslanda Goode Robeson's *Paul Robeson, Negro,*" each take up this issue in different ways, refreshing this familiar discussion through a consideration of the *Bildungsroman,* on the one hand and "life writing," on the other. Both address what Major Jackson terms in a different context, the "pressures of exemplarity." Jackson uses this term to describe the Harlem Renaissance poet, Countee Cullen (who oddly makes no appearance in this volume), who experienced his own pressures "conferred on him in the wake of his early successes" as a "youthful" poet.[8] Such pressures conscripted him and his work into the service of "representing" successful blackness in an overwhelmingly racist nation, but Cullen was not alone in this regard.

While scholars have addressed the ways in which Harlem Renaissance writers responded to this pressure by penning manifestoes of literary independence from various forms of racial constraint – Hughes's "The Negro Artist and the Racial Mountain," most notably – Whalan considers the responses to this pressure in the form of *Bildungsroman*. Several Harlem Renaissance writers found this form appealing, notes Whalan: Arna Bontemps, W. E. B. Du Bois, Jessie Fauset, Langston Hughes, Zora Neale Hurston, James Weldon Johnson, Nella Larsen, Wallace Thurman, and Walter White. In resorting so often to this form, Whalan argues, these writers "modeled and augmented the New Negro movement's prioritization of youth as its central symbolic and political motif," one that gave ballast and energy to some of the most popular manifestoes of the era: Locke's "Negro Youth Speaks," Langston Hughes's "The Negro Artist and the Racial Mountain," and Marita Bonner's "On Being Young, a Woman, and Colored." Yet at the same time, through this form, they registered their ambivalence about (and sometimes resistance to) the cultural pedagogy of an idea of racial uplift with aesthetics at its heart. Together they agonized over the limits and power of "instrumentalizing the aesthetic," and dramatized in their work the "political limits of the aesthetic sphere," perhaps none more so than Nella Larsen in *Quicksand* and Wallace Thurman in *Infants of the Spring*. Even those examples of the *Bildungsroman* less pessimistic than Larsen's and Thurman's still resist the pressures of exemplarity by staking their hopes in "*future* artwork, in the ability of a yet-unrealized novel or painting to help challenge a national discourse of race that seemed so violent and intractable in the present." In other words, in an era that witnessed escalating rates of lynching and compounding racial oppression, any imagined cultural interventions reliant on the power and viability of an "exemplary" racial subject seemed decidedly out of touch.

Sweeney's discussion of Eslanda Goode's biography of her husband, Paul Robeson, shifts the question of "exemplary racial representation" from "youth" to "maturity." Robeson, she notes, was one of that "'aristocracy of talent' and achievement, destined to provide leadership and example in addressing the obstacle of the color line." While Goode's biography seems on the surface to conform to "the creed of the New Negro," meant to perform his exemplarity as "artist, cultural ambassador, and nationalist activist," in the end, the biography, much like the coming-of-age novels Whalan discusses, ultimately abandons the convention.

Indeed, the book, Sweeney argues, becomes in the process of its writing "the vehicle of an iconoclastic intent." As a result, she concludes, "*Paul Robeson, Negro* takes its place as a re-definitional narrative of the Harlem Renaissance, one that complicates the assuredness with which male artists and intellectuals might be cast as exceptional yet representative." A significant aspect of that "re-definitional narrative" for Goode, abandons narrative, incorporating photographic images, reviews, newspaper reports, which together contribute to what Rachel Farebrother terms a "collage aesthetic."[9]

Although print has dominated considerations of the Harlem Renaissance, Sweeney's chapter, as does Caroline Goeser's "The Visual Image in New Negro Renaissance Print Culture," establishes the significance of the visual image in the artistic production of the Harlem Renaissance. In the case of Goode's biography of Robeson, the incorporation of visual artifacts might be read as her resistance to exemplary narratives of racial representation. By contrast, in her discussion of the artistic collaborations between writers and visual artists of the period, Goeser sees these images as answering the call for "new interpretations and portrayals of Black identity and history," without primary regard for audience. Although the illustrations, positioned in active dialogue with the prose and poetry surrounding them, were modernist and experimental, their presence on the pages of the National Association for the Advancement of Colored People's (NAACP) *The Crisis* and the National Urban League's *Opportunity* "embellished messages of racial uplift championed by their editors, W. E. B. Du Bois and Charles S. Johnson." Even if these collaborations between word and image also exemplified for Goeser, a "collage aesthetic," lending them a "modernist" edge, they could still be appropriated for their representational functions, in that they could be counterposed to "the demeaning Black stereotypes that continued to circulate on the pages of modern print culture."

Goeser productively sidelines these questions of representation, and what she terms "embellished messages of racial uplift," preferring to view the illustrations she discusses for their role in making black "modern," for their role in shaping a "newly dynamic and hybrid idiom, composed as a modernist collage of disparate fragments." Employing Farebrother's concept of the "collage aesthetic," Goeser see these illustrations as forming a "new iconography of Black agency," unfettered by prefabricated expectations of black representation. More important, she suggests that these visual illustrations worked to extend the impact of the poetry, essays, and novels within which they are embedded. Although Goeser does not provide enough descriptions, the various visual strategies found in the illustrations of the era are suggestive. Especially suggestive is her discussion of the illustrations for the lynching poems that predominated during the period. Both Countee Cullen's *The Black Christ and Other Poems* (1929) and Langston Hughes's *Scottsboro Limited* (1932) include graphic illustrations likening black lynching victims to the crucified Christ. Such religious iconography served to address contemporary instances of violence and political oppression, illustrating, more broadly, that the millenialist prophecies that inaugurated the Harlem Renaissance had not come to fruition. Many have observed the striking contrasting tones and images between Hughes's poem "Justice" from *Scottsboro Limited*:

> That Justice is a blind goddess
> Is a thing to which we black are wise.
> Her bandage hides two festering sores
> That once perhaps were eyes.[10]

and those in "Youth," which Locke had incorporated into his essay "The New Negro":

> We have tomorrow
> Bright before us
> Like a flame.
>
> Yesterday, a night-gone thing
> A sun-down name.
>
> And dawn today
> Broad arch above the road we came.
> We march! (5)

In a mere few years, Hughes's images of optimism had been replaced by images of justice as a blind justice with festering sores for eyes. It would be mistaken to suggest, however, that this shift was so dramatic, for, despite Locke's announcement of a promising "New Negro" future, many writers associated with the Harlem Renaissance knew that art was powerless to heal the intractable racial problems in the USA. In other words, the overweening optimism, the emancipatory energies, the preoccupation with "newness" reflected in Locke's "The New Negro" were far from representative of the spirit and tone of the Harlem Renaissance, or even for that matter, the tone of Locke's overall anthology. Indeed, other selections in the volume sounded more sobering notes, as regards both the definition and future possibilities of "the New Negro" and the fate of black cultural production, whether in Harlem or beyond.

For roughly a generation now, scholarship on the Harlem Renaissance has done much to complicate Locke's culturalist agenda and to redefine his "New Negro" as a global figure within a world system and thus connected to cultural activities, as well as social and political struggles beyond Harlem and the US nation state. If, from its inception, the Harlem Renaissance was "moulded in a national image," to quote Jak Peake, its image has since come to "reveal a more internationalist and plural history."[11] In "London, New York, and the Black Bolshevik Renaissance: Radical Black Internationalism During the New Negro Renaissance" one of the strongest pieces in the volume, James Smethurst offers a provocative examination of the Harlem Renaissance beyond the bounds of Harlem. The chapter contributes significantly to ongoing research on "black internationalism," which has revitalized Harlem Renaissance studies. This "new mode of thinking about the 'world,'" to borrow from Jak Peake, focuses "less on discrete origins and more on points of contact, cross-fertilization and transculturation."[12] Not only does Smethurst fruitfully examine such points of contact and cross-fertilization, he revises and complicates that aspect of "transnational" studies, which has focused overmuch on "the West" and the reification of the "Atlantic World."

Smethurst considers the "interplay between Black political and cultural activists in Britain and the USA during the New Negro era and the creation of Black internationalist networks," constituting what he terms the "Black Bolshevik Renaissance." In looking eastward, invoking the "Black Bolshevik World" and the "Black Bolshevik Renaissance," Smethurst means to emphasize black writing informed by the October Revolution. Importantly, the revolution does not function in this work merely as an example of sympathy or identification with other oppressed people. Rather, it becomes a node in a "political and cultural network that African and African-descended peoples could join." That network would, in turn, function as "leverage to end colonialism and white supremacy."

Although Smethurst gathers a range of writers in his net – Claude McKay, C. L. R. James, Eric Walrond, among others – I am particularly taken with his discussion of McKay, which deepens our understanding of this restless figure, who never made Harlem his "home," during the heyday of the renaissance. Indeed, it is now axiomatic that perhaps McKay's greatest contribution to the Harlem Renaissance was his global, pan-African sensibility and experience, although this sensibility showed itself in the work of other artists of the period, including Hughes who traveled broadly, touching down in Haiti, France, Africa, and also the Soviet Union. According to Smethurst, McKay, much like other black radical artists and activists, worked to "refigure the symbolic geography of the world so as to decenter the relationship between Europe and the Americas." Read through these new frames, McKay's work takes on dimensions and significance not considered heretofore. Not only does Smethurst introduce us to little-known poems in McKay's corpus, "Ethiopia," and "Exhortation," he compels us to reinterpret the McKay poems we think we know, or at least to see them in more textured light. For example, while "If We Must Die" has been historically interpreted as McKay's treatment of the mass racist US violence during the "Red Summer" of 1919, examined anew through Smethurst's frames, it is just as fruitful to read this sonnet both as an example of "black nationalist resistance," and as an example of McKay's solidarity with a besieged Soviet Union.

Smethurst's chapter illuminates the kind of re-reading and re-interpretation that can result when the movement's central and most canonical figures are read in the round, in this case, the round that is the globe. Such re-interpretations can also result from examining aspects of their work, which has seldom been submitted to close analysis. Such is also the strength of Shane Vogel's chapter, "Alain Locke and the Value of the Harlem Renaissance," which examines Locke's philosophical writings. Of course, students of philosophy have examined Locke on value, but that work has seldom made its way into Harlem Renaissance studies from the literary side. As a result, scholars of the field have neglected to appreciate Locke's own intellectual evolution. Over the course of his career, he significantly expanded the parameters of the Harlem Renaissance and deepened his positions about the relationship between cultural expression and political change, particularly in a world that devalued black art as much as it devalued black people. According to Vogel, Locke sought to intervene in such devaluation in his philosophical work devoted to formulating theories of value. Vogel does here for considerations of Locke what Durkin's chapter does for considerations of Hurston: read aspects of each author's work in relation to others. As Vogel notes, Locke's "academic philosophy and cultural criticism deeply informed one another," in ways that may not be immediately evident when they are read apart from each other.

Locke's theories of value, Vogel argues, "called for a shift from a *racial axiology* to the *axiology of race.*" Whereas the former was "predicated on a racial distinction that holds whiteness as an absolute, unchanging standard by which to measure the beautiful, the good, and the true," the latter describes "how race came to be a marker of value in the first place." For Locke, Vogel suggests, value was not a metaphysical concept, but rather a "practical functional dynamic," derived from lived experiences. Although rooted in the realities of power and domination, cultural value systems could not only coexist, they could be mutually transforming.

Approaching the Harlem Renaissance through Locke's theories of value, Vogel argues, necessarily forces us to rethink various aspects of his evolving project, not least his formulations of the "New Negro." Through the prism of these theories, the New Negro is less an "individual subjectivity, collective figure, or historical formation," than an "endlessly renewable resource," subject to the "process of reinterpretation and revaluation." By extension, the Harlem Renaissance, he adds, must be seen in much the same way. The movement "appears less as a delimited historical period or literary formation than as an ongoing and unending process of transvaluation," an "ever-renewable engagement and refinement of aesthetic, political and spiritual values."

There is certainly much value in Vogel's disinclination to delimit the Harlem Renaissance chronologically. Indeed, other scholars, including William Maxwell, have similarly called for "various models of elongated renaissance time,"[13] but I would still sound a cautionary note, lest we risk losing all meaning and explanatory power in the concept of the "Harlem Renaissance." Is it perhaps less fruitful to extend the chronological boundaries of the movement, in either direction, than it is to continue to discuss the lines of its influence, to establish, as does Sonya Posmentier in this volume, its lasting influence on subsequent artists in the black literary tradition. Yet even this move may have its limits. For example, in tracing the "lasting influence of the New Negro writers on [Gwendolyn] Brooks's poetry," Posmentier argues for continuity between generations of poets "from the Harlem Renaissance or New Negro Renaissance, to the Chicago Renaissance, to the Black Arts Movement . . . to our present day." I would suggest that stretching such continuities across such vast territory can ultimately be just as attenuating as expanding the chronological seams of the period.

Stretching the period's chronological seams becomes far less pressing, in any case, when we consider just how much work on the Harlem Renaissance remains to be done, despite the vast amount of interpretive territory covered in this volume. This fabled era, which James Weldon Johnson termed the "Harlem of story and song, the scene of laughter singing, dancing, and primitive passions"[14] does seem, as Vogel suggests, ever renewable. Nearly a hundred years since the Harlem Renaissance was first heralded, it retains its fascination and appeal for scholars and the general public alike. That appeal grows increasingly more commercial. In recent years, even the "young adult" and children's book industries have capitalized on the cultural appetite for the Harlem Renaissance, publishing such books as Laban Carrick Hill's *Harlem Stomp!: A Cultural History of the*

Harlem Renaissance (2004), Faith Ringgold's *Harlem Renaissance Party* (2015), and Tamra Orr's *The Harlem Renaissance: An African American Cultural Movement* (2018). Amazon.com markets these as texts "frequently bought together." The site markets *Harlem Stomp!* as "the first trade book to bring the Harlem Renaissance alive for young adults!" Praising Ringgold's "bold and vibrant illustrations," which capture the "song and dance" of the period, the blurb on the back cover of *Harlem Renaissance Party* invites young readers to a party:

> Come one! Come all! To a party today in Harlem. Celebrate the great men and women of the Harlem Renaissance. Lonnie and his uncle Bates go on an unforgettable journey back in time to the Harlem Renaissance. Along the way, they meet the famous writers, musicians, artists, and athletes who created this incredible period. And after an exciting day of walking with giants, Lonnie fully understands why the Harlem Renaissance is so important.[15]

These books form a study in contrast to those Katherine Capshaw discusses here in her chapter "Children's Literature of the Harlem Renaissance." She credits Du Bois with spearheading the field of black children's literature, although Jessie Fauset should also be named. The focus of their children's publications was, as many have noted, mature, in that it exposed young readers to such topics as lynching, Haitian revolutionary heroes, as well as the US military occupation of Haiti. The field of black children's literature not only attempted to build and educate a new generation of black citizens – "New Negroes" in formation – but also worked to supplement and respond to educational and textual inequities in the schooling of your black children.

I started this afterword with two questions: "Do we need another book on the Harlem Renaissance" and "What is left to say about it?" If only because each new year seems to bring word of some newly discovered work, long buried in the archives, we are likely to need yet more books. It is fair to say that study of the Harlem Renaissance is likely to remain an open-ended project at least for the foreseeable future.

Notes

1. Eric J. Sundquist, "Red, White, Black and Blue," *Transition*, no. 70 (1996): 94.
2. Hazel Carby, "The Politics of Fiction, Anthropology, and the Folk: Zora Neale Hurston," in *New Essays on Their Eyes Were Watching God*, ed. Michael Awkward (Cambridge: Cambridge University Press, 1990), 80.
3. Ibid., 77, 78.

4. Henry Louis Gates, Jr., "Zora Neale Hurston and the Speakerly Text," in *The Signifying Monkey: A Theory of African-American Literary Criticism* (Oxford: Oxford University Press, 1988), 170–216.

5. Cathy Brigham, "The Talking Frame of Zora Neale Hurston's Talking Book: Storytelling as Dialectic in *Their Eyes Were Watching God*," in *The Harlem Renaissance, 1920–1940: Analysis and Assessment, 1980–1994*, ed. Carl D. Wintz (New York: Garland, 1996), 26, 27, 43.

6. Alain Locke, "The New Negro," in *The New Negro*, ed. Alain Locke (New York: Touchstone, 1997), 16. Hereafter cited parenthetically.

7. Henry Louis Gates, Jr., "The Trope of the New Negro and the Reconstruction of the Image of the Black," *Representations* 24 (Autumn 1988): 132.

8. Major Jackson, "Introduction," in *Countee Cullen: Complete Poems* (New York: Library of America, 2013), 3.

9. Rachel Farebrother, *The Collage Aesthetic in the Harlem Renaissance* (Farnham: Ashgate, 2009).

10. Langston Hughes, "Justice," in *The Collected Poems of Langston Hughes*, ed. Arnold Rampersad (New York: Vintage, 1994), 31.

11. Jak Peake, "'Watching the Waters': Tropic Flows in the Harlem Renaissance, Black Internationalism and Other Currents," *Radical Americas* 3, no. 1 (2018): 35.

12. Ibid., 4.

13. William J. Maxwell, "Questionnaire Response," *Modernism/modernity* 23, no. 3 (2013): 447.

14. James Weldon Johnson, *Along This Way* (1933; New York: Penguin, 1990), 380.

15. This invitation appears on the back cover of Faith Ringgold's *Harlem Renaissance Party* (New York: HarperCollins, 2015).

Bibliography

Gwendolyn Bennett Papers, Schomburg Center for Research in Black Culture.

W. E. B. Du Bois papers. Special Collections and University Archives, University of Massachusetts Amherst Libraries. MS 312.

Alice Dunbar-Nelson Collection, University of Delaware, Newark.

Angelina Weld Grimké Collection, Moorland-Spingarn Research Center, Howard University.

James Weldon Johnson and Grace Nail Johnson Papers, Yale Collection of American Literature, Beinecke Rare Book and Manuscript Library.

James Weldon Johnson Collection. Stuart A. Rose Manuscripts, Archives, and Rare Book Library, Emory University.

Alain Locke papers, Moorland-Spingarn Research Center, Howard University.

May Miller Papers, Stuart A. Rose Manuscript, Archives, and Rare Book Library, Emory University.

Paul and Eslanda Robeson Collection, Moorland-Spingarn Archive, Howard University, Washington, DC.

Adi, Hakim. *Pan-Africanism and Communism: The Communist International, Africa and the Diaspora, 1919–1939*. Trenton: Africa World Press, 2013.

Allen, Edward. "Langston Hughes at the Cinema." In *Modernist Invention: Media Technology and American Poetry*, 206–248. Cambridge: Cambridge University Press, 2020.

Anderson, Eric and Alfred A. Moss, Jr. *Dangerous Donations: Northern Philanthropy and Southern Black Education, 1902–1930*. Columbia: University of Missouri Press, 1999.

Anderson, James D. *The Education of Blacks in the South, 1860–1935*. Chapel Hill: University of North Carolina Press, 1988.

Anderson, Paul Allen. *Deep River: Music and Memory in Harlem Renaissance Thought*. Durham: Duke University Press, 2001.

Andrews, William L. "The Novelization of Voice in Early African American Narrative." *PMLA* 105, no. 1 (1990): 23–34.

"Slave Narratives, 1865–1900." In *The Oxford Handbook of the African American Slave Narrative*, ed. John Ernest, 219–232. New York: Oxford University Press, 2014.

Anonymous. "Claude McKay." *The Liberator* (July 1919): 7. www.marxists.org/h
    istory/usa/culture/pubs/liberator/1919/07/v2n07-w17-jul-1919-liberator.pdf.

Anonymous. "Garvey Reviews Big Negro Parade." *New York Times*, August 2,
    1924. https://search.proquest.com/docview/103300388/398642110B7A434BP
    Q/46?accountid=14664.

Anonymous. "Radicals Ridicule Arms Conference." *New York Times*,
    November 14, 1921. https://search.proquest.com/docview/98578125/9E
    F0258D673C4959PQ/16?accountid=14664.

Anstey, John C. "Anne Spencer: A Conventional, Yet Unconventional, Harlem
    Renaissance Poet." MA thesis, Longwood University, 1999.

Aptheker, Herbert, ed. *The Correspondence of W. E. B. Du Bois: Selections,
    1877–1934*. Vol. I. Amherst: University of Massachusetts Press, 1997.

Armstrong, Louis. *Louis Armstrong: In His Own Words*, ed. Thomas Brothers.
    Oxford: Oxford University Press, 1999.

Baker, Jr., Houston A. *Modernism and the Harlem Renaissance*. Chicago:
    University of Chicago Press, 1987.

   "'The Urge to Adorn': Generational Wit and the Birth of 'The Signifying
    Monkey.'" *Early American Literature* 50, no. 3 (2015): 831–842.

Baldwin, Davarian L. "Introduction: New Negroes Forging a New World." In
    Escape from New York: The New Negro Renaissance Beyond Harlem, ed.
    Davarian Baldwin and Minkah Makalani, 1–27. Minneapolis: University of
    Minnesota Press, 2013.

Baldwin, Davarian L. and Minkah Makalani, eds. *Escape from New York: The New
    Negro Renaissance Beyond Harlem*. Minneapolis: University of Minnesota
    Press, 2013.

Baldwin, Kate A. *Beyond the Color Line and the Iron Curtain: Reading
    Encounters between Black and Red, 1922–1963*. Durham: Duke University
    Press, 2002.

Balshaw, Maria. *Looking for Harlem: Urban Aesthetics in African American
    Literature*. London: Pluto Press, 2000.

Barrett, Lindon. *Blackness and Value: Seeing Double*. Cambridge: Cambridge
    University Press, 1999.

Batiste, Stephanie Leigh. *Darkening Mirrors: Imperial Representation in Depression-
    Era African American Performance*. Durham, NC: Duke University Press, 2011.

Beal, Wesley. *Networks of Modernism: Reorganizing American Narrative*. Iowa
    City: University of Iowa Press, 2015.

Benbow, Mark E. "Birth of a Quotation: Woodrow Wilson and 'Like Writing
    History with Lightning.'" *Journal of the Gilded Age and Progressive Era* 9
    (2010): 509–533.

Bennett, Gwendolyn. "To a Dark Girl," and "Fantasy." In *Caroling Dusk: An
    Anthology of Verse by Negro Poets of the Twenties*, ed. Countee Cullen, 157; 158.
    New York: Harper & Brothers, 1927.

   "The Ebony Flute." *Opportunity* (August 1926): 260–261.

   "Heritage." *Opportunity* (December 1923): 371.

   "Song." In *The New Negro*, ed. Alain Locke, 225. New York: Touchstone, 1997.

"Song." *Palms* (October 1926): 21.

"Street Lamps in Early Spring." *Opportunity* (May 1926): 152.

Bernard, Emily. *Carl Van Vechten and the Harlem Renaissance: A Portrait in Black and White*. New Haven: Yale University Press, 2012.

"The Renaissance and the Vogue." In *The Cambridge Companion to the Harlem Renaissance*, ed. George Hutchinson, 28–40. New York: Cambridge University Press, 2007.

Bernstein, Robin. *Racial Innocence: Performing American Childhood from Slavery to Civil Rights*. New York: New York University Press, 2011.

Bertsch, Andy. "The Melting Pot vs. the Salad Bowl: A call to explore regional cross-cultural differences and similarities within the U.S.A." *Journal of Organizational Culture, Communications and Conflict* 17, no. 1 (2013): 131–148.

Biers, Katherine. "Practices of Enchantment: The Theatre of Zora Neale Hurston." *The Drama Review* 59, no. 4 (2015): 67–82.

Blake, Casey Nelson. *Beloved Community: The Cultural Criticism of Randolph Bourne, Van Wyck Brooks, Waldo Frank, and Lewis Mumford*. Chapel Hill: University of North Carolina Press, 1990.

Blassingame, John W. *Slave Testimony: Two Centuries of Letters, Speeches, Interviews, and Autobiographies*. Baton Rouge: Louisiana State University Press, 1977.

Blount, Marcellus. "The Preacherly Text: African American Poetry and Vernacular Performance." *PMLA* 107, no. 3 (May 1992): 582–593.

Boas, Franz. "Preface" to Zora Neale Hurston, *Mules and Men* [1935]. In *Zora Neale Hurston, Folklore, Memoirs, and Other Writings*, ed. Cheryl A. Wall, n. p. New York: Library of America, 1995.

Boes, Tobias. *Formative Fictions: Nationalism, Cosmopolitanism, and the Bildungsroman*. Ithaca: Cornell University Press, 2012.

"Modernist Studies and the *Bildungsroman*: A Historical Survey of Critical Trends." *Literature Compass* 3, no. 2 (2006): 230–243.

Bond, Horace Mann. "The Legacy of W. E. B. Du Bois." *Freedomways* (Winter 1965): 16–17.

Bontemps, Arna. *Sad-Faced Boy*. Boston: Houghton Mifflin, 1937.

Bontemps, Arna and Langston Hughes. *Popo and Fifina: Children of Haiti*. 1932; New York: Oxford University Press, 1993.

"The Book of the Month." *The Review of Reviews* XVIII (July–December 1898): 84–92.

"The Borzoi Broadside for September 1925." *American Mercury* 6, no. 21 (September 1925): xv–xxii.

Boykoff, Jules and Kaia Sand. "Recasting Poetry: 'The Long Biography of a Poem.'" *Jacket 2* (blog), June 10, 2011. https://jacket2.org/commentary/re casting-poetry-0.

Boyd, Marion. "Letter: Nella Larsen's Story." *Forum* 83, no. 4 (April 1930): 41.

Boyd, Valerie. *Wrapped in Rainbows: The Life of Zora Neale Hurston*. New York: Scribner, 2004.

Boyer, Richard O. "The Hot Bach." In *The Duke Ellington Reader*, ed. Mark Tucker, 214–245. Oxford: Oxford University Press, 1993.

Braddock, Jeremy. "Race: Tradition and Archive in the Harlem Renaissance." *A Handbook of Modernism Studies*, ed. Jean-Michel Rabaté, 87–106. Chichester: Wiley-Blackwell, 2013.

Branley, Edward. "NOLA History: Congo Square and the Roots of New Orleans Music." July 2, 2012. https://gonola.com/things-to-do-in-new-orleans/arts-culture/nola-history-congo-square-and-the-roots-of-new-orleans-music.

Brawley, Benjamin. "The Negro Literary Renaissance." *Southern Workman* (January 1927): 177–184.

"The Negro in American Fiction." *Dial* 60 (1916): 445–450.

Brier, Jennifer, Jim Downs, and Jennifer L. Morgan, eds. *Connexions: Histories of Race and Sex in North America*. Urbana: University of Illinois Press, 2016.

Briggs, Cyril K. "Africa for the Africans." In *African Anti-Colonial Thought*, ed. Cathy Bergin, 82–84. Edinburgh: Edinburgh University Press, 2016.

Brigham, Cathy. "The Talking Frame of Zora Neale Hurston's Talking Book: Storytelling as Dialectic in *Their Eyes Were Watching God*." In *The Harlem Renaissance, 1920–1940: Analysis and Assessment, 1980–1994*, ed. Carl D. Wintz, 26–43. New York: Garland, 1996.

Brittan, Jennifer. "The Terminal: Eric Walrond, the City of Colón, and the Caribbean of the Panama Canal." *American Literary History* 25, no. 2 (Summer 2013), 294–316.

Brooks, Christopher A. and Robert Sims. *Roland Hayes: The Legacy of an American Tenor*. Bloomington: Indiana University Press, 2015.

Brooks, Daphne A. *Bodies in Dissent: Spectacular Performances of Race and Freedom. 1850–1910*. Durham: Duke University Press, 2006.

Brooks, Gwendolyn. "An Aspect of Love, Alive in the Ice and Fire." In *Riot*, 21–22. Detroit, MI: Broadside Press, 1969.

"Gwendolyn Brooks to James Weldon Johnson." March 21, 1938. Box 4, Folder 59. James Weldon Johnson and Grace Nail Johnson Papers.

"Letters." *Time* 98, no. 16 (October 18, 1971): 10.

"Poems." n.d. Box 4, Folder 59. James Weldon Johnson and Grace Nail Johnson Papers.

Report from Part One. Detroit: Broadside Press, 1972.

"Riot." In *Riot*, 9–10. Detroit, MI: Broadside Press, 1969.

"The Third Sermon on the Warpland." In *Riot*, 11–20. Detroit, MI: Broadside Press, 1969.

Brown, Jayna. *Babylon Girls: Black Women Performers and the Shaping of the Modern*. Durham, NC: Duke University Press, 2008.

Brown, Sterling A. "Old Time Tales." *New Masses* (February 25, 1936): 24–25.

Negro Poetry and Drama. No. 7 Bronze Booklet. Washington, DC: Associates in Negro Folk Education, 1937.

"The New Negro in Literature (1925–1955)." In *A Son's Return: Selected Essays of Sterling A. Brown*, ed. Mark A. Sanders, 184–203. Boston: Northeastern University Press, 1996.

Southern Road. New York: Harcourt Brace, 1932.

Brundage, W. Fitzhugh. "Le Réveil de la Louisiane: Memory and Acadian Identity, 1920–1960." In *Where These Memories Grow: History, Memory, and Southern Identity*, ed. W. Fitzhugh Brundage, 271–298. Chapel Hill: University of North Carolina Press, 2000.

The Southern Past: A Clash of Race and Memory. Cambridge, MA: Belknap Press of Harvard University Press, 2005.

Buckley, Jerome H. *Season of Youth: The Bildungsroman from Dickens to Golding*. Cambridge, MA: Harvard University Press, 1974.

Bürger, Peter. *Theory of the Avant-Garde*. Minneapolis: University of Minnesota Press, 1984.

Burke, Inez M. "Two Races." In *Plays and Pageants from the Life of the Negro*, ed. Willis Richardson, 295–302. Washington, DC: Associated Publishers, 1930.

Butler, Judith. *Gender Trouble: Feminism and the Subversion of Identity*. New York: Routledge, 1990.

Byrd, Rudolph P. and Henry Louis Gates, Jr. "Introduction." In *Cane: Authoritative Text, Contexts, Criticism*, ed. Rudolph P. Byrd and Henry Louis Gates, Jr., xix–lxxix. New York: Norton, 2011.

Caddoo, Cara. "Double-Consciousness and the Films of Zora Neale Hurston." In *Theorizing Visual Studies: Writing Through the Discipline*, ed. James Elkins and Kristi McGuire, 107–109. New York: Routledge, 2013.

Cade, John B. "Out of the Mouths of Ex-Slaves." *Journal of Negro History* 20 (1935): 294–337.

Capogna, Frank. "Ekphrasis, Cultural Capital, and the Cultivation of Detachment in T. S. Eliot's Early Poetry." *Journal of Modern Literature* 41, no. 3 (2018): 147–165.

Capshaw, Katharine. "Childhood, the Body, and Race Performance: Early 20th-Century Etiquette Books for Black Children." *African American Review* 40, no. 4 (Winter 2006): 975–811.

Children's Literature of the Harlem Renaissance. Bloomington: Indiana University Press, 2004.

"War, The Black Diaspora, and Anti-Colonialist Journalism: The Case of *Our Boys and Girls*." In *Children's Literature and Culture of the First World War*, ed. Lissa Paul, Rosemary Ross Johnston, and Emma Short, 77–92. New York: Routledge, 2016.

Capshaw, Katharine and Anna Mae Duane, eds. *Who Writes for Black Children? African American Children's Literature before 1900*. Minneapolis: University of Minnesota Press, 2017.

Carby, Hazel. "The Politics of Fiction, Anthropology and the Folk: Zora Neale Hurston." In *New Essays on Their Eyes Were Watching God*, ed. Michael Awkward, 71–90. Cambridge: Cambridge University Press, 1990.

Race Men. Cambridge, MA: Harvard University Press, 1998.

Reconstructing Womanhood: The Emergence of the Afro-American Woman Novelist. New York: Oxford University Press, 1989.

Carroll, Anne Elizabeth. *Word, Image, and the New Negro: Representation and Identity in the Harlem Renaissance.* Bloomington: Indiana University Press, 2005.

Castronovo, Russ. *Beautiful Democracy: Aesthetics and Anarchy in a Global Era.* Chicago: University of Chicago Press, 2007.

Cayer, Jennifer A. "'Roll Yo' Hips - Don't Roll Yo' Eyes': Angularity and Embodied Spectatorship in Zora Neale Hurston's Play, *Cold Keener.*" *Theatre Journal* 60, no. 1 (March 2008): 37–69.

Chapman, Erin D. *Prove It on Me: New Negroes, Sex, and Popular Culture in the 1920s.* New York: Oxford University Press, 2012.

Charnov, Elaine S. "The Performative Visual Anthropology Films of Zora Neale Hurston." *Film Criticism* 23, no. 1 (1998): 38–47.

Chauncey, George. *Gay New York: Gender, Urban Culture, and the Making of the Gay Male World, 1890–1940.* New York: Flamingo, 1995.

Cheng, Anne Anlin. *The Melancholy of Race: Psychoanalysis, Assimilation, and Hidden Grief.* Oxford: Oxford University Press, 2001.

Chude-Sokei, Louis. *The Last "Darky": Bert Williams, Black-on-Black Minstrelsy, and the African Diaspora.* Durham: Duke University Press, 2006.

Clark, John. "Mystery Novel Writer Is Interviewed over the Radio." *Pittsburgh Courier*, January 21, 1933.

Cohen, Harvey G. *Duke Ellington's America.* Chicago: University of Chicago Press, 2010.

Colbert, Soyica Diggs. *The African American Theatrical Body: Reception, Performance, and the Stage.* Cambridge: Cambridge University Press, 2011.

Cole, Carriebel B. "Playtime: Hark, Hark, the Dogs Do Bark, A Nursery Rhyme Dance." *The Brownies' Book*, 1, no. 1 (January 1920): 20–21.

Cole, Jean Lee and Charles Mitchell, "Introduction to *Spears.*" In *Zora Neale Hurston: Collected Plays*, 51. New Brunswick, NJ: Rutgers University Press, 2008.

"Zora Neale Hurston – A Theatrical Life." In *Zora Neale Hurston: Collected Plays*, ed. Jean Lee Cole and Charles Mitchell, xv–xxxi. New Brunswick, NJ: Rutgers University Press, 2008.

Collier, James Lincoln. *Louis Armstrong: An American Genius.* New York: Oxford University Press, 1983.

The Making of Jazz: A Comprehensive History. Boston: Houghton Mifflin, 1978.

Connolly, Brian, and Marisa Fuentes, eds. *History of the Present* 6, no. 2 (2016).

Cooper, Wayne F. *Claude McKay: Rebel Sojourner in the Harlem Renaissance.* Baton Rouge: Louisiana University Press, 1996.

Corbould, Clare. *Becoming African Americans: Black Public Life in Harlem 1919–1939.* Cambridge, MA: Harvard University Press, 2009.

"Streets, Sounds and Identity in Interwar Harlem." *Journal of Social History* 40, no. 4 (2007): 859–894.

Covarrubias, Miguel, and Eric Walrond. "Enter, the New Negro, a Distinctive Type Recently Created by the Coloured Cabaret Belt in New York." *Vanity Fair* 23, no. 4 (December 1924): 60–61.

"The Increasing Vogue of the Negro Revue on Broadway." *Vanity Fair* 23, no. 6 (February 1925): 61.

Cowdery, Mae V. "Dusk," in *Ebony and Topaz: A Collecteana*, ed. Charles S. Johnson, 23. New York: National Urban League, 1927.

"Farewell," *The Crisis* (February 1929): 50.

"Longings," *The Crisis* (December 1927): 337.

We Lift Our Voices and Other Poems. Philadelphia: Alpress, 1936.

"The Young Voice Cries," *Harlem* (November 1928): 14.

Cox, Karen L., *Dixie's Daughters: The United Daughters of the Confederacy and the Preservation of Confederate Culture*. Gainesville: University Press of Florida, 2003.

Crenshaw, Kimberlé. "Why Intersectionality Can't Wait." *The Washington Post*, September 24, 2015. www.washingtonpost.com/news/in-theory/wp/2015/09/24/why-intersectionality-cant-wait/?utm_term=.2559e04c32855.

Cullen, Countee. *The Black Christ and Other Poems*. New York: Harper and Brothers, 1929.

ed. *Caroling Dusk: An Anthology of Verse by Negro Poets of the Twenties*. New York: Harper & Brothers, 1927.

One Way to Heaven. New York: Harper and Brothers, 1932.

Review of *Porgy*. *Opportunity* 3, no. 36 (December 1925): 379.

Cuney-Hare, Maud. *Negro Musicians and their Music*. 1936; New York: Da Capo, 1974.

Dace, Tish, ed. *Langston Hughes: The Contemporary Reviews*. Cambridge: Cambridge University Press, 1997.

Dagbovie, Pero. *The Early Black History Movement, Carter G. Woodson, and Lorenzo Johnston Greene*. Urbana: University of Illinois Press, 2007.

Davis, Angela. *Blues Legacies and Black Feminism: Gertrude "Ma" Rainey, Bessie Smith, and Billie Holiday*. New York: Pantheon Books, 1998.

Davis, Cynthia and Verner D. Mitchell. "Modernism and the Urban Frontier in the Work of Dorothy West and Helene Johnson." In *A Companion to the Harlem Renaissance*, ed. Cherene Sherrard-Johnson, 103–118. Chichester, UK: Wiley-Blackwell, 2015.

Davis, James C. *Eric Walrond: A Life in the Harlem Renaissance and the Transatlantic Caribbean*. New York: Columbia University Press, 2015.

Davis, Thadious M. *Nella Larsen, Novelist of the Harlem Renaissance: A Woman's Life Unveiled*. Baton Rouge: Louisiana State University Press, 1996.

Dean, Michelle. "Passing Through: Nella Larsen made a career of not quite belonging." April 3, 2015. www.laphamsquarterly.org/roundtable/passing-through.

DeFrantz, Thomas F. *Dancing Many Drums: Excavations in African American Dance*. Madison: University of Wisconsin Press, 2002.

Des Jardins, Julie. *Women and the Historical Enterprise in America: Gender, Race, and the Politics of Memory, 1880–1945*. Chapel Hill: University of North Carolina Press, 2003.

Diamond, Elin. "Folk Modernism: Zora Neale Hurston's Gestural Drama." *Modern Drama* 58, no. 1 (Spring 2015): 112–134.

Dickson-Carr, Darryl. *Spoofing the Modern: Satire in the Harlem Renaissance.* Columbia: University of South Carolina Press, 2015.

Domingo, W. A. "Did Bolshevism Stop Race Riots in Russia." In *African American Anti-Colonial Thought, 1917–1937*, ed. Cathy Bergin, 31–34. Edinburgh: Edinburgh University Press, 2016.

"The Tropics in New York." *Survey Graphic* 6, no. 6 (March 1925): 648–650.

Douglas, Aaron and Langston Hughes "Two Artists." *Opportunity* (October 1926): 315.

Douglas, Ann. *Terrible Honesty: Mongrel Manhattan in the 1920s.* New York: Farrar, Straus, and Giroux, 1995.

Duberman, Martin. *Paul Robeson: A Biography.* New York: New Press, 2007.

Du Bois, W. E. B. *Black Flame Trilogy* (1957–61): *The Ordeal of Mansart* (1957; Oxford: Oxford University Press, 2007).

"The Browsing Reader." *The Crisis* 37 (September 1930): 313.

"The Browsing Reader, review of *The Walls of Jericho*." *The Crisis* 35 (June 1928): 374.

"Of Children." *The Crisis* 4, no. 6 (October 1912): 287.

"The Conservation of Races" [1897]. In *Writings*, ed. Nathan Huggins, 815–826. New York: Library of America, 1986.

"Criteria of Negro Art." *The Crisis* 36, no. 2 (October 1926): 290–297.

"Critiques of Carl Van Vechten's *Nigger Heaven*: W. E. B. Du Bois." In *The Portable Harlem Renaissance Reader*, ed. David Levering Lewis, 106–108. New York: Penguin, 1994.

The Dark Princess. 1928; Jackson: University Press of Mississippi, 1995.

Darkwater: Voices from within the Veil. Mineola, NY: Dover, 1999.

Darkwater: Voices from Within the Veil. New York: Harcourt, Brace and Howe, 1920.

"Debit and Credit." *The Crisis* 25, no. 4 (February 1923): 151.

"Five Books." *The Crisis* 33 (January 1927): 152.

The Gift of Black Folk: Negroes in the Making of America. Boston: Stratford, 1924.

"Krigwa Players Little Negro Theater." *The Crisis* 32, no. 3 (July 1926): 134–136.

The Quest of the Silver Fleece. 1911; New York: Dover, 2008.

The Souls of Black Folk, ed. David W. Blight and Robert Gooding-Williams. 1903; Boston: Bedford/St. Martins, 1997.

"The Talented Tenth." In *The Negro Problem: A Series of Articles by Representative American Negroes of To-Day*, 31–75. New York: James Pott & Co., 1903.

"The True Brownies." *The Crisis* 18, no. 6 (October 1919): 285–286.

Writings, ed. Nathan Huggins. New York: Library of America, 1986.

[Du Bois, W. E. B.]. "The Browsing Reader." *The Crisis* 37, no. 4 (April 1930): 129.

duCille, Ann. *The Coupling Convention: Sex, Text, and Tradition in Black Women's Fiction*. Oxford: Oxford University Press, 1993.

Duck, Leigh Anne. "Go There Tuh Know There: Zora Neale Hurston and the Chronotope of the Folk." *American Literary History* 13, no. 2 (Summer 2001): 265–294.

Dunbar-Nelson, Alice *The Quest*. Ts. Box 20, Folder 380, Alice Dunbar-Nelson Collection, University of Delaware, Newark (Act 2.11).

Duncan, Thelma Myrtle. *Sacrifice*. In *Plays and Pageants from the Life of the Negro*, ed. Willis Richardson, 3–24. Washington, DC: Associated Publishers, 1930.

Durkin, Hannah, "Finding Last Middle Passage Survivor Sally 'Redoshi' Smith on the Page and Screen." *Slavery and Abolition*, 40, no. 4 (2019): 631–658.

Early, Gerald. "Pulp and Circumstance: The Story of Jazz in High Places." In *The Jazz Cadence of American Culture*, ed. Robert G. O'Meally, 393–430. New York: Columbia University Press, 1998.

"Three Notes Toward a Cultural Definition of the Harlem Renaissance." *Callaloo* 14, no. 1 (1991): 136–149.

Edwards, Brent Hayes. *The Practice of Diaspora: Literature, Translation, and the Rise of Black Internationalism*. Cambridge, MA: Harvard University Press, 2003.

"The Seemingly Eclipsed Window of Form: James Weldon Johnson's Prefaces." In *The Jazz Cadence of American Culture*, ed. Robert G. O'Meally, 580–601. New York: Columbia University Press, 1998.

"The Uses of Diaspora." *Social Text 66* 19, no. 1 (2001): 45–73.

Edwards, Erica. *Charisma and the Fictions of Black Leadership*. Minneapolis: University of Minnesota Press, 2012.

Eliot, T. S. "Tradition and the Individual Talent." *The Egoist* VI, no. 4 (1919): 54–55.

Ellington, Duke. "Black Brown and Beige: A Tone Parallel to the History of the American Negro." The Duke Ellington Carnegie Hall Concerts: 1943, Prestige Records, 1977. CD.

Enstice, Wayne and Paul Rubin. *Jazz Spoken Here: Conversations with 22 Musicians*. New York: Da Capo Press, 1994.

Esty, Jed. *Unseasonable Youth: Modernism, Colonialism, and the Fiction of Development*. Oxford: Oxford University Press, 2011.

Ewing, K. T. "What Kind of Woman? Alberta Hunter and Expressions of Black Female Sexuality in the Twentieth Century." In *Black Female Sexualities*, ed. Trimiko Melancon and Joanne M. Braxton, 100–112. New Brunswick, NJ: Rutgers University Press, 2015.

Fakinlede, Kayode J. *English-Yoruba, Yoruba-English: Modern Practical Dictionary*. New York: Hippocrene, 2003.

Farebrother, Rachel. *The Collage Aesthetic of the Harlem Renaissance*. Farnham: Ashgate, 2009.

Fauset, Jessie Redmon. "Oriflamme." *The Crisis* 19, no. 3 (January 1920): 128.

Plum Bun. 1928; London: Pandora, 1985.

"Some Notes on Color." *The World Tomorrow* (March 1922): 76–77. Repr. in *Harlem Renaissance: A Gale Critical Companion, Vol. 2*, 365–367. http://enc yjudaica.com/pdf/samples/sp666181.pdf.

There is Confusion. Boston: Northeastern University Press, 1989.

Fearnley, Andrew M. "When the Harlem Renaissance Became Vogue: Periodization and the Organization of Postwar American Historiography." *Modern Intellectual History* 11, no. 1 (2014): 59–87.

Fearnley, Andrew M. and Daniel Matlin. "Introduction." In *Race Capital? Harlem as Setting and Symbol*, ed. Andrew M. Fearnley and Daniel Matlin, 1–23. New York: Columbia University Press, 2019.

Feith, Michel. "The Syncopated African: Constructions of Origins in the Harlem Renaissance (Literature, Music, Visual Arts)." In *Temples for Tomorrow: Looking Back at the Harlem Renaissance*, eds. Geneviève Fabre and Michel Feith, 51–72. Bloomington: Indiana University Press, 2001.

"The First Reader," *New York World*, June 25, 1930, 11.

Fisher, Rudolph. "The City of Refuge." In *The New Negro*, ed. Alain Locke, 57–74. New York: Touchstone, 1997.

The Conjure Man Dies. 1932; London: X Press, 1995.

Walls of Jericho. 1928; Ann Arbor: University of Michigan Press, 1994.

Fitzgerald, F. Scott. *The Great Gatsby*. 1925; New York: Scribner, 2004.

Floyd, Silas X. *Short Stories for Colored People both Old and Young*. Washington, DC: Austin Jenkins, 1920.

Foley, Barbara. *Jean Toomer: Race, Repression, and Revolution*. Urbana: University of Illinois Press, 2014.

Spectres of 1919: Class and Nation in the Making of the New Negro. Urbana: Illinois University Press, 2003.

Foster, Tonya, Amber Rose Johnson, and Davy Knittle. "Not Detainable." PoemTalk, November 16, 2018. https://jacket2.org/podcasts/not-detainable-poemtalk-130.

Frank, Waldo. *Memoirs of Waldo Frank*. Amherst: University of Massachusetts Press, 1973.

Fuentes, Marisa J. *Dispossessed Lives: Enslaved Women, Violence, and the Archive*. Philadelphia: University of Pennsylvania Press, 2016.

Fusco, Katherine. "Sexing Farina: *Our Gang*'s Episodes of Racial Childhood." *PMLA* 133, no. 3 (2018): 526–541.

Gaines, Kevin K. *Uplifting the Race: Black Leadership, Politics, and Culture in the Twentieth Century*. Chapel Hill: University of North Carolina Press, 1996.

Gallego, Mar. *Passing Novels in the Harlem Renaissance: Identity Politics and Textual Strategies*. New Brunswick: Transaction, 2003.

Gates, Jr., Henry Louis. *Figures in Black: Words, Signs, and the "Racial" Self*. Oxford: Oxford University Press, 1987.

The Signifying Monkey: A Theory of African-American Literary Criticism. Oxford: Oxford University Press, 1988.

"The Trope of the New Negro and the Reconstruction of the Image of the Black." *Representations* 24 (Autumn 1988): 129–155.

"Zora Neale Hurston and the Speakerly Text." In *The Signifying Monkey: A Theory of African-American Literary Criticism*, 170–216. Oxford: Oxford University Press, 1988.

Gaunt, Kyra D. *The Games Black Girls Play: Learning the Ropes from Double-Dutch to Hip-Hop*. New York: NYU Press, 2006.

Gibson, Gloria J. "Cinematic Foremothers: Zora Neale Hurston and Eloyce King Patrick Gist." In *Oscar Micheaux and His Circle: African-American Filmmaking and Race Cinema of the Silent Era*, ed. Pearl Bowser, Jane Gaines, and Charles Musser, 195–209. Bloomington: Indiana University Press, 2001.

Giddings, Franklin H. *Readings in Descriptive and Historical Sociology*. New York: Macmillan, 1906.

Gidley, Mick and Ben Gidley. "The Native-American South." In *A Companion to the Literature of the American South*, ed. Richard Gray and Owen Robinson, 166–184. Malden, MA: Blackwell, 2004.

Gilroy, Paul. *The Black Atlantic: Modernity and Double Consciousness*. Cambridge, MA: Harvard University Press, 1993.

Gioia, Ted. *The History of Jazz*. New York: Oxford University Press, 2011.

"Jazz and the Primitive Myth." *The Musical Quarterly* 73, no. 1 (1989): 130–143.

Girard, Melissa. "J. Saunders Redding and the 'Surrender' of African American Women's Poetry." *PMLA* 132, no. 2 (2017): 281–297.

"'Jeweled Bindings': Modernist Women's Poetry and the Limits of Sentimentality." In *The Oxford Handbook of Modern and Contemporary American Poetry*, ed. Cary Nelson, 96–119. New York: Oxford University Press, 2012.

Glavey, Brian. *The Wallflower Avant-Garde: Modernism, Sexuality, and Queer Ekphrasis*. Oxford and New York: Oxford University Press, 2015.

God Struck Me Dead: Religious Conversion Experiences and Autobiographies of Negro Ex-Slaves, Social Science Source Documents No. II. Nashville, TN: Social Science Institute, Fisk University, 1945.

Goeser, Caroline. "Black and Tan: Racial and Sexual Crossings in *Ebony and Topaz*." In *Little Magazines and Modernism: New Approaches*, ed. Suzanne W. Churchill and Adam McKible, 151–175. Aldershot: Ashgate, 2007.

"The Blare of *God's Trombones*: Modernizing Biblical Narratives in the Work of Aaron Douglas." In *Beholding Christ and Christianity in African American Art*, ed. James Romaine and Phoebe Wolfskill, 45–49. University Park: Pennsylvania State University Press, 2017.

Picturing the New Negro: Harlem Renaissance Print Culture and Modern Black Identity. Lawrence: University Press of Kansas, 2007.

Goggin, Jacqueline. *Carter G. Woodson: A Life in Black History*. Baton Rouge: Louisiana State University Press, 1993.

"Countering White Racist Scholarship: Carter G. Woodson and the *Journal of Negro History*." *Journal of Negro History* 68 (1983): 355–375.

Goyal, Yogita. *Romance, Diaspora, and Black Atlantic Literature*. Cambridge: Cambridge University Press, 2010.

Graves, Ralph A. "Louisiana, Land of Perpetual Romance." *National Geographic* LVII (1930): 393–482.

Greene, J. Lee. *Time's Unfading Garden: Anne Spencer's Life and Poetry*. Baton Rouge: Louisiana State University Press, 1977.

Gregory, Montgomery. "The Drama of Negro Life." In *The New Negro*, ed. Alain Locke, 153–160. New York: Touchstone, 1992.

Griffin, Farah Jasmine. *"Who Set You Flowin'?": The African-American Migration Narrative.* New York: Oxford University Press, 1995.

Griffiths, Alison. *Wondrous Difference: Cinema, Anthropology, & Turn-of-the-Century Visual Culture.* New York: Columbia University Press, 2002.

Grimké, Angelina Weld. "A Mona Lisa," and "Grass Fingers." In *Caroling Dusk: An Anthology of Verse by Negro Poets of the Twenties*, ed. Countee Cullen, 42–43; 38. New York: Harper & Brothers, 1927.

"Grown-Ups' Corner." *Brownies' Book* 2, no. 2 (February 1921): 63.

"Guided Hubby to Fame." *The Pittsburgh Courier*, September 27, 1924, 1.

"Guide for the Christmas Book-Buyer." *The Critic* XXXV (July–December 1899): 1145–1164.

Guterl, Matthew Pratt, *The Color of Race in America, 1900–1940.* Cambridge, MA: Harvard University Press, 2001.

Hack, Daniel. *Reaping Something New: African American Transformations of Victorian Literature.* Princeton: Princeton University Press, 2017.

Haidarali, Laila. *Brown Beauty: Color, Sex, and Race from the Harlem Renaissance to World War II.* New York: New York University Press, 2018.

Hammond, John. "Is the Duke Deserting Jazz?" *Jazz*, May 1943, 15. Reprinted in Mark Tucker, *The Duke Ellington Reader*, 172. Oxford: Oxford University Press, 1993.

Handley, Fiona J. L. "Memorializing Race in the Deep South: The 'Good Darkie' Statue, Louisiana, USA." *Public Archaeology* 6 (2007): 98–115.

"Harlem Types: Portraits by Winold Reiss." *Survey Graphic* 6, no. 6 (March 1925): 651–654.

"Harlem: Mecca of the New Negro." *Survey Graphic* 6, no. 6 (March 1925).

Harper and Brothers, Publishers order coupon, *Opportunity: A Journal of Negro Life*, nd, np, Paul and Eslanda Robeson Collection, Moorland-Spingarn Archive, Howard University, Washington, DC (PERC).

Harris, Leonard. "Rendering the Subtext: Subterranean Deconstructive Project." In *The Philosophy of Alain Locke: The Harlem Renaissance and Beyond*, ed. Leonard Harris, 279–289. Philadelphia: Temple University Press, 1989.

Harrison, Hubert. "A New International." In *African Anti-Colonial Thought*, ed. Cathy Bergin, 40–41. Edinburgh: Edinburgh University Press, 2016.

"No Negro Literary Renaissance" [1927]. In *A Hubert Harrison Reader*, ed. Jeffrey B. Perry, 351–354. Middletown, CT: Wesleyan University Press, 2001.

Hartman, Saidiya V. *Scenes of Subjection: Terror, Slavery, and Self-Making in Nineteenth-Century America.* New York: Oxford University Press, 1997.

"Venus in Two Acts." *Small Axe* 26 (2008): 1–14.

Wayward Lives, Beautiful Experiments: Intimate Histories of Social Upheaval. New York: Norton, 2019.

Haviland, Beverly. "Passing from Paranoia to Plagiarism: The Abject Authorship of Nella Larsen." *Modern Fiction Studies* 43, no. 2 (1997): 295–318.

Helton, Laura et al., eds. "The Question of Recovery: Slavery, Freedom, and the Archive." *Social Text* 125, no. 33 (2015).

Hemenway, Robert E. *Zora Neale Hurston: A Literary Biography*. Urbana: University of Illinois Press, 1980.

Henderson, Stephen. *Understanding the New Black Poetry: Black Speech and Black Music as Poetic References*. New York: William Morrow and Company, 1973.

Herron, Carolivia, ed. *Selected Works of Angelina Weld Grimké*. New York: Oxford University Press, 1991.

Higginbotham, Evelyn Brooks. "Rethinking Vernacular Culture: Black Religion and Race Records in the 1920s and 1930s." In *African American Religious Thought: An Anthology*, ed. Cornel West and Eddie S. Glaude, Jr., 978–996. Louisville, KY: Westminster John Knox Press, 2003.

Hill, Constance Valis. *Tap Dancing America: A Cultural History*. Oxford: Oxford University Press, 2010.

Honey, Maureen. *Aphrodite's Daughters: Three Modernist Poets of the Harlem Renaissance*. New Brunswick, NJ: Rutgers University Press, 2016.

   ed. *Shadowed Dreams: Women's Poetry of the Harlem Renaissance*. New Brunswick, NJ: Rutgers University Press, 2006.

Howes, Kelly King and Christine Slovey, eds. *Harlem Renaissance*. Detroit: UXL, 2001.

Huggins, Nathan Irvin. *Harlem Renaissance*. New York: Oxford University Press, 1971.

Hughes, Langston. "Aunt Sue's Stories." *The Crisis* 22, no. 3 (July 1921): 121.

   The Big Sea. 1940; New York: Hill and Wang, 1993.

   "The Blues I'm Playing." In *The Ways of White Folks*, 96–120. London: George Allen and Unwin, 1934.

   "Christ in Alabama." *Contempo: A Review of Ideas and Personalities* (December 1, 1931): 1.

   The Collected Works of Langston Hughes: The Novels: Not Without Laughter and Tambourines to Glory, ed. Dolan Hubbard. 1930; Columbia: University of Missouri, 2001.

   "College Formal: Renaissance Casino." In *The Collected Works of Langston Hughes: The Poems 1951–1967*, ed. Arnold Rampersad, 53. Columbia: University of Missouri, 2001.

   "Harlem and its Negritude." *African Forum* (Spring 1966): 11–20. Repr. in *The Langston Hughes Review* 4, no. 1 (Spring 1985): 29–36.

   "Jazzonia." In *The New Negro*, ed. Alain Locke, 226. New York: Touchstone, 1997.

   "Justice." In *The Collected Poems of Langston Hughes*, ed. Arnold Rampersad, 31. New York: Vintage, 1994.

   "Marl Dust and West Indian Sun." *New York Herald Tribune*, December 5, 1926, 9.

   "The Negro Artist and the Racial Mountain." *The Nation*, June 23, 1926, 692–694. Repr. in *The Norton Anthology of African American Literature*, ed. Henry Louis Gates, Jr. and Nellie Y. McKay, 1311–1314. New York: Norton, 2004.

One-Way Ticket. New York: Alfred A. Knopf, 1949.

"Passing." In *The Ways of White Folks*, 51–55. 1934; New York: Vintage, 1990.

"Slave on the Block." In *The Ways of White Folks*, 19–31. New York: Knopf, 1934.

"The Weary Blues." *Forum* (August 1925): 239.

Hull, Gloria T. *Color, Sex, and Poetry: Three Women Writers of the Harlem Renaissance*. Bloomington: Indiana University Press, 1987.

Hurst, Fannie. "Zora Neale Hurston: A Personality Sketch." *Yale University Library Gazette*, July 1960, 17–22.

Hurston, Zora Neale. "Characteristics of Negro Expression" [1934]. In *Zora Neale Hurston, Folklore, Memoirs, and Other Writings*, ed. Cheryl A. Wall, 830–846. New York: Library of America, 1995.

Color Struck [1926]. In *Zora Neale Hurston: Collected Plays*, ed. Jean Lee Cole and Charles Mitchell, 33–50. New Brunswick, NJ: Rutgers University Press, 2008.

"Dance Songs and Tales from the Bahamas." *The Journal of American Folklore* 43, no. 169 (1930): 294–312.

"Drenched in Light." In *Zora Neale Hurston: The Complete Stories*, 17–25. New York: HarperPerennial, 1995.

Dust Tracks on a Road [1942]. In *Zora Neale Hurston, Folklore, Memoirs, and Other Writings*, ed. Cheryl A. Wall, 557–803. New York: Library of America, 1995.

Every Tongue Got to Confess: Negro Folk-Tales from the Gulf States, ed. Carla Kaplan. New York: HarperCollins, 2001.

The First One [1927]. In *Zora Neale Hurston: Collected Plays*, ed. Jean Lee Cole and Charles Mitchell, 63–74. New Brunswick, NJ: Rutgers University Press, 2008.

"Hoodoo in America." *The Journal of American Folklore* 44, no. 174 (1931): 317–417.

"How It Feels To Be Colored Me" [1928]. In *Zora Neale Hurston, Folklore, Memoirs, and Other Writings*, ed. Cheryl A. Wall, 826–829. New York: Library of America, 1995.

Meet the Mamma [1925]. In *Zora Neale Hurston, Folklore, Memoirs, and Other Writings*, ed. Cheryl A. Wall, 1–32. New York: Library of America, 1995.

Mules and Men [1935]. In *Zora Neale Hurston, Folklore, Memoirs, and Other Writings*, ed. Cheryl A. Wall, 1–267. New York: Library of America, 1995.

"New Children's Games." In *Go Gator and Muddy the Water: Writings by Zora Neale Hurston from the Federal Writers' Project*, ed. Pamela Bordelon, 99–105. New York: Norton.

Spears [1926]. In *Zora Neale Hurston: Collected Plays*, ed. Jean Lee Cole and Charles Mitchell, 51–62. New Brunswick, NJ: Rutgers University Press, 2008.

"Spunk." In *The New Negro*, ed. Alain Locke, 105–111. New York: Touchstone, 1997.

Tell My Horse. Philadelphia: J. B. Lippincott, 1938.

Their Eyes Were Watching God. 1937; Urbana: University of Illinois Press, 1978.

"What White Publishers Won't Print" [1950]. In *Zora Neale Hurston, Folklore, Memoirs, and Other Writings*, ed. Cheryl A. Wall, 950–955. New York: Library of America, 1995.

Hutchinson, George. "Harlem Central," *American Literary History* 23, no. 2 (2011): 405–422.

The Harlem Renaissance in Black and White. Cambridge, MA: Belknap Press of Harvard University Press, 1995.

"Introduction." In Jean Toomer, *Cane*, xiii–xxxii. New York: Penguin Classics, 2019.

"Jean Toomer and American Racial Discourse." In *Interracialism: Black-White Intermarriage in American History, Literature, and Law*, ed. Werner Sollors, 369–390. Oxford: Oxford University Press, 2000.

"Jean Toomer and the New Negroes of Washington." *American Literature* 63 (December 1991): 683–692.

"The Novel of the Negro Renaissance." In *The Cambridge Companion to the African American Novel*, ed. Maryemma Graham, 50–69. Cambridge: Cambridge University Press, 2004.

"Publishers and Publishing Houses." In *Encyclopedia of the Harlem Renaissance*, ed. Cary D. Wintz and Paul Finkelman, 1000–1004. New York: Routledge, 2004.

In Search of Nella Larsen: A Biography of the Color Line. Cambridge, MA: Belknap Press of Harvard University Press, 2006.

Hyest, Jenny. "Anne Spencer's Feminist Modernist Poetics." *Journal of Modern Literature* 38, no. 3 (2015): 129–147.

"Index of Modernist Magazines: *Broom*." http://modernistmagazines.org/ameri can/broom/

Jackson, Angela. *A Surprised Queenhood in the New Black Sun: The Life & Legacy of Gwendolyn Brooks*. Boston: Beacon Press, 2017.

Jackson, Major, ed. *Countee Cullen: Complete Poems*. New York: Library of America, 2013.

"Migration." In *Holding Company: Poems*, Paperback, 8. New York: Norton, 2012.

James, C. L. R. *Toussaint Louverture: The Story of the Only Successful Slave Revolt in History*. Durham: Duke University Press, 2013.

James, Winston. "Harlem's Difference." In *Race Capital? Harlem as Setting and Symbol*, ed. Andrew M. Fearnley and Daniel Matlin, 111–142. New York: Columbia University Press, 2019.

Japtok, Martin. *Growing Up Ethnic: Nationalism and the Bildungsroman: African American and Jewish American Fiction*. Iowa: University of Iowa Press, 2005.

Johnson, Charles S. ed. *Ebony and Topaz: A Collectanea*. New York: National Urban League, 1927.

Johnson, James Weldon. *Along This Way: The Autobiography of James Weldon Johnson*. New York: Viking Press, 1933.

The Autobiography of an Ex-Colored Man, ed. Jacqueline Goldsby. 1912; New York: Norton, 2015.

Black Manhattan. 1930; New York: Arno Press, 1968.

ed. *The Book of American Negro Poetry*. New York: Harcourt, Brace and Company, 1922.

ed. *The Book of American Negro Spirituals*. New York: Viking Press, 1925.

"The Dilemma of the Negro Author." *American Mercury* 15, no. 60 (December 1928): 477–481.

God's Trombones: Seven Negro Sermons in Verse. New York: Viking Press, 1927; repr. New York: Penguin, 1990.

"James Weldon Johnson to Gwendolyn Brooks." April 4, 1938. Box 4, Folder 59. James Weldon Johnson and Grace Nail Johnson Papers.

"Preface." In *The Book of American Negro Poetry*, ed. James Weldon Johnson, vii–xlviii. New York: Harcourt, Brace, 1922.

"Preface." In *The Book of American Negro Spirituals*, ed. James Weldon Johnson, 11–50. New York: Viking, 1925.

"Preface." In *God's Trombones: Seven Negro Sermons in Verse*, 1–11. 1927; New York: Penguin, 1990.

"Preface to the Revised Edition." In *The Book of American Negro Poetry*, ed. James Weldon Johnson, 3–8. New York: Harcourt Brace, 1931.

The Second Book of Negro Spirituals. New York: Viking Press, 1926.

"What the Negro is Doing for Himself." *The Liberator* (June 1918): 29–31. www.marxists.org/history/usa/culture/pubs/liberator/1918/04/v1n04-jun-1918-liberator.pdf

Johnson, Joan Marie. "'Drill into us ... the Rebel tradition': The Contest over Southern Identity in Black and White Women's Clubs, South Carolina, 1898–1930." *Journal of Southern History* 66 (2000): 525–562.

Johnson, Mat and Warren Pleece. *Incognegro: Renaissance #1*. Milwaukie, OR: Dark Horse, 2018.

Kaplan, Carla. "Introduction." In Zora Neale Hurston, *Every Tongue Got To Confess: Negro Folk-tales from the Gulf States*, xxi–xxxi. New York: HarperCollins, 2001.

Kaplan, Carla, ed. *Zora Neale Hurston: A Life in Letters*. New York: Random House, 2002.

Keats, John. "Ode on a Grecian Urn." In John Keats, *The Complete Poems*, ed. John Barnard, 344–346. Harmondsworth: Penguin, 1988.

Kelley, Robin D. G. "Foreword." In Deborah Willis, *Reflections in Black: A History of Black Photographers, 1840 to the Present*, ix–xi. New York: Norton, 2000.

"'We Are Not What We Seem': Rethinking Black Working-Class Opposition in the Jim Crow South." *The Journal of American History* 80, no. 1 (1993): 75–112.

Kemp, Melissa Prunty. "African American Women Poets, the Harlem Renaissance, and Modernism: An Apology." *Callaloo* 36 (2013): 789–801.

Keyser, Catherine. "Review of Mary Chapman, *Making Noise, Making News* and Ellen Gruber Garvey, *Writing with Scissors*." *Journal of Modern Periodical Studies* 6, no. 1 (2015): 85–89.

Klobucar, Gretchen Victoria. "Thinking Outside the (Wooden) Box: A Rhetorical Analysis of the Ethical Complexity of the Uncle Jack Statue." MA thesis, University of North Carolina, 2011.

Knadler, Stephen. "Dis-Abled Citizenship: Narrating the Extraordinary Body in Racial Uplift." *Arizona Quarterly* 69, no. 3 (2013): 99–128.

Knopf. "The Wooings of Jezebel Pettyfer." *The Saturday Review of Literature*, October 3, 1925, 180.

Krasner, David. *A Beautiful Pageant: African American Theatre, Drama, and Performance in the Harlem Renaissance, 1910–1927*. New York: Palgrave, 2002.

Kuenz, Jane. "Modernism, Mass Culture, and the Harlem Renaissance: The Case of Countée Cullen." *Modernism/modernity* 14, no. 3 (2007): 507–515.

Kytle, Ethan J. and Blain Roberts. *Denmark Vesey's Garden: Slavery and Memory in the Cradle of the Confederacy*. New York: New Press, 2018.

Larsen, Nella. "Letter: The Author's Explanation." *Forum* 83, no. 4 (April 1930): 41.
  Quicksand and Passing, ed. Deborah McDowell. 1928; 1929; London: Serpent's Tail, 1989.

Latham, Sean. *The Art of Scandal: Modernism, Libel Law, and the Roman à Clef*. Oxford: Oxford University Press, 2009.

Leland, Robert DeCamp. *Syncopation*. Boston: The Poetry-Drama Company, 1919.

Leonard, Keith D. "African American Women Poets and the Power of the Word." In *The Cambridge Companion to African American Women's Literature*, ed. Angelyn Mitchell and Danielle K. Taylor, 168–186. New York: Cambridge University Press, 2009.
  "Postmodern Soul: The Innovative Nostalgia of Thomas Sayers Ellis." *Contemporary Literature* 56, no. 2 (Summer 2015): 340–371.

Lewis, Charles. "Babbled Slander where the Paler Shades Dwell: Reading Race in *The Great Gatsby* and *Passing*." *LIT: Literature, Interpretation, Theory* 18, no. 2 (2007): 173–191.

Lewis, David Levering. *W. E. B. Du Bois: The Fight for Equality and the American Century, 1919–1963*. New York: Henry Holt, 2000.
  When Harlem Was in Vogue. New York: Penguin, 1997.

Lewis, Earl and Heidi Ardizzone. *Love on Trial: An American Scandal in Black and White*. New York: Norton, 2001.

"'Lift Every Voice and Sing': Whether Anthem or Hymn, Song Invokes Pride." *Atlanta Journal-Constitution*, February 1, 2018. www.ajc.com/news/local/lift-every-voice-and-sing-whether-anthem-hymn-song-invokes-pride/oG3m3HPfeeygasa5bbyaTI/

"Literary Notes." *The Saturday Review*, July 2, 1898, 24.

Löbberman, Dorothea. "Richard Bruce Nugent and the Queer Memory of Harlem." In *Race Capital? Harlem as Setting and Symbol*, ed. Andrew M. Fearnley and Daniel Matlin, 221–240. New York: Columbia University Press, 2019.

Locke, Alain. "To Certain of Our Philistines." *Opportunity* 3, no. 29 (May 1925): 155–157.
  "The Drama of Negro Life," *Theatre Arts Monthly* 10, no. 2 (October 1926): 701–706. Repr. in *The Works of Alain Locke*, ed. Charles Molesworth, 122–126. New York: Oxford University Press, 2012.
  "Enter the New Negro." *Survey Graphic* (March 1925): 631–634.

"Foreword." In *The New Negro: An Interpretation*, ed. Alain Locke, xxv–xxvii. 1925; New York: Touchstone, 1997.

"A Functional View of Value Ultimates" [1945]. In *The Philosophy of Alain Locke: The Harlem Renaissance and Beyond*, ed. Leonard Harris, 81–93. Philadelphia: Temple University Press, 1989.

"Introduction: The Drama of Negro Life." In *Plays of Negro Life: A Source-Book of Native American Drama*, ed. Montgomery Gregory and Alain Locke, n.p. New York: Harper and Brothers, 1927.

"The Legacy of the Ancestral Arts." In *The New Negro: An Interpretation*, ed. Alain Locke, 254–267. 1925; New York: Touchstone, 1997.

"More of the Negro in Art." *Opportunity* 3, no. 36 (December 1925): 363–366.

The Negro and His Music. Washington, DC: Associates in Negro Folk Education, 1936.

"The Negro and the American Stage." *Theatre Arts Monthly* (February 1926): 112–120.

"Negro Music Goes to Par" [1939]. In *The Critical Temper of Alain Locke: A Selection of His Essays in Art and Culture*, ed. Jeffrey C. Stewart, 117–121. 1 New York: Garland Publishing, 1983.

"The Negro: 'New' or Newer: A Retrospective Review of the Literature of the Negro for 1938" [1939]. In *The Critical Temper of Alain Locke: A Selection of His Essays in Art and Culture*, ed. Jeffrey C. Stewart, 271–283. New York: Garland Publishing, 1983.

"The Negro Spirituals." In *The New Negro*, ed. Alain Locke, 199–213. New York: Touchstone, 1997.

"Negro Youth Speaks." *The New Negro*, 47–53. 1925; New York: Simon & Schuster, 1992.

"The New Negro." In *The New Negro: An Interpretation*, ed. Alain Locke, 3–16. 1925; New York: Touchstone, 1997.

The New Negro: An Interpretation. New York: A. and C. Boni, 1925.

The New Negro: An Interpretation. 1925; New York: Touchstone, 1997.

"Pluralism and Intellectual Democracy" [1942]. In *The Philosophy of Alain Locke: The Harlem Renaissance and Beyond*, ed. Leonard Harris, 53–66. Philadelphia: Temple University Press, 1989.

Race Contacts and Interracial Relations: Lectures on the Theory and Practice of Race, ed. Jeffrey C. Stewart. Washington, DC: Howard University Press, 1992.

"Roland Hayes: An Appreciation" [1923]. In *The Critical Temper of Alain Locke: A Selection of His Essays in Art and Culture*, ed. Jeffrey C. Stewart, 103–105. New York: Garland Publishing, 1983.

"Spirituals" [1940]. In *The Critical Temper of Alain Locke: A Selection of His Essays in Art and Culture*, ed. Jeffrey C. Stewart, 123–126. New York: Garland Publishing, 1983.

"Towards a Critique of Negro Music." *Opportunity* 12 (November 1934): 328–331, 365–367. Repr. *The Critical Temper of Alain Locke: A Selection of His Essays in Art and Culture*, ed. Jeffrey C. Stewart, 109–115. New York: Garland Publishing, 1983.

"Value" [*c.* 1935]. In *The Philosophy of Alain Locke: The Harlem Renaissance and Beyond*, ed. Leonard Harris, 111–126. Philadelphia: Temple University Press, 1989.

"Values and Imperatives" [1935]. In *The Philosophy of Alain Locke: The Harlem Renaissance and Beyond*, ed. Leonard Harris, 34–50. Philadelphia: Temple University Press, 1989.

"Who and What is Negro?" [1942]. In *The Critical Temper of Alain Locke: A Selection of His Essays in Art and Culture*, ed. Jeffrey C. Stewart, 309–318. New York: Garland Publishing, 1983.

"This Year of Grace: Outstanding Books of the Year in Negro Literature" [1931]. In *The Critical Temper of Alain Locke: A Selection of His Essays in Art and Culture*, ed. Jeffrey C. Stewart, 205–208. New York: Garland Publishing, 1983.

Lott, Eric. "Blackface and Blackness: The Minstrel Show in American Culture." In *Inside the Minstrel Mask: Readings in Nineteenth-Century Blackface Minstrelsy*, ed. Annemarie Bean, James Vernon Hatch and Brooks McNamara, 3–32. Middletown, CT: Wesleyan University Press, 1996.

Lovett, Louise J. "Forward: A Pageant in Five Episodes." Ts. Box 120–2, Folder 100, William A. Joiner Papers, Moorland-Spingarn Research Center, Howard University, Washington, DC.

Lowell, Amy. *Tendencies in Modern American Poetry*. New York: Macmillan, 1917.

Lynes, Katherine R. "'A real honest-to-cripe jungle': Contested Authenticities in Helene Johnson's 'Bottled.'" *Modernism/modernity* 14, no. 3 (2007): 517–525.

Macfall, Haldane. *The House of the Sorcerer*. Boston: R. G. Badger & Co., 1900. *The Wooings of Jezebel Pettyfer*. New York: A. A. Knopf, 1925.

Mao, Douglas. *Fateful Beauty: Aesthetic Environments, Juvenile Development, and Literature, 1860–1960*. Princeton: Princeton University Press, 2008.

Marrs, Aaron W. "New Introduction." In Ulrich Bonnell Phillips, *A History of Transportation in the Eastern Cotton Belt to 1860*, xv–xxvii. Columbia: University of South Carolina Press, 2011.

Mason, Ernest D. "Deconstruction in the Philosophy of Alain Locke." *Transactions of the Charles S. Peirce Society* 24 (1988): 85–105.

Massood, Paula J. *Making a Promised Land: Harlem in Twentieth-Century Photography and Film*. New Brunswick, NJ: Rutgers University Press, 2013.

Maxwell, William J. "Introduction: Claude McKay – Lyric Poetry in the Age of Cataclysm." In *Complete Poems*, ed. William J. Maxwell, xi–xliv. Urbana: University of Illinois Press, 2004.

"Questionnaire Response." *Modernism/modernity* 23, no. 3 (2013): 446–449.

McBrown, Gertrude Parthenia. *The Picture-Poetry Book*. Washington, DC: Associated Publishers, 1935.

McCarthy, Albert. *Big Band Jazz*. London: Barrie and Jenkins, 1974.

McCluskey, Jr., John. "Aim High and Go Straight: The Grandmother Figure in the Short fiction of Rudolph Fisher." *Black American Literature Forum* 15 (1981): 55–59.

ed. *The City of Refuge: The Collected Stories of Rudolph Fisher*. Columbia: University of Missouri Press, 1987.

McDowell, Deborah. "Introduction: A Question of Power or, The Rearguard Faces Front." In Jessie Fauset, *Plum Bun*, ix–xxiv. London: Pandora, 1985.

McElya, Micki. *Clinging to Mammy: The Faithful Slave in Twentieth-Century America*. Cambridge, MA: Harvard University Press, 2007.

McHenry, Elizabeth. *Forgotten Readers: Recovering the Lost History of African American Literary Societies*. Durham: Duke University Press, 2002.

McKay, Claude. *A Long Way from Home: An Autobiography*. 1937; London: Pluto Press, 1985.

   Amiable with Big Teeth, completed in 1941 and ed. Jean-Christophe Cloutier. New York: Penguin Classics, 2017.

   Banana Bottom. 1933; London: Serpent's Tail, 2005.

   Banjo: A Novel without a Plot. New York: Harper and Brothers, 1929.

   Complete Poems, ed. William J. Maxwell. Urbana: University of Illinois Press, 2004.

   "Garvey as a Negro Moses." *The Liberator* (April 1922): 8–10. www.marxists.org /history/usa/culture/pubs/liberator/1922/04/v5n04-w49-apr-1922-liberator.pdf

   Home to Harlem. New York: Harper and Brothers, 1928.

   "How Black Sees Green and Red." *The Liberator* (June 1921): 17–21. www .marxists.org/history/usa/culture/pubs/liberator/1921/06/v04n06-w39-jun-1 921-liberator.pdf

   "Negro Dancers." In *The New Negro*, ed. Alain Locke, 214–215. New York: Touchstone, 1997.

Meer, Sarah. *Uncle Tom Mania: Slavery, Minstrelsy, and Transatlantic Culture in the 1850s*. Athens: University of Georgia Press, 2005.

Megill, David W. and Paul O. W. Tanner. *Jazz Issues: A Critical History*. Madison, WI: Brown & Benchmark, 1995.

Meier, August and Elliott Rudwick. *Black History and the Historical Profession, 1915–1980*. Urbana: University of Illinois Press, 1986.

Mercer, Kobena. "Romare Bearden, 1964: Collage as Kuntswollen." In *Cosmopolitan Modernisms*, ed. Kobena Mercer, 125–145. Cambridge, MA: MIT Press, 2005.

Michaels, Walter Benn. *Our America: Nativism, Modernism and Pluralism*. Durham, NC: Duke University Press, 1995.

Miller, May. "The Guide Book." Ts. Box 17, Folder 12, May Miller Papers, Stuart A. Rose Manuscript, Archives, and Rare Book Library, Emory University.

   "Riding the Goat." In *Plays and Pageants from the Life of the Negro*, ed. Willis Richardson, 141–176. Washington, DC: Associated Publishers, 1930.

Miller, Monica L. *Slaves to Fashion: Black Dandyism and the Styling of Black Diasporic Identity*. Durham: Duke University Press, 2009.

Miller, Nina. *Making Love Modern: The Intimate Public Worlds of New York's Literary Women*. New York: Oxford University Press, 1999.

Monroe, Harriet. *Poets and Their Art.* New York: Macmillan, 1932.

Moore, Darnell. "Black Radical Love: A Practice." *Public Integrity* 20, no. 4 (2018): 325–328.

Moretti, Franco. *The Way of the World: The Bildungsroman in European Culture.* London: Verso, 1987.

Morrison, Toni. *The Bluest Eye.* 1970; London: Picador, 1994.

　Jazz. London: Picador, 1993.

Morrissette, Noelle. *James Weldon Johnson's Modern Soundscapes.* Iowa City: University of Iowa Press, 2013.

Munby, Jonathan. *Under a Bad Sign: Criminal Self-Representation in African American Popular Culture.* Chicago: University of Chicago Press, 2011.

Murray, Alana D. "Countering the Master Narrative in US Social Studies: Nannie Helen Burroughs and New Narratives in History Education." In *Histories of Social Studies and Race, 1865–2000,* ed. Christine Woyshner and Chara Haeussler Bohan, 99–114. New York: Palgrave, 2012.

Nadell, Martha Jane. *Enter the New Negroes: Images of Race in American Culture.* Cambridge: Harvard University Press, 2004.

Napier, Winston. "Affirming Critical Conceptualism: Harlem Renaissance Aesthetics and the Formation of Alain Locke's Social Philosophy." *The Massachusetts Review* 39, no. 1 (1998): 93–112.

"The Negro in Art: How Shall He Be Portrayed?" *The Crisis* 31, no. 5 (March 1926): 219.

"The Negro in Art: How Shall He Be Portrayed?" *The Crisis* 32, no. 2 (June 1926): 71–73.

News from Brown. "Rudolph Fisher '19, physician and literary wit of the Harlem Renaissance." February 11, 2011. https://news.brown.edu/articles/2011/02/fisher

Newsome, Effie Lee. "Bronze Legacy (To a Brown Boy)." *The Crisis* 24, no. 6 (October 1922): 265.

Ngai, Mae M. *Impossible Subjects: Illegal Aliens and the Making of Modern America.* Princeton: Princeton University Press, 2004.

North, Michael. *The Dialect of Modernism: Race, Language and Twentieth-century Literature.* Oxford: Oxford University Press, 1994.

Nugent, Richard Bruce. *Gentleman Jigger.* Philadelphia: DaCapo, 2008.

　"Smoke, Lilies, and Jade." *Fire!!* (November 1926): 33–39. https://issuu.com/p oczineproject/docs/poczp_fire_1926_readview

Ogren, Kathy J. "Controversial Sounds: Jazz Performance as Theme and Language in the Harlem Renaissance." In *The Harlem Renaissance: Revaluations,* ed. Amritjit Singh, William S. Shiver, and Stanley Brodwin, 159–184. New York: Garland Publishing, 1989.

　The Jazz Revolution: Twenties America and the Meaning of Jazz. New York: Oxford University Press, 1992.

Oler, Andy. "'Their Song filled the Whole Night': *Not Without Laughter,* Hinterlands Jazz, and Rural Modernity." *College Literature* 41, no. 4 (2014): 94–110.

Olson, Liesl. *Chicago Renaissance: Literature and Art in the Midwest Metropolis*. New Haven: Yale University Press, 2017.

Ottley, Roi. "Hectic Harlem: Let's Look at the Record." *Amsterdam News* (New York), February 22, 1936, 13.

Panovka, Rebecca. "A Different Backstory for Zora Neale Hurston's 'Barracoon,'" *Los Angeles Review of Books*, July 7, 2018. https://lareviewofbooks.org/article/different-backstory-for-zora-neale-hurstons-barracoon.

Parfait, Claire, "Rewriting History: The Publication of W. E. B. Du Bois's *Black Reconstruction in America* (1935)." *Book History* 12 (2009): 266–294.

Patterson, Tiffany Ruby. *Zora Neale Hurston and a History of Southern Life*. Philadelphia, PA: Temple University Press, 2005.

Peake, Jak. "'Watching the Waters': Tropic Flows in the Harlem Renaissance, Black Internationalism and Other Currents." *Radical Americas* 3, no. 1 (2018): 1–52. DOI:https://doi.org/10.14324/111.444.ra.2018.v3.1.013.

Peiss, Kathy, *Hope in a Jar: The Making of America's Beauty Culture*. New York: Henry Holt, 1998.

Peterson, Theodore. *Magazines in the Twentieth Century*. Urbana: University of Illinois Press, 1956.

Pfeiffer, Kathleen, ed. *Brother Mine: The Correspondence of Jean Toomer and Waldo Frank*. Urbana: University of Illinois Press, 2010.

"The Limits of Identity in Jessie Fauset's *Plum Bun*." *Legacy* 18, no. 1 (2001): 79–93.

Race Passing and American Individualism. Amherst: University of Massachusetts Press, 2002.

Phillips, Carl. "Brooks's Prosody: Three Sermons on the Warpland." *Poetry Magazine*, Poetry Foundation, July 16, 2019. www.poetryfoundation.org/poetrymagazine/articles/141970/brookss-prosody-three-sermons-on-the-warpland.

Phillips, Michelle H. "The Children of Double Consciousness: From *The Souls of Black Folk* to *The Brownies' Book*." *PMLA* 128, no. 3 (2013): 590–607.

Representations of Childhood in American Modernism. New York: Palgrave, 2016.

Pierce, Clayton. "W. E. B. Du Bois and Caste Education: Racial Capitalist Schooling from Reconstruction to Jim Crow." *American Educational Research Journal* 54, no. 1 (2017): 23–47.

Pinkerton, Steve. "'New Negro' v. 'Niggeratti': Defining and Defiling the Black Messiah." *Modernism/modernity* 20, no. 3 (2013): 539–555.

Plant, Deborah G. *Every Tub Must Sit on its Own Bottom: The Philosophy and Politics of Zora Neale Hurston*. Urbana: University of Illinois Press, 1995.

"Introduction." In Zora Neale Hurston, *Barracoon: The Story of the Last Slave*, xiii–xxv. London: HQ, 2018.

Posmentier, Sonya. *Cultivation and Catastrophe: The Lyric Ecology of Modern Black Literature*. Baltimore: Johns Hopkins University Press, 2017.

Powell, Richard J. "The Aaron Douglas Effect." In *Aaron Douglas: African American Modernist*, ed. Susan Earle, 53–73. New Haven: Yale University Press, 2007.

"Paint that Thing! Aaron Douglas's Call to Modernism." *American Studies* 49, no. 1/2 (2008): 107–119.

Prevots, Naima. *American Pageantry: A Movement for Art and Democracy.* Ann Arbor: UMI Research, 1990.

Pugh, Megan. *American Dancing: From the Cakewalk to the Moonwalk.* New Haven: Yale University Press, 2015.

"A Questionnaire." *The Crisis* 31, no. 4 (February 1926): 165.

Ramazani, Jahan. *A Transnational Poetics.* Chicago: University of Chicago Press, 2009.

Rampersad, Arnold. *The Life of Langston Hughes Vol. I, 1902–1941.* Oxford: Oxford University Press, 1986.

Ransby, Barbara. *Eslanda. The Large and Unconventional Life of Mrs. Paul Robeson.* New Haven: Yale University Press, 2014.

Reed, Ishmael. "The Celtic in Us." *Comparative American Studies* 8, no. 4 (December 2010): 327–336.

"Is Ethnicity Obsolete?" In *The Invention of Ethnicity*, ed. Werner Sollors, 226–269. Oxford: Oxford University Press, 1989.

Mumbo Jumbo. New York: Doubleday, 1972.

Reuter, E. B. "The Changing Status of the Mulatto." In *Ebony and Topaz: A Collectanea*, ed. Charles S. Johnson, 107–110. New York: National Urban League, 1927.

Rich, Alan. "A Bouncy Seventy-Five: Roland Hayes, Despite His Age, Gives Concerts, Teaches and Reminisces." *New York Times*, June 3, 1962, X7.

Richards, Grant. "*The Wooings of Jezebel Pettyfer.* By Haldane Macfall." *The Athenaeum*, no. 3691 (July 23, 1898): 125.

Richards, Sandra L. "Writing the Absent Potential: Drama, Performance, and the Canon of African American Literature." In *Performativity and Performance*, ed. Eve Kosofky Sedgewick and Andrew Parker, 64–88. New York: Routledge, 1995.

Richardson, Willis and May Miller, eds. *Negro History in Thirteen Plays.* Washington, DC: Associated Publishers, 1935.

Richardson, Willis. "Near Calvary." In *Negro History in Thirteen Plays*, ed. Willis Richardson and May Miller, 95–107. Washington, DC: Associated Publishers, 1935.

Riis, Thomas L. *Just Before Jazz: Black Musical Theatre in New York, 1890–1915.* Washington, DC: Smithsonian Institution Press, 1989.

Ringgold, Faith. *Harlem Renaissance Party.* New York: HarperCollins, 2015.

Robeson, Eslanda. *Paul Robeson, Negro.* London: Gollancz, 1930.

Paul Robeson, Negro. New York and London: Harper and Harper, 1930.

Robeson, Paul. "From My Father's Parsonage To My 'Ole Man River' Stage Triumph," *The Sunday Sun*, January, 13, 1929, n.p., PERC.

Robinson, Amy. "Forms of Appearance of Value: Homer Plessy and the Politics of Privacy." In *Performance and Cultural Politics*, ed. Elin Diamond, 239–261. London: Routledge, 1996.

"It Takes One to Know One: Passing and Communities of Common Interest." *Critical Inquiry* 20, no. 4 (1994): 715–736.

Robinson, M. Michelle. *Dreams for Dead Bodies: Blackness, Labor, and the Corpus of American Detective Fiction*. Ann Arbor: University of Michigan Press, 2016.

Rogers, J. A. "Jazz at Home." In *The New Negro*, ed. Alain Locke, 216–224. 1925; New York: Touchstone, 1997.

Rony, Fatimah Tobing. *The Third Eye: Race, Cinema, and Ethnographic Spectacle*. Durham: Duke University Press, 1996.

Rosenberg, Rachel A. "Looking for Zora's *Mule Bone*: The Battle for Artistic Authority in the Hurston-Hughes Collaboration." *Modernism/modernity* 6, no. 2 (1999): 79–105.

Ross, Marlon. *Manning the Race: Reforming Black Men in the Jim Crow Era*. New York: New York University Press, 2004.

Roy, Sneharika. *The Postcolonial Epic: From Melville to Walcott and Ghosh*. London: Routledge, 2018.

Rutter, Emily R. "'Belch the pity! / Straddle the city!': Helene Johnson's Late Poetry and the Rhetoric of Empowerment." *African American Review* 47, no. 4 (2014): 495–509.

Saint-Amour, Paul K. *The Copywrights: Intellectual Property and the Literary Imagination*. Ithaca: Cornell University Press, 2011.

"Introduction: Modernism and the Lives of Copyright." In *Modernism and Copyright*, ed. Paul K. Saint-Amour, 1–38. Oxford: Oxford University Press, 2011.

Saks, Eva. "Representing Miscegenation Law." In *Interracialism: Black-white Intermarriage in American History, Literature, and Law*, ed. Werner Sollors, 61–81. New York: Oxford University Press, 2000.

Sanborn, Geoffrey. *Plagiarama: William Wells Brown and the Aesthetic of Attractions*. New York: Columbia University Press, 2016.

Sanders, Cheryl J. *Saints in Exile: The Holiness-Pentecostal Experience in African American Religion and Culture*. New York: Oxford University Press, 1996.

Sanders, Mark A. "African American Folk Roots and Harlem Renaissance Poetry." In *The Cambridge Companion to the Harlem Renaissance*, ed. George Hutchinson, 96–111. Cambridge: Cambridge University Press, 2007.

"American Modernism and the New Negro Renaissance." In *The Cambridge Companion to American Modernism*, ed. Walter Kalaidjian, 129–156. New York: Cambridge University Press, 2005.

Schiff, David. *The Ellington Century*. Berkeley: University of California Press, 2012.

Schomburg, Arthur. "The Negro Digs Up His Past." In *The New Negro*, ed. Alain Locke, 231–237. 1925; New York: Touchstone, 1997.

Schuyler, George S. *Black No More*, intro. Ishmael Reed. 1931; New York: Modern Library, 1999.

"The Negro-Art Hokum," *The Nation* 122 (June 16, 1926), 662–663. Repr. *The Norton Anthology of African American Literature*, ed. Henry Louis Gates, Jr. and Nellie Y. McKay, 1221–1223. New York: Norton, 2004.

Scott, Bonnie Kime. "Beyond (?) Feminist Recuperative Study." In *Women and Literary History: "For There She Was,"* ed. Katherine Binhammer and Jeanne Wood, 220–234. Newark: University of Delaware Press, 2003.

Scott, Clarissa M. Review of *The Wooings of Jezebel Pettyfer. Opportunity* 4, no. 36 (January 1926): 26–27.

Scott, Emmett J. Review of *The Wooings of Jezebel Pettyfer. The Crisis* 31, no. 1 (November 1925): 32–33.

Sergeant, Elizabeth Shepley. "The Man With His Home in a Rock: Paul Robeson." *The New Republic*, March 3, 1926, 40–44.

Seymour, Bella. "Letter to the Grown-Ups' Corner." *Brownies' Book* 1, no. 2 (February 1920): 45.

Shackelford, Jane Dabney. *The Child's Story of the Negro*. Washington, DC: Associated Publishers, 1938.

"How I Became a Writer." Ms. Jane Dabney Shackelford Collection, Accession Number 800627, D.C. 1, folder 20, Community Archives, Vigo County Public Library, Terre Haute, Ind.

Shaffer, Robert. "Out of the Shadows: The Political Writing of Eslanda Goode Robeson." *Pennsylvania History: A Journal of Mid-Atlantic Studies* 66, no. 1 (1999): 47–64.

Sherrard-Johnson, Cherene. *Dorothy West's Paradise: A Biography of Class and Color*. New Brunswick: Rutgers University Press, 2012.

"Introduction: Harlem as Shorthand: The Persistent Value of the Harlem Renaissance." In *A Companion to the Harlem Renaissance*, ed. Cherene Sherrard-Johnson, 1–14. Chichester, UK: Wiley-Blackwell, 2015.

Portraits of the New Negro Woman: Visual and Literary Culture in the Harlem Renaissance. New Brunswick: Rutgers University Press, 2007.

Sherwood, Marika. *Claudia Jones: A Life in Exile: A Biography*. London: Lawrence & Wishart, 1999.

"The Comintern, the CPGB, Colonies, and Black Britons, 1920–1938." *Science and Society* 60, no. 2 (Summer 1996): 137–163.

Shipton, Alyn. *Hi-De-Ho: The Life of Cab Calloway*. New York: Oxford University Press, 2010.

A New History of Jazz. New York: Continuum, 2001.

Shockley, Evie. *the new black*. Middletown, CT: Wesleyan University Press, 2012.

Renegade Poetics: Black Aesthetics and Formal Innovation in African American Poetry. Iowa City: University of Iowa Press, 2011.

Smethurst, James. *The New Red Negro: The Literary Left and African American Poetry, 1930–1946*. New York: Oxford University Press, 1999.

Snyder, Jeffrey Aaron. *Making Black History: The Color Line, Culture, and Race in the Age of Jim Crow*. Athens: University of Georgia Press, 2018.

Soitos, Stephen F. *The Blues Detective: A Study of African American Detective Fiction*. Amherst: University of Massachusetts Press, 1996.

Sollors, Werner. *Beyond Ethnicity: Consent and Descent in American Culture.* Oxford: Oxford University Press, 1986.

Soto, Michael. "Hemingway Among the Bohemians: A Generational Reading of *The Sun Also Rises.*" *The Hemingway Review* 21, no. 1 (2001): 5–21.

Measuring the Harlem Renaissance: The U.S. Census, African American Identity, and Literary Form. Amherst: University of Massachusetts Press, 2016.

Soumahoro, Maboula. "Story, History, Discourse: Maryse Condé's Segu and Afrodiasporic Historical Narration." In *Toward an Intellectual History of Black Women*, ed. Mia Bay et al., 178–194. Chapel Hill: University of North Carolina Press, 2015.

Southern, Eileen. *The Music of Black Americans: A History.* New York: Norton, 1971.

Spencer, Anne. "The Sévignés." In *Shadowed Dreams: Women's Poetry of the Harlem Renaissance*, 2nd ed., ed. Maureen Honey, 261–262. New Brunswick, NJ: Rutgers University Press, 2006.

Spillers, Hortense J. "Mama's Baby, Papa's Maybe: An American Grammar Book." *Diacritics* 17, no. 2 (1987): 65–81.

Spring, Howard. "Swing." *Grove Music Online.* Accessed August 22, 2019. www.oxfordmusiconline.com/grovemusic/view/10.1093/gmo/9781561592630.001.0001/omo-9781561592630-e-1002258226?rskey=TuUKkI.

Starrett, Vincent. "Haldane Macfall, Novelist." *The Double Dealer* I, no. 5 (May 1921): 186–189.

Stephens, Michelle Ann. *Black Empire: The Masculine Global Imaginary of Caribbean Intellectuals in the United States, 1914–1962.* Durham: Duke University Press, 2005.

Stepto, Robert. *From Behind the Veil: A Study of Afro-American Narrative.* Urbana: University of Illinois Press, 1991.

Stevens, Margaret. *Red International and Black Caribbean Communists in New York City, Mexico and the West Indies, 1919–1939.* London: Pluto Press, 2017.

Stewart, Catherine A. *Long Past Slavery: Representing Race in the Federal Writers' Project.* Chapel Hill: University of North Carolina Press, 2016.

Stewart, Jeffrey C. *The New Negro: The Life of Alain Locke.* New York: Oxford University Press, 2018.

Stowe, Harriet Beecher. "Sojourner Truth, The Libyan Sibyl." *Atlantic* (April 1863). www.theatlantic.com

Sullivan, James D. "Killing John Cabot and Publishing Black: Gwendolyn Brooks's 'Riot.'" *African American Review* 36, no. 4 (2002): 557–569.

Summers, Martin. *Manliness and its Discontents: The Black Middle Class and the Transformation of Masculinity, 1900–1930.* Chapel Hill: University of North Carolina Press, 2004.

Sundquist, Eric. "Red, White, Black, and Blue." *Transitions*, no. 70 (1996): 94–115.

Svoboda, Terese. *Anything That Burns You: A Portrait of Lola Ridge, Radical Poet.* Tucson: Schaffner Press, 2016.

Tate, Claudia, ed. *The Selected Works of Georgia Douglas Johnson*. New York: G. K. Hall, 1997.

Taylor, Yuval. *Zora and Langston: A Story of Friendship and Betrayal*. New York: Norton, 2019.

Teachout, Terry. *Duke Ellington: The Life of Duke Ellington*. London: Robson Press, 2013.

Thaggert, Miriam. "Black Modernist Feminism and This Contemporary Moment: Evie Shockley's *the new black*." *Feminist Modernist Studies* 1, no. 1–2 (2018): 44–50.

Images of Black Modernism: Verbal and Visual Strategies of the Harlem Renaissance. Amherst: University of Massachusetts Press, 2010.

Thiele, Bob. "The Case of Jazz Music." *Jazz*, July 1943, 19–20. Repr. in *The Duke Ellington Reader*, ed. Mark Tucker, 175–177. Oxford: Oxford University Press, 1993.

Thomas, Katrina Dyonne. *Ring Shout, Wheel About: The Racial Politics of Music and Dance in North American Slavery*. Urbana: University of Illinois Press, 2014.

Thomsett, Michael C. *Musical Terms, Symbols and Theory: An Illustrated Dictionary*. Jefferson, NC: McFarland and Company, 1989.

Thorpe, Earl E. *Black Historians: A Critique*. New York: William Morrow, 1971.

Thurman, Wallace. *The Blacker the Berry*. 1929; New York: Scribner, 1996.

ed. *Fire!! A Quarterly Devoted to Younger Negro Artists* (November 1926).

Infants of the Spring. 1932; London: X Press, 1998.

"Letter to William Jourdan Rapp" [*c.* July 1929]. In *The Collected Writings of Wallace Thurman: A Harlem Renaissance Reader*, ed. Amritjit Singh and Daniel M. Scott III, 152–155. New Brunswick: Rutgers University Press, 2003.

"Negro Artists and the Negro." *New Republic*, August 31, 1927, 37–39. Repr. *The Collected Writings of Wallace Thurman*, ed. Amritjit Singh and Daniel M. Scott III, 195–200. New Brunswick: Rutgers University Press, 2003.

Negro Life in New York's Harlem: A Lively Picture of a Popular and Interesting Section. Girard: Haldeman-Julius Publications, 1928.

"A Stranger at the Gates: A Review of *Nigger Heaven* by Carl Van Vechten." *Messenger*, September 1926. In *The Collected Writings of Wallace Thurman: A Harlem Renaissance Reader*, ed. Amritjit Singh and Daniel M. Scott III, 191–192. New Brunswick: Rutgers University Press, 2003.

Toomer, Jean. "The Americans." In *A Jean Toomer Reader: Selected Unpublished Writings*, ed. Frederick L. Rusch, 106–109. Oxford: Oxford University Press, 1993.

Cane, ed. George Hutchinson. 1923; New York: Penguin Classics, 2019.

"Song of the Son." *The Crisis* 23, no. 6 (April 1922): 261.

Trouillot, Michel-Rolph. *Silencing the Past: Power and the Production of History*. Boston: Beacon Press, 1995.

Turner, Lucy Mae. *'Bout Cullud Folkses*. New York: Henry Harrison Pub, 1938.

Untermeyer, Louis. *The New Era in American Poetry*. New York: Henry Holt & Co, 1919.

Unwritten History of Slavery: Autobiographical Account of Negro Ex-Slaves, Social Science Source Documents No. 1. Nashville, TN: Social Science Institute, Fisk University, 1945.

van Notten, Eleonore. *Wallace Thurman's Harlem Renaissance*. Amsterdam: Rodopi, 1994.

van Patten, Nathan. "Organization of Source Material for the Study of American English and American Dialects." *American Speech* 4, no. 6 (1929): 425–429.

Van Vechten, Carl. *Keep A-Inchin' Along: Selected Writings of Carl Van Vechten about Black Art and Letters*, ed. Bruce Kellner. Westport, CT: Greenwood Press, 1979.

   "Moanin' Wid a Sword in Mah Han'." *Vanity Fair* 25, no. 6 (February 1926): 61, 100, 102.

   Nigger Heaven, ed. Kathleen Pfeiffer. 1926; Urbana: University of Illinois Press, 2000.

   The Splendid Drunken Twenties: Selections from the Daybooks, 1922–1930, ed. Bruce Kellner. Urbana: University of Illinois Press, 2003.

Villalongo, William. "Strange Material: Black Pulp!" In *Black Pulp!*, ed. Mark Thomas Gibson and William Villalongo, 8–13. New Haven: Yale School of Art, 2016.

Vogel, Shane. *The Scene of Harlem Cabaret: Race, Sexuality, Performance*. Chicago: University of Chicago Press, 2009.

   "The Sensuous Harlem Renaissance: Sexuality and Queer Culture." In *A Companion to the Harlem Renaissance*, ed. Cherene Sherrard-Johnson, 267–283. Chichester, UK: Blackwell, 2015.

W., G. "Women Who Did and Who Do Yet." *The Egoist* (January 1, 1914): 16–17.

Walker, Aida Overton. "Colored Men and Women on the Stage." *The Colored American Magazine*, October 1905, 571–575.

Walker, Madam C. J. "Advertisement for Egyptian Brown Face Powder and Glossine." *The Crisis* (January 1928).

Walker, Rafael. "Nella Larsen Reconsidered: The Trouble with Desire in *Quicksand* and *Passing*." *MELUS* 41, no. 1 (Spring 2016): 165–192.

Wall, Cheryl A. *The Harlem Renaissance: A Very Short Introduction*. Oxford: Oxford University Press, 2016.

   "Histories and Heresies: Engendering the Harlem Renaissance." *Meridians* 2, no. 1 (2001): 59–76.

   Women of the Harlem Renaissance. Bloomington: Indiana University Press, 1995.

Walrond, Eric. "The Adventures of Kit Skyhead and Mistah Beauty: An All-Negro Evening in the Coloured Cabarets of New York," *Vanity Fair* 24, no. 1 (March 1925): 52, 100.

   "Mr. Macfall's 'Jezebel'." *The Saturday Review of Literature*, May 1, 1926, 756.

   Tropic Death. New York: Liveright, 2015.

Walser, Robert, ed. *Keeping Time: Readings in Jazz History*. Oxford: Oxford University Press, 1999.

"War at Attica: Was There No Other Way?" *Time* 98, no. 13 (September 27, 1971): 22.

Warren, Kenneth. *What Was African American Literature?* Cambridge, MA: Harvard University Press, 2011.

Wedin, Carolyn. *Jessie Redmon Fauset, Black American Writer*. Troy, NY: Whitston Pub. Co., 1981.

Weheliye, Alexander G. "I Am I Be: The Subject of Sonic Afro-Modernity." *boundary* 30, no. 2 (2003): 97–114.

West, Dorothy. "An Unimportant Man." In Dorothy West, *The Richer, the Poorer: Stories, Sketches, and Reminiscences*, 137–160. New York: Random House, 1995.

Whalan, Mark. "Jean Toomer and the Avant-Garde." In *The Cambridge Companion to the Harlem Renaissance*, ed. George Hutchinson, 71–81. Cambridge: Cambridge University Press, 2007.

   ed. *The Letters of Jean Toomer, 1919–1924*. Knoxville: University of Tennessee Press, 2006.

Wheeler, Belinda and Louis J. Parascandola, eds. *Heroine of the Harlem Renaissance and Beyond: Gwendolyn Bennett's Selected Writings*. University Park, PA: Pennsylvania State University Press, 2018.

Wheeler, Laura. "Ruth Is Not Coming Out of College." Illustration in Willis Richardson, "The Deacon's Awakening." *The Crisis* (November 1920): 13.

White, Edward. *The Tastemaker: Carl Van Vechten and the Birth of Modern America*. New York: Farrar, Straus and Giroux, 2014.

White, Walter. *Flight*. 1926; Baton Rouge: Louisiana State University Press, 1998.

Wiegman, Robyn. *American Anatomies: Theorizing Race and Gender*. Durham, NC: Duke University Press, 1995.

Williams, Erika Renée. "A Lie of Omission: Plagiarism in Nella Larsen's *Quicksand*." *African American Review* 45, no. 1–2 (2012): 205–216.

Williams, Daniel G. *Black Skin, Blue Books: African Americans and Wales, 1845–1945*. Cardiff: University of Wales Press, 2012.

   Ethnicity and Cultural Authority: From Arnold to Du Bois. Edinburgh: Edinburgh University Press, 2006.

Williams, Raymond. *The Politics of Modernism: Against the New Conformists*, ed. Tony Pinkney. London: Verso, 1989.

Winn, J. Emmett. *Documenting Racism: African Americans in U.S. Department of Agriculture Documentaries, 1921–42*. New York: Continuum, 2014.

Wintz, Cary and Paul Finkelman. *Encyclopedia of the Harlem Renaissance*. New York: Routledge, 2004.

Wirth, Thomas H. ed. *Gay Rebel of the Harlem Renaissance: Selections from the Work of Richard Bruce Nugent*. Durham: Duke University Press, 2002.

Womack, Jacob. "Luckey Roberts, Willie 'the Lion' Smith, 'Fats' Waller, and James P. Johnson: An Analysis of Historical, Cultural, and Performance Aspects of Stride Piano from 1910 to 1940." PhD diss., West Virginia University, 2013.

Woodley, Jenny. *Art for Equality: The NAACP's Cultural Campaign for Civil Rights.* Lexington: University Press of Kentucky, 2014.

Woodson, Carter G. Letter to Jane Dabney Shackelford, April 7, 1936. Ts. Jane Dabney Shackelford Collection, Accession Number 780222, Series VI, folder 1. Community Archives, Vigo County Public Library, Terre Haute, Ind.

"Two Timely and Useful Books: *Gladiola Garden* and *Word Pictures of the Great*, a New Book." *Negro History Bulletin* 4, no. 9 (June 1941): 202–203.

Wright, Nazera Sadiq. *Black Girlhood in the Nineteenth Century.* Urbana: University of Illinois Press, 2016.

Wright, Richard. "Between Laughter and Tears." *The New Masses*, October 5, 1937, 22–25.

"High Tide in Harlem: Joe Louis as a Symbol of Freedom." In *Speech and Power: The African-American Essay and its Cultural Content From Polemics to Pulpit*, ed. Gerald Early, 153–157. Hopewell, NJ: Ecco Press, 1992.

Yancey, Bessie Woodson. *Echoes from the Hills.* Washington, DC: Associated Publishers, 1939.

Young, John K. *Black Writers, White Publishers: Marketplace Politics in Twentieth-Century African American Literature.* Jackson: University Press of Mississippi, 2006.

Yuhl, Stephanie E. *A Golden Haze of Memory: The Making of Historic Charleston.* Chapel Hill: University of North Carolina Press, 2005.

Zamora, Javier. "Citizenship." In *Unaccompanied*, 63. Port Townsend, Washington: Copper Canyon Press, 2017.

Index